ADVANCE PRAISE FOR AMERICAN DESTINY
NARRATIVE OF A NATION
Second Edition

"American Destiny: Narrative of a Nation *is well written, concise, and designed to meet the needs of the introductory student of American history. It covers complex events with broad strokes and plays on many of the common themes in American history, like American exceptionalism. The book does a great job of distilling a mass of material for the everyday reader.*"

Jeff Littlejohn, Norfolk State University

"*The strength of this book lies in its clear writing style. Carnes and Garraty make sometimes difficult issues understandable, bringing them to the student's level without sacrificing the excellent scholarship. The text presents an excellent balance of political, military, and social history, which keeps readers interested.*"

Donald Whatley, Blinn College

"*This current collaboration of John Garraty, the political history guru, and Mark Carnes, the seeker of social and cultural inclusion, is a great one. The text is designed not to see how much the reader already knows but how much the reader can learn.*"

A. G. Dunston, Eastern Kentucky University

"*The narrative is entertaining and covers subject matter that students will enjoy reading. The 'Re-Viewing the Past' feature makes the book very appealing to the average college freshman or sophomore. It is a feature that I would use on a regular basis.*"

Loyce B. Miles, Hinds Community College

ABOUT THE AUTHORS

$\rightarrow$ ——— $\leftarrow$

Mark C. Carnes received his undergraduate degree from Harvard and his Ph.D. in history from Columbia University, where he studied and trained with Professor John A. Garraty. The Ann Whitney Olin Professor of History at Barnard College, Columbia University, Professor Carnes has chaired both the departments of History and American Studies at Bar-

© 1999 Joel Gordon

John A. Garraty (left) *and Mark C. Carnes* (right).

nard. In addition to this textbook, Carnes and Garraty have co-authored *Mapping America's Past: A Historical Atlas* and are co-general editors of the 24-volume *American National Biography,* for which they were awarded the Waldo Leland Prize of the American Historical Association, the Darmouth Prize of the American Library Association, and the Hawkins Prize of the American Association of Publishers. In addition, Carnes has published numerous books in American social and cultural history, including *Past Imperfect: History According to the Movies* (1995), *Novel History: Historians and Novelists Confront America's Past (and Each Other)* (2001), and *Invisible Giants: 50 Americans That Shaped the Nation but Missed the History Books* (2002). Carnes also created "Reacting to the Past," which won the Theodore Hesburgh Award, sponsored by TIAA-CREF, as the outstanding pedagogical innovation of 2004.

"Garraty preaches a particular doctrine on historical writing, expounding on the details of a complex process whereby the murky abstractions of the past are distilled into clean, clear narrative. He insists that the writer's sole duty is to readers. This literary alchemy is all the more wondrous for being so devoid of artifice," Carnes observes.

MARK C. CARNES
Ann Whitney Olin Professor of History
Barnard College, Columbia University

John A. Garraty holds a Ph.D. from Columbia University and an L.H.D. from Michigan State University, and is Gouverneur Morris Professor Emeritus of History at Columbia. He is the author, co-author, and editor of scores of books and articles, among them biographies of Silas Wright, Henry Cabot Lodge, Woodrow Wilson, George W. Perkins, and Theodore Roosevelt. Along with Mark Carnes, he is co-editor of the *American National Biography*. Garraty has also contributed a volume—*The New Commonwealth*—to the New American Nation series and edited *Quarrels That Shaped the Constitution*. He was a member of the Board of Directors of *American Heritage* magazine and served as both vice president and head of the teaching division of the American Historical Association. His areas of research interest include the Gilded Age, unemployment (in a historical sense), and the Great Depression of the 1930s. Of his collaboration with Carnes on *American Destiny*, Garraty says, "Although this volume is the work of two authors, it is as nearly the product of a single historical sensibility as is possible. Mark's scholarly specialization in cultural and social issues, especially gender, complements mine in politics and the economy. The book has benefited, too, from his special interest in postwar America. Over the many years of our collaborations, one of our favorite topics of discussion has been the craft of historical writing. We share a commitment to clarity and conciseness. We strive to avoid jargon and verbiage. We believe that while the political history of the nation provides a useful narrative framework, its people are what give the story meaning."

JOHN A. GARRATY
Gouverneur Morris Professor of History, Emeritus
Columbia University

Penguin Academics

Volume II • Since 1865

AMERICAN DESTINY
NARRATIVE OF A NATION

Second Edition

MARK C. CARNES
Ann Whitney Olin Professor of History
Barnard College, Columbia University

JOHN A. GARRATY
Gouverneur Morris Professor of History, Emeritus
Columbia University

PEARSON
Longman

New York   Boston   San Francisco
London   Toronto   Sydney   Tokyo   Singapore   Madrid
Mexico City   Munich   Paris   Cape Town   Hong Kong   Montreal

To Our Children:
Stephanie
and
Kathy, Jack, and Sarah

Executive Editor:	Michael Boezi
Development Manager:	Betty Slack
Executive Marketing Manager:	Sue Westmoreland
Media and Supplements Editor:	Kristi Olson
Production Manager:	Ellen MacElree
Project Coordination and Electronic Page Makeup:	Nesbitt Graphics, Inc.
Senior Cover Designer/Manager:	Nancy Danahy
Cover Photo:	The clock on the Chicago Board of Trade Building, Chicago, Illinois. Copyright © Superstock, Inc.
Cartographer:	Mapping Specialists
Photo Researcher:	Photosearch, Inc.
Senior Manufacturing Buyer:	Dennis J. Para
Printer and Binder:	Quebecor World/Eusey
Cover Printer:	Phoenix Color Corps.

Library of Congress Cataloging-in-Publication Data

Carnes, Mark C. (Mark Christopher), 1950–
    American destiny: narrative of a nation / Mark C. Carnes, John A. Garraty — 2nd ed.
        v. cm.
    Includes bibliographic references and index.
    Contents: v. 1. To 1877 — v. 2. Since 1865.
    ISBN 0-321-31636-3 (single v. ed.) — ISBN 0-321-31635-5 (v. 1) — ISBN 0-321-29857-8 (v. 2)
        1. United States—History. I. Garraty, John Arthur, 1920– II. Title.

E178.6.C33 2006
973—dc22   2005040915

Please visit our website at http://www.ablongman.com

ISBN 0-321-31636-3 (Single Volume Edition)
ISBN 0-321-31635-5 (Volume I)
ISBN 0-321-29857-8 (Volume II)

1 2 3 4 5 6 7 8 9 10—QWE— 08 07 06 05

BRIEF CONTENTS

Detailed Contents ix
Maps and Graphs xv
Feature Essays xvii
Preface xix

CHAPTER 16 | RECONSTRUCTION AND THE SOUTH 447

CHAPTER 17 | IN THE WAKE OF WAR 472

CHAPTER 18 | AN INDUSTRIAL GIANT 502

CHAPTER 19 | AMERICAN SOCIETY IN THE INDUSTRIAL AGE 530

CHAPTER 20 | INTELLECTUAL AND CULTURAL TRENDS 556

CHAPTER 21 | POLITICS: LOCAL, STATE, AND NATIONAL 575

CHAPTER 22 | THE AGE OF REFORM 598

CHAPTER 23 | FROM ISOLATION TO EMPIRE 630

CHAPTER 24 | WOODROW WILSON AND THE GREAT WAR 658

CHAPTER 25 | POSTWAR SOCIETY AND CULTURE:
CHANGE AND ADJUSTMENT 689

CHAPTER 26 | THE NEW ERA: 1921–1933 717

CHAPTER 27 | THE NEW DEAL: 1933–1941 741

CHAPTER 28 | WAR AND PEACE 772

CHAPTER 29 | THE AMERICAN CENTURY 799

CHAPTER 30 | FROM CAMELOT TO WATERGATE 827

CHAPTER 31 | SOCIETY IN FLUX 857

CHAPTER 32 | RUNNING ON EMPTY: THE NATION TRANSFORMED 882

CHAPTER 33 | MISDEMEANORS AND HIGH CRIMES 908

Appendix A-1
Credits C-1
Index 1-1

DETAILED CONTENTS

Maps and Graphs xv
Feature Essays xvii
   Re-Viewing the Past
   Debating the Past
Preface xix

CHAPTER 16 | RECONSTRUCTION AND THE SOUTH 447

Presidential Reconstruction 448 • Republican Radicals 450 • Congress Rejects
Johnsonian Reconstruction 451 • The Fourteenth Amendment 452 • The
Reconstruction Acts 453 • Congress Supreme 454 • The Fifteenth Amendment
455 • "Black Republican" Reconstruction: Scalawags and Carpetbaggers 456 •
The Ravaged Land 459 • Sharecropping and the Crop-Lien System 461 • The
White Backlash 463 • Grant as President 465 • The Disputed Election of 1876
466 • The Compromise of 1877 469

CHAPTER 17 | IN THE WAKE OF WAR 472

Congress Ascendant 473 • The Political Aftermath of War 474 • Blacks After
Reconstruction 476 • Booker T. Washington: A "Reasonable" Champion for
Blacks 478 • White Violence and Vengeance 480 • The West After the Civil War
481 • The Plains Indians 482 • Indian Wars 484 • The Destruction of Tribal
Life 486 • The Lure of Gold and Silver in the West 488 • Big Business and the
Land Bonanza 492 • Western Railroad Building 493 • The Cattle Kingdom 496
• Open-Range Ranching 497 • Barbed-Wire Warfare 498

CHAPTER 18 | AN INDUSTRIAL GIANT 502

Essentials of Industrial Growth 502 • Railroads: The First Big Business 503 • Iron,
Oil, and Electricity 506 • Competition and Monopoly: The Railroads 509 •
Competition and Monopoly: Steel 511 • Competition and Monopoly: Oil 512 •
American Ambivalence to Big Business 516 • Reformers: George, Bellamy,
Lloyd, and the Marxists 518 • The Government Reacts to Big Business: Railroad
Regulation 521 • The Government Reacts to Big Business: The Sherman
Antitrust Act 522 • The Labor Union Movement 523 • The American
Federation of Labor 524 • Labor Militancy Rebuffed 526 • Whither America,
Whither Democracy? 528

CHAPTER 19 | AMERICAN SOCIETY IN THE INDUSTRIAL AGE 530
Middle-Class Life 530 • Skilled and Unskilled Workers 531 • Working Women
532 • Farmers 534 • Working-Class Attitudes 535 • Working Your Way Up 536
• The "New" Immigration 537 • New Immigrants Face New Nativism 539 •
The Expanding City and Its Problems 541 • Teeming Tenements 542 • The
Cities Modernize 545 • Leisure Activities: More Fun and Games 547 •
Christianity's Conscience and the Social Gospel 550 • The Settlement Houses
552 • Civilization and Its Discontents 554

CHAPTER 20 | INTELLECTUAL AND CULTURAL TRENDS 556
Publishing 556 • Colleges and Universities 559 • Revolution in the Social
Sciences 562 • Progressive Education 563 • History 564 • Realism in Literature
565 • Mark Twain 567 • William Dean Howells 568 • Henry James 569 • The
Pragmatic Approach 572

CHAPTER 21 | POLITICS: LOCAL, STATE, AND NATIONAL 575
Voting Along Ethnic and Religious Lines 575 • City Bosses 576 • Party Politics:
Sidestepping the Issue 578 • Lackluster Leaders 580 • Crops and Complaints
585 • The Populist Movement 586 • Showdown on Silver 589 • The Depression
of 1893 591 • The Election of 1896 593 • The Meaning of the Election 595

CHAPTER 22 | THE AGE OF REFORM 598
Roots of Progressivism 598 • The Progressive Mind 601 • "Radical" Progressives:
The Wave of the Future 602 • Political Reform: Cities First 603 • Political
Reform: The States 604 • State Social Legislation 604 • Political Reform: The
Woman Suffrage Movement 607 • Political Reform: Income Taxes and Popular
Election of Senators 609 • Theodore Roosevelt: Cowboy in the White House
611 • Roosevelt and Big Business 612 • Roosevelt and the Coal Strike 613 •
TR's Triumphs 615 • Roosevelt Tilts Left 616 • William Howard Taft: The
Listless Progressive, or More Is Less 617 • Breakup of the Republican Party 618
• The Election of 1912 620 • Wilson: The New Freedom 621 • The Progressives
and Minority Rights 624 • Black Militancy 626

CHAPTER 23 | FROM ISOLATION TO EMPIRE 630
Origins of the Large Policy: Coveting Colonies 630 • Toward an Empire in the
Pacific 633 • Toward an Empire in Latin America 636 • The Cuban Revolution
638 • The "Splendid Little" Spanish-American War 641 • Developing a Colonial
Policy 643 • The Anti-Imperialists 645 • The Philippine Insurrection 646 •
Cuba and the United States 647 • The United States in the Caribbean and
Central America 649 • The Open Door Policy 650 • The Panama Canal 652 •
Imperialism Without Colonies 655

CHAPTER 24 | WOODROW WILSON AND THE GREAT WAR 658
Wilson's "Moral" Diplomacy 658 • Europe Explodes in War 660 • Freedom of the
Seas 661 • The Election of 1916 664 • The Road to War 665 • Mobilizing the
Economy 666 • Workers in Wartime 668 • Paying for the War 668 •

Propaganda and Civil Liberties 669 • Wartime Reforms 670 • Women and Blacks in Wartime 671 • Americans: To the Trenches and Over the Top 674 • Preparing for Peace 676 • The Paris Peace Conference and the Versailles Treaty 679 • The Senate Rejects the League of Nations 681 • The Red Scare 683 • The Election of 1920 686

CHAPTER 25 | POSTWAR SOCIETY AND CULTURE: CHANGE AND ADJUSTMENT 689

Closing the Gates to New Immigrants 689 • New Urban Social Patterns 691 • The Younger Generation 692 • The "New" Woman 693 • Popular Culture: Movies and Radio 698 • The Golden Age of Sports 700 • Urban–Rural Conflicts: Fundamentalism 702 • Urban–Rural Conflicts: Prohibition 704 • The Ku Klux Klan 706 • Sacco and Vanzetti 707 • Literary Trends 707 • The "New Negro" 709 • Economic Expansion 711 • The Age of the Consumer 712 • Henry Ford 713 • The Airplane 714

CHAPTER 26 | THE NEW ERA: 1921–1933 717

Harding and "Normalcy" 718 • "The Business of the United States Is Business" 719 • The Harding Scandals 720 • Coolidge Prosperity 721 • Peace Without a Sword 722 • The Peace Movement 723 • The Good Neighbor Policy 724 • The Totalitarian Challenge 724 • War Debts and Reparations 725 • The Election of 1928 727 • Economic Problems 729 • The Stock Market Crash of 1929 730 • Hoover and the Depression 731 • The Economy Hits Bottom 733 • The Depression and Its Victims 736 • The Election of 1932 736

CHAPTER 27 | THE NEW DEAL: 1933–1941 741

The Hundred Days 741 • The National Recovery Administration (NRA) 743 • The Agricultural Adjustment Administration (AAA) 744 • The Tennessee Valley Authority (TVA) 745 • The Unemployed 745 • Literature in the Depression 747 • Three Extremists: Long, Coughlin, and Townsend 748 • The Second New Deal 751 • The Election of 1936 753 • Roosevelt Tries to Undermine the Supreme Court 754 • The New Deal Winds Down 755 • Significance of the New Deal 758 • Women as New Dealers: The Network 759 • Blacks During the New Deal 760 • A New Deal for Indians 762 • The Role of Roosevelt 762 • The Triumph of Isolationism 763 • War Again in Europe 764 • A Third Term for FDR 767 • The Undeclared War 768

CHAPTER 28 | WAR AND PEACE 772

The Road to Pearl Harbor 772 • Mobilizing the Home Front 773 • The War Economy 775 • War and Social Change 776 • African Americans in Time of War 776 • Internment of the Japanese 778 • Women's Contribution to the War Effort 780 • Allied Strategy: Europe First 782 • Germany Overwhelmed 783 • The Naval War in the Pacific 785 • Island Hopping 785 • Building the Atom Bomb 791 • Wartime Diplomacy 794 • Allied Suspicion of Stalin 795 • Yalta and Potsdam 796

CHAPTER 29 | THE AMERICAN CENTURY 799

The Postwar Economy 800 • The Containment Policy 801 • A Turning Point in Greece 801 • The Marshall Plan and the Lesson of History 802 • The Election of 1948 804 • Containing Communism Abroad 807 • Hot War in Korea 808 • The Communist Issue at Home 813 • McCarthyism 814 • Dwight D. Eisenhower 814 • The Eisenhower-Dulles Foreign Policy 816 • McCarthy Self-Destructs 817 • Asian Policy After Korea 817 • Israel and the Middle East 818 • Eisenhower and Khrushchev 819 • Latin America Aroused 820 • The Politics of Civil Rights 821 • The Election of 1960 824

CHAPTER 30 | FROM CAMELOT TO WATERGATE 827

The Cuban Crises 827 • The Vietnam War 830 • "We Shall Overcome": The Civil Rights Movement 831 • Tragedy in Dallas: JFK Assassinated 834 • Lyndon Baines Johnson 836 • The Great Society 836 • Johnson Escalates the War 838 • Opposition to the War 839 • The Election of 1968 839 • Nixon as President: "Vietnamizing" the War 844 • The Cambodian "Incursion" 845 • Détente with Communism 846 • Nixon in Triumph 848 • Domestic Policy Under Nixon 849 • The Watergate Break-in 850 • More Troubles for Nixon 852 • The Judgment on Watergate: "Expletive Deleted" 853

CHAPTER 31 | SOCIETY IN FLUX 857

A Society on the Move 858 • The Advent of Television 858 • At Home and Work 859 • The Growing Middle Class 861 • Religion in Changing Times 862 • The Perils of Progress 864 • The Costs of Prosperity 865 • New Racial Turmoil 866 • Native-Born Ethnics 868 • Rethinking Public Education 870 • Students in Revolt 872 • The Counterculture 874 • The Sexual Revolution 875 • Women's Liberation 878

CHAPTER 32 | RUNNING ON EMPTY: THE NATION TRANSFORMED 882

The Oil Crisis 882 • Ford as President 884 • The Fall of South Vietnam 885 • Ford Versus Carter 885 • The Carter Presidency 886 • A National Malaise 887 • Stagflation: The Weird Economy 887 • Families Under Stress 888 • Cold War or Détente? 890 • The Iran Crisis: Origins 891 • The Iran Crisis: Carter's Dilemma 892 • The Election of 1980 892 • Reagan as President 895 • Four More Years 896 • "The Reagan Revolution" 897 • Change and Uncertainty 898 • AIDS 900 • The New Merger Movement 901 • "A Job for Life": Layoffs Hit Home 902 • A "Bipolar" Economy, a Fractured Society 903 • The Iran-Contra Arms Deal 904

CHAPTER 33 | MISDEMEANORS AND HIGH CRIMES 908

The Election of 1988 908 • Crime and Punishment 909 • "Crack" and Urban Gangs 910 • George H. W. Bush as President 911 • The Collapse of Communism in Eastern Europe 912 • The War in the Persian Gulf 913 • The Deficit Worsens 916 • Enter Bill Clinton 916 • The Election of 1992 917 • A New Start: Clinton 917 • Emergence of the Republican Majority 919 • The Election of 1996 919 • A Racial Divide 920 • Violence and Popular Culture

921 • Clinton Impeached 923 • Clinton's Legacy 924 • The Economic Boom and the Internet 926 • The 2000 Election: George W. Bush Wins by One Vote 927 • Terrorism Intensifies 928 • September 11, 2001 929 • America Fights Back: War in Afghanistan 931 • The Second Iraq War 932 • The Election of 2004 934 • The Imponderable Future 936

APPENDIX A-1
The Declaration of Independence A-3
The Constitution of the United States of America A-6
Amendments to the Constitution A-14
Supplementary Reading A-21
Suggested Web Sites A-47
Present-day United States A-68
Present-day World A-70

CREDITS C-1

INDEX I-1

Maps and Graphs

MAPS	PAGE
The Compromise of 1877	469
Loss of Indian Lands, 1850–2000	488
The West: Cattle, Railroads, and Mining, 1850–1893	496
The Forging of U.S. Steel	513
The Election of 1896	595
The Woman Suffrage Campaign, 1896–1919	610
The Election of 1912	621
The Course of Empire, 1867–1901	636
Spanish-American War, Caribbean Theater	644
The United States in the Caribbean and Central America	650
The U.S. Panama Canal	654
The Western Front, 1918	676
Europe Before World War I	678
Europe After World War I	679
The Tennessee Valley Authority	746
Japanese American Internment Camps	779
The Liberation of Europe	784
World War II, Pacific Theater	790
European Recipients of Marshall Plan, 1948–1952	803
Air Relief to Berlin	805
North Korean Offensive, June–August 1950	811
Southeast Asia, 1954–1975	840
Ratification of the Equal Rights Amendment, 1972–1978	890
The Collapse of Communism in Eastern Europe	912
The Middle East	914
Present-day United States	A-68
Present-day World	A-70

GRAPHS	PAGE
Southern Agriculture	463
Immigration, 1860–1910	539
U-Boat Campaign, 1914–1918	666
Casualties of the Great War	677
Unemployment and Federal Action, 1929–1941	747
High School and College Graduates, 1870–1983	872

FEATURE ESSAYS

RE-VIEWING THE PAST

	PAGE
Titanic	570
Chicago	696
Saving Private Ryan	786

DEBATING THE PAST

	PAGE
Were Reconstruction governments corrupt?	457
Was the frontier exceptionally violent?	490
Were the industrialists "robber barons" or savvy entrepreneurs?	519
Did immigrants assimilate?	543
Did the frontier engender individualism and democracy?	566
Were city governments corrupt and incompetent?	579
Were the progressives forward-looking?	614
Did the United States acquire an overseas empire for moral or economic reasons?	634
Did a stroke sway Wilson's judgment?	684
Was the decade of the 1920s one of self-absorption?	694
What caused the Great Depression?	735
Did the New Deal succeed?	756
Should the United States have used atomic bombs against Japan?	793
Did Truman needlessly exacerbate relations with the Soviet Union?	809
Would JFK have sent a half-million American troops to Vietnam?	841
Did mass culture make life shallow?	876
Did Reagan end the Cold War?	899
Do historians ever get it right?	937

PREFACE

" American Destiny"—these words, so laden with portent, may strike some readers as an unsuitable title for a sober work of history. Such words have been invoked on behalf of countless partisan causes and feverish enthusiasms: in John Louis O'Sullivan's 1845 editorial proclaiming it "our manifest destiny to overspread the continent allotted by Providence for the free development of our yearly multiplying millions"; in Daniel Webster's terse repudiation of the looming sectional crisis: "One country, one constitution, one destiny"; in Walt Whitman's celebration, after that crisis had erupted in civil war, of "one common indivisible destiny for ALL"; and in Franklin D. Roosevelt's speaking during the Great Depression of his generation's "rendezvous with destiny." Modern politicians have found such expressions irresistible; Ronald Reagan—perhaps unwittingly—invoked puritan theology when he told a Republican gathering: "We will achieve our destiny to be a shining city on a hill for all mankind to see."

Even the nation's critics have been obliged to address the popular belief in an American destiny, if only to repudiate it. For instance, in 1853 Henry David Thoreau bristled that the American people might "go their way to their manifest destiny, a filibustering toward heaven by the great western route"; he intended to look in a different direction. In 1862 Frederick Douglass asserted that "the destiny of America" was also the destiny of black Americans. One hundred and one years later, Martin Luther King, Jr., writing from a jail in Birmingham, Alabama, resurrected Douglass's words: Insofar as "the goal of America is freedom," he declared, "our destiny is tied up with America's destiny." Suffragist Elizabeth Cady Stanton similarly feared for the nation unless it allowed each woman to become "arbiter of her own destiny."

But if most Americans have accepted the concept of a national purpose, they have endlessly debated where the nation was headed and the nature of the force impelling it there. Some have discerned the hand of God lifting the nation up—or perhaps hurling it down. Others have claimed that the nation's destiny was dictated by accident of geography or economics, by the "laws" of social evolution or the "spirit" of democratic liberalism, by the "patterns" of demography or "processes" of modernity, and so on. Our book, however, maintains that no single model explains the complexity of American history. Because historians are poor prophets, we make no attempt to peer into the future. For us, the concept of an American destiny describes a pervasive if inchoate longing that has exerted a powerful hold on the American imagination.

The subtitle—"Narrative of a Nation"—may also strike readers as provocative. Some historians object to the subjectivity and sweep of narrative history; others, to the intellectual concept of an American nation. The latter contend that the diverse peoples of the United States cannot be encompassed within the analytical boundaries of a single nation. They point to the wealth of information historians have gathered in recent decades on particular racial and ethnic groups; on the experiences of women in many different social and cultural contexts; on the lives of children, the elderly, and those confronting various physical and emotional challenges; on gays and lesbians, farmers and factory workers, western miners and eastern capitalists, and many more.

The proliferation of this scholarship has shown that "the American people" is so vast a subject that it is beyond comprehension. Consequently, we do not claim to have written a history of "the American people." Rather, we describe how the voices and actions of its many peoples have produced a particular political structure—the United States, a single nation—and how that nation has in turn influenced the lives of everyone.

Narrative history is subjective. We must decide, quite arbitrarily, which stories to tell and how to tell them. Historical sources are incomplete and biased; our judgments more art than science. We have tried, by digging into the muck of the past, to haul out the bits that make sense to us and to present them so as to tell a coherent story. Though some contend that the past is too murky to yield clear meanings, we persist because no one is satisfied with the mud.

Of course, a plausible story may not be good history. We underscore this point by including feature essays on popular movies which, while "based on" true stories, often include a bewildering assortment of historical facts and fictions. We hope that these "Re-Viewing the Past" essays will provide guidance on which of Hollywood's stories contain some measure of truthfulness, which do not, and how viewers can tell the difference. The essays also serve as reminder that all historical narratives are interpretations, and all contain biases of selection, presentation, voice, and argument. When considering the past, people should be critical of what they see—and read.

"Debating the Past" is a new feature in this edition of *American Destiny*. Historians argue about nearly every aspect of the nation's complex past, and each chapter now includes a brief essay on an important historiographical debate. Because such issues are hard to fix in memory, we have provided a photograph or picture to "trigger" the historiographical essay. For example, the question for Chapter 2—"Were puritan communities peaceful?"—is prefaced by a contemporary painting of a seventeenth-century puritan village, with a river meandering through a nearby meadow. The question for Chapter 12—"Did the frontier change women's lives?"—commences with a photograph of a farm woman hauling buffalo chips in a wheelbarrow. Each essay concludes with a list of the major works cited. Our final debate—"Do historians ever get it right?" (Chapter 33)—poses a question that we hope will stimulate discussion.

People have always looked to the past, whether chronicling a hunt for mammoth beasts in a cave painting or recounting the foundation stories of their civilizations in the Bible or the Mahabharata. Our lives have grown out of the rich fabric of the past, many of whose elements cannot be readily analyzed or even discerned. For us, a less elusive element, but surely an important one, is the American nation, itself the product of the myriad actions, ideas, and forces described in the following pages. By considering its past, we better understand ourselves—and perhaps our own destiny.

MARK C. CARNES
JOHN A. GARRATY

16

RECONSTRUCTION AND THE SOUTH

On April 5, 1865, Abraham Lincoln visited Richmond, Virginia. The fallen Confederate capital lay in ruins, sections blackened by fire, but the president was able to walk the streets unmolested and almost unattended. Everywhere black people crowded around him worshipfully; some fell to their knees as he passed, crying "Glory, Hallelujah," hailing him as a messiah. Even white townspeople seemed to have accepted defeat without resentment.

A few days later, in Washington, Lincoln delivered an important speech on Reconstruction, urging compassion and open-mindedness. On April 14 he held a Cabinet meeting at which postwar readjustment was considered at length. That evening, while Lincoln was watching a performance of the play *Our American Cousin* at Ford's Theater, a half-mad actor, John Wilkes Booth, slipped into the president's box and shot him in the back of the head with a small pistol. Early the next morning, without having regained consciousness, Lincoln died.

The murder was part of a complicated plot organized by die-hard pro-Southerners. Seldom have fanatics displayed so little understanding of their own interests, for with Lincoln perished the South's best hope for a mild peace. After his body had been taken home to Illinois, the national mood hardened; apparently the awesome drama was still unfolding—retribution and a final humbling of the South were inevitable.

⑤

PRESIDENTIAL RECONSTRUCTION

Despite its bloodiness, the Civil War had caused less intersectional hatred than might have been expected. Although civilian property was often seized or destroyed, the invading armies treated the southern population with forbearance, both during the war and after Appomattox. While confederate President Davis was ensconced in Richmond behind Lee's army, Northerners boasted that they would "hang Jeff Davis to a sour apple tree," and when he was captured in Georgia in May 1865, he was at once clapped into irons preparatory to being tried for treason and murder. But feeling against Davis subsided quickly. In 1867 the military turned him over to the civil courts, which released him on bail. He was never brought to trial. A few other Confederate officials spent short periods behind bars, but the only Southerner executed for war crimes was Major Henry Wirz, the commandant of Andersonville military prison.

The legal questions related to bringing the defeated states back into the Union were extremely complex. Since Southerners believed that secession was legal, logic should have compelled them to argue that they were out of the Union and would thus have to be formally readmitted. Northerners should have taken the contrary position, for they had fought to prove that secession was illegal. Yet the people of both sections did just the opposite. Senator Charles Sumner and Congressman Thaddeus Stevens, in 1861 uncompromising expounders of the theory that the Union was indissoluble, now insisted that the Confederate states had "committed suicide" and should be treated like "conquered provinces." Lincoln believed the issue a "pernicious abstraction" and tried to ignore it.

The process of readmission began in 1862, when Lincoln reappointed provisional governors for those parts of the South that had been occupied by federal troops. On December 8, 1863, he issued a proclamation setting forth a general policy. With the exception of high Confederate officials and a few other special groups, all Southerners could reinstate themselves as United States citizens by taking a simple loyalty oath. When, in any state, a number equal to 10 percent of those voting in the 1860 election had taken this oath, they could set up state government. Such governments had to be republican in form, must recognize the "permanent freedom" of the slaves, and must provide for education for blacks. The plan, however, did not require that blacks be given the right to vote.

The "Ten Percent Plan" reflected Lincoln's lack of vindictiveness and his political wisdom. He realized that any government based on such a small minority of the population would be, as he put it, merely "a tangible nucleus which the remainder . . . may rally around as fast as it can," a sort of puppet regime, like the paper government established in those sections of Virginia under federal control.[1] The regimes established under this plan in Tennessee, Louisiana, and Arkansas bore, in the president's mind, the same relation to finally reconstructed states that an egg bears to a chicken. "We shall sooner have the fowl by hatching

---

[1] *By approving the separation of the western counties that had refused to secede, this government provided a legal pretext for the creation of West Virginia.*

Andrew Johnson in 1855, from a painting by William Cooper. From origins even more lowly than Lincoln's, Johnson had risen to be congressman, governor of Tennessee, and United States senator. He was able and ambitious but fundamentally unsure of himself, as could be seen in his boastfulness and stubbornness.

it than by smashing it," he remarked. He knew that eventually representatives of the southern states would again be sitting in Congress, and he wished to lay the groundwork for a strong Republican party in the section. Yet he realized that Congress had no intention of seating representatives from the "10 percent" states at once.

The Radicals in Congress disliked the 10 percent plan, partly because of its moderation and partly because it enabled Lincoln to determine Union policy toward the recaptured regions. In July 1864 they passed the Wade-Davis bill, which provided for constitutional conventions only after a majority of the others in a southern state had taken a loyalty oath. Confederate officials and anyone who had "voluntarily borne arms against the United States" were barred from voting in the election or serving at the convention. Besides prohibiting slavery, the new state constitutions would have to repudiate Confederate debts. Lincoln disposed of the Wade-Davis bill with a pocket veto and there matters stood when Andrew Johnson became president following the assassination.

Lincoln had picked Johnson for a running mate in 1864 because he was a border-state Unionist Democrat and something of a hero as a result of his courageous service as military governor of Tennessee. His political strength came from the poor whites and yeomen farmers of eastern Tennessee, and he was fond of extolling the common man and attacking "stuck-up aristocrats."

Thaddeus Stevens called Johnson a "rank demagogue" and a "damned scoundrel," and it is true that Johnson was a masterful rabble-rouser. But few men of his generation labored so consistently on behalf of small farmers. Free homesteads, public education, absolute social equality—such were his objectives. The father of communism, Karl Marx, a close observer of American affairs at this time, wrote approvingly of Johnson's "deadly hatred of the oligarchy."

Johnson was a Democrat, but because of his record and his reassuring penchant for excoriating southern aristocrats, the Republicans in Congress were ready to cooperate with him. "Johnson, we have faith in you," said Senator Ben Wade, author of the Wade-Davis bill, the day after Lincoln's death. "By the gods, there will be no trouble now in running the government!"

Johnson's reply, "Treason must be made infamous," delighted the Radicals, but the president proved temperamentally unable to work with them. Like Randolph of Roanoke, his antithesis intellectually and socially, opposition was his specialty; he soon alienated every powerful Republican in Washington.

Radical Republicans listened to Johnson's diatribes against secessionists and the great planters and assumed that he was anti-southern. Nothing could have been further from the truth. He had great respect for states' rights and he shared most of his poor white Tennessee constituents' contempt of blacks. "Damn the negroes, I am fighting these traitorous aristocrats, their masters," he told a friend during the war. "I wish to God," he said on another occasion, "every head of a family in the United States had one slave to take the drudgery and menial service off his family."

The new president did not want to injure or humiliate all white Southerners. He issued an amnesty proclamation only slightly more rigorous than Lincoln's. It assumed, correctly enough, that with the war over most southern voters would freely take the loyalty oath; thus it contained no 10 percent clause. More classes of Confederates, including those who owned taxable property in excess of $20,000, were excluded from the general pardon. By the time Congress convened in December 1865, all the southern states had organized governments, ratified the Thirteenth Amendment abolishing slavery, and elected senators and representatives. Johnson promptly recommended these new governments to the attention of Congress.

REPUBLICAN RADICALS

Johnson's proposal had no chance in Congress. The Thirteenth Amendment had the effect of increasing the representation of the southern states in Congress because it made the Three-fifths Compromise meaningless. Henceforth those who had been slaves would be counted as whole persons in apportioning seats in the House of Representatives. If Congress seated the Southerners, the balance of power might swing to the Democrats. To expect the Republicans to surrender power in such a fashion was unrealistic. Former Copperheads gushing with extravagant praise for Johnson put them instantly on guard.

Southern voters had provoked northern resentment by their choice of congressmen. Georgia elected Alexander H. Stephens, vice president of the Confederacy, to the Senate, although he was still in a federal prison awaiting trial for treason! Several dozen men who had served in the Confederate Congress had been elected to either the House or the Senate, together with four generals and many other high officials. The southern people understandably selected locally respected and experienced leaders, but it was equally reasonable that these choices would sit poorly with Northerners.

Finally, the so-called Black Codes enacted by southern governments to control former slaves alarmed the North. These varied in severity from state to state, but all, as one planter admitted, set out to keep the blacks "as near to a state of bondage as possible." Blacks could not bear arms, be employed in occupations other than farming and domestic service, or leave their jobs without forfeiting back pay. The Mississippi code required them to sign labor contracts for the year in January, and, in addition, drunkards, vagrants, beggars, "common nightwalkers," and even "mischief makers" and persons who "misspend what they earn" and who could not pay the stiff fines assessed for such misbehavior were to be "hired out . . . at public outcry" to the white persons who would take them for the shortest period in return for paying the fines. Such laws, apparently designed to get around the Thirteenth Amendment, outraged Northerners.

CONGRESS REJECTS JOHNSONIAN RECONSTRUCTION

President Johnson's attitude speeded the swing toward the Radical position. Congress passed a bill expanding and extending the Freedmen's Bureau, which had been established in March 1865 to care for refugees. The bureau, a branch of the War Department, was already exercising considerable coercive and supervisory power in the South. Now Congress sought to add to its authority in order to protect the black population. Although the bill had wide support, Johnson vetoed it, arguing that it was an unconstitutional extension of military authority in peacetime. Congress then passed a Civil Rights Act that, besides declaring specifically that blacks were citizens of the United States, denied the states the power to restrict their rights to testify in court, to make contracts for their labor, and to hold property. In other words, it put teeth in the Thirteenth Amendment.

Once again the president refused to go along, although his veto was sure to drive more moderates into the arms of the Radicals. On April 9, 1866, Congress repassed the Civil Rights Act by a two-thirds majority, the first time in American history that a major piece of legislation became law over the veto of a president. This event marked a revolution in the history of Reconstruction. Thereafter Congress, not President Johnson, had the upper hand.

The president misread northern opinion. He believed that Congress had no right to pass laws affecting the South before southern representatives had been readmitted to Congress. However, in the light of the refusal of most southern whites to grant any real power or responsibility to the freedmen (an attitude that Johnson did not condemn), the public would not accept this point of view. Johnson placed his own judgment over that of the overwhelming majority of northern voters, and this was a great error, morally and tactically. By encouraging white Southerners to resist efforts to improve the lot of blacks, Johnson played into the hands of the Radicals.

The Radicals encountered grave problems in fighting for their program. Northerners might object to the Black Codes and to seating "rebels" in Congress, but few believed in racial equality. Between 1865 and 1868, Wisconsin, Minnesota, Connecticut, Nebraska, New Jersey, Ohio, Michigan, and Pennsylvania all rejected bills granting blacks the vote.

Thus, while the Radicals sought partisan advantage in their battle with Johnson and sometimes played on war-bred passions in achieving their ends, they were taking large political risks in defense of genuinely held principles. One historian has aptly called them the "moral trustees" of the Civil War.

THE FOURTEENTH AMENDMENT

In June 1866 Congress submitted to the states a new amendment to the Constitution. The Fourteenth Amendment was, in the context of the times, a truly radical measure. Never before had newly freed slaves been granted significant political rights. For example, in the British Caribbean sugar islands, where slavery had been abolished in the 1830s, stiff property qualifications and poll taxes kept freedmen from voting. The Fourteenth Amendment was also a milestone along the road to the centralization of political power in the United States because it reduced the power of all the states. In this sense it confirmed the great change wrought by the Civil War: the growth of a more complex, more closely integrated social and economic structure requiring closer national supervision. Few people understood this aspect of the amendment at the time.

First the amendment supplied a broad definition of American citizenship: "All persons born or naturalized in the United States, and subject to the jurisdiction thereof, are citizens of the United States and of the State wherein they reside." Obviously this included blacks. Then it struck at discriminatory legislation like the Black Codes: "No State shall make or enforce any law which shall abridge the privileges or immunities of citizens of the United States; nor shall any State deprive any person of life, liberty, or property, without due process of law." The next section attempted to force the southern states to permit blacks to vote. If a state denied the vote to any class of its adult male citizens, its representation was to be reduced proportionately. Under another clause, former federal officials who had served the Confederacy were barred from holding either state or federal office unless specifically pardoned by a two-thirds vote of Congress. Finally, the Confederate debt was repudiated.

While the amendment did not specifically outlaw segregation or prevent a state from disenfranchising blacks, the southern states would have none of it.

Without them the necessary three-fourths majority of the states could not be obtained.

President Johnson vowed to make the choice between the Fourteenth Amendment and his own policy the main issue of the 1866 congressional elections. He embarked on "a swing around the circle" to rally the public to his cause. He failed dismally. Northern women objected to the implication in the amendment that black men were more fit to vote than white women, but a large majority of northern voters was determined that African Americans must have at least formal legal equality. The Republicans won better than two-thirds of the seats in both houses, together with control of all the northern state governments. Johnson emerged from the campaign discredited, the Radicals stronger and determined to have their way. The southern states, Congressman James A. Garfield of Ohio said in February 1867, have "flung back into our teeth the magnanimous offer of a generous nation. It is now our turn to act."

THE RECONSTRUCTION ACTS

Had the southern states been willing to accept the Fourteenth Amendment, coercive measures might have been avoided. Their recalcitrance and continuing indications that local authorities were persecuting blacks finally led to the passage, on March 2, 1867, of the First Reconstruction Act. This law divided the former Confederacy—exclusive of Tennessee, which had ratified the Fourteenth Amendment—into five military districts, each controlled by a major general. It gave these officers almost dictatorial power to protect the civil rights of "all persons," maintain order, and supervise the administration of justice. To rid themselves of military rule, the former states were required to adopt new state constitutions guaranteeing blacks the right to vote and disenfranchising broad classes of ex-Confederates. If the new constitutions proved satisfactory to Congress, and if the new governments ratified the Fourteenth Amendment, their representatives would be admitted to Congress and military rule ended. Johnson's veto of the act was easily overridden.

Although drastic, the Reconstruction Act was so vague that it proved unworkable. Military control was easily established. But in deference to moderate Republican views, the law had not spelled out the process by which the new constitutions were to be drawn up. Southern whites preferred the status quo, even under army control, to enfranchising blacks and retiring their own respected leaders. They made no effort to follow the steps laid down in the law. Congress therefore passed a second act, requiring the military authorities to register voters and supervise the election of delegates to constitutional conventions. A third act further clarified procedures.

Still white Southerners resisted. The laws required that the constitutions be approved by a majority of the registered voters. Simply by staying away from the polls, whites prevented ratification in state after state. At last, in March 1868, a full year after the First Reconstruction Act, Congress changed the rules again.

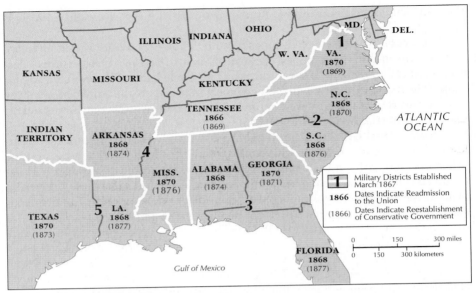

Return to the Union During Reconstruction

The constitutions were to be ratified by a majority of the voters. In June 1868 Arkansas, having fulfilled the requirements, was readmitted to the Union, and by July a sufficient number of states had ratified the Fourteenth Amendment to make it part of the Constitution. But it was not until July 1870 that the last southern state, Georgia, qualified to the satisfaction of Congress.

CONGRESS SUPREME

To carry out this program in the face of determined southern resistance required a degree of single-mindedness over a long period seldom demonstrated by an American legislature. A series of measures passed between 1866 and 1868 increased the authority of Congress over the army, over the process of amending the Constitution, and over Cabinet members and lesser appointive officers. Even the Supreme Court was affected. Its size was reduced and its jurisdiction over civil rights cases limited. Finally, in a showdown caused by emotion more than by practical considerations, the Republicans attempted to remove President Johnson from office.

The chief issue was the Tenure of Office Act of 1867, which prohibited the president from removing officials who had been appointed with the consent of the Senate without first obtaining Senate approval. In February 1868 Johnson "violated" this act by dismissing Secretary of War Edwin M. Stanton, who had been openly in sympathy with the Radicals for some time. The House, acting under the procedure set up in the Constitution for removing the president, promptly impeached him before the bar of the Senate, Chief Justice Salmon P. Chase presiding.

In the trial, Johnson's lawyers easily established that he had removed Stanton only in an effort to prove the Tenure of Office Act unconstitutional. They demonstrated that the act did not protect Stanton to begin with, since it gave Cabinet members tenure "during the term of the President by whom they may have been appointed," and Stanton had been appointed in 1862, during Lincoln's first term!

Nevertheless the Radicals pressed the charges (11 separate articles) relentlessly. To the argument that Johnson had committed no crime, the learned Senator Sumner retorted that the proceedings were "political in character" rather than judicial. Thaddeus Stevens, directing the attack on behalf of the House, warned the senators that although "no corrupt or wicked motive" could be attributed to Johnson, they would "be tortured on the gibbet of everlasting obloquy" if they did not convict him. Tremendous pressure was applied to the handful of Republican senators who were unwilling to disregard the evidence.

Seven of them resisted to the end, and the Senate failed by a single vote to convict Johnson. This was probably fortunate. The trial weakened the presidency, but if Johnson had been forced from office on such flimsy grounds, the independence of the executive might have been permanently undermined. Then the legislative branch would have become supreme.

THE FIFTEENTH AMENDMENT

The failure of the impeachment did not affect the course of Reconstruction. The president was acquitted on May 16, 1868. A few days later, the Republican National Convention nominated General Ulysses S. Grant for the presidency. At the Democratic convention Johnson had considerable support, but the delegates nominated Horatio Seymour, a former governor of New York. In November Grant won an easy victory in the Electoral College, 214 to 80, but the popular vote was close: 3 million to 2.7 million. Although he would probably have carried the Electoral College in any case, Grant's margin in the popular vote was supplied by southern blacks enfranchised under the Reconstruction acts, about 450,000 of whom supported him. On the other hand, Grant had carried Indiana by fewer than 10,000 votes and lost New York by a similar number. If blacks in these and other closely divided states had voted, Republican strength would have been greatly enhanced.

Suddenly Congress blossomed with suffrage amendments. After considerable bickering over details, the Fifteenth Amendment was sent to the states for ratification in February 1869. It forbade all the states to deny the vote to anyone "on account of race, color, or previous condition of servitude." Once again nothing was said about denial of the vote on the basis of sex, which caused feminists, such as Elizabeth Cady Stanton, to be even more outraged than they had been by the Fourteenth Amendment.

Most southern states, still under federal pressure, ratified the amendment swiftly. The same was true in most of New England and in some western states.

Bitter battles were waged in Connecticut, New York, Pennsylvania, and the states immediately north of the Ohio River, but by March 1870 most of them had ratified the amendment and it became part of the Constitution.

The debates occasioned by these conventions show that partisan advantage was not the only reason why voters approved black suffrage at last. The unfairness of a double standard of voting, North and South, the contribution of black soldiers during the war, and the hope that by passing the amendment the strife of Reconstruction could finally be ended all played a part.

When the Fifteenth Amendment went into effect, President Grant called it "the greatest civil change and . . . the most important event that has occurred since the nation came to life." The American Anti-Slavery Society formally dissolved itself, its work apparently completed. "The Fifteenth Amendment confers upon the African race the care of its own destiny," Radical Congressman James A. Garfield wrote proudly after the amendment was ratified. "It places their fortunes in their own hands."

"BLACK REPUBLICAN" RECONSTRUCTION: SCALAWAGS AND CARPETBAGGERS

The Radicals had at last succeeded in imposing their will on the South. Throughout the region former slaves had real political influence; they voted, held office, and exercised the "privileges" and enjoyed the "immunities" guaranteed them by the Fourteenth Amendment. Almost to a man they voted Republican.

The spectacle of blacks not five years removed from slavery in positions of power and responsibility attracted much attention at the time and has since been examined exhaustively by historians. But the real rulers of the "black Republican" governments were white: the "scalawags"—Southerners willing to cooperate with the Republicans because they accepted the results of the war and wished to advance their own interests—and the "carpetbaggers"—Northerners who went to the South as idealists to help the freed slaves, as employees of the federal government, or more commonly as settlers hoping to improve themselves.

The scalawags were by far the more numerous. A few were prewar politicians or well-to-do planters, men such as the Mississippi planter John L. Alcorn and Joseph E. Brown, the Confederate governor of Georgia. General James Longstreet, one of Lee's most important lieutenants, was another prominent Southerner who cooperated with the Republicans. But most were people who had supported the Whig party before the secession crisis and who saw the Republicans as the logical successors of the Whigs.

The carpetbaggers were a particularly varied lot. Most had mixed motives for coming south and personal gain was certainly among them. But so were opposition to slavery and the belief that blacks deserved to be treated decently and given a chance to get ahead in the world.

Many northern blacks became carpetbaggers: former Union soldiers, missionaries from northern black churches, and also teachers, lawyers, and other

DEBATING THE PAST

Were Reconstruction governments corrupt? Racist depictions of Reconstruction were common. This one by Thomas Nast was entitled "Colored Rule in a Reconstructed (?) State" and appeared in the influential *Harper's Weekly* (1874). The harsh assessment of Reconstruction persisted. In 1902 Columbia historian William A. Dunning declared that free slaves were mere children, incapable of holding office. Such views informed D. W. Griffith's 1915 film, *The Birth of a Nation.* In 1910 W. E. B. Du Bois, an African American scholar, was the first to applaud Reconstruction for broadening educational opportunities and democratizing government, but few historians concurred. In the 1960s, as the civil rights movement was gaining momentum, more scholars came out in support of Reconstruction. Kenneth Stampp (1965) emphasized the Reconstruction governments' attempts to protect freedmen; that same year, Joel Williamson turned Dunning's thesis on its head and endorsed nearly all aspects of Reconstruction. More recent scholars have generally taken a moderate position: Reconstruction may have failed, but its accomplishments under difficult circumstances of white opposition were substantial; see, for example, Eric Foner (1988). Certain facts are beyond argument. Black officeholders were neither numerous nor inordinately influential. None was ever elected governor of a state; fewer than a dozen and a half during the entire period served in Congress. Blacks held many minor offices and were influential in southern legislatures, although (except in South Carolina) they never made up the majority.

William A. Dunning, *Reconstruction and the Constitution* (1902), W. E. B. Du Bois, *Black Reconstruction in America* (1935), Kenneth Stampp, *The Peculiar Institution* (1965), Joel Williamson, *After Slavery* (1965), Eric Foner, *Reconstruction* (1988).

During Reconstruction, 14 blacks won election to the House of Representatives and two, Hiram Revels and Blanche K. Bruce, served in the Senate. Revels, at far left, won the Mississippi Senate seat that Jefferson Davis had once held. He later became president of Alcorn University. Congressman R. Brown Elliot, at far right, had been educated at Eton in England.

members of the small northern black professional class. Many of these became officeholders, but like southern black politicians their influence was limited.

In South Carolina and elsewhere, blacks proved in the main able and conscientious public servants: able because the best tended to rise to the top in such a fluid situation and conscientious because most of those who achieved importance sought eagerly to demonstrate the capacity of their race for self-government. Even at the local level, where the quality of officials was usually poor, there was little difference in the degree of competence displayed by white and black officeholders. In power, the blacks were not vindictive; by and large they did not seek to restrict the rights of ex-Confederates.

Not all black legislators and administrators were paragons of virtue. In South Carolina, despite their control of the legislature, they broke up into factions repeatedly and failed to press for laws that would improve the lot of poor black farm workers. The "black Republican" governments displayed qualities that grew directly from the ignorance and political inexperience of the former slaves. There was a tragicomic aspect to the South Carolina legislature during these years, its many black members—some dressed in old frock coats, others in rude farm clothes—rising to points of order and personal privilege without reason, discoursing ponderously on subjects they did not understand. But those who complained about the ignorance and irresponsibility of blacks conveniently forgot that the tendency of nineteenth-century American democracy was away from educational, financial, or any other restrictions on the franchise. Thousands of white Southerners were as illiterate and uncultured as the freedmen, yet no one suggested depriving them of the ballot.

In fact, the Radical southern governments accomplished a great deal. They spent money freely but not entirely wastefully. Tax rates zoomed, but the money financed the repair and expansion of the South's dilapidated railroad network, rebuilt crumbling levees, and expanded social services. Before the Civil War, southern planters possessed a disproportionate share of political as well as economic power, and they spent relatively little public money on education and public services of all kinds.

During Reconstruction an enormous gap had to be filled, and it took money to fill it. The Freedmen's Bureau made a major contribution. Northern religious and philanthropic organizations also did important work. Eventually, however, the state governments established and supported hospitals, asylums, and systems of free public education that, while segregated, greatly benefited everyone, whites as well as blacks. Much state money was also spent on economic development: land reclamation, repairing and expanding the war-ravaged railroads, maintaining levees.

The former slaves grasped eagerly at the opportunities to learn. Schools and other institutions were supported chiefly by property taxes, and these, of course, hit well-to-do planters hard. Hence much of the complaining about the "extravagance" of Reconstruction governments concealed traditional selfish objections to paying for public projects. Eventually the benefits of expanded government services to the entire population became clear, and when white supremacy was reestablished, most of the new services remained in force, and the corruption and inefficiency inherited from the carpetbagger governments continued.

THE RAVAGED LAND

The South's grave economic problems complicated the rebuilding of its political system. The section had never been as prosperous as the North, and wartime destruction left it desperately poor by any standard. In the long run the abolition of slavery released immeasurable quantities of human energy previously stifled, but the immediate effect was to create confusion. Freedom to move without a pass, to "see the world," was one of the former slaves' most cherished benefits of emancipation. Understandably, many at first equated legal freedom with freedom from having to earn a living, a tendency reinforced for a time by the willingness of the Freedmen's Bureau to provide rations and other forms of relief in war-devastated areas. Most, however, soon accepted the fact that they must earn a living; a small plot of land of their own ("40 acres and a mule") would complete their independence.

This objective was forcefully supported by the relentless Congressman Thaddeus Stevens, whose hatred of the planter class was pathological. "The

The Freedmen's Bureau built 4329 schools, attended by some 250,000 former slaves, in the postwar South. Many of the teachers in these schools were abolitionists or missionaries from New England. The schools drew African Americans of all ages, from children to grandparents, who were eager for the advantages offered by education.

property of the chief rebels should be seized," he stated. If the lands of the richest "70,000 proud, bloated and defiant rebels" were confiscated, the federal government would obtain 394 million acres. Every adult male ex-slave could easily be supplied with 40 acres. The beauty of his scheme, Stevens insisted, was that "nine-tenths of the [southern] people would remain untouched." Dispossessing the great planters would make the South "a safe republic," its lands cultivated by "the free labor of intelligent citizens." If the plan drove the planters into exile, "all the better."

Aside from its vindictiveness, the proposals of Stevens and other extremists were simplistic. Land without tools, seed, and other necessities would have done the freedmen little good. Congress did throw open 46 million acres of poor-quality federal land in the South to blacks under the Homestead Act, but few settled on it. Establishing former slaves on small farms with adequate financial aid would have been of incalculable benefit to them. This would have been practicable, but extremely expensive. It was not done.

The former slaves therefore had either to agree to work for their former owners or strike out on their own. White planters, influenced by the precipitous decline of sugar production in Jamaica and other Caribbean islands that had followed the abolition of slavery there, expected freed blacks to be incapable of self-directed effort. If allowed to become independent farmers, they would either starve to death or descend into barbarism. Of course the blacks did neither. True, the output of cotton and other southern staples declined precipitously after slavery was abolished. Observers soon came to the conclusion that a free black produced much less than a slave had produced. "You can't get only about two-thirds as much out of 'em now as you could when they were slaves," an Arkansas planter complained.

However, the decline in productivity was not caused by the inability of free blacks to work independently. They simply chose no longer to work like slaves. They let their children play instead of forcing them into the fields. Mothers devoted more time to childcare and housework, less to farm labor. Elderly blacks worked less.

The family life of former slaves was changed in other ways. Male authority increased when husbands became true heads of families. (Under slavery the ultimate responsibility for providing for women and children was the master's.) When blacks became citizens, the men acquired rights and powers denied to all women, such as the right to hold public office and serve on juries. Similarly, black women became more like white women, devoting themselves to separate "spheres" where their lives revolved around housekeeping and child rearing.

SHARECROPPING AND THE CROP-LIEN SYSTEM

Quite swiftly, a new agricultural system known as sharecropping emerged. Instead of cultivating the land by gang labor as in antebellum times, planters broke up their estates into small units and established on each unit a black family. The planter provided housing, agricultural implements, draft animals, seed, and other supplies, and the family provided labor. The crop was divided between planter and laborer, usually on a fifty-fifty basis. If the landlord supplied only land and housing, the laborer got a larger share. This was called share tenancy.

Sharecropping gave blacks the day-to-day control of their lives that they craved and the hope of earning enough to buy a small farm. But few blacks succeeded in this goal. As late as 1880 blacks owned less than 10 percent of the agricultural land in the South, although they made up more than half of the region's farm population. Mississippi actually prohibited the purchase of farmland by blacks.

Many white farmers in the South were also trapped by the sharecropping system and by white efforts to keep blacks in a subordinate position. New fencing laws kept them from grazing livestock on undeveloped land, a practice common before the Civil War. But the main cause of southern rural poverty for whites as well as for blacks was the lack of enough capital to finance the sharecropping system. Like their colonial ancestors, the landowners had to borrow against October's harvest to pay for April's seed. Thus the crop-lien system developed.

Under the crop-lien system, both landowner and sharecropper depended on credit supplied by local bankers, merchants, and storekeepers for everything from seed, tools, and fertilizer to overalls, coffee, and salt. Crossroads stores proliferated, and a new class of small merchants appeared. The prices of goods sold

After the Civil War, most blacks worked as sharecroppers on land owned by whites. In this photograph, black sharecroppers pick cotton, a major cash crop of the South with the owner of the land getting a share of the crop (crop-lien). The crop-lien system injured everyone. Diversified farming would have reduced the farmers' need for cash, preserved the fertility of the soil, and, by placing a premium on imagination and shrewdness, aided the best of them to rise in the world. Because the price for cotton remained low, sharecroppers often fell into debt and were tied to the land almost as tightly as under slavery.

on credit were high, adding to the burden borne by the rural population. The small southern merchants were almost equally victimized by the system, for they also lacked capital, bought goods on credit, and had to pay high interest rates.

Seen in broad perspective, the situation is not difficult to understand. The South, drained of every resource by the war, was competing for funds with the North and West, both vigorous and expanding and therefore voracious consumers of capital. Reconstruction, in the literal sense of the word, was accomplished chiefly at the expense of the standard of living of the producing classes. The crop-lien system and the small storekeeper were only agents of an economic process dictated by national, perhaps even worldwide, conditions.

Compared with the rest of the country, progress in the South was slow. Just before the Civil War cotton harvests averaged about 4 million bales. During the conflict, output fell to about half a million, and the former Confederate states did not enjoy a 4-million-bale year again until 1870. In contrast, national wheat production in 1859 was 175 million bushels and in 1878, 449 million. About 7000 miles of railroad were built in the South between 1865 and 1879; in the rest of the nation nearly 45,000 miles of track were laid.

But in the late 1870s, cotton production revived. It soon regained, and thereafter long retained, its title as "king" of the southern economy. This was true in large measure because of the crop-lien system.

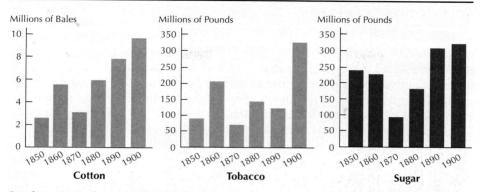

Southern Agriculture, 1850–1900
Cotton production recovered to its prewar level by 1880, but tobacco and sugar production lagged. Not until 1900 did tobacco growers have a better year than they had in 1860. The years following 1870 saw a general downward trend in wholesale prices for farm commodities. (Statistics are for the 11 states of the Confederacy.)

The South made important gains in manufacturing after the war. The tobacco industry, stimulated by the sudden popularity of the cigarette, expanded rapidly. Virginia and North Carolina tobacco towns like Richmond, Lynchburg, and Durham flourished. The exploitation of the coal and iron deposits of northeastern Alabama in the early 1870s made a boomtown of Birmingham. The manufacture of cotton cloth increased, productive capacity nearly doubling between 1865 and 1880. Yet the mills of Massachusetts alone had eight times the capacity of the entire South in 1880. Despite the increases, the South's share of the national output of manufactured goods declined sharply during the Reconstruction era.

THE WHITE BACKLASH

Radical southern governments could sustain themselves only as long as they had the support of a significant proportion of the white population, for except in South Carolina and Louisiana, the blacks were not numerous enough to win elections alone. The key to survival lay in the hands of the wealthy merchants and planters, mostly former Whigs. People of this sort had nothing to fear from black economic competition. Taking a broad view, they could see that improving the lot of the former slaves would benefit all classes.

Southern white Republicans used the Union League of America, a patriotic club founded during the war, to control the black vote. Employing secret rituals, exotic symbols, and other paraphernalia calculated to impress unsophisticated people, they enrolled the freedmen in droves and marched them to the polls en masse.

Powerless to check the League by open methods, dissident Southerners established a number of secret terrorist societies, bearing such names as the Ku Klux

Klan, the Knights of the White Camelia, and the Pale Faces. The most notorious of these organizations was the Klan, which originated in Tennessee in 1866. At first it was purely a social club, but by 1868 it had been taken over by vigilante types dedicated to driving blacks out of politics, and it was spreading rapidly across the South. Sheet-clad nightriders roamed the countryside, frightening the impressionable and chastising the defiant. Klansmen, using a weird mumbo jumbo and claiming to be the ghosts of Confederate soldiers, spread horrendous rumors and published broadsides designed to persuade the freedmen that it was unhealthy for them to participate in politics.

When intimidation failed, the Klansmen resorted to force. After being whipped by one group in Tennessee, a recently elected justice of the peace reported: "They said they had nothing particular against me . . . but they did not intend any nigger to hold office." In hundreds of cases the KKK murdered their opponents, often in the most gruesome manner.

Congress struck at the Klan with three Force Acts (1870–1871), which placed elections under federal jurisdiction and imposed fines and prison sentences on persons convicted of interfering with any citizen's exercise of the franchise. Troops were dispatched to areas where the Klan was strong, and by 1872 the federal authorities had arrested enough Klansmen to break up the organization.

Nevertheless the Klan contributed substantially to the destruction of Radical regimes in the South. Its depredations weakened the will of white Republicans (few of whom really believed in racial equality), and it intimidated many blacks, who gave up trying to exercise their rights. The fact that the army had to be called in to suppress it was a glaring illustration of the weakness of the Reconstruction governments.

Gradually it became respectable to intimidate black voters. Beginning in Mississippi in 1874, terrorism spread through the South. Instead of hiding behind masks and operating in the dark, these terrorists donned red shirts, organized into military companies, and paraded openly. Mississippi redshirts seized militant blacks and whipped them publicly. Killings were frequent. When blacks dared to fight back, heavily armed whites put them to rout. In other states similar results followed.

Before long the blacks learned to stay home on election day. One by one, "Conservative" parties—Democratic in national affairs—took over southern state governments. Intimidation was only a partial explanation of this development. The increasing solidarity of whites, northern and southern, was equally significant.

The North had subjected the South to control from Washington while preserving state sovereignty in the North itself. In the long run this discrimination proved unworkable. Many Northerners had supported the Radical policy only out of irritation with President Johnson. After his retirement their enthusiasm waned. The war was fading into the past and with it the worst of the anger it had generated.

Northern voters could still be stirred by references to the sacrifices Republicans had made to save the Union and by reminders that the Democratic party was the organization of rebels, Copperheads, and the Ku Klux Klan. "If the Devil himself were at the helm of the ship of state," wrote the novelist Lydia Maria Child in 1872, "my conscience would not allow me to aid in removing him to make room for the Democratic party." Yet emotional appeals could not convince Northerners that it was still necessary to maintain a large army in the South. In 1869 the occupying forces were down to 11,000 men. After Klan disruption and intimidation had made a farce of the 1874 elections in Mississippi, Governor Ames appealed to Washington for help. President Grant's attorney general, Edwards Pierrepont, refused to act. "The whole public are tired out with these autumnal outbreaks in the South," he told Ames. "Preserve the peace by the forces of your own state."

Nationalism was reasserting itself. Had not Washington and Jefferson been Virginians? Was not Andrew Jackson Carolina-born? Since most Northerners had little real love or respect for blacks, their interest in racial equality flagged once they felt reasonably certain that blacks would not be re-enslaved if left to their own devices in the South.

Another, much subtler force was also at work. The prewar Republican party had stressed the common interest of workers, manufacturers, and farmers in a free and mobile society, a land of equal opportunity where all could work in harmony. Southern whites had insisted that laborers must be disciplined if large enterprises were to be run efficiently. By the 1870s, as large industrial enterprises developed in the northern states, the thinking of business leaders changed—the southern argument began to make sense to them, and they became more sympathetic to the southern demand for more control over "their" labor force.

GRANT AS PRESIDENT

Other matters occupied the attention of northern voters. The expansion of industry and the rapid development of the West, stimulated by a new wave of railroad building, loomed more important to many than the fortunes of the former slaves. Beginning in 1873, when a stock market panic struck at public confidence, economic difficulties plagued the country for nearly a decade. Heated controversies arose over tariff policy, with western agricultural interests seeking to force reductions from the high levels established during the war, and over the handling of the wartime greenback paper money, with debtor groups and many manufacturers favoring further expansion of the supply of dollars and conservative merchants and bankers arguing for retiring the greenbacks in order to return to a "sound" currency.

More damaging to the Republicans was the failure of Ulysses S. Grant to live up to expectations as president. His most serious weakness as president was his failure to deal effectively with economic and social problems, but the one that injured him and the Republicans most was his inability to cope with government corruption. The worst of the scandals—such as the Whiskey Ring affair, which implicated Grant's private secretary, Orville E. Babcock, and cost the government millions in tax revenue, and the corruption of Secretary of War William W.

Belknap in the management of Indian affairs—did not become public knowledge during Grant's first term. However, in 1872 Republican reformers, alarmed by rumors of corruption and disappointed by Grant's failure to press for civil service reform, organized the Liberal Republican party and nominated Horace Greeley, the able but eccentric editor of the *New York Tribune,* for president.

The Liberal Republicans were mostly well-educated, socially prominent types—editors, college presidents, economists, along with a sprinkling of businessmen and politicians. Their liberalism was of the laissez-faire variety; they were for low tariffs and sound money, and against what they called "class legislation," meaning measures benefiting particular groups, whether labor unions or railroad companies or farm organizations. Nearly all had supported Reconstruction at the start, but by the early 1870s most were including southern blacks among the special interests that ought to be left to their own devices. Their observation of urban corruption and of unrestricted immigration led them to disparage universal suffrage, which, one of them said, "can only mean in plain English the government of ignorance and vice."

The Democrats also nominated Greeley in 1872, although he had devoted his political life to flailing the Democratic party in the *Tribune.* That surrender to expediency, together with Greeley's temperamental unsuitability for the presidency, made the campaign a fiasco for the reformers. Grant triumphed easily, with a popular majority of nearly 800,000.

Nevertheless, the defection of the Liberal Republicans hurt the Republican party in Congress. In the 1874 elections, no longer hampered as in the presidential contest by Greeley's notoriety and Grant's fame, the Democrats carried the House of Representatives. It was clear that the days of military rule in the South were ending. By the end of 1875 only three southern states—South Carolina, Florida, and Louisiana—were still under Republican control.

The Republican party in the South was "dead as a doornail," a reporter noted. He reflected the opinion of thousands when he added: "We ought to have a sound sensible republican . . . for the next President as a measure of safety; but only on the condition of absolute noninterference in Southern local affairs, for which there is no further need or excuse."

THE DISPUTED ELECTION OF 1876

Against this background the presidential election of 1876 took place. Since corruption in government was the most widely discussed issue, the Republicans passed over their most attractive political personality, the dynamic James G. Blaine, Speaker of the House of Representatives, who had been connected with some chicanery involving railroad securities. Instead they nominated Governor Rutherford B. Hayes of Ohio, a former general with an untarnished reputation. The Democrats picked Governor Samuel J. Tilden of New York, a wealthy lawyer who had attracted national attention for his part in breaking up the Tweed Ring in New York City.

This cartoon—"A Strong Man at the Head of Government"—pokes fun at Grant, whose presidency was weighed down with scandal. Grant did not cause the corruption, nor did he participate in the remotest way in the rush to "fatten at the public trough," as the reformers of the day might have put it. But he did nothing to prevent the scandals that disgraced his administration. Out of a misplaced belief in the sanctity of friendship, he protected some of the worst culprits and allowed calculating tricksters to use his good name and the prestige of his office to advance their own interests at the country's expense. "Mistakes have been made, as all can see and I admit," Grant conceded in his final report to Congress.

In November early returns indicated that Tilden had carried New York, New Jersey, Connecticut, Indiana, and all the southern states, including Louisiana, South Carolina, and Florida, where Republican regimes were still in control. This seemed to give him 203 electoral votes to Hayes's 165, and a popular plurality in the neighborhood of 250,000 out of more than 8 million votes cast. However, Republican leaders had anticipated the possible loss of Florida, South Carolina, and Louisiana and were prepared to use their control of the election machinery in those states to throw out sufficient Democratic ballots to alter the results if doing so would change the national outcome. Realizing that the electoral votes of those states were exactly enough to elect their man, they telegraphed their henchmen on the scene, ordering them to go into action. The local Republicans then invalidated Democratic ballots in wholesale lots and filed returns showing Hayes the winner. Naturally the local Democrats protested vigorously and filed their own returns.

The Constitution provides (Article II, Section 1) that presidential electors must meet in their respective states to vote and forward the results to "the Seat of the Government." There, it adds, "the President of the Senate shall, in the Presence of the Senate and House of Representatives, open all the Certificates, and the Votes shall then be counted." But who was to do the counting? The House was Democratic, the Senate Republican; neither would agree to allow the other to do the job. On January 29, 1877, scarcely a month before inauguration day, Congress created an electoral commission to decide the disputed cases.

Evidence presented before the commission revealed a disgraceful picture of election shenanigans. On the one hand, in all three disputed states Democrats had clearly cast a majority of the votes; on the other, it was unquestionable that many blacks had been forcibly prevented from voting.

In truth, both sides were shamefully corrupt. The governor of Louisiana was reported willing to sell his state's electoral votes for $200,000. The Florida election board was supposed to have offered itself to Tilden for the same price. "That seems to be the standard figure," Tilden remarked ruefully.

Most modern authorities take the view that in a fair election the Republicans would have carried South Carolina and Louisiana but that Florida would have gone to Tilden, giving him the election, 188 electoral votes to 181. In the last analysis, this opinion has been arrived at simply by counting white and black noses: Blacks were in the majority in South Carolina and Louisiana. Amid the tension and confusion of early 1877, however, even a Solomon would have been hard-pressed to judge rightly amid the rumors, lies, and contradictory statements, and the electoral commission was not composed of Solomons. The Democrats had some hopes that Justice Bradley would be sympathetic to their case, for he was known to be opposed to harsh Reconstruction policies. On the eve of the commission's decision in the Florida controversy, he was apparently ready to vote in favor of Tilden. But the Republicans subjected him to tremendous political pressure. When he read his opinion on February 8, it was for Hayes. Thus, by a vote of 8 to 7, the commission awarded Florida's electoral votes to the Republicans.

The rest of the proceedings was routine. The commission assigned all the disputed electoral votes (including one in Oregon where the Democratic governor had seized on a technicality to replace a single Republican elector with a Democrat) to Hayes.

Democratic institutions, shaken by the South's refusal to go along with the majority in 1860 and by the suppression of civil rights during the rebellion, and further weakened by military intervention and the intimidation of blacks in the South during Reconstruction, seemed now a farce. According to Tilden's campaign manager, angry Democrats in 15 states, chiefly war veterans, were readying themselves to march on Washington to force the inauguration of Tilden. Tempers flared in Congress, where some spoke ominously of a filibuster that would prevent the recording of the electoral vote and leave the country, on March 4, with no president at all.

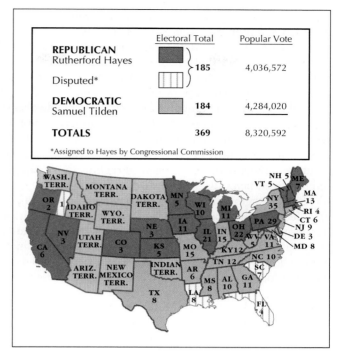

	Electoral Total	Popular Vote
REPUBLICAN Rutherford Hayes	} 185	4,036,572
Disputed*		
DEMOCRATIC Samuel Tilden	184	4,284,020
TOTALS	369	8,320,592

*Assigned to Hayes by Congressional Commission

The Compromise of 1877

THE COMPROMISE OF 1877

Forces for compromise had been at work behind the scenes in Washington for some time. Although northern Democrats threatened to fight to the last ditch, many southern Democrats were willing to accept Hayes if he would promise to remove the troops and allow the southern states to manage their internal affairs by themselves. Ex-Whig planters and merchants who had reluctantly abandoned the carpetbag governments and who sympathized with Republican economic policies hoped that by supporting Hayes they might contribute to the restoration of the two-party system that had been destroyed in the South during the 1850s. Ohio Congressman James A. Garfield urged Hayes to find "some discreet way" of showing these Southerners that he favored "internal improvements." Hayes replied: "Your views are so nearly the same as mine that I need not say a word."

Tradition has it that a great compromise between the sections was worked out during a dramatic meeting at the Wormley Hotel[2] in Washington on February 26. Actually the negotiations were drawn out and informal, and the Wormley conference was but one of many. With the tacit support of many Democrats, the electoral vote was counted by the president of the Senate on March 2, and Hayes was declared elected, 185 votes to 184.

---

[2]*Ironically, the hotel was owned by James Wormley, reputedly the wealthiest black in Washington.*

Like all compromises, this agreement was not entirely satisfactory; like most, it was not honored in every detail. Hayes recalled the last troops from South Carolina and Louisiana in April. He appointed a former Confederate general, David M. Key of Tennessee, postmaster general and delegated to him the congenial task of finding Southerners willing to serve their country as officials of a Republican administration. But the alliance of ex-Whigs and northern Republicans did not flourish; the South remained solidly Democratic. The major significance of the compromise, one of the great intersectional political accommodations of American history, was that it ended Reconstruction and inaugurated a new political order in the South. More than the Constitutional amendments and federal statutes, this new regime would shape the destinies of the four million freedmen.

For most, this future was to be bleak. Forgotten in the North, manipulated and then callously rejected by the South, rebuffed by the Supreme Court, voiceless in national affairs, they and their descendants were condemned in the interests of sectional harmony to lives of poverty, indignity, and little hope. Meanwhile, the rest of the United States continued its golden march toward wealth and power.

MILESTONES

1863	Lincoln announces "Ten Percent Plan" for Reconstruction
1865	Federal government sets up Freedmen's Bureau
	Lee surrenders at Appomattox Court House
	Lincoln is assassinated; Andrew Johnson becomes president
	Johnson issues amnesty proclamation
	States ratify Thirteenth Amendment abolishing slavery
1865–1866	Southern states enact Black Codes
1866	Civil Rights Act passes over Johnson's veto
	Johnson campaigns for his Reconstruction policy
1867	First Reconstruction Act puts former Confederacy under military rule
	Tenure of Office Act protects Senate appointees
1868	House of Representatives impeaches Johnson
	Fourth Reconstruction Act requires a majority of Southern voters to ratify state consititutions
	Senate acquits Johnson
	States ratify Fourteenth Amendment extending rights to freed slaves
	Ulysses S. Grant is elected president
	Ku Klux Klan uses intimidation and force throughout South
1870	States ratify Fifteenth Amendment granting black suffrage
1870–1871	Force (Ku Klux Klan) Act destroys Klan
1872	Liberal Republican party nominates Horace Greeley for president
	Grant is reelected president
1876	Rutherford B. Hayes runs against Samuel Tilden in disputed presidential election
1877	Electoral Commission awards disputed votes to Rutherford B. Hayes who becomes president
	Hayes agrees to Compromise of 1877

17

IN THE WAKE OF WAR

After Appomattox the immense resources of the United States, combined with the high value most Americans assigned to work and achievement, made the people strongly materialistic. From colonial times they had assumed that prosperity was the natural state of things, and they had shown an inordinate respect for wealth. The Civil War further encouraged the glorification of money and the things it could buy. The North's capacity to produce the tools of war had helped preserve the Union; the role of businessmen and manufacturers in winning the struggle was clear to every soldier from General Grant to the lowliest private.

After the failures of Reconstruction, Americans seemed even more enamored of material values. They were tired of sacrifice, eager to act for themselves. Never especially noted for their sophistication, taste, or interest in preserving the resources of the country, the people now tolerated the grossest kind of waste and seemed to care little about corruption in high places, so long as no one interfered with their personal pursuit of profit. Mark Twain, raised in an earlier era, called this a Gilded Age, dazzling on the surface, base metal below. A later writer, Vernon Parrington, named the period the Great Barbecue, a time when everyone rushed to gobble up the national inheritance like hungry picnickers crowding around the savory roast at one of the big political outings common in those years.

CONGRESS ASCENDANT

A succession of weak presidents presided over the White House after the Civil War. Although the impeachment proceedings against Andrew Johnson had failed, Congress dominated the government. Within Congress, the Senate generally overshadowed the House of Representatives. In his novel *Democracy* (1880), the cynical Henry Adams wrote that the United States had a "government of the people, by the people, for the benefit of Senators." Critics called the Senate a "rich man's club," and it did contain many millionaires, among them Leland Stanford, founder of the Central Pacific Railroad; the mining tycoon James G. "Bonanza" Fair of Nevada; Philetus Sawyer, a self-made Wisconsin lumberman; and Nelson Aldrich of Rhode Island, whose wealth derived from banking and a host of corporate connections. However, the true sources of the Senate's influence lay in the long tenure of many of its members (which enabled them to master the craft of politics), in the fact that it was small enough to encourage real debate, and in its long-established reputation for wisdom, intelligence, and statesmanship.

The House of Representatives, on the other hand, was one of the most disorderly and inefficient legislative bodies in the world. "As I make my notes," a reporter wrote in 1882 while sitting in the House gallery,

> I see a dozen men reading newspapers with their feet on their desks. . . . "Pig Iron" Kelley of Pennsylvania has dropped his newspaper and is paring his fingernails. . . . The vile odor of . . . tobacco . . . rises from the two-for-five-cents cigars in the mouths of the so-called gentlemen below. . . . They chew, too! Every desk has a spittoon of pink and gold china beside it to catch the filth from the statesman's mouth.

The great political parties professed undying enmity to each other, but they seldom took clearly opposing positions on the questions of the day. Democrats were separated from Republicans more by accidents of geography, religious affiliation, ethnic background, and emotion than by economic issues. Questions of state and local importance, unrelated to national politics, often determined the outcome of congressional elections and thus who controlled the federal government.

The fundamental division between Democrats and Republicans was sectional, a result of the Civil War. The South, after the political rights of blacks had been drastically circumscribed, became heavily Democratic. Most of New England was solidly Republican. Elsewhere the two parties stood in fair balance, although the Republicans tended to have the advantage. A preponderance of the well-to-do, cultured Northerners were Republicans. Perhaps in reaction to this concentration, immigrants, Catholics, and—except for blacks—other minority groups tended to vote Democratic. But there were so many exceptions that these generalizations are of little practical importance. German and Scandinavian immigrants usually voted Republican; many powerful business leaders supported the Democrats.

The bulk of the people—farmers, laborers, shopkeepers, white-collar work-ers—distributed their ballots fairly evenly between the two parties in most elec-tions; the balance of political power after 1876 was almost perfect—"the most spectacular degree of equilibrium in American history." Between 1856 and 1912 the Democrats elected a president only twice (1884 and 1892), but most contests were extremely close. Majorities in both the Senate and the House fluctuated continually. Between 1876 and 1896 the "dominant" Republican party con-trolled both houses of Congress and the presidency at the same time for only one 2-year period.

THE POLITICAL AFTERMATH OF WAR

Four issues obsessed politicians in these years. The first was the "bloody shirt." The term, which became part of the language after a Massachusetts congressman dramatically displayed to his colleagues in the House the blood-stained shirt of an Ohio carpetbagger who had been flogged by terrorists in Mississippi, referred to the tactic of reminding the electorate of the northern states that the men who had taken the South out of the Union and precipitated the Civil War had been Democrats and that they and their descendants were still Democrats. Should their party regain power, former rebels would run the government and undo all the work accomplished at such sacrifice during the war. "Every man that endeav-ored to tear down the old flag," a Republican orator proclaimed in 1876, "was a Democrat. Every man that tried to destroy this nation was a Democrat. . . . The man that assassinated Abraham Lincoln was a Democrat. . . . Soldiers, every scar you have on your heroic bodies was given you by a Democrat."

Every scoundrel or incompetent who sought office under the Republican banner waved the bloody shirt in order to divert the attention of northern voters from his own shortcomings, and the technique worked so well that many decent candidates could not resist the temptation to employ it in close races. Nothing, of course, so effectively obscured the real issues of the day.

Intimately related to the issue of the bloody shirt was the question of rights for blacks. Throughout this period Republicans vacillated between trying to build up their organization in the South by appealing to black voters—which re-quired them to make sure that blacks in the South could vote—and trying to win conservative white support by stressing economic issues such as the tariff. When the former strategy seemed wise, they waved the bloody shirt with vigor; in the latter case, they piously announced that the blacks' future was "as safe in the hands of one party as it is in the other."

The question of veterans' pensions also bore a close relationship to the bloody shirt issue. Following the Civil War, Union soldiers founded the Grand Army of the Republic (GAR). By 1890 the organization had a membership of 409,000. The GAR put immense pressure on Congress, first for aid to veterans with service-connected disabilities, then for those with any disability, and eventu-ally for all former Union soldiers. Republican politicians played on the emotions of the former soldiers by waving the bloody shirt, but the tough-minded leaders of the GAR demanded that they prove their sincerity by treating in open-handed fashion the warriors whose blood had stained the shirt.

The second perennial issue in post–Civil War politics was the tariff. Despite considerable loose talk about free trade, almost no one in the United States except for a handful of professional economists, most of them college professors, believed in eliminating duties on imports. Manufacturers desired protective tariffs to keep out competing products, and a majority of their workers were convinced that wage levels would fall if goods produced by cheap foreign labor entered the United States untaxed. Many farmers supported protection, although almost no competing agricultural products were being imported. Congressman William McKinley of Ohio, who reputedly could make reciting a tariff schedule sound like poetry, stated the majority opinion in the clearest terms: high tariffs foster the growth of industry and thus create jobs. "Reduce the tariff and labor is the first to suffer," he said.

The third political issue in this period was currency reform. During the Civil War, the government, faced with obligations it could not meet by taxing or borrowing, suspended specie payments and issued about $450 million in paper money. The greenbacks did not command the full confidence of a people accustomed to money readily convertible into gold or silver. Greenbacks seemed to threaten inflation, for how could one trust the government not to issue them in wholesale lots to avoid passing unpopular tax laws? Thus, when the war ended, strong sentiment developed for withdrawing the greenbacks from circulation and returning to a bullion standard. "By a law resting on the concurring judgment . . . of mankind in all ages and countries, the precious metals have been the measure of value," one politician wrote. "That law can no more be repealed by act of Congress than the law of gravitation."

In fact, beginning during Reconstruction, prices declined sharply. The deflation increased the real income of bondholders and other creditors but injured debtors. Farmers were particularly hard hit, for many of them had borrowed heavily during the wartime boom to finance expansion.

Currency reform was a political issue of real significance. Many groups supported some kind of currency inflation. A National Greenback party nominated Peter Cooper, an iron manufacturer, for president in 1876. Cooper received only 81,000 votes, but a new Greenback Labor party polled over a million in 1878, electing 14 congressmen. However, the major parties refused to confront each other over the currency issue. While Republicans professed to be the party of sound money, most western Republicans favored expansion of the currency. And while one wing of the Democrats flirted with the Greenbackers, the conservative, or "Bourbon," Democrats favored deflation as much as Republicans did. Under various administrations steps were taken to increase or decrease the amount of money in circulation, but the net effect on the economy was not significant.

The fourth major political issue of these years was civil service reform. That the federal bureaucracy needed overhauling nearly everyone agreed. As American society grew larger and more complex, the government necessarily took on more functions. The need for professional administration increased. The number of federal employees rose from 53,000 in 1871 to 256,000 at the end of the century. Corruption flourished; waste and inefficiency were the normal state of affairs. The collection of tariff duties offered perhaps the greatest opportunity for corruption. The New York Custom House, one observer wrote in 1872, teemed with "corrupting merchants and their clerks and runners, who think that all men can be bought, and . . . corrupt swarms [of clerks], who shamelessly seek their price."

With a succession of relatively ineffective presidents and a Congress that squandered its energies on private bills, pork-barrel projects, and other trivia, the administration of the government was strikingly inefficient.

Every honest observer could see the need for reform, but the politicians refused to surrender the power of dispensing government jobs to their lieutenants without regard for their qualifications. They argued that patronage was the lifeblood of politics, that parties could not function without armies of loyal political workers, and that the workers expected and deserved the rewards of office when their efforts were crowned with victory at the polls. Typical was the attitude of the New York assemblyman who, according to Theodore Roosevelt, had "the same idea about Public Life and the Civil Service that a vulture has of a dead sheep." When reformers suggested establishing the most modest kind of professional, nonpartisan civil service, politicians of both parties subjected them to every kind of insult and ridicule even though both the Democratic and Republican parties regularly wrote civil service reform planks into their platforms.

BLACKS AFTER RECONSTRUCTION

Minorities were treated with callousness and contempt in the postwar decades. That the South would deal harshly with the former slaves once federal control was relaxed probably should have been expected. Men like Governor Wade Hampton of South Carolina had promised to respect black civil rights. "We . . . will secure to every citizen, the lowest as well as the highest, black as well as white, full and equal protection in the enjoyment of all his rights under the Constitution," Hampton said in 1877. This pledge was not kept.

President Hayes had urged blacks to trust southern whites. A new Era of Good Feelings had dawned, he announced after making a goodwill tour of the South shortly after his inauguration. By December 1877 he had been sadly disillusioned. "By state legislation, by frauds, by intimidation, and by violence of the most atrocious character, colored citizens have been deprived of the right of suffrage," he wrote in his diary. However, he did nothing to remedy the situation. Frederick Douglass called Hayes's policy "sickly conciliation."

Hayes's successors in the 1880s did no better. "Time is the only cure," President James Garfield said, thereby confessing that he had no policy at all. President Chester Arthur gave federal patronage to antiblack groups in an effort to split the Democratic South. In President Grover Cleveland's day blacks had scarcely a friend in high places, North or South. In 1887 Cleveland explained to

An 1887 cartoon indicting the Senate for closely attending to the Big (read, fat) Trusts rather than to the needs of the public (whose "entrance" to the Senate is "closed"). Drawn by Joseph Keppler, a caricaturist who was born and trained in Germany, this type of grotesque satire greatly influenced late nineteenth-century American comic arts.

a correspondent why he opposed "mixed schools." Expert opinion, the president said, believed "that separate schools were of much more benefit for the colored people." Hayes, Garfield, and Arthur were Republicans, Cleveland a Democrat; party made little difference. Both parties subscribed to hypocritical statements about equality and constitutional rights, and neither did anything to implement them.

For a time blacks were not totally disenfranchised in the South. Rival white factions tried to manipulate them, and corruption flourished as widely as in the machine-dominated wards of the northern cities. In the 1890s, however, the southern states, led by Mississippi, began to deprive blacks of the vote despite the Fifteenth Amendment. Poll taxes raised a formidable economic barrier, one that also disenfranchised many poor whites. Literacy tests completed the work; a number of states provided a loophole for illiterate whites by including an "understanding" clause whereby an illiterate person could qualify by demonstrating an ability to explain the meaning of a section of the state constitution when an election official read it to him. Blacks who attempted to take the test were uniformly declared to have failed it.

In *Plessy* v. *Ferguson* (1896), the Supreme Court ruled that even in places of public accommodation, such as railroads and, by implication, schools, segregation was legal as long as facilities of equal quality were provided. "If one race be inferior to the other socially, the Constitution of the United States cannot put them upon the same plane." In a noble dissent in the *Plessy* case, Justice John

Marshall Harlan protested this line of argument. "Our Constitution is color-blind," he said. "The arbitrary separation of citizens, on the basis of race . . . is a badge of servitude wholly inconsistent with civil freedom. . . . The two races in this country are indissolubly linked together, and the interests of both require that the common government of all shall not permit the seeds of race hatred to be planted under the sanction of law."

More than half a century was to pass before the Court came around to Harlan's reasoning and reversed the *Plessy* decision. Meanwhile, total segregation was imposed throughout the South. Separate schools, prisons, hospitals, recreational facilities, and even cemeteries were provided for blacks, and these were almost never equal to those available to whites.

Most Northerners supported the government and the Court. Newspapers presented a stereotyped, derogatory picture of blacks, no matter what the circumstances. Northern magazines, even high-quality publications such as *Harper's, Scribner's,* and *The Century,* repeatedly made blacks the butt of crude jokes.

The southern insistence on segregating the public schools, buttressed by the separate but equal decision of the Supreme Court in *Plessy* v. *Ferguson,* imposed a crushing financial burden on poor, sparsely settled communities, and the dominant opinion that blacks were not really educable did not encourage these communities to make special efforts in their behalf.

BOOKER T. WASHINGTON: A "REASONABLE" CHAMPION FOR BLACKS

Southern blacks reacted to this deplorable situation in a variety of ways. Some sought redress in racial pride and what would later be called black nationalism. Some became so disaffected that they tried to revive the African colonization movement. "Africa is our home," insisted Bishop Henry M. Turner, a huge, plainspoken man who had served as an army chaplain during the war and as a member of the Georgia legislature during Reconstruction. "Every man that has the sense of an animal must see there is no future in this country for the Negro." Another militant, T. Thomas Fortune, editor of the New York *Age* and founder of the Afro-American League (1887), called on blacks to demand full civil rights, better schools, and fair wages and to fight against discrimination of every sort. "Let us stand up like men in our own organization," he urged. "If others use . . . violence to combat our peaceful arguments, it is not for us to run away from violence."

For a time, militancy and black separatism won few adherents among southern blacks. For one thing, life was better than it had been under slavery. Segregation actually helped southern blacks who became barbers, undertakers, restaurateurs, and shopkeepers because whites were reluctant to supply such services to blacks. Even when whites competed with black businesses, the resentment caused by segregation led blacks to patronize establishments run by people of their own race. According to the most conservative estimates, the living stan-

Photograph of a 1902 history class at Tuskegee Institute, a coeducational school for African Americans in east-central Alabama. Booker T. Washington was its principal from its incorporation in 1881 until his death in 1915. It is now Tuskegee University.

dard of the average southern black more than doubled between 1865 and 1900. But this only made many southern whites more angry and vindictive.

This helps explain the tactics of Booker T. Washington, one of the most extraordinary Americans of that generation. Washington had been born a slave in Virginia in 1856. Laboriously he obtained an education, supporting himself while a student by working as a janitor. In 1881, with the financial help of northern philanthropists, he founded Tuskegee Institute in Alabama. His experiences convinced Washington that blacks must lift themselves up by their own bootstraps but that they must also accommodate themselves to white prejudices. A persuasive speaker and a brilliant fund-raiser, he soon developed a national reputation as a "reasonable" champion of his race. (In 1891 Harvard awarded him an honorary degree.)

In 1895 Washington made a now-famous speech to a mixed audience at the Cotton States International Exposition in Atlanta. To the blacks he said: "Cast down your bucket where you are," by which he meant stop fighting segregation and second-class citizenship and concentrate on learning useful skills. "Dignify and glorify common labor," he urged. "Agitation of questions of racial equality is the extremest folly." Progress up the social and economic ladder would come not from "artificial forcing" but from self-improvement. "There is as much dignity in tilling a field as in writing a poem."

Washington asked the whites of what he called "our beloved South" to lend the blacks a hand in their efforts to advance themselves. If you will do so, he promised, you will be "surrounded by the most patient, faithful, law-abiding, and unresentful people that the world has seen."

This "Atlanta Compromise" delighted white Southerners and won Washington financial support in every section of the country. He became one of the most powerful men in the United States, consulted by presidents, in close touch with business and philanthropic leaders, and capable of influencing in countless unobtrusive ways the fate of millions of blacks.

Blacks responded to the compromise with mixed feelings. Accepting Washington's approach might relieve them of many burdens and dangers. Being obsequious might, like discretion, be the better part of valor. But Washington was asking them to give up specific rights in return for vague promises of future help. The cost was high in surrendered personal dignity and lost hopes of obtaining real justice.

Washington's career illustrates the terrible dilemma that American blacks have always faced: the choice between confrontation and accommodation. This choice was particularly difficult in the late nineteenth century.

Washington chose accommodation. Today it is easy to condemn him as a toady but it is difficult to see how, during his time, a more aggressive policy could have succeeded. One can even interpret the Atlanta Compromise as a subtle form of black nationalism; in a way, Washington was not urging blacks to accept inferiority and racial slurs but to ignore them. His own behavior lends force to this view, for his method of operating was indeed subtle, even devious. In public he minimized the importance of civil and political rights and accepted separate but equal facilities—if they were truly equal. Behind the scenes he lobbied against restrictive measures, marshaled large sums of money to fight test cases in the courts, and worked hard in northern states to organize the black vote and make sure that black political leaders got a share of the spoils of office. He may not have been an admirable man, but he was a useful one. His defects point up more the unlovely aspects of the age than those of his own character.

WHITE VIOLENCE AND VENGEANCE

By the time of the Atlanta Compromise, however, Washington's calls for "sagacious silence," as one black militant put it, could scarcely be heard over the anguished cries of black victims of white violence. For decades, some southern whites had tried to replace the legal subjugation of slavery with psychological subjugation through terror. "They had to have a license to kill anything but a nigger," a black Southerner recalled. "We was always in season." Each year from 1890 through 1910, nearly a hundred blacks were lynched.

These numbers, which omit those blacks who were executed after biased though nominally legal trials, fail to tell the whole story of the intensification of violence against blacks. An example was the lynching in 1899 of Sam Hose in a town outside Atlanta. Hose, a black laborer, killed his boss in self-defense. He was seized by a white mob and chained to a tree. His ears, fingers, toes, and genitals were cut off and his face was skinned. Then, while still alive, he was doused with kerosene and set on fire. A crowd numbering in the thousands watched, in the words of one newspaper account, "with unfeigning satisfaction." The dead man's body parts were auctioned: small bones went for 25 cents; his liver, "crisply cooked," for 10 cents.

White fears were excited by feverish rumors of black males as rapists and predators. "There is a black vampire hovering over our beloved North Carolina," Rebecca Strowd warned the White Government Leagues in 1898. Violence and violent rhetoric succeeded in disfranchising southern black men and driving them, often literally, out of public spaces. Ironically, this created an opportunity for black women to fill the leadership void, taking increasingly prominent roles as spokespersons in religious and reform associations.

The public activities of black women reformers and of white supremacists such as Rebecca Strowd contradicted ideals of feminine domesticity, but their arguments affirmed middle-class sensibilities. Thus black women insisted that whites uphold Christian brotherhood, while women such as Strowd called on white men to do their duty in protecting their womenfolk. By advancing middle-class ideology, however, these women distanced themselves from the working classes of both races. Few male sharecroppers or industrial workers could hope to earn enough to enable their wives to devote themselves exclusively to the home or to the cultivation of middle-class proprieties. And many working-class women, having sampled the independence of paid work, were unconvinced of the appeal of domesticity.

THE WEST AFTER THE CIVIL WAR

Many parts of the West had as large a percentage of foreign-born residents as the populous eastern states—nearly a third of all Californians were foreign-born, as were more than 40 percent of Nevadans and over half the residents of Idaho and Arizona. There were, of course, large populations of Spanish-speaking Americans of Mexican origin all over the Southwest. Chinese and Irish laborers were pouring into California by the thousands, and there were substantial numbers of Germans in Texas. Germans, Scandinavians, and other Europeans were also numerous on the High Plains east of the Rockies.

Although the image of the West as the land of great open spaces is accurate enough, the region contained several bustling cities. San Francisco, with a population approaching 250,000 in the late 1870s, had long outgrown its role as a rickety boomtown where the forty-niners bought supplies and squandered whatever wealth they had sifted from the streams of the Sierras. Though still an important warehouse and supply center, the city had become the commercial and financial heart of the Pacific Coast and a center of light manufacturing, food processing, and machine shops. Denver, San Antonio, and Salt Lake City were far smaller, but growing rapidly and equally "urban."

There was, in short, no one West, no typical Westerner. If the economy was predominantly agricultural and extractive, it was also commercial and entering the early stages of industrial development. The seeds of such large enterprises as

Wells Fargo, Levi Strauss, and half a dozen important department store empires were sown in the immediate postwar decades.

Beginning in the mid-1850s a steady flow of Chinese migrated to the United States, most of them to the west coast. About four or five thousand came each year, until the negotiation of the Burlingame Treaty of 1868, the purpose of which was to provide cheap labor for railroad construction crews. Thereafter the annual influx more than doubled, although before 1882 it exceeded 20,000 only twice. When the railroads were completed and the Chinese began to compete with native workers, a great cry of resentment went up on the west coast. Riots broke out in San Francisco in 1877. Chinese workers were called "groveling worms," "more slavish and brutish than the beasts that roam the fields." The California constitution of 1879 denied the right to vote to any "native of China" along with idiots, the insane, and persons convicted of "any infamous crime."

When Chinese immigration increased in 1882 to nearly 40,000, the protests reached such a peak that Congress passed a law prohibiting all Chinese immigration for ten years. Later legislation extended the ban indefinitely.

THE PLAINS INDIANS

For 250 years the Indians had been driven back steadily, yet on the eve of the Civil War they still inhabited roughly half the United States. By the time of Hayes's inauguration, however, the Indians had been shattered as independent peoples, and in another decade the survivors were penned up on reservations, the government committed to a policy of extinguishing their way of life.

In 1860 the survivors of most of the eastern tribes were living peacefully in Indian Territory, what is now Oklahoma. In California the forty-niners had made short work of the local tribes. Elsewhere in the West—in the deserts of the Great Basin between the Sierras and the Rockies, in the mountains themselves, and on the semiarid, grass-covered plains between the Rockies and the edge of white civilization in eastern Kansas and Nebraska—nearly a quarter of a million Indians dominated the land.

By far the most important lived on the High Plains. From the Blackfoot of southwestern Canada and the Sioux of Minnesota and the Dakotas to the Cheyenne of Colorado and Wyoming and the Comanche of northern Texas, the Plains tribes possessed a generally uniform culture. All lived by hunting the hulking American bison, or buffalo, which ranged over the Plains by the millions. The buffalo provided the Indians with food, clothing, and even shelter, for the famous Indian tepee was covered with hides. On the treeless Plains, dried buffalo dung was used for fuel. The buffalo was also an important symbol in Indian religion.

Although they seemed the epitome of freedom, pride, and self-reliance, the Plains Indians had begun to fall under the sway of white power. They eagerly adopted the products of the more technically advanced culture—cloth, metal tools, weapons, cheap decorations. However, the most important thing the whites gave them had nothing to do with technology: It was the horse.

After the start of the gold rush the need to link the East with California meant that the tribes were pushed aside. Deliberately the government in

An Oglala Sioux named Kills Two painted this portrayal of an Indian horse dance. Horses were vital to survival for the Sioux, as their inclusion in such ceremonies demonstrates.

Washington prepared the way. In 1851 Thomas Fitzpatrick—an experienced mountain man, a founder of the Rocky Mountain Fur Company, scout for the first large group of settlers to Oregon in 1841 and for American soldiers in California during the Mexican War, and now an Indian agent—summoned a great "council" of the tribes. About 10,000 Indians, representing nearly all the Plains tribes, gathered that September at Horse Creek, 37 miles east of Fort Laramie, in what is now Wyoming.

The Indians respected Fitzpatrick, who had recently married a woman who was half Indian. At Horse Creek he persuaded each tribe to accept definite limits to its hunting grounds. For example, the Sioux nations were to stay north of the Platte River, and the Cheyenne and Arapaho were to confine themselves to the Colorado foothills. In return the Indians were promised gifts and annual payments. This policy, known as "concentration," was designed to cut down on intertribal warfare and—far more important—to enable the government to negotiate separately with each tribe. It was the classic strategy of divide and conquer.

Although it made a mockery of diplomacy to treat Indian tribes as though they were European powers, the United States maintained that each tribe was a sovereign nation, to be dealt with as an equal in solemn treaties. Both sides knew that this was not the case. When Indians agreed to meet in council, they were tacitly admitting defeat. They seldom drove hard bargains or broke off negotiations. Moreover, tribal chiefs had only limited power; young braves frequently refused to respect agreements made by their elders.

INDIAN WARS

The government showed little interest in honoring agreements with Indians. No sooner had the Kansas-Nebraska bill become law than the Kansas, Omaha, Pawnee, and Yankton Sioux tribes began to feel pressure for further concessions of territory. A gold rush into Colorado in 1859 sent thousands of greedy prospectors across the Plains to drive the Cheyenne and Arapaho from land guaranteed them in 1851. By 1860 most of Kansas and Nebraska had been cleared. Other trouble developed in the Sioux country. Thus it happened that in 1862, after federal troops had been pulled out of the West for service against the Confederacy, most of the Plains Indians rose up against the whites. For five years intermittent but bloody clashes kept the entire area in a state of alarm.

This was guerrilla warfare, with all its horror and treachery. In 1864 a party of Colorado militia fell on an unsuspecting Cheyenne community at Sand Creek and killed an estimated 450. "Kill and scalp all, big and little," Colonel J. M. Chivington, a minister in private life, told his men. A white observer described the scene: "They were scalped, their brains knocked out; the men used their knives, ripped open women, clubbed little children, knocked them in the head with their guns, beat their brains out, mutilated their bodies in every sense of the word."

In turn the Indians slaughtered dozens of isolated white families, ambushed small parties, and fought many successful skirmishes against troops and militia. They achieved their most notable triumph in December 1866, when the Oglala Sioux, under their great chief Red Cloud, wiped out a party of 82 soldiers under Captain W. J. Fetterman. Red Cloud fought ruthlessly, but only when goaded by the construction of the Bozeman Trail, a road through the heart of the Sioux hunting grounds in southern Montana.[1]

In 1867 the government tried a new strategy. The "concentration" policy had evidently not gone far enough. All the Plains Indians would be confined to two small reservations, one in the Black Hills of the Dakota Territory, the other in Oklahoma, and forced to become farmers. At two great conclaves held in 1867 and 1868 at Medicine Lodge Creek and Fort Laramie, the principal chiefs yielded to the government's demands.

Many Indians refused to abide by these agreements. With their whole way of life at stake, they raged across the Plains like a prairie fire—and were almost as destructive.

That a relative handful of "savages," without central leadership, could hold off the cream of the army, battle-hardened in the Civil War, can be explained by the character of the vast, trackless country and the ineptness of many American military commanders. Indian leadership was also poor in that few chiefs were capable of organizing a campaign or following up an advantage. But the Indians made superb guerrillas. Every observer called them the best cavalry soldiers in

---

[1]*Fetterman had boasted that with 80 cavalrymen he could ride the entire length of the Bozeman Trail. When he tried, however, he blundered into an ambush.*

the world. Armed with stubby, powerful bows capable of driving an arrow clear through a bull buffalo, they were a fair match for troops equipped with carbines and Colt revolvers. Expertly they led pursuers into ambushes, swept down on unsuspecting supply details, stole up on small parties the way a mountain lion stalks a grazing lamb. They could sometimes be rounded up, as when General Philip Sheridan herded the tribes of the Southwest into Indian Territory in 1869. But once the troops withdrew, braves began to melt away into the emptiness of the surrounding grasslands. The distinction between "treaty" Indians, who had agreed to live on the new reservations, and the "nontreaty" variety shifted almost from day to day. Trouble flared here one week, next week somewhere else, perhaps 500 miles away. No less an authority than General William Tecumseh Sherman testified that a mere 50 Indians could often "checkmate" 3000 soldiers.

If one concedes that no one could reverse the direction of history or stop the invasion of Indian lands, then some version of the "small reservation" policy would probably have been best for the Indians. Had they been guaranteed a reasonable amount of land and adequate subsidies and allowed to maintain their way of life, they might have accepted the situation and ceased to harry the whites.

Whatever chance that policy had was weakened by the government's poor administration of Indian affairs. In dealing with Indians, nineteenth-century Americans displayed a grave insensitivity. After 1849 the Department of the Interior supposedly had charge of tribal affairs. Most of its agents systematically cheated the Indians. One, heavily involved in mining operations on the side, diverted goods intended for his charges to his private ventures. When an inspector looked into his records, he sold him shares in a mine. That worthy in turn protected himself by sharing some of the loot with the son of the commissioner of Indian affairs. Army officers squabbled frequently with Indian agents over policy, and an "Indian Ring" in the Department of the Interior system typically stole funds and supplies intended for the reservation Indians. "No branch of the national government is so spotted with fraud, so tainted with corruption . . . as this Indian Bureau," Congressman Garfield charged in 1869.

President Grant wished to place the reservations under army control, but the Indians opposed this. They fared no better around army camps than on the reservations. In 1869 Congress created a nonpolitical Board of Indian Commissioners to oversee Indian affairs, but the bureaucrats in Washington stymied the commissioners at every turn.

In 1874 gold was discovered in the Black Hills Indian reservation. By the next winter thousands of miners had invaded the reserved area. Already alarmed by the approach of crews building the Northern Pacific Railroad, the Sioux once again went on the warpath. Joining with nontreaty tribes to the west, they concentrated in the region of the Bighorn River, in southern Montana Territory.

The summer of 1876 saw three columns of troops in the field against them. The commander of one column, General Alfred H. Terry, sent ahead a small detachment of the Seventh Cavalry under Colonel George A. Custer with orders to locate the Indians' camp and then block their escape route into the inaccessible

Bighorn Mountains. Custer was vain and rash, and vanity and rashness were grave handicaps when fighting Indians. Grossly underestimating the number of the Indians, he decided to attack directly with his tiny force of 264 men. At the Little Bighorn late in June he found himself surrounded by 2500 Sioux under Rain-in-the-Face, Crazy Horse, and Sitting Bull. He and all his men died on the field.

Because it was so one-sided, "Custer's Last Stand" was not a typical battle, although it may be taken as symbolic of the Indian warfare of the period in the sense that it was characterized by bravery, foolhardiness, and a tragic waste of life. The battle greatly heartened the Indians, but it did not gain them their cause. That autumn, short of rations and hard-pressed by overwhelming numbers of soldiers, they surrendered and returned to the reservation.

THE DESTRUCTION OF TRIBAL LIFE

After Little Bighorn, the fighting slackened. Two factors were chiefly responsible: the building of transcontinental railroads and the destruction of the buffalo. An estimated 13 to 15 million head of buffalo had roamed the Plains in the mid-1860s. Then the slaughter began. Thousands were butchered to feed the gangs of laborers engaged in building the Union Pacific Railroad. Thousands more fell before the guns of sportsmen. Buffalo hunting became a fad, and a brisk demand developed for buffalo rugs and mounted buffalo heads. Railroads made the Army a far more efficient force. Troops and supplies could be moved swiftly when trouble with the tribes erupted. The railroads also contributed to the decimation of the buffalo by running excursion trains for hunters; even the shameful practice of gunning down the beasts directly from railroad cars was allowed.

The discovery in 1871 of a way to make commercial use of buffalo hides completed the tragedy. In the next three years about 9 million head were killed; after another decade the animals were almost extinct. No more efficient way could have been found for destroying the Plains Indians. The disappearance of the bison left them starving and homeless.

By 1887 the tribes of the mountains and deserts beyond the Plains had also given up the fight. Typical of the heartlessness of the government's treatment of these peoples was that afforded the Nez Percé of Oregon and Idaho, who were led by the remarkable Chief Joseph. After outwitting federal troops in a campaign across more than a thousand miles of rough country, Joseph finally surrendered in October 1877. The Nez Percé were then settled on "the malarial bottoms of the Indian Territory" in far-off Oklahoma.

The last Indians to abandon the unequal battle were the relentless Apache of the Southwest, who finally yielded on the capture of their leader, Geronimo, in 1886.

By the 1880s, the advance of whites into the Plains had become, in the words of one congressman, as irresistible "as that of Sherman's to the sea." Greed for land lay behind the pressure, but large numbers of disinterested people, including most of those who deplored the way the Indians had been treated in the past, believed that the only practical way to solve the "Indian problem" was to persuade

A mound of buffalo skulls. In 1870 an estimated 30 million buffalo roamed the Plains; by 1900, there were fewer than 1000. During eight months from 1867–1868, William F. Cody (Buffalo Bill) killed 4280 buffalo, which fed construction crews for the Union Pacific railroad. Tourists also took up buffalo hunting, often shooting from trains. The depletion of the buffalo, which provided the Plains Indians with meat and hides, was a major source of conflict with whites.

the Indians to abandon their tribal culture and live on family farms. The "wild" Indian must be changed into a "civilized" member of "American" society.

To accomplish this goal Congress passed the Dawes Severalty Act of 1887. Tribal lands were to be split up into individual allotments. To keep speculators from wresting the allotments from the Indians while they were adjusting to their new way of life, the land could not be disposed of for 25 years. Funds were to be appropriated for educating and training the Indians, and those who accepted allotments, took up residence "separate from any tribe," and "adopted the habits of civilized life" were to be granted United States citizenship.

The sponsors of the Severalty Act thought they were effecting a fine humanitarian reform. "We must throw some protection over [the Indian]," Senator Henry L. Dawes declared. "We must hold up his hand." But no one expected all the Indians to accept allotments at once, and for some years little pressure was put on any to do so. The law was a statement of policy rather than a set of specific rules and orders. "Too great haste . . . should be avoided," Indian

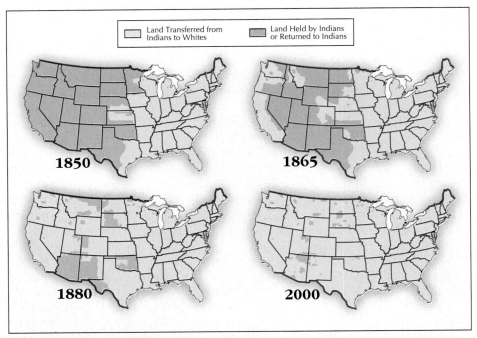

Loss of Indian Lands, 1850–2000

Commissioner John Atkins explained. "Character, habits, and antecedents cannot be changed by enactment."

The Dawes Act had disastrous results in the long run. It assumed that Indians could be transformed into small agricultural capitalists by an act of Congress. It shattered what was left of the Indians' culture without enabling them to adapt to white ways. Moreover, unscrupulous white men systematically tricked many Indians into leasing their allotments for a pittance, and local authorities often taxed Indian lands at excessive rates. In 1934, after about 86 million of the 138 million acres assigned under the Dawes Act had passed into white hands, the government returned to a policy of encouraging tribal ownership of Indian lands.

THE LURE OF GOLD AND SILVER IN THE WEST

The natural resources of the nation were exploited in these decades even more ruthlessly and thoughtlessly than were its human resources. Americans had long regarded the West as a limitless treasure to be grasped as rapidly as possible, and after 1865 they engrossed its riches still faster and in a wider variety of ways. From the mid-1850s to the mid-1870s thousands of gold-crazed prospectors fanned out through the Rockies, panning every stream and hacking furiously at every likely outcropping from the Fraser River country of British Columbia to

Tucson in southern Arizona, from the eastern slopes of the Sierras to the Great Plains.

Gold and silver were scattered throughout the area, though usually too thinly to make mining profitable. Whenever anyone made a "strike," prospectors, the vast majority utterly without previous experience but driven by what a mining journal of the period called an "unhealthy desire" for sudden wealth, flocked to the site, drawn by rumors of stream beds gleaming with gold-rich gravel and of nuggets the size of men's fists. For a few months the area teemed with activity. Towns of 5000 or more sprang up overnight; improvised roads were crowded with people and supply wagons. Claims were staked out along every stream and gully. Then, usually, expectations faded in the light of reality: high prices, low yields, hardship, violence, and deception. The boom collapsed and the towns died as quickly as they had risen. A few would have found wealth, the rest only backbreaking labor and disappointment—until tales of another strike sent them dashing feverishly across the land on another golden chase.

In the spring of 1858 it was on the Fraser River in Canada that the horde descended, 30,000 Californians in the vanguard. The following spring, Pikes Peak in Colorado attracted the pack, experienced California prospectors ("yonder siders") mixing with "greenhorns" from every corner of the globe. In June 1859 came the finds in Nevada, where the famous Comstock Lode yielded ores worth nearly $4000 a ton. In 1861, while men in the settled areas were laying down their tools to take up arms, the miners were racing to the Idaho panhandle, hoping to become millionaires overnight. The next year the rush was to the Snake River valley, then in 1863 and 1864 to Montana. In 1874 to 1876 the Black Hills in the heart of the Sioux lands were inundated.

The sudden prosperity of the mining towns attracted every kind of shady character—according to one forty-niner "rascals from Oregon, pickpockets from New York, accomplished gentlemen from Europe, interlopers from Lima and Chile, Mexican thieves, gamblers from no particular spot, and assassins manufactured in Hell." Gambling dens, dance halls, saloons, and brothels mushroomed wherever precious metal was found.

Law enforcement was a constant problem. Much of the difficulty lay in the antisocial attitudes of the miners themselves. Gold and silver dominated people's thoughts and dreams, and few paid much attention to the means employed in accumulating this wealth. Storekeepers charged outrageous prices; claim holders "salted" worthless properties with nuggets in order to swindle gullible investors. Ostentation characterized the successful, braggadocio those who failed. During the administration of President Grant, Virginia City, Nevada, was at the peak of its vulgar prosperity, producing an average of $12 million a year in ore. Built on the richness of the Comstock Lode ($306 million in gold and silver was extracted from the Comstock in 20 years), it had 25 saloons before it had 4000 people. By the 1870s its mountainside site was disfigured by ugly, ornate mansions where successful mine operators ate from fine china and swilled champagne as though it were water.

In 1873, after the discovery of the Big Bonanza, a seam of rich ore more than 50 feet thick, the future of Virginia City seemed boundless. Other discoveries

DEBATING THE PAST

Was the frontier exceptionally violent? In 1882 the *New York Daily Graphic* described Jesse James *(left)* as "the most renowned murderer and robber of his age." Here he is shown with members of his gang, each holding a rifle and wearing a holster and pistol, a stereotypical expression of gun violence in the frontier West.

Several decades ago historians challenged the notion that the western frontier was exceptionally violent. Robert Dykstra observed that most of the frontier was devoted to agriculture, and that such communities were peaceable. John Unruh, Jr., and John Reid were struck by how few crimes occurred during the difficult, long months of the overland trail.

Some historians have approached this issue by compiling comparative statistics of homicides per 100,000 population (the standard way that federal crime statistics are now expressed). In 1985, when Miami had a homicide rate of 33, the highest in the nation, Roger D. McGrath found that a California mining camp had a rate of 116 in the 1870s and 1880s. John Boessenecker found that in 1851 Los Angeles County had a staggering rate of 1240. Clare McKenna, Jr., arrived at a similar conclusion based on statistics for rural California. Critics, however, rejected the methodology. They note that in a frontier town of 100 people, a single murder generates a fearful homicide rate of 1000. Little wonder that Jesse James was perceived as a one-gang crime wave.

Robert R. Dykstra, *The Cattle Towns* (1968), John Unruh, Jr., *The Plains Across* (1979), John Reid, *Law for the Elephant* (1980), Roger D. McGrath, *Gunfighters, Highwaymen & Vigilantes* (1985), John Boessenecker, *Gold Dust and Gunsmoke* (1999), Clare V. McKenna, Jr., *Race and Homicide in Nineteenth-Century California* (2002). McKenna found that most homicides were somehow bound up with alcohol, while David Courtwright, *Violent Land* (1996), believed that high levels of violence were due to the relative absence of the restraining hand of women in frontier communities. See also David Peterson del Mar, *Beaten Down: A History of Interpersonal Violence in the West* (2002).

shortly thereafter indicated to optimists that the mining boom in the West would continue indefinitely. The finds in the Black Hills district in 1875 and 1876, heralding deposits yielding eventually $100 million, led to the mushroom growth of Deadwood, home of Wild Bill Hickok, Deadwood Dick, Calamity Jane, and such lesser-known characters as California Jack and Poker Alice. The West continued to yield much gold and silver, especially silver, but big corporations produced nearly all of it. The mines around Deadwood were soon controlled by one large company, Homestake Mining. Butte, Montana, was similarly dominated by Anaconda Mining.

This is the culminating irony of the history of the mining frontier: Shoestring prospectors, independent and enterprising, made the key discoveries. They established local institutions and supplied the West with much of its color and folklore. But the stockholders of large corporations, many of whom had never seen a mine, made off with the lion's share of the wealth. Those whose worship of gold was direct and incessant, the prospectors who peopled the mining towns and gave the frontier its character, mostly died poor, still seeking a prize as elusive if not as illusory as the pot of gold at the end of the rainbow.

Though marked by violence, fraud, greed, and lost hopes, the gold rushes had valuable results. The most obvious was the new metal itself, which bolstered the financial position of the United States during and after the Civil War. Quantities of European goods needed for the war effort and for postwar economic development were paid for with the yield of the new mines. Gold and silver also caused a great increase of interest in the West. A valuable literature appeared, part imaginative, part reportorial, describing the mining camps and the life of the prospectors. These works fascinated contemporaries (as they have continued to fascinate succeeding generations when adapted to the motion picture and to television). Mark Twain's *Roughing It* (1872), based in part on his experiences in the Nevada mining country, is the most famous example of this literature.

Each new strike and rush, no matter how fleeting, brought permanent settlers along with the prospectors: farmers, cattlemen, storekeepers, teamsters, lawyers, and ministers. The boomtowns had to import everything from bread, meat, and liquor to building materials and tools of every sort. Without the well-worn trails blazed by earlier hunters and migrants headed for Oregon and California, and of freighting companies equipped to haul heavy loads over long distances, the towns could not have existed. Some of the gold seekers saw from the start that a better living could be made supplying the needs of prospectors than looking for the elusive metal. Others, failing to find mineral wealth, took up whatever occupation they could rather than starve or return home empty-handed. In every mining town—along with the saloons and brothels—schools, churches, and newspaper offices sprang up.

The mines also speeded the political organization of the West. Colorado and Nevada became territories in 1861, Arizona and Idaho in 1863, Montana in 1864. Although Nevada was admitted to the Union before it had 60,000 residents (in 1864, to ratify the Thirteenth Amendment and help reelect Lincoln), most of these territories did not become states for decades. But because of the miners, the framework for future development was early established.

BIG BUSINESS AND THE LAND BONANZA

While the miners were engrossing the mineral wealth of the West, other interests were snapping up the region's choice farmland. Presumably the Homestead Act of 1862 had ended the reign of the speculator and the large landholder. An early amendment to the act even prevented husbands and wives from filing separate claims. The West, land reformers had assumed, would soon be dotted with 160-acre family farms.

These reformers were doomed to disappointment. Most landless Americans were too poor to become farmers even when they could obtain land without cost. The expense of moving a family to the ever-receding frontier exceeded the means of many, and the cost of a plow, hoes and scythes, draft animals, a wagon, a well, fencing, and of building the simplest house, might come to $1000—a formidable barrier. As for the industrial workers for whom the free land was supposed to provide a "safety valve," they had neither the skills nor the inclination to become farmers. Homesteaders usually came from districts not far removed from frontier conditions. And despite the intent of the law, speculators often managed to obtain large tracts. They hired men to stake out claims, falsely swear that they had fulfilled the conditions laid down in the law for obtaining legal title, and then deed the land over to their employers.

Had the land laws been better drafted and more honestly enforced, it is still unlikely that the policy of granting free land to small homesteaders would have succeeded. Aside from the built-in difficulties faced by small-scale agriculturalists in the West, too many people in every section were eager to exploit the nation's land for their own profit. Immediately after the Civil War, Congress reserved 47.7 million acres of public land in the South for homesteaders, stopping all cash sales in the region. But in 1876 this policy was reversed and the land thrown open. Speculators flocked to the feast in such numbers that the Illinois Central Railroad ran special trains from Chicago to Mississippi and Louisiana. Between 1877 and 1888 over 5.6 million acres were sold; much of the land was covered with valuable pine and cypress.

However they attained their acres, frontier farmers of the 1870s and 1880s grappled with novel problems as they pushed across the Plains with their families. The soil was rich, but the climate, especially in the semiarid regions beyond 98° longitude, made agriculture frequently difficult and often impossible. Blizzards, floods, grasshopper plagues, and prairie fires caused repeated heartaches, but periodic drought and searing summer heat were the worst hazards, destroying the hopes and fortunes of thousands.

Despite the hazards of Plains agriculture, the region became the breadbasket of America in the decades following the Civil War. By 1889 Minnesota topped the nation in wheat production, and ten years later four of the five leading wheat states lay west of the Mississippi. The Plains also accounted for heavy percentages of the nation's other cereal crops, together with immense quantities of beef, pork, and mutton.

Like other exploiters of the nation's resources, farmers took whatever they could from the soil with little heed for preserving its fertility and preventing erosion. The consequent national loss was less apparent because it was diffuse and slow to assume drastic proportions, but it was nonetheless real.

WESTERN RAILROAD BUILDING

Further exploitation of land resources by private interests resulted from the government's policy of subsidizing western railroads. Here was a clear illustration of the conflict between the idea of the West as a national heritage to be disposed of to deserving citizens and the concept of the region as a cornucopia pouring forth riches to be gathered up and carted off by anyone powerful and determined enough to take them. When it came to a choice between giving a particular tract to railroads or to homesteaders, the homesteaders nearly always lost out. On the other hand, the swift development of western railroads was essential if farmers, miners, and cattle ranchers were to prosper.

Unless the government had been willing to build the transcontinental lines itself—and this was unthinkable in an age dominated by belief in individual exploitation—some system of subsidy was essential. Private investors would not hazard the huge sums needed to lay tracks across hundreds of miles of rugged, empty country when traffic over the road could not possibly profit for many years. It might appear that subsidizing construction by direct outlays of public funds would have been adopted, but that idea had few supporters. Most voters were wary of entrusting the dispensing of large sums to politicians. Grants of land seemed a sensible way of financing construction. The method avoided direct outlays of public funds, for the companies could pledge the land as security for bond issues or sell it directly for cash.

Federal land grants to railroads began in 1850 with those allotted to the Illinois Central. Over the next two decades about 49 million acres were given to various lines indirectly in the form of grants to the states, but the most lavish gifts of the public domain were those made directly to builders of intersectional trunk lines. These roads received more than 155 million acres, although about 25 million acres reverted to the government because some companies failed to lay the required miles of track. About 75 percent of this land went to aid the construction of four transcontinental railroads: the Union Pacific–Central Pacific line, running from Nebraska to San Francisco, completed in 1869; the Atchison, Topeka and Santa Fe, running from Kansas City to Los Angeles by way of Santa Fe and Albuquerque, completed in 1883; the Southern Pacific, running from San Francisco to New Orleans by way of Yuma and El Paso, completed in 1883; and the Northern Pacific, running from Duluth, Minnesota, to Portland, Oregon, completed in 1883.

The Pacific Railway Act of 1862 established the pattern for these grants. It gave the builders of the Union Pacific and Central Pacific railroads 5 square miles of public land on each side of their right-of-way for each mile of track laid. The land was allotted in alternate sections, forming a pattern like a checker-board, the squares of one color representing railroad property, the other govern-ment property. Presumably this arrangement benefited the entire nation since half the land close to the railroad remained in public hands.

Historians have argued at length about the fairness of the land-grant system. No railroad corporation grew wealthy directly from the sale of its lands, which were sold at prices averaging between $2 and $5 an acre. Collectively the roads took in between $400 million and $500 million from this source, but only over the course of a century. Land-grant lines encouraged the growth of the West by advertising their property widely and by providing cheap transportation for prospective settlers and efficient shipping services for farmers. They were re-quired by law to carry troops and handle government business free or at reduced rates, which saved the government millions over the years. At the same time the system imposed no effective restraints on how the railroads used the funds raised with federal aid. Being able to lay track with money obtained from land grants, the operators tended to be extravagant and often downright corrupt.

The construction of the Central Pacific in the 1860s illustrates how the sys-tem encouraged extravagance. The line was controlled by four businessmen: Collis P. Huntington ("scrupulously dishonest" but an excellent manager); Leland Stanford, a Sacramento grocer and politician; Mark Hopkins, a hardware merchant; and Charles Crocker, a hulking, relentless driver of men who had come to California during the gold rush and made a small fortune as a merchant. The Central Pacific and the Union Pacific were given, in addition to their land grants, loans in the form of government bonds—from $16,000 to $48,000 for each mile of track laid, depending on the difficulty of the terrain. The two lines competed with each other for the subsidies, the Central Pacific building eastward from Sacramento, the Union Pacific westward from Nebraska. They put huge crews to work grading and laying track, bringing up supplies over the already completed road. The Union Pacific employed Civil War veterans and Irish immi-grants; the Central, Chinese immigrants.

This plan favored the Union Pacific. While the Central Pacific was inching up the gorges and granite of the mighty Sierras, the Union Pacific was racing across the level plains laying 540 miles of track between 1865 and 1867. Once beyond the Sierras, the Central Pacific would have easy going across the Nevada–Utah plateau country, but by then it might be too late to prevent the Union Pacific from making off with most of the government aid.

Crocker managed the Central Pacific construction crews. He wasted huge sums by working through the winter in the High Sierras. Often the men labored in tunnels dug through 40-foot snowdrifts to get at the frozen ground. To speed construction of the Summit Tunnel, Crocker had a shaft cut down from above so that crews could work out from the middle as well as in from each end. In 1866, over the most difficult terrain, he laid 28 miles of track, at a cost of more than $280,000 a mile. Experts later estimated that 70 percent of this sum could have been saved had speed not been a factor. Such wastefulness made economic sense to Huntington, Stanford, Hopkins, and Crocker because of the profits they were

Chinese workers building a railroad trestle in the Sierras (1877). "Without them," Leland Stanford, president of the Central Pacific Railroad said, "it would be impossible to complete the western portion of this great national highway." Some Chinese were drawn from the gold fields further north, and others were imported from China, under five-year contracts with the railroads in which they were paid $10 or $12 a month.

making through the Central Pacific's construction company and because of the gains they could count on once they reached the flat country beyond the Sierras, where costs would amount to only half the federal aid.

Crocker's herculean efforts paid off. The mountains were conquered, and then the crews raced across the Great Basin to Salt Lake City and beyond. The meeting of the rails—the occasion of a national celebration—took place at Promontory, north of Ogden, Utah, on May 10, 1869. Leland Stanford drove the final ceremonial golden spike with a silver hammer.[2] The Union Pacific had built 1086 miles of track, the Central 689 miles.

In the long run the wasteful way in which the Central Pacific was built hurt the railroad severely. It was ill constructed, over grades too steep and around curves too sharp, and burdened with debts that were too large. Steep grades meant that heavier, more expensive locomotives burning more coal were needed to pull lighter loads—a sure way to lower profits. Such was the fate of nearly all the railroads constructed with the help of government subsidies.

The only transcontinental railroad built without land grants was the Great Northern, running from St. Paul, Minnesota, to the Pacific. Spending private capital, its guiding genius, James J. Hill, was compelled to build economically and to plan carefully. As a result, his was the only transcontinental line to weather the depression of the 1890s without going into bankruptcy.

---

[2] *A mysterious "San Francisco jeweler" passed among the onlookers, taking orders for souvenir watch chains that he proposed to make from the spike at $5 each.*

THE CATTLE KINGDOM

While miners were digging out the mineral wealth of the West and railroaders were taking possession of much of its land, another group was exploiting endless acres of its grass. For 20 years after the Civil War cattlemen and sheep raisers dominated huge areas of the High Plains, making millions of dollars by grazing their herds on lands they did not own.

Columbus brought the first cattle to the New World in 1493, on his second voyage, and later conquistadores took them to every corner of Spain's American empire. Mexico proved to be so well suited to cattle raising that many were allowed to roam loose. They multiplied rapidly, and by the late eighteenth century what is now southern Texas harbored enormous herds. The beasts interbred with nondescript "English" cattle, brought into the area by settlers from the United States, to produce the Texas longhorn. Hardy, wiry, ill-tempered, and fleet, with horns often attaining a spread of 6 feet, these animals were far from ideal as beef cattle and almost as hard to capture as wild horses, but they existed in southern Texas by the millions, most of them unowned.

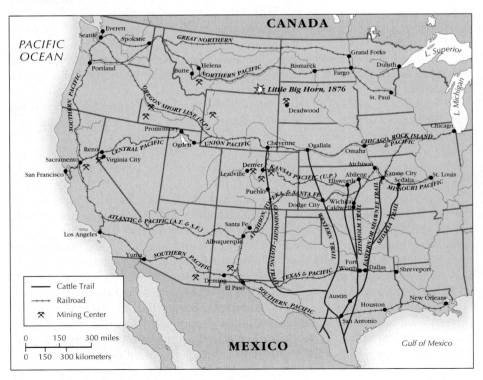

The West: Cattle, Railroads, and Mining, 1850–1893

The lack of markets and transportation explains why Texas cattle were lightly regarded. But conditions were changing. Industrial growth in the East was causing an increase in the urban population and a consequent rise in the demand for food. At the same time, the expansion of the railroad network made it possible to move cattle cheaply over long distances. As the iron rails inched across the Plains, astute cattlemen began to do some elementary figuring. Longhorns could be had locally for $3 and $4 a head. In the northern cities they would bring ten times that much, perhaps even more. Why not round them up and herd them northward to the railroads, allowing them to feed along the way on the abundant grasses of the Plains? The land was unoccupied and owned by the federal government. Anyone could drive cattle across it without paying a fee or asking anyone's permission. The grass the cattle ate on the way swiftly renewed itself.

In 1866 a number of Texans drove large herds northward toward Sedalia, Missouri, railhead of the Missouri Pacific. This route took the herds through wooded and settled country and across Indian reservations, which provoked many difficulties. At the same time Charles Goodnight and Oliver Loving successfully drove 2000 head in a great arc west to the New Mexico Territory and then north to Colorado.

The next year the drovers, inspired by a clever young Illinois cattle dealer named Joseph G. McCoy and other entrepreneurs, led their herds north by a more westerly route, across unsettled grasslands, to the Kansas Pacific line at Abilene, Kansas, which McCoy described as "a very small, dead place, consisting of about one dozen log huts." They earned excellent profits, and during the next five years about 1.5 million head made the "long drive" over the Chisholm Trail to Abilene, where they were sold to ranchers, feedlot operators, and the agents of eastern meatpackers. Other shipping points sprang up as the railroads pushed westward. According to the best estimates 10 million head were driven north before the practice ended in the mid-1880s.

OPEN-RANGE RANCHING

Soon cattlemen discovered that the hardy Texas stock could survive the winters of the northern Plains. Attracted by the apparently limitless forage, they began to bring up herds to stock the vast regions where the buffalo had so recently roamed. Introducing pedigreed Hereford bulls, they improved the stock without weakening its resistance to harsh conditions. By 1880 some 4.5 million head had spread across the sea of grass that ran from Kansas to Montana and west to the Rockies.

The prairie grasses offered ranchers a bonanza almost as valuable as the gold mines. Open-range ranching required actual ownership of no more than a few acres along some watercourse. In this semiarid region, control of water enabled a rancher to dominate all the surrounding area back to the divide separating his range from the next stream without investing a cent in the purchase of land. His cattle, wandering freely on the public domain, fattened on grass owned by all the people, to be turned into beefsteak and leather for the profit of the rancher.

With the demand for meat rising and transportation cheap, princely fortunes could be made in a few years. Capitalists from the East and from Europe began to pour funds into the business. Eastern "dudes" like Theodore Roosevelt, a young New York assemblyman who sank over $50,000 in his Elkhorn Ranch in the Dakota Territory in 1883, bought up cattle as a sort of profitable hobby. (Roosevelt, clad in buckskin and bearing a small armory of rifles and six-shooters, made quite a splash in Dakota, but not as a rancher.) Soon large outfits such as the Nebraska Land and Cattle Company, controlled by British investors, and the Union Cattle Company of Wyoming, a $3 million corporation, dominated the business, just as large companies had taken over most of the important gold and silver mines.

Unlike other exploiters of the West's resources, cattle ranchers did not at first injure or reduce any public resource. Grass eaten by their stock annually renewed itself; droppings from the animals enriched the soil. Furthermore, ranchers poached on the public domain because there was no reasonable way for them to obtain legal possession of the large areas necessary to raise cattle on the Plains. Federal land laws made no allowance for the special conditions of the semiarid West.

A system to take account for those conditions was soon devised by Major John Wesley Powell, later the director of the United States Geological Survey. His *Report on the Lands of the Arid Region of the United States* (1879) suggested that western lands be divided into three classes: irrigable lands, timber lands, and "pasturage" lands. On the pasturage lands the "farm unit" ought to be at least 2560 acres (four sections), Powell urged. Groups of these units should be organized into "pasturage districts" in which the ranchers "should have the right to make their own regulations for the division of lands, the use of the water . . . and for the pasturage of lands in common or in severalty."

BARBED-WIRE WARFARE

Congress refused to change the land laws in any basic way, and this had two harmful effects. First, it encouraged fraud: Those who could not get title to enough land honestly turned to subterfuge. The Desert Land Act (1877) allowed anyone to obtain 640 acres in the arid states for $1.25 an acre provided the owner irrigated part of it within three years. Since the original claimant could transfer the holding, the ranchers set their cowboys and other hands to filing claims, which were then signed over to them. Over 2.6 million acres were taken up under the act, and according to the best estimate, 95 percent of the claims were fraudulent—no sincere effort was made to irrigate the land.

Second, overcrowding became a problem that led to serious conflicts, even killings, because no one had uncontestable title to the land. The leading ranchers banded together in cattlemen's associations to deal with overcrowding and with such problems as quarantine regulations, water rights, and thievery. In most cases these associations devised effective and sensible rules, but their functions

In 1885 masked Nebraskans seeking access to water posed for photographer S. D. Butcher, who captioned the picture "Settlers taking the law into their own hands: Cutting 15 miles of the Brighton Ranch fence."

would better have been performed by the government, as such matters usually are.

To keep other ranchers' cattle from those sections of the public domain they considered their own, the associations and many individuals began to fence huge areas. This was possible only because of the invention in 1874 of barbed wire by Joseph F. Glidden, an Illinois farmer. By the 1880s thousands of miles of the new fencing had been strung across the Plains, often across roads and in a few cases around entire communities. "Barbed-wire wars" resulted, fought by rancher against rancher, cattleman against sheepman, herder against farmer. The associations tried to police their fences and to punish anyone who cut their wire. Posted signs gave dire warnings to trespassers. "The Son of a Bitch who opens this fence had better look out for his scalp," one such sign announced, another fine statement of the philosophy of the age.

By stringing so much wire the cattlemen were unwittingly destroying their own way of doing business. On a truly open range, cattle could fend for themselves, instinctively finding water during droughts, drifting safely downwind before blizzards. Barbed wire prevented their free movement. During winter storms these slender strands became as lethal as high-tension wires: the drifting cattle piled up against them and died by the thousands.

The boom times were ending. Overproduction was driving down the price of beef; expenses were on the rise; many sections of the range were badly overgrazed. The dry summer of 1886 left the stock in such poor condition as winter approached that the *Rocky Mountain Husbandman* urged its readers to sell their cattle despite the prevailing low prices rather than "endanger the whole herd by having the range overstocked."

Some ranchers took this advice; those who did not made a fatal error. Winter that year arrived early and with unparalleled fury. Blizzards raged and temperatures plummeted far below zero. Cattle crowded into low places only to be engulfed in giant snowdrifts; barbed wire took a fearful toll. When spring finally came, the streams were choked with rotting carcasses. Between 80 and 90 percent of all cattle on the range were dead. "We have had a perfect smashup all through the cattle country," Theodore Roosevelt wrote sadly in April 1887 from Elkhorn Ranch.

That cruel winter finished open-range cattle-raising. The large companies were bankrupt; many independent operators, Roosevelt among them, became discouraged and sold out. When the industry revived, it was on a smaller, more efficiently organized scale. The fencing movement continued, but now ranchers enclosed only the land they actually owned. It then became possible to bring in pedigreed bulls to improve the breed. Cattle-raising, like mining before it, ceased to be an adventure in rollicking individualism and became a business.

By the late 1880s the bonanza days of the West were over. No previous frontier had caught the imagination of Americans so completely as the Great West, with its heroic size, its awesome emptiness, its massive, sculptured beauty. Most of what Walter Prescott Webb, author of the classic study *The Great Plains* (1931) called the "primary windfalls" of the region—the furs, the precious metals, the forests, the cattle, and the grass—had been snatched up by first comers and by individuals already wealthy. Big companies were taking over all the West's resources. The frontier was no more.

But the frontier never existed except as an intellectual construction among white settlers and those who wrote about them. To the Indians, the land was simply home. The "conquest of the frontier" was thus an appealing evasion: it transformed the harmful actions and policies of the nation into an expression of human progress, the march westward of "civilization."

"Civilization," though, was changing. The nation was becoming more powerful, richer, and larger, and its economic structure more complex and diversified as the West yielded its treasures. But the East, and especially eastern industrialists and financiers, was increasingly dominating the economy of the entire nation.

MILESTONES

1859	Discovery of the Comstock Lode lures miners west
1864	Chivington massacre of Cheyenne
1869	Union Pacific Railroad completed
	Board of Indian Commissioners established
1876	Sioux slaughter Custer's cavalry at Battle of Little Bighorn
1877	Desert Land Act favors ranchers
1879	Major Powell's *Report on the Lands of the Arid Region* suggests division of West
1881	Booker T. Washington founds Tuskegee Institute for blacks
1886–1887	Blizzards end open-range ranching
1887	Dawes Severalty Act splits tribal lands
1890–1900	Blacks are deprived of the vote in the South
1895	Booker T. Washington urges self-improvement in Atlanta Compromise speech
1896	Supreme Court upholds doctrine of "separate but equal" facilities in *Plessy* v. *Ferguson*

18

AN INDUSTRIAL GIANT

When the Civil War began, the country's industrial output, while important and increasing, did not approach that of major European powers. By the end of the century the United States had become far and away the colossus among world manufacturers, dwarfing the production of Great Britain and Germany. The world had never seen such a remarkable example of rapid economic growth. The value of American manufactured products rose from $1.8 billion in 1859 to over $13 billion in 1899. Modern economists estimate that the output of goods and services in the country (the gross national product, or GNP) increased by 44 percent between 1874 and 1883 and continued to expand in succeeding years. This growth was not confined to the Northeast. Wisconsin, for example, underwent a major transformation between 1873 and 1893. An economy based on grain and lumber became a mainly urban-centered industrial economy. The consequences for the nation's political institutions, if less visible, were equally profound.

ESSENTIALS OF INDUSTRIAL GROWTH

American manufacturing flourished for many reasons. New natural resources were discovered and exploited steadily, thereby increasing opportunities. These opportunities, in turn, attracted the brightest and most energetic of a vigorous and expanding population. The growth of the country added constantly to the size of the national market, and protective tariffs shielded that market from foreign competition. Foreign capital, however, entered the market freely, in part because tariffs kept out so many foreign goods.

The dominant spirit of the time encouraged businessmen to maximum effort by emphasizing progress, yet it also produced a generation of Robber Barons. The energetic search for wealth led to corrupt business practices such as stock manipulation, bribery, and cutthroat competition and ultimately to "combinations in restraint of trade," a kind of American euphemism for monopoly. European immigrants provided the additional labor needed by expanding industry; 2.5 million arrived in the 1870s, twice that number in the 1880s. These immigrants saw America as a land of opportunity, and for many, probably most, it was that indeed. But for others, emigrating to the United States meant a constant struggle for survival; dreary, often unhealthy living conditions; and grinding poverty.

It was a period of rapid advance in basic science, and technicians created a bountiful harvest of new machines, processes, and power sources that increased productivity in many industries and created new industries as well. In agriculture there were what one contemporary expert called "an endless variety of cultivators," better harvesters and binding machines, and combines capable of threshing and bagging 450 pounds of grain a minute. An 1886 report of the Illinois Bureau of Labor Statistics claimed that "new machinery has displaced fully 50 percent of the muscular labor formerly required to do a given amount of work in the manufacture of agricultural implements." Of course that also meant that many farm families were "displaced" from their homes and livelihoods, and it made farmers dependent on the vagaries of distant markets and powerful economic forces they could not control.

As a result of improvements in the milling of grain, packaged cereals appeared on the American breakfast table. The commercial canning of food, spurred by the "automatic line" canning factory, expanded so rapidly that by 1887 a writer in *Good Housekeeping* could say: "Housekeeping is getting to be ready made, as well as clothing." The Bonsack cigarette-rolling machine created a new industry that changed the habits of millions. George B. Eastman created still another with his development of mass-produced, roll photographic film and the simple but efficient Kodak camera. The perfection of the typewriter by the Remington company in the 1880s revolutionized the way office work was performed. But even some of these inventions were mixed blessings. The harm done by the popularity of cigarettes, for example, needs no explanation.

RAILROADS: THE FIRST BIG BUSINESS

Railroads were important first as an industry in themselves. Fewer than 35,000 miles of track existed when Lee laid down his sword at Appomattox in 1865. Ten years later railroad mileage exceeded 74,000 and the skeleton of the network was complete. Over the next two decades the skeleton was fleshed out. In 1890 the mature but still-growing system took in over $1 billion in passenger and freight revenues. (The federal government's income in 1890 was only $403 million.) The value of railroad properties and equipment was more than $8.7 billion. The national railroad debt of $5.1 billion was almost five times the national debt of $1.1 billion! By 1900 the nation had 193,000 miles of track.

The emphasis in railroad construction after 1865 was on organizing integrated systems. The lines had high fixed costs: taxes, interest on their bonds, maintenance of track and rolling stock, and salaries of office personnel. A short train with half-empty cars required almost as many workers and as much fuel to operate as a long one jammed with freight or passengers. To earn profits the railroads had to carry as much traffic as possible. They therefore spread out feeder lines to draw business to their main lines the way the root network of a tree draws water into its trunk.

Before the Civil War, passengers and freight could travel by rail from beyond Chicago and St. Louis to the Atlantic coast, but only after the war did true interregional trunk lines appear. In 1861, for example, the New York Central ran from Albany to Buffalo. One could proceed from Buffalo to Chicago, but on a different company's trains. In 1867 the New York Central passed into the hands of "Commodore" Cornelius Vanderbilt, who had made a large fortune in the shipping business. Vanderbilt already controlled lines running from Albany to New York City; now he merged these properties with the New York Central. In 1873 he integrated the Lake Shore and Michigan Southern into his empire and two years later the Michigan Central. At his death in 1877 the New York Central operated a network of over 4500 miles of track between New York City and most of the principal cities of the Midwest.

While Vanderbilt was putting together the New York Central complex, Thomas A. Scott was fusing roads to Cincinnati, Indianapolis, St. Louis, and Chicago to his Pennsylvania Railroad, which linked Pittsburgh and Philadelphia. In 1871 the Pennsylvania line obtained access to New York; soon it reached Baltimore and Washington. By 1869 another important system, the Erie, extended from New York to Cleveland, Cincinnati, and St. Louis. Soon thereafter it too tapped the markets of Chicago and other cities. In 1874 the Baltimore and Ohio rail line also obtained access to Chicago.

The transcontinental railroads were trunk lines from the start; the emptiness of the western country would have made short lines unprofitable, and builders quickly grasped the need for direct connections to eastern markets and thorough integration of feeder lines.

The dominant system builder of the Southwest was Jay Gould, a soft-spoken, unostentatious-looking man who was in fact ruthless, cynical, and aggressive. Another railroad president once called Gould a "perfect eel." Gould took over the Kansas Pacific, running from Denver to Kansas City, and consolidated it with the Union Pacific and the Missouri Pacific, a line from Kansas City to St. Louis. Often he put together such properties merely to unload them on other railroads at a profit, but his grasp of the importance of integration was sound.

In the Northwest, Henry Villard, a German-born former newspaperman, constructed another great complex based on his control of the Northern Pacific. James J. Hill controlled the Great Northern system, still another western network.

The Civil War had highlighted the need for thorough railroad connections in the South. Shortly after the conflict the Chesapeake and Ohio opened a direct line from Norfolk, Virginia, to Cincinnati. By the late 1880s, the Richmond and West Point Terminal Company controlled an 8558-mile network. Like other southern trunk lines such as the Louisville and Nashville and the Atlantic Coast Line, this system was controlled by northern capitalists.

The trunk lines interconnected and thus had to standardize many of their activities. This, in turn, led to the standardization of other aspects of life. The present system of time zones was developed in 1883 by the railroads. The standard track gauge (4 feet 8½ inches) was established in 1886. Standardized car coupling and braking mechanisms, standard signal systems, even standard methods of accounting were essential to the effective functioning of the network.

The lines sought to work out fixed rates for carrying different types of freight, charging more for valuable manufactured goods than for bulky products like coal or wheat, and they agreed to permit rate concessions to shippers when necessary to avoid hauling empty cars. In other words, they charged what the traffic would bear. However, by the 1880s the men who ran the railroads had come to recognize the advantages of cooperating with one another to avoid "senseless" competition. Railroad management was becoming a kind of profession, with certain standard ways of doing things, even with its own professional journals and with regional organizations such as the Eastern Trunk Line Association and the Western Traffic Association.

To speed the settlement of new regions, the land-grant railroads sold land cheaply and on easy terms, for sales meant future business as well as current income. They offered reduced rates to travelers interested in buying farms and set up "bureaus of immigration" that distributed brochures describing the wonders of the new country. Their agents greeted immigrants at the eastern ports and tried to steer them to railroad property. They sent agents who were usually themselves immigrants—often ministers—all over Europe to recruit prospective settlers.

Technological advances in railroading accelerated economic development in complex ways. In 1869 George Westinghouse invented the air brake. By enabling an engineer to apply the brakes to all cars simultaneously (formerly each car had to be braked separately by its own conductor or brakeman), this invention made possible revolutionary increases in the size of trains and the speed at which they could safely operate. The sleeping car, invented in 1864 by George Pullman, now came into its own.

To pull the heavier trains, more powerful locomotives were needed. They in turn produced a call for stronger and more durable rails to bear the additional weight. Steel, itself reduced in cost because of technological developments, supplied the answer, for steel rails outlasted iron by many years despite the use of much heavier equipment.

A close tie developed between the railroads and the nation's telegraph network, dominated by the Western Union Company. Commonly the railroads allowed Western Union to string wires along their rights-of-way, and they transported telegraphers and their equipment without charge. In return they received free telegraphic service, important for efficiency and safety.

The Union Railroad Station in Montgomery, Alabama, designed by Henry Hobson Richardson, the nation's foremost architect of the era. Richardson borrowed ideas from the past—the arches evoked the early Middle Ages—but adapted them to contemporary purposes. This building's massiveness and horizontal lines hinted at the power and reach of the railroads.

IRON, OIL, AND ELECTRICITY

The transformation of iron manufacturing affected the nation almost as much as railroad development. Output rose from 920,000 tons in 1860 to 10.3 million tons in 1900, but the big change came in the development of ways to mass-produce steel. In its pure form (wrought iron) the metal is tough but relatively soft. Ordinary cast iron, which contains large amounts of carbon and other impurities, is hard but brittle. Steel, which contains 1 or 2 percent carbon, combines the hardness of cast iron with the toughness of wrought iron. For nearly every purpose—structural girders for bridges and buildings, railroad track, machine tools, boiler plate, barbed wire—steel is immensely superior to other kinds of iron.

But steel was so expensive to manufacture that it could not be used for bulky products until the invention in the 1850s of the Bessemer process, perfected independently by Henry Bessemer, an Englishman, and William Kelly of Kentucky. Bessemer and Kelly discovered that a stream of air directed into a mass of molten iron caused the carbon and other impurities to combine with oxygen and burn off. When measured amounts of carbon, silicon, and manganese were then added, the brew became steel. What had been a rare metal could now be produced by the hundreds and thousands of tons. The Bessemer process and the open-hearth method, a slower but more precise technique that enabled producers to sample the molten mass and thus control quality closely, were introduced commercially in the 1860s. In 1870, 77,000 tons of steel were manufactured; by 1890, that had expanded to nearly 5 million tons. Such growth would have been impossible without the huge supplies of iron ore in the United States and the coal necessary to fire the furnaces that refined it. In the 1870s the great iron fields rimming Lake Superior began to yield their treasures. The enormous iron concentrations of the Mesabi region made a compass needle spin like a top. Mesabi ores could be mined with steam shovels, almost like gravel.

Pittsburgh, surrounded by vast coal deposits, became the iron and steel capital of the country, the Minnesota ores reaching it by way of steamers on the Great Lakes and rail lines from Cleveland. Other cities in Pennsylvania and Ohio were important producers, and a separate complex, centering on Birmingham, Alabama, developed to exploit local iron and coal fields.

The petroleum industry expanded even more spectacularly than iron and steel. Edwin L. Drake drilled the first successful well in Pennsylvania in 1859. During the Civil War, production ranged between 2 million and 3 million barrels a year. By 1890 the figure had leaped to about 50 million barrels.

Before the invention of the gasoline engine and the automobile, the most important petroleum product was kerosene, which was burned in lamps. Refiners heated crude oil in large kettles and, after the volatile elements had escaped, condensed the kerosene in coils cooled by water. The heavier petroleum tars were discarded.

Technological advances came rapidly. By the early 1870s, refiners had learned how to "crack" petroleum by applying high temperatures to the crude oil in order to rearrange its molecular structure, thereby increasing the percentage of kerosene yielded. By-products such as naphtha, gasoline (used in vaporized form as an illuminating gas), rhigolene (a local anesthetic), cymogene (a coolant for refrigerating machines), and many lubricants and waxes began to appear on the market. At the same time a great increase in the supply of crude oil—especially after the German-born chemist Herman Frasch perfected a method for removing sulfur from low-quality petroleum—drove prices down.

These circumstances put a premium on refining efficiency. Larger plants using expensive machinery and employing skilled technicians became more important. In the mid-1860s only three refineries in the country could process 2000 barrels of crude oil a week; a decade later plants capable of handling 1000 barrels a day were common.

Two other important new industries were the telephone and electric light businesses. Both were typical of the period, being products of technical advances and intimately related to the growth of a high-speed, urban civilization that put great stress on communication. The telephone was invented in 1876 by Alexander Graham Bell, who had been led to the study of acoustics through his interest in the education of the deaf. The invention soon proved its value. By 1900 there were almost 800,000 telephones in the country, twice the total for all Europe. The American Telephone and Telegraph Company, a consolidation of over 100 local systems, dominated the business.

When Western Union realized the importance of the telephone, it tried for a time to compete with Bell by developing a machine of its own. The man it commissioned to devise this machine was Thomas A. Edison, but Bell's patents

"A sneeze captured on film"—the first copyrighted movie (1894). In 1889 Thomas A. Edison conceived of a machine that would do for the eye what the phonograph did for the ear. Over the next two years, Edison invented two separate devices—a camera to take a rapid sequence of pictures and a machine to view them called a Kinetoscope. In 1893 he developed reliable film for his camera. The motion picture industry was born.

proved unassailable. Edison had already made a number of contributions toward solving what he called the "mysteries of electrical force," including a multiplex telegraph capable of sending four messages over a single wire at the same time. At Menlo Park, New Jersey, he built the prototype of the modern research laboratory, where specific problems could be attacked on a mass scale by a team of trained specialists. During his lifetime he took out more than 1000 patents, dealing with machines as varied as the phonograph, the motion-picture projector, the storage battery, and the mimeograph.

Edison's most significant achievement was the incandescent lamp, or electric light bulb. Others before him had experimented with the idea of producing light by passing electricity through a filament in a vacuum. Always, however, the filaments quickly burned out. Edison tried hundreds of fibers before producing, in

1879, a carbonized filament that would glow brightly in a vacuum tube for as long as 170 hours without crumbling. At Christmastime he decorated the grounds about his laboratory with a few dozen of the new lights. People flocked by the thousands to see this miracle of the "Wizard of Menlo Park." The inventor boasted that soon he would be able to illuminate entire towns, even great cities like New York.

He was true to his promise. In 1882 his Edison Illuminating Company opened a power station in New York City and began to supply current for lighting to 85 consumers, including the *New York Times* and the banking house of J. P. Morgan and Company. Soon central stations were springing up everywhere until, by 1898, there were about 3000 in the country.

The substitution of electric for steam power in factories was as liberating as that of steam for waterpower before the Civil War. Small, safe electric motors replaced dangerous and cumbersome mazes of belts and wheels. The electric power industry expanded rapidly. By the early years of the twentieth century almost 6 billion kilowatt-hours of electricity were being produced annually. Yet this was only the beginning.

COMPETITION AND MONOPOLY: THE RAILROADS

During the post–Civil War era, expansion in industry went hand in hand with concentration. The principal cause of this trend, aside from the obvious economies resulting from large-scale production and the growing importance of expensive machinery, was the downward trend of prices after 1873. The deflation, which resulted mainly from the failure of the money supply to keep pace with the rapid increase in the volume of goods produced, affected agricultural goods as well as manufactures, and it lasted until 1896 or 1897.

Contemporaries believed that they were living through a "great depression." That label is misleading, for output expanded almost continuously, and at a rapid rate, until 1893, when production slumped and a true depression struck the country. Falling prices, however, kept a steady pressure on profit margins, and this led to increased production and thus to intense competition for markets.

According to the classical economists, competition advanced the public interest by keeping prices low and ensuring the most efficient producer the largest profit. Up to a point it accomplished these purposes in the years after 1865, but it also caused side effects that injured both the economy and society as a whole. Railroad managers, for instance, found it impossible to enforce "official" rate schedules and maintain their regional associations once competitive pressures mounted. In 1865 it had cost from 96 cents to $2.15 per 100 pounds, depending on the class of freight, to ship goods from New York to Chicago. In 1888 rates ranged from 35 cents to 75 cents.

Competition cut deeply into railroad profits, causing the lines to seek desperately to increase volume. They did so chiefly by reducing rates still more, on a selective basis. They gave rebates (secret reductions below the published rates) to large shippers in order to capture their business. Giving discounts to those who shipped in volume made economic sense: It was easier to handle freight in carload lots than in smaller units. So intense was the battle for business, however, that the roads often made concessions to big customers far beyond what the economics of bulk shipment justified. In the 1870s the New York Central regularly reduced the rates charged important shippers by 50 to 80 percent. One large Utica dry-goods merchant received a rate of 9 cents while others paid 33 cents. Two big New York City grain merchants paid so little that they soon controlled the grain business of the entire city.

Railroad officials disliked rebating but found no way to avoid the practice. "Notwithstanding my horror of rebates," the president of a New England trunk line told one of his executives in discussing the case of a brick manufacturer, "bill at the usual rate, and rebate Mr. Cole 25 cents a thousand." In extreme cases the railroads even gave large shippers drawbacks, which were rebates on the business of the shippers' competitors! Besides rebating, railroads issued passes to favored shippers, built sidings at the plants of important companies without charge, and gave freely of their landholdings to attract businesses to their territory. "The force of competition," a railroad man explained, "is one that no carrying corporation can withstand and before which the managing officers of a corporation are helpless." James F. Joy of the Chicago, Burlington, and Quincy made the same point more bluntly: "Unless you prepare to defend yourselves," he advised the president of the Michigan Central, "you will be boarded by pirates in all quarters."

To make up for losses forced on them by competitive pressures, railroads charged higher rates at waypoints along their tracks where no competition existed. Frequently it cost more to ship a product a short distance than a longer one. Rochester, New York, was served only by the New York Central. In the 1870s it cost 30 cents to transport a barrel of flour from Rochester to New York City, a distance of 350 miles. At the same time flour could be shipped from Minneapolis to New York, a distance of well over 1000 miles, for only 20 cents a barrel. One Rochester businessman told a state investigating committee that he could save 18 cents a hundredweight by sending goods to St. Louis by way of New York, where several carriers competed for the traffic, even though, in fact, the goods might come back through Rochester over the same tracks on the way to St. Louis!

Although cheap transportation stimulated the economy, few people benefited from cutthroat competition. Small shippers—and all businessmen in cities and towns with limited rail outlets—suffered; railroad discrimination speeded the concentration of industry in large corporations located in major centers. The instability of rates even troubled interests like the Midwestern flour millers who benefited from the competitive situation, for it hampered planning. Nor could manufacturers who received rebates be entirely happy, since few could be sure that some other producer was not getting a larger reduction.

Probably the worst sufferers were the railroads themselves. The loss of revenue resulting from rate cutting, combined with inflated debts, put most of them in grave difficulty when faced with a downturn in the business cycle. In 1876 two-fifths of all railroad bonds were in default; three years later 65 lines were bankrupt. Wits called Samuel J. Tilden, the 1876 Democratic presidential candidate, "the Great Forecloser" because of his work reorganizing bankrupt railroads at this time. Since the public would not countenance bankrupt railroads going out of business, these companies were placed in the hands of court-appointed receivers. The receivers, however, seldom provided efficient management and had no funds at their disposal for new equipment.

During the 1880s the major roads responded to these pressures by building or buying lines in order to create interregional systems. These were the first giant corporations, capitalized in the hundreds of millions of dollars. Their enormous cost led to another wave of bankruptcies when a true depression struck in the 1890s.

The consequent reorganizations brought most of the big systems under the control of financiers, notably J. Pierpont Morgan and such other private bankers as Kuhn, Loeb of New York and Lee, Higginson of Boston.

Critics called the reorganizations "Morganizations." Representatives of the bankers sat on the board of every line they saved and their influence was predominant. They consistently opposed rate wars, rebating, and other competitive practices. In effect, control of the railroad network became centralized, even though the companies maintained their separate existences and operated in a seemingly independent manner. When Morgan died in 1913, "Morgan men" dominated the boards of the New York Central; the Erie; the New York, New Haven, and Hartford; the Southern; the Pere Marquette; the Atchison, Topeka and Santa Fe; and many other lines.

COMPETITION AND MONOPOLY: STEEL

The iron and steel industry was also intensely competitive. Despite the trend toward higher production, demand varied erratically from year to year, even from month to month. In good times producers built new facilities, only to suffer heavy losses when demand declined. The forward rush of technology put a tremendous emphasis on efficiency; expensive plants quickly became obsolete. Improved transportation facilities allowed manufacturers in widely separated places to compete with one another.

The kingpin of the industry was Andrew Carnegie. Carnegie was born in Scotland and came to the United States in 1848 at the age of 12. His first job, as a bobbin boy in a cotton mill, brought him $1.20 a week, but his talents perfectly fitted the times and he rose rapidly: to Western Union messenger boy, to telegrapher, to private secretary, to railroad manager. He saved his money, made some shrewd investments, and by 1868 had an income of $50,000 a year.

At about this time he decided to specialize in the iron business. Carnegie possessed great talent as a salesman, boundless faith in the future of the country, an uncanny knack of choosing topflight subordinates, and enough ruthlessness to survive in the iron and steel jungle. Where other steelmen built new plants in good times, he preferred to expand in bad times, when it cost far less to do so. During the 1870s, he later recalled, "many of my friends needed money. . . . I bought out five or six of them. That is what gave me my leading interest in this steel business."

Carnegie grasped the importance of technological improvements. Slightly skeptical of the Bessemer process at first, once he became convinced of its practicality he adopted it enthusiastically. In 1875 he built the J. Edgar Thomson Steel Works, named after a president of the Pennsylvania Railroad, his biggest customer. He employed chemists and other specialists and was soon making steel from iron oxides that other manufacturers had discarded as waste. He was a merciless competitor. When a plant manager announced: "We broke all records for making steel last week," Carnegie replied: "Congratulations! Why not do it every week?" Carnegie sold rails by paying "commissions" to railroad purchasing agents, and he was not above reneging on a contract if he thought it profitable and safe to do so.

By 1890 the Carnegie Steel Company dominated the industry, and its output increased nearly tenfold during the next decade. Profits soared. Alarmed by his increasing control of the industry, the makers of finished steel products such as barbed wire and tubing considered pooling their resources and making steel themselves. Carnegie, his competitive temper aroused, threatened to manufacture wire, pipes and other finished products. A colossal steel war seemed imminent.

However, Carnegie longed to retire in order to devote himself to philanthropic work. He believed that great wealth entailed social responsibilities and that it was a disgrace to die rich. When J. P. Morgan approached him through an intermediary with an offer to buy him out, he assented readily. In 1901 Morgan put together United States Steel, the "world's first billion-dollar corporation." This combination included all the Carnegie properties, the Federal Steel Company (Carnegie's largest competitor), and such important fabricators of finished products as the American Steel and Wire Company, the American Tin Plate Company, and the National Tube Company. Vast reserves of Minnesota iron ore and a fleet of Great Lakes ore steamers were also included. U.S. Steel was capitalized at $1.4 billion, about twice the value of its component properties but not necessarily an overestimation of its profit-earning capacity. The owners of Carnegie Steel received $492 million, of which $250 million went to Carnegie himself.

COMPETITION AND MONOPOLY: OIL

The pattern of fierce competition leading to combination and monopoly is well illustrated by the history of the petroleum industry. Irresistible pressures pushed the refiners into a brutal struggle to dominate the business. Production of crude oil, subject to the uncertainties of prospecting and drilling, fluctuated constantly and without regard for need. In general, output surged far ahead of demand.

By the 1870s the chief oil-refining centers were Cleveland, Pittsburgh, Baltimore, and the New York City area. Of these Cleveland was the fastest growing, chiefly because the New York Central and Erie railroads competed fiercely for its oil trade and the Erie Canal offered an alternative route.

The Standard Oil Company of Cleveland, founded in 1870 by a 31-year-old merchant named John D. Rockefeller, emerged as the giant among the refiners. Rockefeller exploited every possible technical advance and employed fair means

The Forging of U.S. Steel

and foul to persuade competitors either to sell out or to join forces. By 1879 he controlled 90 percent of the nation's oil-refining capacity along with a network of oil pipelines and large reserves of petroleum in the ground.

Standard Oil emerged victorious from the competitive wars because Rockefeller and his associates were the toughest and most imaginative fighters as well as the most efficient refiners in the business. In addition to obtaining from the railroads a 10 percent rebate and drawbacks on its competitors' shipments, Standard Oil cut prices locally to force small independents to sell out or face ruin. Since kerosene was sold in grocery stores, Standard supplied its own outlets with meat, sugar, and other products at artificially low prices to help crush the stores that handled other brands of kerosene. The company employed spies to track down the customers of independents and offer them oil at bargain prices. Bribery was also a Standard practice; the reformer Henry Demarest Lloyd quipped that the company had done everything to the Pennsylvania legislature except refine it.

Although a bold planner and a daring taker of necessary risks, Rockefeller was far too orderly and astute to enjoy the free-swinging battles that plagued his industry. Born in an upstate New York village in 1839, he settled in Cleveland in 1855 and became a produce merchant. During the Civil War he invested in a local refinery and by 1865 was engaged full time in the oil business.

Like Carnegie, Rockefeller was an organizer; he knew little about the technology of petroleum. His forte was meticulous attention to detail: stories are told of his ordering the number of drops of solder used to seal oil cans reduced from 40 to 39 and of his insisting that the manager of one of his refineries account for 750 missing barrel bungs. Not miserliness but a profound grasp of the economies of large-scale production explain this behavior.

Rockefeller competed ruthlessly not primarily to crush other refiners but to persuade them to join with him, to share the business peaceably and rationally so that all could profit. Competition was obsolescent, he argued, though no more effective competitor than he ever lived.

Having achieved his monopoly, Rockefeller stabilized and structured it by creating a new type of business organization, the trust. Standard Oil was an Ohio corporation, prohibited by local law from owning plants in other states or holding stock in out-of-state corporations. As Rockefeller and his associates took over dozens of companies with facilities scattered across the country, serious legal and managerial difficulties arose. How could these many organizations be integrated with Standard Oil of Ohio?

A rotund, genial little Pennsylvania lawyer named Samuel C. T. Dodd came up with an answer to this question in 1879.[1] The stock of Standard of Ohio and of all the other companies that the Rockefeller interests had swallowed up was turned over to nine trustees, who were empowered to "exercise general supervision" over all the properties. In exchange, stockholders received trust certificates, on which dividends were paid. This seemingly simple device brought order to the petroleum business. Competition almost disappeared; prices steadied; profits skyrocketed. By 1892 John D. Rockefeller was worth over $800 million.

The Standard Oil Trust was not a corporation. It had no charter, indeed no legal existence at all. For many years few people outside the organization knew that it existed. The form they chose persuaded Rockefeller and other Standard

---

[1]*The trust formula was not "perfected" until 1882.*

A regally attired John D. Rockefeller, astride a barrel from his Standard Oil refinery, his crown encircled by the railroads he controlled. His actual attire was considerably less conspicuous.

Oil officials that without violating their consciences, they could deny under oath that Standard Oil of Ohio owned or controlled other corporations "directly or indirectly through its officers or agents." The trustees controlled these organizations—and Standard of Ohio too!

After Standard Oil's duplicity was revealed during a New York investigation in 1888, the word *trust,* formerly signifying a fiduciary arrangement for the protection of the interests of individuals incompetent or unwilling to guard them themselves, became a synonym for monopoly. However, from the company's point of view, monopoly was not the purpose of the trust—that had been achieved before the device was invented. Centralization of the management of diverse and far-flung operations in the interest of efficiency was its chief function. Standard Oil headquarters in New York became the brain of a complex network where information from salaried managers in the field was collected and digested, where top managerial decisions were made, and whence orders went out to armies of drillers, refiners, scientists, and salesmen.

The pattern of competition leading to dominance by a few great companies was repeated in many businesses. In life insurance an immense expansion took place after the Civil War, stimulated by the development of a new type of group policy, the "tontine," by Henry B. Hyde of the Equitable Life Company.[2] High-pressure salesmanship prevailed; agents gave rebates to customers by shaving their own commissions; companies stole crack agents from their rivals and raided new territories. They sometimes invested as much as 96 percent of the first year's premiums in obtaining new business. By 1900, after three decades of fierce competition, three giants dominated the industry—Equitable, New York Life, and Mutual Life, each with approximately $1 billion of insurance in force.

In retailing, the period saw the growth of urban department stores. In 1862 Alexander T. Stewart had built an eight-story emporium in New York City that covered an entire block and employed 2000 persons. John Wanamaker in Philadelphia and Marshall Field in Chicago headed similar establishments by the 1880s, and there were others. These department stores advertised heavily, stressing low prices, efficient service, and money-back guarantees. High volume made for large profits. Here is how one of Field's biographers described his methods:

> His was a one-price store, with the price plainly marked on the merchandise. Goods were not misrepresented, and a reputation for quality merchandise and for fair and honest dealing was built up. . . . Courtesy toward customers was an unfailing rule.

AMERICAN AMBIVALENCE TO BIG BUSINESS

The expansion of industry and its concentration in fewer and fewer hands changed the way many people felt about the role of government in economic and social affairs. On the one hand, they professed to believe strongly in a government policy of noninterference, or laissez-faire. "'Things regulate themselves' . . . means, of course, that God regulates them by his general laws," Professor Francis Bowen of Harvard wrote in his *American Political Economy* (1870).

Certain intellectual currents encouraged this type of thinking. Charles Darwin's *The Origin of Species* was published in 1859, and by the 1870s his theory of evolution was beginning to influence opinion in the United States. That nature had ordained a kind of inevitable progress, governed by the natural selection of those individual organisms best adapted to survive in a particular environment, seemed eminently reasonable to most Americans, for it fit well with their own experiences. "Let the buyer beware; that covers the whole business," the sugar magnate Henry O. Havemeyer explained to an investigating committee. "You cannot wet-nurse people from the time they are born until the time they die. They have to wade and get stuck, and that is the way men are educated."

---

[2]*A tontine policy paid no dividends for a stated period of years. The heirs of the policyholder who died received the face value but no dividends. At the end of the tontine period, survivors collected not only their own dividends but those of the unfortunates who had died or permitted their policies to lapse. This was psychologically appealing, since it stressed living rather than dying and added an element of gambling to insurance.*

This reasoning was similar to that of the classical economists and was thus at least as old as Adam Smith's *Wealth of Nations* (1776). But it appeared to supply a hard scientific substitute for Smith's somewhat vague "invisible hand" as an explanation of why free competition advanced the common good.

Yale professor William Graham Sumner sometimes used the survival-of-the-fittest analogy in teaching undergraduates. "Professor," one student asked Sumner, "don't you believe in any government aid to industries?" "No!" Sumner replied, "It's root, hog, or die." The student persisted: "Suppose some professor of political science came along and took your job away from you. Wouldn't you be sore?" "Any other professor is welcome to try," Sumner answered promptly. "If he gets my job, it is my fault. My business is to teach the subject so well that no one can take the job away from me." Sumner's argument described what came to be known as *social Darwinism,* the belief that the activities of people, that is, their business and social relationships, were governed by the Darwinian principle that "the fittest" will always "survive" if allowed to exercise their capacities without restriction.

But the fact that Americans disliked powerful governments in general and strict regulation of the economy in particular had never meant that they objected to all government activity in the economic sphere. Banking laws, tariffs, internal-improvement legislation, and the granting of public land to railroads are only the most obvious of the economic regulations enforced in the nineteenth century by both the federal government and the states. Americans saw no contradiction between government activities of this type and the free enterprise philosophy, for such laws were intended to release human energy and thus increase the area in which freedom could operate. Tariffs stimulated industry and created new jobs, railroad grants opened up new regions for development, and so on.

The growth of huge industrial and financial organizations and the increasing complexity of economic relations frightened people yet made them at the same time greedy for more of the goods and services the new society was turning out. To many, the great new corporations and trusts resembled Frankenstein's monster—marvelous and powerful but a grave threat to society.

To some extent public fear of the industrial giants reflected concern about monopoly. If Standard Oil dominated oil refining, it might raise prices inordinately at vast cost to consumers. Charles Francis Adams, Jr., expressed this feeling in the 1870s: "In the minds of the great majority, and not without reason, the idea of any industrial combination is closely connected with that of monopoly, and monopoly with extortion."

Although in isolated cases monopolists did raise prices unreasonably, generally they did not. On the contrary, prices tended to fall until by the 1890s a veritable "consumer's millennium" had arrived. Far more important in causing resentment was the fear that the monopolists were destroying economic opportunity and threatening democratic institutions. It was not the wealth of tycoons like Carnegie and Rockefeller and Morgan so much as their influence that worried people. In the face of the growing disparity between rich and poor, could republican institutions survive? "The belief is common," wrote Charles Francis

Adams's brother Henry as early as 1870, "that the day is at hand when corporations . . . will ultimately succeed in directing government itself."

As criticism mounted, business leaders rose to their own defense. Rockefeller described in graphic terms the chaotic conditions that plagued the oil industry before the rise of Standard Oil: "It seemed absolutely necessary to extend the market for oil . . . and also greatly improve the process of refining so that oil could be made and sold cheaply, yet with a profit. We proceeded to buy the largest and best refining concerns and centralized the administration of them with a view to securing greater economy and efficiency." Carnegie, in an essay published in 1889, insisted that the concentration of wealth was necessary if humanity was to progress, softening this "Gospel of Wealth" by insisting that the rich must use their money "in the manner which . . . is best calculated to produce the most beneficial results for the community." The rich man was merely a trustee for his "poorer brethren," Carnegie said, "bringing to their service his superior wisdom, experience, and ability to administer." Lesser tycoons echoed these arguments.

The voices of the critics were louder if not necessarily more influential. Many clergymen denounced unrestrained competition, which they considered un-Christian. The new class of professional economists (the American Economic Association was founded in 1885) tended to repudiate laissez-faire. State aid, Richard T. Ely of Johns Hopkins University wrote, "is an indispensable condition of human progress."

REFORMERS: GEORGE, BELLAMY, LLOYD, AND THE MARXISTS

The popularity of a number of radical theorists reflects public feeling in the period. In 1879 Henry George, a California journalist, published *Progress and Poverty,* a forthright attack on the uneven distribution of wealth in the United States. George argued that labor was the true and only source of capital. Observing the speculative fever of the West, which enabled landowners to reap profits merely by holding property while population increased, George proposed a property tax that would confiscate this "unearned increment." The value of land depended on society and should belong to society; allowing individuals to keep this wealth was the major cause of the growing disparity between rich and poor, George believed.

George's "single tax," as others called it, would bring in so much money that no other taxes would be necessary, and the government would have plenty of funds to establish new schools, museums, theaters, and other badly needed social and cultural services. While the single tax on property was never adopted, George's ideas attracted enthusiastic attention. Single tax clubs sprang up throughout the nation, and *Progress and Poverty* became a best-seller.

Even more spectacular was the reception afforded *Looking Backward, 2000–1887,* a utopian novel written in 1888 by Edward Bellamy. This book,

Debating the Past

Were the industrialists "robber barons" or savvy entrepreneurs? The Biltmore Estate in Asheville, North Carolina *(left)*, was completed in 1895 by George Vanderbilt; it required 1000 workers to build the house.

Such wealth caused consternation at the time, and a later generation of historians picked up on the issue. In 1934 biographer Matthew Josephson, writing during the nation's worst depression, blamed the late nineteenth-century industrialists—robber barons, in his words—for the evident flaws in the economy. But in 1942, when the United States was at war and its industries were out-producing Nazi Germany and Japan, historians Thomas C. Cochran and William Miller contended that the late-nineteenth-century industrialists had exhibited skill and daring.

Historians subsequently shifted focus from the character of the entrepreneurs to the systems they built. In the early 1960s Alfred D. Chandler, Jr. argued that the great industrialists, in response to the demands of burgeoning urban markets, created the requisite large-scale industrial enterprises.

Other historians countered that much of the nation's industrial growth was achieved not by the huge corporations and their famous owners, but by small firms (John N. Ingham, 1991) or by mid-level managers (Oliver Zunz, 1990).

Most historians concede that the industrialists often put their fortunes to good use. The critics of Andrew Carnegie, for example, may have studied in one of the scores of libraries he donated to communities, such as that in Tuskegee, Alabama *(right)*.

Matthew Josephson, *The Robber Barons* (1934), Thomas C. Cochran and William Miller, *The Age of Enterprise* (1942), Alfred D. Chandler, Jr., *Strategy and Structure* (1962), John N. Ingham, *Making Iron and Steel* (1991), Oliver Zunz, *Making America Corporate* (1990).

which sold over a million copies in its first few years, described a future America that was completely socialized, all economic activity carefully planned. Bellamy compared nineteenth-century society to a lumbering stagecoach upon which the favored few rode in comfort while the mass of the people hauled them along life's route. Occasionally one of the toilers managed to fight his way onto the coach; whenever a rider fell from it, he had to join the multitude dragging it along.

Such, Bellamy wrote, was the working of the vaunted American competitive system. He suggested that the ideal socialist state, in which all citizens shared equally, would arrive without revolution or violence. The trend toward consolidation would continue, he predicted, until one monster trust controlled all economic activity. At this point everyone would realize that nationalization was essential.

A third influential attack on monopoly came from Henry Demarest Lloyd, whose *Wealth Against Commonwealth* appeared in 1894. Lloyd, a journalist of independent means, devoted years to preparing a denunciation of the Standard Oil Company. Marshaling masses of facts and vivid examples of Standard's evildoing, he assaulted the trust at every point. Although in his zeal Lloyd sometimes distorted and exaggerated the evidence to make his indictment more effective—"Every important man in the oil, coal and many other trusts ought today to be in some one of our penitentiaries," he wrote in a typical overstatement—as a polemic his book was peerless. His forceful but uncomplicated arguments and his copious references to official documents made *Wealth Against Commonwealth* utterly convincing to thousands. The book was more than an attack on Standard Oil. Lloyd denounced the application of Darwin's concept of survival of the fittest to economic and social affairs, and he condemned laissez-faire policies as leading directly to monopoly.

The popularity of these books indicates that the trend toward monopoly in the United States worried many. But despite the drastic changes suggested in their pages, none of these writers questioned the underlying values of the middle-class majority. They insisted that reform could be accomplished without serious inconvenience to any individual or class. In *Looking Backward* Bellamy pictured the socialists of the future gathered around a radiolike gadget in a well-furnished parlor listening to a minister delivering an inspiring sermon.

Nor did most of their millions of readers seriously consider trying to apply the reformers' ideas. Henry George ran for mayor of New York City in 1886 and lost narrowly to Abram S. Hewitt, a wealthy iron manufacturer, but even if he had won, he would have been powerless to apply the single tax to metropolitan property. The national discontent was apparently not as profound as the popularity of these works might suggest. If John D. Rockefeller became the bogeyman of American industry because of Lloyd's attack, no one prevented him from also becoming the richest man in the United States.

By the 1870s the ideas of European socialists were beginning to penetrate the United States, and in 1877 a Socialist Labor party was founded. The first serious attempt to explain the ideas of German political philosopher Karl Marx to Americans was Laurence Gronlund's *The Cooperative Commonwealth*, which was published in 1884, two years before Marx's *Das Kapital* was translated into English.

Capitalism, Gronlund claimed, contained the seeds of its own destruction. The state ought to own all the means of production. Competition was "Established Anarchy," middlemen were "parasites," speculators "vampires." "Capital and Labor," he wrote in one of the rare humorous lines in his book, "are just as harmonious as roast beef and a hungry stomach." Yet like other harsh critics of that day, Gronlund expected the millennium to arrive in a peaceful, indeed orderly manner. The red flag of socialism, he said, "has no relation to blood." The movement could accommodate "representatives of all classes," even "thoughtful" middleman parasites.

THE GOVERNMENT REACTS TO BIG BUSINESS: RAILROAD REGULATION

Political action related to the growth of big business came first on the state level and dealt chiefly with the regulation of railroads. Even before the Civil War, a number of New England states established railroad commissions to supervise lines within their borders; by the end of the century, 28 states had such boards.

Strict regulation was largely the result of agitation by the National Grange of the Patrons of Husbandry. The Grange, founded in 1867 by Oliver H. Kelley, was created to provide social and cultural benefits for isolated rural communities. As it spread and grew in influence—14 states had Granges by 1872 and membership reached 800,000 in 1874—the movement became political too. "Granger" candidates, often not themselves farmers (many local businessmen resented such railroad practices as rebating), won control of a number of state legislatures in the West and South. Granger-controlled legislatures established "reasonable" maximum rates and outlawed "unjust" discrimination. The legislature also set up a commission to enforce the laws and punish violators.

The railroads protested, insisting that they were being deprived of property without due process of law. In *Munn* v. *Illinois* (1877), a case that involved a grain elevator whose owner had refused to comply with a state warehouse act, the Supreme Court upheld the constitutionality of this kind of act. Any business that served a public interest, such as a railroad or a grain warehouse, was subject to state control, the justices ruled. Legislatures might fix maximum charges; if the charges seemed unreasonable to the parties concerned, they should direct their complaints to the legislatures or to the voters, not to the courts.

Regulation of the railroad network by the individual states was inefficient, and in some cases the commissions were incompetent and even corrupt. To alleviate such abuses, Congress in 1877 passed the Interstate Commerce Act. All charges made by railroads "shall be reasonable and just," the act stated. Rebates, drawbacks, the long-and-short-haul evil, and other competitive practices were declared unlawful, and so were their monopolistic counterparts—pools and traffic-sharing agreements. Railroads were required to publish schedules of rates and forbidden to change them without due public notice. Most important, the law established an Interstate Commerce Commission (ICC), the first federal regulatory board, to supervise the affairs of railroads, investigate complaints, and issue cease and desist orders when the roads acted illegally.

The Interstate Commerce Act broke new ground, yet it was neither a radical nor a particularly effective measure. Its terms contradicted one another, some being designed to stimulate, others to penalize, competition. The new commission had less power than the law seemed to give it. It could not fix rates, only bring the roads to court when it considered rates unreasonably high. Such cases could be extremely complicated; applying the law "was like cutting a path through a jungle." With the truth so hard to determine and the burden of proof on the commission, the courts in nearly every instance decided in favor of the railroads.

Nevertheless, by describing so clearly the right of Congress to regulate private corporations engaged in interstate commerce, the Interstate Commerce Act challenged the philosophy of laissez-faire. Later legislation made the commission more effective. The commission also served as the model for a host of similar federal administrative authorities, such as the Federal Communications Commission (1934).

THE GOVERNMENT REACTS TO BIG BUSINESS: THE SHERMAN ANTITRUST ACT

As with railroad legislation, the first antitrust laws originated in the states, but they were southern and western states with relatively little industry, and most of the statutes were vaguely worded and ill-enforced. Federal action came in 1890 with the passage of the Sherman Antitrust Act. Any combination "in the form of trust or otherwise" that was "in restraint of trade or commerce among the several states, or with foreign nations" was declared illegal. Persons forming such combinations were subject to fines of $5000 and a year in jail. Individuals and businesses suffering losses because of actions that violated the law were authorized to sue in the federal courts for triple damages.

Where the Interstate Commerce Act sought to outlaw the excesses of competition, the Sherman Act was supposed to restore competition. If businessmen joined together to "restrain" (monopolize) trade in a particular field, they should be punished and their deeds undone. "The great thing this bill does," Senator George Frisbie Hoar of Massachusetts explained, "is to extend the common-law principle . . . to international and interstate commerce." This was important because the states ran into legal difficulties when they tried to use the common law to restrict corporations engaged in interstate activities.

In fact, the Supreme Court quickly weakened the Sherman Act. In *United States v. E. C. Knight Company* (1895) it held that the American Sugar Refining Company had not violated the law by taking over a number of important competitors. Although the Sugar Trust now controlled about 98 percent of all sugar refining in the United States, it was not restraining trade. "Doubtless the power to control the manufacture of a given thing involves in a certain sense the control of its disposition," the Court said in one of the greatest feats of judicial understatement of all time. "Although the exercise of that power may result in bringing the operation of commerce into play, it does not control it, and affects it only incidentally and indirectly."

If the creation of the Sugar Trust did not violate the Sherman Act, it seemed unlikely that any other combination of manufacturers could be convicted under the law. However, in several cases in 1898 and 1899 the Supreme Court ruled that agreements to fix prices or divide markets did violate the Sherman Act.

These decisions precipitated a wave of outright mergers in which a handful of large companies swallowed up hundreds of smaller ones. Presumably mergers were not illegal. When, some years after his retirement, Andrew Carnegie was asked by a committee of the House of Representatives to explain how he had dared participate in the formation of the U.S. Steel Corporation, he replied: "Nobody ever mentioned the Sherman Act to me, that I remember."

THE LABOR UNION MOVEMENT

At the time of the Civil War only a small percentage of the American workforce was organized, and most union members were cigarmakers, printers, carpenters, and other skilled artisans, not factory hands. Aside from ironworkers, railroad workers, and miners, few industrial laborers belonged to unions. Nevertheless the union was the workers' response to the big corporation: a combination designed to eliminate competition for jobs and to provide efficient organization for labor.

After 1865 the growth of national craft unions, which had been stimulated by labor dissatisfaction during the Civil War, quickened perceptibly. In 1866 a federation of these organizations, the National Labor Union, was founded and by the early 1870s many new trades, notably in railroading, had been unionized.

Most of the leaders of these unions were visionaries who were out of touch with the practical needs and aspirations of workers. They opposed the wage system, strikes, and anything that increased the laborers' sense of being members of the working class. A major objective was the formation of worker-owned cooperatives.

Far more remarkable was the Knights of Labor, a curious organization founded in 1869 by a group of Philadelphia garment workers headed by Uriah S. Stephens. Like so many labor organizers of the period, Stephens was a reformer of wide interests rather than a man dedicated to the specific problems of industrial workers. He, his successor Terence V. Powderly, and many other leaders of the Knights would have been thoroughly at home in the labor organizations of the Jacksonian era. Like the Jacksonians, they supported political objectives that had no direct connection with working conditions, such as currency reform and the curbing of land speculation. They rejected the idea that workers must resign themselves to remaining wage earners. By pooling their resources, working people could advance up the economic ladder and enter the capitalist class. "There is no good reason," Powderly wrote in his autobiography, *The Path I Trod,* "why labor cannot, through cooperation, own and operate mines, factories, and railroads." The leading Knights saw no contradiction between their denunciation of "soulless" monopolies and "drones" like bankers and lawyers and their talk of "combining all branches of trade in one common brotherhood." Such muddled thinking led the Knights to attack the wage system and to frown on strikes as "acts of private warfare."

Under Powderly, secrecy was discarded. Between 1882 and 1886 successful strikes by local "assemblies" against western railroads, including one against the

Here Jay Gould, perhaps the most vilified of the "robber barons," is depicted as a spider amidst a web of control bound by the telegraph lines of Western Union. Alfred Chandler, Jr., as noted in the feature Debating the Past on page 519, took a more positive look at the nation's industrialists. He credited Gould with salvaging the Union Pacific Railroad, building his own railroad company (Missouri Pacific), and rationalizing the nation's communications system.

hated Jay Gould's Missouri Pacific, brought recruits by the thousands. The membership passed 42,000 in 1882, 110,000 in 1885, and in 1886 it soared beyond the 700,000 mark. Alas, sudden prosperity was too much for the Knights. Its national leadership was unable to control local groups. A number of poorly planned strikes failed dismally, and the public was alienated by sporadic acts of violence and intimidation. Disillusioned recruits began to drift away.

Circumstances largely fortuitous caused the collapse of the organization. By 1886 the movement for the eight-hour day had gained wide support among workers, including many who did not belong to unions. Several hundred thousand (estimates vary) were on strike in various parts of the country by May of that year. In Chicago, a center of the eight-hour movement, about 80,000 workers were involved, and a small group of anarchists was trying to take advantage of the excitement to win support.

When a striker was killed in a fracas at the McCormick Harvesting Machine Company, the anarchists called a protest meeting on May 4, at Haymarket Square. Police intervened to break up the meeting, and someone—his identity was never established—hurled a bomb into their ranks. Seven policemen were killed and many others injured.

THE AMERICAN FEDERATION OF LABOR

Although the anarchists were the immediate victims of the resulting public indignation and hysteria—seven were condemned to death and four eventually executed—organized labor, especially the Knights, suffered heavily. No tie between

This famous depiction of the Haymarket bombing (1886), which appeared in Harper's Weekly, *suggests that the police were being fired on. In actuality, the bomb exploded after the crowd had begun to disperse. Then the police began firing into the crowd.*

the Knights and the bombing could be established, but the union had been closely connected with the eight-hour agitation, and the public tended to associate it with violence and radicalism. Its membership declined as suddenly as it had risen, and soon it ceased to exist as a force in the labor movement.

The Knights' place was taken by the American Federation of Labor (AFL), a combination of national craft unions established in 1886. In a sense the AFL was a reactionary organization. Its principal leaders, Adolph Strasser and Samuel Gompers of the Cigarmakers Union, were, like the founders of the Knights of Labor, originally interested in utopian social reforms. They even toyed with the idea of forming a workers' political party. Experience, however, soon led them to concentrate on organizing skilled workers and fighting for "bread-and-butter" issues such as higher wages and shorter hours. "Our organization does not consist of idealists," Strasser explained to a congressional committee. "We do not control the production of the world. That is controlled by the employers. . . . I look first to cigars."

The AFL accepted the fact that most workers would remain wage earners all their lives and tried to develop in them a sense of common purpose and pride in their skills and station. Strasser and Gompers paid great attention to building a strong organization of dues-paying members committed to unionism as a way of improving their lot. Rank-and-file AFL members were naturally eager to win wage increases and other benefits, but most also valued their unions for the companionship they provided, the sense of belonging to a group. In other words, despite statements such as Strasser's, unions, in and out of the AFL, were a kind of club as well as a means of defending and advancing their members' material interests.

The chief weapon of the federation was the strike, which it used to win concessions from employers and to attract recruits. Gompers, president of the AFL almost continuously from 1886 until his death in 1924, encouraged workers to make "intelligent use of the ballot" in order to advance their interests. The federation worked for such things as eight-hour days, employers' liability, and mine-safety laws, but it avoided direct involvement in politics. "I have my own philosophy and my own dreams," Gompers once told a left-wing French politician, "but first and foremost I want to increase the workingman's welfare year by year . . . . The French workers waste their economic force by their political divisions."

Gompers's approach to labor problems produced solid, if unspectacular, growth for the AFL. Unions with a total of about 150,000 members formed the federation in 1886. By 1892 the membership had reached 250,000, and in 1901 it passed the million mark.

LABOR MILITANCY REBUFFED

The stress of the AFL on the strike weapon reflected rather than caused the increasing militancy of labor. Workers felt themselves threatened from all sides: the growing size and power of their corporate employers; the substitution of machines for human skills; the invasion of foreign workers willing to accept substandard wages. At the same time they had tasted some of the material benefits of industrialization and had learned the advantages of concerted action.

The average employer behaved like a tyrant when dealing with his workers. He discharged them arbitrarily when they tried to organize unions; he hired scabs to replace strikers; he frequently failed to provide the most rudimentary protection against injury on the job. Some employers, Carnegie for example, professed to approve of unions, but almost none would bargain with labor collectively. To do so, they argued, would be to deprive workers of their freedom to contract for their own labor in any way they saw fit.

The industrialists of the period were not all ogres; they were as alarmed by the rapid changes of the times as their workers, and since they had more at stake materially, they were probably more frightened by the uncertainties. Deflation, technological change, and intense competition kept even the most successful under constant pressure.

Thus capital and labor were often spoiling for a fight, frequently without fully understanding why. When labor troubles developed, they tended to be bitter, even violent. In 1877 a great railroad strike convulsed much of the nation. It began on the Baltimore and Ohio system in response to a wage cut and spread to other eastern lines and then throughout the West until about two-thirds of the railroad mileage of the country had been shut down. Violence broke out, rail yards were put to the torch, dismayed and frightened businessmen formed militia companies to patrol the streets of Chicago and other cities. Eventually President Hayes sent federal troops to the trouble spots to restore order, and the strike collapsed. There had been no real danger of revolution, but the violence and destruction of the strike had been without precedent in America.

The disturbances of 1877 were a response to a business slump, those of the next decade a response to good times. Twice as many strikes occurred in 1886 as in any previous year. Even before the Haymarket bombing centered the country's attention on labor problems, the situation had become so disturbing that President Grover Cleveland, in the first presidential message devoted to labor problems, had urged Congress to create a voluntary arbitration board to aid in settling labor disputes—a remarkable suggestion for a man of Cleveland's conservative, laissez-faire approach to economic issues.

In 1892 a violent strike broke out among silver miners at Coeur d'Alene, Idaho, and a far more important clash shook Andrew Carnegie's Homestead steel plant near Pittsburgh when strikers attacked 300 private guards brought in to protect strikebreakers. Seven guards were killed at Homestead and the rest forced to "surrender" and march off ignominiously. The Homestead affair was part of a struggle between capital and labor in the steel industry. Steel producers insisted that the workers were holding back progress by resisting technological advances, while the workers believed that the company was refusing to share the fruits of more efficient operation fairly. The strike was precipitated by the decision of company officials to crush the union at all costs. The final defeat, after a five-month walkout, of the 24,000-member Amalgamated Association of Iron and Steel Workers, one of the most important elements in the AFL, destroyed unionism as an effective force in the steel industry and set back the progress of organized labor all over the country.

As in the case of the Haymarket bombing, the activities of radicals on the fringe of the dispute turned the public against the steelworkers. The boss of Homestead was Henry Clay Frick, a tough-minded foe of unions who was determined to "teach our employees a lesson." Frick made the decision to bring in strikebreakers and to employ Pinkerton detectives to protect them. During the course of the strike, Alexander Berkman, an anarchist, burst into Frick's office and attempted to assassinate him. Frick was only slightly wounded, but the attack brought him much sympathy and unjustly discredited the strikers.

The most important strike of the period took place in 1894. It began when the workers at George Pullman's Palace Car factory outside Chicago walked out in protest against wage cuts. (While reducing wages, Pullman insisted on holding the line on rents in the company town of Pullman; when a delegation called on him to remonstrate, he refused to give in and had three of the leaders fired.) Some Pullman workers belonged to the American Railway Union, headed by Eugene V. Debs. After the strike had dragged along for weeks, the union voted to refuse to handle trains with Pullman cars. The union was perfectly willing to handle mail trains, but the owners refused to run trains unless they were made up of a full complement of cars.

When Pullman cars were added to mail trains, the workers refused to move them. The resulting railroad strike tied up trunk lines running in and out of Chicago. The railroad owners appealed to President Cleveland to send troops to preserve order. On the pretext that the soldiers were needed to ensure the movement of the mails, Cleveland agreed. When Debs defied a federal injunction to end the walkout, he was jailed for contempt and the strike was broken.

WHITHER AMERICA, WHITHER DEMOCRACY?

Each year more of the nation's wealth and power seemed to fall into fewer hands. As with the railroads, other industries were being influenced, if not completely dominated, by bankers. The firm of J. P. Morgan and Company controlled many railroads; the largest steel, electrical, agricultural machinery, rubber, and shipping companies; two life insurance companies; and a number of banks. By 1913 Morgan and the Rockefeller National City Bank group between them could name 341 directors to 112 corporations worth over $22.2 billion. The "Money Trust," a loose but potent fraternity of financiers, seemed fated to become the ultimate monopoly.

Centralization unquestionably increased efficiency, at least in industries that used a great deal of expensive machinery to turn out goods for the mass market, and in those where close coordination of output, distribution, and sales was important. The public benefited immensely from the productive efficiency of the new empires. Living standards rose.

But the trend toward giantism raised doubts. With ownership falling into fewer hands, what would be the ultimate effect of big business on American democracy? What did it mean for ordinary people when a few tycoons possessed huge fortunes and commanded such influence even on Congress and the courts?

The crushing of the Pullman strike demonstrated the power of the courts to break strikes by issuing injunctions. And the courts seemed only concerned with protecting the interests of the rich and powerful. Particularly ominous for organized labor was the fact that the federal government based its request for the injunction that broke the strike on the Sherman Antitrust Act, arguing that the American Railway Union was a combination in restraint of trade. An indirect result of the Pullman strike was that while serving his sentence for contempt, Eugene Debs was visited by a number of prominent socialists who sought to convert him to their cause. One gave him a copy of Karl Marx's *Capital,* which he found too dull to finish, but he did read *Looking Backward* and *Wealth Against Commonwealth.* In 1897 he became a socialist.

MILESTONES

1859	First oil well is drilled in Pennsylvania
	Charles Darwin publishes *The Origin of Species*
1868	Carnegie Steel Company is formed
1869	George Westinghouse invents air brake
	Garment workers found Knights of Labor
1870–1890	Railroad trunk lines are completed
1876	Alexander Graham Bell invents telephone
1877	Great railroad strike convulses nation
	Munn v. *Illinois* upholds state regulatory laws
1879	Thomas Edison invents electric light bulb
	Reformer Henry George publishes *Progress and Poverty*
1884	Marxist Laurence Gronlund publishes *The Cooperative Commonwealth*
1886	Anarchists clash with police in Chicago's Haymarket bombing
	Craft unions found American Federation of Labor (AFL)
1887	Interstate Commerce Act regulates railroads
1888	Edward Bellamy publishes utopian novel *Looking Backward*
1889	Philanthropist Andrew Carnegie publishes "Gospel of Wealth"
1890	Sherman Antitrust Act outlaws monopolies
1892	Seven Pinkerton guards are killed in Homestead steel strike
1894	Eugene V. Debs leads American Railway Union in Pullman strike
	Henry Demarest Lloyd condemns laissez-faire in *Wealth Against Commonwealth*
1895	*U.S.* v. *E.C. Knight Company* weakens Sherman Antitrust Act
1901	J. P. Morgan forms U.S. Steel, "world's first billion-dollar corporation"

19

AMERICAN SOCIETY IN THE INDUSTRIAL AGE

The industrialization that followed the Civil War profoundly affected every aspect of American life. New machines, improvements in transportation and communication, the appearance of the great corporation with its uncertain implications for the future—all made deep impressions on the shape and character of American society. The growth of cities and the influx of tens of thousands of immigrants who knew little about urban life and who neither spoke nor understood English transformed the immigrants and the world they inhabited.

The United States was fast becoming a modern nation. Some found this alarming. Physician George M. Beard contended that "modern civilization" overloaded the human nervous system the way burning too many of Thomas Edison's light bulbs would overload an electrical circuit. On the other hand, Edward Bellamy saw the future as a "paradise of order, equity, and felicity." Most Americans took a more balanced view, believing that the modern world encompassed new possibilities as well as perils. The future beckoned, and yet it also menaced.

MIDDLE-CLASS LIFE

"This middle-class country had got a middle-class president, at last," Ralph Waldo Emerson had noted with satisfaction when Lincoln took office in 1861. Emerson did not endorse an economic class so much as a set of values that were, pointedly, antithetical to those of the antebellum South. Middle-class culture took the best aspects of romanticism—the enshrinement of human potential, the restless striving for personal betterment, the zest for competition and excitement—and tempered them with a passion for self-control and regularity.

But the Civil War sapped middle-class culture of its reforming zeal. The vital energy that had spawned a host of antebellum reform movements became transmuted into greater mass; the fervor of the individual was channeled into institutions. American society and culture underwent a process of "incorporation," as the predominant form of the business world seeped deep into the American consciousness.

Historians had long claimed that family relations were stiff and, in matters pertaining to sexuality, downright prudish. One witless historian imagined that intercourse occurred "in a dark bedroom into which the husband would creep to create his offspring in silence while the wife endured the connection in a coma." But diaries and letters provide ample proof that many couples experienced emotionally intense and sexually fulfilling relationships. Elaborate and protracted courtship rituals, which doubtless proved frustrating, intensified the expression of love by delaying its gratification. Middle-class mothers at the end of the century had two or three children, four or five fewer than their grandmothers. Their families were smaller mostly because they married later in life and practiced abstinence, though during the last half of the century there was a "commercial explosion," as one scholar termed it, in the dissemination of contraceptive devices and the practice of abortion.

The children in middle-class families, while much treasured, were carefully supervised. Upwardly striving parents were much concerned about the status and prospects of their children's marriage partners, but it was no longer considered proper to interfere with "the course of true love" for any materialistic or purely social reason.

While most women remained home to supervise their children, men worked away from home, in shops and offices. Members of the professions and the large and diffuse groups of shopkeepers, small manufacturers, skilled craftsmen, and established farmers that made up the middle class lived in varying degrees of comfort. A family with an annual income of $1000 in the 1880s would have no need to skimp on food, clothing, or shelter. When Professor Woodrow Wilson moved with his family to Wesleyan University in 1888, he was able to rent a large house and employ two full-time servants on his salary of $2500 a year. Indeed, at this time, about a quarter of all urban families employed at least one servant.

SKILLED AND UNSKILLED WORKERS

Wage earners felt the full force of the industrial tide, being affected in countless ways—some beneficial, others unfortunate. As manufacturing and mining became more important, the number of workers in these fields multiplied rapidly: from 885,000 in 1860 to more than 3.2 million in 1890. While workers lacked much sense of solidarity, they exerted a far larger influence on society at the turn of the century than they had in the years before the Civil War.

More efficient methods of production enabled them to increase their output, making possible a rise in their standard of living. The working day still tended to approximate the hours of daylight, but it was shortening perceptibly by the 1880s, at least in many occupations. In 1860 the average workday had been 11 hours, but by 1880 only one worker in four labored more than 10 hours and radicals were beginning to talk about 8 hours as a fair day's work.

This generalization, however, conceals some important differences. Skilled industrial workers—such types as railroad engineers and conductors, machinists, and iron molders—were quite well off in most cases. But it was still true that unskilled laborers could not earn enough to maintain a family decently by their own efforts alone.

Industrialization created problems for workers beyond the obvious one of earning enough money to support themselves. By and large, skilled workers, always better off than the unskilled, improved their positions relatively, despite the increased use of machinery. Furthermore, when machines took the place of human skills, jobs became monotonous. Mechanization undermined both the artisans' pride and their bargaining power with their employers. As expensive machinery became more important, the worker seemed less important. Machines more than workers controlled the pace of work and its duration. The time clock regulated the labor force more rigidly than the most exacting foreman. The length of the workday may have declined, but the pace of work and the danger involved in working around heavy, high-speed machinery increased accordingly.

As businesses grew larger, personal contact between employer and hired hand tended to disappear. Relations between them became less human, more businesslike, and ruthless. On the other hand, large enterprises usually employed a higher percentage of managerial and clerical workers than smaller companies, thus providing opportunities for more "blue-collar" workers to rise in the industrial hierarchy. But the trend toward bigness made it more difficult for workers to rise from the ranks of labor to become manufacturers themselves, as Andrew Carnegie, for example, had done during the Civil War era.

Another problem for workers was that industrialization tended to accentuate swings of the business cycle. On the upswing something approaching full employment existed, but in periods of depression unemployment became a problem that affected workers without regard for their individual abilities. It is significant that the word *unemployment* (though not, of course, the condition itself) was a late-nineteenth-century invention.

WORKING WOMEN

Women continued to supply a significant part of the industrial working force. But now many more of them were working outside their homes; the factory had almost completely replaced the household as the seat of manufacturing.[1] Textile mills and "the sewing trades" absorbed a large percentage of women, but in all fields women were paid substantially lower wages than men.

---

[1] *However, at least half of all working women were domestic servants.*

The glove counter at Rike's Department Store in Dayton, Ohio (1893). Shopping was an excuse for middle-class women to venture from the home into public. Rike's department store was decorated much like the Victorian home: potted ferns, stuffed animals, and carpeted stairways. The salesgirl (far right) was obliged to leave the home to work. She spent much of her income to "keep up appearances" to enable her to mix with middle-class shoppers.

Women found many new types of work in these years, a fact commented on by the *New York Times* as early as 1869. They made up the overwhelming majority of salespersons and cashiers in the big new department stores. Store managers considered women more polite, easier to control, and more honest than male workers, all qualities especially valuable in the huge emporiums. Over half of the more than 1700 employees in A. T. Stewart's New York store were women.

Educated, middle-class women also dominated the new profession of nursing that developed alongside the expanding medical profession and the establishment of large urban hospitals. To nearly all doctors, to most men, and indeed to many women of that day, nursing seemed the perfect female profession since it required the same characteristics that women were thought to have by nature: selflessness, cleanliness, kindliness, tact, sensitivity, and submissiveness to male control.

Middle-class women did replace men as teachers in most of the nation's grade schools, and they also replaced men as clerks and secretaries and operators of the new typewriters in government departments and in business offices. Most men with the knowledge of spelling and grammar that these positions required had better opportunities and were uninterested in office work, so women high school graduates, of whom there was an increasing number, filled the gap.

Both department store clerks and "typewriters" (as they were called) earned more money than unskilled factory workers, and working conditions were more pleasant. Opportunities for promotion for women, however, were rare; managerial posts in these fields remained almost exclusively in the hands of men.

FARMERS

Long the backbone of American society, independent farmers and the agricultural way of life were rapidly being left behind in the race for wealth and status. The number of farmers and the volume of agricultural production continued to rise, but agriculture's relative place in the national economy was declining. Between 1860 and 1890 the number of farms rose from 2 million to 4.5 million; wheat output leaped from 173 million bushels to 449 million, cotton from 5.3 million bales to 8.5 million. The rural population increased from 25 million to 40.8 million. Yet industry was expanding far faster, and the urban population, quadrupling in the period, would soon overtake and pass that of the countryside.

Farmers were not all affected by economic developments in the same way. Because of the steady decline of the price level, those in newly settled regions were usually worse off than those in older areas since they had to borrow money to get started and were therefore burdened with fixed interest charges that became harder to meet each year. In the 1870s farmers in Illinois and Iowa suffered most—which accounts for the strength of the Granger movement in that region. Except as a purely social organization, the Grange had little importance in eastern states, where rapidly expanding urban markets made farmers relatively prosperous. A typical eastern farm family raising wheat and other grains and perhaps some livestock worked hard but made a good living. Such a family might employ a neighbor's daughter to help with housework, milking, and similar chores and a "hired hand" whose work was mainly in the fields.

By the late 1880s farmers in the old Middle West had also become better established. Even when prices dipped and a general depression gripped the country, they were able to weather the bad times nicely by taking advantage of lower transportation costs, better farm machinery, and new fertilizers and insecticides to increase output and by shifting from wheat to the production of corn, oats, hogs, and cattle, which had not declined so drastically in price.

On the agricultural frontier from Texas to the Dakotas, and through the states of the old Confederacy, farmers were less fortunate. The burdens of the crop-lien system kept thousands of southern farmers in poverty, while on the Plains life was a succession of hardships. The first settlers in western Kansas, Nebraska, and the Dakotas took up land along the rivers and creeks, where they found enough timber for home building, fuel, and fencing. Later arrivals had to build houses of the tough prairie sod and depend on hay, sunflower stalks, and buffalo dung for fuel.

A sod house in North Dakota, 1896. Individual "bricks" of sod were hewn from the ground and stacked in layers to build such houses. The roof was made of timber packed with branches, twigs, straw, and more sod. This house was expanded with a room made of planed lumber (right). Sod houses were quite cool in summer and warm in winter, although excess moisture was always a problem.

Frontier farm families had always had to work hard and endure the hazards of storm, drought, and insect plagues, along with isolation and loneliness. But all these burdens were magnified on the prairies and the High Plains. Life was particularly hard for farm women, who, in addition to childcare and housework, performed endless farm chores—milking cows, feeding livestock, raising vegetables, and so on. "I . . . am set and running every morning at half-past four o'clock, and run all day, often until half-past eleven P.M.," one farm woman explained. "Is it any wonder I have become slightly demoralized?"

WORKING-CLASS ATTITUDES

Social workers and government officials made many efforts in the 1880s and 1890s to find out how working people felt about all sorts of matters connected with their jobs. Their reports reveal a wide spectrum of opinion. To the question, asked of two Wisconsin carpenters, "What new laws, in your opinion, ought to be enacted?" one replied: "Keep down strikes and rioters. Let every man attend to his own business." But the other answered: "Complete nationalization of land and all ways of transportation. Burn all government bonds. A graduated income tax. . . . Abolish child labor and [pass] any other act that capitalists say is wrong."

Every variation of opinion between these extremes was expressed by working people in many sections and in many kinds of work. In 1881 a female textile worker in Lawrence, Massachusetts, said to an interviewer: "If you will stand by the mill, and see the people coming out, you will be surprised to see the happy, contented look they all have."

Despite such remarks and the general improvement in living standards, it is clear, if only from the large number of bitter strikes of the period, that there was a considerable dissatisfaction among industrial workers. Writing in 1885, the labor leader Terence V. Powderly reported that "a deep-rooted feeling of discontent pervades the masses."

The discontent had many causes. For some, poverty was still the chief problem, but for others, rising aspirations triggered discontent. Workers were confused about their destiny; the tradition that no one of ability need remain a hired hand died hard. They wanted to believe their bosses and the politicians when those worthies voiced the old slogans about a classless society and the community of interest of capital and labor. "Our men," William Vanderbilt of the New York Central Railroad said in 1877, "feel that, although I . . . may have my millions and they the rewards of their daily toil, still we are about equal in the end. If they suffer, I suffer, and if I suffer, they cannot escape."

WORKING YOUR WAY UP

To study mobility in a large industrial country is extraordinarily difficult. Americans in the late nineteenth century believed their society offered great opportunities for individual advancement, and to prove it they pointed to men like Andrew Carnegie and to other poor boys who accumulated large fortunes. How general was the rise from rags to riches (or even to modest comfort) is another question.

Americans had been on the move, mostly, of course, in a westward direction, since the colonial period, but studies of census records show that there was considerable geographic mobility in urban areas throughout the last half of the nineteenth century and into the twentieth. Most investigations reveal that only about half the people recorded in one census were still in the same place ten years later. The nation had a vast reservoir of rootless people. For many, the way to move up in the world was to move on.

In most of the cities studied, mobility was accompanied by some economic and social improvement. On the average, about a quarter of the manual laborers traced rose to middle-class status during their lifetimes, and the sons of manual laborers were still more likely to improve their place in society. In New York City about a third of the Italian and Jewish immigrants of the 1890s had risen from unskilled to skilled jobs a decade later. Even in Newburyport, Massachusetts, a town that was something of an economic backwater, most laborers made some progress, though far fewer rose to skilled or white-collar positions than in more prosperous cities.

Such progress was primarily the result of the economic growth the nation was experiencing and of the energy and ambition of the people, native-born and immigrant alike, who were pouring into the cities in such numbers. The public education system gave an additional boost to the upwardly mobile.

The history of American education after about 1870 reflects the impact of social and economic change. Although Horace Mann, Henry Barnard, and others had laid the foundations for state-supported school systems, most of these systems became compulsory only after the Civil War, when the growth of cities provided the concentration of population and financial resources necessary for economical mass education. In the 1860s about half the children in the country were getting some formal education, but this did not mean that half the children were attending school at any one time.

Thereafter, steady growth and improvement took place. Attendance in the public schools increased from 6.8 million in 1870 to 15.5 million in 1900, a remarkable expansion even when allowance is made for the growth of the population. More remarkable still, during a time when prices were declining steadily, public expenditures for education nearly quadrupled. A typical elementary school graduate, at least in the cities, could count on having studied, besides the traditional "Three Rs," history, geography, a bit of science, drawing, and physical training.

Industrialization created many demands for vocational and technical training; both employers and unskilled workers quickly grasped the possibilities. Science courses were taught in some of the new high schools, but secondary education was still assumed to be only for those with special abilities and youths whose families did not require that they immediately become breadwinners. As late as 1890 fewer than 300,000 of the 14.3 million children attending public and private schools had progressed beyond the eighth grade and nearly a third of these were attending private institutions.

Education certainly helped young people to rise in the world, but progress from rags to real riches was far from common. Carnegies were rare. A study of the family backgrounds of 200 late-nineteenth-century business leaders revealed that nearly all of them grew up in well-to-do middle-class families. They were far better educated than the general run, and most were members of one or another Protestant church.

The unrealistic expectations inspired by the rags-to-riches myth more than the absence of real opportunity probably explains why so many workers, even when expressing dissatisfaction with life as it was, continued to subscribe to such middle-class values as hard work and thrift—that is, they continued to hope.

THE "NEW" IMMIGRATION

Industrial expansion increased the need for labor, and this in turn powerfully stimulated immigration. Between 1866 and 1915 about 25 million foreigners entered the United States. Industrial growth alone does not explain the influx. The launching in 1858 of the English liner *Great Eastern,* which was nearly 700 feet from stem to stern and weighed about 19,000 tons, opened a new era in transatlantic travel. Although most immigrants traveled in steerage, which was cramped and almost totally lacking in anything that could be considered an amenity, the

Atlantic crossing, once so hazardous, became safe and speedy with the perfection of the steamship. Competition between the great packet lines such as Cunard, North German Lloyd, and Holland-America drove down the cost of the passage, and advertising by the lines further stimulated traffic.

"Push" pressures as well as these "pull" factors had much to do with this "new" immigration. Improvements in transportation produced unexpected and disruptive changes in the economies of many European countries. Cheap wheat from the United States, Russia, and other parts of the world poured into Europe, bringing disaster to farmers throughout Europe. The spreading industrial revolution and the increased use of farm machinery led to the collapse of the peasant economy of central and southern Europe. For rural inhabitants this meant the loss of self-sufficiency, the fragmentation of landholdings, unemployment, and for many the decision to make a new start in the New World.

Political and religious persecutions pushed still others into the migrating stream, but the main reason for immigration remained the desire for economic betterment. "In America," a British immigrant reported, "you get pies and puddings."

While immigrants continued to people the farms of America, industry absorbed an ever-increasing number of the newcomers. In 1870 one industrial worker in three was foreign-born. When congressional investigators examined 21 major industries early in the new century, they discovered that well over half of the labor force had not been born in the United States.

Before 1882, when—in addition to the Chinese—criminals, and persons adjudged mentally defective or liable to become public charges were excluded, entry into the United States was almost unrestricted. Indeed, until 1891 the Atlantic coast states, not the federal government, exercised whatever controls were imposed on newcomers. Even when federally imposed, medical inspection was perfunctory. Public health officials boasted that with "one glance" at each arrival, the inspectors could "take in six details, namely the scalp, face, neck, hands, gait and general condition, both mental and physical." Only those who failed this "test" were examined more closely. On average, only 1 immigrant in 50 was ultimately rejected.

Private agencies, philanthropic and commercial, served as a link between the new arrivals and employers looking for labor. Until the Foran Act of 1885 outlawed the practice, a few companies brought in skilled workers under contract, advancing them passage money and collecting it in installments from their paychecks, a system somewhat like the indentured servitude of colonial times. Numerous nationality groups assisted (and sometimes exploited) their compatriots by organizing "immigrant banks" that recruited labor in the old country, arranged transportation, and then housed the newcomers in boardinghouses in the United States while finding them jobs. The *padrone* system of the Italians and Greeks was typical. The *padrone,* a sort of contractor who agreed to supply gangs of unskilled workers to companies for a lump sum, usually signed on immigrants unfamiliar with American wage levels at rates that ensured him a healthy profit.

Immigration, 1860–1910
In this graph, Germany is counted as a part of northern and western Europe. Note the new immigration from southern and eastern Europe in the early 1900s.

Beginning in the 1880s, the spreading effects of industrialization in Europe caused a shift in the sources of American immigration from northern and western to southern and eastern sections of the Continent. In 1882, 789,000 immigrants entered the United States; more than 350,000 came from Great Britain and Germany, only 32,000 from Italy, and fewer than 17,000 from Russia. In 1907—the all-time peak year, with 1,285,000 immigrants—Great Britain and Germany supplied fewer than half as many as they had 25 years earlier, while Russia and Italy were supplying eleven times as many as then. Up to 1880, only about 200,000 southern and eastern Europeans had migrated to America. Between 1880 and 1910, approximately 8.4 million arrived.

NEW IMMIGRANTS FACE NEW NATIVISM

The "new" immigrants, like the "old" Irish of the 1840s and 1850s, were mostly peasants. They also seemed more than ordinarily clannish; southern Italians typically called all people outside their families *forestieri,* "foreigners." Old-stock Americans thought them harder to assimilate, and in fact many were. Some Italian immigrants, for example, were unmarried men who had come to the United States to earn enough money to buy a farm back home. Such people made hard and willing workers but were not much concerned with being part of an American community.

These "birds of passage" were a substantial minority, but the immigrant who saved in order to bring his wife and children or his younger brothers and sisters to America was more typical. In addition, thousands of immigrants came as family groups and intended to remain. Some, like the eastern European Jewish migrants, were refugees who were almost desperately eager to become Americans, although of course they retained and nurtured much of their traditional culture.

Cultural differences among immigrants were often large and had important effects on their relations with native-born Americans and with other immigrant groups. Italians who settled in the city of Buffalo, for example, adjusted relatively smoothly to urban industrial life because of their close family and kinship ties. Poverty, unemployment, females holding jobs outside the home, and other traumas that might have been expected to disrupt family relationships apparently had little effect. Polish immigrants in Buffalo, having different traditions, found adjustment more difficult.

German American and Irish American Catholics had different attitudes that caused them to clash over such matters as the policies of the Catholic University in Washington. Although (or perhaps because) the Haymarket anarchists were German-born, in 1887 one prominent German American denounced the Knights of Labor as a hotbed of radicalism—and was said to have claimed that it was dominated by "Irish ignoramuses." Controversies erupted between Catholic and Protestant German Americans, between Greek American groups supporting various political factions in their homeland, and so on.

Confused by such differences and conflicts, many "older" Americans concluded, wrongly but understandably, that the new immigrants were incapable of becoming good citizens and should be kept out. During the 1880s, large numbers of social workers, economists, and church leaders, worried by the problems that arose when so many poor immigrants flocked into cities already bursting at the seams, began to believe that some restriction should be placed on the incoming human tide. The directors of charitable organizations, which bore the burden of aiding the most unfortunate immigrants, complained that their resources were being exhausted by the needs of the flood.

Social Darwinists and people obsessed with pseudoscientific ideas about "racial purity" also found the new immigration alarming. Misunderstanding the findings of the new science of genetics, they attributed the social problems associated with mass immigration to supposed physiological characteristics of the newcomers. Forgetting that earlier Americans had accused pre–Civil War Irish and German immigrants of similar deficiencies, they decided that the peoples of southern and eastern Europe were racially (and therefore permanently) inferior to "Nordic" and "Anglo-Saxon" types and ought to be kept out.

Workers, fearing the competition of people with low living standards and no bargaining power, spoke out against the "enticing of penniless and unapprised immigrants . . . to undermine our wages and social welfare." In 1883 the president of the Amalgamated Iron and Steel Workers told a Senate committee that Hungarian, Polish, Italian, and other immigrants "can live where I think a decent man would die; they can live on . . . food that other men would not touch." A Wisconsin iron worker put it this way: "Immigrants work for almost nothing and seem to be able to live on wind—something I can not do."

After the Exclusion Act of 1882 and the almost meaningless 1885 ban on importing contract labor, no further restrictions were imposed on immigration until the twentieth century. Strong support for a literacy test for admission developed in the 1890s, pushed by a new organization, the Immigration Restriction League. Since there was much more illiteracy in the southeastern quarter of Europe than in the northwestern, such a test would discriminate without seeming to do so on national or racial grounds. A literacy test bill passed both houses of Congress in 1897, but President Cleveland vetoed it. Such a "radical departure"

Contemporary cartoonists reflected the "new nativist" attitude against unrestricted immigration. Frank Beard's 1885 drawing shows anarchists, socialists, and members of the Mafia (indicated here as the Black Hand) arriving from the sewers of Europe and being resisted by Columbia and her watchdogs "Law" and "Order."

from the "generous and free-handed policy" of the past, Cleveland said, was unjustified. He added, perhaps with tongue in cheek, that a literacy requirement would not keep out "unruly agitators," who were only too adept at reading and writing.

THE EXPANDING CITY AND ITS PROBLEMS

Americans who favored restricting immigration made much of the fact that so many of the newcomers crowded into the cities, aggravating problems of housing, public health, crime, and immorality. Immigrants concentrated in the cities because the jobs created by expanding industry were located there. So, of course, did native-born Americans; the proportion of urban dwellers had been steadily increasing since about 1820.

It is important to keep in mind that population density is not necessarily related to the existence of large cities. In the late nineteenth century there were areas in Asia as large as the United States that were as densely populated as Belgium and England yet overwhelmingly rural. The United States by any standard was sparsely populated, but well before the Civil War it had become one of the most urban nations in the world.

Industrialization does not entirely explain the growth of nineteenth-century cities. All the large American cities began as commercial centers, and the development of huge metropolises like New York and Chicago would have been impossible without the national transportation network. But by the final decades of the century, the expansion of industry had become the chief cause of city growth. Thus the urban concentration continued; in 1890 one person in three lived in a city, by 1910 nearly one in two.

A steadily increasing proportion of the urban population was made up of immigrants. In 1890 the foreign-born population of Chicago almost equaled the total population of Chicago in 1880; a third of all Bostonians and a quarter of all Philadelphians were immigrants; and four out of five residents of New York City were either foreign-born or the children of immigrants.

After 1890 the immigrant concentration became even more dense. The migrants from eastern and southern Europe lacked the resources to travel to the agriculturally developing regions (to say nothing of the sums necessary to acquire land and farm equipment). As the concentration progressed it fed upon itself, for all the eastern cities developed many ethnic neighborhoods, in each of which immigrants of one nationality congregated. Lonely, confused, often unable to speak English, the Italians, the Greeks, the Polish and Russian Jews, and other immigrants tended to settle where their predecessors had settled.

Most newcomers intended to become United States citizens, to be absorbed in the famous American "melting pot." But they also wanted to maintain their traditional culture. They supported "national" churches and schools. Newspapers in their native languages flourished, as did social organizations of all sorts. Each great American city became a Europe in microcosm. New York City, the great *entrepôt,* had a Little Italy; Polish, Greek, Jewish, and Bohemian quarters; and even a Chinatown.

Observing the immigrants' attachment to "foreign" values and institutions, numbers of "natives" accused the newcomers of resisting Americanization and blamed them for urban problems. The immigrants were involved in these problems, but the rapidity of urban expansion explains the troubles associated with city life far more fully than the high percentage of foreigners.

TEEMING TENEMENTS

The cities were suffering from growing pains. Sewer and water facilities frequently could not keep pace with skyrocketing needs. By the 1890s the tremendous growth of Chicago had put such a strain on its sanitation system that the Chicago River had become virtually an open sewer, and the city's drinking water contained such a high concentration of germ-killing chemicals that it tasted like creosote. In the 1880s all the sewers of Baltimore emptied into the sluggish Back Basin, and according to the journalist H. L. Mencken, every summer the city smelled "like a billion polecats." Fire protection became less and less adequate; garbage piled up in the streets faster than it could be carted away; and the streets themselves crumbled beneath the pounding of heavy traffic. Urban growth

DEBATING THE PAST

Did immigrants assimilate? In this 1909 photograph, immigrant children at Ellis Island hold American flags as they share a ride in an "Uncle Sam" wagon. Did they and their parents readily adjust to life in the United States?

In 1951 historian Oscar Handlin thought not. He asserted that immigrants were "uprooted" from the lives they had known and "replanted" in "strange ground, among strangers, where strange manners prevailed." Many were shattered by the experience, which accounted for rampant crime, ruptured families, and social disorder in tenement districts.

But subsequent studies found that many immigrants adapted well. John Bodnar (1985) pointedly described immigrants as "transplanted" rather than "uprooted." When challenged by new situations, they "forged a culture, a constellation of behavioral and thought patterns which would offer them explanations, order, and a prescription for how to live with their lives." Sometimes they modified traditional institutions to serve new purposes; sometimes they created new ones, such as ethnic clubs and parochial schools. The diversity of immigrant experiences was reflected in the *Harvard Encyclopedia of American Ethnic Groups* (1980), edited by Handlin and Stephen Thernstrom. The trend toward specialized studies of different groups prompted Arthur M. Schlesinger, Jr. (1992) to bemoan his profession's role in the "disuniting of America."

In short, each child in "Uncle Sam's" wagon experienced life in his or her own way; but they were in for the ride together.

Oscar Handlin, *The Uprooted*, 1951, John Bodnar, *The Transplanted* (1985), Arthur M. Schlesinger, Jr., *The Disuniting of America* (1992). Other studies anticipating Bodnar's thesis are Francis G. Courvares, *The Remaking of Pittsburgh* (1984), Humbert S. Nelli, *Italians in Chicago* (1970), Alan Dawley, *Class and Community* (1976), and Virginia Yans-McLaughlin, *Family and Community: Italian Immigrants in Buffalo* (1977). Ronald Takaki, *A Different Mirror* (1993) endorses the multiculturalist approach. See also Roger Daniels, *Guarding the Golden Door: American Immigration Policy and Immigrants since 1882* (2004).

Impoverished immigrant families, like the one in this 1889 Jacob Riis photograph, often lived in tiny windowless rooms in crowded tenement districts. Riis devised a "flash bulb" for indoor photographs in poorly illuminated rooms like this one.

proceeded with such speed that new streets were laid out more rapidly than they could be paved. Chicago had more than 1400 miles of dirt streets in 1890.

People poured into the great cities faster than housing could be built to accommodate them. The influx into areas already densely packed in the 1840s became unbearable as rising property values and the absence of zoning laws conspired to make builders use every possible foot of space, squeezing out light and air ruthlessly in order to wedge in a few additional family units.

Substandard living quarters aggravated other evils such as disease and the disintegration of family life, with its attendant mental anguish, crime, and juvenile delinquency. The bloody New York City riots of 1863, though sparked by dislike of the Civil War draft and of blacks, reflected the bitterness and frustration of thousands jammed together amid filth and threatened by disease. A citizens' committee seeking to discover the causes of the riots expressed its amazement after visiting the slums "that so much misery, disease, and wretchedness can be huddled together and hidden . . . unvisited and unthought of, so near our own abodes."

New York City created a Metropolitan Health Board in 1866, and a state tenement house law the following year made a feeble beginning at regulating city housing. Another law in 1879 placed a limit on the percentage of lot space that could be covered by new construction and established minimal standards of plumbing and ventilation. The magazine *Plumber and Sanitary Engineer* sponsored a contest to pick the best design for a tenement that met these specifications. The winner of the competition was James E. Ware, whose plan for a "dumbbell" apartment house managed to crowd from 24 to 32 four-room apartments on a plot of ground only 25 by 100 feet.

Despite these efforts in 1890 more than 1.4 million persons were living on Manhattan Island, and in some sections the population density exceeded 900 persons per acre. The unhealthiness of the tenements was notorious. No one knows exactly, but as late as 1900 about three quarters of the residents of New York City's Lower East Side lacked indoor toilets and had to use backyard outhouses to relieve themselves. One noxious corner became known as the "lung block" because of the prevalence of tuberculosis among its inhabitants. In 1900 three out of five babies born in one poor district of Chicago died before their first birthday.

Equally frightening was the impact of overcrowding on the morals of tenement dwellers. The number of prison inmates in the United States increased by 50 percent in the 1880s, and the homicide rate nearly tripled, most of the rise occurring in cities. Driven into the streets by the squalor of their homes, slum youths formed gangs bearing names like Alley Gang, Rock Gang, and Hell's Kitchen Gang. From petty thievery and shoplifting they graduated to housebreaking, bank robbery, and murder. According to Jacob Riis, when the leader of the infamous Whyo Gang, convicted of murder, confessed his sins to a prison chaplain, "his father confessor turned pale . . . though many years of labor as chaplain of the Tombs had hardened him to such rehearsals."

Slums bred criminals—the wonder was that they bred so few. They also drove well-to-do residents into exclusive sections and to the suburbs. From Boston's Beacon Hill and Back Bay to San Francisco's Nob Hill, the rich retired into their cluttered mansions and ignored conditions in the poorer parts of town.

THE CITIES MODERNIZE

As American cities grew larger and more crowded, thereby aggravating a host of social problems, practical forces operated to bring about improvements. Once the relationship between polluted water and disease was fully understood, everyone saw the need for decent water and sewage systems. While some businessmen profited from corrupt dealings with the city machines, more of them wanted efficient and honest government in order to reduce their tax bills. City dwellers of all classes resented dirt, noise, and ugliness, and in many communities public-spirited groups formed societies to plant trees, clean up littered areas, and develop recreational facilities. When one city undertook improvements, others tended to follow suit, spurred on by local pride and the booster spirit.

Gradually the basic facilities of urban living were improved. Streets were paved, first with cobblestones and wood blocks and then with smoother, quieter asphalt. Gaslight, then electric arc lights, and finally Edison's incandescent lamps brightened the cities after dark, making law enforcement easier, stimulating night life, and permitting factories and shops to operate after sunset.

Urban transportation underwent enormous changes. Until the 1880s, horse-drawn cars running on tracks set flush with the street were the main means of urban public transportation. In 1860 New York City's horsecars were carrying about 100,000 passengers a day. But horsecars had serious drawbacks. Enormous numbers of horses were needed, and feeding and stabling the animals was costly. Their droppings (10 pounds per day per horse) became a major source of urban pollution. That is why the invention of the electric trolley car in the 1880s put an end to horsecar transportation. Trolleys were cheaper and less unsightly than horsecars and quieter than steam-powered trains.

A retired naval officer, Frank J. Sprague, installed the first practical electric trolley line in Richmond, Virginia, in 1887–1888. At once other cities seized on the trolley. Lines soon radiated outward from the city centers, bringing commuters and shoppers from the residential districts to the business district. Without them the big-city department stores could not have flourished as they did. By 1895 some 850 lines were busily hauling city dwellers over 10,000 miles of track, and mileage tripled in the following decade. As with other new enterprises, ownership of street railways quickly became centralized until a few big operators controlled the trolleys of more than 100 eastern cities and towns.

Streetcars changed the character of big-city life. Before their introduction urban communities were limited by the distances people could conveniently walk to work. The "walking city" could not easily extend more than 2½ miles from its center. Streetcars increased this radius to 6 miles or more, which meant that the area of the city expanded enormously. Dramatic population shifts resulted as the better-off moved away from the center in search of air and space, abandoning the crumbling, jam-packed older neighborhoods to the poor. Thus economic segregation speeded the growth of ghettos. Older peripheral towns that had maintained some of the self-contained qualities of village life were swallowed up, becoming metropolitan centers.

As time passed, each new area, originally peopled by rising economic groups, tended to become crowded and then to deteriorate. By extending their tracks beyond the developed areas, the streetcar companies further speeded suburban growth because they assured developers, bankers, builders, and middle-class home buyers of efficient transport to the center of town. By keeping fares low (5 cents a ride was standard) the lines enabled poor people to "escape" to the countryside on holidays.

Advances in bridge design, notably the perfection of the steel-cable suspension bridge by John A. Roebling, aided the ebb and flow of metropolitan populations. The Brooklyn Bridge described by a poet as "a weird metallic Apparition . . . the cables, like divine messages from above . . . cutting and dividing into innumerable musical spaces the nude immensity of the sky," was Roebling's triumph. Completed in 1883 at a cost of $15 million, it was soon carrying more than 33 million passengers a year over the East River between Manhattan and Brooklyn.

Efforts to relieve the congestion in slum districts made little headway. In Brooklyn Alfred T. White established Home Buildings, a 40-family model tene-

On Sundays in the late nineteenth century, city people crowded into streetcars and thronged to the countryside. Enticed by this taste of bucolic splendor, many chose to live in the suburbs and take the streetcars to work downtown. Soon, the population density of the suburbs resembled that of the cities.

ment in 1877; eventually he expanded the experiment to include 267 apartments. Each unit had plenty of light and air and contained its own sink and toilet. Ellen Collins developed a smaller project in Manhattan's Fourth Ward in the 1890s. These model tenements were self-sustaining, but of necessity they yielded only modest returns. The landlords were essentially philanthropists; their work had no significant impact on urban housing in the nineteenth century.

LEISURE ACTIVITIES: MORE FUN AND GAMES

By bringing together large numbers of people, cities made possible many kinds of social activity difficult or impossible to maintain in rural areas. Cities remained unsurpassed as centers of artistic and intellectual life. New York was the outstanding example, as seen in its many theaters and in the founding of the American Museum of Natural History (1870), the Metropolitan Museum of Art (1870), and the Metropolitan Opera (1883), but other cities were equally hospitable to such endeavors. Boston's Museum of Fine Arts, for example, was founded in 1870 and the Boston Symphony in 1881.

Of course less sophisticated forms of recreation also flourished in the urban environment. From 1865 to 1885 the number of breweries in Massachusetts quadrupled. It is only a slight exaggeration to say that in crowded urban centers there was a saloon on every corner; during the last third of the century the number of saloons in the country tripled. Saloons were strictly male working-class institutions, usually decorated with pictures and other mementos of sports heroes, the bar perhaps under the charge of a retired pugilist.

For workingmen the saloon was a kind of club, a place to meet friends, exchange news and gossip, gamble, and eat, as well as to drink beer and whiskey. Saloons also flourished because factory owners and other employers of large numbers of workers tended to forbid the consumption of alcohol on their premises. In addition, the gradual reduction of the workday left men with more free time, which may explain why vaudeville and burlesques, the latter described by one straightlaced critic as a "disgraceful spectacle of padded legs juggling and tight-laced wriggling," also proliferated.

Calvinist-inspired opposition to sports as a frivolous waste of valuable time was steadily evaporating, replaced among the upper and middle classes by the realization that games like golf and tennis were "healthy occupation[s] for mind and body." Bicycling became a fad, both as a means of getting from place to place in the ever-expanding cities and as a form of exercise and recreation.

Many of the new streetcar companies built picnic grounds and amusement parks at their outer limits. In good weather thousands seeking to relax after a hard day's work flocked to these "trolley parks" to enjoy a fresh-air meal or patronize the shooting galleries, merry-go-rounds, and "freak shows."

The postwar era also saw the first important development of spectator sports, again because cities provided the concentrations of population necessary to support them. Curious relationships developed between upper- and working-class interests and between competitive sports as pure enjoyment for players and spectators and sports as something to bet on. Horse racing had strictly upper-class origins, but racetracks attracted huge crowds of ordinary people more intent on picking a winner than on improving the breed.

Professional boxing offers an even better example. It was in a sense a hobby of the rich, who sponsored favorite gladiators, offered prizes, and often wagered large sums on the matches. But the audiences were made up overwhelmingly of young working-class males, from whose ranks most of the fighters emerged. The gambling and also the brutality of the bloody, bare-knuckle character of the fights caused many communities to outlaw boxing, a fact that added to the appeal of the sport for some.

The first widely popular pugilist was the legendary "Boston Strong Boy," John L. Sullivan, who became heavyweight champion in 1882 by disposing of one Paddy Ryan in nine rounds. Sullivan was an immensely powerful man whose idea of fighting, according to his biographer, "was simply to hammer his opponent into unconsciousness," something he did repeatedly during his ten-year reign. Sullivan became an international celebrity and made and lost large sums during this period. He was also the beneficiary of patronage in such forms as a diamond belt worth $10,000 presented to him by some of his admirers. Yet box-

Luna Park at Coney Island was a vast living theatre, in which the strollers were both spectators and actors. At night, a quarter million electric lights turned Luna Park into what its designer, Frederic Thompson, called "a different world—a dream world, perhaps a nightmare world—where all is bizarre and fantastic."

ing remained a raffish, clandestine occupation. One of Sullivan's important fights took place in France, on the estate of Baron Rothschild, yet when it ended both he and his opponent were arrested.

Three major team games, baseball, football, and basketball, developed in something approaching their modern form during the last quarter of the century. Various forms of what became baseball were played long before that time. Organized teams, in most cases made up of upper-class amateurs, first emerged in the 1840s, but the game only became truly popular during the Civil War, when it was a major form of camp recreation for the troops.

After the war professional teams began to appear (the first, the Cincinnati Red Stockings, paid players between $800 and $1400 for the season), and in 1876 teams in eight cities formed the National League. The American League followed in 1901. After a brief period of rivalry, the two leagues made peace in 1903, the year of the first World Series.

Organized play led to codification of the rules and improvements in technique and strategy, for example, the development of "minor" leagues; impartial umpires calling balls and strikes and ruling on close plays; the use of catcher's masks and padded gloves; the invention of various kinds of curves and other erratic pitches (often enhanced by "doctoring" the ball). As early as the 1870s, baseball was being called "the national game" and losing all upper-class connotations. Important games attracted crowds in the tens of thousands; betting became a problem. Despite its urban origins, its broad green fields and dusty base paths gave the game a rural character that only recently has begun to fade away.

Nobody "invented" baseball, but both football and basketball owe their present form to individuals. James Naismith's invention of basketball is undisputed. In 1891, while a student at a YMCA school, he attached peach baskets to the edge of an elevated running track in the gymnasium and drew up what are still the basic rules of the game. The first basketball was a soccer ball. The game was popular from the start, but because it was played indoors it was not an important spectator sport until much later.

Football was not created by one person in the way that basketball was; it evolved out of English rugby. For many decades it remained almost entirely a college sport (and thus played almost entirely by upper- and middle-class types). Organized collegiate sports dated back to before the Civil War; the first intercollegiate matches were rowing races between Harvard and Yale students. The first intercollege football game occurred when Princeton defeated Rutgers in 1869, and by the 1880s college football had become extremely popular.

Spectator sports had little appeal to women at this time and indeed for decades thereafter. And few women participated in organized athletics. Sports were "manly" activities; a woman might ride a bicycle, play croquet and perhaps a little tennis, but to display any concentrated interest in excelling in a sport was considered unfeminine.

CHRISTIANITY'S CONSCIENCE AND THE SOCIAL GOSPEL

The modernization of the great cities was not solving most of the social problems of the slums. As this fact became clear, a number of urban religious leaders began to take a hard look at the situation. Traditionally, American churchmen had insisted that where sin was concerned there were no extenuating circumstances. To the well-to-do they preached the virtues of thrift and hard work; to the poor they extended the possibility of a better existence in the next world; to all they stressed one's responsibility for one's own behavior—and thus for one's own salvation. Such a point of view brought meager comfort to residents of slums. Consequently, the churches lost influence in the poorer sections. Furthermore, as better-off citizens followed the streetcar lines out from the city centers, their church leaders followed them.

An increasing proportion of the residents of the blighted districts were Catholics, and the Roman church devoted much effort to distributing alms, maintaining homes for orphans and old people, and other forms of social welfare. But church leaders seemed unconcerned with the social causes of the blight; they were deeply committed to the idea that sin and vice were personal, poverty an act of God. They deplored the rising tide of crime, disease, and destitution among their coreligionists, yet they failed to see the connection between these evils and the squalor of the slums. "Intemperance is the great evil we have to overcome," wrote the president of the leading Catholic charitable organization, the Society of St. Vincent de Paul. "It is the source of the misery for at least three-fourths of the families we are called upon to visit and relieve."

The conservatism of most Protestant and Catholic clergymen did not prevent some earnest preachers from working directly to improve the lot of the city poor. Some followed the path blazed by Dwight L. Moody, a lay evangelist who became famous throughout America and Great Britain in the 1870s. A gargantuan figure weighing nearly 300 pounds, Moody conducted a vigorous campaign to persuade the denizens of the slums to cast aside their sinful ways. He went among them full of enthusiasm and God's love and made an impact no less powerful than that of George Whitefield during the Great Awakening of the eighteenth century or Charles Grandison Finney in the first part of the nineteenth. The evangelists founded mission schools in the slums and tried to provide spiritual and recreational facilities for the unfortunate. They were prominent in the establishment of American branches of the YMCA (1851) and the Salvation Army (1880).

However, the evangelists paid little heed to the causes of urban poverty and vice, believing that faith in God would enable the poor to transcend the material difficulties of life. For a number of Protestant clergymen who had become familiar with the slums, a different approach seemed called for. Slum conditions caused the sins and crimes of the cities; the wretched human beings who committed them could not be blamed, these ministers argued. They began to preach a "Social Gospel" that focused on improving living conditions rather than on saving souls. If people were to lead pure lives, they must have enough to eat, decent homes, and opportunities to develop their talents. Social Gospelers advocated civil service reform, child labor legislation, regulation of big corporations, and heavy taxes on incomes and inheritances.

The most influential preacher of the Social Gospel was probably Washington Gladden. At first, Gladden, who was raised on a Massachusetts farm, had opposed all government interference in social and economic affairs, but his experiences as a minister in Springfield, Massachusetts, and Columbus, Ohio, exposed him to the realities of life in industrial cities, and his views changed. In *Applied Christianity* (1886) and in other works he defended labor's right to organize and strike and denounced the idea that supply and demand should control wage rates. He favored factory inspection laws, strict regulation of public utilities, and other reforms.

Gladden never questioned the basic values of capitalism. But by the 1890s a number of ministers had gone all the way to socialism. The Reverend William D. P. Bliss of Boston, for example, believed in the kind of welfare state envisioned by Edward Bellamy in *Looking Backward*. He founded the Society of Christian

Socialists (1889) and edited a radical journal, *The Dawn*. In addition to nationalizing industry, Bliss and other Christian Socialists advocated government unemployment relief programs, public housing and slum clearance projects, and other measures designed to aid the city poor.

Nothing so well reveals the receptivity of the public to the Social Gospel as the popularity of Charles M. Sheldon's novel *In His Steps* (1896), one of America's all-time best-sellers. Sheldon, a minister in Topeka, Kansas, described what happened in the mythical city of Raymond when a group of leading citizens decided to live truly Christian lives, asking themselves "What would Jesus do?" before adopting any course of action. Naturally the tone of Raymond's society was immensely improved, but basic social reforms followed quickly. The Rectangle, a terrible slum area, "too dirty, too coarse, too sinful, too awful for close contact," became the center of a great reform effort. One of Raymond's "leading society heiresses" undertook a slum clearance project, and a concerted attack was made on drunkenness and immorality. The moral regeneration of the entire community was soon accomplished.

THE SETTLEMENT HOUSES

Although millions read *In His Steps,* its effect, and that of other Social Gospel literature, was merely inspirational. On the practical level, a number of earnest souls began to grapple with slum problems by organizing what were known as settlement houses. These were community centers located in poor districts that provided guidance and services to all who would use them. The settlement workers, most of them idealistic, well-to-do young people, lived in the houses and were active in neighborhood affairs.

The prototype of the settlement house was London's Toynbee Hall, founded in the early 1880s; the first American example was the Neighborhood Guild, opened on the Lower East Side of New York in 1886 by Dr. Stanton Coit. By the turn of the century 100 had been established, the most famous being Jane Addams's Hull House in Chicago (1889), Robert A. Woods's South End House in Boston (1892), and Lillian Wald's Henry Street Settlement in New York (1893).

While some men were active in the movement, the most important settlement house workers were women fresh from college—the first generation of young women to experience the trauma of having developed their capacities only to find that society offered them few opportunities to use them. The settlements provided an outlet for their hopes and energies, and they seized upon the work avidly. An English social reformer who visited Hull House around the turn of the century described the residents as "strong-minded energetic women, bustling about their various enterprises" and "earnest-faced self-subordinating and mild-mannered men who slide from room to room apologetically."

The settlement workers tried to interpret American ways to the new immigrants and to create a community spirit in order to teach, in the words of one of them, "right living through social relations." Unlike most charity workers, who

This portrait of Jane Addams was completed in 1896 by Alice Kellog Tyler, who worked as an artist at Hull House.

acted out of a sense of upper-class responsibility toward the unfortunate, they expected to benefit morally and intellectually themselves by experiencing a way of life far different from their own and by obtaining "the first-hand knowledge the college classroom cannot give."

In Boston Robert A. Woods organized clubs to get the youngsters of the South End off the streets, helped establish a restaurant where a meal could be had for 5 cents, acted as an arbitrator in labor disputes, and lobbied for laws tightening up the franchises of public utility companies. In Chicago Jane Addams developed an outstanding cultural program that included classes in music and art and an excellent "little theater" group. Hull House soon boasted a gymnasium, a day nursery, and several social clubs. Addams also worked tirelessly and effectively for improved public services and for social legislation of all kinds. She even got herself appointed garbage inspector in her ward and hounded local landlords and the garbage contractor until something approaching decent service was established.

A few critics considered the settlement houses mere devices to socialize the unruly poor by teaching them the "punctilios of upper-class propriety," but almost everyone appreciated their virtues. By the end of the century the Catholics, laggard in entering the arena of practical social reform, were joining the movement, partly because they were losing many communicants to socially minded Protestant churches. The first Catholic-run settlement house was founded in 1898 in an Italian district of New York. Two years later Brownson House in Los Angeles, catering chiefly to Mexican immigrants, threw open its doors.

With all their accomplishments, the settlement houses seemed to be fighting a losing battle. "Private beneficence," Jane Addams wrote of Hull House, "is totally inadequate to deal with the vast numbers of the city's disinherited." As a tropical forest grows faster than a handful of men armed with machetes can cut it down, so the slums, fed by an annual influx of hundreds of thousands, blighted new areas more rapidly than the intrepid settlement house workers could clean up old ones. It became increasingly apparent that the wealth and authority of the state must be brought to bear in order to keep abreast of the problem.

CIVILIZATION AND ITS DISCONTENTS

As the nineteenth century died, the majority of the American people, especially those comfortably well-off, the residents of small towns, the shopkeepers, and some farmers and skilled workers, remained confirmed optimists and uncritical admirers of their civilization. However, blacks, immigrants, and others who failed to share equitably in the good things of life, along with a growing number of humanitarian reformers, found little to cheer about and much to lament in their increasingly industrialized society. Giant monopolies flourished despite federal restrictions. The gap between rich and poor appeared to be widening, while the slum spread its poison and the materially successful made a god of their success. Human values seemed in grave danger of being crushed by impersonal forces typified by the great corporations.

In 1871 Walt Whitman, usually so full of extravagant praise for everything American, had called his fellow countrymen the "most materialistic and money-making people ever known":

> I say we had best look our times and lands searchingly in the face, like a physician diagnosing some deep disease. Never was there, perhaps, more hollowness of heart than at present, and here in the United States.

Harvard professor Henry Adams, was critical of the way his contemporaries had become moneygrubbers. "All one's friends," he complained, along with church and university leaders and other educated people, "had joined the banks to force submission to capitalism."

Of course intellectuals often tend to be critical of the world they live in, whatever its nature; Thoreau denounced materialism and the worship of progress in the 1840s as vigorously as any late nineteenth-century prophet of gloom. But the voices of the dissatisfied were rising. Despite the many benefits that industrialization had made possible, it was by no means clear around 1900 that the American people were really better off under the new dispensation.

MILESTONES

1858	English launch transatlantic liner *Great Eastern*
1870	Metropolitan Museum of Art and American Museum of Natural History open in New York City
1876	Eight teams form National Baseball League
1880	American branch of Salvation Army is founded
1880s	"New" immigration begins
1882	John L. Sullivan wins heavyweight boxing championship
	Exclusion Act bans Chinese immigrants
1883	Roebling completes Brooklyn Bridge
1885	Foran Act outlaws importing contract skilled labor
1888	Richmond, Virginia opens first urban electric streetcar system
1889	Jane Addams founds Hull House
1896	Charles M. Sheldon asks "What would Jesus do?" in best-selling *In His Steps*
1897	Cleveland vetoes Congress's literacy test bill

20

INTELLECTUAL AND CULTURAL TRENDS

Industrialization altered the way Americans thought at the same time that it transformed their ways of making a living. Technological advances revolutionized the communication of ideas more drastically than they did the transportation of goods or the manufacture of steel. The materialism that permeated American attitudes toward business also affected contemporary education and literature, while Charles Darwin's theory of evolution influenced American philosophers, lawyers, and historians profoundly.

New ideas about how children should be educated and what they should be taught emerged along with new methods of communicating information to adults. As society became more complex, the need for specialized training increased, with the result that higher education became more important. Americans began to make significant contributions both in the "hard" sciences, such as chemistry and physics, and in the relatively new "soft" social sciences, such as psychology, political science, and sociology. A new literary flowering comparable to the "renaissance" of the 1840s and 1850s occurred in the 1870s and 1880s. By the end of the century America had finally emerged intellectually from the shadow of Europe.

PUBLISHING

Millions of Americans profited from the proliferation of public libraries. By the end of the century nearly all the states supported libraries. Private donors, led by the steel industrialist Andrew Carnegie, contributed millions to the cause. In 1900 over 1700 libraries in the United States had collections of more than 5000 volumes.

Photograph of the first Remington typewriter, 1874. The typewriter was the idea of Christopher Sholes, a tinkerer at a machine shop in Milwaukee, Wisconsin. He put printer's type at the end of little rods, which struck a flat plate on which had been placed a sheet of carbon paper. E. Remington, a gun manufacturer in Ilion, New York, decided to build Sholes's "type-writer."

Newspapers were an even more important means of disseminating information and educating the masses. Here new technology supplied the major incentive for change. The development by Richard Hoe and Stephen Tucker of the web press (1871), which printed simultaneously on both sides of paper fed into it from large rolls, and Ottmar Mergenthaler's linotype machine (1886), which cast rows of type as needed directly from molten metal, cut printing costs dramatically. Machines for making paper out of wood pulp reduced the cost of newsprint to a quarter of what it had been in the 1860s. By 1895 machines were printing, cutting, and folding 32-page newspapers at a rate of 24,000 an hour.

The telegraph and transoceanic cables wrought a similar transformation in the gathering of news. Press associations, led by the New York Associated Press, flourished; the syndicated article appeared; and a few publishers—Edward W. Scripps was the first—began to acquire chains of newspapers.

Population growth and better education created an ever-larger demand for printed matter. At the same time, the integration of the economy enabled manufacturers to sell their goods all over the country. Advertising became important, and sellers soon learned that newspapers and magazines were excellent means of placing their products before millions of eyes. Advertising revenues soared just when new machines and general expansion were making publishing an expensive business. The day of the journeyman printer-editor ended. Rich men such as the railroad magnate Jay Gould and the mining tycoon George Hearst invested heavily in newspapers in the postwar decades.

John Singer Sargent's 1905 portrait of Joseph Pulitzer. On his death six years later, Pulitzer's will provided for the endowment of the Columbia School of Journalism and the establishment of Pulitzer Prizes for journalism, letters, and other categories.

Publishers tended to be conservative, but reaching the masses meant lowering intellectual and cultural standards, appealing to emotions, and adopting popular, sometimes radical, causes. Cheap, mass-circulation papers had first appeared in the 1830s and 1840s, the most successful being the *Sun,* the *Herald,* and the *Tribune* in New York, the *Philadelphia Public Ledger,* and the *Baltimore Sun.* None of them much exceeded a circulation of 50,000 before the Civil War. The first publisher to reach a truly massive audience was Joseph Pulitzer, a Hungarian-born immigrant who made a first-rate paper of the *St. Louis Post-Dispatch.* In 1883 Pulitzer bought the *New York World,* a sheet with a circulation of perhaps 20,000. Within a year he was selling 100,000 copies daily, and by the late 1890s the *World*'s circulation regularly exceeded 1 million.

"The *World* is the people's newspaper," Pulitzer boasted, and in the sense that it interested men and women of every sort, he was correct. Pulitzer's methods were quickly copied by competitors, especially William Randolph Hearst, who purchased the *New York Journal* in 1895 and soon outdid the *World* in sensationalism. But no other newspaperman of the era approached Pulitzer in originality, boldness, and the knack of reaching the masses without abandoning seriousness of purpose and basic integrity.

Growth and ferment also characterized the magazine world. In 1865 there were about 700 magazines in the country, by the turn of the century more than 5000. Until the mid-1880s, few of the new magazines were in any way unusual. A handful of serious periodicals, such as the *Atlantic Monthly, Harper's,* and *The*

Century, dominated the field. They were staid in tone and conservative in political caste. Articles on current affairs, a good deal of fiction and poetry, historical and biographical studies, and similar material filled their pages, and many of them justly prided themselves on the quality of their illustrations. Although they had great influence, none approached mass circulation because of the limited size of the upper-middle-class audience they aimed at. *The Century* reached a peak in the 1880s of about 250,000 when it published a series of articles on Civil War battles by famous commanders, but it could not sustain that level. A circulation of 100,000 was considered good for such magazines.

COLLEGES AND UNIVERSITIES

The same forces that were affecting the dissemination of information were also altering higher education and professional training. The number of colleges rose from about 350 to 500 between 1878 and 1898, and the student body roughly tripled. Despite this growth, less than 2 percent of the college-age population attended college, but the aspirations of the nation's youth were rising, and more and more parents had the financial means necessary for fulfilling them.

More significant than the expansion of the colleges were the alterations in their curricula and in the atmosphere permeating the average campus. In 1870 most colleges remained what they had been in the 1830s: small, limited in their offerings, intellectually stagnant. The ill-paid professors were seldom scholars of stature. Thereafter, change came like a flood tide. State universities proliferated; the federal government's land-grant program in support of training in "agriculture and the mechanic arts," established under the Morrill Act of 1862, came into its own; wealthy philanthropists poured fortunes into old institutions and founded new ones; educators introduced new courses and adopted new teaching methods; professional schools of law, medicine, education, business, journalism, and other specialties increased in number.

In the forefront of reform was Harvard, the oldest and most prestigious college in the country. In the 1860s it possessed an excellent faculty, but teaching methods were antiquated and the curriculum had remained almost unchanged since the colonial period. In 1869, however, a dynamic president, the chemist Charles W. Eliot, undertook a transformation of the college. Eliot introduced the elective system, gradually eliminating required courses and expanding offerings in such areas as modern languages, economics, and the laboratory sciences. For the first time, students were allowed to borrow books from the library!

An even more important development in higher education was the founding of Johns Hopkins in 1876. This university was one of many established in the period by wealthy industrialists; its benefactor, the Baltimore merchant Johns Hopkins, had made his fortune in the Baltimore and Ohio Railroad. Its distinctiveness, however, was due to the vision of Daniel Coit Gilman, its first president.

Gilman modeled Johns Hopkins on the German universities, where meticulous research and freedom of inquiry were the guiding principles. In staffing the institution, he sought scholars of the highest reputation, scouring Europe as well

The earliest colleges were "vocational," their chief purpose being to furnish clergy for the colonists. The colonists, most of whom were farmers, would have been astonished by Cornell University's school of agriculture, whose purpose was to teach the vocation of farming. At the left of the picture are some of the school's experimental gardens.

as America in his search for talent and offering outstanding men high salaries for that time—up to $5000 for a professor, roughly ten times the income of a skilled artisan. Gilman promised his teachers good students and ample opportunity to pursue their own research (which explains why so many Hopkins professors repeatedly turned down attractive offers from other universities).

Johns Hopkins specialized in graduate education. In the generation after its founding, it turned out a remarkable percentage of the most important scholars in the nation, including Woodrow Wilson in political science, John Dewey in philosophy, Frederick Jackson Turner in history, and John R. Commons in economics.

The example of Johns Hopkins encouraged other wealthy individuals to endow universities offering advanced work. Clark University in Worcester, Massachusetts, founded by Jonas Clark, a merchant and real estate speculator, opened its doors in 1889. Its president, G. Stanley Hall, had been a professor of psychology at Hopkins, and he built the new university in that institution's image. More important was John D. Rockefeller's creation, the University of Chicago (1892). The president of the University of Chicago, William Rainey Harper, was a brilliant biblical scholar—he received his Ph.D. from Yale at the age of 18—and an imaginative administrator. The new university, he told Rockefeller, should be designed "with the example of Johns Hopkins before our eyes." Chicago soon offered first-class graduate and undergraduate education. During its first year there were 120 instructors for fewer than 600 students, and despite fears that the mighty tycoon Rockefeller would enforce his social and economic views on the institution, academic freedom was the rule.

Advances in women's higher education opened up new fields of study for women. Here, a group of Smith College students with picks and hammers set out for a geology field trip in the 1880s.

State and federal aid to higher education expanded rapidly. The Morrill Act, granting land to each state at a rate of 30,000 acres for each senator and representative, provided the endowments that gave many important modern universities, such as Illinois, Michigan State, and Ohio State, their start. While the federal assistance was earmarked for specific subjects, the land-grant colleges offered a full range of courses, and all received additional state funds. The land-grant universities adopted new ideas quickly. They were coeducational from the start, and most developed professional schools and experimented with extension work and summer programs.

Typical of the better state institutions was the University of Michigan, which reached the top rank among the nation's universities during the presidency of James B. Angell (1871–1909). Like Eliot at Harvard, Angell expanded the undergraduate curriculum and strengthened the law and medical schools. He encouraged graduate studies, seeking to make Michigan "part of the great world of scholars," and sought ways in which the university could serve the general community.

Important advances were made in women's higher education. Beginning with Vassar College, which opened its doors to 300 women students in 1865, the opportunity for young women to pursue serious academic work gradually expanded. Wellesley and Smith, both founded in 1875, completed the so-called Big Three women's colleges. Together with the already established Mount Holyoke, and with Bryn Mawr (1885), Barnard (1889), and Radcliffe (1893), they became known as the Seven Sisters.

The only professional careers easily available to women were nursing, teaching, and the new area called social work. Nevertheless, the remarkable women that these institutions trained were conscious of their uniqueness and determined to demonstrate their capabilities. They provided most of the leaders of the early twentieth-century drive for equal rights for women.

Not all the changes in higher education were beneficial. The elective system led to superficiality; students gained a smattering of knowledge of many subjects and mastered none. For example, 55 percent of the Harvard class of 1898 took elementary courses and no others during their four years of study. Intensive graduate work often produced narrowness of outlook and research monographs on trivial subjects. Attempts to apply the scientific method in fields such as history and economics often enticed students into making smug (and preposterous) claims to objectivity and definitiveness.

The gifts of rich industrialists sometimes came with strings, and college boards of trustees tended to be dominated by businessmen who sometimes attempted to impose their own social and economic beliefs on faculty members. Although few professors lost their positions because their views offended trustees, at many institutions trustees exerted constant nagging pressures that limited academic freedom and scholarly objectivity. At state colleges, politicians often interfered in academic affairs, even treating professorships as part of the patronage system.

Thorstein Veblen pointed out in his caustic study of *The Higher Learning in America* (1918) that "the intrusion of businesslike ideals, aims and methods" harmed the universities in countless subtle ways. Size alone—the verbose Veblen called it "an executive weakness for spectacular magnitude"—became an end in itself, and the practical values of education were exalted over the humanistic. When universities grew bigger, administration became more complicated and the prestige of administrators rose inordinately. At many institutions professors came to be regarded as mere employees of the governing boards. In 1893 the members of the faculty of Stanford University were officially classified as personal servants of Mrs. Leland Stanford, widow of the founder. This was done in good cause—the Stanford estate was tied up in probate court and the ruling made it possible to pay professors out of Mrs. Stanford's allowance for household expenses—but that such a procedure was even conceivable must have appalled the scholarly world.

Thus higher education reflected American values, with all their strengths and weaknesses. A complex society required a more professional and specialized education for its youth; the coarseness and the rampant materialism and competitiveness of the era inevitably found expression in the colleges and universities.

REVOLUTION IN THE SOCIAL SCIENCES

In the social sciences a close connection existed between the practical issues of the age and the achievements of the leading thinkers. The application of the theory of evolution to every aspect of human relations, the impact of industrialization on society—such topics were of intense concern to American economists, sociologists, and historians. An understanding of Darwin increased the already strong interest in studying the development of institutions and their interactions with one another. Controversies over trusts, slum conditions, and other problems drew scholars out of their towers and into practical affairs.

Social scientists were impressed by the progress being made in the physical and biological sciences. They eagerly applied the scientific method to their own specialties, hoping thereby to arrive at objective truths in fields that by nature were essentially subjective.

Among the economists something approaching a revolution took place in the 1880s. The classical school, which maintained that immutable natural laws governed all human behavior and which used the insights of Darwin only to justify unrestrained competition and laissez-faire, was challenged by a group of young economists who argued that as times changed, economic theories and laws must be modified in order to remain relevant. Richard T. Ely, another of the scholars who made Johns Hopkins a font of new ideas in the 1880s, summarized the thinking of this group in 1885. "The state [is] an educational and ethical agency whose positive aid is an indispensable condition of human progress," Ely proclaimed. Laissez-faire was outmoded and dangerous. Economic problems were basically moral problems; their solution required "the united efforts of Church, state and science." The proper way to study these problems was by analyzing actual conditions, not by applying abstract laws or principles.

A similar revolution struck sociology in the mid-1880s. Prevailing opinion up to that time rejected the idea of government interference with the organization of society. The influence of the English social Darwinist, Herbert Spencer, who objected even to public schools and the postal system, was immense. Spencer and his American disciples, among them Edward L. Youmans, editor of *Popular Science Monthly,* twisted the ideas of Darwin to mean that society could be changed only by the force of evolution, which moved with cosmic slowness. "You and I can do nothing at all," Youmans told the reformer Henry George. "It's all a matter of evolution. Perhaps in four or five thousand years evolution may have carried men beyond this state of things."

PROGRESSIVE EDUCATION

Traditionally, American teachers had emphasized the three Rs and relied on strict discipline and rote learning. Typical of the pedagogues of the period was the Chicago teacher, described by a reformer in the 1890s, who told her students firmly: "Don't stop to think, tell me what you know!" Yet new ideas were attracting attention. According to a German educator, Johann Friedrich Herbart, teachers could best arouse the interest of their students by relating new information to what they already knew; good teaching called for professional training, psychological insight, enthusiasm, and imagination, not merely facts and a birch rod. At the same time, evolutionists were pressing for a kind of education that would help children to "survive" by adapting to the demands of their environment.

Forward-looking educators seized on these ideas because dynamic social changes were making the old system increasingly inadequate. Settlement house workers discovered that slum children needed training in handicrafts, good citizenship, and personal hygiene as much as in reading and writing. They were appalled by the local schools, which suffered from the same diseases—filth, overcrowding, rickety construction—that plagued the tenements, and by school systems that were controlled by machine politicians who doled out teaching positions to party hacks and other untrained persons. They argued that school playgrounds, nurseries, kindergartens, and adult education programs were essential in communities where most women worked and many people lacked much formal education. "We are impatient with the schools which lay all stress on reading and writing," Jane Addams declared. This type of education "fails to give the child any clew to the life about him." The philosopher who summarized and gave direction to these forces was John Dewey, a professor at the University of Chicago. Dewey was concerned with the implications of evolution—indeed, of all science—for education. Essentially his approach was ethical. Was the nation's youth being properly prepared for the tasks it faced in the modern world? He thought not.

"Education," Dewey insisted in *The School and Society* (1899), a work in which he described and defended his theories, was "the fundamental method of social progress and reform." To seek to improve conditions merely by passing laws was "futile." Moreover, in an industrial society the family no longer performed many of the educational functions it had carried out in an agrarian society. Farm children learn about nature, about work, about human character in countless ways denied to children in cities. The school can fill the gap by becoming "an embryonic community . . . with types of occupations that reflect the life of the larger society." At the same time, education should center on the child, and new information should be related to what the child already knows. Children's imagination, energy, and curiosity are tools for broadening their outlook and increasing their store of information. Finally, the school should become an instrument for social reform, "saturating [the child] with the spirit of service" and helping to produce a "society which is worthy, lovely, and harmonious." Education, in other words, ought to build character and teach good citizenship as well as transmit knowledge.

The School and Society created a stir, and Dewey immediately assumed leadership of what in the next generation was called progressive education. Although the gains made in public education before 1900 were more quantitative than qualitative and the philosophy dominant in most schools was not very different at the end of the century from that prevailing in Horace Mann's day, change was in the air. The best educators of the period were full of optimism, convinced that the future was theirs.

HISTORY

Evolution, too, influenced the study of history. Many scholars of the origins and evolution of political institutions concluded, after much "scientific" study of old charters and law codes, that the roots of democracy were to be found in the customs of the ancient tribes of northern Europe. This theory of the "Teutonic origins" of democracy, which has since been thoroughly discredited, fitted well with the prejudices of people of British stock, and it provided ammunition for those who favored restricting immigration and for those who argued that blacks were inferior beings.

Out of this work, however, came an essentially democratic concept, the frontier thesis of Frederick Jackson Turner, still another scholar trained at Johns Hopkins. Turner's essay "The Significance of the Frontier in American History" (1893) argued that the frontier experience, through which every section of the country had passed, had affected the thinking of the people and the shape of American institutions. The isolation of the frontier and the need during each successive westward advance to create civilization anew, Turner wrote, account for the individualism of Americans and the democratic character of their society. Nearly everything unique in our culture could be traced to the existence of the frontier, he claimed.

Turner, and still more his many disciples, made too much of his basic insights. Life on the frontier was not as democratic as Turner believed, and it certainly does not "explain" American development as completely as he said it did. Nevertheless, his work showed how important it was to investigate the evolution of institutions, and it encouraged historians to study social and economic, as well as purely political, subjects. If the claims of the new historians to objectivity and definitiveness were absurdly overstated, their emphasis on thoroughness, exactitude, and impartiality did much to raise standards in the profession. Perhaps the finest product of the new scientific school, a happy combination of meticulous scholarship and literary artistry, was Henry Adams's nine-volume *History of the United States During the Administrations of Jefferson and Madison.*

REALISM IN LITERATURE

When what Mark Twain called the Gilded Age began, American literature was dominated by the romantic mood. All the important writers of the 1840s and 1850s except Hawthorne, Thoreau, and Poe were still living. Longfellow stood at the height of his fame, and the lachrymose Susan Warner—"tears on almost every page"—continued to turn out stories in the style of her popular *The Wide, Wide World.* Romanticism, however, had lost its creative force; most writing in the decade after 1865 was sentimental trash pandering to the preconceptions of middle-class readers. Magazines like the *Atlantic Monthly* overflowed with stories about fair ladies worshiped from afar by stainless heroes, women coping selflessly with drunken husbands, and poor but honest youths rising through various combinations of virtue and diligence to positions of wealth and influence. Most writers of fiction tended to ignore the eternal conflicts inherent in human nature and the social problems of the age; polite entertainment and pious moralizing appeared to be their only objectives.

The patent unreality, even dishonesty, of contemporary fiction eventually caused a reaction. The most important forces giving rise to the Age of Realism

DEBATING THE PAST

Did the frontier engender individualism and democracy? This 1887 photograph depicts a family in Custer County, Nebraska. Their optimism is indicated by the fact that they have begun to build a house *(center)*; yet their isolation suggests their vulnerability, as does the dugout *(upper left)* they now live in. Were such people self-reliant individualists or needy dependents?

In 1893 historian Frederick Jackson Turner argued that the boundless expanses of the frontier gave rise to democracy, individualism and "withal that buoyancy and exuberance which comes with freedom." Insofar as the frontier was then receding before the advance of urbanization and industrialization, Turner's readers had cause for alarm. Historians adopting Turner's analysis—and there were many—were generally pessimistic about the prospects for American democracy.

Philosopher John Dewey (1922) was among those who dissented. He argued that rather than promoting democracy, the frontier had a "depressing effect upon the free life of inquiry and criticism." Other scholars insisted that democracy flourished not in the West but in urban and industrial areas. In subsequent decades scholars challenged Turner's assertions that frontier peoples were self-sufficient and their democratic institutions vital.

Richard White (1991) insisted that the West, more so than any other region, had been "historically a dependency of the federal government." Donald Worster (1992) contended that its predominant economy—cattle raising and irrigation agriculture—was developed mostly by large corporations.

And even if the frontier promoted democratic sensibilities, this came at the cost of dispossessing the Indians—missing from the photograph—who had previously ranged over this land.

Donald Worster, *Under Western Skies* (1992), Richard White, *"It's Your Misfortune and None of My Own"* (1991), Peggy Pascoe, *Relations of Rescue: The Search for Female Moral Authority in the American West, 1874–1939* (1990), Patricia Limerick, *Legacy of Conquest* (1988), and Elliot West, *The Contested Plains* (1998).

were those that were transforming every other aspect of American life: industrialism, with its associated complexities and social problems; the theory of evolution, which made people more aware of the force of the environment and the basic conflicts of existence; the new science, which taught dispassionate, empirical observation. Novelists undertook the examination of social problems such as slum life, the conflict between capital and labor, and political corruption. They created multidimensional characters, depicted persons of every social class, used dialect and slang to capture the flavor of particular types, and fashioned painstaking descriptions of the surroundings into which they placed their subjects. The romantic novel did not disappear. General Lew Wallace's *Ben Hur* (1880) and Frances Hodgson Burnett's *Little Lord Fauntleroy* (1886) were bestsellers. But by 1880 realism was the point of view of the finest literary talents in the country.

MARK TWAIN

While it was easy to romanticize the West, that region lent itself to the realistic approach. Almost of necessity, novelists writing about the West described coarse characters from the lower levels of society and dealt with crime and violence. It would have been difficult indeed to write a genteel romance about a mining camp. The outstanding figure of western literature, the first great American realist, was Mark Twain.

Twain, whose real name was Samuel L. Clemens, was born in 1835. He grew up in Hannibal, Missouri, on the banks of the Mississippi. After mastering the printer's trade and working as a riverboat pilot, he went west to Nevada in 1861. The wild, rough life of Virginia City fascinated him, but prospecting got him nowhere, and he became a reporter for the *Territorial Enterprise*. Soon he was publishing humorous stories about the local life under the nom de plume Mark Twain. In 1865, while working in California, he wrote "The Celebrated Jumping Frog of Calaveras County," a story that brought him national recognition. A tour of Europe and the Holy Land in 1867 to 1868 led to *The Innocents Abroad* (1869), which made him famous.

Twain's greatness stemmed from his keen reportorial eye and ear, his eagerness to live life to the full, his marvelous sense of humor, and his ability to be at once in society and outside it, to love humanity yet be repelled by human vanity and perversity. He epitomized the zest and adaptability of his age and also its materialism. No contemporary pursued the almighty dollar more zealously. An inveterate speculator, he made a fortune with his pen and lost it in foolish business ventures. Twain died a dark pessimist, surrounded by adulation yet alone, an alien and a stranger in the land he loved and knew so well.

Twain excelled every contemporary in the portrayal of character. In *Huckleberry Finn* (1884), his masterpiece, his portrait of the slave Jim, loyal, patient, naive, yet withal a man, is unforgettable. When Huck takes advantage of Jim's credulity merely for his own amusement, the slave turns from him coldly and says: "Dat truck dah is trash; en trash is what people is dat puts dirt on de head er dey fren's en makes 'em ashamed." And there is Huck Finn himself, full of devilry, romantic, amoral—up to a point—and at bottom the complete realist. When Miss Watson tells him he can get anything he wants by praying for it, he makes the effort, is disillusioned, and concludes: "If a body can get anything they pray for, why don't Deacon Winn get back the money he lost on pork? . . . Why can't Miss Watson fat up? No, I says to myself, there ain't nothing in it."

Whether directly, as in *The Innocents Abroad* and in his fascinating account of the world of the river pilot, *Life on the Mississippi* (1883), or when transformed by his imagination in works of fiction such as *Tom Sawyer* (1876) and *A Connecticut Yankee in King Arthur's Court* (1889), Mark Twain always put much of his own experience and feeling into his work. "The truth is," he wrote in 1886, "my books are mainly autobiographies." A story, he told a fellow author, "must be written with the blood out of a man's heart." Twain's achievement was magnificent. Rough and uneven like the man himself, his works catch more of the spirit of the age he named than those of any other writer.

WILLIAM DEAN HOWELLS

Twain's realism was far less self-conscious than that of his longtime friend William Dean Howells. Like Twain, Howells, who was born in Ohio in 1837, had little formal education. He learned the printer's trade from his father and became a reporter for the *Ohio State Journal*. In 1860 he wrote a campaign biography of Lincoln and was rewarded with an appointment as consul in Venice. His sketches in *Venetian Life* (1866) were a product of this experience. After the Civil War he worked briefly for *The Nation* in New York and then moved to Boston, where he became editor of the *Atlantic Monthly*. In 1886 he returned to New York as editor of *Harper's*.

A long series of novels and much literary criticism poured from Howells's pen over the next 30 years. While he insisted on treating his material honestly, he was not at first a critic of society, being content to write about what he called "the smiling aspects" of life. Realism to Howells meant concern for the complexities of individual personalities and faithful description of the genteel, middle-class world he knew best.

Besides a sharp eye and an open mind, Howells had a real social conscience. Gradually he became aware of the problems that industrialization had created. In 1885, in *The Rise of Silas Lapham*, he dealt with some of the ethical conflicts faced by businessmen in a competitive society. The harsh public reaction to the Haymarket bombing in 1886 stirred him, and he threw himself into a futile campaign to prevent the execution of the anarchist suspects. Thereafter he moved rapidly toward the left; soon he was calling himself a socialist. "After fifty years of optimistic content with 'civilization' . . . I now abhor it, and feel that it is coming out all wrong in the end, unless it bases itself anew on a real equality," he wrote. But he added immediately: "Meanwhile I wear a fur-lined overcoat, and live in all the luxury my money can buy." In *A Hazard of New Fortunes* (1890), he attempted to portray the whole range of metropolitan life, weaving the destinies of a dozen interesting personalities from diverse sections and social classes.

The book represents a triumph of realism in its careful descriptions of various sections of New York and the ways of life of rich and poor, in the intricacy of its characters, and in its rejection of sentimentality and romantic love.

His own works were widely read, and Howells was also the most influential critic of his time. He helped bring the best contemporary foreign writers, including Tolstoy, Dostoevsky, Ibsen, and Zola, to the attention of readers in the United States, and he encouraged many important young American novelists, among them Stephen Crane, Theodore Dreiser, Frank Norris, and Hamlin Garland.

Some of these writers went far beyond Howells's realism to what they called naturalism. Many, like Twain and Howells, began as newspaper reporters. Working for a big-city daily in the 1890s was sure to teach anyone a great deal about the dark side of life. Naturalist writers believed that the human being was essentially an animal, a helpless creature whose fate was determined by environment. Their world was Darwin's world—mindless, without mercy or justice. They wrote chiefly about the most primitive emotions—lust, hate, greed. In *Maggie, A Girl of the Streets* (1893), Stephen Crane described the seduction, degradation, and eventual suicide of a young woman, all set against the background of a sordid slum; in *The Red Badge of Courage* (1895), he captured the pain and humor of war. In *McTeague* (1899), Frank Norris told the story of a brutal, dull-witted dentist who murdered his greed-crazed wife with his bare fists.

HENRY JAMES

Henry James was very different in spirit and background from the tempestuous naturalists. Born to wealth, reared in a cosmopolitan atmosphere, twisted in some strange way while still a child and unable to achieve satisfactory relationships with women, James spent most of his mature life in Europe, writing novels, short stories, plays, and volumes of criticism. Although far removed from the world of practical affairs, he was preeminently a realist, determined, as he once said, "to leave a multitude of pictures of my time" for the future to contemplate. He admired the European realists and denounced the "floods of tepid soap and water which under the name of novels are being vomited forth" by the romancers.

Although he preferred living in the cultivated surroundings of London high society, James yearned for the recognition of his fellow Americans almost as avidly as Mark Twain. However, he was incapable of modifying his rarefied, overly subtle manner of writing. Most serious writers of the time admired his books, and he received many honors, but he never achieved widespread popularity. His major theme was the clash of American and European cultures, his primary interest the close-up examination of wealthy, sensitive, yet often corrupt persons in a cultivated but far from polite society.

James's reputation, greater today than in his lifetime, rests more on his highly refined accounts of the interactions of individuals and their environment and his masterful commentaries on the novel as a literary form than on his ability

Re-Viewing the Past

Titanic

James Cameron's *Titanic* was a blockbuster. He made audiences feel what it was like to be on the ship. When the deck tilted to the right, viewers leaned to the left; many gasped as the ship plunged into the icy depths. What sent a shiver down the spine was the knowledge that real people had experienced what was being depicted on the screen.

Cameron well understood the audience's craving to relive a true story. By showing footage of the actual HMS *Titanic* on the floor of the Atlantic, fish gliding silently through its barnacle-encrusted wreckage, he reminded audiences that what they were seeing had actually happened. He spent scores of millions of dollars devising computer-enhanced techniques to ensure that his *Titanic* looked like the one that went down in the North Atlantic on the night of April 14–15, 1912.

But Cameron's *Titanic* was more than a disaster movie. It was also the story of two young people who fall in love. The romance begins when Jack (Leonardo DiCaprio), a struggling artist, spots Rose (Kate Winslet), a wealthy socialite, climbing over the railing and peering despondently into the water below. Obliged to marry a contemptuous (and contemptible) snob, she is miserable. Jack, from a lower deck, scrambles up and persuades her to forego the plunge.

As a reward for saving Rose, Jack is invited to dine with Rose's table. At dinner, Rose appraises Jack more carefully—and is impressed. He looks good in a tuxedo, displays plenty of moxie, and possesses artistic talent ("Jack, you see things!"). She proposes that she pose for him in the nude. A few hours later they venture below decks and, in anticipation of the courtship rituals of future decades, locate an automobile, climb inside, and rip off each other's clothes. Soon the car is bouncing. The windows steam up, and a hand leaves an imprint, fingers outstretched in ecstasy.

Minutes later they are cooled off when the ship has its close encounter of the icy kind. Jack—young, vital, alive—perishes in the frigid

waters; but he has imparted to Rose a gift of love, and thus of life. This tale of young lovers, held apart by society, is a nautical "Romeo and Juliet," a brief, pure instant of love, tragically ended by death.

If Cameron's *Titanic* is a love story for the ages, it was also frozen in a particular place and in a particular time. Much as Cameron spent millions to show the ship as it really was, he took similar pains to give a convincing rendering of New York society, especially its clothing, silverware, and social conventions.

Of the latter, the most significant for the story are the elaborate rituals of Victorian courtship. Rose seeks to break free from her impending marriage partly because she despises her fiancé, but also because marriage to him constitutes the final, irreversible step into the gilded cage of a society lady. Jack's presence at dinner with the "best" of society underscores the shallow materialism of this upper crust and its preoccupation with wealth, its disdain for those who lack both, its absurd rules of etiquette, and its repressive attitudes toward sexuality. Viewers of the movie, looking through Rose's eyes, may wonder how such rituals ever came to be.

Some had existed for centuries. The idealization of courtly love and pure womanhood was commonplace in medieval literature; in the early nineteenth century novelist Jane Austen described the subtle interplay of money and romance in England. But the rituals of New York society in the Gilded Age were characterized by sumptuous and public displays of wealth—glittering balls, and extravagant "Grand Tours" of Europe.

This new mode of courtship was largely the creation of Mrs. John Jacob Astor, wife of one of New York's wealthiest businessmen, and her friends. After the Civil War, industrialization and urbanization were generating new wealth and destroying the old at a dizzying pace. While prominent businessmen and investment bankers were devising institutions to impose order on industrial chaos, their wives were regularizing its social elite. They endeavored to determine who

Leonardo DiCaprio and Kate Winslet as lovers on the Titanic.

A young society couple courting in New York, about 1914.

should be admitted to New York's "best" families—and who should not.

By controlling entrance into society, women such as Mrs. Astor (and her imitators in nearly every city in the nation) also determined the disposition, through marriage and inheritance, of the nation's largest fortunes. Society women possessed power.

Although the system was created and supervised by mature women, it demanded the compliance of adolescent girls. The process began when a mother took her daughter on a round of visits to society women, to whom they would present their "calling cards." If mother and daughter were judged suitable, they would be invited in for tea; if the girl behaved with decorum (and if her father's assets proved sound), she would be invited to balls and other formal events. At or near her sixteenth birthday, her parents would hold a ball in her honor—in New York the event usually took place at Delmonico's restaurant—marking her "debut" into society. She wore a white gown symbolizing her virginity. A male relative presented her formally to the prominent women. Now she could accept male suitors.

This highly stylized—almost tribal—ritual brought young women to the threshold of womanhood. Marriage awaited beyond the door. Many eagerly anticipated the acquisition of adult status and the social power it entailed. Others regarded this rite with terror. (Novelist Edith Wharton remembered her debut as a "long cold agony of shyness.") In the early twentieth century, some young women began to rebel. Elsie Clews, daughter of a Wall Street banker, refused to wear corsets. When her

mother wasn't looking, she took off her veil and white gloves. She subsequently scandalized Newport—the fashionable Rhode Island summer resort for society's wealthy—by going swimming with a young man without a chaperone (but not without a bathing suit). To her mother's dismay, Clews delayed marriage and went to Barnard College; eventually she became a respected anthropologist (Elsie Clews Parsons).

Kate Winslet's "Rose" was, like Elsie Clews, a prematurely "modern" woman. But Clews tore off only her veil and white gloves, not all her clothes; she dispensed with the rituals of courtship, not its substance. Even in the waning years of the Victorian era, few wealthy young women succumbed to impoverished men, however earnest and appealing.

Victorian courtship was necessarily protracted. Young women did not unburden themselves to strangers; and even to friends, especially of the opposite sex, the process of revealing one's inner feelings unfolded slowly, often after a series of tests and trials. Letters and diaries show that, over time, these personal revelations often led to sexual intimacies. Nowadays many people regard Victorian marriages as unfeeling and stiff; but many Victorians maintained that their personal intimacies were the more delicious for having been long delayed.

Cameron's *Titanic* looked like the past; but the heart of the movie is Jack and Rose's whirlwind romance. While Rose's story addresses some of the anxieties of young society women, it more closely resembles the courtship patterns of Hollywood today than the experiences of young people at the beginning of the last century.

as a storyteller. Few major writers have been more long-winded, more prone to circumlocution. Yet few have been so dedicated to their art, possessed of such psychological penetration, or so successful in producing a large body of important work.

THE PRAGMATIC APPROACH

It would have been remarkable indeed if the intellectual ferment of the late nineteenth century had not affected contemporary ideas about the meaning of life, the truth of revealed religion, moral values, and similar fundamental problems. In particular the theory of evolution, so important in altering contemporary views of science, history, and social relations, produced significant changes in American thinking about religious and philosophical questions.

Evolution posed an immediate challenge to religion: If Darwin was correct, the biblical account of the creation was obviously untrue and the idea that the human race had been formed in God's image was highly unlikely. A bitter controversy erupted, described by President Andrew D. White of Cornell in *The Warfare of Science with Theology in Christendom* (1896). While millions continued to believe in the literal truth of the Bible, among intellectuals, lay and clerical, victory went to the evolutionists because, in addition to the arguments of the geologists and the biologists, scholars were throwing light on the historical origins of the Bible, showing it to be of human rather than divine inspiration.

The effects of Darwinism on philosophy were less dramatic but in the end more significant. Fixed systems and eternal truths were difficult to justify in a world that was constantly evolving. By the early 1870s a few philosophers had begun to reason that ideas and theories mattered little except when applied to specifics.

"Nothing justifies the development of abstract principles but their utility in enlarging our concrete knowledge of nature," wrote Chauncey Wright, secretary of the American Academy of Arts and Sciences. In "How to Make Our Ideas Clear" (1878), Wright's friend Charles S. Peirce, an amazingly versatile and talented albeit obscure thinker, argued that concepts could be fairly understood only in terms of their practical effects. Once the mind accepted the truth of evolution, Peirce believed, logic required that it accept the impermanence even of scientific laws. There was, he wrote, "an element of indeterminacy, spontaneity, or absolute chance in nature."

This startling philosophy, which Peirce called pragmatism, was presented in more understandable language by William James, brother of the novelist. James was one of the most remarkable persons of his generation. Educated in London, Paris, Bonn, and Geneva—as well as at Harvard—he studied painting, participated in a zoological expedition to South America, earned a medical degree, and was professor at Harvard successively of comparative anatomy, psychology, and finally philosophy. His *Principles of Psychology* (1890) may be said to have established that discipline as a modern science. His *Varieties of Religious Experience* (1902), which treated the subject from both psychological and philosophical

Henry James (left), *a novelist of exquisite perception, withdrew from America to Europe; his brother, William* (right) *shook off a bout of depression in his twenties, propounded pragmatism, a philosophy that eschewed abstraction, and criticized aesthetes such as his brother:* "There is no more contemptible type of human character than that of the nerveless sentimentalist and dreamer, who spends his life in a weltering sea of sensibility and emotion, but who never does a manly concrete deed."

points of view, helped thousands of readers reconcile their religious faith with their increasing knowledge of psychology and the physical universe.

Although he was less rigorous a logician than Peirce, James's wide range and his verve and imagination as a writer made him by far the most influential philosopher of his time. He rejected the deterministic interpretation of Darwinism and all other one-idea explanations of existence. Belief in free will was one of his axioms; environment might influence survival, but so did the *desire* to survive, which existed independent of surrounding circumstances. Even truth was relative; it did not exist in the abstract but *happened* under particular circumstances. What a person thought helped to make thought occur, or come true. The mind, James wrote in a typically vivid phrase, has "a vote" in determining truth. Religion was true, for example, because people were religious.

The pragmatic approach inspired much of the reform spirit of the late nineteenth century and even more of that of the early twentieth. James's hammer blows shattered the laissez-faire extremism of Herbert Spencer. In "Great Men and Their Environment" (1880) James argued that social changes were brought about by the actions of geniuses whom society had selected and raised to positions of power, rather than by the impersonal force of the environment. Such reasoning fitted the preconceptions of rugged individualists yet encouraged those dissatisfied with society to work for change. Educational reformers like John Dewey, the institutionalist school of economists, settlement house workers, and other reformers adopted pragmatism eagerly. James's philosophy did much to revive the buoyant optimism that had characterized the pre–Civil War reform movement.

Yet pragmatism brought Americans face-to-face with somber problems. While relativism made them optimistic, it also bred insecurity, for there could be no certainty, no comforting reliance on any eternal value in the absence of absolute truth. Pragmatism also seemed to suggest that the end justified the means, that what worked was more important than what ought to be. At the time of James's death in 1910, the *Commercial and Financial Chronicle* pointed out that the pragmatic philosophy was helpful to businessmen in making decisions. By emphasizing practice at the expense of theory, the new philosophy encouraged materialism, anti-intellectualism, and other unlovely aspects of the American character. And what place had conventional morality in such a system? Perhaps pragmatism placed too much reliance on the free will of human beings, ignoring their capacity for selfishness and self-delusion.

The people of the new century found pragmatism a heady wine. They would quaff it freely and enthusiastically—down to the bitter dregs.

MILESTONES

1862	Morrill Act establishes land-grant colleges
1865	Vassar College is founded for women
1869	Charles W. Eliot becomes Harvard's president, undertakes transformation of college by introducing elective system and expanding offerings
1876	Johns Hopkins University is founded to specialize in graduate education
1883	Joseph Pulitzer purchases *New York World*
1884	Mark Twain publishes *Huckleberry Finn*
1886	Ottmar Mergenthaler invents linotype machine
	William Dean Howells becomes editor of *Harper's*
1890	William James publishes *Principles of Psychology*
1893	Frederick Jackson Turner publishes " Significance of the Frontier in American History"
1895	William Randolph Hearst purchases the *New York Journal*
1899	John Dewey publishes *The School and Society*

21

⇥ ⇤

POLITICS: LOCAL, STATE, AND NATIONAL

uring the last third of the nineteenth century, American politics reflected changes in economic and social institutions in the United States. The public spectacles of typical antebellum politics—parades down Main Street and debates in Court House squares—were being superseded by new institutions. Mass circulation newspapers, themselves a product of new machines and distribution systems, became increasingly effective in shaping public opinion. Exactly what the parties stood for, however, was often difficult to determine. American political parties have nearly always avoided clear-cut stands on controversial questions in order to appeal to as wide a segment of the electorate as possible, but in the last quarter of the nineteenth century, their equivocations assumed abnormal proportions. This was due in part to the precarious balance of power between them. No party dared declare itself too clearly on any question lest it drive away more voters than it attracted.

VOTING ALONG ETHNIC AND RELIGIOUS LINES

The major parties had national committees, and delegates met in national conventions every four years to select their presidential candidates and draft "platforms," but they remained essentially separate state organizations. Professionals spent far more time dealing with local people and local issues than they did thinking about tariffs and money policy and other matters of broad national concern. They had to understand how different kinds of people felt about such matters if they wanted to win their support. In many parts of the country, that meant entering a veritable maze of diverse and often conflicting interests. People's ethnic backgrounds, their religious affiliations, whether they lived in cities or on farms, how they felt about the Civil War, and countless aspects of their lives that had no apparent relationship to national political issues affected whether they voted Republican or Democratic.

The politicians of the period were not shy about explaining why people voted the way they did. Senator George Frisbie Hoar of Massachusetts, for example, offered such an analysis in an 1889 magazine article. The Republicans, he wrote, were "the men who do the work of piety and charity in our churches . . . who administer our school systems . . . who own and till their own farms . . . who perform skilled labor . . . who went to the war . . . who paid the debt, and kept the currency sound, and saved the nation's honor." The Democrats, he went on, were "the old slave-owner and slave-driver, the saloon-keeper, the ballot-box-stuffer, the Ku-Klux, the criminal class of the great cities, and men who cannot read or write."

Despite the partisan character of Hoar's analysis, it contained an element of truth; a more disinterested observer, James Bryce, wrote in *The American Commonwealth* that at least in the North "the best people" were Republicans, whereas a "vast ignorant fluctuating mass of people" were Democrats. But if Hoar or even Bryce were correct, the Republicans would have swept the northern states at every election, which they assuredly did not.

Local and state issues interacted with religious and ethnic backgrounds to affect political attitudes. Prohibition, public education, and other matters subject to state and local control that seemed to have little or no relation to religion were in fact questions on which voters split along religious and ethnic lines. All these tangles influenced the way political leaders devised their strategies and chose candidates for office. Moreover, how voters felt about local issues almost invariably affected how they voted in national elections.

CITY BOSSES

City governments were influenced by the religious and ethnic character of the inhabitants and further complicated by the special problems of late-nineteenth-century urban life: rapid, helter-skelter growth; the influx of European immigrants; the need to develop costly transportation, sanitation, and other public utility systems; and the crime and corruption that the size, confusion, and anonymity incidental to urban existence fostered.

The movement to the suburbs of large numbers of middle-class city people who might have been expected to supply the political leadership needed to deal with these problems created a vacuum of sorts, a vacuum that was filled by political bosses, with their informal but powerful "machines."

The immigrants who flocked into American cities in the 1880s and early 1890s made up much of the "vast ignorant fluctuating mass" that Bryce was referring to in his description of party alignments. They were largely of peasant stock, and having come from societies unacquainted with democracy, they had no experience with representative government. The tendency of urban workers to move frequently in search of better jobs further lessened the likelihood that they would develop political influence independently.

Furthermore, the difficulties of life in the slums bewildered and often overwhelmed newcomers, both native- and foreign-born. Hopeful, but passive and naive, they could hardly be expected to take a broad view of social problems when so beset by personal ones. This enabled shrewd urban politicians—most of them in this period of Irish origin, the Irish being the first-comers among the migrants and, according to mobility studies, more likely to stay put—to take command of the city masses and march them in obedient phalanxes to the polls.

Most city machines were loose-knit neighborhood organizations headed by ward bosses, not tightly geared hierarchical bureaucracies ruled by a single leader. Timothy "Big Tim" Sullivan of New York's Lower East Side and Michael "Hinky Dink" Kenna of Chicago's First Ward were typical of the breed. Sullivan, Kenna, and others like them performed many useful services for people they liked to think of as their constituents. They found jobs for new arrivals and distributed food and other help to all in bad times. Anyone in trouble with the law could obtain at least a hearing from the ward boss, and often, if the crime was minor or due to ignorance, the difficulty was quietly "fixed" and the culprit was sent off with a word of caution. Sullivan provided turkey dinners for 5000 or more homeless people each Christmas, distributed new shoes to the poor children of his district on his birthday, and arranged summer boat rides and picnics for young and old alike. At any time of year the victim of some sudden disaster could turn to the local clubhouse for help. Informally, probably without consciously intending to do so, the bosses educated the immigrants in the complexities of American civilization, helping them to leap the gulf between the almost medieval society of their origins and the modern industrial world.

The price of such aid—the bosses were not altruists—was unquestioning political support, which the bosses converted into cash. In New York, Sullivan levied tribute on gambling, had a hand in the liquor business, and controlled the issuance of peddlers' licenses. When he died in 1913, he was reputedly worth $1 million. Yet he and others like him were immensely popular; 25,000 grieving constituents followed Big Tim's coffin on its way to the grave.

The more visible and better-known city bosses played even less socially justifiable roles than the ward bosses. Their principal technique for extracting money from the public till was the kickback. To get city contracts, suppliers were made to pad their bills and, when paid for their work with funds from the city treasury, turn over the excess to the politicians. Similarly, operators of streetcar lines, gas and electricity companies, and other public utilities were compelled to pay huge bribes to obtain favorable franchises.

The most notorious of the nineteenth-century city bosses was William Marcy Tweed, whose "Tweed Ring" extracted tens of millions of dollars from New York City during the brief period 1869 to 1871. Tweed was swiftly jailed. More typical was Richard Croker, who ruled New York's Tammany Hall organization from the mid-1880s to the end of the century. Croker held a number of local offices, but his power rested on his position as chairman of the Tammany Hall finance committee. Although more concerned than Tweed with the social and economic services that machines provided, Croker was primarily a corrupt political manipulator; he accumulated a large fortune and owned a mansion and a stable of racehorses, one of which was good enough to win the English Derby.

Despite their welfare work and their popularity, most bosses were essentially thieves. Efforts to romanticize them as the Robin Hoods of industrial society grossly distort the facts. However, the system developed and survived because too many middle-class city dwellers were indifferent to the fate of the poor. Except during occasional reform waves, few tried to check the politicos' greed.

Many substantial citizens shared at least indirectly in the corruption. The owners of tenements were interested in crowding as many rent payers as possible into their buildings. Utility companies seeking franchises preferred a system that enabled them to buy favors. Honest citizens who had no selfish stake in the system and who were repelled by the sordidness of city government were seldom sufficiently concerned to do anything about it. When young Theodore Roosevelt decided to seek a political career in 1880, his New York socialite friends laughed in his face. They told him, Roosevelt wrote in his autobiography, "that politics were 'low'; that the organizations were not controlled by 'gentlemen'; that I would find them run by saloonkeepers, horse-car conductors, and the like."

PARTY POLITICS:
SIDESTEPPING THE ISSUE

As for national politics, with the Democrats invincible in the South and the Republicans predominant in New England and most of the states beyond the Mississippi, the outcome of presidential elections was usually determined in a handful of populous states: New York (together with its satellites, New Jersey and Connecticut), Ohio, Indiana, and Illinois. The fact that opinion in these states on important questions such as the tariff and monetary policy was divided and that every imaginable religious and ethnic interest was represented in the electorate goes far to explain why the parties hesitated to commit themselves on issues. In every presidential election, Democrats and Republicans concentrated their heaviest guns on these states. Of the eighteen Democrats and Republicans nominated for president in the nine elections between 1868 and 1900, only three were not from New York, Ohio, Indiana, or Illinois, and all three lost.

The level of political morality was abysmal. Mudslinging, character assassination, and plain lying were standard practice; bribery was routine. Drifters and other dissolute citizens were paid in cash—or more often in free drinks—to vote the party ticket. The names of persons long dead were solemnly inscribed in voting registers, their votes cast by impostors. During the 1880 campaign the

DEBATING THE PAST

Were city governments corrupt and incompetent? This 1871 cartoon lampoons "Boss Tweed" for crushing a helpless New York City.

James Bryce (1888), a British observer, described municipal government as "the one conspicuous failure of the United States." Two years later Andrew D. White, president of Cornell, called American city governments "the worst in Christendom—the most expensive, the most inefficient, and the most corrupt." In 1904 journalist Lincoln Steffens's *The Shame of the Cities* offered a searing denunciation of municipal corruption throughout the nation, a view with which most historians long concurred. As late as 1974, Ernest S. Griffith characterized nine-teenth-century municipal governments as cesspools of corruption and inefficiency.

But by then, other scholars were considering the nineteenth-century city governments in a more favorable light. During the 1960s many cities were plagued by race riots and be-set with financial woes. They struggled merely to maintain the hospitals, museums, or-phanages, waterworks, and sewage and transit systems that had been built by presumably incompetent municipal governments during the Gilded Age. In *The Unheralded Triumph* (1984), a book whose thesis is carried in its title, Jon Teaford applauded municipal leaders of the late nineteenth century for building the complex infrastructure of rapidly growing cities. Historians such as John Buenker (1973) also observed that while the bosses often pilfered public monies, they also provided essential services for needy immigrants.

Corrupt bosses like Tweed stuck their hands deep into city coffers; but their thumbs failed to keep down those who did the work of building the great cities.

James Bryce, *The American Commonwealth* (1888), Jon C. Teaford, *The Unheralded Triumph: City Government in America, 1860–1900* (1984), Ernest S. Griffith, *A History of American City Government* (1974), John Buenker, *Urban Liberalism and Progressive Reform* (1973).

Democratic national chairman, hearing that the Republicans were planning to transport Kentuckians into Indiana to vote illegally in that crucial state, urged Indiana Democrats to "check this outrageous fraud." Then, perhaps seeking an easier solution to the problem, he added: "If necessary . . . keep even with them." Since, as this incident demonstrates, both parties indulged in these tactics, their efforts often canceled each other's, yet presidents were sometimes made and un-made in this sordid fashion.

LACKLUSTER LEADERS

The leading statesmen of the period showed as little interest in important contemporary questions as the party hacks who made up the rank and file of their organizations. Consider the presidents.

Rutherford B. Hayes, elected president in 1876, came to office with a distinguished record. He attended Kenyon College and Harvard Law School before settling down to practice in Cincinnati. Although he had a family to support, he volunteered for service in the Union army within weeks after the first shell fell on Fort Sumter. Hayes was wounded at South Mountain on the eve of Antietam and later served under Sheridan in the Shenandoah Valley campaign of 1864. Entering the army as a major, he emerged a major general. In 1864 he was elected to Congress; four years later he became governor of Ohio, serving three terms altogether. The Republicans nominated him for president in 1876 because of his reputation for honesty and moderation, and his election, made possible by the Compromise of 1877, seemed to presage an era of sectional harmony and political probity.

Outwardly Hayes had a sunny disposition; inwardly, in his own words, he was sometimes "nervous to the point of disaster." Despite his geniality, he was utterly without political glamour. He accounted himself a civil service reformer,

A former officer under General Philip Sheridan, Rutherford B. Hayes was sympathetic to the plight of southern blacks, but, like many northern politicians of his generation, took no action to stop the racist oppression.

being opposed to the collection of political contributions from federal officeholders. Hayes complained about the South's failure to treat blacks decently after the
withdrawal of federal troops, but he took no action. He worked hard for civil
service reform, yet failed to achieve the "thorough, rapid, and complete" change
he had promised. In most matters, he was content to "let the record show that he
had made the requests."

Hayes's successor, James A. Garfield, elected president in 1880, was cut
down by an assassin's bullet in July 1881, just four months after his inauguration. Even in that short time, however, his ineffectiveness had been demonstrated.
During the war Garfield fought at Shiloh and later at Chickamauga. In two years
he rose from lieutenant colonel to major general. In 1863 he won a seat in
Congress, where his oratorical and managerial skills brought him to prominence
in the affairs of the Republican party.

Garfield was studious and industrious and had wide-ranging interests. His
weakness was indecisiveness—what an admirer described as a "want of certainty."

Although eager to improve the efficiency of the government and resentful of
the "intellectual dissipation" resulting from time wasted listening to the countless appeals of office seekers, he often wilted under pressure from the spoilsmen.
Only on fiscal policy did he take a firm stand: He opposed categorically all inflationary schemes.

Political patronage proved to be Garfield's undoing. Garfield had been a
compromise choice at the 1880 Republican convention. The party then was split
into two factions; competition for office was the main reason for their rivalry.

Garfield's election precipitated a great battle over patronage, the new president standing in a sort of no-man's-land between the factions. But he infuriated
one group by resisting its schemes for patronage. In July 1881 an unbalanced
job-seeker—a lawyer named Charles J. Guiteau—shot Garfield in the
Washington railroad station. After lingering for weeks, the president died on
September 19.

Garfield's assassination elevated Chester A. Arthur to the presidency. A New
York lawyer and abolitionist, Arthur became an early convert to the Republican
party and rose rapidly in its local councils. In 1871 Grant gave him the juiciest
political plum in the country, the collectorship of the Port of New York, which he
held until removed by Hayes in 1878 for refusing to keep his hands out of party
politics.

The vice presidency was the only elective position that Arthur had ever held.
Before Garfield's death, he had paid little attention to questions like the tariff and
monetary policy, being content to take in fees ranging upward of $50,000 a year
as collector of the port and to oversee the operations of the New York customs
office, with its hordes of clerks and laborers. (During Arthur's tenure, the novelist Herman Melville was employed as an "outdoor inspector" by the custom
house.) Of course, Arthur was an unblushing defender of the spoils system,
though in fairness it must be said that he was personally honest and an excellent
administrator.

James A. Garfield, mortally wounded. After failing to locate the bullet, surgeons called in Alexander Graham Bell, the famous inventor. Bell conceived of a device, pictured here, that anticipated the mine detector. Bell's machine failed to locate the bullet, however, perhaps because the metal bed springs interfered with its operation. Garfield died, either from the bullet or the surgeon's unsuccessful attempts to extricate it.

The tragic circumstances of his elevation to the presidency sobered Arthur considerably. Although he was a genial, convivial man, perhaps overly fond of good food and flashy clothes, he comported himself with great dignity as president. He handled patronage matters with restraint, and he gave at least nominal support to the movement for civil service reform, which had been strengthened by the public's indignation at Garfield's assassination. In 1883 Congress passed the Pendleton Act, "classifying" about 10 percent of all government jobs and creating the bipartisan Civil Service Commission to administer competitive examinations for these positions. The law made it illegal to force officeholders to make political contributions and empowered the president to expand the list of classified positions at his discretion.

As an administrator Arthur was systematic, thoughtful, businesslike, and at the same time cheerful and considerate. Just the same, he too was a political failure. He made relatively little effort to push his program through Congress and satisfied neither of the factions of the Republican party. He did not seek a second term in 1884.

The 1884 election brought the Democrat Grover Cleveland to the White House. Cleveland grew up in western New York. After studying law, he settled in Buffalo. Although somewhat lacking in the social graces and in intellectual pretensions, he had a basic integrity that everyone recognized; when a group of reformers sought a candidate for mayor in 1881, he was a natural choice. His success in Buffalo led to his election as governor of New York in 1882.

In the governor's chair his no-nonsense attitude toward public administration endeared him to civil service reformers at the same time that his basic conservatism pleased businessmen. When he vetoed a popular bill to force a reduction of the fares charged by the New York City elevated railway on the ground that it was an unconstitutional violation of the company's franchise, his reputation soared. Here was a man who cared more for principle than for the adulation of the multitude, a man who was courageous, honest, hardworking, and eminently sound. The Democrats nominated him for president in 1884.

The election revolved around personal issues, for the platforms of the parties were almost identical. On the one hand, the Republican candidate, the dynamic James G. Blaine, had an immense following, but his reputation had been soiled by the publication of the "Mulligan letters," which connected him with the corrupt granting of congressional favors to the Little Rock and Fort Smith Railroad. On the other hand, it came out during the campaign that Cleveland, a bachelor, had fathered an illegitimate child. Instead of debating public issues, the Republicans chanted the ditty

> *Ma! Ma! Where's my pa?*
> *Gone to the White House,*
> *Ha! Ha! Ha!*

to which the Democrats countered

> *Blaine, Blaine, James G. Blaine,*
> *The continental liar from the State of Maine.*

Blaine lost more heavily in the mudslinging than Cleveland, whose quiet courage in saying, "Tell the truth" when his past was brought to light contrasted favorably with Blaine's glib and unconvincing denials. A significant group of eastern Republicans, known as mugwumps, campaigned for the Democrats.[1] However, Blaine ran a strong race against a general pro-Democratic trend; Cleveland won the election by fewer than 25,000 votes. The change of 600 ballots in New York would have given that state, and the presidency, to his opponent.

As a Democrat, Cleveland had no stomach for refighting the Civil War. Civil service reformers overestimated his commitment to their cause, for he believed in

---

[1]*The mugwumps considered themselves reformers, but on social and economic questions nearly all of them were very conservative. They were sound-money proponents and advocates of laissez-faire. Reform to them consisted almost entirely of doing away with corruption and making the government more efficient.*

President Grover Cleveland and Frances Folsom in 1888. The couple had married two years earlier; he was 48, and she, 21, the youngest First Lady. Her popularity blunted criticisms that Cleveland, a bachelor, had earlier fathered an illegitimate child. When he lost the 1888 election, his wife predicted that she would return as First Lady. Four years later, she did.

rotation in office. He would not summarily dismiss Republicans, but he thought that when they had served four years, they "should as a rule give way to good men of our party." He did, however, insist on honesty and efficiency regardless of party. As a result, he made few poor appointments.

Toward the end of his term Cleveland bestirred himself and tried to provide constructive leadership on the tariff question. The government was embarrassed by a large revenue surplus, which Cleveland hoped to reduce by cutting the duties on necessities and on raw materials used in manufacturing. He devoted his entire annual message of December 1887 to the tariff, thereby focusing public attention on the subject. When worried Democrats reminded him that an election was coming up and that the tariff might cause a rift in the organization, he replied simply: "What is the use of being elected or re-elected, unless you stand for something?"

In that contest, Cleveland obtained a plurality of the popular vote, but his opponent, Benjamin Harrison, grandson of President William Henry Harrison, carried most of the key northeastern industrial states by narrow margins, thereby obtaining a comfortable majority in the electoral college, 233 to 168.

Although intelligent and able, Harrison was too reserved to make a good politician. One observer called him a "human iceberg." During the Civil War he fought under Sherman at Atlanta and won a reputation as a stern, effective disciplinarian. In 1876 he ran unsuccessfully for governor of Indiana, but in 1881 was elected to the Senate.

Harrison believed ardently in protective tariffs, and no more flamboyant waver of the bloody shirt existed. Harrison professed to favor civil service reform, but fashioned an unimpressive record on the question. He appointed the vigorous young reformer Theodore Roosevelt to the Civil Service Commission and then proceeded to undercut him systematically. Before long the frustrated Roosevelt was calling the president a "cold blooded, narrow minded, prejudiced, obstinate, timid old psalm singing Indianapolis politician."

Under Harrison, Congress distinguished itself by expending, for the first time in a period of peace, more than $1 billion in a single session. It raised the tariff to an all-time high. The Sherman Antitrust Act was also passed.

Harrison had little to do with the fate of any of these measures. By and large he failed, as one historian has said, to give the people "magnetic and responsive leadership." The Republicans lost control of Congress in 1890, and two years later Grover Cleveland swept back into power, defeating Harrison by more than 350,000 votes.

CROPS AND COMPLAINTS

The emptiness of American politics may well have stemmed from the complacency of the middle-class majority. The country was growing; no foreign enemy threatened it; the poor were mostly recent immigrants, blacks, and others with little influence, who were easily ignored by those in comfortable circumstances. However, one important group in society suffered increasingly as the years rolled by: the farmers. Out of their travail came the force that finally, in the 1890s, brought American politics face to face with the problems of the age.

After the Civil War, farmers did well. Harvests were bountiful and wheat prices high, with wheat selling at over a dollar a bushel in the early 1870s. Well into the 1880s farmers on the Plains experienced boom conditions. In that decade the population of Kansas increased by 43 percent, that of Nebraska by 134 percent, that of the Dakotas by 278 percent. Land prices rose and farmers borrowed money to expand their farms.

In the 1890s disaster struck. First came a succession of dry years and poor harvests. Then farmers in Australia, Canada, Russia, and Argentina took advantage of improvements in transportation to sell their produce in European markets that had relied on American foodstuffs. The price of wheat fell to about 60 cents a bushel. Cotton, the great southern staple, which sold for more than 30 cents a pound in 1866 and 15 cents in the early 1870s, at times in the 1890s fell below 6 cents.

The tariff on manufactured goods appeared to aggravate the farmers' predicament and so did the domestic marketing system, which enabled a multitude of middlemen to gobble up a large share of the profits of agriculture. The shortage of credit, particularly in the South, was an additional burden.

The downward swing of the business cycle in the early 1890s completed the devastation. Settlers who had paid more for their lands than they were worth and borrowed money at high interest rates to do so found themselves squeezed relentlessly. Thousands lost their farms and returned eastward, penniless and dispirited. The population of Nebraska increased by fewer than 4000 persons in the entire decade of the 1890s.

THE POPULIST MOVEMENT

The agricultural depression triggered a new outburst of farm radicalism, the Alliance movement. Alliances were organizations of farmers' clubs, most of which had sprung up during the bad times of the late 1870s. The first Knights of Reliance group was founded in 1877 in Lampasas County, Texas. As the Farmers Alliance, this organization gradually expanded in northeastern Texas, and after 1885 it spread rapidly throughout the cotton states. Alliance leaders stressed cooperation. Their co-ops bought fertilizer and other supplies in bulk and sold them at fair prices to members. They sought to market their crops cooperatively but could not raise the necessary capital from banks, with the result that some of them began to question the workings of the American financial and monetary system. They became economic and social radicals in the process. A similar though less influential Alliance movement developed in the North.

The alliances adopted somewhat differing policies, but all agreed that agricultural prices were too low, that transportation costs were too high, and that something was radically wrong with the nation's financial system. "There are three great crops raised in Nebraska," an angry rural editor proclaimed in 1890. "One is a crop of corn, one is a crop of freight rates, and one a crop of interest. One is produced by farmers who by sweat and toil farm the land. The other two are produced by men who sit in their offices and behind their bank counters and farm the farmers." All agreed on the need for political action if the lot of the agriculturalist was to be improved.

Although the state alliances of the Dakotas and Kansas joined the Southern Alliance in 1889, for a time local prejudices and conflicting interests prevented the formation of a single national organization. Northern farmers mostly voted Republican, Southerners Democratic, and resentments created during the Civil War lingered in all sections. Cotton-producing Southerners opposed the protective tariff; most Northerners, fearing the competition of foreign grain producers, favored it. Railroad regulation and federal land policy seemed vital questions to Northerners; financial reform loomed most important in southern eyes. Northerners were receptive to the idea of forming a third party, while Southerners, wedded to the one-party system, preferred working to capture local Democratic machines.

The farm groups entered local politics in the 1890 elections. Convinced of the righteousness of their cause, they campaigned with tremendous fervor. The results were encouraging. In the South, Alliance-sponsored gubernatorial candidates won in Georgia, Tennessee, South Carolina, and Texas; eight southern legislatures fell under Alliance control, and forty-four representatives and three senators committed to Alliance objectives were sent to Washington. In the West, Alliance candidates swept Kansas and captured a majority in the Nebraska legislature and enough seats in Minnesota and South Dakota to hold the balance of power between the major parties.

Such success, coupled with the reluctance of the Republicans and Democrats to make concessions to their demands, encouraged Alliance leaders to create a new national party. By uniting southern and western farmers, they succeeded in breaking the sectional barrier erected by the Civil War. If they could recruit industrial workers, perhaps a real political revolution could be accomplished. In February 1892, farm leaders, representatives of the Knights of Labor, and various professional reformers, some 800 in all, met at St. Louis. They organized the People's, or Populist, party, and issued a call for a national convention to meet at Omaha in July.

That convention nominated General James B. Weaver of Iowa for president (with a one-legged Confederate veteran as his running mate) and drafted a platform that called for a graduated income tax and national ownership of railroads and the telegraph and telephone systems. It also advocated a "subtreasury" plan that would permit farmers to keep nonperishable crops off the market when prices were low. Under this proposal the government would make loans in the form of greenbacks to farmers, secured by crops held in storage in federal warehouses. When prices rose, the farmers could sell their crops and repay the loans. To combat deflation further, the platform demanded the unlimited coinage of silver and an increase in the money supply "to no less than $50 per capita."

To make the government more responsive to public opinion, the Populists urged the adoption of the initiative and referendum procedures and the election of U.S. senators by popular vote. To win the support of industrial workers, their platform denounced the use of Pinkerton detectives in labor disputes and backed the eight-hour day and the restriction of "undesirable" immigration.

The appearance of the new party was the most exciting and significant aspect of the presidential campaign of 1892, which saw Harrison and Cleveland refighting the election of 1888. The Populists put forth a host of colorful spellbinders: Tom Watson, a Georgia congressman whose temper was such that on one occasion he administered a beating to a local planter with the man's own riding crop; William A. Peffer, a senator from Kansas whose long beard and grave demeanor gave him the look of a Hebrew prophet; "Sockless Jerry" Simpson of Kansas, unlettered but full of grassroots shrewdness and wit, a former Greenbacker, and an admirer of the single tax doctrine of Henry George; Ignatius Donnelly, the "Minnesota Sage," who claimed to be an authority on science, economics, and Shakespeare (he believed that Francis Bacon wrote the plays) and whose widely read novel, *Caesar's Column* (1891), pictured an America of the

Mary Elizabeth Lease was a prominent Populist, noted for her rallying cry urging farmers to "raise less corn and more hell."

future wherein a handful of plutocrats tyrannized masses of downtrodden workers and serfs.

In the one-party South, Populist strategists sought to wean black farmers away from the ruling Democratic organization. Southern black farmers had their own Colored Alliance, and even before 1892 their leaders had worked closely with the white alliances. Nearly 100 black delegates had attended the Populist convention at St. Louis. Of course, the blacks would be useless to the party if they could not vote; therefore, white Populist leaders opposed the southern trend toward disfranchising African Americans and called for full civil rights for all.

In the Northwest, the Populists assailed the "bankers' conspiracy" in unbridled terms. Donnelly, running for governor of Minnesota, made 150 speeches, vowing to make the campaign "the liveliest ever seen" in the state.

The results proved disappointing. Tom Watson lost his seat in Congress, and Donnelly ran a poor third in the Minnesota gubernatorial race. The Populists did sweep Kansas. They elected numbers of local officials in other western states and cast over a million votes for General Weaver. But the effort to unite white and black farmers in the South failed miserably. Conservative Democrats, while continuing with considerable success to attract black voters, played on racial fears cruelly, insisting that the Populists sought to undermine white supremacy. Since most white Populists saw the alliance with blacks as at best a marriage of convenience, this argument had a deadly effect. Elsewhere, even in the old centers of the Granger movement, the party made no significant impression. Urban workers remained aloof.

To this hostile cartoonist, the Populist party was a patchwork coalition of farmers' alliances, urban laborers, prohibitionists, socialists, anarchists, Grangers, and Greenbackers, who were all floating a platform of "lunacy."

By standing firmly for conservative financial policies, Cleveland attracted considerable Republican support and won a solid victory over Harrison in the electoral college, 277 to 145. Weaver's electoral vote was 22.

SHOWDOWN ON SILVER

One conclusion that politicians reached after analyzing the 1892 election was that the money question, particularly the controversy over the coinage of silver, was of paramount interest to the voters. Despite the wide-ranging appeal of the Populist platform, most of Weaver's strength came from the silver-mining states.

In truth, the issue of gold versus silver was superficial; the important question was what, if anything, should be done to check the deflationary spiral. The declining price level benefited people with fixed incomes and injured most others. Industrial workers profited from deflation except when depression caused unemployment.

By the early 1890s, discussion of federal monetary policy revolved around the coinage of silver. Traditionally, the United States had been on a bimetallic standard. Both gold and silver were coined, the number of grains of each in the dollar being adjusted periodically to reflect the commercial value of the two metals. The discovery of numerous gold mines in California in the 1840s and 1850s

In Kansas in 1893 a Populist governor and a Populist-controlled Senate invalidated the election of some Republicans in the Kansas House of Representatives, giving the Populists control of that body, too. The displaced Republicans, denied seats, smashed their way into the capitol building with this sledgehammer and ousted the Populists, who decided to meet in a separate building. Each proclaimed itself to be the true legislature of Congress and passed its own laws. Eventually the Kansas Supreme Court decided in favor of the Republican legislature and disbanded the Populist gathering.

depressed the price of gold relative to silver. By 1861, a silver dollar could be melted down and sold for $1.03. No miner took silver to the mint to be stamped into coin. In a short time, silver dollars were withdrawn and only gold dollars circulated. However, an avalanche of silver from the mines of Nevada and Colorado gradually depressed the price until, around 1874, it again became profitable for miners to coin their bullion. Alas, when they tried to do so, they discovered that the Coinage Act of 1873, taking account of the fact that no silver had been presented to the mint in years, had demonetized the metal.

Silver miners denounced this "Crime of '73." Inflationists joined them in demanding a return to bimetallism. They knew that if more dollars were put into circulation, the value of each dollar would decline; that is, prices and wages would rise. Conservatives, still fighting the battle against inflationary greenback paper money, resisted strongly. The result was a series of compromises. In 1878 the Bland-Allison Act authorized the purchase of between $2 and $4 million of silver a month at the market price, but this had little inflationary effect because the government consistently purchased the minimum amount. The commercial price of silver continued to fall. In 1890 the Sherman Silver Purchase Act required the government to buy 4.5 million *ounces* of silver monthly, but in the face of increasing supplies the price of silver fell still further. By 1894, a silver coin weighed 32 times more than a gold one.

The compromises satisfied no one. Silver miners grumbled because their bullion brought in only half what it had in the early 1870s. Debtors noted angrily that because of the general decline in prices, the dollars they used to meet their obligations were worth more than twice as much as in 1865. Advocates of the gold standard feared that unlimited silver coinage would be authorized, "destroying the value of the dollar."

THE DEPRESSION OF 1893

Both the silverites and "gold bugs" warned of economic disaster if their policies were not followed. Then, in 1893, after the London banking house of Baring Brothers collapsed, a financial panic precipitated a worldwide industrial depression. In the United States hundreds of cotton mills and iron foundries closed, never to reopen. During the harsh winter of 1893–1894, millions were without jobs. Discontented industrial workers added their voices to the complaints of the Midwestern farmers.

President Cleveland believed that the controversy over silver had caused the depression by shaking the confidence of the business community and that all would be well if the country returned to a single gold standard. He summoned a special session of Congress, and by exerting immense political pressure he obtained the repeal of the Sherman Silver Purchase Act in October 1893. All that this accomplished was to split the Democratic party, its southern and western wings deserting him almost to a man.

During 1894 and 1895, while the nation floundered in the worst depression it had ever experienced, a series of events further undermined public confidence. In the spring of 1894 several "armies" of the unemployed, the most imposing led by Jacob S. Coxey, an eccentric Ohio businessman, marched on Washington to demand relief. Coxey wanted the government to undertake a program of federal public works and to authorize local communities to exchange non-interest-bearing bonds with the Treasury for $500 million in paper money, the funds to be used to hire unemployed workers to build roads. The scheme, Coxey claimed, would pump money into the economy, provide work for the jobless, and benefit the entire nation by improving transportation facilities.

When Coxey's group of demonstrators, perhaps 500 in all, reached Washington, he and two other leaders were arrested for trespassing on the grounds of the Capitol. Their followers were dispersed by club-wielding policemen. This callous treatment convinced many Americans that the government had little interest in the suffering of the people, an opinion strengthened when Cleveland, in July 1894, used federal troops to crush the Pullman strike.

The next year the Supreme Court handed down several reactionary decisions. In *United States* v. *E. C. Knight Company* it refused to employ the Sherman Antitrust Act to break up the Sugar Trust. In *Pollock* v. *Farmers' Loan and Trust Company* it invalidated a federal income tax law despite the fact that a similar measure levied during the Civil War had been upheld by the Court in *Springer* v. *United States* (1881). Throughout 1894 the Treasury's supply of gold dwindled as worried citizens exchanged greenbacks (now convertible into gold) for hard money and foreign investors cashed in large amounts of American securities. The government tried to sell bonds for gold to bolster the reserve, but the gold reserve continued to melt away. Early in 1895 it touched a low point of $41 million.

At this juncture a syndicate of bankers headed by J. P. Morgan turned the tide by underwriting a $62 million bond issue, guaranteeing that half the gold would come from Europe. This caused a great public outcry; the spectacle of the nation being saved from bankruptcy by a private banker infuriated millions.

These events, together with the continuing depression, discredited the Cleveland administration. As the presidential election of 1896 approached, with the Populists demanding unlimited coinage of silver, the major parties found it impossible to continue straddling the money question. The Populist vote had increased by 42 percent in the 1894 congressional elections. Southern and western Democratic leaders feared that they would lose their following unless Cleveland was repudiated. Western Republicans, led by Senator Henry M. Teller of Colorado, were threatening to bolt to the Populists unless their party came out for silver coinage. After a generation of political equivocation, the major parties had to face an important issue squarely.

The Republicans, meeting to choose a candidate at St. Louis in June 1896, announced for the gold standard. "We are unalterably opposed to every measure calculated to debase our currency or impair the credit of our country," the platform declared. "We are therefore opposed to the free coinage of silver. . . . The existing gold standard must be maintained." The party then nominated Ohio's William McKinley for president. McKinley, best known for his staunch advocacy of the protective tariff yet highly regarded by labor, was expected to run strongly in the Midwest and the East.

The Democratic convention met in July at Chicago. The pro-gold Cleveland element made a hard fight, but the silverites swept them aside. The high point came when a youthful Nebraskan named William Jennings Bryan spoke for silver against gold, for western farmers against the industrial East. Bryan's every sentence provoked ear-shattering applause. He ended with a marvelous figure of speech that set the tone for the coming campaign. "You shall not press down upon the brow of labor this crown of thorns," he warned, bringing his hands down suggestively to his temples. "You shall not crucify mankind upon a cross of gold!" Dramatically, he extended his arms to the side, the very figure of the crucified Christ.

The convention promptly adopted a platform calling for "the free and unlimited coinage of both silver and gold at the present legal ratio of 16 to 1" and went on to nominate Bryan, who was barely 36 years old, for president.

This action put tremendous pressure on the Populists. If they supported the Democrat Bryan, they risked losing their party identity; if they nominated another candidate, they would ensure McKinley's election. In part because the delegates could not find a person of stature willing to become a candidate against Bryan, the Populist convention nominated him, seeking to preserve the party identity by substituting Watson for the Democratic vice-presidential nominee, Arthur Sewall of Maine.

William Jennings Bryan's "Cross of Gold" speech inspired this cartoonist's caricature of it as "plagiarized from the Bible." Bryan's speech in favor of bimetallism was, in fact, studded with religious references. He described the unlimited coinage of silver and gold as a "holy cause" supported by those who built churches "where they praise their Creator."

THE ELECTION OF 1896

Never did a presidential campaign raise such intense emotions. The Republicans from the silver-mining states swung solidly behind Bryan. But many solid-money Democrats, especially in the Northeast, refused to accept the decision of the Chicago convention. Cleveland professed to be "so dazed by the political situation that I am in no condition for speech or thought on the subject." Many others adopted the policy of Governor David B. Hill of New York, who said, "I am a Democrat still—very still."

At the start the Republicans seemed to have everything in their favor. Bryan's youth and relative lack of political experience—two terms in the House—contrasted unfavorably with McKinley's distinguished war record, his long service in Congress and as governor of Ohio, and his reputation for honesty and good judgment. The severe depression operated in favor of the party out of power, although by repudiating Cleveland the Democrats escaped much of the burden of explaining away his errors. The newspapers came out almost unanimously for the Republicans. Important Democratic papers such as the *New York World*, the *Boston Herald*, the *Baltimore Sun*, the *Chicago Chronicle*, and the *Richmond Times* supported McKinley editorially and even slanted news stories against the

Democrats. The Democrats had very little money and few well-known speakers to fight the campaign.

But Bryan proved a formidable opponent. Casting aside tradition, he took to the stump personally, traveling 18,000 miles and making over 600 speeches. He was one of the greatest of orators. A big, handsome man with a voice capable of carrying without strain to the far corners of a great hall yet equally effective before a cluster of listeners at a rural crossroads, he projected an image of absolute sincerity without appearing fanatical or argumentative. At every major stop on his tour, huge crowds assembled.

McKinley's campaign was managed by a new type of politician, Marcus Alonzo Hanna, an Ohio businessman. In a sense Hanna was a product of the Pendleton Civil Service Act. When deprived of the contributions of officeholders, the parties turned to business for funds, and Hanna was one of the first leaders with a foot in both camps. Politics fascinated him, and despite his wealth and wide interests, he was willing to labor endlessly at the routine work of political organization.

Hanna aspired to be a kingmaker and early fastened on McKinley, whose charm he found irresistible, as the vehicle for satisfying his ambition. He spent about $100,000 of his own money on the preconvention campaign. His attitude toward the candidate, one mutual friend observed, was "that of a big, bashful boy toward the girl he loves."

Before most Republicans realized how effective Bryan was on the stump, Hanna perceived the danger and sprang into action. Since the late 1880s the character of political organization had been changing. The Civil Service Act was also cutting down on the number of jobs available to reward campaign workers. At the same time, the new mass circulation newspapers and the nationwide press associations were increasing the pressure on candidates to speak openly and often on national issues. This trend put a premium on party organization and consistency—the old political trick of speaking out of one side of the mouth to one audience and out the other to a different audience no longer worked very well.

Hanna, who was certain that money was the key to political power, raised an enormous campaign fund. When businessmen hesitated to contribute, he used a combination of persuasiveness and intimidation to pry open their purses. Banks and insurance companies were "assessed" a percentage of their assets, big corporations a share of their receipts, until some $3.5 million had been collected.

Hanna disbursed these funds with efficiency and imagination. He sent 1500 speakers into the doubtful districts and blanketed the land with 250 million pieces of campaign literature, printed in a dozen languages. "He has advertised McKinley as if he were a patent medicine," Theodore Roosevelt, never at a loss for words, exclaimed.

Incapable of competing with Bryan as a swayer of mass audiences, McKinley conducted a "front-porch campaign." Superficially the proceedings were delightfully informal. From every corner of the land, groups representing various regions, occupations, and interests descended on McKinley's unpretentious frame house in Canton, Ohio. Gathering on the lawn—the grass was soon reduced to mud, the fence stripped of pickets by souvenir hunters—the visitors paid their

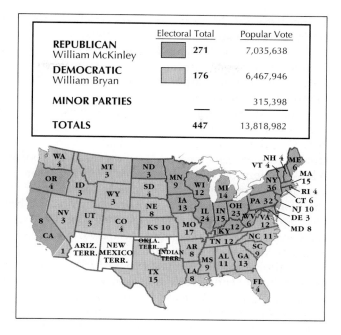

	Electoral Total	Popular Vote
REPUBLICAN William McKinley	271	7,035,638
DEMOCRATIC William Bryan	176	6,467,946
MINOR PARTIES	—	315,398
TOTALS	447	13,818,982

The Election of 1896

compliments to the candidate and heard him deliver a brief speech, while beside him on the porch his aged mother and adoring invalid wife listened with rapt attention. Then there was a small reception, during which the delegates were given an opportunity to shake their host's hand.

Despite the air of informality, these performances were carefully staged. The delegations arrived on a tightly coordinated schedule worked out by McKinley's staff and the railroads, which operated cut-rate excursion trains to Canton from all over the nation. McKinley was fully briefed on the special interests and attitudes of each group, and the speeches of delegation leaders were submitted in advance. Often his secretary amended these remarks, and on occasion McKinley wrote the visitors' speeches himself. His own talks were carefully prepared, each calculated to make a particular point. All were reported fully in the newspapers. Thus without moving from his doorstep, McKinley met thousands of people from every section of the country.

These tactics worked admirably. On election day McKinley collected 271 electoral votes to Bryan's 176, the popular vote being 7,036,000 to 6,468,000.

THE MEANING OF THE ELECTION

During the campaign, some frightened Republicans had laid plans for fleeing the country if Bryan were elected, and belligerent ones, such as Theodore Roosevelt, then police commissioner of New York City, readied themselves to meet the "social revolutionaries" on the battlefield. McKinley's victory sent such people into transports of joy. Most conservatives concluded that the way of life they so fervently admired had been saved for all time.

However heartfelt, such sentiments were not founded on fact. With workers standing beside capitalists and with the farm vote split, it cannot be said that the election divided the nation class against class or that McKinley's victory saved the country from revolution.

Far from representing a triumph for the status quo, the election marked the coming of age of modern America. The battle between gold and silver, which everyone had considered so vital, had little real significance. The inflationists seemed to have been beaten, but new discoveries of gold in Alaska and South Africa and improved methods of extracting gold from low-grade ores soon led to a great expansion of the money supply. In any case, within two decades the system of basing the volume of currency on bullion had been abandoned. Bryan and the "political" Populists who supported him, supposedly the advance agents of revolution, were oriented more toward the past than the future; their ideal was the rural America of Jefferson and Jackson.

McKinley, for all his innate conservatism, was capable of looking ahead toward the new century. His approach was national where Bryan's was basically parochial. Though never daring and seldom imaginative, McKinley was able to deal pragmatically with current problems. Before long, as the United States became increasingly an exporter of manufactures, he would even modify his position on the tariff. And no one better reflected the spirit of the age than Mark Hanna, the outstanding political realist of his generation. Far from preventing change, the outcome of the election of 1896 made possible still greater changes as the United States moved into the twentieth century.

MILESTONES

1873	Congress suspends the coining of silver ("Crime of '73")
1876	Rutherford B. Hayes is elected president
1877	Farmers Alliance movement is founded
1878	Bland-Allison Act authorizes government silver purchases
1880	James Garfield is elected president
1881	Garfield is assassinated; Grover Cleveland becomes president
1883	Pendleton Act creates Civil Service Commission
1884	"Mugwump" Republicans support Democratic candidate Cleveland in 1884 presidential campaign
	Grover Cleveland is elected president
1887	Cleveland delivers tariff message
1888	Benjamin Harrison is elected president
1890	Sherman Silver Purchase Act requires government silver purchase
1892	People's (Populist) Party is founded
	Cleveland is elected president a second time
1893	Sherman Silver Purchase Act is repealed
1893	Panic of 1893 causes industrial depression
1894	Coxey's Army marches to Washington to demand relief
1895	Supreme Court declares federal income tax unconstitutional (*Pollock* v. *Farmers' Loan and Trust Company*)
	J. P. Morgan raises $62 million in gold for the U.S. Treasury
1896	William Jennings Bryan delivers "Cross of Gold" speech
	William McKinley is elected president

22

THE AGE OF REFORM

The period bounded roughly by the end of the nineteenth century and American entry into World War I in 1917 is usually called the progressive era. Like all such generalizations about complex subjects, this title involves a great simplification. Whether *progressive* is taken to mean "tending toward change" or "improvement" or is merely used to suggest an attitude of mind, it was neither a unique nor a universal characteristic of the early years of the twentieth century. Progressive elements had existed in earlier periods and did not disappear when the first American soldiers took ship for France. In important ways the progressivism of the time was a continuation of the response to industrialism that began after the Civil War. Historians have scoured the sources trying to define and explain the progressive era, without satisfying everyone. Nevertheless the term *progressive* provides a useful description of this exciting and significant period of American history.

ROOTS OF PROGRESSIVISM

The progressives were never a single group seeking a single objective. The movement sprang from many sources. One was the fight against corruption and inefficiency in government, which began with the Liberal Republicans of the Grant era and was continued by the mugwumps of the 1880s. The struggle for civil service reform was only the first skirmish in this battle; the continuing power of corrupt political machines and the growing influence of large corporations and their lobbyists on municipal and state governments outraged thousands of citizens and led them to seek ways of purifying politics and making the machinery of government at all levels responsive to the majority rather than to special-interest groups.

Progressivism also had roots in the effort to regulate and control big business, which characterized the Granger and Populist agitation of the 1870s and 1890s. The failure of the Interstate Commerce Act to end railroad abuses and of the Sherman Antitrust Act to check the growth of large corporations became increasingly apparent after 1900. The return of prosperity after the depression of the 1890s encouraged reformers by removing the inhibiting fear, so influential in the 1896 presidential campaign, that an assault on the industrial giants might lead to the collapse of the economy.

Between 1897 and 1904 the trend toward concentration in industry accelerated. Such new giants as Amalgamated Copper (1899), U.S. Steel (1901), and International Harvester (1902) attracted most of the attention, but even more alarming were the overall statistics. In a single year (1899) more than 1200 firms were absorbed in mergers, the resulting combinations being capitalized at $2.2 billion. By 1904 there were 318 industrial combinations in the country with an aggregate capital of $7.5 billion. People who considered bigness inherently evil demanded that the huge new "trusts" be broken up or at least strictly controlled.

Settlement house workers and other reformers concerned about the welfare of the urban poor made up a third battalion in the progressive army. This was an area in which women made the most important contributions. The working and living conditions of slum dwellers remained abominable, and the child labor problem was particularly acute; in 1900 about 1.7 million children under the age of 16 were working full time—more than the membership of the American Federation of Labor. In addition, laws regulating the hours and working conditions of women in industry were far from adequate, and almost nothing had been done, despite the increased use of dangerous machinery in the factories, to enforce safety rules or to provide compensation or insurance for workers injured on the job. As the number of professionally competent social workers grew, the movement for social welfare legislation gained momentum.

America was becoming more urban, more industrial, more mechanized, more centralized—in short, more complex. This trend put a premium on efficiency and cooperation. It seemed obvious to the progressives that people must become more socially minded, the economy more carefully organized.

By attracting additional thousands of sympathizers to the general cause of reform, the return of prosperity after 1896 fueled the progressive movement. Good times made people more tolerant and generous. As long as profits were on the rise, the average employer did not object if labor improved its position too. Middle-class Americans who had been prepared to go to the barricades in the event of a Bryan victory in 1896 became conscience-stricken when they compared their own comfortable circumstances with those of the "huddled masses" of immigrants and native-born poor.

Giant industrial and commercial corporations undermined not so much the economic well-being as the ambitions and sense of importance of the middle class. What owner of a small mill or shop could now hope to rise to the heights

Orchard Street, a tenement district in lower Manhattan, New York. The unpaved street, ankle deep in mud, is lined with garbage. The sidewalks are packed with makeshift stalls and wagons, loaded with food, clothing, and other commodities for sale. Reformers worried that the congestion and filth of such streets constituted a health hazard. But many people who lived there enjoyed the sociability of the crowded streets; note that the man at the lower left is smiling.

attained by Carnegie or merchants like John Wanamaker and Marshall Field? The growth of large labor organizations worried such types. In general, character and moral values seemed less influential; organizations—cold, impersonal, heartless—were coming to control business, politics, and too many other aspects of life.

Protestant pastors accustomed to the respect and deference of their flocks found their moral leadership challenged by materialistic congregations who did not even pay them decent salaries. College professors worried about their institutions falling under the sway of wealthy trustees who had little interest in or respect for learning. Lawyers had been "the aristocracy of the United States," James Bryce recalled in 1905; they were now merely "a part of the great organized system of industrial and financial enterprise."

The middle classes could support reform measures without feeling that they were being very radical because they were resisting change and because the intellectual currents of the time harmonized with their ideas of social improvement and the welfare state. The new doctrines of the social scientists, the Social Gospel religious leaders, and the philosophers of pragmatism provided a favorable climate for progressivism.

One of McClure's *magazine's most effective muckrakers, Ida Tarbell, brought to her investigative journalism the well-trained mind of an historian and the indignation of a daughter whose father was done in by big business, specifically the Standard Oil Company.*

As the diffuse progressive army gradually formed its battalions, a new journalistic fad brought the movement into focus. For many years magazines had been publishing articles discussing current political, social, and economic problems. Henry Demarest Lloyd's first blast at the Standard Oil monopoly appeared in the *Atlantic Monthly* in 1881. Over the years the tempo and forcefulness of this type of literature increased. Then, in the fall of 1902, *McClure's* began two particularly hard-hitting series of articles, one on Standard Oil by Ida Tarbell, the other on big-city political machines by Lincoln Steffens. These articles provoked much comment; soon many were clamoring to get copies of the magazine.

Other editors jumped to adopt the McClure formula. A small army of professional writers soon flooded the periodical press with denunciations of the insurance business, the drug business, college athletics, prostitution, sweatshop labor, political corruption, and dozens of other subjects. This type of article inspired Theodore Roosevelt, with his gift for vivid language, to compare the journalists to "the Man with the Muck-Rake" in John Bunyan's *Pilgrim's Progress*, whose attention was so fixed on the filth at his feet that he could not notice the "celestial crown" that was offered him in exchange. Roosevelt's characterization grossly misrepresented the literature of exposure, but the label *muckraking* was thereafter affixed to the type. Despite its literal connotations, *muckraker* became a term of honor.

THE PROGRESSIVE MIND

Progressives sought to arouse the conscience of "the people" in order to "purify" American life. They believed that the source of society's evils lay in the structure of its institutions, not in the weaknesses or sinfulness of individuals. Therefore, local, state, and national government must be made more responsive to the will of citizens who stood for the traditional virtues.

When government had been thus reformed, then it must act; whatever its virtues, laissez-faire was obsolete. Businessmen, especially big businessmen, must be compelled to behave fairly, their acquisitive drives curbed in the interests of justice and equal opportunity for all. The weaker elements in society—women, children, the poor, the infirm—must be protected against unscrupulous power.

Many progressives who desired to improve the living standards of industrial workers rejected the proposition that workers could help themselves best by organizing powerful national unions. They found it difficult to cooperate with actual working people, who seemed to them unrefined and narrow-minded. Union leaders favored government action to outlaw child labor and restrict immigration but adopted a laissez-faire attitude toward wages-and-hours legislation; they preferred to win these objectives through collective bargaining, thereby justifying their own existence. Many who favored "municipal socialism" (public ownership of streetcar lines, waterworks, and other local utilities) adamantly opposed national ownership of railroads. Progressives stressed individual freedom yet gave strong backing to the drive to deprive the public of its right to drink alcoholic beverages.

The progressives never challenged the fundamental principles of capitalism, nor did they attempt a basic reorganization of society. They would have little to do with the socialist brand of reform. Wisconsin was the most progressive of states, but its leaders never cooperated with the Socialist party of Milwaukee. When socialists threatened to win control of Los Angeles in 1911, California progressives made common cause with reactionary groups in order to defeat them. Many progressives were anti-immigrant, and only a handful had anything to offer blacks, surely the most exploited group in American society.

"RADICAL" PROGRESSIVES: THE WAVE OF THE FUTURE

Some people espoused more radical views. The hard times of the 1890s and the callous reactions of conservatives to the victims of that depression pushed many toward Marxist socialism. In 1900 the labor leader Eugene V. Debs ran for president on the Socialist ticket. He polled fewer than 100,000 votes. When he ran again in 1904 he got more than 400,000, and in later elections still more. Labor leaders hoping to organize unskilled workers in heavy industry were increasingly frustrated by the craft orientation of the American Federation of Labor, and some saw in socialism a way to win rank-and-file backing.

In 1905 Debs; William "Big Bill" Haywood of the Western Federation of Miners; Mary Harris "Mother" Jones, a former organizer for the United Mine Workers; Daniel De Leon of the Socialist Labor party; and a few others organized a new union: the Industrial Workers of the World (IWW). The IWW was openly anticapitalist. The preamble to its constitution began: "The working class and the employing class have nothing in common."

But the IWW never attracted many ordinary workers. Haywood, its most prominent leader, was usually a general in search of an army. His forte was attracting attention to spontaneous strikes by unorganized workers, not the patient recruiting of workers and the pursuit of practical goals. Shortly after the founding of the IWW, he was charged with complicity in the murder of an antiunion governor of Idaho after an earlier strike but was acquitted. In 1912 he was closely involved in a bitter and at times bloody strike of textile workers in Lawrence, Massachusetts, which was settled with some benefit to the strikers, and in a strike the following winter and spring by silk workers in Paterson, New Jersey, which was a failure.

POLITICAL REFORM: CITIES FIRST

Beginning in the late 1890s progressives mounted a massive assault on dishonest and inefficient urban governments. In San Francisco a group headed by Fremont Older, a newspaperman, and Rudolph Spreckels, a wealthy sugar manufacturer, broke the machine of Mayor Abe Ruef, one of the most powerful bosses in the nation; Ruef ended up in jail. In Toledo, Ohio, Samuel M. "Golden Rule" Jones was elected mayor in 1897 and succeeded in arousing the citizenry against the corrupt officials. Other important progressive mayors were Tom L. Johnson of Cleveland, whose administration Lincoln Steffens called the best in the United States; Seth Low and later John P. Mitchell of New York; and Hazen S. Pingree of Detroit.

City reformers could seldom destroy the machines without changing urban political institutions. Some cities obtained "home rule" charters that gave them greater freedom from state control in dealing with local matters. Many created research bureaus that investigated government problems in a scientific and nonpartisan manner. A number of middle-sized communities (Galveston, Texas, was the prototype) experimented with a system that integrated executive and legislative powers in the hands of a small elected commission, thereby concentrating responsibility and making it easier to coordinate complex activities. Out of this experiment came the city manager system, under which the commissioners appointed a professional manager to administer city affairs on a nonpartisan basis. Dayton, Ohio, which adopted the plan after a flood devastated the town in 1913, offers the best illustration of the city manager system in the progressive era.

Once the political system had been made responsive to the desires of the people, the progressives hoped to use it to improve society itself. Many cities experimented with "gas and water socialism," taking over public utility companies and operating them as departments of the municipal government. Under "Golden Rule" Jones, Toledo established a minimum wage for city employees, built playgrounds and golf courses, and moderated its harsh penal code. Mayor Seth Low improved New York's public transportation system and obtained passage of the tenement house law of 1901. Mayor Tom Johnson forced a fare cut to 3 cents on the Cleveland street railways.

POLITICAL REFORM: THE STATES

To carry out this kind of change required the support of state legislatures since all municipal government depends on the authority of a sovereign state. Such approval was often difficult to obtain—local bosses were usually entrenched in powerful state machines, and rural majorities insensitive to urban needs controlled most legislatures. Therefore the progressives had to strike at inefficiency and corruption at the state level too.

During the first decade of the new century, Robert M. La Follette, one of the most remarkable figures of the age, transformed Wisconsin, the progressive state par excellence. La Follette was born in Primrose, Wisconsin, in 1855. He had served three terms as a Republican congressman (1885–1891) and developed a reputation as an uncompromising foe of corruption before being elected governor in 1900. That the people would always do the right thing if properly informed and inspired was the fundamental article of his political faith. "Machine control is based upon misrepresentation and ignorance," La Follette said. "Democracy is based upon knowledge." His own career seemed to prove his point, for in his repeated clashes with the conservative Wisconsin Republican machine, he won battle after battle by vigorous grassroots campaigning.

Despite the opposition of railroad and lumbering interests, as governor La Follette secured passage of a direct primary system for nominating candidates, a corrupt practices act, and laws limiting campaign expenditures and lobbying activities. In power he became something of a boss himself. He made ruthless use of patronage, demanded absolute loyalty of his subordinates, and often stretched, or at least oversimplified, the truth when presenting complex issues to the voters.

Reform administrations swept into office in Iowa and Arkansas (1901); Oregon (1902); Minnesota, Kansas, and Mississippi (1904); New York and Georgia (1906); Nebraska (1909); and New Jersey and Colorado (1910). In some cases the reformers were Republicans, in others Democrats, but in all the example of Wisconsin was influential. By 1910, fifteen states had established legislative reference services, most of them staffed by personnel trained in Wisconsin. The direct primary system became almost universal.

Some states went beyond Wisconsin in striving to make their governments responsive to the popular will. In 1902 Oregon began to experiment with the initiative, a system by which a bill could be forced on the attention of the legislature by popular petition, and the referendum, a method for allowing the electorate to approve measures rejected by their representatives and to repeal measures that the legislature had passed. Eleven states, most of them in the West, legalized these devices by 1914.

STATE SOCIAL LEGISLATION

The first state laws aimed at social problems long preceded the progressive era, but most were either so imprecise as to be unenforceable or, like the Georgia law "limiting" textile workers to eleven hours a day, so weak as to be ineffective. In

1874 Massachusetts restricted the working hours of women and children to ten per day, and by the 1890s many other states, mostly in the East and Midwest, had followed suit. Illinois passed an eight-hour law for women workers in 1893. A New York law of 1882 struck at the sweatshops of the slums by prohibiting the manufacture of cigars on premises "occupied as a house or residence."

As part of this trend, some states established special rules for workers in hazardous industries. But before 1900 the collective impact of such legislation was not impressive. Powerful manufacturers and landlords often succeeded in defeating the bills or rendering them innocuous. The federal system further complicated the task of obtaining effective legislation.

The Fourteenth Amendment to the Constitution, although enacted to protect the civil rights of blacks, imposed a revolutionary restriction on the states by forbidding them to "deprive any person of life, liberty, or property without due process of law." Since much state social legislation represented new uses of coercive power that conservative judges considered dangerous and unwise, the Fourteenth Amendment gave them an excuse to overturn the laws on the grounds that they deprived someone of liberty or property.

As stricter and more far-reaching laws were enacted, many judges, sensing what they took to be a trend toward socialism and regimentation, adopted an increasingly narrow interpretation of state authority to regulate business. In 1905 the United States Supreme Court declared in the case of *Lochner* v. *New York* that a New York ten-hour act for bakers deprived the bakers of the liberty of working as long as they wished and thus violated the Fourteenth Amendment. Justice Oliver Wendell Holmes, Jr., wrote a famous dissenting opinion in this case. If the people of New York believed that the public health was endangered by bakers working long hours, he reasoned, it was not the Court's job to overrule them.

Nevertheless, the progressives continued to battle for legislation to use state power against business. Women played a particularly important part in these struggles. Sparked by the National Child Labor Committee, organized in 1904, reformers over the next ten years obtained laws in nearly every state banning the employment of young children and limiting the hours of older ones. Many of these laws were poorly enforced, yet when Congress passed a federal child labor law in 1916, the Supreme Court declared it unconstitutional.[1]

By 1917 nearly all the states had placed limitations on the hours of women industrial workers, and about ten had set minimum wage standards for women. But once again federal action that would have extended such regulation to the entire country did not materialize. A minimum wage law for women in the District of Columbia was overturned by the Court in *Adkins* v. *Children's Hospital* (1923).

---

[1]*A second child labor law, passed in 1919, was also thrown out by the Court, and a child labor amendment, submitted in 1924, failed to achieve ratification by the necessary three-quarters of the states.*

Orphans on the steps of an orphanage, 1911. From 1854 to 1929, nearly 200,000 orphans or abandoned children from eastern cities were sent on "orphan trains" to live with farming families in the Midwest. Billy the Kid was one of the less successful "orphan train" placements.

Laws protecting workers against on-the-job accidents were also enacted by many states. Disasters like the 1911 fire in New York City, in which nearly 150 women perished because the Triangle shirtwaist factory had no fire escapes, led to the passage of stricter municipal building codes and factory inspection acts. By 1910 most states had modified the common-law principle that a worker accepted the risk of accident as a condition of employment and was not entitled to compensation if injured unless it could be proved that the employer had been negligent. Gradually the states adopted accident insurance plans, and some began to grant pensions to widows with small children. Most manufacturers favored such measures, if for no other reason than that they regularized procedures and avoided costly lawsuits.

The passage of so much state social legislation sent conservatives scurrying to the Supreme Court for redress. Such persons believed that no government had the power to deprive either workers or employers of the right to negotiate any kind of labor contract they wished. The decision of the Supreme Court in *Lochner* v. *New York* seemed to indicate that the justices would adopt this point of view. When an Oregon law limiting women laundry workers to ten hours a day was challenged in *Muller* v. *Oregon* (1908), Florence Kelley and Josephine Goldmark of the Consumers' League persuaded Louis D. Brandeis to defend the statute before the Court.

The Consumers' League, whose slogan was "investigate, agitate, legislate," was probably the most effective of the many women's reform organizations of the period. With the aid of league researchers, Brandeis prepared a remarkable brief stuffed with economic and sociological evidence indicating that long hours damaged both the health of individual women and the health of society. This nonlegal evidence greatly impressed the justices, who upheld the constitutionality of the Oregon law. "Woman's physical structure, and the functions she performs in consequence thereof, justify special legislation," they concluded. After 1908 the right of states to protect women, children, and workers performing danger-ous and unhealthy tasks by special legislation was widely accepted. The use of the "Brandeis brief" technique to demonstrate the need for such legislation be-came standard practice.

Progressives also launched a massive if ill-coordinated attack on problems related to monopoly. The variety of regulatory legislation passed by the states be-tween 1900 and 1917 was almost infinite. Wisconsin enacted a graduated per-sonal income tax, forced corporations to bear a larger share of the cost of gov-ernment, created an industrial commission to enforce the state's labor and factory legislation, and established a conservation commission, headed by Charles R. Van Hise, president of the University of Wisconsin.

A similar spate of legislation characterized the brief reign of Woodrow Wilson as governor of New Jersey (1911–1913). Urged on by the relentless Wilson, the legislature created a commission to fix rates and set standards for railroad, gas, electric, and telephone corporations, enacted storage and food in-spection laws, and passed seven bills (the "Seven Sisters" laws) tightening the state's loose controls over corporations. Economic reforms in other states were less spectacular but impressive in the mass. However, piecemeal state regulation failed to solve the problems of an ever more complex economy. The most signifi-cant battles for economic reform were fought in Congress.

POLITICAL REFORM: THE WOMAN SUFFRAGE MOVEMENT

On the national level the progressive era saw the culmination of the struggle for woman suffrage. The shock occasioned by the failure of the Fourteenth and Fifteenth Amendments to give women the vote after the Civil War continued to embitter most leaders of the movement. But it resulted in a split among feminists. One group, the American Woman Suffrage Association (AWSA), focused on the vote question alone. The more radical National Woman Suffrage Association (NWSA), led by Elizabeth Cady Stanton and Susan B. Anthony, concerned itself with many issues of importance to women as well as suffrage. The NWSA put the immediate interests of women ahead of everything else. It was deeply in-volved in efforts to unionize women workers, yet it did not hesitate to urge women to be strikebreakers if they could get better jobs by doing so.

Aside from their lack of unity, feminists were handicapped in the late nine-teenth century by Victorian sexual inhibitions, which most of their leaders shared. Even under the best of circumstances, dislike of male-dominated society

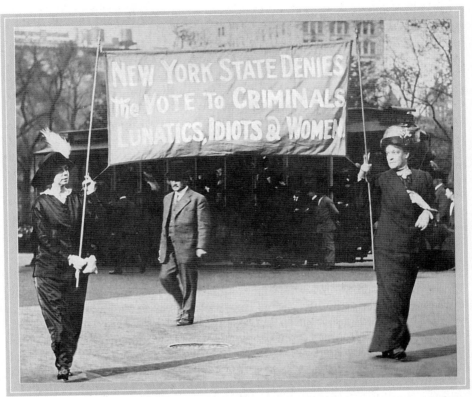

A banner in a 1911 woman's suffrage parade carries one of the longest-standing arguments in favor of women getting the vote.

is hard enough to separate from dislike of men. At a time when sex was an unmentionable topic in polite society, some of the most militant advocates of women's rights probably did not understand their own feelings. Most feminists, for example, opposed contraception, insisting that birth control by any means other than abstinence would encourage what they called masculine lust. The Victorian idealization of female "purity" and the popular image of women as the revered guardians of home and family further confused many reformers. And the trend of nineteenth-century scientific thinking influenced by the Darwinian concept of biological adaptation led to the conclusion that the female personality was different from that of the male and that the differences were inherent, not culturally determined.

These ideas and prejudices enticed feminists into a logical trap. If women were morally superior to men—a tempting conclusion—giving women the vote would improve the character of the electorate. Society would benefit because politics would become less corrupt, war a thing of the past. "City housekeeping has failed," said Jane Addams of Hull House in arguing for the reform of municipal government, "partly because women, the traditional housekeepers, have not been consulted."

The trouble with this argument (aside from the fact that opponents could easily demonstrate that in states where women did vote, governments were no better or worse than elsewhere) was that it surrendered the principle of equality. In the long run this was to have serious consequences for the women's movement, although the immediate effect of the purity argument was probably to advance the suffragists' cause.

By the early twentieth century there were signs of progress. In 1890 the two major women's groups combined as the National American Woman Suffrage Association (NAWSA). Stanton and Anthony were the first two presidents of the association. The NAWSA made winning the right to vote its main objective and concentrated on a state-by-state approach. Wyoming gave women the vote in 1869, and Utah, Colorado, and Idaho had been won over to women's suffrage by 1896. The 1911 election in California was crucial. Fifteen years earlier, California voters had rejected the measure. But in 1911, despite determined opposition from saloonkeepers, the proposal passed, though just barely. Within three years, most other Western states fell into line. For the first time, large numbers of working-class women began to agitate for the vote. In 1917, bosses at New York City's Tammany Hall, who had engineered the defeat of woman suffrage in that state two years earlier, concluded that passage was inevitable and threw their support to the measure, which passed.

The suffragists then shifted the campaign back to the national level, the lead taken by a new organization, the Congressional Union, headed by Alice Paul and the wealthy reformer Alva Belmont. When President Wilson refused to support the idea of a constitutional amendment granting women the vote, militant women picketed the White House. A number of them, including the daughter of Thomas Bayard, a former senator and secretary of state, were arrested and sentenced to sixty days in the workhouse. This roused a storm of criticism, and Wilson quickly pardoned the picketers. After some hesitation the NAWSA stopped concentrating on the state-by-state approach and began to campaign for a constitutional amendment. Pressure on Congress mounted steadily. The amendment finally won congressional approval in 1919. By 1920 the necessary three-quarters of the states had ratified the Nineteenth Amendment; the long fight was over.

POLITICAL REFORM: INCOME TAXES AND POPULAR ELECTION OF SENATORS

The progressive reform drive also found expression in the Sixteenth Amendment to the Constitution, authorizing federal income taxes, and the Seventeenth, which required the popular election of senators, both ratified in 1913.

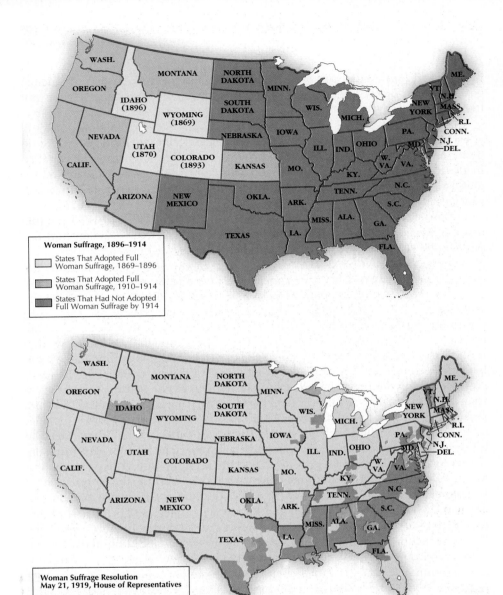

Woman Suffrage, 1896–1914

- States That Adopted Full Woman Suffrage, 1869–1896
- States That Adopted Full Woman Suffrage, 1910–1914
- States That Had Not Adopted Full Woman Suffrage by 1914

WASH. — MONTANA — NORTH DAKOTA — MINN. — ME. — VT. — N.H. — NEW YORK — MASS. — R.I. — CONN. — N.J. — DEL.
OREGON — IDAHO (1896) — SOUTH DAKOTA — WIS. — MICH. — PA. — MD. — W. VA. — VA.
NEVADA — WYOMING (1869) — NEBRASKA — IOWA — ILL. — IND. — OHIO — KY.
UTAH (1870) — COLORADO (1893) — KANSAS — MO. — TENN. — N.C. — S.C.
CALIF. — ARIZONA — NEW MEXICO — OKLA. — ARK. — MISS. — ALA. — GA.
— TEXAS — LA. — FLA.

Woman Suffrage Resolution May 21, 1919, House of Representatives

- Yes
- No
- Not Voting

The Woman Suffrage Campaign, 1869–1919

In 1869 Wyoming, while still a territory, voted to give women the vote. The next year, after Mormon leader Brigham Young endorsed woman suffrage, Utah followed. Then came Colorado (1893) and Idaho (1896), frontier states that sought to attract women settlers. In 1911, by a margin of 3587 votes, California endorsed woman suffrage, and within three years the remainder of the western states had done so, too. World War I stimulated support for the Woman Suffrage (Nineteenth) Amendment. The May 21, 1919 vote in the House of Representatives shows that most of the opposing votes came from southern congressmen who believed that woman suffrage would be the first step securing the vote for blacks.

No other important alterations of the national political system were made during the progressive era. Although some twenty states passed presidential primary laws, the cumbersome method of electing presidents was not changed.

THEODORE ROOSEVELT: COWBOY IN THE WHITE HOUSE

On September 6, 1901, an anarchist named Leon Czolgosz shot President McKinley during a public reception at the Pan-American Exposition at Buffalo, New York. Eight days later McKinley died and Vice President Theodore Roosevelt became president of the United States. His ascension to the presidency marked the beginning of a new era in national politics.

Although only forty-two years old, by far the youngest president in the nation's history up to that time, Roosevelt brought solid qualifications to the office. Son of a well-to-do New York merchant, he had graduated from Harvard in 1880 and studied law briefly at Columbia, though he did not obtain a degree. In addition to political experience that included three terms in the New York assembly, six years on the United States Civil Service Commission, two years as police commissioner of New York City, another as assistant secretary of the navy, and a term as governor of New York, he had been a rancher in the Dakota Territory and a soldier in the Spanish-American War. He was also a well-known historian: His *Naval War of 1812* (1882), begun during his undergraduate days at Harvard, and his four-volume *Winning of the West* (1889–1896) were valuable works of scholarship, and he had written two popular biographies and other books as well. Politically, he had always been a loyal Republican. He rejected the mugwump heresy in 1884, despite his distaste for Blaine, and during the tempestuous 1890s he vigorously denounced populism, Bryanism, and "labor agitators."

Nevertheless, Roosevelt's elevation to the presidency alarmed many conservatives, and not without reason. He did not fit their conception, based on a composite image of the chief executives from Hayes to McKinley, of what a president should be like. He seemed too undignified, too energetic, too outspoken, too unconventional. It was one thing to have operated a cattle ranch, another to have captured a gang of rustlers at gunpoint; one thing to have run a metropolitan police force, another to have roamed New York slums in the small hours to catch patrolmen fraternizing with thieves and prostitutes; one thing to have commanded a regiment, another to have killed a Spaniard personally.

Roosevelt had been a sickly child, plagued by asthma and poor eyesight, and he seems to have spent much of his adult life compensating for the sense of inadequacy that these troubles bred in him. He repeatedly carried his displays of physical stamina and personal courage and his love of athletics and big-game hunting to preternatural lengths. Henry Adams, who watched Roosevelt's development over the years with a mixture of fear and amusement, said that he was "pure act."

Had Roosevelt been the impetuous hothead that conservatives feared, he would have plunged ahead without regard for their feelings and influence.

The original stuffed bear, introduced as a toy in 1903. About the same time president "Teddy" Roosevelt, a big game hunter, refrained from shooting a bear cub. A cartoon rendering of that cub resembled the new toy, which people began referring to as "Teddy's Bears"—soon shortened to "Teddy Bears."

Instead he moved slowly and often got what he wanted by using his executive power rather than by persuading Congress to pass new laws. His domestic program included some measure of control of big corporations, more power for the Interstate Commerce Commission (ICC), and the conservation of natural resources. By consulting congressional leaders and following their advice not to bring up controversial matters like the tariff and currency reform, he obtained a modest budget of new laws.

The Newlands Act (1902) funneled the proceeds from land sales in the West into federal irrigation projects. The Department of Commerce and Labor, which was to include a Bureau of Corporations with authority to investigate industrial combines and issue reports, was established. The Elkins Railroad Act of 1903 strengthened the ICC's hand against the railroads by making the receiving as well as the granting of rebates illegal and by forbidding the roads to deviate in any way from their published rates.

ROOSEVELT AND BIG BUSINESS

Roosevelt soon became known as a trustbuster, and in the sense that he considered the monopoly problem the most pressing issue of the times, this was accurate to an extent. But he did not believe in breaking up big corporations indiscriminately. Regulation seemed the best way to deal with large corporations because, he said, industrial giantism "could not be eliminated unless we were willing to turn back the wheels of modern progress."

With Congress unwilling to pass a stiff regulatory law, Roosevelt resorted to the Sherman Act to get at the problem. Although the Supreme Court decision in the Sugar Trust case seemed to have emasculated that law, in 1902 he ordered the Justice Department to bring suit against the Northern Securities Company.

The announcement of the suit caused consternation in the business world. Attorney General Philander C. Knox pressed the case vigorously, and in 1904 the Supreme Court ordered the dissolution of the Northern Securities Company.

Roosevelt then ordered suits against the meat packers, the Standard Oil Trust, and the American Tobacco Company. His stock among progressives rose, yet he had not embarrassed the conservatives in Congress by demanding new antitrust legislation.

The president went out of his way to assure cooperative corporation magnates that he was not against size per se. At a White House conference in 1905, Roosevelt and Elbert H. Gary, chairman of the board of U.S. Steel, reached a "gentlemen's agreement" whereby Gary promised "to cooperate with the Government in every possible way." The Bureau of Corporations would conduct an investigation of U.S. Steel, Gary allowing it full access to company records. Roosevelt in turn promised that if the investigation revealed any corporate malpractices, he would allow Gary to set matters right voluntarily, thereby avoiding an antitrust suit. He reached a similar agreement with the International Harvester Company two years later.

ROOSEVELT AND THE COAL STRIKE

Roosevelt made remarkable use of his executive power during the anthracite coal strike of 1902. In June the United Mine Workers (UMW), led by John Mitchell, laid down their picks and demanded higher wages, an eight-hour day, and recognition of the union. Most of the anthracite mines were owned by railroads. Two years earlier the miners had won a 10 percent wage increase in a similar strike, chiefly because the owners feared that labor unrest might endanger the election of McKinley. Now the coal companies were dead set against further concessions; when the men walked out, they shut down the mines and prepared to starve the strikers into submission.

The strike dragged on through summer and early fall. The miners conducted themselves with great restraint, avoiding violence and offering to submit their claims to arbitration. As the price of anthracite soared with the approach of winter, sentiment in their behalf mounted.

The owners' spokesman, George F. Baer of the Reading Railroad, proved particularly inept at public relations. Baer stated categorically that God was on the side of management, but when someone suggested asking an important Roman Catholic prelate to arbitrate the dispute, he replied icily: "Anthracite mining is a business and not a religious, sentimental or academic proposition."

Roosevelt shared the public's sympathy for the miners, and the threat of a coal shortage alarmed him. Early in October he summoned both sides to a

DEBATING THE PAST

Were the progressives forward-looking? "Jack and the Wall Street Giants" shows a diminutive Teddy Roosevelt taking on the titans of Wall Street, among them railroad barons James J. Hill and Jay Gould and financier J. P. Morgan. The cartoon anticipates the familiar argument—that the progressives sought genuine change. But it also suggests that the prospects for victory were poor. Note that TR stands alone. By the 1930s, when the nation was mired in depression, many blamed the progressives. In 1932 John Chamberlain published a "Farewell to Reform" that excoriated progressive leaders for failing to check the power of the trusts. That failure, Richard Hofstadter (1955) declared, was rooted in their psychology. The progressives, mostly members of the middle class and the declining old elites, felt threatened by the increasing power and status of the new tycoons, many of them coarse, domineering, and fond of vulgar display. The antics of machine politicians who made a mockery of the traditions of duty, service, and patriotism associated with statesmanship also troubled them. They sought to restore "familiar and traditional ideals," and their nostrums were as old-fashioned as their goals. Revisionist historians such as Gabriel Kolko (1963) pushed Hofstadter's argument still further: the progressives never sought meaningful reform in the first place. They endorsed government regulation to prevent anarchic economic competition, and they hoped to ameliorate the plight of workers to forestall revolution. Their "progressivism" was in fact the "triumph of conservatism." Daniel Rodgers (1998) was among the many who insisted that this portrait was overdrawn. The progressives in the United States were not much different from reformers at that time in Europe. All shared a dynamic rhetoric; all sought to counteract the increasing concentration of industrial power; none met with great success. In the cartoon TR is armed only with the sword of "Public Service." Did he mean to preach to the giants or slay them?

John Chamberlain, *Farewell to Reform* (1932), Richard Hofstadter, *The Age of Reform* (1955), Gabriel Kolko, *The Triumph of Conservatism* (1963), Allen Weinstein, *The Decline of Socialism in America* (1967), Robert Wiebe, *The Search for Order* (1967), Daniel Rodgers, *Atlantic Crossings* (1998).

conference in Washington and urged them as patriotic Americans to sacrifice any "personal consideration" for the "general good." His action enraged the coal operators, for they believed he was trying to force them to recognize the union. They refused even to speak to the UMW representatives at the conference and demanded that Roosevelt end the strike by force and bring suit against the union under the Sherman Act. Mitchell, aware of the immense prestige that Roosevelt had conferred on the union by calling the conference, cooperated fully with the president.

The attitudes of management and of the union further strengthened public support for the miners. Encouraged by this state of affairs, Roosevelt took a bold step: He announced that unless a settlement was reached promptly, he would order federal troops into the anthracite regions, not to break the strike but to seize and operate the mines.

The threat of government intervention brought the owners to terms. The miners would return to the pits and all issues between them and the coal companies would be submitted for settlement to a commission appointed by Roosevelt. Both sides accepted the arrangement, and the men went back to work. In March 1903 the commission granted the miners a 10 percent wage increase and a nine-hour workday.

To the public the incident seemed a perfect illustration of the progressive spirit—in Roosevelt's words, everyone had received a "square deal." In fact the results were by no means so clear-cut. The miners gained relatively little and the companies lost still less, for they were not required to recognize the UMW and the commission also recommended a 10 percent increase in the price of coal, ample compensation for the increased wage costs. The president was the main winner. The public acclaimed him as a fearless, imaginative, public-spirited leader. Without calling on Congress for support, he had expanded his own authority and hence that of the federal government. His action marked a major forward step in the evolution of the modern presidency.

TR's TRIUMPHS

By reviving the Sherman Act, settling the coal strike, and pushing moderate reforms through Congress, Roosevelt ensured that he would be reelected president in 1904. Progressives, if not captivated, were at least pleased by his performance. Conservative Republicans offered no serious objection. Sensing that Roosevelt had won over the liberals, the Democrats nominated a conservative, Judge Alton B. Parker of New York, and bid for the support of eastern industrialists.

This strategy failed, for businessmen continued to eye the party of Bryan with intense suspicion. They preferred, as the *New York Sun* put it, "the impulsive candidate of the party of conservatism to the conservative candidate of the party which the business interests regard as permanently and dangerously impulsive." Despite his resentment at Roosevelt's attack on the Northern Securities Company, J. P. Morgan contributed $150,000 to the Republican campaign. Other tycoons gave with equal generosity. Roosevelt swept the country, carrying even the normally Democratic border states of Maryland and Missouri.

Encouraged by the landslide and the increasing militancy of progressives, Roosevelt pressed for more reform legislation. His most imaginative proposal was a plan to make the District of Columbia a model progressive community. He suggested child labor and factory inspection laws and a slum clearance program, but Congress refused to act. Likewise, his request for a minimum wage for railroad workers was rejected.

He had greater success when he proposed still another increase in the power of the Interstate Commerce Commission. Rebating remained a serious problem.

With progressive state governors demanding federal action and farmers and manufacturers, especially in the Midwest, clamoring for relief against discriminatory rates, Roosevelt was ready by 1905 to make railroad legislation his major objective. The ICC should be empowered to fix rates, not merely to challenge unreasonable ones. It should have the right to inspect the private records of the railroads since fair rates could not be determined unless the true financial condition of the roads was known.

Because these proposals struck at rights that businessmen considered sacrosanct, many congressmen balked. But Roosevelt applied presidential pressure, and in June 1906 the Hepburn bill became law. It gave the commission the power to inspect the books of railroad companies, to set maximum rates (once a complaint had been filed by a shipper), and to control sleeping car companies, owners of oil pipelines, and other firms engaged in transportation. In all, the Hepburn Act made the ICC a more powerful and more active body.

Congress also passed meat inspection and pure food and drug legislation. In 1906 Upton Sinclair published *The Jungle,* a devastating exposé of the filthy conditions in the Chicago slaughterhouses. Sinclair was more interested in writing a socialist tract than he was in meat inspection, but his book, a best-seller, raised a storm against the packers. After Roosevelt read *The Jungle* he sent two officials to Chicago to investigate. Their report was so shocking, he said, that its publication would "be well-nigh ruinous to our export trade in meat." He threatened to release the report, however, unless Congress acted. After a hot fight, the meat inspection bill passed. The Pure Food and Drug Act, forbidding the manufacture and sale of adulterated and fraudulently labeled products, rode through Congress on the coattails of this measure.

Roosevelt has probably received more credit than he deserves for these laws. He compromised with opponents of meat inspection cheerfully, despite his loud denunciations of the evils under attack. "As now carried on the [meat-packing] business is both a menace to health and an outrage on decency," he said: "No legislation that is not drastic and thoroughgoing will be of avail." Yet he went along with the packers' demand that the government pay the costs of inspection, though he believed that "the only way to secure efficiency is by the imposition upon the packers of a fee." Nevertheless, the end results were positive and in line with his conception of the public good.

To advanced liberals Roosevelt's achievements seemed limited when placed beside his professed objectives and his smug evaluations of what he had done. How could he be a reformer and a defender of established interests at the same time? Roosevelt found no difficulty in holding such a position.

ROOSEVELT TILTS LEFT

As the progressive movement advanced, Roosevelt advanced with it. He never accepted all the ideas of what he called its "lunatic fringe," but he took steadily more liberal positions. He always insisted that he was not hostile to business interests, but when those interests sought to exploit the national domain, they had no more implacable foe. Conservation of natural resources was dear to his heart and probably his most significant achievement as president. He placed some 150 million acres of forest lands in federal reserves, and he strictly enforced the laws governing grazing, mining, and lumbering.

In 1908 Roosevelt came out in favor of federal income and inheritance taxes, stricter regulation of interstate corporations, and reforms designed to help industrial workers. He denounced "the speculative folly and the flagrant dishonesty" of "malefactors of great wealth," further alienating conservative, or Old Guard, Republicans, who resented the attacks on their integrity implicit in Roosevelt's statements. When the president began criticizing the courts, the last bastion of conservatism, he lost all chance of obtaining further reform legislation. As he said himself, during his last months in office "stagnation continued to rage with uninterrupted violence."

WILLIAM HOWARD TAFT: THE LISTLESS PROGRESSIVE, OR MORE IS LESS

But Roosevelt remained popular and politically powerful; before his term ended, he chose William Howard Taft, his secretary of war, to succeed him and easily obtained Taft's nomination. William Jennings Bryan was again the Democratic candidate. Campaigning on Roosevelt's record, Taft carried the country by well over a million votes, defeating Bryan 321 to 162 in the Electoral College.

Taft was intelligent, experienced, and public spirited; he seemed ideally suited to carry out Roosevelt's policies. Born in Cincinnati in 1857, educated at Yale, he had served as an Ohio judge, as solicitor general of the United States under Benjamin Harrison, and then as a federal circuit court judge before accepting McKinley's assignment to head the Philippine Commission in 1900. His success as civil governor of the Philippines led Roosevelt to make him secretary of war in 1904.

Taft supported the Square Deal loyally. This, together with his mentor's ardent endorsement, won him the backing of most progressive Republicans. Yet the Old Guard liked him too; although outgoing, he had none of the Roosevelt impetuosity and aggressiveness. His genial personality and his obvious desire to avoid conflict appealed to moderates.

However, Taft lacked the physical and mental stamina required of a modern chief executive. Although not lazy, he weighed over 300 pounds and needed to rest this vast bulk more than the job allowed. He liked to eat in leisurely fashion, to idle away mornings on the golf course, to take an afternoon nap. Campaigning bored him; speech making seemed a useless chore. He supported many progressive measures, but he never absorbed the progressive spirit.

Taft honestly wanted to carry out most of Roosevelt's policies. He enforced the Sherman Act vigorously and continued to expand the national forest reserves. He signed the Mann-Elkins Act of 1910, which empowered the ICC to suspend rate increases without waiting for a shipper to complain and established the Commerce Court to speed the settlement of railroad rate cases. An eight-hour day for all persons engaged in work on government contracts, mine safety legislation, and several other reform measures received his approval. He even summoned Congress into special session specifically to reduce tariff duties—something that Roosevelt had not dared to attempt.

But Taft had been disturbed by Roosevelt's sweeping use of executive power. "We have got to work out our problems on the basis of law," he insisted. Whereas Roosevelt had excelled at maneuvering around congressional opposition and at finding ways to accomplish his objectives without waiting for Congress to act, Taft adamantly refused to use such tactics. His restraint was in many ways admirable, but it reduced his effectiveness.

In 1910 Taft got into difficulty with the conservationists. Although he believed in husbanding natural resources carefully, he did not like the way Roosevelt had circumvented Congress in adding to the forest reserves. He demanded, and eventually obtained, specific legislation to accomplish this purpose. The issue that aroused the conservationists concerned the integrity of his secretary of the interior, Richard A. Ballinger. A less than ardent conservationist, Ballinger returned to the public domain certain waterpower sites that the Roosevelt administration had withdrawn on the legally questionable ground that they were to become ranger stations. Ballinger's action alarmed Chief Forester Gifford Pinchot, the darling of the conservationists. When Pinchot learned that Ballinger intended to validate the shaky claim of mining interests to a large tract of coal-rich land in Alaska, he launched an intemperate attack on the secretary.

In the Ballinger-Pinchot controversy Taft felt obliged to support his own man. The coal lands dispute was complex, and Pinchot's charges were exaggerated. It was certainly unfair to call Ballinger "the most effective opponent the conservation policies have yet had." When Pinchot, whose own motives were partly political, persisted in criticizing Ballinger, Taft dismissed the chief forester. He had no choice under the circumstances, but a more adept politician might have found some way of avoiding a showdown.

BREAKUP OF THE REPUBLICAN PARTY

One ominous aspect of the Ballinger-Pinchot affair was that Pinchot was a close friend of Theodore Roosevelt. After Taft's inauguration, Roosevelt had gone off to hunt big game in Africa, bearing in his baggage an autographed photograph of his protégé and a touching letter of appreciation, in which the new president said: "I can never forget that the power I now exercise was a voluntary transfer from you to me." For months, as he trudged across Africa, guns blazing, Roosevelt was out of touch with affairs in the United States. As soon as he emerged from the wilderness in March 1910, bearing more than 3000 trophies, including 9 lions, 5 elephants, and 13 rhinos, he was caught up in the squabble between the progressive members of his party and its titular head. Pinchot met him in Italy, laden with injured innocence and a packet of angry letters from various progressives. TR's intimate friend Senator Henry Cabot Lodge, essentially a conservative, barraged him with messages, the gist of which was that Taft was lazy and inept and that Roosevelt should prepare to become the "Moses" who would guide the party "out of the wilderness of doubt and discontent" into which Taft had led it.

Roosevelt hoped to steer a middle course, but Pinchot's complaints impressed him. Taft had decided to strike out on his own, he concluded. "No man must render such a service as that I rendered Taft and expect the individual . . . not in the end to become uncomfortable and resentful," he wrote Lodge sadly. Taft sensed the former president's coolness and was offended.

Perhaps the resulting rupture was inevitable. The Republican party was dividing into two factions, the progressives and the Old Guard. Forced to choose between them, Taft threw in his lot with the Old Guard. Roosevelt backed the progressives. Speaking at Osawatomie, Kansas, in August 1910, he came out for a comprehensive program of social legislation, which he called the New Nationalism. Besides attacking "special privilege" and the "unfair money-getting" practices of "lawbreakers of great wealth," he called for a broad expansion of federal power. "The betterment we seek must be accomplished," he said, "mainly through the National Government."

The final break came in October 1911, when the president ordered an antitrust suit against U.S. Steel. Roosevelt opposed breaking up large corporations. "The effort at prohibiting all combination has substantially failed," Taft said. "The way out lies . . . in completely controlling them." He was prepared to enforce the Sherman Act "or die in the attempt." But what angered Roosevelt was Taft's emphasis in the suit on U.S. Steel's absorption of the Tennessee Coal and Iron Company, which Roosevelt had unofficially authorized during the panic of 1907. The government's antitrust brief made Roosevelt appear to have been either an abettor of monopoly or, far worse, a fool who had been duped by the steel corporation. Early in 1912 he declared himself a candidate for the Republican presidential nomination.

Roosevelt plunged into the preconvention campaign with typical energy. He was almost uniformly victorious in states that held presidential primaries, carrying even Ohio, Taft's home state. However, the president controlled the party machinery and entered the national convention with a small majority of the delegates. Since some Taft delegates had been chosen under questionable circumstances, the Roosevelt forces challenged the right of 254 of them to their seats. The Taft-controlled credentials committee, paying little attention to the evidence, gave all but a few of the disputed seats to the president, who then won the nomination on the first ballot.

Had Roosevelt swallowed his resentment and bided his time, Taft would almost certainly have been defeated in the election, and the 1916 Republican nomination would have been Roosevelt's for the asking. But he was understandably outraged by the ruthless manner in which the Taft "steamroller" had overridden his forces. When his leading supporters urged him to organize a third party, and when two of them, George W. Perkins, formerly a partner of the banker J. P. Morgan, and the publisher Frank Munsey, offered to finance the campaign, Roosevelt agreed to make the race.

In August, amid scenes of hysterical enthusiasm, the first convention of the Progressive party met at Chicago and nominated him for president. Announcing that he felt "as strong as a bull moose," Roosevelt delivered a stirring "confession of faith," calling for strict regulation of corporations, a tariff commission, national presidential primaries, minimum wage and workers' compensation laws, the elimination of child labor, and many other reforms.

THE ELECTION OF 1912

The Democrats made the most of the opportunity offered by the Republican schism. Had they nominated a conservative or allowed Bryan a fourth chance, they would probably have ensured Roosevelt's election. Instead, after battling through forty-six ballots at their convention in Baltimore, they nominated Woodrow Wilson, who had achieved a remarkable liberal record as governor of New Jersey. Incidentally, Wilson was one of three southern candidates for the nomination, further evidence that the sectional conflicts of Reconstruction had been forgotten.

Although as a political scientist Wilson had criticized the status quo and taken a pragmatic approach to the idea of government regulation of the economy, he had objected strongly to Bryan's brand of politics. In 1896 he voted for the Gold Democratic party candidate instead of Bryan. But by 1912, influenced partly by ambition and partly by the spirit of the times, he had been converted to progressivism. He called his brand of reform the New Freedom.

The federal government could best advance the cause of social justice, Wilson reasoned, by eradicating the special privileges that enabled the "interests" to flourish. Where Roosevelt had lost faith in competition as a way of protecting the public against monopolies, Wilson insisted that competition could be restored. The government must break up the great trusts, establish fair rules for doing business, and subject violators to stiff punishments. Thereafter, the free enterprise system would protect the public from exploitation without destroying individual initiative and opportunity.

Roosevelt's reasoning was perhaps theoretically more sound. He called for a New Nationalism. Laissez-faire made less sense than it had in earlier times. The complexities of the modern world seemed to call for a positive approach, a plan, the close application of human intelligence to social and economic problems.

To choose between the New Nationalism and the New Freedom, between the dynamic Roosevelt and the idealistic Wilson, was indeed difficult. Thousands grappled with this problem before going to the polls, but partisan politics determined the outcome of the election. Taft got the hard-core Republican vote but lost the progressive wing of the party to Roosevelt. Wilson had the solid support of both conservative and liberal Democrats. As a result, Wilson won an easy victory in the Electoral College, receiving 435 votes to Roosevelt's 88 and Taft's 8. The popular vote was Wilson, 6,286,000; Roosevelt, 4,126,000; and Taft, 3,484,000.

If partisan politics had determined the winner, the election was nonetheless an overwhelming endorsement of progressivism. The temper of the times was

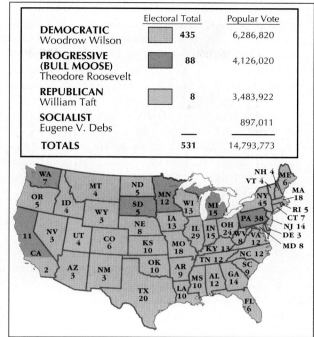

	Electoral Total	Popular Vote
DEMOCRATIC Woodrow Wilson	435	6,286,820
PROGRESSIVE (BULL MOOSE) Theodore Roosevelt	88	4,126,020
REPUBLICAN William Taft	8	3,483,922
SOCIALIST Eugene V. Debs		897,011
TOTALS	531	14,793,773

The Election of 1912

The fourth-largest vote getter in the election of 1912 was Eugene V. Debs of the Socialist party, who gained nearly 900,000 popular votes (or approximately 6 percent of the total popular vote) but no electoral votes.

shown by the 897,000 votes for Eugene Debs, who was again the Socialist candidate. Altogether, professed liberals amassed over 11 million of the 15 million ballots cast. Wilson was a minority president, but he took office with a clear mandate to press forward with further reforms.

WILSON: THE NEW FREEDOM

No one ever rose more suddenly or spectacularly in American politics than Woodrow Wilson. In the spring of 1910 he was president of Princeton University; he had never held or even run for public office. In the fall of 1912 he was president-elect of the United States. Yet if his rise was meteoric, in a very real sense he had devoted his life to preparing for it. He was born in Staunton, Virginia, in 1856, the son of a Presbyterian minister. As a student he became interested in political theory, dreaming of representing his state in the Senate. He studied law solely because he thought it the best avenue to public office, and when he discovered that he did not like legal work, he took a doctorate at Johns Hopkins in political science.

For years Wilson's political ambitions appeared doomed to frustration. He taught at Bryn Mawr, then at Wesleyan, finally at his alma mater, Princeton. He wrote several influential books, among them *Congressional Government* and *The State,* and achieved an outstanding reputation as a teacher and lecturer. In

Woodrow Wilson, presiding over the 1906 Princeton commencement, with steel magnate cum educational philanthropist Andrew Carnegie firmly in tow.

1902 he was chosen president of Princeton and soon won a place among the nation's leading educators. He revised the curriculum, introducing many new subjects and insisting that students pursue an organized and integrated course of study. He instituted the preceptorial system, which placed the students in close intellectual and social contact with their teachers. He attracted outstanding young scholars to the Princeton faculty.

Wilson was an immediate success as president. Since Roosevelt's last year in office Congress had been almost continually at war with the executive branch and with itself. Legislative achievements had been few. Now a small avalanche of important measures received the approval of the lawmakers. In October 1913 the Underwood Tariff brought the first significant reduction of duties since before the Civil War. To compensate for the expected loss of revenue, the act provided for a graduated tax on personal incomes.

Two months later the Federal Reserve Act gave the country a central banking system for the first time since Jackson destroyed the Bank of the United States. The measure divided the nation into twelve banking districts, each under the supervision of a Federal Reserve bank, a sort of bank for bankers. All national banks in each district and any state banks that wished to participate had to invest 6 percent of their capital and surplus in the reserve bank, which was empowered to exchange (the technical term is *rediscount*) paper money, called Federal Reserve notes, for the commercial and agricultural paper that member banks took in as security from borrowers. The volume of currency was no longer at the mercy of the supply of gold or any other particular commodity.

The crown and nerve center of the system was the Federal Reserve Board in Washington, which appointed a majority of the directors of the Federal Reserve banks and had some control over rediscount rates (the commission charged by the reserve banks for performing the rediscounting function). The board provided a modicum of public control over the banks, but the effort to weaken the power of the great New York banks by decentralizing the system proved ineffective. Nevertheless, a true central banking system was created.

When inflation threatened, the reserve banks could raise the rediscount rate, discouraging borrowing and thus reducing the amount of money in circulation. In bad times it could lower the rate, making it easier to borrow and injecting new dollars into the economy. Much remained to be learned about the proper management of the money supply, but the nation finally had a flexible yet safe currency.

In 1914 Congress passed two important laws affecting corporations. One created the Federal Trade Commission (FTC) to replace Roosevelt's Bureau of Corporations. In addition to investigating corporations and publishing reports, this nonpartisan board could issue cease-and-desist orders against "unfair" trade practices brought to light through its research. The law did not define the term *unfair,* and the commission's rulings could be taken on appeal to the federal courts, but the FTC was nonetheless a powerful instrument for protecting the public against the trusts.

The second measure, the Clayton Antitrust Act, made certain specific business practices illegal, including price discrimination that tended to foster monopolies; "tying" agreements, which forbade retailers from handling the products of a firm's competitors; and the creation of interlocking directorates as a means of controlling competing companies. The officers of corporations could be held individually responsible if their companies violated the antitrust laws.

The Democrats controlled both houses of Congress for the first time since 1890 and were eager to make a good record, but Wilson's imaginative and aggressive use of presidential power was decisive. He called the legislators into special session in April 1913 and appeared before them to lay out his program; he was the first president to address Congress in person since John Adams. Then he followed the course of administration bills closely. He had a private telephone line installed between the Capitol and the White House. Administration representatives haunted the cloakrooms and lobbies of both houses. Cooperative congressmen began to receive notes of praise and encouragement, recalcitrant ones stern demands for support, often pecked out on the president's own portable typewriter. When lobbyists tried to frustrate his plans for tariff reform by bringing pressure to bear on key senators, he made a dramatic appeal to the people. "The public ought to know the extraordinary exertions being made by the lobby in Washington," he told reporters. "Only public opinion can check and destroy it." The voters responded so strongly that the Senate passed the tariff bill substantially as Wilson desired it.

There were limits to Wilson's progressivism, limits imposed partly by his temperament and partly by his philosophy. He objected as strenuously to laws granting special favors to farmers and workers as to those benefiting the tycoons. When a bill was introduced in 1914 making low-interest loans available to farmers, he refused to support it. "It is unwise and unjustifiable to extend the credit of the Government to a single class of the community," he said. He considered the provision exempting unions from the antitrust laws equally unsound. Nor would he push for a federal law prohibiting child labor; such a measure would be unconstitutional, he believed. He also refused to back the constitutional amendment giving the vote to women.

By the end of 1914 Wilson's record, on balance, was positive but distinctly limited. The president believed that the major progressive goals had been achieved; he had no plans for further reform. Many other progressives thought that a great deal more remained to be done.

THE PROGRESSIVES AND MINORITY RIGHTS

On one important issue, race relations, Wilson was distinctly reactionary. With a mere handful of exceptions, the progressives exhibited strong prejudices against people of color and against certain categories of whites as well. Many were as unsympathetic to immigrants from Asia and eastern and southern Europe as any of the "conservative" opponents of immigration in the 1880s and 1890s. The Gentlemen's Agreement excluding Japanese immigrants was reached in 1907 at the height of the progressive movement.

American Indians were also affected by the progressives' racial attitudes. Where the sponsors of the Dawes Act (1887) had assumed that Indians were inherently capable of adopting the ways of "civilized" people, in the progressive period the tendency was to write Indians off as fundamentally inferior and to assume that they would make second-class citizens at best. A leading muckraker, Ray Stannard Baker, who was far more sympathetic to blacks than most progressives, dismissed Indians as pathetic beings, "eating, sleeping, idling, with no more thought of the future than a white man's child." In 1902 Congress passed the Dead Indian Land Act, which made it easier for Indians to sell allotments that they had inherited, and in 1906 another law further relaxed restrictions on land sales. Efforts to improve the education of Indian children continued, but most progressives assumed that only vocational training would help them. Theodore Roosevelt knew from his experiences as a rancher in the Dakota Territory that Indians could be as energetic and capable as whites, but he considered these "exceptional." As for the rest, it would be many generations before they could be expected to "move forward" enough to become "ordinary citizens," Roosevelt believed.

To say that African Americans did not fare well at the hands of progressives would be a gross understatement. Populist efforts to unite white and black farmers in the southern states had led to the imposition of further repressive measures. Segregation became more rigid, white opposition to black voting more monolithic. In 1900 the body of a Mississippi black was dug up by order of the state legislature and reburied in a segregated cemetery; in Virginia in 1902 the

Although lynchings were common after the Civil War, by the 1890s they had become public spectacles. Sometimes special "excursion" trains were scheduled, employers released workers, and families would bring picnics to the event. This lynching, viewed by a crowd of 10,000, took place at Paris, Texas, in 1893.

daughter of Robert E. Lee was arrested for riding in the black section of a railroad car. "Insult is being added to injury continually," a black journalist in Alabama complained. "Have those in power forgotten that there is a God?"

Many progressive women, still smarting from the insult to their sex entailed in the Fourteenth and Fifteenth Amendments and eager to attract southern support for their campaign for the vote, adopted racist arguments. They contrasted the supposed corruption and incompetence of black voters with their own "purity" and intelligence. Southern progressives of both sexes argued that disfranchising blacks would reduce corruption by removing from unscrupulous white politicians the temptation to purchase black votes!

The typical southern attitude toward the education of blacks was summed up in a folk proverb: "When you educate a Negro, you spoil a good field hand." In 1910 only about 8000 black children in the entire South were attending high schools. Despite the almost total suppression of black rights, lynchings continued to occur; between 1900 and 1914 more than 1100 blacks were murdered by mobs, most (but not all) in the southern states. In the rare cases in which local prosecutors brought the lynchers to trial, juries almost without exception brought in verdicts of not guilty.

Booker T. Washington was shaken by this trend, but he could find no way to combat it. The times were passing him by. He appealed to his white southern "friends" for help but got nowhere. Increasingly he talked about the virtues of rural life, the evils of big cities, and the uselessness of higher education for black people. By the turn of the century a number of young, well-educated blacks, most of them Northerners, were breaking away from his accommodationist leadership.

BLACK MILITANCY

William E. B. Du Bois was the most prominent of the militants. Du Bois was born in Great Barrington, Massachusetts, in 1868. His father, a restless wanderer of Negro and French Huguenot stock, abandoned the family, and young William grew up on the edge of poverty. Neither accepted nor openly rejected by the overwhelmingly white community, he devoted himself to his studies, showing such brilliance that his future education was ensured by scholarships: to Fisk University, then to Harvard, then to the University of Berlin. In 1895 Du Bois became the first American black to earn a Ph.D. in history from Harvard; his dissertation was *The Suppression of the African Slave Trade* (1896).

Personal success and "acceptance" by whites did not make the proud and sensitive Du Bois complacent. Outraged by white racism and the willingness of many blacks to settle for second-class citizenship, he set out to make American blacks proud of their color—"Beauty is black," he said—and of their African origins and culture.

Like Washington, Du Bois wanted blacks to lift themselves up by their own bootstraps. They must establish their own businesses, run their own newspapers and colleges, write their own literature; they must preserve their identity rather than seek to amalgamate themselves into a society that offered them only crumbs and contempt. At first he cooperated with Washington, but in 1903, in the essay "Of Mr. Booker T. Washington and Others," he subjected Washington's "attitude of adjustment and submission" to polite but searching criticism. Washington had asked blacks to give up political power, civil rights, and the hope of higher education, not realizing that "voting is necessary to modern manhood, that . . . discrimination is barbarism, and that black boys need education as well as white boys." Washington "apologizes for injustice," Du Bois charged. "He belittles the emasculating effects of caste distinctions, and opposes the higher training and ambitions of our brightest minds." Du Bois deemed this totally wrong. "The way for a people to gain their reasonable rights is not by voluntarily throwing them away."

Du Bois was not an uncritical admirer of the ordinary American black. He believed that "immorality, crime, and laziness" were common vices. Quite properly he blamed the weaknesses of blacks on the treatment afforded them by whites, but his approach to the solution of racial problems was frankly elitist. "The Negro race," he wrote, "is going to be saved by its exceptional men," what he called the "talented tenth" of the black population. After describing in vivid detail how white mistreatment had corrupted his people, Du Bois added loftily: "A saving remnant continually survives and persists, continually aspires, continually shows itself in thrift and ability and character."

A striking likeness of W. E. B. Du Bois drawn by Winold Reiss when Du Bois was in his fifties.

Whatever his prejudices, Du Bois exposed both the weaknesses of Washington's strategy and the callousness of white American attitudes. Accommodation was not working. Washington was praised, even lionized by prominent southern whites, yet when Theodore Roosevelt invited him to a meal at the White House they exploded with indignation, and Roosevelt, although not personally prejudiced, meekly backtracked, never repeating his "mistake." He defended his record by saying, "I have stood as valiantly for the rights of the negro as any president since Lincoln." That, sad to relate, was true enough.

Not mere impatience but despair led Du Bois and a few like-minded blacks to meet at Niagara Falls in July 1905 and to issue a stirring list of demands: the unrestricted right to vote, an end to every kind of segregation, equality of economic opportunity, higher education for the talented, equal justice in the courts, and an end to trade-union discrimination. This Niagara movement did not attract mass support, but it did stir the consciences of some whites, many of them the descendants of abolitionists, who were also becoming disenchanted by the failure of accommodation to provide blacks with real opportunity.

In 1909, the centennial of the birth of Abraham Lincoln, a group of these liberals, including the newspaperman Oswald Garrison Villard (grandson of William Lloyd Garrison), the social worker Jane Addams, the philosopher John Dewey, and the novelist William Dean Howells, founded the National Association for the Advancement of Colored People (NAACP). The organization was dedicated to the eradication of racial discrimination. Its leadership was predominantly white in the early years, but Du Bois became a national officer and the editor of its journal, *The Crisis*.

A turning point had been reached. After 1909 virtually every important leader, white and black alike, rejected the Washington approach. More and more, blacks turned to the study of their past in an effort to stimulate pride in their heritage.

This militancy produced few results in the Progressive Era. Theodore Roosevelt behaved no differently than earlier Republican presidents; he courted blacks when he thought it advantageous, turned his back when he did not. When he ran for president on the Progressive ticket in 1912, he pursued a "lily-white" policy, hoping to break the Democrats' monopoly in the South. By trusting in "[white] men of justice and of vision," Roosevelt argued in the face of decades of experience to the contrary, "the colored men of the South will ultimately get justice."

The southern-born Wilson was actively hostile to blacks. During the 1912 campaign he appealed to them for support and promised to "assist in advancing the interest of their race" in every possible way. Once elected, he refused even to appoint a privately financed commission to study the race problem. Southerners dominated his administration and Congress; as a result, blacks were further degraded. No fewer than thirty-five blacks in the Atlanta post office lost their jobs. In Washington employees in many government offices were rigidly segregated, and those who objected were summarily discharged.

Du Bois, who had supported Wilson in 1912, attacked administration policy in *The Crisis*. In November 1914 the militant editor of the *Boston Guardian*, William Monroe Trotter, a classmate of Du Bois at Harvard and a far more caustic critic of the Washington approach, led a delegation to the White House to protest the segregation policy of the government. When Wilson accused him of blackmail, Trotter lost his temper, and an ugly confrontation resulted. The mood of black leaders had changed completely.

By this time the Great War had broken out in Europe. Soon every American would feel its effects, blacks perhaps more than any other group. In November 1915, a year almost to the day after Trotter's clash with Wilson, Booker T. Washington died. One era had ended; a new one was beginning.

MILESTONES

1890	American Woman Suffrage Association and National Woman Suffrage Association unite to form National American Woman Suffrage Association (NAWSA)
1900	Robert La Follette is elected governor of Wisconsin
1901	McKinley is assassinated; Theodore Roosevelt becomes president
1902	Roosevelt helps settle anthracite coal strike
	Oregon adopts initiative system for proposing legislation
1904	Northern Securities case revives Sherman Antitrust Act
	National Child Labor Committee is established
	Theodore Roosevelt is elected president
1905	Anticapitalist Industrial Workers of the World (IWW) is founded
1906	Hepburn Act strengthens Interstate Commerce Commission
	Upton Sinclair exposes Chicago slaughterhouses in *The Jungle*
1907	U.S. Steel absorbs Tennessee Coal and Iron Company
1908	*Muller* v. *Oregon* upholds law limiting women's work hours
	William Howard Taft is elected president
1909	National Association for the Advancement of Colored People (NAACP) is founded
1910	Ballinger-Pinchot controversy deepens Roosevelt-Taft rift
1911	Roosevelt delivers speech outlining his New Nationalism program
1912	Roosevelt runs for president on Progressive ticket
	Democrat Woodrow Wilson is elected president
1913	Sixteenth Amendment authorizes federal income taxes
	Seventeenth Amendment provides direct election of U.S. senators
	Underwood Tariff reduces duties
	Federal Reserve Act creates a central banking system
1914	Federal Trade Commission (FTC) is created to protect against trusts
	Clayton Antitrust Act regulates business
1920	Nineteenth Amendment guarantees women the right to vote

23

FROM ISOLATION TO EMPIRE

In the decades following the Civil War, Americans were occupied with exploiting the West and building their great industrial machine. They gave little thought to foreign affairs. Even some American statesmen were curiously disinterested. In 1885 Secretary of State Thomas F. Bayard declared that he looked upon the political intrigues of Europe "with impatience and contempt." During the 1888 presidential campaign Benjamin Harrison reflected a widely held belief when he said that the United States was "an apart nation" and so it should remain. James Bryce made the same point in *The American Commonwealth*. "Happy America," he wrote, stood "apart in a world of her own . . . safe even from menace."

ORIGINS OF THE LARGE POLICY: COVETING COLONIES

The nation's interests elsewhere in the world gradually increased. During the Civil War, France had established a protectorate over Mexico, installing the Archduke Maximilian of Austria as emperor. In 1866 Secretary of State William H. Seward demanded that the French withdraw, and the United States moved 50,000 soldiers to the Rio Grande. While fear of American intervention was only one of many reasons for their action, the French pulled their troops out of Mexico during the winter of 1866–1867. Mexican nationalists promptly seized and executed Maximilian. In 1867, at the instigation of Seward, the United States purchased Alaska from Russia for $7.2 million, thereby ridding the continent of another foreign power.

In 1867 the aggressive Seward acquired the Midway Islands in the western Pacific, which had been discovered in 1859 by an American naval officer, N. C. Brooks. Seward also made overtures toward annexing the Hawaiian Islands, and he looked longingly at Cuba. In 1870 President Grant submitted to the Senate a treaty annexing the Dominican Republic. He applied tremendous pressure in an effort to obtain ratification, thus forcing a "great debate" on extracontinental expansion. Expansionists stressed the wealth and resources of the country, the markets it would provide, even its "salubrious climate." But the arguments of the opposition proved more persuasive. The distance of the Dominican Republic from the continent and its crowded, dark-skinned population of what one congressman called "semi-civilized, semi-barbarous men who cannot speak our language" made annexation unattractive. The treaty was rejected. Seward had to admit that there was no significant support in the country for his expansionist plans.

The internal growth that preoccupied Americans eventually led them to look outward. By the late 1880s the country was exporting a steadily increasing share of its agricultural and industrial output. Exports, only $450 million in 1870, passed the billion-dollar mark early in the 1890s. Imports increased at a rate only slightly less spectacular.

The character of foreign trade was also changing: Manufactures loomed ever more important among exports until in 1898 the country shipped abroad more manufactured goods than it imported. By this time American steelmakers could compete with producers anywhere in the world. In 1900 one American firm received a large order for steel plates from a Glasgow shipbuilder, and another won contracts for structural steel to be used in constructing bridges for the Uganda Railroad in British East Africa. When a member of Parliament questioned the colonial secretary about the latter deal, the secretary replied: "Tenders [bids] were invited in the United Kingdom . . . [but] one of the American tenders was found to be considerably the lowest in every respect and was therefore accepted." When American industrialists became conscious of their ability to compete with Europeans in far-off markets, they took more interest in world affairs, particularly during periods of depression, when domestic consumption fell.

Shifting intellectual currents further altered the attitudes of Americans. Darwin's theories, applicable by analogy to international relations, gave the concept of manifest destiny a new plausibility. Darwinists like the historian John Fiske argued that the American democratic system of government was so clearly the world's "fittest" that it was destined to spread peacefully over "every land on the earth's surface." In *Our Country* (1885) Josiah Strong found racist and religious justifications for American expansionism, again based on the theory of evolution. The Anglo-Saxon race, centered now in the United States, possessed "an instinct or genius for colonization," Strong claimed. "God, with infinite wisdom and skill is training the Anglo-Saxon race for . . . the final competition of races." Soon American civilization would "move down upon" Mexico and all Latin America and "out upon the islands of the sea, over upon Africa and beyond." "Can anyone doubt," Strong asked, "that the result of this . . . will be 'the survival of the fittest'?"[1]

The completion of the conquest of the American West encouraged Americans to consider expansion beyond the seas. "For nearly 300 years the dominant fact in American life has been expansion," declared Frederick Jackson Turner, propounder of the frontier thesis. "That these energies of expansion will no longer operate would be a rash prediction." Turner and writers who advanced other expansionist arguments were much influenced by foreign thinking.

Finally, military and strategic arguments were advanced to justify adopting a "large" policy. The powerful Union army had been demobilized rapidly after Appomattox; in the 1880s only about 25,000 men were under arms, their chief occupation fighting Indians in the West.

Half the navy, too, had been scrapped after the war, and the remaining ships were obsolete. While other nations were building steam-powered iron warships, the United States still depended on wooden sailing vessels. In 1867 a British naval publication accurately described the American fleet as "hapless, broken-down, tattered [and] forlorn."

Although no foreign power menaced the country, the decrepit state of the navy vexed many of its officers and led one of them, Captain Alfred Thayer Mahan, to develop a startling theory about the importance of sea power. He explained his theory in two important books, *The Influence of Sea Power Upon History* (1890) and *The Influence of Sea Power Upon the French Revolution and Empire* (1892). According to Mahan, history proved that a nation with a powerful navy and the overseas bases necessary to maintain it would be invulnerable in war and prosperous in time of peace. Applied to the current American situation, this meant that in addition to building a modern fleet, the United States should obtain a string of coaling stations and bases in the Caribbean, annex the Hawaiian Islands, and cut a canal across Central America.

Writing at a time when the imperialist-minded European nations showed signs of extending their influence in South America and the Pacific islands, Mahan attracted many influential disciples. One was Congressman Henry Cabot Lodge of Massachusetts, a prominent member of the Naval Affairs Committee. Lodge had married into a navy family and was close with the head of the new Naval War College, Commodore Stephen B. Luce. In 1883 he helped push through Congress an act authorizing the building of three steel warships, and he consistently advocated expanding and modernizing the fleet. Elected to the Senate in 1893, Lodge pressed for expansionist policies, basing his arguments on Mahan's strategic concepts. "Sea power," Lodge proclaimed, "is essential to the greatness of every splendid people." Lodge's friend Theodore Roosevelt was another ardent supporter of the "large" policy, but he had little influence until McKinley appointed him assistant secretary of the navy in 1897.

---

[1] In later writings Strong insisted that by "fittest" he meant "social efficiency," not "mere strength."

TOWARD AN EMPIRE IN THE PACIFIC

The interest of the United States in the Pacific and East Asia began in the late eighteenth century, when the first American merchant ship dropped anchor in the harbor of Canton, China. After the Treaty of Wanghia (1844), American merchants in China enjoyed many privileges and trade expanded rapidly. Missionaries began to flock into the country—in the late 1880s, over 500 were living there.

The Hawaiian Islands were an important way station on the route to China, and by 1820 merchants and missionaries were making contacts there. As early as 1854 a movement to annex the islands to the United States existed, although it foundered because Hawaii insisted on being admitted to the Union as a state. Commodore Matthew Perry's expedition to Japan led to the signing of a commercial treaty (1858) that opened several Japanese ports to American traders.

The United States pursued a policy of cooperating with the European powers in expanding commercial opportunities in East Asia. In Hawaii the tendency was to claim a special position but to accept the fact that Europeans also had interests in the islands. This state of affairs did not change radically following the Civil War. Despite Chinese protests over the exclusion of their nationals from the United States after 1882, American commercial privileges in China were not disturbed.

American influence in Hawaii increased steadily; the descendants of missionary families, most of them engaged in raising sugar, dominated the Hawaiian monarchy. While they made no overt effort to make the islands an American colony, all the expansionist ideas of the era—manifest destiny, Darwinism, Josiah Strong's racist and religious assumptions, and the relentless force of American commercial interests—pointed them in that direction. In 1875 a reciprocity treaty admitted Hawaiian sugar to the United States free of duty in return for a promise to yield no territory to a foreign power. When this treaty was renewed in 1887, the United States obtained the right to establish a naval base at Pearl Harbor. In addition to occupying Midway, America obtained a foothold in the Samoan Islands in the South Pacific.

During the 1890s American interest in the Pacific area steadily intensified. Conditions in Hawaii had much to do with this. The McKinley Tariff Act of 1890, discontinuing the duty on raw sugar and compensating American producers of cane and beet sugar by granting them a bounty of 2 cents a pound, struck Hawaiian sugar growers hard, for it destroyed the advantage they had gained in the reciprocity treaty.

The following year the death of the complaisant King Kalakaua brought Queen Liliuokalani, a determined nationalist, to the throne. Placing herself at the head of a "Hawaii for the Hawaiians" movement, she abolished the existing constitution under which the white minority had pretty much controlled the islands and attempted to rule as an absolute monarch. The resident Americans then staged a coup. In January 1893, with the connivance of the U.S. minister, John L. Stevens, who ordered 150 marines from the cruiser *Boston* into Honolulu, they

DEBATING THE PAST

Did the United States acquire an overseas empire for moral or economic reasons? The American flag, second from left, flies over a warehouse in Guangzhou on the south coast of China in the late nineteenth century. The second photo, dated 1898, is of a family of Presbyterian missionaries in Beijing, attended by Chinese servants. In an influential work, diplomat and historian George F. Kennan (1951) contended that expansionist policies during these years were animated by excessive morality and idealism. McKinley went to war with Spain over the injustice of its colonial rule in Cuba, and he claimed to colonize the Philippines to "educate the Filipinos, and uplift and Christianize them."

During the 1960s and 1970s, however, revisionist historians argued that expansionist schemes were not in the least motivated by idealism. William A. Williams (1972) claimed that American policymakers sought profitable economic penetration of underdeveloped areas. Their subsidiary aim was to encourage these countries to "modernize," that is, to remake themselves in the image of the United States. The Open Door policy, in Williams's view, was not unrealistic and by no means a failure—indeed, it was too successful. He criticized American policy because of its harmful effects on underdeveloped countries. The policy, Williams contended, was "tragic" rather than evil, because its creators were not evil but possessed only limited vision. They did not recognize the contradictions in their ideas and values. They saw American expansion as beneficial to all concerned—and not exclusively in materialistic terms. They genuinely believed that they were exporting democracy along with capitalism and industrialization. Yet while U.S. statesmen abroad certainly sought to fill the warehouses, records show that they spent most of their time speaking with American missionaries and attending to their problems. Religious and moral considerations did matter.

George F. Kennan, *American Diplomacy* (1951), William Appleman Williams, *The Tragedy of American Diplomacy* (1972).

Sugar planters deposed Hawaii's Queen Liliuokalani, a determined nationalist, in 1893 and requested United States annexation. This 1887 portrait of Queen Liliuokalani was taken in London during Queen Victoria's jubilee.

deposed Queen Liliuokalani and set up a provisional government. Stevens recognized their regime at once, and the new government sent a delegation to Washington to seek a treaty of annexation.

In the closing days of the Harrison administration such a treaty was negotiated and sent to the Senate, but when Cleveland took office in March, he withdrew it. The new president disapproved of the way American troops had been used to overthrow the monarchy. He sent a special commissioner, James H. Blount, to Hawaii to investigate. When Blount reported that the Hawaiians opposed annexation, the president dismissed Stevens and attempted to restore Queen Liliuokalani. Since the provisional government was by that time firmly entrenched, this could not be accomplished peacefully. Because Cleveland was unwilling to use force against the Americans in the islands, however much he objected to their actions, he found himself unable to do anything. The revolutionary government of Hawaii remained in power, independent yet eager to be annexed.

The Hawaiian debate continued sporadically over the next four years. It provided a thorough airing of the question of overseas expansion. Fears that another power—Great Britain or perhaps Japan—might step into the void created by Cleveland's refusal to act alarmed those who favored annexation. When the Republicans returned to power in 1897, a new annexation treaty was negotiated,

The Course of Empire, 1867–1901

but domestic sugar producers now threw their weight against it, and the McKinley administration could not obtain the necessary two-thirds majority in the Senate. Finally, in July 1898, after the outbreak of the Spanish-American War, Congress annexed the islands by joint resolution, a procedure requiring only a simple majority vote.

TOWARD AN EMPIRE IN LATIN AMERICA

As early as 1869 President Grant had come out for an American-owned canal across the isthmus of Panama, in spite of the fact that the United States had agreed in the Clayton-Bulwer Treaty with Great Britain (1850) that neither nation would "obtain or maintain for itself any exclusive control" over an interoceanic canal. In 1880, when the French engineer Ferdinand de Lesseps organized a company to build a canal across the isthmus, President Hayes announced that the United States would not permit a European power to control such a waterway. "The policy of the country is a canal under American control," he announced, another blithe disregard of the Clayton-Bulwer agreement.

When Cleveland returned to power in 1893, the possibility of trouble in Latin America seemed remote, for he had always opposed imperialistic ventures. Yet scarcely two years later the United States was again on the verge of war in South America as a result of a crisis in Venezuela, and before this issue was settled Cleveland had made the most powerful claim to American hegemony in the hemisphere ever uttered. The tangled borderland between Venezuela and British Guiana (present-day Guyana) had long been in dispute, Venezuela demanding more of the region than it was entitled to and Great Britain making exaggerated claims and imperiously refusing to submit the question to arbitration.

There was considerable latent anti-British feeling in the United States. By taking the Venezuelan side in the boundary dispute, Cleveland would be defending a weak neighbor against a great power, a position certain to evoke a popular response. "Turn this Venezuela question up or down, North, South, East or West, and it is a winner" one Democrat advised the president.

Cleveland did not resist the temptation to intervene. In July 1895 he ordered Secretary of State Richard Olney to send a near ultimatum to the British. By occupying the disputed territory, Olney insisted, Great Britain was invading Venezuela and violating the Monroe Doctrine. Quite gratuitously, he went on to boast: "Today the United States is practically sovereign on this continent, and its fiat is law upon the subjects to which it confines its interposition." Unless Great Britain responded promptly by agreeing to arbitration, the president would call the question to the attention of Congress.

The note threatened war, but the British ignored it for months. They did not take the United States seriously as a world power, and with reason, for the American navy, although expanding, could not hope to stand up against the British, who had 50 battleships, 25 armored cruisers, and many smaller vessels. When Lord Salisbury, the prime minister and foreign secretary, finally replied, he rejected outright the argument that the Monroe Doctrine had any status under international law and refused to arbitrate what he called the "exaggerated pretensions" of the Venezuelans.

While Olney's note had been belligerent, Salisbury's reply was supercilious and caustic. Cleveland was furious. On December 17, 1895, he asked Congress for authority to appoint an American commission to determine the correct line between British Guiana and Venezuela. When that had been done, he added, the United States should "resist by every means in its power" the appropriation by Great Britain of any territory "we have determined of right belongs to Venezuela." Congress responded at once, unanimously appropriating $100,000 for the boundary commission. Popular approval was almost universal.

Great Britain agreed to arbitrate the boundary. The war scare subsided; soon Olney was talking about "our inborn and instinctive English sympathies" and offering "to stand side by side and shoulder to shoulder with England in . . . the defense of human rights." When the boundary tribunal awarded nearly all the disputed region to Great Britain, whatever ill feeling the surrender may have occasioned in that country faded away. Instead of leading to war, the affair marked the beginning of an era of Anglo-American friendship. It had the unfortunate effect, however, of adding to the long-held American conviction that the nation could get what it wanted in international affairs by threat and bluster—a dangerous illusion.

THE CUBAN REVOLUTION

On February 10, 1896, scarcely a week after Venezuela and Great Britain had signed the treaty ending their dispute, General Valeriano Weyler arrived in Havana from Spain to take up his duties as governor of Cuba. His assignment to this post was occasioned by the guerrilla warfare that Cuban nationalist rebels had been waging for almost a year. Weyler, a tough and ruthless soldier, set out to administer Cuba with "a salutary rigor." He began herding the rural population into wretched "reconcentration" camps to deprive the rebels of food and recruits. Resistance in Cuba hardened.

Public sympathy in the United States went to the Cubans, who seemed to be fighting for liberty and democracy against an autocratic Old World power. Most newspapers supported the rebels; labor unions, veterans' organizations, many Protestant clergymen, a great majority of American blacks, and important politicians in both major parties demanded that the United States aid their cause. Rapidly increasing American investments in Cuban sugar plantations, now approaching $50 million, were endangered by the fighting and by the social chaos sweeping across the island.

Cuban propagandists in the United States played on American sentiments cleverly. When reports, often exaggerated, of the cruelty of "Butcher" Weyler and the horrors of his reconcentration camps filtered into America, the cry for action intensified. In April 1896 Congress adopted a resolution suggesting that the revolutionaries be granted the rights of belligerents. Since this would have been akin to formal recognition, Cleveland would not go that far, but he did exert diplomatic pressure on Spain to remove the causes of the rebels' complaints, and he offered the services of his government as mediator. The Spanish rejected the suggestion. For a time the issue subsided. The election of 1896 deflected American attention from Cuba, and then McKinley refused to take any action that might disturb Spanish-American relations. Business interests—except those with holdings in Cuba—backed McKinley, for they feared that a crisis would upset the economy, which was just beginning to pick up after the depression. In Cuba General Weyler made some progress toward stifling rebel resistance.

American expansionists, however, continued to demand intervention, and the press, especially Joseph Pulitzer's *New York World* and William Randolph Hearst's *New York Journal,* competing fiercely to increase circulation, kept resentment alive with tales of Spanish atrocities. McKinley remained adamant. Although he warned Spain that Cuba must be pacified, and soon, his tone was friendly and he issued no ultimatum. A new government in Spain relieved the situation by recalling Weyler and promising partial self-government to the Cubans.

Instability in Latin America led many to speculate that the United States would play an increasingly dominant role in the region. In Louis Dalrymple's 1895 cartoon, Uncle Sam wins the affection of the damsel Cuba as Spanish misrule and native insurgency lay waste to each other.

In a message to Congress in December 1897, McKinley urged that Spain be given "a reasonable chance to realize her expectations" in the island.

His hopes were doomed, primarily because Spain failed to "realize her expectations." The fighting in Cuba continued. When riots broke out in Havana in January 1898, McKinley ordered the battleship *Maine* to Havana harbor to protect American citizens.

Shortly thereafter Hearst's *New York Journal* printed a letter written to a friend in Cuba by the Spanish minister in Washington, Dupuy de Lôme. The letter had been stolen by a spy. De Lôme, an experienced but arrogant diplomat, failed to appreciate McKinley's efforts to avoid intervening in Cuba. In the letter he characterized the president as a *politicastro*, or "small-time politician," which was a gross error, and a "bidder for the admiration of the crowd," which was equally insulting though somewhat closer to the truth. Americans were outraged, and de Lôme's hasty resignation did little to soothe their feelings.

Then, on February 15, the *Maine* exploded and sank in Havana harbor, 260 of the crew perishing in the disaster. Interventionists in the United States accused Spain of having destroyed the ship and clamored for war. The willingness of Americans to blame Spain indicates the extent of anti-Spanish opinion in the United States by 1898. No one has ever discovered what actually happened. A naval court of inquiry decided that the vessel had been sunk by a submarine mine, but it now seems more likely that an internal explosion destroyed the

The explosion of the Maine *in Havana harbor, killing 260 men, caused much speculation in the newspapers and across the nation as to its cause. Many Americans pointed the finger at Spain, a reaction that typified American sentiment toward the Spanish in 1898. What really caused the explosion remains unknown.*

Maine. The Spanish government could hardly have been foolish enough to commit an act that would probably bring American troops into Cuba.

With admirable courage, McKinley refused to panic; but he could not resist the wishes of millions of citizens that something be done to stop the fighting and allow the Cubans to determine their own fate. Spanish pride and Cuban patriotism had taken the issue of peace or war out of the president's hands. Spain could not put down the rebellion, and it would not yield to the nationalists' increasingly extreme demands. To have granted independence to Cuba might have caused the Madrid government to fall, might even have led to the collapse of the monarchy, for the Spanish public was in no mood to surrender. The Cubans, sensing that the continuing bloodshed aided their cause, refused to give the Spanish regime room to maneuver. After the *Maine* disaster, Spain might have agreed to an armistice had the rebels asked for one, and in the resulting negotiations it might well have given up the island. The rebels refused to make the first move. The fighting continued, bringing the United States every day closer to intervention.

The president faced a dilemma. Most of the business interests of the country, to which he was particularly sensitive, opposed intervention. His personal feelings were equally firm. "I have been through one war," he told a friend. "I have seen the dead piled up, and I do not want to see another." Congress, however, seemed determined to act. When he submitted a restrained report on the sinking of the *Maine,* the Democrats in Congress, even most of those who had supported Cleveland's policies, gleefully accused him of timidity.

McKinley spent a succession of sleepless nights; sedatives brought him no repose. Finally, early in April, the president drafted a message asking for authority to use the armed forces "to secure a full and final termination of hostilities" in Cuba.

At the last moment the Spanish government seemed to yield; it ordered its troops in Cuba to cease hostilities. McKinley passed this information on to Congress along with his war message, but he gave it no emphasis and did not try to check the march toward war. To seek further delay would have been courageous but not necessarily wiser. Merely to stop fighting was not enough. The Cuban nationalists now insisted on full independence, and the Spanish politicians were unprepared to abandon the last remnant of their once-great American empire. If the United States took Cuba by force, the Spanish leaders might save their political skins; if they meekly surrendered the island, they were done for.

THE "SPLENDID LITTLE" SPANISH-AMERICAN WAR

On April 20, 1898, Congress, by joint resolution, recognized the independence of Cuba and authorized the use of the armed forces to drive out the Spanish. An amendment proposed by Senator Henry M. Teller disclaiming any intention of adding Cuban territory to the United States passed without opposition. Four days later Spain declared war on the United States.

The Spanish-American War was fought to free Cuba, but the first action took place on the other side of the globe, in the Philippine Islands. Weeks earlier, Theodore Roosevelt, at the time assistant secretary of the navy, had alerted Commodore George Dewey, who was in command of the United States Asiatic Squadron located at Hong Kong, to move against the Spanish base at Manila if war came. Dewey had acted promptly, drilling his gun crews, taking on supplies, giving his gleaming white ships a coat of battle-gray paint, and establishing secret contacts with the Filipino nationalist leader, Emilio Aguinaldo. When word of the declaration of war reached him, Dewey steamed from Hong Kong across the South China Sea with four cruisers and two gunboats. On the night of April 30 he entered Manila Bay, and at daybreak he opened fire on the Spanish fleet at 5000 yards. His squadron made five passes, each time reducing the range; when the smoke had cleared, all ten of Admiral Montojo's ships had been destroyed. Not a single American was killed in the engagement.

Dewey immediately asked for troops to take and hold Manila, for now that war had been declared, he could not return to Hong Kong or put in at any other neutral port. McKinley took the fateful step of dispatching some 11,000 soldiers and additional naval support. On August 13 these forces, assisted by Filipino irregulars under Aguinaldo, captured Manila.

Admiral Dewey aboard the Olympia, *directing the attack on the Spanish fleet at Manila Bay, which Dewey suspected of being mined. Dewey's nephew, who commanded a supply ship with the fleet, proposed to lead the way into the bay. "Billy," responded Dewey, "mines or no mines, I am leading the squadron in myself." But Dewey's squadron had arrived before the harbor had been mined and it entered unharmed.*

Meanwhile, in Cuba, the United States had won a swift and total victory, though more because of the weakness of the Spanish armed forces than because of the power or efficiency of the American. When the war began, the U.S. regular army consisted of about 28,000 men. This tiny force was bolstered by 200,000 hastily enlisted volunteers. In May an expeditionary force gathered at Tampa, Florida. That hamlet was inundated by the masses of men and supplies that descended upon it. Entire regiments sat without uniforms or weapons while hundreds of freight cars jammed with equipment lay forgotten on sidings. Army management was abominable, rivalry between commanders a serious problem. Aggressive units like the regiment of "Rough Riders" raised by Theodore Roosevelt, who had resigned his navy department post to become a lieutenant colonel of volunteers, scrambled for space and supplies, shouldering aside other units to get what they needed. "No words could describe . . . the confusion and lack of system and the general mismanagement of affairs here," the angry Roosevelt complained.

Since a Spanish fleet under Admiral Pascual Cervera was known to be in Caribbean waters, no invading army could safely embark until the fleet could be located. On May 29 American ships found Cervera at Santiago harbor, on the eastern end of Cuba, and established a blockade. In June a 17,000-man expeditionary force commanded by General William Shafter landed at Daiquiri, east of Santiago, and pressed quickly toward the city, handicapped more by its own bad staff work than by the enemy, though the Spanish troops resisted bravely. The Americans sweated through Cuba's torrid summer in heavy wool winter uniforms, ate "embalmed beef" out of cans, and fought mostly with old-fashioned rifles using black powder cartridges that marked the position of each soldier with a puff of smoke whenever he pulled the trigger. On July 1 they broke through undermanned Spanish defenses and stormed San Juan Hill, the intrepid Roosevelt at the forefront. ("Are you afraid to stand up while I am on horseback?" Roosevelt demanded of one soldier.)

With Santiago harbor in range of American artillery, Admiral Cervera had to run the blockade. On July 3 his black-hulled ships, flags proudly flying, steamed forth from the harbor and fled westward along the coast. Like hounds after rabbits, five American battleships and two cruisers, commanded by Rear Admiral William T. Sampson and Commodore Winfield Scott Schley, ran them down. In four hours the entire Spanish force was destroyed by a hail of 8-inch and 13-inch projectiles (the size of artillery shells refers to their diameter). Damage to the American ships was superficial; only one American seaman lost his life in the engagement.

The end then came abruptly. Santiago surrendered on July 17. A few days later, other U.S. troops completed the occupation of Puerto Rico. On August 12, one day before the fall of Manila, Spain agreed to get out of Cuba and to cede Puerto Rico and an island in the Marianas (Guam) to the United States. The future of the Philippines was to be settled at a formal peace conference, convening in Paris on October 1.

DEVELOPING A COLONIAL POLICY

Although the Spanish resisted surrendering the Philippines at Paris, they had been so thoroughly defeated that they had no choice. The decision hung rather on the outcome of a conflict over policy within the United States. The war, won at so little cost militarily, produced problems far larger than those it solved.[2] The nation had become a great power in the world's eyes. The annexation of Hawaii and other overseas bases intensified the conviction of European leaders that the United States was determined to become a major force in international affairs.

But were the American people determined to exercise that force? The debate over taking the Philippine Islands throws much light on their attitudes. The imagination of Americans had been captured by the trappings of empire, not by its essence. It was titillating to think of a world map liberally sprinkled with

[2]More than 5000 Americans died as a result of the conflict, but fewer than 400 fell in combat. The others were mostly victims of yellow fever, typhoid, and other diseases.

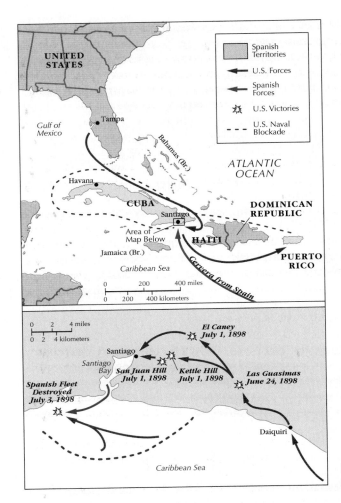

Spanish-American War, Caribbean Theater

American flags and of the economic benefits that colonies might bring, but most citizens were not prepared to join in a worldwide struggle for power and influence. They entered blithely on adventures in far-off regions without facing the implications of their decision.

Since the United States (in the Teller Amendment) had renounced any claim to Cuba, even though the island had long been desired by expansionists, logic dictated that a similar policy be applied to the Philippines, a remote land few Americans had ever thought about before 1898. But expansionists were eager to annex the entire archipelago. Even before he had learned to spell the name, Senator Lodge was saying that "the Phillipines [sic] mean a vast future trade and wealth and power," offering the nation a greater opportunity "than anything that has happened . . . since the annexation of Louisiana."

President McKinley adopted a more cautious stance, but he too favored "the general principle of holding on to what we can get." A speaking tour of the Midwest in October 1898, during which he experimented with varying degrees of commitment to expansionism, convinced him that the public wanted the islands. Business opinion had shifted dramatically during the war. Business leaders were now calling the Philippines the gateway to the markets of East Asia.

① THE ANTI-IMPERIALISTS

The war had produced a wave of unifying patriotic feeling. It greatly furthered reconciliation between the North and the South; two major generals, for example, were Confederate veterans. But victory raised new divisive questions. An important minority objected strongly to the U.S. acquisition of overseas possessions. Persons as different in interest and philosophy as the tycoon Andrew Carnegie and the labor leader Samuel Gompers, as the venerable Republican Senator George Frisbie Hoar of Massachusetts and "Pitchfork Ben" Tillman, the southern Democratic firebrand, together with the writers Mark Twain and William Dean Howells, the reformers Lincoln Steffens and Jane Addams, and the educators Charles W. Eliot of Harvard and David Starr Jordan of Stanford united in opposing annexation of the Philippines.

The anti-imperialists insisted that since no one would consider statehood for the Philippines, it would be unconstitutional to annex them. It was a violation of the spirit of the Declaration of Independence to govern a foreign territory without the consent of its inhabitants, Senator Hoar argued; by taking over "vassal states" in "barbarous archipelagoes" the United States was "trampling . . . on our own great Charter, which recognizes alike the liberty and the dignity of individual manhood."

McKinley was not insensitive to this appeal to idealism and tradition, which was the fundamental element in the anti-imperialist argument. But he rejected it. Labor leaders particularly feared the competition of "the Chinese, the Negritos, and the Malays" who presumably would flood into the United States if the Philippines were taken. More compelling to McKinley was the absence of any practical alternative to annexation. Public opinion would not sanction restoring Spanish authority in the Philippines or allowing some other power to have them. That the Filipinos were sufficiently advanced and united socially to form a stable government if granted independence seemed unlikely. Senator Hoar believed that "for years and for generations, and perhaps for centuries, there would have been turbulence, disorder and revolution" in the islands if they were left to their own devices.

Strangely—for he was a kind and gentle man—Hoar faced this possibility with equanimity. McKinley was unable to do so. The president searched the depths of his soul and could find no solution but annexation. Of course the state of public feeling made the decision easier, and he probably found the idea of presiding over an empire appealing. Certainly the commercial possibilities did not escape him. In the end it was with a heavy sense of responsibility that he ordered the American peace commissioners to insist on acquiring the Philippines. To salve the feelings of the Spanish the United States agreed to pay $20 million for the archipelago, but it was a forced sale, accepted by Spain under duress.

The peace treaty faced a hard battle in the U.S. Senate, where a combination of partisan politics and anticolonialism made it difficult to amass the two-thirds majority necessary for ratification. McKinley had shrewdly appointed three senators, including one Democrat, to the peace commission. This predisposed many members of the upper house to approve the treaty, but the vote was close. William Jennings Bryan, titular head of the Democratic party, could probably have prevented ratification had he urged his supporters to vote nay. The question should be decided, Bryan said, "not by a minority of the Senate but by a majority of the people" at the next presidential election. Perplexed by Bryan's stand, a number of Democrats allowed themselves to be persuaded by the expansionists' arguments and by McKinley's judicious use of patronage; the treaty was ratified in February 1899 by a vote of 57 to 27.

THE PHILIPPINE INSURRECTION

The national referendum that Bryan had hoped for never materialized. Bryan himself confused the issue in 1900 by making free silver a major plank in his platform, thereby driving conservative anti-imperialists into McKinley's arms. Moreover, early in 1899 the Filipino nationalists under Aguinaldo, furious because the United States would not withdraw, took up arms. A savage guerrilla war resulted, one that cost far more in lives and money than the "splendid little" Spanish-American conflict.

Like all conflicts waged in tangled country chiefly by small, isolated units surrounded by a hostile civilian population, neither side displayed much regard for the "rules" of war. Goaded by sneak attacks and instances of cruelty to captives, American soldiers, most of whom had little respect for Filipinos to begin with, responded in kind. Civilians were rounded up, prisoners tortured, property destroyed. Horrifying tales of rape, arson, and murder by U.S. troops filtered into the country, providing ammunition for the anti-imperialists. "You seem to have about finished your work of civilizing the Filipinos," Andrew Carnegie wrote angrily to one of the American peace commissioners. "About 8000 of them have been completely civilized and sent to Heaven. I hope you like it." In fact, far more than 8000 Filipinos lost their lives during the conflict, which raged for three years. More than 70,000 American soldiers had to be sent to the islands before the resistance was crushed, and about as many of them lost their lives as had perished in the Cuban conflict.

A commission that had been sent to the Philippines by McKinley in 1899 before the fighting started to study the problem attributed the insurrection to the ambitions of the nationalist leaders and recommended that the Philippines be granted independence at an indefinite future date. In 1900 McKinley sent an-

Emilio Aguinaldo, shown here with his young son, commanded Filipino insurgents who worked with Commodore Dewey to help overthrow Spanish rule of the Philippines in 1898. He later took up arms against the United States in a brutal three-year struggle when President McKinley opposed granting independence to the islands.

other commission, this one headed by William Howard Taft, a federal judge, to establish a government. Taft, a warmhearted, affable man, took an instant liking to the Filipinos, and his policy of encouraging them to participate in the territorial government attracted many converts. In July 1901 he became the first civilian governor of the Philippines.

Actually, McKinley's reelection in 1900 settled the Philippine question so far as most Americans were concerned. Anti-imperialists still claimed that it was unconstitutional to take over territories without the consent of the local population. Their reasoning, while certainly not unsound, was unhistorical. No American government had seriously considered the wishes of the American Indians, the French and Spanish settlers in Louisiana, the Eskimos of Alaska, or the people of Hawaii when it had seemed in the national interest to annex new lands.

CUBA AND THE UNITED STATES

Nevertheless, grave constitutional questions arose as a result of the acquisitions that followed the Spanish-American War. McKinley acted with remarkable independence in handling the problems involved in expansion. He set up military governments in Cuba, Puerto Rico, and the Philippines without specific congressional authority. But eventually both Congress and the Supreme Court took a hand in shaping colonial policy. In 1900 Congress passed the Foraker Act, establishing a civil government for Puerto Rico. It did not give the Puerto Ricans either American citizenship or full local self-government, and it placed a tariff on Puerto Rican products imported into the United States.

While the most heated arguments raged over Philippine policy, the most difficult colonial problems concerned the relationship between the United States and Cuba, for there idealism and self-interest clashed painfully. Despite the desire of most Americans to get out of Cuba, an independent government could not easily be created. Order and prosperity did not automatically appear when the red and gold ensigns of Spain were hauled down from the flagstaffs of Havana and Santiago.

The insurgent government was feeble, corrupt, and oligarchic, the Cuban economy in a state of collapse, life chaotic. The first Americans entering Havana found the streets littered with garbage and the corpses of horses and dogs. All public services were at a standstill; it seemed essential for the United States, as McKinley said, to give "aid and direction" until "tranquillity" could be restored.

When McKinley established a military government for Cuba late in 1898, it was soon embroiled with local leaders. Then an eager horde of American promoters descended on Cuba in search of profitable franchises and concessions. Congress put a stop to this exploitation by forbidding all such grants as long as the occupation continued.

In the end the United States did withdraw, after doing a great deal to modernize sugar production, improve sanitary conditions, establish schools, and restore orderly administration. In November 1900 a Cuban constitutional convention met at Havana and proceeded without substantial American interference or direction to draft a frame of government. The chief restrictions imposed by this document on Cuba's freedom concerned foreign relations; at the insistence of the United States, it authorized American intervention whenever necessary "for the preservation of Cuban independence" and "the maintenance of a government adequate for the protection of life, property, and individual liberty." Cuba had to promise to make no treaty with a foreign power compromising its independence and to grant naval bases on its soil to the United States.

The Cubans, after some grumbling, accepted this arrangement, known as the Platt Amendment. It had the support of most American opponents of imperialism. The amendment was a true compromise: it safeguarded American interests while granting to the Cubans real self-government on internal matters. In May 1902 the United States turned over the reins of government to the new republic. The next year the two countries signed a reciprocity treaty tightening the economic bonds between them.

True friendship did not result. Although American troops occupied Cuba only once more, in 1906, and then at the specific request of Cuban authorities, the United States repeatedly used the threat of intervention to coerce the Cuban government. American economic penetration proceeded rapidly and without regard for the well-being of the Cuban peasants, many of whom lived in a state of peonage on great sugar plantations. Nor did the Americans' good intentions make up for their tendency to consider themselves innately superior to the Cubans and to overlook the fact that Cubans did not always wish to adopt American customs and culture.

THE UNITED STATES IN THE CARIBBEAN AND CENTRAL AMERICA

If the purpose of the Spanish-American War had been to bring peace and order to Cuba, the Platt Amendment was a logical step. The same purpose soon necessitated a further extension of the principle, for once the United States accepted the role of protector and stabilizer in parts of the Caribbean and Central America, it seemed desirable, for the same economic, strategic, and humanitarian reasons, to supervise the entire region.

The Caribbean and Central American countries were economically underdeveloped, socially backward, politically unstable, and desperately poor. Everywhere a few families owned most of the land and dominated social and political life. Most of the people were uneducated peasants, many of whom were little better off than slaves. Rival cliques of wealthy families struggled for power, force being the usual method of effecting a change in government. Most of the meager income of the average Caribbean state was swallowed up by the military or diverted into the pockets of the current rulers.

In 1903, after Theodore Roosevelt had become president, the Dominican Republic defaulted on bonds totaling some $40 million. When European investors urged their governments to intervene, Roosevelt announced that under the Monroe Doctrine the United States could not permit foreign nations to intervene in Latin America. But, he added, Latin American nations should not be allowed to escape their obligations. "If we intend to say 'Hands off' . . . sooner or later we must keep order ourselves," he told Secretary of War Elihu Root.

The president did not want to make a colony of the Dominican Republic. "I have about the same desire to annex it as a gorged boa constrictor might have to swallow a porcupine wrong-end-to," he said. He therefore arranged for the United States to take charge of the Dominican customs service—the one reliable source of revenue in that poverty-stricken country. Fifty-five percent of the customs duties would be devoted to debt payment, the remainder turned over to the Dominican government to care for its internal needs. Roosevelt defined his policy, known as the Roosevelt Corollary to the Monroe Doctrine, in a message to Congress in December 1904. "Chronic wrongdoing" in Latin America, he stated with his typical disregard for the subtleties of complex affairs, might require outside intervention. Since, under the Monroe Doctrine, no other nation could step in, the United States must "exercise . . . an international police power."

In the short run this policy worked admirably. Dominican customs were honestly collected for the first time and the country's finances put in order. The

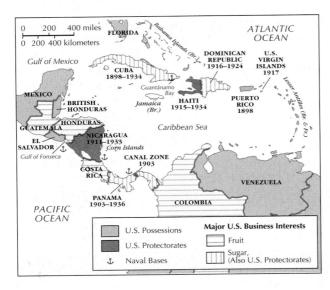

The United States in the Caribbean and Central America
Puerto Rico was ceded by Spain to the United States after the Spanish-American War; the Virgin Islands were bought from Denmark; the Canal Zone was leased from Panama. The ranges of dates following Cuba, the Dominican Republic, Haiti, Nicaragua, and Panama cover those years during which the United States either had troops in occupation or in some other way (such as financial) had a protectorate relationship with that country.

presence of American warships in the area provided a needed measure of political stability. In the long run, however, the Roosevelt Corollary caused a great deal of resentment in Latin America, for it added to nationalist fears that the United States wished to exploit the region for its own benefit.

THE OPEN DOOR POLICY

Coincidental with the Cuban rebellion of the 1890s, a far greater upheaval had convulsed the ancient empire of China. In 1894–1895 Japan easily defeated China in a war over Korea. Alarmed by Japan's aggressiveness, the European powers hastened to carve out for themselves new spheres of influence along China's coast. After the annexation of the Philippines, McKinley's secretary of state, John Hay, urged on by business leaders fearful of losing out in the scramble to exploit the Chinese market, tried to prevent the further absorption of China by the great powers.

For the United States to join in the dismemberment of China was politically impossible because of anti-imperialist feeling, so Hay sought to protect American interests by clever diplomacy. In a series of "Open Door" notes (1899) he asked the powers to agree to respect the trading rights of all countries and to impose no discriminatory duties within their spheres of influence. Chinese tariffs should continue to be collected in these areas and by Chinese officials.

The replies to the Open Door notes were at best noncommittal, yet Hay blandly announced in March 1900 that the powers had "accepted" his suggestions! Thus he could claim to have prevented the breakup of the Chinese empire and protected the right of Americans to do business freely in its territories. In reality nothing had been accomplished; the imperialist nations did not extend their political control of China only because they feared that by doing so they might precipitate a major war among themselves. Nevertheless, Hay's action marked a revolutionary departure from the traditional American policy of isolation, a bold advance into the complicated and dangerous world of international power politics.

Within a few months of Hay's announcement the Open Door policy was put to the test. Chinese nationalists, angered by the spreading influence of foreign governments, launched the so-called Boxer Rebellion. They swarmed into Beijing and drove foreigners behind the walls of their legations, which were placed under siege. For weeks, until an international rescue expedition (which included 2500 American soldiers) broke through to free them, the fate of the foreigners was unknown. Fearing that the Europeans would use the rebellion as a pretext for further expropriations, Hay sent off another round of Open Door notes announcing that the United States believed in the preservation of "Chinese territorial and administrative entity" and in "the principle of equal and impartial trade with all parts of the Chinese Empire." This broadened the Open Door policy to include all China, not merely the European spheres of influence.

In time the United States would pay a heavy price for this unrealistic attitude, but in the decade following 1900 its policy of diplomatic meddling unbacked by bayonets worked fairly well. Japan attacked Russia in a quarrel over Manchuria, smashing the Russian fleet in 1905 and winning a series of battles on the mainland. Japan was not prepared for a long war, however, and suggested to President Roosevelt that an American offer to mediate would be favorably received.

Eager to preserve the nice balance in East Asia, which enabled the United States to exert influence without any significant commitment of force, Roosevelt accepted the hint. In June 1905 he invited the belligerents to a conference at Portsmouth, New Hampshire. At the conference the Japanese won title to Russia's sphere around Port Arthur and a free hand in Korea, but when they demanded Sakhalin Island and a large money indemnity, the Russians balked. Unwilling to resume the war, the Japanese settled for half of Sakhalin and no money.

The Treaty of Portsmouth was unpopular in Japan, and the government managed to place the blame on Roosevelt, who had supported the compromise. Ill feeling against Americans increased in 1906 when the San Francisco school board, responding to local opposition to the influx of cheap labor from Japan, instituted a policy of segregating Asian children in a special school. Japan protested, and President Roosevelt persuaded the San Franciscans to abandon segregation in exchange for his pledge to cut off further Japanese immigration. He accomplished this through a "Gentlemen's Agreement" (1907) in which the Japanese promised not to issue passports to laborers seeking to come to America. Discriminatory legislation based specifically on race was thus avoided. However, the atmosphere between the two countries remained charged. Japanese resentment at American racial prejudice was great; many Americans talked fearfully of the "yellow peril."

Theodore Roosevelt was preeminently a realist in foreign relations. "Don't bluster," he once said. "Don't flourish a revolver, and never draw unless you intend to shoot." In East Asia he failed to follow his own advice. He considered the situation in that part of the world fraught with peril. The Philippines, he said, were "our heel of Achilles," indefensible in case of a Japanese attack. He suggested privately that the United States ought to "be prepared for giving the islands independence . . . much sooner than I think advisable from their own standpoint."

Yet while Roosevelt did not appreciably increase American naval and military strength in East Asia, neither did he stop trying to influence the course of events in the area, and he took no step toward withdrawing from the Philippines. He sent the fleet on a world cruise to demonstrate its might to Japan but knew well that this was mere bluff. "The 'Open Door' policy," he advised his successor, "completely disappears as soon as a powerful nation determines to disregard it." Nevertheless he allowed the belief to persist in the United States that the nation could influence the course of East Asian history without risk or real involvement.

THE PANAMA CANAL

In the Caribbean region American policy centered on building an interoceanic canal across Central America. Expanding interests in Latin America and East Asia made a canal necessary, a truth pointed up during the war with Spain by the two-month voyage of USS *Oregon* from California waters around South America to participate in the action against Admiral Cervera's fleet at Santiago. The first step was to get rid of the old Clayton-Bulwer Treaty with Great Britain, which barred the United States from building a canal on its own. In 1901 Lord Pauncefote, the British ambassador, and Secretary of State John Hay negotiated an agreement abolishing the Clayton-Bulwer pact and giving the United States the right to build and, by implication, fortify a waterway across the isthmus. The United States agreed in turn to maintain any such canal "free and open to the vessels of commerce and of war of all nations."

One possible canal route lay across the Colombian province of Panama, where the French-controlled New Panama Canal Company had taken over the franchise of the old De Lesseps company. Although only fifty miles separated the oceans in Panama, the terrain there was rugged and the climate unhealthy. While the French company had sunk much money into the project, it had little to show for its efforts aside from some rough excavations. A second possible route ran across Nicaragua. This route was about 200 miles long but was relatively easy since much of it traversed Lake Nicaragua and other natural waterways.

President McKinley appointed a commission to study the alternatives. It reported that the Panamanian route was technically superior, but recommended building in Nicaragua because the New Panama Canal Company was asking $109 million for its assets, which the commission valued at only $40 million. Lacking another potential purchaser, the French company lowered its price to $40 million, and after a great deal of clever propagandizing by Philippe Bunau-

Varilla, a French engineer with heavy investments in the company, President Roosevelt settled on the Panamanian route.

In January 1903 Secretary of State Hay negotiated a treaty with Tomás Herrán, the Colombian chargé d'affaires in Washington. In return for a 99-year lease on a zone across Panama 6 miles wide, the United States agreed to pay Colombia $10 million and an annual rent of $250,000. The Colombian senate, however, unanimously rejected this treaty, in part because it did not adequately protect Colombian sovereignty over Panama and in part because it hardly seemed fair that the New Panama Canal Company should receive $40 million for its frozen assets and Colombia only $10 million. The government demanded $15 million directly from the United States, plus $10 million of the company's share.

A little more patience might have produced a mutually satisfactory settlement, but Roosevelt looked on the Colombians as highwaymen who were "mad to get hold of the $40,000,000 of the Frenchmen." ("You could no more make an agreement with the Colombian rulers," Roosevelt later remarked, "than you could nail currant jelly to a wall.") When Panamanians, egged on by the French company, staged a revolution in November 1903, Roosevelt ordered the cruiser *Nashville* to Panama. Colombian government forces found themselves looking down the barrels of the guns of the *Nashville* and shortly thereafter eight other American warships. The revolution succeeded.

Roosevelt instantly recognized the new Republic of Panama. Secretary Hay and the new "Panamanian" minister, Bunau-Varilla, then negotiated a treaty granting the United States a zone 10 miles wide in perpetuity, on the same terms as those rejected by Colombia. Within the Canal Zone the United States could act as "the sovereign of the territory . . . to the entire exclusion of . . . the Republic of Panama." The United States guaranteed the independence of the republic. The New Panama Canal Company then received its $40 million, including a substantial share for Bunau-Varilla.

Historians have condemned Roosevelt for his actions in this shabby affair, and with good reason. It was not that he fomented the revolution, for he did not. Separated from the government at Bogotá by an impenetrable jungle, the people of Panama province had long wanted to be free of Colombian rule. Since an American-built canal would bring a flood of dollars and jobs to the area, they were prepared to take any necessary steps to avoid having the United States shift to the Nicaraguan route. Nor was it that Roosevelt prevented Colombia from suppressing the revolution. He sinned, rather, in his disregard of Latin American sensibilities. He referred to the Colombians as "dagoes" and insisted smugly that he was defending "the interests of collective civilization" when he overrode their opposition to his plans. "They cut their own throats," he said. "They tried to hold us up; and too late they have discovered their criminal error."

If uncharitable, Roosevelt's analysis was not entirely inaccurate, yet it did not justify his haste in taking Panama under his wing. "Have I defended myself?" Roosevelt asked Secretary of War Root. "You certainly have, Mr. President," Root retorted. "You were accused of seduction and you have conclusively proved

The U.S. Panama Canal
Following many negotiations, construction on the Panama Canal began in 1904. After many delays and hardships, it was completed in 1914.

that you were guilty of rape." Throughout Latin America, especially as national-ist sentiments grew stronger, Roosevelt's intolerance and aggressiveness in the canal incident bred resentment and fear.

In 1921 the United States made amends by giving Colombia $25 million. Colombia in turn recognized the independence of the Republic of Panama, but Panama was independent only in name because the United States controlled the canal. Meanwhile, the first vessels passed through the canal in 1914—and American hegemony in the Caribbean expanded. Yet even in that strategically vi-tal area there was more show than substance to American strength. The navy ruled Caribbean waters largely by default, for it lacked adequate bases in the re-gion. In 1903, as authorized by the Cuban constitution, the United States ob-tained an excellent site for a base at Guantanamo Bay, but before 1914 Congress appropriated only $89,000 to develop it.

Roosevelt's successor, William Howard Taft, tried to influence events in the Caribbean without intervening militarily. He called this policy "dollar diplo-macy," reasoning that economic penetration would bring stability to underdevel-oped areas and power and profit to the United States without the government's having to commit troops or spend public funds.

When Nicaragua defaulted on its foreign debt in 1911, the U.S. State Department arranged for American bankers to reorganize Nicaraguan finances and manage the customs service. Although the government truthfully insisted that it did not "cover an inch of territory south of the Rio Grande," dollar diplo-

President Theodore Roosevelt on a steam shovel at the Culebra cut in Panama. The setting caused him to think of the Spanish conquistadors and English explorers who had preceded him in the region. He observed that while nothing remained of their efforts, the Panama Canal was the "greatest engineering feat of the ages" and would last as long as "our civilization."

macy provoked further apprehension in Latin America. Efforts to establish similar arrangements in Honduras, Costa Rica, and Guatemala all failed. In Nicaragua orderly administration of the finances did not bring internal peace. In 1912, 2500 American marines and sailors were sent to Nicaragua to put down a revolution.

U.S. economic penetration proceeded briskly. American investments in Cuba reached $500 million by 1920, and smaller but significant investments were made in the Dominican Republic and in Haiti. In Central America the United Fruit Company accumulated large holdings in banana plantations, railroads, and other ventures. Other firms plunged heavily into Mexico's rich mineral resources.

IMPERIALISM WITHOUT COLONIES

The United States deserves fair marks for effort in its foreign relations following the Spanish-American War, barely passable marks for performance, and failing marks for results. If imperialism is defined narrowly as a policy of occupying and governing foreign lands, American imperialism lasted for a very short time. With trivial exceptions, all the American colonies—Hawaii, the Philippines, Guam, Puerto Rico, the Guantanamo base, and the Canal Zone—were obtained between 1898 and 1903. Both the U.S. government and American businessmen showed little interest in finding out what the people of Cuba wanted from life. They assumed that the Cubans wanted what everybody (read "Americans") wanted and, if by some strange chance this was not the case, that it was best to give it to them anyway. Dollar diplomacy had two main objectives, the avoidance of violence and the economic development of Latin America; it paid small heed to how peace was maintained and how the fruits of development were distributed. The policy was self-defeating, for in the long run stability depended on the support of local people, and this was seldom forthcoming.

By the eve of World War I the United States had become a world power and had assumed what it saw as a duty to guide the development of many countries with traditions far different from its own. The American people, however, did not understand what world power involved. While they stood ready to extend their influence into distant lands, they did so with little awareness of the implications of their behavior for themselves or for other peoples. The national psychology, if such a term has any meaning, remained fundamentally isolationist. Americans understood that their wealth and numbers made their nation strong and that geography made it virtually invulnerable. Thus they proceeded to do what they wanted to do in foreign affairs, limited more by their humanly flexible consciences than by any rational analysis of the probable consequences. This policy seemed safe enough—in 1914.

MILESTONES

1850 Britain and United States sign Clayton-Bulwer Treaty concerning interoceanic canal

1858 Commercial treaty with Japan opens several ports to American trade

1867 United States buys Alaska from Russia

1875 Reciprocity treaty increases U.S. influence in Hawaii

1885 Josiah Strong justifies expansionism in *Our Country*

1890 Alfred T. Mahan fuels American imperialism in *The Influence of Sea Power*

1893 United States helps sugar planters depose Queen Liliuokalani of Hawaii

1895 United States supports Venezuela in European border dispute over British Guiana

1898 *Maine* explodes in Havana harbor

Spanish-American war breaks out

Dewey defeats Spanish fleet at Battle of Manila Bay

Theodore Roosevelt leads Rough Riders at the Battle of San Juan Hill

United States annexes Hawaii

1899 Hays's Open Door notes safeguard U.S. access to China trade

1900 Platt Amendment gives United States naval stations and right to intervene in Cuba

1901 Hay-Pauncefote agreement gives United States rights to build interoceanic canal

1902 Europeans accept Monroe Doctrine during Venezuela bond dispute

1904 Roosevelt Corollary to Monroe Doctrine gives United States "international police power"

1907 "Gentlemen's Agreement" curtails Japanese immigration

24

WOODROW WILSON AND
THE GREAT WAR

oodrow Wilson's approach to foreign relations was well intentioned
and idealistic but somewhat confused. He knew that the United States
had no wish to injure any foreign state and assumed that all nations
would recognize this fact and cooperate. He wanted to help the republics of
Latin America achieve stable democratic governments and improve the living
conditions of their people. Imperialism was, in his eyes, immoral. But he felt
obliged to sustain and protect American interests abroad. The maintenance of
the Open Door in China and the completion of the Panama Canal were as important to him as they had been to Theodore Roosevelt.

Wilson's view of foreign nations was shortsighted and provincial. Like nineteenth-century Christian missionaries, he wanted to spread the gospel of
American democracy, to lift and enlighten the unfortunate and the ignorant—but
in his own way. "I am going to teach the South American republics to elect good
men!" he told one British diplomat.

WILSON'S "MORAL" DIPLOMACY

Wilson set out to raise the moral tone of American foreign policy by denouncing
dollar diplomacy. Encouraging bankers to lend money to countries like China, he
said, implied the possibility of "forcible interference" if the loans were not re-
paid, and that would be "obnoxious to the principles upon which the government of our people rests." To seek special economic concessions in Latin
America was "unfair" and "degrading." The United States would deal with
Latin American nations "upon terms of equality and honor."

In certain small matters Wilson succeeded in conducting American diplomacy on this idealistic basis. When the Japanese attempted in the notorious Twenty-One Demands (1915) to reduce China almost to the status of a Japanese protectorate, he persuaded them to modify their conditions slightly.

Where more important interests were concerned, Wilson sometimes failed to live up to his promises. Because of the strategic importance of the Panama Canal, he was unwilling to tolerate "unrest" anywhere in the Caribbean. Within months of his inauguration he was pursuing the same tactics circumstances had forced on Roosevelt and Taft. The Bryan-Chamorro Treaty of 1914, which gave the United States an option to build a canal across Nicaragua, made that country virtually an American protectorate and served to maintain in power an unpopular dictator, Adolfo Díaz.

 An example of missionary diplomacy with much more serious results occurred in Mexico. In 1911 a liberal coalition overthrew the dictator Porfirio Díaz and Francisco Madero became president. Soon thereafter one of Madero's generals, Victoriano Huerta, seized power and had his former chief murdered. Most European states recognized Huerta's new government, but Wilson, appalled by Madero's murder, refused to do so. "I will not recognize a government of butchers," he declared. This was unconventional; nations do not ordinarily consider the means by which a foreign regime has come to power before deciding to establish diplomatic relations.

Wilson brought enormous pressure to bear against Huerta. He dragooned the British into withdrawing recognition. He dickered with other Mexican factions. He demanded that Huerta hold free elections as the price of American mediation in the continuing civil war. Huerta would not yield an inch.

The tense situation exploded in April 1914, when a small party of American sailors was arrested in the port of Tampico, Mexico. When the Mexican government refused to supply the apology demanded by the sailors' commander, Wilson fastened on the affair as an excuse for sending troops into Mexico.

The invasion took place at Veracruz, whence Winfield Scott had launched the assault on Mexico City in 1847. Instead of meekly surrendering the city, the Mexicans resisted tenaciously, suffering 400 casualties before falling back. This bloodshed caused dismay throughout Latin America. Huerta, hard-pressed by Mexican opponents, abdicated. On August 20, 1914, General Venustiano Carranza entered Mexico City in triumph.

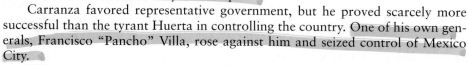 Carranza favored representative government, but he proved scarcely more successful than the tyrant Huerta in controlling the country. One of his own generals, Francisco "Pancho" Villa, rose against him and seized control of Mexico City.

Wilson now made a monumental blunder. Villa professed to be willing to cooperate with the United States, and Wilson, taking him at his word, gave him his support. However, Villa was little more than an ambitious bandit with no other objective than personal power. Carranza, though no radical, was committed to social reform. Fighting back, Carranza drove Villa's forces into the northern provinces.

Wilson finally realized the extent of Carranza's influence in Mexico, and in October 1915 he recognized the Carranza government. Still his Mexican troubles were not over. Early in 1916, Villa, seeking to undermine Carranza by forcing the United States to intervene, stopped a train in northern Mexico and killed sixteen American passengers in cold blood. Then he crossed into New Mexico and burned the town of Columbus, killing nineteen. Having learned his lesson, Wilson would have preferred to bear even this assault in silence, but public opinion forced him to send American troops under General John J. Pershing across the border in pursuit of Villa.

Villa proved impossible to catch. Cleverly he drew Pershing deeper and deeper into Mexico, and this alarmed Carranza, who insisted that the Americans withdraw. Several clashes occurred between Pershing's men and Mexican regulars, and for a brief period in June 1916 war seemed imminent. Wilson now acted bravely and wisely. Early in 1917 he recalled Pershing's force, leaving the Mexicans to work out their own destiny.

Missionary diplomacy in Mexico had produced mixed but in the long run beneficial results. By opposing Huerta, Wilson had surrendered to his prejudices, yet he had also helped the real revolutionaries even though they opposed his acts. His bungling bred anti-Americanism in Mexico, but by his later restraint in the face of stinging provocations, he permitted the constitutionalists to consolidate their power.

EUROPE EXPLODES IN WAR

On June 28, 1914, in the Austro-Hungarian provincial capital of Sarajevo, Gavrilo Princip, a young student, assassinated the Archduke Franz Ferdinand, heir to the imperial throne. Princip was a member of the Black Hand, a Serbian terrorist organization. He was seeking to further the cause of Serbian nationalism. Instead his rash act precipitated a general European war. Within little more than a month, following a complex series of diplomatic challenges and responses, two great coalitions, the Central Powers (chiefly Germany, Austria-Hungary, and Ottoman Turkey) and the Allied Powers (chiefly Great Britain, France, and Russia), were locked in a brutal struggle that brought one era in world history to a close and inaugurated another.

There were good reasons why the United States sought to remain neutral in this conflict, which contemporaries were soon to call the Great War. Over a third of the 92 million U.S. inhabitants were either European-born or the children of European immigrants. Sentimental ties bound them to the lands of their ancestors. American involvement would create new internal stresses in a society already strained by the task of assimilating so many diverse groups. War was also an affront to the prevailing progressive spirit, which assumed that human beings were reasonable, high-minded, and capable of settling disputes peaceably. Along with the traditional American fear of entanglement in European affairs, these were ample reasons for remaining aloof.

Although most Americans hoped to keep out of the war, nearly everyone was partial to one side or the other. People of German or Austrian descent, about 8

During World War I, advancing armies unloosed ferocious artillery barrages to destroy deeply entrenched enemy positions. Before the Third Battle of Ypres, the British fired four and a half million shells at German defenses, pulverizing the landscape. But as the British moved forward they became mired in mud (above); they lost 300,000 men in the action. Few Americans perceived the special horrors of this type of warfare.

million in number, and the nation's 4.5 million Irish Americans, motivated chiefly by hatred of the British, sympathized with the Central Powers. The majority of the people, however, influenced by bonds of language and culture, preferred an Allied victory, and when the Germans launched a mighty assault across neutral Belgium in an effort to outflank the French armies, many Americans were outraged.

As the war progressed, the Allies cleverly exploited American prejudices by such devices as publishing exaggerated tales of German atrocities against Belgian civilians. A supposedly impartial study of these charges by the widely respected James Bryce, author of *The American Commonwealth*, portrayed the Germans as ruthless barbarians. The Germans also conducted a propaganda campaign in the United States, but they labored under severe handicaps and won few converts.

FREEDOM OF THE SEAS

Propaganda did not basically alter American attitudes; far more important were questions arising out of trade and commerce. Under international law, neutrals could trade freely with any belligerent. Americans were prepared to do so, but because the British fleet dominated the North Atlantic, they could not. The situation was similar to the one that had prevailed during the Napoleonic Wars. The British declared nearly all commodities, even foodstuffs, to be contraband of war. They forced neutral merchant ships into British or French ports in order to search them for goods headed for the enemy. Many cargoes were confiscated, often without payment. American firms that traded with the Central Powers were "blacklisted," which meant that no British subject could deal with them. When Americans protested, the British answered that in a battle for survival, they dared not adhere to old-fashioned rules of international law.

Although British tactics frequently exasperated Wilson, they did not result in the loss of innocent lives. He never considered taking as drastic a step as an embargo. To allow the British to make the rules meant siding against the Central Powers. Yet to insist on the old rules (which had never been strictly obeyed in wartime) meant siding against the Allies because that would have deprived them of much of the value of their naval superiority. *Nothing* the United States might do would be truly impartial.

Wilson's own sentiments made it doubly difficult for him to object strenuously to British practices. No American admired British institutions and culture more extravagantly. "Everything I love most in the world is at stake," he confessed privately to the British ambassador. A German victory "would be fatal to our form of Government and American ideals."

The immense expansion of American trade with the Allies made an embargo unthinkable. While commerce with the Central Powers fell to a trickle, that with the Allies soared from $825 million in 1914 to over $3.2 billion in 1916. An attempt to limit this commerce would have raised a storm; to have eliminated it would have caused a catastrophe. Munitions makers and other businessmen did not want the United States to enter the war. Neutrality suited their purposes admirably.

Britain and France soon exhausted their ready cash, and by early 1917 they had borrowed well over $2 billion. Although these loans violated no principle of international law, they fastened the United States more closely to the Allies' cause.

During the first months of the Great War, the Germans were not especially concerned about neutral trade or American goods because they expected to crush the Allied armies quickly. When their first swift thrust into France was blunted along the Marne River, only twenty miles from Paris, and the war became a bloody stalemate, they began to challenge the Allies' control of the seas. Unwilling to risk their battleships and cruisers against the much larger British fleet, they resorted to a new weapon, the submarine, commonly known as the U-boat (for *Unterseeboot*). German submarines played a role in World War I not unlike that of American privateers in the Revolution and the War of 1812: They ranged the seas stealthily in search of merchant ships. However, submarines could not operate under the ordinary rules of war, which required that a raider stop its prey, examine its papers and cargo, and give the crew and passengers time to get off in lifeboats before sending it to the bottom. When surfaced,

NOTICE!

TRAVELLERS intending to embark on the Atlantic voyage are reminded that a state of war exists between Germany and her allies and Great Britain and her allies; that the zone of war includes the waters adjacent to the British Isles; that, in accordance with formal notice given by the Imperial German Government, vessels flying the flag of Great Britain, or of any of her allies, are liable to destruction in those waters and that travellers sailing in the war zone on ships of Great Britain or her allies do so at their own risk.

IMPERIAL GERMAN EMBASSY

WASHINGTON, D. C., APRIL 22, 1915.

Three weeks before the Lusitania *was torpedoed, this notice appeared in the classified sections of Washington newspapers.*

U-boats were vulnerable to the deck guns that many merchant ships carried; they could even be sunk by ramming, once they had stopped and put out a boarding party. Therefore, they commonly launched their torpedoes from below the surface without warning, often resulting in a heavy loss of life.

In February 1915 the Germans declared the waters surrounding the British Isles a zone of war and announced that they would sink without warning all enemy merchant ships encountered in the area. Since Allied vessels sometimes flew neutral flags to disguise their identity, neutral ships entering the zone would do so at their own risk. This statement was largely bluff, for the Germans had only a handful of submarines at sea; but they were feverishly building more.

Wilson—perhaps too hurriedly, considering the importance of the question—warned the Germans that he would hold them to "strict accountability" for any loss of American life or property resulting from violations of "acknowledged [neutral] rights on the high seas." He did not distinguish clearly between losses incurred through the destruction of *American* ships and those resulting from the sinking of other vessels. The issue acquired significance on May 7,

1915, when the submarine *U–20* sank the British liner *Lusitania* off the Irish coast. Nearly 1200 persons, including 128 Americans, lost their lives.

The torpedoing of the *Lusitania* caused as profound and emotional a reaction in the United States as that following the destruction of the *Maine* in Havana harbor. Wilson, like McKinley in 1898, was shocked, but he kept his head. He demanded that Germany disavow the sinking, indemnify the victims, and promise to stop attacking passenger vessels. When the Germans quibbled about these points, he responded with further diplomatic correspondence rather than with an ultimatum.

In one sense, this was sound policy. It would have been difficult for the German government to back down before a U.S. ultimatum. In addition, if Wilson had forced a showdown, he would have alienated a large segment of American opinion. After dragging out the controversy for nearly a year, the German government apologized and agreed to pay an indemnity.

In November 1915 Wilson at last began to press for increased military and naval expenditures. Nevertheless, he continued to vacillate. He dispatched a sharp note protesting Allied blacklisting of American firms, and to his confidant, Colonel Edward M. House, he called the British "poor boobs!"

THE ELECTION OF 1916

Part of Wilson's hesitation in 1916 resulted from the political difficulties he faced in his fight for reelection. He had won the presidency in 1912 only because the Republican party had split in two. Now Theodore Roosevelt, the chief defector, had become so incensed by Wilson's refusal to commit the United States to the Allied cause that he was ready to support almost any Republican in order to guarantee the president's defeat. At the same time, many progressives were complaining about Wilson's unwillingness to work for further domestic reforms. Unless he could find additional support, he seemed likely to be defeated. He attacked the problem by wooing the progressives. In January 1916 he appointed Louis D. Brandeis to the Supreme Court. In addition to being an advanced progressive, Brandeis was the first Jewish American appointed to the Court. Wilson's action won him many friends among people who favored fair treatment for minority groups. In July he bid for the farm vote by signing the Farm Loan Act to provide low-cost loans based on agricultural credit. Shortly thereafter, he approved the Keating-Owen Child Labor Act barring goods manufactured by the labor of children under sixteen from interstate commerce, and a workers' compensation act for federal employees.

The key issue in the campaign was American policy toward the warring powers. Wilson intended to stress preparedness, which he was now wholeheartedly supporting. However, during the Democratic convention, the delegates shook the hall with cheers whenever orators referred to the president's success in keeping the country out of the war. "He Kept Us Out of War" became the Democratic slogan.

To his credit, Wilson made no promises. "I can't keep the country out of war," he told one member of his Cabinet. "Any little German lieutenant can put us into the war at any time by some calculated outrage." His attitude undoubtedly cost him the votes of extremists on both sides, but it won the backing of thousands of moderates.

The combination of progressivism and the peace issue placed the Democrats on substantially equal terms with the Republicans, who nominated Charles Evans Hughes. Thereafter, personal factors probably tipped the balance. Hughes was very stiff (Theodore Roosevelt called him a bearded Woodrow Wilson) and an ineffective speaker; he offended a number of important politicians, especially in crucial California, where he inadvertently snubbed the popular progressive governor, Hiram Johnson; and he equivocated on a number of issues. Nevertheless, on election night he appeared to have won, having carried nearly all the East and Midwest. Late returns gave Wilson California, however, and with it victory by the narrow margin of 277 to 254 in the Electoral College. He led Hughes in the popular vote, 9.1 million to 8.5 million.

THE ROAD TO WAR

Encouraged by his triumph, appalled by the continuing slaughter on the battle-fields, fearful that the United States would be dragged into the conflagration, Wilson made one last effort to end the war by negotiation. In 1915 and again in 1916 he had sent his friend Colonel House on secret missions to London, Paris, and Berlin to try to mediate among the belligerents. Each mission had proved fruitless, but after another long season of bloodshed, perhaps the powers would listen to reason.

Wilson, on January 22, 1917, delivered a moving speech aimed at "the people of the countries now at war" more than at their governments. Any settlement imposed by a victor, he declared, would breed hatred and more wars. There must be "peace without victory," based on the principles that all nations were equal and that every nationality should determine its own form of government. He mentioned, albeit vaguely, disarmament and freedom of the seas, and he suggested the creation of some kind of international organization to preserve world peace. "There must be not a balance of power, but a community of power," he said, and he added, "I am speaking for the silent mass of mankind everywhere."

This noble appeal met a tragic fate. The Germans had already decided to unleash their submarines against all vessels headed for Allied ports. After February 1, any ship in the war zone would be attacked without warning. Possessed now of more than 100 U-boats, the German military leaders had convinced themselves that they could starve the British people into submission and reduce the Allied armies to impotence by cutting off the flow of American supplies. The United States would probably declare war, but the Germans believed that they could overwhelm the Allies before the Americans could get to the battlefields in force. In 1917, after the German military leaders had made this decision, events

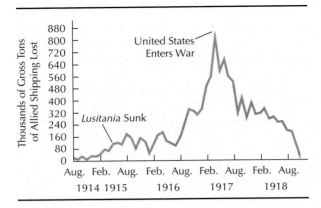

U-Boat Campaign, 1914–1918

moved relentlessly, almost uninfluenced by the actors who presumably controlled the fate of the world. In February and March, German U-boats sank more ships, including several passenger liners. On April 2, Wilson asked Congress to declare war. Germany, he said, was guilty of "throwing to the winds all scruples of humanity." "The world must be made safe for democracy." Two days later, Congress declared war by a vote of 82–6 in the Senate, and 373–50 in the House.

MOBILIZING THE ECONOMY

America's entry into the Great War determined its outcome. The Allies were running out of money and supplies; their troops, decimated by nearly three years in the trenches, were exhausted, disheartened, and rebellious. In February and March 1917, U-boats sent over a million tons of Allied shipping to the bottom of the Atlantic. The outbreak of the Russian Revolution in March 1917, at first lifting the spirits of the Western democracies, led to the Bolshevik takeover under Lenin. The Russian armies collapsed; by December 1917 Russia was out of the war and the Germans were moving masses of men and equipment from the eastern front to France. Without the aid of the United States, it is likely that the war would have ended in 1918 on terms dictated from Berlin. Instead American men and supplies helped contain the Germans' last drives and then push them back to final defeat.

Still, it was a close Allied victory, for the United States entered the war little better prepared to fight than it had been in 1898. The conversion of American industry to war production had to be organized and carried out without prearrangement. Confusion and waste resulted. The hurriedly designed shipbuilding program was an almost total fiasco. The big guns that backed up American soldiers in 1918 were made in France and Great Britain; of the 8.8 million rounds of artillery ammunition fired by American troops, a mere 8000 were manufactured in the United States. Congress authorized the manufacture of 20,000 airplanes, but only a handful, mostly British-designed planes made in America, got to France.

The problem of mobilization was complicated. It took Congress six weeks of hot debate merely to decide on conscription. Only in September 1917, nearly six months after the declaration of war, did the first draftees reach the training camps, and it is hard to see how Wilson could have speeded this process appreciably. He wisely supported the professional soldiers, who insisted that he resist the appeals of politicians who wanted to raise volunteer units, even rejecting, at considerable political cost, Theodore Roosevelt's offer to raise an entire army division.

Wilson was a forceful and inspiring war leader once he grasped what needed to be done. He displayed both determination and unfailing patience in the face of frustration and criticism. Raising an army was only a small part of the job. The Allies had to be supplied with food and munitions, and immense amounts of money had to be collected.

After several false starts, Wilson placed the task in the hands of the War Industries Board (WIB). The board was given almost dictatorial power to allocate scarce materials, standardize production, fix prices, and coordinate American and Allied purchasing. Evaluating the mobilization effort raises interesting historical questions. The antitrust laws were suspended and producers were encouraged, even compelled, to cooperate with one another. Government regulation went far beyond what the New Nationalists had envisaged in 1912.

As for the New Freedom variety of laissez-faire, it had no place in a wartime economy. The nation's railroads, strained by immensely increased traffic, became progressively less efficient. A monumental tie-up in December and January 1917–1918 finally persuaded Wilson to appoint Secretary of the Treasury William G. McAdoo director-general of the railroads, with power to run the roads as a single system. McAdoo's Railroad Administration pooled all railroad equipment, centralized purchasing, standardized accounting practices, and raised wages and passenger rates.

Wilson accepted the kind of government-industry agreement developed under Theodore Roosevelt that he had denounced in 1912. Prices were set by the WIB at levels that allowed large profits—U.S. Steel, for example, despite high taxes, cleared over half a billion dollars in two years. It is at least arguable that producers would have turned out just as much even if compelled to charge lower prices.

The history of industrial mobilization was the history of the entire home front effort in microcosm: marvels were performed, but the task was so gigantic and unprecedented that a full year passed before an efficient system had been devised, and many unforeseen results occurred.

The problem of mobilizing agricultural resources was solved more quickly, and this was fortunate because in April 1917 the British had on hand only a six-week supply of food. As food administrator Wilson appointed Herbert Hoover, a mining engineer who had headed the Belgian Relief Commission earlier in the war. Acting under powers granted by the Lever Act of 1917, Hoover set the price of wheat at $2.20 a bushel in order to encourage production. He established a government corporation to purchase the entire American and Cuban sugar crop, which he then doled out to American and British refiners. To avoid rationing he organized a campaign to persuade consumers to conserve food voluntarily. One slogan ran "If U fast U beat U boats"; another, "Serve beans by all means." "Wheatless Mondays" and "meatless Tuesdays" were the rule, and although no law compelled their observance, the public responded patriotically.

Without subjecting its own citizens to serious inconvenience, the United States increased food exports from 12.3 million tons to 18.6 million tons. Farmers, of course, profited greatly. Their real income went up nearly 30 percent between 1915 and 1918.

WORKERS IN WARTIME

With the army siphoning so many men from the labor market and with immigration reduced to a trickle, unemployment disappeared and wages rose. Although the cost of living soared, imposing hardships on people with fixed incomes, the boom produced unprecedented opportunities.

The War Labor Policies Board, chaired by Felix Frankfurter of the Harvard Law School, set wages-and-hours standards for each major war industry. Since these were determined in consultation with employers and representatives of labor, they speeded the unionization of workers by compelling management, even in antiunion industries like steel, to deal with labor leaders. Union membership rose by 2.3 million during the war.

Trends in the steel industry reflected the improvement of wartime labor earnings. Wages of unskilled steelworkers more than doubled. Thousands of southern blacks, attracted by jobs in big-city factories, flocked into the steel towns. Union organizers made inroads in many plants, and by the summer of 1918 they were preparing an all-out effort to unionize the industry. If the world was to be made safe for democracy, they argued, there must be "economic democracy [along] with political democracy."

PAYING FOR THE WAR

Wilson managed the task of financing the war effectively. The struggle cost the United States about $33.5 billion, not counting pensions and other postwar expenses. About $7 billion of this was lent to the Allies,[1] but since this money was spent largely in America, it contributed to the national prosperity.

Over two-thirds of the cost of the war was met by borrowing. Five Liberty and Victory Loan drives, spurred by advertising, parades, and other appeals to patriotism, persuaded people to open their purses. Industrialists, eager to instill

---

[1] *In 1914 Americans owed foreigners about $3.8 billion. By 1919 Americans were owed $12.5 billion by Europeans alone.*

in their employees a sense of personal involvement in the war effort, conducted campaigns in their plants. Some went so far as to threaten "A Bond or Your Job," but more typical was the appeal of the managers of the Gary, Indiana, plant of U.S. Steel, who published bond advertisements in six languages in order to reach their immigrant workers.

In addition to borrowing, the government collected about $10.5 billion in taxes during the war. A steeply graduated income tax took more than 75 percent of the incomes of the wealthiest citizens. A 65 percent excess-profits tax and a 25 percent inheritance tax were also enacted. Thus although many individuals made fortunes from the war, its cost was distributed far more equitably than during the Civil War.

PROPAGANDA AND CIVIL LIBERTIES

Wilson was preeminently a teacher and preacher, a specialist in the transmission of ideas and ideals. He excelled at mobilizing public opinion and inspiring Americans to work for the better world he hoped would emerge from the war. In April 1917 he created the Committee on Public Information (CPI), headed by the journalist George Creel. Soon 75,000 speakers were deluging the country with propaganda prepared by hundreds of CPI writers. They pictured the war as a crusade for freedom and democracy, the Germans as a bestial people bent on world domination.

A large majority of the nation supported the war enthusiastically. But thousands of persons—German-Americans and Irish-Americans, for example; people of pacifist leanings such as Jane Addams, the founder of Hull House; and some who thought both sides in the war were wrong—still opposed American involvement. Creel's committee and a number of unofficial "patriotic" groups allowed their enthusiasm for the conversion of the hesitant to become suppression of dissent.

Although Wilson spoke in defense of free speech, his actions opposed it. He signed the Espionage Act of 1917, which imposed fines of up to $10,000 and jail sentences ranging to twenty years on persons convicted of aiding the enemy or obstructing recruiting, and he authorized the postmaster general to ban from the mails any material that seemed treasonable or seditious.

In May 1918, again with Wilson's approval, Congress passed the Sedition Act, which made "saying anything" to discourage the purchase of war bonds a crime, with the proviso that investment counselors could still offer "bona fide and not disloyal advice" to clients. The law also made it illegal to "utter, print, write, or publish any disloyal, profane, scurrilous, or abusive language" about the government, the Constitution, or the uniform of the army or navy. Socialist periodicals such as *The Masses* were suppressed, and Eugene V. Debs was sentenced to ten years in prison for making an antiwar speech. Ricardo Flores Magón, an anarchist, was sentenced to twenty years in jail for publishing a statement criticizing Wilson's Mexican policy, an issue that had nothing to do with the war.

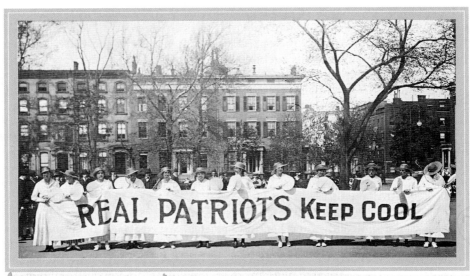

These members of the Woman's Peace party urge Wilson to find a way to stay out of the war in Europe. They are carrying fans to reinforce their message.

These laws went far beyond what was necessary to protect the national interest. Citizens were jailed for suggesting that the draft law was unconstitutional and for criticizing private organizations like the Red Cross and the YMCA. One woman was sent to prison for writing, "I am for the people, and the government is for the profiteers."

The Supreme Court upheld the constitutionality of the Espionage Act in *Schenck* v. *United States* (1919), a case involving a man who had mailed circulars to draftees urging them to refuse to report for induction into the army. Free speech has its limits, Justice Oliver Wendell Holmes, Jr., explained. No one has the right to cry, "Fire!" in a crowded theater. When there is a "clear and present danger" that a particular statement would threaten the national interest, it can be repressed by law. In peacetime Schenck's circulars would be permissible, but not in time of war.

WARTIME REFORMS

The American mobilization experience was part and product of the progressive era. The work of the progressives at the national and state levels in expanding government functions in order to deal with social and economic problems provided precedents and conditioned the people for the all-out effort of 1917 and 1918. Social and economic planning and the management of huge business operations by public boards and committees got their first practical tests. College professors, technicians, and others with complex skills entered government service en masse. The federal government for the first time actively entered such fields as housing and labor relations.

Many progressives believed that the war was creating the sense of common purpose that would stimulate the people to act unselfishly to benefit the poor and to eradicate social evils. Patriotism and public service seemed at last united. Secretary of War Newton D. Baker, a prewar urban reformer, expressed this attitude in supporting a federal child labor law: "We cannot afford, when we are losing boys in France, to lose children in the United States."

Men and women of this sort worked for a dozen causes only remotely related to the war effort. The woman's suffrage movement was brought to fruition, as was the campaign against alcohol. Both the Eighteenth Amendment, outlawing the manufacture, sale, import, and export of alcoholic beverages, and the Nineteenth, giving women the vote, were adopted at least in part because of the war. Reformers began to talk about health insurance. The progressive campaign against prostitution and venereal disease gained strength, winning the enthusiastic support both of persons worried about inexperienced local girls being seduced by the soldiers and of those concerned lest prostitutes lead innocent soldiers astray. One of the latter type claimed to have persuaded "over 1000 fallen women" to promise not to go near any army camps.

WOMEN AND BLACKS IN WARTIME

Although a number of prominent feminists were pacifists, most supported the war enthusiastically, moved by patriotism and the belief that opposition to the war would doom their hopes of gaining the vote. They also expected that the war would open up many kinds of high-paying jobs to women. To some extent it did; about a million women replaced men in uniform, but the numbers actually engaged in war industries were small (about 6000 found jobs making airplanes, for example), and the gains were fleeting. When the war ended, most women who were engaged in industrial work either left their jobs voluntarily or were fired to make room for returning veterans. Some women went overseas as nurses, and a few served as ambulance drivers and YMCA workers.

Most unions were unsympathetic to the idea of enrolling women, and the government did little to encourage women to do more for the war effort than prepare bandages, knit warm clothing for soldiers, participate in food conservation programs, and encourage people to buy war bonds. There was a Women in Industry Service in the Department of Labor and a Woman's Committee of the Council of National Defense, but both served primarily as window dressing for the Wilson administration. The final report of another wartime agency, issued in 1919, admitted that few women war workers had been paid as much as men and that women had been promoted more slowly than men, were not accepted by unions, and were discharged promptly when the war ended.

The wartime "great migration" of southern blacks to northern cities where jobs were available brought them important economic benefits. Actually, the emigration of blacks from the former slave states began with emancipation, but the

Women workers at the Dupont factory in Old Hickory, Tennessee in 1917. They are forming smokeless gunpowder into long strips, which will then be cut to be used in artillery shells and other armaments.

mass exodus that many people had expected was slow to materialize. Between 1870 and 1890 only about 80,000 blacks moved to northern cities. Compared with the influx from Europe and from northern farms, this number was inconsequential. The black proportion of the population of New York City, for example, fell from over 10 percent in 1800 to under 2 percent in 1900.

Around the turn of the century, as the first postslavery generation reached maturity and as southern repression increased, the northward movement quickened—about 200,000 blacks migrated between 1890 and 1910. Then, after 1914, the war boom drew blacks north in a flood. The African American population of New York City rose from 92,000 to 152,000; that of Chicago from 44,000 to 109,000; that of Detroit from 5700 to 41,000.

Life for the newcomers was difficult; many whites resented them; workers feared them as potential strikebreakers yet refused to admit them into their unions. In East St. Louis, Illinois, where employers had brought in large numbers of blacks in an attempt to discourage local unions from striking for higher wages, a bloody riot erupted during the summer of 1917 in which nine whites and an undetermined number of blacks were killed. As in peacetime, the Wilson administration was at worst antagonistic and at best indifferent to blacks' needs and aspirations.

When manufacturers in East Saint Louis (Illinois) sought to weaken labor unions by hiring African American workers from Mississippi and western Tennessee, the white workers went on a rampage. When the dust had cleared, much of East Saint Louis had burned down and several dozen blacks and a few whites were dead. Here several National Guardsmen lead a black to safety.

There were two black regiments in the regular army and a number of black national guard units when the war began, and once these outfits were brought up to combat strength, no more volunteers were accepted. Indeed, at first no blacks were conscripted; Southerners in particular found the thought of giving large numbers of guns to blacks and teaching them how to use them most disturbing. However, blacks were soon drafted, and once they were, a larger proportion of them than whites were taken. One Georgia draft board exempted more than 500 of 815 white registrants and only 6 of the 202 blacks in its jurisdiction before its members were relieved of their duties. After a riot in Texas in which black soldiers killed seventeen white civilians, black recruits were dispersed among many camps for training to lessen the possibility of trouble.

In the military service, all blacks were placed in segregated units. Only a handful were commissioned officers. Despite the valor displayed by black soldiers in the Civil War and the large role they played in the Spanish-American War, where five blacks had won the Congressional Medal of Honor, most blacks, even those sent overseas, were assigned to labor battalions, working as stevedores and common laborers. But many fought and died for their country. Altogether about 200,000 served overseas. There were black Red Cross nurses in France, and some blacks held relatively high posts in government agencies in

Washington, the most important being Emmett J. Scott, who was special assistant for Negro affairs in the War Department.

W. E. B. Du Bois supported the war wholeheartedly. He praised Wilson for making, at last, a strong statement against lynching, which had increased to a shocking extent during the previous decade. He even went along with the fact that the handful of black officer candidates were trained in a segregated camp. "Let us," he wrote in *The Crisis,* "while the war lasts, forget our special grievances and close ranks shoulder to shoulder with our fellow citizens and the allied nations that are fighting for democracy."

Many blacks condemned Du Bois's accommodationism (which he promptly abandoned when the war ended), but most saw the war as an opportunity to demonstrate their patriotism and prove their worth. For the moment the prevailing mood was one of optimism. "We may expect to see the walls of prejudice gradually crumble"—this was the common attitude of blacks in 1917 and 1918. If winning the war would make the world safe for democracy, surely blacks in the United States would be better off when it was won. Whether or not this turned out to be so was (and still is) a matter of opinion.

AMERICANS: TO THE TRENCHES AND OVER THE TOP

All activity on the home front had one ultimate objective: defeating the Central Powers on the battlefield. This was accomplished. The navy performed with special distinction. In April 1917, German submarines sank more than 870,000 tons of Allied shipping; after April 1918, monthly losses never reached 300,000 tons. The decision to send merchant ships across the Atlantic in convoys screened by destroyers made the reduction possible. Checking the U-boats was essential because of the need to transport American troops to Europe. Slightly more than 2 million soldiers made the voyage safely.

The first units of the American Expeditionary Force (AEF), elements of the regular army commanded by General John J. Pershing, reached Paris on Independence Day, 1917. They took up positions on the front near Verdun in October. Not until the spring of 1918, however, did the American "doughboys" play a significant role in the fighting, though their mere presence boosted French and British morale.

Pershing insisted on maintaining his troops as independent units; he would not allow them to be filtered into the Allied armies as reinforcements. This was part of a perhaps unfortunate general policy that reflected America's isolationism. (Wilson always referred to the other nations fighting Germany as "associates," not as "allies.")

In March 1918 the Germans launched a great spring offensive, their armies strengthened by thousands of veterans from the Russian front. By late May they had reached a point on the Marne River near the town of Château-Thierry, only fifty miles from Paris. Early in June the AEF fought its first major engagements, driving the Germans back from Château-Thierry and Belleau Wood.

A recruiting poster for the "True Sons of Freedom," which encouraged African Americans to enlist. In fact, some 350,000 black Americans served in segregated units during the Great War. Several such units fought alongside French units, and 171 African Americans were awarded the French Legion of Honor, an award for courageous military service.

In this fighting only about 27,500 Americans saw action, and they suffered appalling losses. Nevertheless, when the Germans advanced again in the direction of the Marne in mid-July, 85,000 Americans were in the lines that withstood their charge. Then, in the major turning point of the war, the Allied armies counterattacked. Some 270,000 Americans participated, helping to flatten the German bulge between Reims and Soissons. By late August the American First Army, 500,000 strong, was poised before the Saint-Mihiel salient, a deep extension of the German lines southeast of Verdun. On September 12 this army, buttressed by French troops, struck and in two days wiped out the salient.

Late in September began the greatest American engagement of the war. No fewer than 1.2 million doughboys drove forward west of Verdun into the Argonne Forest. For over a month of indescribable horror they inched ahead through the tangle of the Argonne and the formidable defenses of the Hindenburg line, while to the west, French and British armies staged similar drives. In this one offensive the AEF suffered 120,000 casualties. Finally, on November 1, they broke the German center and raced toward the vital Sedan-Mézières railroad. On November 11, with Allied armies advancing on all fronts, the Germans signed the armistice, ending the fighting.

The Western Front, 1918

PREPARING FOR PEACE

The fighting ended on November 11, 1918, but the shape of the postwar world remained to be determined. European society had been shaken to its foundations. Confusion reigned. People wanted peace yet burned for revenge. Millions faced starvation. Other millions were disillusioned by the seemingly purposeless sacrifices of four years of horrible war. Communism—to some an idealistic promise of human betterment, to others a commitment to rational economic and social planning, to still others a danger to individual freedom, toleration, and democracy—having conquered Russia, threatened to envelop Germany and much of the defunct Austro-Hungarian Empire, perhaps even the victorious Allies. How could stability be restored? How could victory be made worth its enormous cost?

Woodrow Wilson had grasped the significance of the war while most statesmen still thought that triumph on the battlefield would settle everything automatically. As early as January 1917 he had realized that victory would be wasted if the winners permitted themselves the luxury of vengeance. Such a policy would disrupt the balance of power and lead to economic and social chaos. The victors must build a better society, not punish those they believed had destroyed the old.

In a speech to Congress on January 8, 1918, Wilson outlined a plan, known as the Fourteen Points, designed to make the world "fit and safe to live in." The peace treaty should be negotiated in full view of world opinion, not in secret. It should guarantee the freedom of the seas to all nations, in war as in peacetime. It should tear down barriers to international trade, provide for a drastic reduction of armaments, and establish a colonial system that would take proper account of

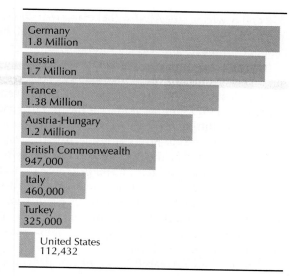

Germany
1.8 Million

Russia
1.7 Million

France
1.38 Million

Austria-Hungary
1.2 Million

British Commonwealth
947,000

Italy
460,000

Turkey
325,000

United States
112,432

Casualties of the Great War

the interests of the native peoples concerned. European boundaries should be re-drawn so that no substantial group would have to live under a government not of its own choosing.

Wilson's Fourteen Points for a fair peace lifted the hopes of people everywhere. After the guns fell silent, however, the vagueness and inconsistencies in his list became apparent. Complete national self-determination was impossible in Europe; there were too many regions of mixed population for every group to be satisfied. Self-determination, like the war itself, also fostered the spirit of nationalism that Wilson's dream of international organization, a league of nations, was designed to de-emphasize. Furthermore, the Allies had made territorial commitments to one another in secret treaties that ran counter to the principle of self-determination, and they were not ready to give up all claims to Germany's colonies. Freedom of the seas in wartime posed another problem; the British flatly refused to accept the idea. In every Allied country, millions rejected the idea of a peace without indemnities. They expected to make the enemy pay for the war, hoping, as Sir Eric Geddes, first lord of the Admiralty, said, to squeeze Germany "as a lemon is squeezed—until the pips squeak."

Wilson assumed that the practical benefits of his program would compel opponents to fall in line. He had the immense advantage of seeking nothing for his own country and the additional strength of being leader of the one important nation to emerge from the war richer and more powerful than it had been in 1914.

Yet this combination of altruism, idealism, and power was his undoing; it intensified his tendency to be overbearing and undermined his judgment. He had never found it easy to compromise. Once, when he was president of Princeton, he got into an argument over some abstract question with a professor while shooting a game of pool. To avoid acrimony, the professor finally said: "Well, Doctor Wilson, there are two sides to every question." "Yes," Wilson answered, "a right side and a wrong side." Now, believing that the fate of humanity hung on his actions, he was unyielding. Always a preacher, he became in his own mind a prophet—almost, one fears, a kind of god.

Wilson then came to a daring decision: He would personally attend the conference as a member of the United States Peace Commission. This was a precedent-shattering step, for no president had ever left American territory while in office. (Taft, who had a summer home on the St. Lawrence River in Canada, never vacationed there during his term, believing that to do so would be unconstitutional.)

Wilson probably erred in going to Paris, but not because of the novelty or possible illegality of the act. By going, he was turning his back on obvious domestic problems. Western farmers believed that they had been discriminated against during the war, since wheat prices had been controlled while southern cotton had been allowed to rise unchecked from seven cents a pound in 1914 to thirty-five cents in 1919. The administration's drastic tax program had angered many businessmen. Labor, despite its gains, was restive in the face of reconversion to peacetime conditions.

Wilson had increased his political difficulties by making a partisan appeal for the election of a Democratic Congress in 1918. Republicans, who had in many instances supported his war program more loyally than the Democrats, considered the action a gross affront. The appeal failed; the Republicans won majorities in both houses. Wilson appeared to have been repudiated at home at

Europe Before World War I

the very moment that he set forth to represent the nation abroad. Most important, Wilson intended to break with the isolationist tradition and bring the United States into a league of nations. Such a revolutionary change would require explanation; he should have undertaken a major campaign to convince the American people of the wisdom of this step.

THE PARIS PEACE CONFERENCE AND THE VERSAILLES TREATY

Wilson arrived in Europe a world hero. He toured England, France, and Italy briefly and was greeted ecstatically almost everywhere. The reception tended to increase his sense of mission and to convince him, in the fashion of a typical progressive, that whatever the European politicians might say about it, "the people" were behind his program.

When the conference settled down to its work, control quickly fell into the hands of the so-called Big Four: Wilson, Prime Minister David Lloyd George of Great Britain, Premier Georges Clemenceau of France, and Prime Minister Vittorio Orlando of Italy. Wilson stood out in this group but did not dominate it. His principal advantage in the negotiations was his untiring industry. He alone of the leaders tried to master all the complex details of the task.

Europe After World War I

The 78-year-old Clemenceau cared only for one thing: French security. He viewed Wilson cynically, saying that since mankind had been unable to keep God's Ten Commandments, it was unlikely to do better with Wilson's Fourteen Points. Lloyd George's approach was pragmatic and almost cavalier. He sympathized with much that Wilson was trying to accomplish but found the president's frequent sermonettes about "right being more important than might, and justice being more eternal than force" incomprehensible. "If you want to succeed in politics," Lloyd George advised a British statesman, "you must keep your conscience well under control." Orlando, clever, cultured, a believer in international cooperation but inflexible where Italian national interests were concerned, was not the equal of his three colleagues in influence. He left the conference in a huff when they failed to meet all his demands.

The conference labored from January to May 1919 and finally brought forth the Versailles Treaty. American liberals whose hopes had soared at the thought of a peace based on the Fourteen Points found the document abysmally disappointing.

The peace settlement failed to carry out the principle of self-determination completely. It gave Italy a large section of the Austrian Tyrol, though the area contained 200,000 people who considered themselves Austrians. Other German-speaking groups were incorporated into the new states of Poland and Czechoslovakia.

The victors forced Germany to accept responsibility for having caused the war—an act of senseless vindictiveness as well as a gross oversimplification—and to sign a "blank check," agreeing to pay for all damage to civilian properties and even future pensions and other indirect war costs. This reparations bill, as finally determined, amounted to $33 billion. Instead of attacking imperialism, the treaty attacked German imperialism; instead of seeking a new international social order based on liberty and democracy, it created a great-power entente designed to crush Germany and to exclude Bolshevik Russia from the family of nations. It said nothing about freedom of the seas, the reduction of tariffs, or disarmament.

Wilson himself backtracked on his pledge to honor the right of self-determination. For example, Point 12 of the Fourteen Points called for the "autonomous development" of Arab peoples who had lived under Ottoman rule. But Wilson had second thoughts about their self-determination. Secretary of State Lansing worried about the "danger of putting such ideas into the minds of certain races," particularly the "Mohammedans of Syria and Palestine." Wilson reluctantly deleted explicit references to self-determination from the postwar settlements. Arab leaders seethed. Similarly, Ho Chi Minh, a young Vietnamese nationalist, was embittered by the failure at Versailles to deliver his people from French colonial rule. He decided to become a communist revolutionary. The repercussions of Arab and Vietnamese discontent, though far removed from American interests at the time, would be felt in full force much later.

Wilson expected the League of Nations to make up for all the inadequacies of the Versailles Treaty. Once the League had begun to function, problems like freedom of the seas and disarmament would solve themselves, he argued, and the relaxation of trade barriers would surely follow. The League would arbitrate international disputes, act as a central body for registering treaties, and employ military and economic sanctions against aggressor nations. Each member promised (Article 10) to protect the "territorial integrity" and "political independence" of all other members. No nation could be made to go to war against its will, but Wilson emphasized that all were *morally* obligated to carry out League decisions. By any standard, Wilson had achieved a remarkably moderate peace, one full of hope for the future. Except for the war guilt clause and the heavy reparations imposed on Germany, he could be justly proud of his work.

THE SENATE REJECTS THE LEAGUE OF NATIONS

When Wilson returned from France, he finally directed his attention to the task of winning public approval of his handiwork. A large majority of the people probably favored the League of Nations in principle, though few understood all its implications or were entirely happy with every detail. Wilson had persuaded the Allies to accept certain changes in the original draft to mollify American opposition. No nation could be forced to accept a colonial mandate, and "domestic questions" such as tariffs and the control of immigration and the Monroe Doctrine were excluded from League control.

Many senators found these modifications insufficient. Even before the peace conference ended, thirty-seven Republican senators signed a manifesto, devised by Henry Cabot Lodge of Massachusetts, opposing Wilson's League and demanding that the question of an international organization be put off until "the urgent business of negotiating peace terms with Germany" had been completed. Wilson rejected this suggestion icily. Further alterations were out of the question. "Anyone who opposes me . . . I'll crush!" he told one Democratic senator. "I shall consent to nothing. The Senate must take its medicine." Thus the stage was set for a monumental test of strength between the president and the Republican majority in the Senate.

Partisanship, principle, and prejudice clashed mightily in this contest. A presidential election loomed. Should the League prove a success, the Republicans wanted to be able to claim a share of the credit, but Wilson refused to allow them to participate in drafting the document. Alarm at the possible sacrifice of American sovereignty to an international authority led many Republicans to urge modification of the League covenant. Personal dislike of Wilson and his high-handed methods motivated others to oppose the League. The intense desire of the people to secure an end to the long war made Republican leaders hesitate before voting down the Versailles Treaty, but they could not reject the League without rejecting the treaty.

Wilson could count on the Democratic senators almost to a man, but he had to win over many Republicans to obtain the two-thirds majority necessary for ratification. Republican opinion divided roughly into three segments. At one extreme were some dozen "irreconcilables," led by the shaggy-browed William E. Borah of Idaho, an able and kindly person of progressive leanings but an uncompromising isolationist. Borah claimed that he would vote against the League even if Jesus Christ returned to earth to argue in its behalf, and most of his followers were equally inflexible. At the other extreme stood another dozen "mild" reservationists who were in favor of the League but who hoped to alter it in minor ways, chiefly for political purposes. In the middle were the "strong" reservationists, senators willing to go along with the League only if American sovereignty were fully protected and if it were made clear that their party had played a major role in fashioning the final document.

Senator Lodge, the leader of the Republican opposition, was a haughty, rather cynical, intensely partisan individual. He possessed a keen intelligence, a mastery of parliamentary procedure, and, as chairman of the Senate Foreign Relations Committee, a great deal of power. Although not an isolationist, he had little faith in the League. He also had a profound distrust of Democrats, especially Wilson, whom he considered a hypocrite and a coward. The president's pious idealism left him cold.

Lodge belonged to the strong reservationist faction. His own proposals, known as the Lodge Reservations, fourteen in number to match Wilson's Fourteen Points, limited U.S. obligations to the League and stated in unmistakable terms the right of Congress to decide when to honor these obligations. The most important reservation applied to Article 10 of the League covenant, which committed signatories to protect the political independence and territorial integrity of all member nations. Wilson had rightly called Article 10 "the heart of the Covenant." One of Lodge's reservations made it inoperable so far as the United States was concerned "unless in any particular case the Congress . . . shall by act or joint resolution so provide."

Lodge performed brilliantly, if somewhat unscrupulously, in uniting the three Republican factions behind his reservations. He got the irreconcilables to agree to them by conceding their right to vote against the final version in any event, and he held the mild reservationists in line by modifying some of his demands and stressing the importance of party unity. Reservations—as distinct from amendments—would not have to win the formal approval of other League members. In addition, the Lodge proposals dealt forthrightly with the problem of reconciling traditional concepts of national sovereignty with the new idea of world cooperation. Supporters of the League could accept them without sacrifice of principle. Wilson, however, refused to agree. "Accept the Treaty with the Lodge reservations?" the president snorted when a friendly senator warned him that he must accept a compromise. "Never! Never!"

This foolish intransigence seems almost incomprehensible in a man of Wilson's intelligence and political experience. In part his hatred of Lodge accounts for it, in part his faith in his League. His physical condition in 1919 also played a role. At Paris he had suffered a violent attack of indigestion that was probably a symptom of a minor stroke. Thereafter, many observers noted small changes in his personality, particularly increased stubbornness and a loss of good judgment. Instead of making concessions, the president set out early in September on a nationwide speaking crusade to rally support for the League. In three weeks, Wilson traveled some 10,000 miles by train and gave forty speeches, some of them brilliant. But they had little effect on senatorial opinion, and the effort drained his last physical reserves. On September 25, after an address in Pueblo, Colorado, he collapsed. The rest of the trip had to be canceled. A few days later, in Washington, he suffered a severe stroke that partially paralyzed his left side.

For nearly two months the president was almost totally cut off from affairs of state, leaving supporters of the League leaderless while Lodge maneuvered the reservations through the Senate. Gradually, popular attitudes toward the League shifted. The arguments of the irreconcilables persuaded many citizens that Wilson had made too sharp a break with America's isolationist past and that the Lodge Reservations were therefore necessary. Other issues connected with the reconversion of society to a peacetime basis increasingly occupied the public mind.

A coalition of Democratic and moderate Republican senators could easily have carried the treaty. That no such coalition was organized was Wilson's fault. Lodge obtained the simple majority necessary to add his reservations to the treaty merely by keeping his own party united. When the time came for the final roll call on November 19, Wilson, bitter and emotionally distraught, urged the Democrats to vote for rejection. "Better a thousand times to go down fighting than to dip your colors to dishonorable compromise," he explained to his wife. Thus the amended treaty failed, thirty-five to fifty-five, the irreconcilables and the Democrats voting against it. Lodge then allowed the original draft without his reservations to come to a vote. Again the result was defeat, thirty-eight to fifty-three. Only one Republican cast a ballot for ratification.

Dismayed but not yet crushed, friends of the League in both parties forced reconsideration of the treaty early in 1920. Neither Lodge nor Wilson would yield an inch. Lodge, who had little confidence in the effectiveness of any league of nations, was under no compulsion to compromise. Wilson, who believed that the League was the world's best hope, did have such a compulsion. Yet he would not compromise either, and this ensured the Treaty's defeat.

Wilson's behavior is further evidence of his physical and mental decline. Had he died or stepped down, the treaty, with reservations, would almost certainly have been ratified. When the Senate balloted again in March, half the Democrats voted for the treaty with the Lodge Reservations. The others, mostly southern party regulars, joined the irreconcilables. Together they mustered thirty-five votes, seven more than the one-third that meant defeat.

THE RED SCARE

Everyone wanted peace, but wartime tensions did not subside; apparently people continued to need some release for the aggressive drives they had formerly focused on the Germans. Most Americans drew invidious comparisons between the lot of the unemployed soldier who had risked his life for a dollar a day and that of the striker who had drawn fat wages during the war in perfect safety.

DEBATING THE PAST

Did a stroke sway Wilson's judgment? Wilson's refusal to accept some of Lodge's reservations to the League of Nations ensured its defeat; and without the participation of the young new superpower, the League was likely doomed to failure. Was Wilson's refusal motivated by principle or personal pique?

Historians such as Arthur Link (1957) maintained that Lodge's reservations would have emasculated the League. Because "half a League" was worse than none at all, Wilson was right to have stood firm. Wilson's critics described his actions as little more than a temper tantrum, like a child who destroys a favorite toy. George Kennan (1951) thought Wilson's judgment was beclouded by foolish and impractical moral imperatives.

These pictures suggest another interpretation. The first shows Wilson at his inauguration in 1912; the second, at his last cabinet meeting in 1919, after he had suffered a major stroke. Edwin Weinstein (1981), a physician, found that Wilson's stroke had been more debilitating than had been reported. His impaired physical condition had probably contributed to Wilson's obdurate refusal to compromise.

Arthur Link, *Wilson the Diplomatist* (1957), George Kennan, *American Diplomacy* (1951), Edwin Weinstein, *A Medical and Psychological Biography* (1981).

The activities of radicals in the labor movement led millions of citizens to associate unionism and strikes with the new threat of communist world revolution. Although there were only a relative handful of communists in the United States, Russia's experience persuaded many people that a tiny minority of ruthless revolutionaries could take over a nation of millions if conditions were right. Communists appointed themselves the champions of workers; labor unrest attracted them magnetically. When strikes broke out, some accompanied by violence, many people interpreted them as communist-inspired preludes to revolution.

Organized labor in America had seldom been truly radical. The Industrial Workers of the World (IWW) had made little impression in most industries. But some labor leaders had been attracted to socialism, and many Americans failed to distinguish between the common ends sought by communists and socialists and the entirely different methods by which they proposed to achieve those ends. When a general strike paralyzed Seattle in February 1919, the fact that a pro-communist had helped organize it sent shivers down countless conservative spines. When the radical William Z. Foster began a drive to organize the steel industry at about this time, the fears became more intense. In September 1919 a total of 343,000 steelworkers walked off their jobs, and in the same month the Boston police went on strike. Violence marked the steel strike, and the suspension of police protection in Boston led to looting and fighting that ended only when Governor Calvin Coolidge (who might have prevented the strike had he acted earlier) called out the National Guard.

During the same period a handful of terrorists caused widespread alarm by attempting to murder various prominent persons, including John D. Rockefeller, Justice Oliver Wendell Holmes, Jr., and Attorney General A. Mitchell Palmer. Although the terrorists were anarchists and anarchism had little in common with communism, many citizens lumped all extremists together and associated them with a monstrous assault on society.

What aroused the public even more was the fact that most radicals were not American citizens. Wartime fear of alien saboteurs easily transformed itself into peacetime terror of foreign radicals. In place of Germany, the enemy became the lowly immigrant, usually an Italian or a Jew or a Slav and usually an industrial worker. In this muddled way, radicalism, unionism, and questions of racial and national origins combined to make many Americans believe that their way of life was in imminent danger. Thus the "red scare" was born.

Attorney General Palmer was the key figure in the resulting purge. He had been a typical progressive, a supporter of the League of Nations and such reforms as woman suffrage and child labor legislation. But pressure from Congress and his growing conviction that the communists really were a menace led him to join the "red hunt." Soon he was saying of the radicals: "Out of the sly and crafty eyes of many of them leap cupidity, cruelty, insanity, and crime; from their lopsided faces, sloping brows, and misshapen features may be recognized the unmistakable criminal type."

In August 1919, Palmer established within the Department of Justice the General Intelligence Division, headed by J. Edgar Hoover, to collect information about clandestine radical activities. In November, Justice Department agents in a dozen cities swooped down on the meeting places of an anarchist organization known as the Union of Russian Workers. More than 650 persons, many of them unconnected with the union, were arrested but in only 43 cases could evidence be found to justify deportation.

Nevertheless, the public reacted so favorably that Palmer, thinking now of winning the 1920 Democratic presidential nomination, planned an immense roundup of communists. He obtained 3000 warrants, and on January 2, 1920,

The "red scare" that followed the Great War caused panic and new racial violence throughout the nation. Paranoid delusions of "dangerous aliens" and "foreign subversives" were prevalent, as this cartoon demonstrates.

his agents, reinforced by local police and self-appointed vigilantes, struck simultaneously in 33 cities.

About 6000 persons were taken into custody, many of them citizens and therefore not subject to the deportation laws, many others unconnected with any radical cause. Some were held incommunicado for weeks while the authorities searched for evidence against them. In a number of cases, individuals who went to visit prisoners were themselves thrown behind bars on the theory that they too must be communists. Hundreds of suspects were jammed into filthy "bullpens," beaten, and forced to sign "confessions."

The public tolerated these wholesale violations of civil liberties because of the supposed menace of communism. Gradually, however, protests began to be heard, first from lawyers and liberal magazines, then from a wider segment of the population. No revolutionary outbreak had taken place. Of 6000 seized in the Palmer raids, only 556 proved liable to deportation. The widespread ransacking of communists' homes and meeting places produced mountains of inflammatory literature but only three pistols. Within a few months, the red scare subsided.

THE ELECTION OF 1920

Wilson still hoped for vindication at the polls in the presidential election, which he sought to make a "great and solemn referendum" on the League. He would have liked to run for a third term, but in his enfeebled condition he attracted no support among Democratic leaders. The party nominated James M. Cox of Ohio.

Cox favored joining the League, but the election did not produce the referendum on the new organization that Wilson desired. The Republicans, whose candidate was another Ohioan, Senator Warren G. Harding, equivocated shamelessly on the issue. The election turned on other matters, largely emotional. Disillusioned by the results of the war, many Americans had had their fill of idealism. They wanted, apparently, to end the long period of moral uplift and reform agitation that had begun under Theodore Roosevelt and return to what Harding called "normalcy."

To the extent that the voters were expressing opinions on Wilson's League, their response was overwhelmingly negative. Senator Harding, a strong reservationist, swept the country, winning over 16.1 million votes to Cox's 9.1 million. In July 1921, Congress formally ended the war with the Central Powers by passing a joint resolution.

The defeat of the League was a tragedy both for Wilson, whose crusade for a world order based on peace and justice ended in failure, and for the world, which was condemned to endure another, still more horrible and costly war. Perhaps this dreadful outcome could not have been avoided. Had Wilson compromised and Lodge behaved like a statesman instead of a politician, the United States would have joined the League, but it might well have failed to respond when called on to meet its obligations. As events soon demonstrated, the League powers acted timidly and even dishonorably when challenged by aggressor nations.

Yet it might have been different had the Senate ratified the Versailles Treaty. What was lost when the treaty failed was not peace but the possibility of peace, a tragic loss indeed.

MILESTONES

1914	United States invades Veracruz, Mexico
	Great War begins in Europe
1915	German U-boat torpedoes *Lusitania*
	United States recognizes Carranza government in Mexico
1916	Wilson appoints Louis D. Brandeis to Supreme Court
	"Pancho" Villa burns Columbus, New Mexico
	Wilson is reelected president
1917	Russian Revolution begins
	United States declares war on Central Powers
	Herbert Hoover is named food administrator
1918	Sedition Act limits freedom of speech
	Wilson announces Fourteen Points
	Republicans gain control of both houses of Congress
	Armistice ends the Great War
1919	Steel workers strike
	Red Scare culminates in Palmer raids
	Big Four meet at Paris Peace Conference
	Senate rejects Versailles Treaty and League of Nations
	Wilson suffers massive stroke
1920	Senate again rejects Versailles Treaty and League of Nations
	Warren Harding is elected president

25

POSTWAR SOCIETY AND CULTURE: CHANGE AND ADJUSTMENT

The Great War seemed to many of those who lived through it a turning point in history, the real division separating the nineteenth from the new twentieth century. Actually most of what seemed new to the people of the 1920s had begun to appear well before 1917, and the changes they noticed were still going on. They were in the midst of adjusting to new social, cultural, and economic forces, forces that were to shape their lives and those of their children and grandchildren.

CLOSING THE GATES TO NEW IMMIGRANTS

The ending of the red scare did not herald the disappearance of xenophobia. It was perhaps inevitable and possibly wise that some limitation be placed on the entry of immigrants into the United States after the war. An immense backlog of prospective migrants had piled up during the conflict, and the desperate postwar economic condition of Europe led hundreds of thousands to seek better circumstances in the United States. Immigration increased from 110,000 in 1919 to 430,000 in 1920 and to 805,000 in 1921, with every prospect of continuing to rise.

In 1921 Congress, reflecting a widespread prejudice against eastern and southern Europeans, passed an emergency act establishing a quota system. Each year 3 percent of the number of foreign-born residents of the United States in 1910 (about 350,000 persons) might enter the country. Each country's quota was based on the number of its nationals in the United States in 1910. This meant

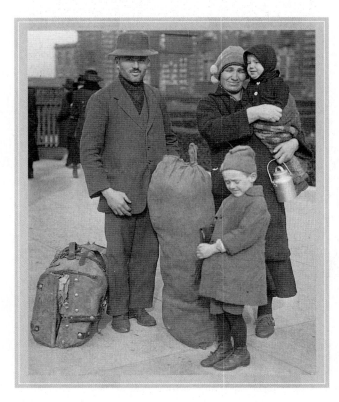

"Give me your tired, your poor, your huddled masses yearning to breathe free, the wretched refuse of your teeming shore"—these words of Emma Lazarus, inscribed at the base of the Statue of Liberty, tell only part of the story. Most immigrants were young and hopeful, like this family at Ellis Island; many were resolute and ambitious. The restriction of immigration during the 1920s, conceived to exclude misfits, also deprived the nation of such as these.

that only a relative handful of the total would be from southern and eastern Europe. In 1924 the quota was reduced to 2 percent and the base year shifted to 1890, thereby lowering further the proportion of southern and eastern Europeans admitted.

In 1929 Congress established a system that allowed only 150,000 immigrants a year to enter the country. (In recent years, that annual number of legal immigrants has been increased to 700,000.) Each national quota was based on the supposed origins of the entire white population of the United States in 1920, not merely on the foreign-born. Here is an example of how the system worked:

$$\frac{\text{Italian quota}}{150,000} = \frac{\text{Italian-origin population, 1920}}{\text{White population, 1920}}$$

$$\frac{\text{Italian quota}}{150,000} = \frac{3,800,000}{95,500,000}$$

$$\text{Italian quota} = 6000 \text{ (approximately)}$$

The system was complicated and unscientific, for no one could determine with accuracy the "origins" of millions of citizens. More seriously, it ignored America's long history of constantly changing ethnic heterogeneity. The motto *E Pluribus Unum,* conceived to represent the unity of the original 13 states, applied even more appropriately to the blending of different cultures into one nationality. The new law sought to freeze the mix, to turn the American melting pot into a kind of gigantic ice cube.

The United States had closed the gates. The National Origins Act caused the foreign-born percentage of the population to fall from about 13 percent in 1920 to 4.7 percent in 1970. (In comparison, in 2005 over 11 percent of the population was foreign born.) Instead of an open, cosmopolitan society eager to accept, in Emma Lazarus's stirring line, the "huddled masses yearning to breathe free," America now became committed to preserving a homogeneous, "Anglo-Saxon" population.

Distaste for the "new" immigrants from eastern Europe, many of whom were Jewish, expanded into a more general anti-Semitism in the 1920s. American Jews, whether foreign-born or native, were subjected to increasing discrimination, not because they were slow in adopting American ways but because (being ambitious and hardworking, as immigrants were supposed to be) many of them were getting ahead in the world somewhat more rapidly than expected. Prestigious colleges like Harvard, Yale, and Columbia that had in the past admitted Jews based on their academic records now imposed unofficial but effective quotas. Medical schools also established quotas, and no matter how talented, most young Jewish lawyers and bankers could find places only in so-called Jewish firms.

NEW URBAN SOCIAL PATTERNS

The census of 1920 revealed that for the first time a majority of Americans (54 million in a population of 106 million) lived in "urban" rather than "rural" places. These figures are somewhat misleading when applied to the study of social attitudes because the census classified anyone in a community of 2500 or more as urban. Of the 54 million "urban" residents in 1920, over 16 million lived in villages and towns of fewer than 25,000 persons and the evidence suggests strongly that a large majority of them held ideas and values more like those of rural citizens than like those of city dwellers. But the truly urban Americans, the one person in four who lived in a city of 100,000 or more—and particularly the nearly 16.4 million who lived in metropolises of at least half a million—were increasing steadily in number and influence. More than 19 million persons moved from farms to cities in the 1920s, and the population living in centers of 100,000 or more increased by about a third.

Earlier differences between working-class and middle-class family structures persisted. In 1920 about a quarter of the American women who were working were married, but less than 10 percent of all married women were working. Middle-class married women who worked were nearly all either childless or highly paid professionals who were able to employ servants. Most male skilled workers now earned enough to support a family in modest comfort so long as they could work steadily, but an unskilled laborer still could not. Wives in most such families helped out, usually by taking in laundry or doing piecework sewing for jobbers.

By the 1920s the idea of intrafamily democracy had emerged. In such families, husbands and wives would deal with each other as equals, which given existing conditions meant sharing housework and childcare, downplaying male authority, and stressing mutual satisfaction in sexual and other matters. On the one hand, they should be friends and lovers, not merely housekeepers, earners of money, and producers of children. On the other hand, advocates of these companionate relationships believed that there was nothing particularly sacred about marriage; divorce should be made easier for couples who did not get along, provided they did not have children.

The growth of large cities further loosened social constraints on sexuality. Amid the sea of people who surged down the streets or into the subways, the solitary individual acquired a freedom derived from anonymity. (For further perspective on urban life, see the Re-Viewing the Past essay "*Chicago*," pp. 696–697.) Homosexuals, in particular, developed a set of identifying signals and fashioned a distinctive culture in parks, cafeterias, nightclubs, and rooming houses of big cities. Because most others wrongly assumed that male homosexuality was characterized by effeminacy, they were unaware of the extent of the emerging gay culture.

THE YOUNGER GENERATION

The Great War profoundly affected the generation born around the turn of the century. It had raised, and its outcome dashed, their hopes for the future. Now the narrowness and prudery of so many of their elders and the stuffy conservatism of nearly all politicians seemed not merely old-fashioned but ludicrous. The actions of red-baiters and reactionaries led them to exaggerate the importance of their right to express themselves in bizarre ways. Their models and indeed some of their leaders were the prewar Greenwich Village bohemians.

The 1920s has been described as the Jazz Age, the era of "flaming youth," when young people danced to syncopated "African" rhythms, careened about the countryside in automobiles in search of pleasure and forgetfulness, and made gods of movie stars and professional athletes. This view of the period bears a superficial resemblance to reality. "Younger people," one observer noted in 1922, were attempting "to create a way of life free from the bondage of an authority that has lost all meaning." But if they differed from their parents and grandparents, it was primarily because young people were adjusting to more profound and more rapid changes in their world than their grandparents could have imagined.

For young people during the 1920s relations between the sexes were becoming more relaxed and uninhibited. Respectable young women smoked cigarettes, something previously done in public only by prostitutes and bohemian types. They cast off heavy corsets, wore lipstick and "exotic" perfumes, and shortened both their hair and their skirts, the latter rising steadily from instep to ankle to calf to knee and beyond as the decade progressed. For decades female dressmakers and beauty salon proprietors had sold their own beauty products and potions. By 1920, however, new cosmetic corporations, managed primarily by men, appropriated the products and marketing strategies of local women entrepreneurs and catered to national mass markets.

Conservatives bemoaned what they described as the breakdown of moral standards, the fragmentation of the family, and the decline of parental authority—all with some reason. Nevertheless, society was not collapsing. Much of the rebelliousness of the young, like their particular style of dress, was faddish in nature, in a sense a kind of youthful conformity. This was particularly true of college students. Elaborate rituals governed every aspect of their extracurricular life, which was consuming a steadily larger share of most students' time and energy. Fraternity and sorority initiations, "proms," attendance at Saturday afternoon football games, styles of dress, and college slang, seemingly aspects of independence and free choice, were nearly everywhere shaped and controlled by peer pressure.

But young people's new ways of relating to one another, while influenced by the desire to conform, were not mere fads and were not confined to people under 30. This can be seen most clearly in the birth control movement, the drive to legalize the use of contraceptives.

THE "NEW" WOMAN

The young people of the 1920s were more open about sex and perhaps more sexually precocious than the young had been before the war. This does not mean that most of them engaged in sexual intercourse before marriage or that they tended to marry earlier. Single young people might "believe in" birth control, but relatively few (at least by modern standards) had occasion to practice it. Contraception was a concern of married people, and particularly of married women.

The leading American proponent of birth control in the 1920s, actually the person who coined the term, was Margaret Sanger, one of the less self-centered Greenwich Village bohemians. Before the war she was a political radical, a friend of Eugene Debs, "Big Bill" Haywood, and the anarchist Emma Goldman. Gradually, however, her attention focused on the plight of the poor women she encountered while working as a nurse; many of these women, burdened by large numbers of children, knew nothing about contraception. Sanger began to write articles and pamphlets designed to enlighten them, but when she did so she ran afoul of the Comstock Act of 1873, an antiobscenity law that banned the distribution of information about contraception from the mails. She was frequently in trouble with the law, but she was persistent to the edge of fanaticism. In 1921 she founded the American Birth Control League and two years later a research center.

The medical profession, though wary of the issue, gave some support to the birth control movement, as did the eugenicists, who claimed that unless the fecundity of "unfit" types (people others might describe simply as poor) was

DEBATING THE PAST

Was the decade of the 1920s one of self-absorption? This magazine cover is a stereotypical expression of the Roaring Twenties: a chic young woman, knee exposed, smoking, drinking, and cavorting with a gin-toting cad in a roadster.

The decade was scarcely over when Frederick Lewis Allen indicted it in *Only Yesterday* (1931), an immediate best-seller. In his view young people believed that "life was futile and nothing much mattered." So they occupied themselves with "tremendous trifles" such as mah-jongg, jazz, and illicit booze. Of the wider world, they cared little. In 1937 Samuel Eliot Morison and Henry Steele Commager added a political gloss to Allen's cultural pessimism. Because people were "weary of reform and disillusioned by the crusade of democracy," they drifted toward conservatism.

Two important works were published in 1955. John Higham referred to the "tribal twenties" as a time when Americans attempted to "close the gates" of immigration, and Richard Hofstadter derided the decade as an insignificant "entr'acte" bracketed by the more consequential eras of progressivism and New Deal reform.

William Leuchtenburg (1958) sought to balance these assessments: there was much more to the decade than "raccoon coats and bathtub gin." While conceding that politicians had failed to solve problems of state authority, industrial concentration, and mass culture, they had not done much worse than the progressives. (Recall Debating the Past, p. 614.)

In later decades leftist scholars such as Roland Marchand (1985) associated the 1920s with the triumph of advertising and consumption, part of a "cultural hegemony" that promoted sales to ensure corporate profits. On the other hand, Kathy Peiss (1998) was among a group of scholars who insisted that consumption could add depth and richness to life. She found, for example, that in purchasing cosmetics women partook of the "pleasures of fantasy and desire."

George Chauncey (1994) championed the self-absorption—self-expression?—of gays who, left mostly to themselves, exulted in a remarkably open homosexual culture in the big cities.

Frederick Lewis Allen, *Only Yesterday* (1931), Samuel Eliot Morison and Henry Steele Commager, *The Growth of the American Republic* (1937), John Higham, *Strangers in the Land* (1955), Richard Hofstadter, *The Age of Reform* (1955), William Leuchtenburg, *The Perils of Prosperity* (1958), Roland Marchand, *Advertising the American Dream* (1985), T. J. Jackson Lears, *Fables of Abundance* (1995), Warren I. Susman, *Culture as History* (1984), Kathy Peiss, *Hope in a Jar* (1998), George Chauncey, *Gay New York* (1994).

This photograph of Margaret Sanger was taken during her trial in January 1917. Having opened the nation's first birth control clinic in Brooklyn, New York, she was convicted of disseminating information on contraception and served 30 days in prison. Friends had advised Sanger to dress conservatively and affect a "Madonna type" persona, much as she appeared here, with her son. Despite her demure clothing, her eyes express her characteristic assertiveness.

curbed, "race suicide" would result. Sanger accepted support wherever it could be found; by the end of the decade she was no longer on the cutting edge of the movement or even a very radical feminist. But by that time resistance to the use of contraception was crumbling.

Other gender-based restrictions and limitations of particular importance to women also seemed to be breaking down. The divorce laws had been modified in most states. More women were taking jobs, attracted by the expanding demand for clerks, typists, salespeople, receptionists, telephone operators, and similar service-oriented occupations. Over 10.6 million women were working by the end of the decade, in contrast with 8.4 million in 1920. The Department of Labor's Women's Bureau, outgrowth of a wartime agency, was founded in 1920 and was soon conducting investigations of the working conditions women faced in different industries and how various laws affected them.

But most of these gains were illusory. Relaxation of the strict standards of sexual morality did not eliminate the double standard. More women worked, but most of the jobs they held were still menial or of a kind that few men wanted: domestic service, elementary school teaching, clerical work, selling behind a counter. One of the worst blows fell in 1923 when in the case of *Adkins* v. *Children's Hospital*, the Supreme Court declared a federal law that limited the hours of work for women in the District of Columbia unconstitutional.

Re-Viewing the Past

Chicago

Chicago (2003) is a tale of illicit sex, booze, and "all that jazz." The characters played by Renée Zellweger and Catherine Zeta-Jones aspire to cabaret stardom. Each is married, each is having an affair, each is jilted, and each shoots her wayward lover because "he had it coming." The newspapers gleefully promote their stories. From prison, while awaiting trial for murder, the women compete to garner the most headlines, courting the fame that will boost their careers. Richard Gere, who plays their celebrity lawyer, "razzle dazzles" all Chicago (including both juries) and gets the women acquitted. *Chicago* is a musical. It does not claim to be history. Trial lawyers do not tap dance upon the judge's bench, nor do prisoners tango on death row. The movie, however, is based on a true story; and both the movie and the story illuminate important aspects of the Roaring Twenties.

On March 11, 1924 Walter Law, an automobile salesman, was found slumped against the steering wheel of a car in downtown Chicago. He was dead from a gunshot wound to the head. A pistol and an empty bottle of gin were on the floor. The car was registered to Belva Gaertner, a twice-divorced cabaret singer known as Belle Brown. Police hurried to her rooming house and peppered her with questions.

Catherine Zeta-Jones and Renée Zellweger.

"We went driving, Mr. Law and I," she told them. The couple had stopped at the Bingham "café," bought a bottle of gin (illegally, since this was during Prohibition), and drove around town. "I don't know what happened next," she declared. During the interrogation Gaertner paced nervously, perhaps for good reason: Her clothes were soaked with blood. She was charged with murder.

On April 3, police received a phone call that a man had attempted to rape a young married woman and that she had shot him. The woman was Beulah Annan, who worked at a laundry. At her apartment, police found Harry Kalstedt dead from a gunshot wound. Mrs. Annan insisted that she had acted in self-defense, and her husband supported her story. But police hammered away at the fact that Kalstedt had worked at the same laundry as Mrs. Annan, and that he had been shot in the back. Mrs. Annan eventually confessed that the two had been having an affair and that, when he threatened to dump her, she shot him. For two hours, as he lay dying, she drank cocktails and listened to a recording of "Hula Lou," a foxtrot about a Hawaiian girl "with more sweeties than a dog has fleas."

Maurine Watkins, a young reporter, covered both stories for the *Chicago Tribune*. Murder had long been a staple of local journalism, but Watkins recognized the extraordinary appeal of this story: jazz, booze, and two comely "lady murderesses," as Watkins termed them. While awaiting trial in prison, the women provided Watkins with splendid quotes.

Gaertner told Watkins that she was innocent. "No woman can love a man enough to kill him," she explained. "There are always plenty more." She added: "Gin and guns—either one is bad enough, but together they get you in a dickens of a mess." When the grand jury ruled that she could be tried for murder, Gaertner was irritated. "That was bum," she snapped. She called the jurors "narrow-minded old birds—bet they

Belva Gaertner and Beulah Annan, "lady murderesses."

never heard a jazz band in their lives. Now, if I'm tried, I want worldly men, broad-minded men, men who know what it is to get out a bit. Why, no one like that would convict me!"

During the trial, Annan's attorney pointed to "this frail little girl, struggling with a drunken brute." On May 25, after deliberating less than two hours, the all-male jury acquitted her of the crime. (Justice in those days was swift; in Illinois, too, it was devoid of women, who did not gain the right to serve on juries until 1939.) Two weeks after Annan's trial, Gaertner was also found not guilty. "Another pretty woman gone free," muttered the prosecutor. Watkins noted that four other women remained on death row, but none were as "stylish" or "pretty" as Gaertner and Annan.

Unlike the movie's "lady murderesses," Annan and Gaertner did not team up in a cabaret act. Annan had a nervous breakdown, was institutionalized, and died in 1928. Of Gaertner's subsequent life, little is known. Watkins abandoned journalism and entered Yale drama school. In 1926 she wrote *Chicago*, a comedy derived from the Gaertner and Annan trials, and it ran on Broadway for 172 performances. The next year Cecil B. De Mille adapted the play as a silent movie. In 1975 director Bob Fosse bought the rights to *Chicago* and created the Broadway musical on which the 2003 movie was based.

The "lady murderesses" became part of the lore of the Roaring Twenties; the story seemed to confirm the fears of traditionalists. One min-

ister warned about jazz's "wriggling movement and sensuous stimulation" of the body's "sensory center." Short, bobbed, or marcelled hair was similarly worrisome, because it signified a young woman's break from convention. Silk stockings, skirts that exposed the knees, and straight dresses that de-emphasized the waist further suggested that women's bodies were not meant solely for childbirth. The movie makes all of these points with suitable salaciousness.

The movie also echoes widespread concerns about city life. Several months after the acquittal of Gaertner and Annan, *Literary Digest* warned "country girls" of the moral dangers of large cities. Such criticisms of the modern city echoed the judgments of sociologists, especially those of "the Chicago school" of urban sociology, headed by Robert Park of the University of Chicago. The Chicago sociologists contended that large cities shattered traditional bonds of family and community and fostered crime and deviance.

Scholars now recognize that the portrait of urban city life as propounded by "the Chicago school"—and by movies such as *Chicago*—was overdrawn. Urbanization did not shatter family and ethnic ties. Neighborliness and community persisted even in blighted tenement districts. Few people cast off social conventions, much less succumbed to murderous impulses. In short, Belva Gaertner and Beulah Annan were good copy, and stories such as theirs helped make that celebrated decade roar, but most folks painted the town less vividly, if at all.

When they competed for jobs with men, women usually received much lower wages. Efforts to get the American Federation of Labor to take up the issue failed; few of the unions in the federation admitted women.

The 1920s proved disillusioning to feminists, who now paid a price for their single-minded pursuit of the right to vote in the progressive era. After the ratification of the Nineteenth Amendment, Carrie Chapman Catt was exultant: "We are no longer petitioners," she announced, "but free and equal citizens." Many activists, assuming the battle won, lost interest in agitating for change. They believed that the suffrage amendment had given them the one weapon needed to achieve whatever women still lacked. In fact, it soon became apparent that women did not vote as a bloc. Many married women voted for the candidates their husbands supported.

When radical feminists discovered that voting did not automatically bring true equality, they founded the Women's party and began campaigning for an equal rights amendment. Their dynamic leader, Alice Paul, disdained specific goals such as disarmament, ending child labor, and liberalized birth control. Total equality for women was the one objective. The party considered protective legislation governing the hours and working conditions of women discriminatory. This caused the so-called social feminists, who believed that children and working women needed the protection provided by such laws, to break away.

The Women's party never attracted a wide following, but only partly because of the split with the social feminists. Many of the younger radical women, like the bohemians of the progressive era, were primarily concerned with their personal freedom to behave as they wished; politics did not interest them. But a more important reason was that nearly all the radicals failed to see that questions of gender—the attitudes that men and women *were taught* to take toward each other, not immutable physical or psychological differences—stood in the way of sexual equality. Many more women joined the more moderate League of Women Voters, which attempted to mobilize support for a broad spectrum of reforms, some of which had no specific connection to the interests of women as such. The entire women's movement lost momentum. The battle for the equal rights amendment persisted through the 1930s, but it was lost. By the end of that decade the movement was moribund.

POPULAR CULTURE: MOVIES AND RADIO

The postwar decade saw immense changes in popular culture. Unlike the literary flowering of the era (see page 707), these changes seemed in tune with the times, not a reaction against them. This was true in part because they were products as much of technology as of human imagination.

The first motion pictures were made around 1900, but the medium only came into its own after the Great War. The early films, such as the eight-minute epic *The Great Train Robbery* (1903), were brief, action-packed, and unpretentious. Professional actors and most educated people viewed them with amused contempt. But their success was instantaneous with recent immigrants and many other slum dwellers. In 1912 there were nearly 13,000 movie houses in the United States, more than 500 in New York City alone. Many of these places were converted stores called nickelodeons because the admission charge was only 5 cents.

In the beginning the mere recording of movement seemed to satisfy the public, but success led to rapid technical and artistic improvements and consequently to more cultivated audiences. D. W. Griffith's 12-reel *Birth of a Nation* (1915) was a particularly important breakthrough in both areas, although Griffith's sympathetic treatment of the Ku Klux Klan of Reconstruction days angered blacks and white liberals.

By the mid-1920s the movie industry, centered in Hollywood, California, was the fourth largest in the nation in capital investment. Films moved from the nickelodeons to converted theaters. So large was the audience that movie "palaces" seating several thousand people sprang up in the major cities. *Daily* ticket sales averaged more than 10 million. With the introduction of talking movies, *The Jazz Singer* (1927) being the first of significance, and color films a few years later, the motion picture reached technological maturity. Costs and profits mounted; by the 1930s million-dollar productions were common.

Charlie Chaplin was the greatest film star of the era. His characterization of the sad-eyed little tramp with his toothbrush moustache and his cane, tight frock coat, and baggy trousers became famous throughout the world. Chaplin's films were superficially unpretentious; they seemed even in the 1920s old-fashioned, aimed at the lower-class audiences that had first found the movies magical. But his work proved both universally popular and enduring; he was perhaps the greatest comic artist of all time. The animated cartoon, perfected by Walt Disney in the 1930s, was a lesser but significant cinematic achievement; Mickey Mouse, Donald Duck, and other Disney cartoon characters gave endless delight to millions of children.

Even more pervasive than the movies in its effects on the American people was radio. Wireless transmission of sound was developed in the late nineteenth century by many scientists in Europe and the United States. During the war radio was put to important military uses and was strictly controlled, but immediately thereafter the airwaves were thrown open to everybody.

Radio was briefly the domain of hobbyists, thousands of "hams" broadcasting in indiscriminate fashion. Even under these conditions, the manufacture of radio equipment became a big business. In 1920 the first commercial station (KDKA in Pittsburgh) began broadcasting, and by the end of 1922 over 500 stations were in operation. In 1926 the National Broadcasting Company, the first continentwide network, was created.

It took little time for broadcasters to discover the power of the new medium. When one pioneer interrupted a music program to ask listeners to phone in requests, the station received 3000 calls in an hour. The immediacy of radio explained its tremendous impact. As a means of communicating the latest news, it had no peer; beginning with the broadcast of the 1924 presidential nominating

Would women believe the claims of cosmetics advertisements? "Kissproof" promised to make a woman's lips "pulsate with the very spirit of reckless, irrepressible youth." In a 1927 survey of housewives in Columbus, Ohio, Pond's Company found that two-thirds of the women could not even recall the company's advertisements. Younger women, however, were more impressionable. When the J. Walter Thompson advertising agency asked Vassar students to describe cosmetics, they unconsciously used the exact phrases from advertising copy—proof of its power.

conventions, all major public events were covered live. Advertisers seized on radio too; it proved to be as effective a way to sell soap as to transmit news.

In 1927 Congress limited the number of stations and parceled out wavelengths to prevent interference. Further legislation in 1934 established the Federal Communications Commission (FCC), with power to revoke the licenses of stations that failed to operate in the public interest. But the FCC placed no effective controls on programming or on advertising practices.

THE GOLDEN AGE OF SPORTS

The extraordinary popularity of sports in the postwar period can be explained in a number of ways. People had more money to spend and more free time to fill. Radio was bringing suspenseful, play-by-play accounts of sports contests into millions of homes, thus encouraging tens of thousands to want to see similar events with their own eyes. New means of persuasion developed by advertisers to sell lipstick, breakfast cereal, and refrigerators were applied with equal success to sporting events and to the athletes who participated in them.

There had been great athletes before; indeed probably the greatest all-around athlete of the twentieth century was Jim Thorpe, a Sac and Fox Indian who won both the pentathlon and the decathlon at the 1912 Olympic Games, made Walter Camp's All-American football team in 1912 and 1913, then played major league baseball for several years before becoming a pioneer founder and player in the National Football League. But what truly made the 1920s a golden age was a co-incidence—the emergence in a few short years of a remarkable collection of what today would be called superstars.

In football there was the University of Illinois's Harold "Red" Grange, who averaged over 10 yards a carry during his college career and who in one incredible quarter during the 1924 game between Illinois and Michigan carried the ball four times and scored a touchdown each time, gaining in the process 263 yards. In prize fighting, heavyweight champion Jack Dempsey, the "Manassas Mauler," knocked out a succession of challengers in bloody battles only to be deposed in 1927 by "Gentleman Gene" Tunney, who gave him a 15-round boxing lesson and then, according to Tunney's own account, celebrated by consuming "several pots of tea."

During the same years William "Big Bill" Tilden dominated tennis, winning the national singles title every year from 1920 to 1925 along with nearly every other tournament he entered. Beginning in 1923, Robert T. "Bobby" Jones ruled over the world of golf with equal authority, his climactic achievement being his capture of the amateur and open championships of both the United States and Great Britain in 1930.

A few women athletes dominated their sports during this Golden Age in similar fashion. In tennis Helen Wills was three times United States singles champion and the winner of the women's singles at Wimbledon eight times in the late 1920s and early 1930s. The swimmer Gertrude Ederle, holder of 18 world records by the time she was 17, swam the English Channel on her second attempt, in 1926. She was not only the first woman to do so, but she did it faster than any of the four men who had previously made it across.

However, the sports star among stars was "the Sultan of Swat," baseball's Babe Ruth.[1] Ruth not only dominated baseball, he changed it from a game ruled by pitchers and low scores to one in which hitting was more greatly admired. Originally himself a brilliant pitcher, his incredible hitting ability made him more valuable in the outfield, where he could play every day. Before Ruth, John "Home Run" Baker was the most famous slugger; his greatest annual home run total was 12, achieved shortly before the Great War. Ruth hit 29 in 1919 and 54 in 1920, his first year with the New York Yankees. By 1923 he was so feared that pitchers intentionally walked him more than half the times he appeared at the plate.

The achievements of these and other outstanding athletes had a cumulative effect. New stadiums were built, and they were filled by "the largest crowds that ever witnessed athletic sports since the fall of Rome." Record crowds paying unprecedented sums attended all sorts of events.

---

[1] *His full name was George Herman Ruth, but the nickname Babe, given to him early in his career, was what everyone called him.*

Newly built Yankee Stadium, on opening day of the 1923 baseball season. Babe Ruth hit his first home run and soon Yankee Stadium was dubbed "the House that Ruth Built." That year, perhaps his best, Ruth hit 41 home runs, batted .393, and drew 170 walks. He got on base more than half the times he appeared at the plate. Ruth's feats matched the colossal appearance of Yankee Stadium, whose arches evoked the imperial grandeur of ancient Rome.

URBAN–RURAL CONFLICTS: FUNDAMENTALISM

These were buoyant times for people in tune with the times—the young, the devil-may-care, factory workers with money in their pockets, many different types. But nearly all of them were city people. However, the tensions and hostilities of the 1920s exaggerated an older rift in American society—the conflict between urban and rural ways of life. To many among the scattered millions who tilled the soil and among the millions who lived in towns and small cities, the new city-oriented culture seemed sinful, overly materialistic, and unhealthy. To them change was something to be resented and resisted.

Yet there was no denying its fascination. Made even more aware of the appeal of the city by radio and the automobile, farmers and townspeople coveted the comfort and excitement of city life at the same time that they condemned its vices. Rural society proclaimed the superiority of its ways at least in part to protect itself from temptation. Change, omnipresent in the postwar world, must be resisted even at the cost of individualism and freedom.

One expression of this resistance was a resurgence of religious fundamentalism. Although it was especially prevalent among Baptists and Methodists, fundamentalism was primarily an attitude of mind, profoundly conservative, rather than a religious idea. Fundamentalists rejected the theory of evolution as well as advanced hypotheses on the origins of the universe.

What made crusaders of the fundamentalists, however, was their resentment of modern urban culture. Although in some cases they harassed liberal ministers, their religious attitudes had little public significance; their efforts to impose their views on public education were another matter. The teaching of evolution must be prohibited, they insisted. Throughout the 1920s they campaigned vigorously for laws banning discussion of Darwin's theory in textbooks and classrooms. By 1929 five southern states had passed laws prohibiting the teaching of evolution in the public schools.

The fundamentalists won a minor victory in 1925, when Tennessee passed a law forbidding instructors in the state's schools and colleges to teach "any theory that denies the story of the Divine Creation of man as taught in the Bible." Although the bill passed both houses by big majorities, most legislators voted aye only because they dared not expose themselves to charges that they disbelieved the Bible. Educators in the state, hoping to obtain larger school appropriations from the legislature, hesitated to protest.

On learning of the passage of this act, the American Civil Liberties Union announced that it would finance a test case challenging its constitutionality if a Tennessee teacher would deliberately violate the statute. Urged on by friends, John T. Scopes, a young biology teacher in Dayton, reluctantly agreed to do so. He was arrested. A battery of nationally known lawyers came forward to defend him, and the state obtained the services of William Jennings Bryan. The "Monkey Trial" became an overnight sensation.

Clarence Darrow, chief counsel for the defendant, stated the issue clearly. "Scopes isn't on trial," he said, "civilization is on trial. The prosecution is opening the doors for a reign of bigotry equal to anything in the Middle Ages. No man's belief will be safe if they win." The comic aspects of the trial obscured this issue. Big-city reporters like H. L. Mencken of the *Baltimore Evening Sun* flocked to Dayton to make sport of the fundamentalists. Scopes's conviction was a foregone conclusion; after the jury rendered its verdict, the judge fined him $100.

Nevertheless the trial exposed the danger of the fundamentalist position. The high point came when Bryan agreed to testify as an expert witness on the Bible. In a sweltering courtroom, both men in shirtsleeves, the lanky, rough-hewn Darrow cross-examined the aging champion of fundamentalism, exposing his childlike faith and his scientific ignorance. Bryan admitted to believing that Eve had been created from Adam's rib and that a whale had swallowed Jonah. "I believe in a God that can make a whale and can make a man and make both do what He pleases," he explained.

The Monkey Trial ended badly for nearly everyone concerned. Scopes moved away from Dayton; the judge, John Raulston, was defeated when he sought reelection; Bryan died in his sleep a few days after the trial. But fundamentalism continued to flourish, not only in the nation's backwaters but also in many cities, brought there by rural people in search of work. In retrospect, even the heroes of

At the Scopes Monkey trial, this open-air stall offers anti-evolution books, such as those by William Jennings Bryan and another title, "Hell & the High School."

the Scopes trial—science and freedom of thought—seem somewhat less stainless than they did to liberals at the time. The account of evolution in the textbook used by Scopes was far from satisfactory, yet it was advanced as unassailable fact. The book also contained statements that to the modern mind seem at least as bigoted as anything that Bryan said at Dayton. In a section on the "Races of Man," for example, it described Caucasians as "the highest type of all . . . represented by the civilized white inhabitants of Europe and America."

URBAN–RURAL CONFLICTS: PROHIBITION

The conflict between the countryside and the city was fought on many fronts, and in one sector the rural forces achieved a quick victory. This was the Eighteenth Amendment, ratified in 1919, which prohibited the manufacture, transportation, and sale of alcoholic beverages. Although there were some big-city advocates of prohibition, the Eighteenth Amendment, in the words of one historian marked a triumph of the "Corn Belt over the conveyor belt."

This "experiment noble in purpose," as Herbert Hoover called it, achieved a number of socially desirable results. It reduced the national consumption of alcohol from 2.6 gallons per capita in the period just before the war to less than 1 gallon in the early 1930s. Arrests for drunkenness fell off sharply, as did deaths from alcoholism. Fewer workers squandered their wages on drink. If the drys had been willing to legalize beer and wine, the experiment might have worked.

During Prohibition, rival gangs in many big cities contended for control of the lucrative (and illegal) sale of liquor. On Valentine's Day, 1929, Al Capone's gangsters, in police uniforms, barged into a garage at 2122 North Clark Street, Chicago, lined up the members of the George "Bugs" Moran gang, and shot them. Three months later Capone spent a year in prison for carrying a concealed weapon. He was later sentenced to 11 years in prison for income tax fraud, though he attained early release for good behavior.

Instead, by insisting on total abstinence, they drove thousands of moderates to violate the law. Strict enforcement became impossible, especially in the cities.

In areas where sentiment favored prohibition strongly, liquor remained difficult to find. Elsewhere, anyone with sufficient money could obtain it easily. Smuggling became a major business, *bootlegger* a household word. Private individuals busied themselves learning how to manufacture "bathtub gin." Many druggists issued prescriptions for alcohol with a free hand. The manufacture of wine for religious ceremonies was legal, and consumption of sacramental wine jumped by 800,000 gallons during the first two years of prohibition. The saloon disappeared, replaced by the speakeasy, a supposedly secret bar or club, operating under the benevolent eye of the local police.

That the law was often violated does not mean that it was ineffective, any more than violations of laws against theft and murder mean that those laws are ineffective. Although gangsters such as Alphonse "Scarface Al" Capone of Chicago were engaged in the liquor traffic, their "organizations" existed before the passage of the Eighteenth Amendment. But prohibition widened already serious rifts in the social fabric of the country. Besides undermining public morality by encouraging hypocrisy, it almost destroyed the Democratic party as a national organization. Democratic immigrants in the cities hated it, but southern Democrats sang its praises, often while continuing to drink (the humorist Will Rogers quipped that Mississippi would vote dry "as long as the voters could stagger to the polls").

THE KU KLUX KLAN

The most horrible manifestation of the social malaise of the 1920s was the revival of the Ku Klux Klan. This new Klan, founded in 1915 by William J. Simmons, a former preacher, admitted only native-born white Protestants. The distrust of foreigners, blacks, Catholics, and Jews implicit in this regulation explains why it flourished in the social climate that spawned religious fundamentalism, immigration restriction, and prohibition. In 1920 two unscrupulous publicity agents, Edward Y. Clarke and Elizabeth Tyler, got control of the movement and organized a massive membership drive, diverting a major share of the initiation fees into their own pockets. In a little over a year they enrolled 100,000 recruits, and by 1923 they claimed the astonishing total of 5 million.

The Klan had relatively little appeal in the Northeast or in metropolitan centers in other parts of the country, but it found many members in middle-sized cities and in the small towns and villages of midwestern and western states like Indiana and Oregon. The scapegoats in such regions were immigrants, Jews, and especially Catholics. The rationale was an urge to return to an older, supposedly finer America and to stamp out all varieties of nonconformity. Klansmen "watched everybody," themselves safe from observation behind their masks and robes. They persecuted gamblers, "loose" women, violators of the prohibition laws, and anyone who happened to differ from them on religious questions or who belonged to a "foreign race."

The very success of the Klan led to its undoing. Factionalism sprang up, and rival leaders squabbled over the large sums that had been collected from the membership. The cruel and outrageous behavior of the organization roused both

A Ku Klux Klan initiation ceremony photographed in Kansas in the 1920s. During its peak influence at mid-decade, Klan endorsement was essential to political candidates in many areas of the West and Midwest. Campaigning for reelection in 1934, an Indiana congressman testified, "I was told to join the Klan, or else."

liberals and conservatives in every part of the country. And of course its victims joined forces against their tormentors. When the powerful leader of the Indiana Klan, a middle-aged reprobate named David C. Stephenson, was convicted of assaulting and causing the death of a young woman, the rank and file abandoned the organization in droves. The Klan remained influential for a number of years, contributing to the defeat of the Catholic Alfred E. Smith in the 1928 presidential election, but it ceased to be a dynamic force after 1924. By 1930 it had only some 9000 members.

SACCO AND VANZETTI

The excesses of the fundamentalists, the xenophobes, the Klan, the red-baiters, and the prohibitionists disturbed American intellectuals profoundly. More and more they became alienated, bitter, and contemptuous of those who appeared to control the country. Yet their alienation came at the very time that society was subjected to complex economic, political, and technological challenges that required the attention of people with brains and sophistication. This compounded the confusion and disillusionment characteristic of the period.

Nothing demonstrates this fact as clearly as the Sacco-Vanzetti case. In April 1920 two men in South Braintree, Massachusetts, killed a paymaster and a guard in a daring daylight robbery of a shoe factory. Shortly thereafter Nicola Sacco and Bartolomeo Vanzetti were charged with the crime, and in 1921 they were convicted of murder. Sacco and Vanzetti were anarchists and Italian immigrants. Their trial was a travesty of justice. The presiding judge, Webster Thayer, conducted the proceedings like a prosecuting attorney; privately he referred to the defendants as "those anarchist bastards."

The case became a cause célèbre. Prominent persons throughout the world protested, and for years Sacco and Vanzetti were kept alive by efforts to obtain a new trial. Vanzetti's quiet dignity and courage in the face of death wrung the hearts of millions. "You see me before you, not trembling," he told the court. "I never commit a crime in my life. . . . I am so convinced to be right that if you could execute me two times, and if I could be reborn two other times, I would live again and do what I have done already." When, in August 1927, the two were at last electrocuted, the disillusionment of American intellectuals with prevailing values was profound. Some historians, impressed by modern ballistic studies of Sacco's gun, now suspect that he, at least, may have been guilty. Nevertheless, the truth and the shame remain: Sacco and Vanzetti paid with their lives for being radicals and aliens, not for any crime.

LITERARY TRENDS

The literature of the 1920s reflects the disillusionment of the intellectuals. The prewar period had been an age of hopeful experimentation in the world of letters. But the progressive era writers, along with most other intellectuals, were beginning to abandon this view by about 1912. The wasteful horrors of the Great

War and then the antics of the fundamentalists and the cruelty of the red-baiters and the Klan turned them into critics of society. After the war the poet Ezra Pound dropped his talk of an American Renaissance and wrote instead of a "botched civilization."

The symbol of the lost generation, in his own mind as well as to his contemporaries and to later critics, was F. Scott Fitzgerald. Born to modest wealth in St. Paul, Minnesota, in 1896, Fitzgerald attended Princeton and served in the army during the Great War. He rose to sudden fame in 1920 when he published *This Side of Paradise,* a somewhat sophomoric novel that appealed powerfully to college students and captured the fears and confusions of the lost generation. In *The Great Gatsby* (1925), a more mature work, Fitzgerald dissected a modern millionaire—coarse, unscrupulous, jaded, in love with another man's wife. Gatsby's tragedy lay in his dedication to a woman who, Fitzgerald made clear, did not merit his passion. He lived in "the service of a vast, vulgar, meretricious beauty," and in the end he understood this himself.

The tragedy of *The Great Gatsby* was related to Fitzgerald's own. Pleasure-loving and extravagant, he squandered the money earned by *This Side of Paradise.* He descended into the despair of alcoholism and ended his days as a Hollywood scriptwriter.

Many young American writers and artists became expatriates in the 1920s. They flocked to Rome, Berlin, and especially Paris, where they could live cheaply and escape what seemed to them the "conspiracy against the individual" prevalent in their own country. Ernest Hemingway was the most talented of the expatriates. He had served in the Italian army during the war and been grievously wounded (in spirit as well as in body). He settled in Paris in 1922 to write. His first novel, *The Sun Also Rises* (1926), portrayed the café world of the expatriate and the rootless desperation, amorality, and sense of outrage at life's meaninglessness that obsessed so many in those years. In *A Farewell to Arms* (1929) he drew on his military experiences to describe the confusion and horror of war.

Hemingway's books were best-sellers and he became a legend in his own time, but his style rather than his ideas explains his towering reputation. Few novelists have been as capable of suggesting powerful emotions and action in so few words. Mark Twain and Stephen Crane were his models; Gertrude Stein, a writer and revolutionary genius, his teacher. But his style was his own, direct, simple, taut, sparse.

Edith Wharton was of the New York aristocracy. She was educated by tutors and governesses and never went to college. To counteract what she called "the creeping darkness of neurasthenia," she traveled frequently to Europe, eventually chose to live there, and took up writing. In Paris at the outset of the Great War, she threw herself into war-related charities. But after the war, she retreated from the jangling energy of postwar life and culture. "I am steeping myself in the nineteenth century," she explained to a friend, "like taking refuge in a mighty temple." The product of her retreat, *The Age of Innocence* (1920), offered a penetrating portrait of an unsettlingly serene if vanished world. *The Nation* remarked that Wharton had described the wealthy of old New York "as familiarly as if she loved them and as lucidly as if she hated them." Though the younger novelists of the decade often dismissed her work as uninventive and dowdy, and she theirs as unformed and thin, her judgment has proven the more enduring.

Sinclair Lewis was probably the most popular American novelist of the 1920s. Like Fitzgerald, his first major work brought him instant fame and notoriety—and for the same reason. *Main Street* (1920) portrayed the smug ignorance and bigotry of the American small town so accurately that even Lewis's victims recognized themselves; his title became a symbol for provinciality and middle-class meanness of spirit. In *Babbitt* (1922), he created what many people considered the typical businessman of the 1920s, gregarious, a "booster," blindly orthodox in his political and social opinions, a slave to every cliché, and full of loud self-confidence but under the surface a bumbling, rather timid fellow who would have liked to be better than he was but dared not try.

Lewis was preeminently a product of the 1920s. When times changed, he could no longer portray society with such striking verisimilitude; none of his later novels approached the level of *Main Street* and *Babbitt*. When critics noticed this, Lewis became bewildered, almost disoriented. He died in 1951 a desperately unhappy man.

As significant as the creation of new literature was the innovation in its distribution. In 1926 a New York advertising man founded the Book-of-the-Month Club. As originally conceived, subscribers to the "club" agreed to buy one new book each month, none costing more than $3, to be chosen by a jury of five prominent writers. The idea caught fire and by the end of the decade it had over 110,000 members. The club introduced thousands to new writers, especially women, including Edna Ferber, Gertrude Stein, and Pearl Buck. But it otherwise tended to hold to familiar formulas. The omission of Hemingway, Faulkner, and Fitzgerald from the club's offerings is striking. With good reason critics complained that the club imposed a "literary dictatorship" on the middlebrow masses.

THE "NEW NEGRO"

The postwar reaction brought despair for many blacks. Aside from the barbarities of the Klan, they suffered from the postwar middle-class hostility to labor (and from the persistent reluctance of organized labor to admit black workers into its ranks). The increasing presence of southern blacks in northern cities also caused conflict. Some 393,000 settled in New York, Pennsylvania, and Illinois in the 1920s, most of them in New York City, Philadelphia, and Chicago. The black population of New York City more than doubled between 1920 and 1930.

In earlier periods blacks in northern cities had tended to live together, but in small neighborhoods scattered over large areas. Now the tendency was toward concentration in what came to be called ghettos.

Coming after the hopes inspired by wartime gains, the disappointments of the 1920s produced a new militancy among many blacks. In 1919 W. E. B. Du

Bois wrote in *The Crisis*: "We are cowards and jackasses if . . . we do not marshal every ounce of our brain and brawn to fight . . . against the forces of hell in our own land." He increased his commitment to black nationalism, organizing a series of Pan African Conferences in an effort—futile, as it turned out—to create an international black movement.

Du Bois never made up his mind whether to work for integration or black separatism. Such ambivalence never troubled Marcus Garvey, a West Indian whose Universal Negro Improvement Association attracted hundreds of thousands of followers in the early 1920s. Garvey had nothing but contempt for whites, for light-skinned blacks like Du Bois, and for organizations such as the NAACP, which sought to bring whites and blacks together to fight segregation and other forms of prejudice. "Back to Africa" was his slogan; the black man must "work out his salvation in his motherland." (Paradoxically, Garvey's ideas won the enthusiastic support of the Ku Klux Klan and other white racist groups.)

Garvey's message was naive, but it served to build racial pride among the masses of poor and unschooled blacks. He dressed in elaborate braided uniforms, wore a plumed hat, drove about in a limousine. Both God and Christ were black, he insisted. He organized black businesses of many sorts, including a company that manufactured black dolls. He established a corps of Black Cross nurses and a Black Star Line Steamship Company to transport blacks back to Africa.

The ghettos produced compensating advantages for blacks. One effect, not fully utilized until later, was to increase their political power by enabling them to elect representatives to state legislatures and to Congress and to exert considerable influence in closely contested elections. More immediately, city life stimulated self-confidence; despite their horrors, the ghettos offered economic opportunity, political rights, and freedom from the everyday debasements of life in the South. The ghetto was a black world where black men and women could be themselves.

Black writers, musicians, and artists found in the ghettos both an audience and the "spiritual emancipation" that unleashed their capacities. Jazz, the great popular music of the age, was largely the creation of black musicians working in New Orleans before the turn of the century. By the 1920s it had spread throughout the country and to most of the rest of the world. White musicians and white audiences took it up—in a way it became a force for racial tolerance and understanding.

Jazz meant improvisation, and both players and audiences experienced in it a kind of liberation. Jazz was the music of the 1920s in part because it expressed the desire of so many people to break with tradition and throw off conventional restraints. Surely this helps to explain why it was so important to blacks.

Harlem, the largest black community in the world, became in the 1920s a cultural capital, center of the "Harlem Renaissance." Black newspapers and magazines flourished along with theatrical companies and libraries. Du Bois opened *The Crisis* to young writers and artists, and a dozen "little" magazines sprang up. Langston Hughes, one of the best poets of the era, described the exhilaration of his first arrival in this city within a city, a magnet for every black intellectual and artist. "Harlem! I . . . dropped my bags, took a deep breath, and felt happy again."

With some exceptions, African American writers like Hughes did not share in the disillusionment that afflicted so many white intellectuals. The persistence of prejudice angered them and made them militant. But to be militant, one must be at some level hopeful. Sociologists and psychologists (for whom the ghettos were indispensable social laboratories) were demonstrating that environment rather than heredity was preventing black economic progress. Together with the achievements of creative blacks, which for the first time were being appreciated by large numbers of white intellectuals, these discoveries seemed to herald the eventual disappearance of racial prejudice.

Black separatist Marcus Garvey and his followers were one of many factions of the black movement during the 1920s and 1930s. Other groups, such as the NAACP, worked to bring blacks and whites together, rather than segregating them further.

ECONOMIC EXPANSION

Despite the turmoil of the times and the dissatisfactions expressed by some of the nation's best minds, the 1920s was an exceptionally prosperous decade. Business boomed, real wages rose, unemployment declined. The United States was as rich as all Europe; perhaps 40 percent of the world's total wealth lay in American hands. Little wonder that business leaders and other conservatives described the period as a "new era."

The prosperity rested on many bases, one of which was the friendly, hands-off attitude of the federal government, which bolstered the confidence of the business community. The Federal Reserve Board kept interest rates low, a further stimulus to economic growth. Pent-up wartime demand helped to power the boom; the construction business in particular profited from a series of extremely busy years. The continuing mechanization and rationalization of industry provided a more fundamental stimulus to the economy. From heavy road-grading equipment and concrete mixers to devices for making cigars and glass tubes, from pneumatic tools to the dial telephone, machinery was replacing human hands at an ever more rapid rate. Industrial output almost doubled between 1921 and 1929 without any substantial increase in the industrial labor force. Greater use of power, especially of electricity, also encouraged expansion—by 1929 the United States was producing more electricity than the rest of the world combined.

THE AGE OF THE CONSUMER

The growing ability of manufacturers to produce goods meant that great effort had to be made to create new consumer demands. Advertising and salesmanship were raised almost to the status of fine arts. Bruce Barton, one of the advertising "geniuses" of the era, wrote a best-selling book, *The Man Nobody Knows* (1925), in which he described Jesus as the "founder of modern business," the man who "picked up twelve men from the bottom ranks . . . and forged them into an organization that conquered the world."

Producers concentrated on making their goods more attractive and on changing models frequently to entice buyers into the market. The practice of selling goods on the installment plan helped bring expensive items within the reach of the masses. Inventions and technological advances created new or improved products: radios, automobiles, electric appliances such as vacuum cleaners and refrigerators, gadgets like cigarette lighters, and new forms of entertainment like motion pictures. These influences interacted much as the textile industry in the early nineteenth century and the railroad industry after the Civil War had been the "multipliers" of their times.

Undoubtedly the automobile had the single most important impact on the nation's economy in the 1920s. Although well over a million cars a year were being regularly produced by 1916, the real expansion of the industry came after 1921. Output reached 3.6 million in 1923 and fell below that figure only twice during the remainder of the decade. By 1929, 23 million private cars clogged the highways, an average of nearly one per family.

The auto industry created industries that manufactured tires and spark plugs and other products. It consumed immense quantities of rubber, paint, glass, nickel, and petroleum products. It triggered a gigantic road-building program: there were 387,000 miles of paved roads in the United States in 1921, 662,000 miles in 1929. Thousands of persons found employment in filling stations, roadside stands, and other businesses catering to the motoring public. The tourist industry profited, and the shift of population from the cities to the suburbs was accelerated.

The automobile made life more mobile yet also more encapsulated. It changed recreational patterns and family life. It created a generation of tinkerers and amateur mechanics and explorers. In addition, it profoundly affected the way Americans thought. It gave them a freedom never before imagined. The owner of the most rickety jalopy could travel further, faster, and far more comfortably than a monarch of old with his pureblooded steeds and gilded coaches.

These benefits were real and priceless. But cars became important symbols. They gave their owners the feeling of power and status that a horse gave to a medieval knight. According to some authorities the typical American cared more about owning an automobile than a house.

In time there were undesirable, even dangerous results of the automotive revolution: roadside scenery disfigured by billboards, gas stations, and other enterprises aimed at satisfying the traveler's needs; horrendous traffic jams; soaring

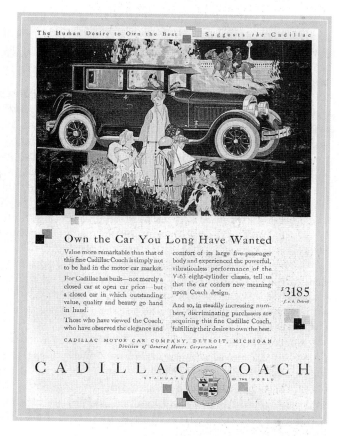

The Human Desire to Own the Best   Suggests *the* Cadillac

Own the Car You Long Have Wanted

Value more remarkable than that of this fine Cadillac Coach is simply not to be had in the motor car market.

For Cadillac has built—not merely a closed car at open car price—but a closed car in which outstanding value, quality and beauty go hand in hand.

Those who have viewed the Coach, who have observed the elegance and

comfort of its large five-passenger body and experienced the powerful, vibrationless performance of the V-63 eight-cylinder chassis, tell us that the car confers new meaning upon Coach design.

And so, in steadily increasing numbers, discriminating purchasers are acquiring this fine Cadillac Coach, fulfilling their desire to own the best.

$3185
f. o. b. Detroit

CADILLAC MOTOR CAR COMPANY, DETROIT, MICHIGAN
Division of General Motors Corporation

CADILLAC COACH
STANDARD   OF THE WORLD

This 1925 magazine advertisement for a Cadillac Coach shows how twentieth-century businesses sought to link nineteenth-century symbols of wealth (horseback riding, the coat-of-arms of nobility, flower gardens) with symbolic expressions of modernity, encapsulated by the independence of short-haired, fashionably dressed young women.

accident rates; air pollution; the neglect of public transportation, which was an important cause of the deterioration of inner cities. All these disadvantages were noticed during the 1920s, but in the springtime of the new industry they were discounted. The automobile seemed an unalloyed blessing—part toy, part tool, part symbol of American freedom, prosperity, and individualism.

HENRY FORD

The person most responsible for the growth of the automobile industry was Henry Ford, a self-taught mechanic from Greenfield, Michigan. Ford was neither a great inventor nor one of the true automobile pioneers. He was not even the first person to manufacture a good low-priced car (that being the achievement of Ransom E. Olds, producer of the "Merry Oldsmobile"). Ford's first brilliant insight was to "get the prices down to the buying power." Through mass production, cars could be made cheaply enough to put them within reach of the ordinary citizen. In 1908 he designed the Model T Ford, a simple, tough box on wheels. In a year he proved his point by selling 11,000 Model T's. Relentlessly cutting costs and increasing efficiency with the assembly line system, he expanded production at an unbelievable rate. By 1925 he was turning out more than 9000 cars a day, one approximately every 10 seconds, and the price of the Model T had been reduced below $300.

Ford's second insight was the importance of high wages in stimulating output (and selling more automobiles). The assembly line simplified the laborer's task and increased the pace of work; at the same time it made each worker much more productive. Jobs became boring and fatiguing, absenteeism and labor turnover serious problems. To combat this difficulty, in 1914 Ford established the $5 day, an increase of about $2 over prevailing wages. The rate of turnover in his plant fell 90 percent, and although critics charged that he recaptured his additional labor costs by speeding up the line, his policy had a revolutionary effect on wage rates. Later he raised the minimum to $6 and then to $7 a day.

Ford's profits soared along with sales; since he owned the entire company, he became a billionaire. He also became an authentic folk hero: his homespun style, his dislike of bankers and sophisticated society, and his intense individualism endeared him to millions. He stood as a symbol of the wonders of the American system—he had given the nation a marvelous convenience at a low price, at the same time enriching himself and raising the living standards of his thousands of employees.

Success made Ford stubborn. The Model T remained essentially unchanged for nearly 20 years. Other companies, notably General Motors, were soon turning out better vehicles for very little more money. Customers, increasingly affluent and style-conscious, began to shift to Chevrolets and Chryslers. Finally, in 1927, Ford shut down all operations for 18 months in order to retool for the Model A. His competitors rushed in during this period to fill the vacuum. Although his company continued to make a great deal of money, Ford never regained the dominant position he had held for so long.

Ford was enormously uninformed, yet—because of his success and the praise the world heaped on him—he did not hesitate to speak out on subjects far outside his area of competence, from the evils of drink and tobacco to medicine and international affairs. He developed political ambitions and published virulent anti-Semitic propaganda. He said he would not give 5 cents for all the art in the world.

THE AIRPLANE

Henry Ford was also an early manufacturer of airplanes, and while the airplane industry was not economically important in the 1920s, its development in that decade laid the basis for changes in lifestyles and attitudes at least as momentous as those produced by the automobile. The invention of the internal combustion gasoline engine, with its extremely high ratio of power to weight, made the airplane possible, which explains why the early experiments with "flying machines" took place at about the same time that the prototypes of the modern automobile were being manufactured. Wilbur and Orville Wright made their famous flight at Kitty Hawk, North Carolina, in 1903, five years before Ford produced his Model T. Another pair of brothers, Malcolm and Haimes Lockheed, built their Model G, one of the earliest commercial planes (commercial in the sense that they used it to take passengers up at $5 a ride) in 1913.

The Great War speeded the advance of airplane technology, and most of the planes built in the 1920s were intended for military use. Practical commercial air travel was long delayed. Aerial acrobats, parachute jumpers, wing walkers, and other daredevils who put on shows at county fairs and similar places where crowds gathered were the principal civilian aviators of the 1920s. They "barn-stormed" from town to town, living the same kind of inbred, encapsulated lives that circus people did, their chief rewards being the sense of independence and pride that the successful performance of their highly skilled but risky trade provided.

The great event of the decade for aviation, still an achievement that must strike awe in the hearts of reflective persons, was Charles A. Lindbergh's nonstop flight from New York to Paris in May 1927. It took more than 33 hours for Lindbergh's single-engine *Spirit of St. Louis* to cross the Atlantic, a formidable physical achievement for the pilot as well as an example of skill and courage. When the public learned that the intrepid "Lucky Lindy" was handsome, modest, uninterested in converting his new fame into cash, and a model of propriety (he neither drank nor smoked), his role as American hero was ensured. It was a role Lindbergh detested—one biographer has described him as "by nature solitary"—but could not avoid.

Lindbergh's flight enormously increased public interest in flying, but it was a landmark in aviation technology as well. The day of routine passenger flights was at last about to dawn. In July 1927, a mere two months after the *Spirit of St. Louis* touched down at Le Bourget Field in France, William E. Boeing of Boeing Air Transport began flying passengers and mail between San Francisco and Chicago, using the M–40, a plane of his own design and manufacture. Early in 1928 he changed the company name to United Aircraft and Transport. Two years later Boeing produced the first all-metal low-wing plane and, in 1933, the twin-engine 247, a prototype for many others.

In retrospect the postwar era seems even more a period of transition than it appeared to most people at the time. Rarely had change come so swiftly, and rarely had old and new existed side by side in such profusion. Creativity and reaction, hope and despair, freedom and repression—the modern world in all its unfathomable complexity was emerging.

MILESTONES

1903	Wright brothers fly at Kitty Hawk, N.C.
1908	Henry Ford designs Model T automobile
1914	Ford establishes $5 day for autoworkers
1919	Eighteenth Amendment outlaws alcoholic beverages (Prohibition)
	Nineteenth Amendment gives women right to vote
1920	Sinclair Lewis publishes *Main Street*
	First commercial radio station, KDKA, begins broadcasting
1920s	Black culture flourishes in Harlem Renaissance
1921	Margaret Sanger founds American Birth Control League
1923	Supreme Court overturns law limiting women's work hours *(Adkins v. Children's Hospital)*
1924	Ku Klux Klan membership peaks
1925	Scopes is convicted for teaching evolution
	F. Scott Fitzgerald publishes *The Great Gatsby*
1926	Gertrude Ederle swims English Channel
	Ernest Hemingway publishes *The Sun Also Rises*
	Charles Lindbergh flies solo across Atlantic
	Sacco and Vanzetti are executed
	The Jazz Singer is first motion picture with sound
	Jack Dempsey loses heavyweight boxing title to Gene Tunney

26

THE NEW ERA: 1921–1933

The men who presided over the government of the United States from 1921 to 1933 were Warren G. Harding, Calvin Coolidge, and Herbert Hoover. Harding was a newspaperman by trade, publisher of the *Marion Star,* with previous political experience as a legislator and lieutenant governor in his home state, Ohio, and as a United States senator. No president, before or since, looked more like a statesman; few were less suited for running the country.

Coolidge was a taciturn, extremely conservative New Englander with a long record in Massachusetts politics climaxed by his inept but much admired suppression of the Boston police strike while governor. Harding referred to him as "that little fellow from Massachusetts." Coolidge preferred to follow public opinion and hope for the best. "Mr. Coolidge's genius for inactivity is developed to a very high point," the correspondent Walter Lippmann wrote. "It is a grim, determined, alert inactivity, which keeps Mr. Coolidge occupied constantly."[1] Hoover was best known for his work as food administrator during the Great War and for his many speeches about "progressive individualism" delivered while serving as secretary of commerce under Harding and Coolidge.

---

[1]*Coolidge was physically delicate, being plagued by chronic stomach trouble. He required 10 or 11 hours of sleep a day.*

HARDING AND "NORMALCY"

Harding won the 1920 Republican nomination because the party convention could not decide between General Leonard Wood, who represented the Theodore Roosevelt progressives, and Frank Lowden, governor of Illinois. Harding's genial nature and lack of strong convictions made him attractive to many of the politicos after eight years of the headstrong Wilson. During the campaign he exasperated sophisticates by his ignorance and imprecision. He coined the famous vulgarism *normalcy* as a substitute for the word *normality*; referred, during a speech before a group of actors, to Shakespeare's play "Charles the Fifth," and committed numerous other blunders. "Why does he not get a private secretary who can clothe . . . his 'ideas' in the language customarily used by educated men?" one Boston gentleman demanded of Senator Lodge, who was strongly supporting Harding. Lodge, ordinarily a stickler for linguistic exactitude, replied acidly that he found Harding a paragon by comparison with Wilson, "a man who wrote English very well without ever saying anything." A large majority of the voters, untroubled by the candidate's lack of erudition, shared Lodge's confidence that Harding would be a vast improvement over Wilson.

As president, Harding tuned the most important government departments over to efficient administrators of impeccable reputation: Charles Evans Hughes

Warren G. Harding looked presidential, and his voice was suitably deep and resonant. Yet he lacked mental agility and discipline. Republican Senator Frank Brandegee explained Harding's nomination by proclaiming him "the best of the second-raters," and thus the natural compromise between contending factions in the party.

as Secretary of State, Herbert Hoover as Secretary of Commerce, Andrew Mellon as Secretary of the Treasury, and Henry C. Wallace as Secretary of Agriculture. He kept track of what these men did but seldom initiated policy in their areas. However, Harding gave many other offices, including some of major importance, to the unsavory "Ohio Gang" headed by Harry M. Daugherty, whom he named Attorney General.

The president was too kindly, too well-intentioned, and too unambitious to be dishonest. He appointed corrupt officials like Daugherty, Secretary of the Interior Albert B. Fall, Director of the Mint "Ed" Scobey, and Charles R. Forbes, head of the new Veterans Bureau, out of a sense of personal obligation or because they were old friends who shared his taste for poker and liquor. Before 1921 he had enjoyed officeholding; but in the White House he found only misery. "The White House is a prison," he complained. "I can't get away from the men who dog my footsteps. I am in jail."

"The Business of the United States Is Business"

Secretary of the Treasury Mellon, multimillionaire banker and master of the aluminum industry, dominated the administration's domestic policy. Mellon set out to lower the taxes of the rich, reverse the low-tariff policies of the Wilson period, return to the laissez-faire philosophy of McKinley, and reduce the national debt by cutting expenses and administrating the government more efficiently.

In principle his program had considerable merit, yet Mellon carried his policies to unreasonable extremes. He proposed eliminating inheritance taxes and reducing the tax on high incomes by two-thirds, but he opposed lower rates for taxpayers earning less than $66,000 a year, apparently not realizing that economic expansion required greater mass consumption as well. Freeing the rich from "oppressive" taxation, he argued, would enable them to invest more in potentially productive enterprises, the success of which would create jobs for ordinary people.

Mellon's tax and tariff program ran into stiff opposition from midwestern Republicans and southern Democrats, who combined to form the so-called farm bloc. The farm bloc represented a kind of conservative populism, economic grievances combining with a general prejudice against "Wall Street financiers" and rich industrialists to unite agriculture against "the interests." Mellon epitomized everything the farm bloc disliked and their representatives in Congress pared back most of his proposals.

Mellon nevertheless succeeded in balancing the budget and reducing the national debt by an average of over $500 million a year. So committed were the Republican leaders to retrenchment that they even resisted the demands of veterans, organized in the politically potent American Legion, for an "adjusted compensation" bonus.

That the business community heartily approved the policies of Harding and Coolidge is not surprising. Both presidents were uncritical advocates of the business point of view. "We want less government in business and more business in government," Harding pontificated, to which Coolidge added, "The business of the United States is business." Harding and Coolidge used their power of appointment to convert regulatory bodies like the Interstate Commerce Commission (ICC) and the Federal Reserve Board into probusiness agencies that ceased almost entirely to restrict the activities of the industries they were supposed to be controlling.

THE HARDING SCANDALS

At least Mellon was honest. That could not be said of Daugherty and the Ohio Gang. The worst scandal involved Secretary of the Interior Fall, a former senator. In 1921 Fall arranged with the complaisant Secretary of the Navy Edwin Denby for the transfer to the Interior Department of government oil reserves being held for the future use of the navy. He then leased these properties to private oil companies. Edward L. Doheny's Pan-American Petroleum Company got the Elk Hills reserve in California; the Teapot Dome reserve in Wyoming was turned over to Harry F. Sinclair's Mammoth Oil Company. When critics protested, Fall explained that it was necessary to develop the Elk Hills and Teapot Dome properties because adjoining private drillers were draining off the navy's oil. Nevertheless, in 1923 the Senate ordered a full-scale investigation, conducted by Senator Thomas J. Walsh of Montana. It soon came out that Doheny had "lent" Fall $100,000 in hard cash, handed over secretly in a "little black bag." Sinclair had given Fall over $300,000 in cash and negotiable securities.

Although the three culprits escaped conviction on the charge of conspiring to defraud the government, Sinclair was sentenced to nine months in jail for contempt of the Senate and for tampering with a jury, and Fall was fined $100,000 and given a year in prison for accepting a bribe. In 1927 the Supreme Court revoked the leases and the two reserves were returned to the government.

The public still knew little of the scandals when, in June 1923, Harding left Washington on a speaking tour that included a visit to Alaska. His health was poor and his spirits low, for he had begun to understand how his "Goddamn friends" had betrayed him. On the return trip from Alaska, he came down with what his physician, an incompetent crony whom he had made surgeon general of the United States, diagnosed as ptomaine poisoning resulting from his having eaten a tainted Japanese crab. In fact the president had suffered a heart attack. He died in San Francisco on August 2.

Few presidents have been more deeply mourned by the people at the moment of their passing. Harding's kindly nature, his very ordinariness, increased his human appeal. Three million people viewed his coffin as it passed across the country. When the scandals came to light, sadness turned to scorn and contempt.

COOLIDGE PROSPERITY

Had he lived, Harding might well have been defeated in 1924 because of the scandals. Vice President Coolidge, unconnected with the troubles and not the type to surround himself with cronies of any kind, seemed the ideal person to clean out the corrupt officials.

Coolidge soon became the darling of the conservatives. His admiration for businessmen and his devotion to laissez-faire knew no limit. "The man who builds a factory builds a temple," he said in all seriousness. "The Government can do more to remedy the economic ills of the people by a system of rigid economy in public expenditures than can be accomplished through any other action." Andrew Mellon, whom he kept on as secretary of the treasury, became his mentor in economic affairs.

Coolidge won the 1924 Republican nomination easily. The Democrats, badly split, required 103 ballots to choose a candidate. The southern wing, dry, anti-immigrant, pro-Klan, had fixed on William G. McAdoo, Wilson's secretary of the treasury. The eastern, urban, wet element supported Governor Alfred E. Smith of New York, child of the slums, a Catholic who had compiled a distinguished record in social welfare legislation. After days of futile politicking, the party compromised on John W. Davis, a conservative corporation lawyer closely allied with the Morgan banking interests.

Dismayed by the conservatism of Coolidge and Davis, Robert M. La Follette, backed by the farm bloc, the Socialist party, the American Federation of Labor, and numbers of intellectuals, entered the race as the candidate of a new Progressive party. The Progressives adopted a neopopulist platform calling for the nationalization of railroads, the direct election of the president, the protection of labor's right to bargain collectively, and other reforms.

Calvin Coolidge's quiet presidential style was a sharp contrast to the outspoken Warren Harding. When Coolidge died in 1933, humorist Dorothy Parker remarked, "How could they tell?"

The situation was almost exactly the opposite of 1912, when one conservative had run against two liberals and had been swamped. Coolidge received 15.7 million votes, Davis 8.4 million, La Follette 4.8 million. In the Electoral College La Follette won only his native Wisconsin; Coolidge defeated Davis, 382 to 136. Conservatism was clearly the dominant mood of the country.

While Coolidge reigned, complacency was the order of the day. "The country," the president reported to Congress in 1928, "can regard the present with satisfaction, and anticipate the future with optimism."

PEACE WITHOUT A SWORD

Presidents Harding and Coolidge handled foreign relations in much the same way they managed domestic affairs. Harding deferred to senatorial prejudice against executive domination in the area and let Secretary of State Charles Evans Hughes make policy. Coolidge adopted a similar course. In directing foreign relations, they faced the obstacle of a resurgent isolationism. The carnage and apparent senselessness of the Great War convinced millions that the only way to be sure it would not happen again was to "steer clear" of "entanglements." That these famous words had been used by Washington and Jefferson in vastly different contexts did not deter the isolationists of the 1920s from attributing to them the same authority they gave to Scripture. On the other hand, far-flung American economic interests, the need for both raw materials for industry and foreign markets for America's growing surpluses of agricultural and manufactured goods, made close attention to and involvement in developments all over the world unavoidable.

Isolationist sentiments, therefore, did not deter the government from seeking to advance American interests abroad. The Open Door concept remained predominant; the State Department worked to obtain opportunities in underdeveloped countries for exporters and investors, hoping both to stimulate the American economy and to bring stability to "backward" nations. Although this policy sometimes roused local resentments because of the tendency of the United States to support entrenched elites while the mass of peasants and city workers lived in poverty, it also resulted in a further retreat from active interventionism.

The first important diplomatic event of the period revealed a great deal about American foreign policy after the Great War. During the war, Japan had greatly increased its influence in the Far East, especially in Manchuria, the northeastern province of warlord-dominated China. To maintain the Open Door in China, it would be necessary to check Japanese expansion. But there was little hope of restoring the old spheres of influence, which the mass of Chinese people bitterly resented. In addition, Japan, the United States, and Great Britain were engaged in expensive naval building programs, a competition none of them really wanted but from which each dared not withdraw.

In November 1921, hoping to reach a general agreement with China, Japan, and the Europeans that would keep China open to the commerce of all and slow the armaments race, Secretary of State Hughes convened a conference in

Washington. By the following February the Washington Conference had drafted three major treaties and a number of lesser agreements: the Five Power Treaty, the Four-Power Treaty, and the Nine-Power Treaty. These treaties committed major nations—including the United States—to refrain from aggression and excessive military buildups. But the treaties were uniformly toothless. The signers of the Four-Power Treaty—the United States, Great Britain, Japan, and France—agreed only to consult in case of aggression in the Pacific; they made no promises to help one another or to restrict their own freedom of action. As President Harding assured the Senate, "there [was] no commitment to armed force, no alliance, no written or moral obligation to join in defense."

The United States entered into all these agreements without realizing their full implications and not really prepared to play an active part in Far Eastern affairs. "We have no favorites in the present dog fight in China," the head of the Far Eastern division of the State Department wrote of the civil war going on there in 1924. "They all look alike to us." The Japanese soon realized that the United States would not do much to defend its interests in China.

THE PEACE MOVEMENT

The Americans of the 1920s wanted peace but would neither surrender their prejudices and dislikes nor build the defenses necessary to make it safe to indulge these passions. "The people have had all the war, all the taxation, and all the military service that they want," President Coolidge announced in 1925.

Peace societies flourished, among them the Carnegie Endowment for International Peace, designed "to hasten the abolition of war, the foulest blot upon our civilization," and the Woodrow Wilson Foundation, aimed at helping "the liberal forces of mankind throughout the world . . . who intend to promote peace by the means of justice." In 1923 Edward W. Bok, retired editor of the *Ladies' Home Journal,* offered a prize of $100,000 for the best workable plan for preserving international peace. He was flooded with suggestions.

The culmination of this illusory faith in preventing war by criticizing it came with the signing of the Kellogg-Briand Pact in 1928. The treaty was born in the fertile brain of French Foreign Minister Aristide Briand, who was eager to collect allies against possible attack by a resurgent Germany. In 1927 Briand proposed to Secretary of State Frank B. Kellogg that their countries agree never to go to war with each other. Kellogg found the idea as repugnant as any conventional alliance, but American isolationists and pacifists found the suggestion fascinating. They plagued Kellogg with demands that he negotiate such a treaty.

To extricate himself from this situation, Kellogg suggested that the pact be broadened to include all nations. Now Briand was angry. Like Kellogg, he saw how meaningless such a treaty would be, especially when Kellogg insisted that it be hedged with a proviso that "every nation is free at all times . . . to defend its territory from attack and it alone is competent to decide when circumstances require war in self-defense." Nevertheless, Briand too found public pressures irresistible. In August 1928, at Paris, diplomats from 15 nations bestowed upon one another an "international kiss," condemning "recourse to war for the solution of international controversies" and renouncing war "as an instrument of national policy." Seldom has so unrealistic a promise been made by so many intelligent people. Yet most Americans considered the Kellogg-Briand Pact a milestone in the history of civilization: The Senate, habitually so suspicious of international commitments, ratified it 85 to 1.

THE GOOD NEIGHBOR POLICY

The conflict between the desire to avoid foreign entanglements and the desire to advance American economic interests is well illustrated by events in Latin America. In dealing with this part of the world, Harding and Coolidge performed neither better nor worse than Wilson had. In the face of continued radicalism and instability in Mexico, which caused Americans with interests in land and oil rights to suffer heavy losses, President Coolidge acted with forbearance. His appointment of Dwight W. Morrow, a patient, sympathetic ambassador, resulted in an improvement in Mexican-American relations. The Mexicans were able to complete their social and economic revolution in the 1920s without significant interference by the United States.

Under Coolidge's successor, Herbert Hoover, the United States began at last to treat Latin American nations as equals. Hoover reversed Wilson's policy of trying to teach them "to elect good men." The Clark Memorandum (1930), written by Undersecretary of State J. Reuben Clark, disassociated the right of intervention in Latin America from the Roosevelt Corollary. The corollary had been an improper extension of the Monroe Doctrine, Clark declared. The right of the United States to intervene depended rather on "the doctrine of self-preservation."

The distinction seemed slight to Latin Americans, but since it seemed unlikely that the existence of the United States could be threatened in the area, it was important. By 1934 the marines who had been occupying Nicaragua, Haiti, and the Dominican Republic had all been withdrawn and the United States had renounced the right to intervene in Cuban affairs, thereby abrogating the Platt Amendment to the Cuban constitution. Unfortunately, the United States did little to try to improve social and economic conditions in the Caribbean region, so the underlying envy and resentment of "rich Uncle Sam" did not disappear.

THE TOTALITARIAN CHALLENGE

The futility and danger of isolationism were exposed in September 1931 when the Japanese, long dominant in Chinese Manchuria, marched in an army and converted the province into a puppet state named Manchukuo. This action violated both the Kellogg-Briand and Nine-Power pacts. China, now controlled by General Chiang Kai-shek, appealed to the League of Nations and to the United States for help. Neither would intervene. When League officials asked about the possibility of American cooperation in some kind of police action, President Hoover refused to consider either economic or military reprisals. The United

Japanese troops advance through the ruins of the Chinese city of Shanghai in March 1932, a year after Japan had seized Manchuria. Five years later, Japan embarked on the conquest of all China.

States was not a world policeman, he said. The Nine-Power and Kellogg-Briand treaties were "solely moral instruments."

The League sent a commission to Manchuria to investigate. Henry L. Stimson, Hoover's secretary of state, announced (the Stimson Doctrine) that the United States would never recognize the legality of seizures made in violation of American treaty rights. This proclamation served only to irritate the Japanese.

In January 1932 Japan attacked Shanghai, the bloody battle marked by the indiscriminate bombing of residential districts. When the League at last officially condemned their aggressions, the Japanese withdrew from the organization and extended their control of northern China. The lesson of Manchuria was not lost on Adolf Hitler, who became chancellor of Germany on January 30, 1933.

WAR DEBTS AND REPARATIONS

The democracies did not take a strong stand against Japan in part because they were quarreling about other matters. Particularly divisive was the controversy over war debts—those of Germany to the Allies and those of the Allies to the United States. The United States had lent more than $10 billion to its comrades in arms. Since most of this money had been spent on weapons and other supplies in the United States, it might well have been considered part of America's contribution to the war effort. The public, however, demanded full repayment—with interest. "These were loans, not contributions," Secretary of the Treasury Mellon firmly declared.

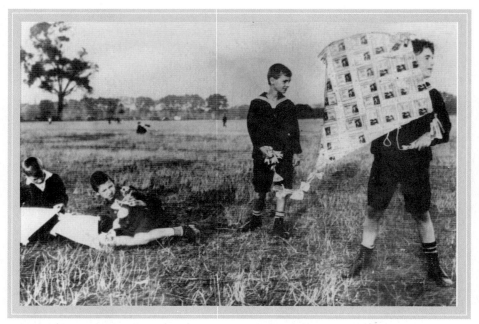

Because of hyperinflation, German bank notes were worth little more than the paper they were printed on. These German boys use them to make a kite.

Repayment of such a sum was virtually impossible. In the first place, the money had not been put to productive use. Dollars lent to build factories or roads might be expected to earn profits for the borrower, but those devoted to the purchase of shells only destroyed wealth. Furthermore, the American protective tariff reduced the ability of the Allies to earn the dollars needed to pay the debts.

The Allies tried to load their obligations to the United States, along with the other costs of the war, on the backs of the Germans. They demanded that the Germans pay reparations amounting to $33 billion. If this sum were collected, they declared, they could rebuild their economies and obtain the international exchange needed to pay their debts to the United States. But Germany was reluctant even to try to pay such huge reparations, and when Germany defaulted, so did the Allies.

Everyone shared the blame: the Germans because they resorted to a runaway inflation that reduced the mark to less than one trillionth of its prewar value, at least in part in hopes of avoiding their international obligations; the Americans because they refused to recognize the connection between the tariff and the debt question; the Allies because they made little effort to pay even a reasonable proportion of their obligations.

In 1924 an international agreement, the Dawes Plan, provided Germany with a $200 million loan designed to stabilize its currency. Germany agreed to pay about $250 million a year in reparations. In 1929 the Young Plan further scaled down the reparations bill. In practice, the Allies paid the United States about what they collected from Germany. Since Germany got the money largely from private American loans, the United States would have served itself and the rest of the world far better had it written off the war debts at the start. In any case, in the late 1920s Americans stopped lending money to Germany, the Great Depression struck, Germany defaulted on its reparations payments, and the Allies then gave up all pretense of meeting their obligations to the United States. The last token payments were made in 1933. All that remained was a heritage of mistrust and hostility.

THE ELECTION OF 1928

Meanwhile, dramatic changes had occurred in the United States. The climax of Coolidge prosperity came in 1928. The president—somewhat cryptically, as was his wont—decided not to run again, and Secretary of Commerce Hoover, whom he detested, easily won the Republican nomination. Hoover was the intellectual leader, almost the philosopher, of the New Era. American capitalists, he believed, had learned to curb their selfish instincts. Voluntary trade associations could create "codes of business practice and ethics that would eliminate abuses and make for higher standards."

Although stiff and uncommunicative and entirely without experience in elective office, Hoover made an admirable candidate in 1928. His roots in the Midwest and West (Iowa-born, he was raised in Oregon and educated at Stanford University in California) neatly balanced his outstanding reputation among eastern business tycoons. He took a "modern" approach to both capital and labor; businessmen should cooperate with one another and with their workers too. He opposed both union busting and trustbusting. His career as a mining engineer had given him a wide knowledge of the world, yet he had become highly critical of Europe—which disarmed the isolationists, who might otherwise have suspected that his long years abroad had made him an effete cosmopolite.

The Democrats, having had their fill of factionalism in 1924, could no longer deny the nomination to Governor Al Smith. Superficially, Smith was Hoover's antithesis. Born and raised in New York's Lower East Side slums, affable, witty, determinedly casual of manner, he had been schooled in machine politics by Tammany Hall. He was a Catholic, Hoover a Quaker, a wet where Hoover supported prohibition; he dealt easily with people of every race and nationality, while Hoover had little interest in and less knowledge of blacks and immigrants. However, like Hoover, Smith managed to combine a basic conservatism with humanitarian concern for the underprivileged. As adept in administration as Hoover, he was equally uncritical of the American capitalist system.

Unwilling to challenge the public's complacent view of Coolidge prosperity, the Democrats adopted a conservative platform. Franklin D. Roosevelt, who ran

Herbert Hoover relaxes during the 1928 presidential campaign. "That man has been offering me advice for the last five years," President Coolidge said of his secretary of commerce, "all of it bad."

for governor of New York at Smith's urging in 1928, charged that Hoover's expansion of the functions of the Department of Commerce had been at least mildly socialistic. This strategy failed miserably. Nothing Smith could do or say was capable of convincing many businessmen that he was a better choice than Hoover. His Catholicism, his brashness, his criticism of prohibition, his machine connections, and his urban background hurt him in rural areas, especially in the normally Democratic South.

In the election Hoover won a smashing triumph, 444 to 87 in the Electoral College, 21.4 million to 14 million in the popular vote. All the usually Democratic border states and even North Carolina, Florida, and Texas went to the Republicans, along with the entire West and the Northeast save for Massachusetts and Rhode Island.

After this defeat the Democratic party appeared on the verge of extinction. Nothing could have been further from the truth. The religious question and his big-city roots had hurt Smith, but the chief reason he lost was prosperity—and the good times were soon to end. Hoover's overwhelming victory also concealed a political realignment that was taking place. Working-class voters in the cities, largely Catholic and unimpressed by Coolidge prosperity, had swung heavily to the Democrats. In 1924 the 12 largest cities had been solidly Republican; in 1928 all went Democratic. In agricultural states like Iowa, Smith ran far better than Davis had in 1924, for Coolidge's vetoes of bills designed to raise farm prices had caused considerable resentment. A new coalition of urban workers and dissatisfied farmers was in the making.

ECONOMIC PROBLEMS

The American economic system of the 1920s had grave flaws. Certain industries did not share in the good times. The coal business, suffering from the competition of petroleum, entered a period of decline. Cotton and woolen textiles also lagged because of the competition of new synthetics, principally rayon. Industry began to be plagued by falling profit margins and chronic unemployment.

The movement toward consolidation in industry, somewhat checked during the latter part of the progressive era, resumed; by 1929, 200 corporations controlled nearly half the nation's corporate assets. General Motors, Ford, and Chrysler turned out nearly 90 percent of all American cars and trucks. Four tobacco companies produced over 90 percent of the cigarettes. One percent of all financial institutions controlled 46 percent of the nation's banking business. Even retail merchandising, traditionally the domain of the small shopkeeper, reflected the trend. The A & P food chain expanded from 400 stores in 1912 to 17,500 in 1928. The Woolworth chain of five-and-ten-cent stores experienced similar growth.

Most large manufacturers, aware that bad public relations resulting from the unbridled use of monopolistic power outweighed any immediate economic gain, sought stability and "fair" prices rather than the maximum profit possible at the moment. "Regulated" competition was the order of the day, dominance by a few large manufacturers the typical situation. The trade association movement flourished; producers formed voluntary organizations to exchange information, discuss policies toward government and the public, and "administer" prices in their industry. Usually the largest corporation, such as U.S. Steel in the iron and steel business, became the "price leader," its competitors, some themselves giants, following slavishly.

The success of the trade associations depended in part on the attitude of the federal government, for such organizations might well have been attacked under the antitrust laws. Their defenders, including President Harding, argued that the associations made business more efficient and prevented violent fluctuations of prices and production. Secretary of Commerce Hoover put the facilities of his department at the disposal of the associations. "We are passing from a period of extremely individualistic action into a period of associational activities," Hoover stated. After Coolidge became president, the Antitrust Division of the Justice Department itself encouraged the trade associations to cooperate in ways that had previously been considered violations of the Sherman Anti-Trust Act.

Even more important to the trade associations were the good times. With profits high and markets expanding, the most powerful producers could afford to share the bounty with smaller, less efficient competitors.

The weakest element in the economy was agriculture. Farm prices slumped and farmers' costs mounted. Besides having to purchase expensive machinery in order to compete, farmers were confronted by high foreign tariffs and in some cases quotas on the importation of foodstuffs. As crop yields per acre rose, chiefly because of the increased use of chemical fertilizers, agricultural prices fell further.

Despite the efforts of the farm bloc, the government did little to improve the situation. President Harding opposed direct aid to agriculture as a matter of principle. "Every farmer is a captain of industry," he declared. "The elimination of competition among them would be impossible without sacrificing that fine individualism that still keeps the farm the real reservoir from which the nation draws so many of the finest elements of its citizenship." During his administration Congress strengthened the laws regulating railroad rates and grain exchanges and made it easier for farmers to borrow money, but it did nothing directly to increase agricultural income. Nor did the high tariffs on agricultural produce have much effect. Being forced to sell their surpluses abroad, farmers found that world prices depressed domestic prices despite the tariff wall.

Thus the unprecedented prosperity rested on unstable foundations. The problem was mainly one of maldistribution of resources. Productive capacity raced ahead of buying power. Too large a share of the profits was going into too few pockets. The 27,000 families with the highest annual incomes in 1929 received as much money as the 11 million with annual incomes of under $1500, the minimum sum required at that time to maintain a family decently. High earnings and low taxes permitted huge sums to pile up in the hands of individuals who did not invest the money productively. A good deal of it went into stock market speculation, which led to the "big bull market" and eventually to the Great Depression.

THE STOCK MARKET CRASH OF 1929

In the spring of 1928, prices on the New York Stock Exchange, already at a historic high, began to surge ahead. As the presidential campaign gathered momentum, the market increased its upward pace, stimulated by the candidates' efforts to outdo each other in praising the marvels of the American economic system. "Glamour" stocks skyrocketed—Radio Corporation of America rose from under 100 to 400 between March and November. A few conservative brokers expressed alarm, warning that most stocks were grossly overpriced. The majority scoffed at such talk. "Be a bull on America," they urged. "Never sell the United States short."

During the first half of 1929 stock prices climbed still higher. A mania for speculation swept the country, thousands of small investors putting their savings in common stocks. Then, in September the market wavered. Amid volatile fluctuations stock averages eased downward. Most analysts contended that the stock exchange was "digesting" previous gains. A Harvard economist expressed the prevailing view when he said that stock prices had reached a "permanently high plateau" and would soon resume their advance.

On October 24 a wave of selling sent prices spinning. Nearly 13 million shares changed hands—a record. Bankers and politicians rallied to check the decline, as they had during the Panic of 1907. J. P. Morgan, Jr. rivaled the efforts of his father in that earlier crisis. President Hoover assured the people that "the business of the country . . . is on a sound and prosperous basis." But on October 29, the bottom seemed to drop out. More than 16 million shares were sold, prices plummeting. The boom was over.

HOOVER AND THE DEPRESSION

The collapse of the stock market did not cause the Depression; stocks rallied late in the year, and business activity did not begin to decline significantly until the spring of 1930. The Great Depression was a worldwide phenomenon caused chiefly by economic imbalances resulting from the chaos of the Great War. In the United States too much wealth had fallen into too few hands, with the result that consumers were unable to buy all the goods produced. The trouble came to a head mainly because of the easy-credit policies of the Federal Reserve Board and the Mellon tax structure, which favored the rich. Its effects were so profound and prolonged because the politicians (and for that matter the professional economists) did not fully understand what was happening or what to do about it.

The chronic problem of underconsumption operated to speed the downward spiral. Unable to rid themselves of mounting inventories, manufacturers closed plants and laid off workers, thereby causing demand to shrink further. Automobile output fell from 4.5 million units in 1929 to 1.1 million in 1932. When Ford closed his Detroit plants in 1931, some 75,000 workers lost their jobs, and the decline in auto production affected a host of suppliers and middlemen as well.

The financial system cracked under the strain. More than 1300 banks closed their doors in 1930, 3700 more during the next two years. Each failure deprived thousands of persons of funds that might have been used to buy goods; when the Bank of the United States in New York City became insolvent in December 1930, 400,000 depositors found their savings immobilized. And of course the industrial depression worsened the depression in agriculture by further reducing the demand for American foodstuffs. Every economic indicator reflected the collapse. New investments declined from $10 billion in 1929 to $1 billion in 1932, and the national income fell from over $80 billion to under $50 billion in the same brief period. Unemployment, under 1 million at the height of the boom, rose to at least 13 million.

President Hoover was an intelligent man, experienced in business matters and knowledgeable in economics. His program for ending the Depression evolved gradually. At first he called on businessmen to maintain prices and wages. The government should cut taxes in order to increase consumers' spendable income, institute public works programs to stimulate production and create jobs for the unemployed, lower interest rates to make it easier for businesses to borrow in order to expand, and make loans to banks and industrial corporations threatened with collapse and to homeowners unable to meet mortgage payments. The president also proposed measures making it easier for farmers to borrow money, and he suggested that the government should support cooperative farm marketing schemes designed to solve the problem of overproduction. He called for an expansion of state and local relief programs and urged all who could afford it to give more to charity. Above all he tried to restore public confidence. The economy was basically healthy; the Depression was only a minor downturn; prosperity was "just around the corner."

Although Hoover's plans were theoretically sound, they failed to check the economic slide, in part because of curious limitations in his conception of how they should be implemented. He placed far too much reliance on his powers of persuasion and the willingness of citizens to act in the public interest without legal compulsion. He urged manufacturers to maintain wages and keep their factories in operation, but the manufacturers, under the harsh pressure of economic realities, soon slashed wages and curtailed output sharply. He permitted the Federal Farm Board (created under the Agricultural Marketing Act of 1929) to establish semipublic stabilization corporations with authority to buy up surplus wheat and cotton, but he refused to countenance crop or acreage controls. The stabilization corporations poured out hundreds of millions of dollars without checking falling agricultural prices because farmers increased production faster than the corporations could buy up the excess for disposal abroad.

Hoover resisted proposals to shift responsibility from state and local agencies to the federal government, despite the fact—soon obvious—that they lacked the resources to cope with the emergency. By 1932 the federal government, with Hoover's approval, was spending $500 million a year on public works projects, but because of the decline in state and municipal construction, the total public outlay fell nearly $1 billion below what it had been in 1930. More serious was his refusal, on constitutional grounds, to allow federal funds to be used for the relief of individuals. State and municipal agencies and private charities must take care of the needy.

Unfortunately the Depression was drying up the sources of private charities just as the demands on these organizations were expanding. State and municipal agencies were swamped just when their capacities to tax and borrow were shrinking. By 1932 more than 40,600 Boston families were on relief (compared with 7400 families in 1929); in Chicago 700,000 persons—40 percent of the workforce—were unemployed. Only the national government possessed the power and the credit to deal adequately with the crisis.

Yet Hoover would not act. He set up a committee to coordinate local relief activities but insisted on preserving what he called "the principles of individual and local responsibility." For the federal government to take over relief would "lead to the super-state where every man becomes the servant of the state and real liberty is lost."

As time passed and the Depression worsened, Hoover put more stress on the importance of balancing the federal budget, reasoning that since citizens had to live within their limited means in hard times, the government should set a good example. This policy was counterproductive; by reducing its expenditures the government made the Depression worse, which reduced federal revenue further. By June 1931 the budget was nearly $500 million in the red.

Hoover understood the value of pumping money into a stagnant economy. He might have made a virtue of necessity. The difficulty lay in the fact that nearly all "informed" opinion believed that a balanced budget was essential to recovery. The most prestigious economists insisted on it; so did business leaders, labor leaders, and even most socialists. In 1932, when the House of Representatives refused to vote a tax increase, the Democratic Speaker compelled reconsideration of the bill by asking those "who do not want to balance the budget to rise." Not a single member did so. As late as 1939 a public opinion poll revealed that over 60 percent of the people (even 57.5 percent of the unemployed) favored reducing government expenditures to balance the budget. When Hoover said, "prosperity cannot be restored by raids on the public Treasury," he was mistaken, but it is equally wrong to criticize him for failing to understand what almost no one understood in the 1930s.

Much of the contemporary criticism of Hoover and a good deal of that heaped on him by later historians was unfair. Yet his record as president shows that he was too rigidly wedded to a particular theory of government to cope effectively with the problems of the day. Since these problems were in a sense insoluble—no one possessed enough knowledge to understand entirely what was wrong or enough authority to enforce corrective measures—flexibility and a willingness to experiment were essential to any program aimed at restoring prosperity. Hoover lacked these qualities. He was his own worst enemy, being too uncompromising to get on well with the politicians and too aloof to win the confidence and affection of ordinary people. He had too much faith in himself and his plans. When he failed to achieve the results he anticipated, he attracted, despite his devotion to duty and his concern for the welfare of the country, not sympathy but scorn.

THE ECONOMY HITS BOTTOM

During the spring of 1932, as the economy sounded the depths, thousands of Americans faced starvation. In Philadelphia during an 11-day period when no relief funds were available, hundreds of families existed on stale bread, thin soup, and garbage. In the nation as a whole, only about one-quarter of the unemployed were receiving any public aid. In Birmingham, Alabama, landlords in poor districts gave up trying to collect rents, preferring, one Alabama congressman told a Senate committee, "to have somebody living there free of charge rather than to have the house . . . burned up for fuel [by scavengers]." Many people were evicted, and they often gathered in ramshackle communities constructed of packing boxes, rusty sheet metal, and similar refuse on swamps, garbage dumps, and other wasteland. People began to call these places "Hoovervilles."

Thousands of tramps roamed the countryside begging and scavenging for food. At the same time, food prices fell so low that farmers burned corn for fuel. In Iowa and Nebraska farmers organized "farm holiday" movements, refusing to ship their crops to market in protest against the 31-cent-a-bushel corn and 38-cent wheat. They blocked roads and rail lines, dumped milk, overturned trucks,

Evicted from their homes, many unemployed gravitated to vacant industrial property, where they erected hovels from scraps of lumber, tarpaper, and cardboard. This shantytown is on the outskirts of Seattle.

and established picket lines to enforce their boycott. The world seemed to have been turned upside down. Professor Felix Frankfurter of the Harvard Law School remarked only half humorously that henceforth the terms B.C. and A.D. would mean "Before Crash" and "After Depression."

The national mood ranged from apathy to resentment. In 1931 federal immigration agents and local groups in the Southwest began rounding up Mexican Americans and deporting them. Some of those returned to Mexico had entered the United States illegally; others had come in properly. Unemployed Mexicans were ejected because they might become public charges, those with jobs because they were presumably taking bread from the mouths of citizens. "Capitalism is dying," the socialist theologian Reinhold Niebuhr remarked in 1932, "and . . . it ought to die."

In June and July 1932, 20,000 World War veterans marched on Washington to demand immediate payment of their "adjusted compensation" bonuses. When Congress rejected their appeal, some 2000 refused to leave, settling in a jerrybuilt camp of shacks and tents at Anacostia Flats, a swamp bordering the Potomac River. President Hoover, alarmed, charged incorrectly that the "Bonus Army" was largely composed of criminals and radicals and sent troops into the Flats to

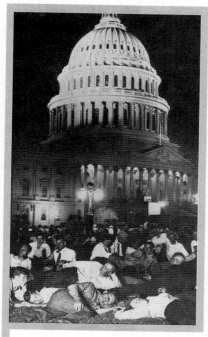

DEBATING THE PAST

What caused the Great Depression? Here some 20,000 "bonus army" marchers camped outside the U.S. Capitol seeking assistance. Most were unemployed. What had caused the depression that threw so many out of work?

The first historian of the Depression wrote about it before it happened, or so some claimed. In the *Communist Manifesto* (1848) Karl Marx and Friedrich Engels had predicted that advanced industrial capitalism would lead to overproduction, wars of imperial expansion, and worsening economic depressions. The Great Depression after 1929 lent credibility to the Marxist explanation. As the Depression persisted through the decade, more historians embraced the Marxist paradigm.

But the economic revival following World War II indicated that either Marx was wrong or that capitalistic industrialism had not yet matured. Most historians now looked elsewhere for the cause of the Depression.

In 1954 economist John K. Galbraith focused on a mania for speculative investment in stocks, aggravated by easy credit policies. Other historians blamed federal policies, such as the high Smoot-Hawley tariff and the Federal Reserve's untimely constriction of credit immediately after the crash. Such measures made things worse, but none were of such a magnitude to have plunged the nation into a depression. Robert Sobel (1968) saw "no causal relationship between the events of late October 1929 and the great depression."

John Garraty (1986) showed that the Great Depression affected much of the world simultaneously. Government policies in many nations contributed to global collapse, but no one nation or policy caused it.

John K. Galbraith, *The Great Crash* (1954), Robert Sobel, *The Great Bull Market* (1968), Peter Temin, *Did Monetary Forces Cause the Great Depression?* (1976), John A. Garraty, *The Great Depression* (1986).

disperse it with bayonets, tear gas, and tanks. The task was accomplished amid much confusion; fortunately no one was killed. The protest had been aimless and not entirely justified, yet the spectacle of the United States government chasing unarmed veterans with tanks appalled the nation.

The unprecedented severity of the Depression led some persons to favor radical economic and political changes. The disparity between the lots of the rich and the poor, always a challenge to democracy, became more striking and engendered considerable bitterness. "Unless something is done to provide employment," two labor leaders warned Hoover, "disorder . . . is sure to arise. . . . There is a growing demand that the entire business and social structure be changed because of the general dissatisfaction with the present system."

The Communist party gained few converts among farmers and industrial workers, but a considerable number of intellectuals, alienated by the trends of the 1920s, responded positively to the communists' emphasis on economic planning and the total mobilization of the state to achieve social goals. Even the cracker-barrel humorist Will Rogers was impressed by reports of the absence of serious unemployment in Russia. "All roads lead to Moscow," the former muckraker Lincoln Steffens wrote.

THE DEPRESSION AND ITS VICTIMS

The Depression affected the families of the jobless in many ways. It caused a dramatic drop in the birthrate, from 27.7 per thousand population in 1920 to 18.4 per thousand in the early 1930s, the lowest in American history. Sometimes it strengthened family ties. Some unemployed men spent more time with their children and helped their wives with cooking and housework. Others, however, became impatient when their children demanded attention, refused to help around the house, sulked, or took to drink.

The influence of wives in families struck by unemployment tended to increase, and in this respect women suffered less psychologically from the Depression. They were usually too busy trying to make ends meet to become apathetic. But the way they used this influence varied. Some wives were sympathetic, others scornful, when the "breadwinner" came home with empty hands. When the wife of an unemployed man managed to find a job, the result could be either gratitude and pride or bitter resentment on the man's part, resentment or a sense of liberation on the woman's.

Children often caused strains in families. Parental authority declined when there was less money available to supply children's needs. Some youngsters became angry when their allowance was cut or when told they could not have something they particularly wanted. Some adolescents found part-time jobs to help out. Others refused to go to school. If there is any generalization about the effects of the Depression on family relations it is probably an obvious one—where relationships were close and loving they became stronger, where they were not, the results could be disastrous.

THE ELECTION OF 1932

As the end of his term approached, President Hoover seemed to grow daily more petulant and pessimistic. The Depression, coming after 12 years of Republican rule, probably ensured a Democratic victory in any case, but his attitude as the election neared alienated many voters and turned defeat into rout.

Confident of victory, the Democrats chose Governor Franklin Delano Roosevelt of New York as their presidential candidate. Roosevelt owed his nomination chiefly to his success as governor. Under his administration, New York

This photograph by Dorothea Lange captures the despair of a typical migrant California family during the depression. Many women had no other choice but to stay in tent cities or makeshift shelters with their children while their husbands searched for work.

had led the nation in providing relief for the needy and had enacted an impressive program of old-age pensions, unemployment insurance, and conservation and public power projects. In 1928, while Hoover was carrying New York against Smith by a wide margin, Roosevelt won election by 25,000 votes. In 1930 he swept the state by a 700,000-vote majority, double the previous record. He also had the advantage of the Roosevelt name (he was a distant cousin of the inimitable TR), and his sunny, magnetic personality contrasted favorably with that of the glum and colorless Hoover.

Roosevelt was far from being a radical. Although he had supported the League of Nations while campaigning for the vice presidency in 1920, during the 1920s he had not seriously challenged the basic tenets of Coolidge prosperity. He never had much difficulty adjusting his views to prevailing attitudes. For a time he even served as head of the American Construction Council, a trade association. Indeed, his life before the Depression gave little indication that he understood the aspirations of ordinary people or had any deep commitment to social reform.

Roosevelt was born to wealth and social status in Dutchess County, New York, in 1882. Pampered in childhood by a doting yet domineering mother, he was educated at the exclusive Groton School and then at Harvard. Ambition as much as the desire to render public service motivated his career in politics; even after an attack of polio in 1921 left him badly crippled in both legs, he refused to abandon his hopes for high office. During the 1920s he was a hardworking member of the liberal wing of his party. He supported Smith for president in 1924 and 1928.

Two boys, barefoot, at a clinic in Arkansas. In 1914 a Rockefeller Foundation study determined that hookworm, which caused debilitating anemia in the rural South, commonly entered the body through the feet. Although Arkansas legislators denounced the study as a plot to make its children buy northern shoes, the Rockefeller Foundation persisted in the campaign, which was backed by federal health officials in the 1930s.

To some observers Roosevelt seemed rather a lightweight intellectually. When he ran for the vice presidency, the *Chicago Tribune* commented: "If he is Theodore Roosevelt, Elihu Root is Gene Debs, and Bryan is a brewer." Twelve years later many critics judged him too irresolute, too amiable, too eager to please all factions to be a forceful leader. Herbert Hoover thought he was "ignorant but well-meaning," and the political analyst Walter Lippmann, in a now-famous observation, called him "a pleasant man who, without any important qualifications for the job, would very much like to be President."

Despite his physical handicap—he could walk only a few steps, and then only with the aid of steel braces and two canes—Roosevelt was a marvelous campaigner. He traveled back and forth across the country, radiating confidence and good humor even when directing his sharpest barbs at the Republicans. Like every great political leader, he took as much from the people as he gave them, understanding the causes of their confusion and sensing their needs. "I have looked into the faces of thousands of Americans," he told a friend. "They have the frightened look of lost children. . . . They are saying: 'We're caught in something we don't understand; perhaps this fellow can help us out.'"

Voters responded in a similar manner. "The people," one member of the Hoover administration noted, "seem to be lifting eager faces to Franklin Roosevelt, having the impression that he is talking intimately to them." But this man then added: "I am glad of his enthusiasm and buoyance but it cannot escape the sense that he really does not understand the full meaning of his own recitations."

Roosevelt soaked up information and ideas from a thousand sources—from professors like Raymond Moley and Rexford Tugwell of Columbia, from politicians like the Texan vice-presidential candidate, John N. Garner, from social workers, businessmen, and lawyers. To those seeking specific answers to the questions of the day, he was seldom satisfying. On such vital matters as farm

A vigorous-looking Franklin D. Roosevelt campaigning for the presidency in 1932. His vice-presidential running mate, John N. Garner, and the conveniently placed post allowed the handicapped candidate to stand when greeting voters along the way.

policy, the tariff, and government spending, he equivocated, contradicted himself, or remained silent.

Roosevelt called for a "re-appraisal of values," a "New Deal." Instead of adhering to conventional limits on the extent of federal power, the government should do whatever was necessary to protect the unfortunate and advance the public good. Lacking concrete answers, Roosevelt advocated a point of view rather than a plan: "The country needs bold, persistent experimentation. It is common sense to take a method and try it. If it fails, admit it frankly and try another. But above all, try something."

The popularity of this approach was demonstrated in November. Hoover, who had lost only eight states in 1928, won only six, all in the Northeast, in 1932. Roosevelt amassed 22.8 million votes to Hoover's 15.8 million and carried the Electoral College, 472 to 59.

During the interval between the election and Roosevelt's inauguration in March 1933, the Great Depression reached its lowest point. The holdover "lame duck" Congress, last of its kind, proved incapable of effective action.[2] President

---

[2]*The Twentieth Amendment (1933) provided for convening new Congresses in January instead of the following December. It also advanced the date of the president's inauguration from March 4 to January 20.*

Hoover, perhaps understandably, hesitated to institute changes without the cooperation of his successor. Roosevelt, for equally plausible reasons, refused to accept responsibility before assuming power officially. The nation, curiously apathetic in the face of so much suffering, drifted aimlessly, like a sailboat in a flat calm.

MILESTONES

1921–1922	Washington Conference tries to slow arms race
1923	President Harding dies; Coolidge becomes president
	Teapot Dome and other Harding scandals are exposed
1924	Dawes Plan restructures German reparations payments
	National Origins Act establishes immigration quotas
	Coolidge is elected president
1928	Fifteen nations sign Kellogg-Briand Pact to "outlaw" war
	Herbert Hoover is elected president
1929	New York Stock Exchange crash ends big bull market; Great Depression begins
	Young Plan further reduces German reparations
1930	Clark Memorandum renounces Roosevelt Corollary to Monroe Doctrine
	Hawley-Smoot tariff raises duties on foreign manufactures
	Ten-year Dust Bowl begins in South and Midwest
1931	Japan invades Manchuria
	Hoover imposes moratorium on war debts
1932	Federal troops disperse Bonus Marchers in Washington, D.C.
	Reconstruction Finance Corporation (RFC) lends to banks, railroads, insurance companies
	Franklin Delano Roosevelt is elected president
1933	Japan withdraws from League of Nations

27

---→ ✦ ←---

THE NEW DEAL:
1933–1941

As the date of Franklin Roosevelt's inauguration approached, the banking system completely disintegrated. Starting in the rural West and spreading to major cities like Detroit and Baltimore, a financial panic swept the land. Depositors lined up before the doors of even the soundest institutions, desperate to withdraw their savings. Hundreds of banks were forced to close. In February, to check the panic, the governor of Michigan declared a "bank holiday," shutting every bank in the state for eight days. Maryland, Kentucky, California, and a number of other states followed suit; by inauguration day four-fifths of the states had suspended all banking operations. Other issues loomed, especially war clouds over Europe and east Asia, but few Americans could look much beyond their own immediate, and increasingly dire, economic prospects.

THE HUNDRED DAYS

Something drastic had to be done. The most conservative business leaders were as ready for government intervention as the most advanced radicals. Partisanship, while not disappearing, was for once subordinated to broad national needs. A sign of this change came in February, even before Roosevelt took office, when Congress submitted to the states the Twenty-first Amendment, putting an end to prohibition. Before the end of the year the necessary three-quarters of the states had ratified it, and the prohibition era was over.

But it was unquestionably Franklin D. Roosevelt who provided the spark that reenergized the American people. His inaugural address reassured the

Well-wishers greet the president at Warm Springs, Georgia, in 1933. Franklin's "first-class temperament" compensated for his "second-class intellect," Justice Oliver Wendell Holmes famously observed.

country and at the same time stirred it to action. "The only thing we have to fear is fear itself. . . . This Nation asks for action, and action now. . . . I assume unhesitatingly the leadership of this great army of our people. . . ." Many such lines punctuated the brief address, which concluded with a stern pledge: "In the event that Congress shall fail . . . I shall not evade the clear course of duty that will then confront me. I shall ask the Congress for the one remaining instrument to meet the crisis—broad Executive power to wage a war against the emergency."

Roosevelt had the power and the will to act but no comprehensive plan of action. He and his eager congressional collaborators proceeded in a dozen directions at once, sometimes wisely, sometimes not, often at cross-purposes with themselves and one another. One of the first administration measures was the Economy Act, which reduced the salaries of federal employees by 15 percent and cut various veterans' benefits. Such belt-tightening measures could only make the Depression worse.

On March 5 Roosevelt declared a nationwide bank holiday and placed an embargo on the exportation of gold. To explain the complexities of the banking problem to the public, Roosevelt delivered the first of his "fireside chats" over a national radio network. "I want to talk for a few minutes with the people of the

United States about banking," he explained. His warmth and steadiness reassured millions. A plan for reopening the banks under Treasury Department licenses was devised, and soon most of them were functioning again, public confidence in their solvency restored. This solved the problem, but it also determined that banks would remain private institutions. Reform, not revolutionary change, had been decided upon at the very start of Roosevelt's presidency.

In April Roosevelt took the country off the gold standard, hoping thereby to cause prices to rise. Before the session ended, Congress established the Federal Deposit Insurance Corporation (FDIC) to guarantee bank deposits. It also forced the separation of investment banking and commercial banking concerns while extending the power of the Federal Reserve Board over both types of institutions, and it created the Home Owners Loan Corporation (HOLC) to refinance mortgages and prevent foreclosures.[1]

THE NATIONAL RECOVERY ADMINISTRATION (NRA)

Problems of unemployment and industrial stagnation had high priority during the Hundred Days. Congress appropriated $500 million for relief of the needy, and it created the Civilian Conservation Corps to provide jobs for men between the ages of 18 and 25 in reforestation and other conservation projects. To stimulate industry, Congress passed one of its most controversial measures, the National Industrial Recovery Act (NIRA). Besides establishing the Public Works Administration with authority to spend $3.3 billion, this law permitted manufacturers to draw up industrywide codes of "fair business practices." Under the law producers could agree to raise prices and limit production without violating the antitrust laws. The law gave workers the protection of minimum wage and maximum hours regulations and guaranteed them the right "to organize and bargain collectively through representatives of their own choosing," an immense stimulus to the union movement.

The act created a government agency, the National Recovery Administration (NRA), to supervise the drafting and operation of the business codes. Drafting posed difficult problems, first because each industry insisted on tailoring the agreements to its special needs and second because most manufacturers were unwilling to accept all the provisions of Section 7a of the law, which guaranteed workers the right to unionize and bargain collectively. While thousands of employers agreed to the pledge "We Do Our Part" in order to receive the Blue Eagle symbol of NRA, many were more interested in the monopolistic aspects of the act than in boosting wages and encouraging unionization. In practice, the largest manufacturers in each industry drew up the codes.

The effects of the NIRA were both more and less than the designers of the system had intended. In a sense it tried to accomplish the impossible—to change

---

[1]In 1934 this task was transferred to the new Securities and Exchange Commission, which was given broad authority over the activities of stock exchanges.

the very nature of business ethics and control the everyday activities of millions of individual enterprises. At the practical level, it did not end the Depression. There was a brief upturn in the spring of 1933, but the expected revival of industry did not take place; in nearly every case the dominant producers in each industry used their power to raise prices and limit production rather than to hire more workers and increase output.

Labor leaders used the NIRA to persuade workers that Roosevelt wanted them to join unions—which was something of an overstatement. In 1935, because the craft-oriented AFL had displayed little enthusiasm for enrolling unskilled workers on an industrywide basis, John L. Lewis, together with officials of the garment trade unions, formed the Committee for Industrial Organization (CIO) and set out to rally workers in each of these mass-production industries into one union without regard for craft lines. Since a union containing all the workers in a factory was easier to organize and direct than separate craft unions, this was a far more effective way of unionizing factory labor. The AFL expelled these unions, however, and in 1938 the CIO became the Congress of Industrial Organizations. Soon it rivaled the AFL in size and importance.

THE AGRICULTURAL ADJUSTMENT ADMINISTRATION (AAA)

Roosevelt was more concerned about the plight of the farmers than that of any other group because he believed that the nation was becoming overcommitted to industry. The Agricultural Adjustment Act of May 1933 combined compulsory restrictions on production with government subsidies to growers of wheat, cotton, tobacco, pork, and a few other staple crops. The money for these payments was raised by levying processing taxes on middlemen such as flour millers. The object was to lift agricultural prices to "parity" with industrial prices, the ratio in most cases being based on the levels of 1909–1914, when farmers had been reasonably prosperous. In return for withdrawing part of their land from cultivation, farmers received "rental" payments from the Agricultural Adjustment Administration (AAA).

Thereafter, limitation of acreage proved sufficient to raise some agricultural prices considerably. Tobacco growers benefited, and so did those who raised corn and hogs. The price of wheat also rose, though more because of bad harvests than because of the AAA program. But dairy farmers and cattlemen were hurt by the law, as were the railroads (which had less freight to haul) and, of course, consumers. Many farmers insisted that the NRA was raising the cost of manufactured goods more than the AAA was raising the prices they received for their crops. "While the farmer is losing his pants to his creditors," one Iowan complained, "NRA is rolling up his shirt. [Soon] we'll have a nudist colony."

A far more serious weakness of the program was its effect on tenant farmers and sharecroppers, many of whom lost their livelihoods when owners took land out of production to obtain AAA payments. In addition many landowners substituted machinery for labor. In the Cotton Belt farmers purchased more than

100,000 tractors during the 1930s. Each could do the work of several tenant or sharecropping families. Yet acreage restrictions and mortgage relief helped thousands of others. The law was a remarkable attempt to bring order to the chaotic agricultural economy. One New Deal official called it "the greatest single experiment in economic planning under capitalist conditions ever attempted by a democracy in times of peace." This was an overstatement. The AAA was a drastic change of American policy, but foreign producers of coffee, sugar, tea, rubber, and other staples had adopted the same techniques of restricting output and subsidizing growers well before the United States did.

THE TENNESSEE VALLEY AUTHORITY (TVA)

Another achievement of the Hundred Days was the creation of the Tennessee Valley Authority (TVA). During the Great War the government had constructed a hydroelectric plant at Muscle Shoals, Alabama, to provide power for factories manufacturing synthetic nitrate explosives. After 1920 farm groups and public power enthusiasts, led by Senator George W. Norris of Nebraska, had blocked administration plans to turn these facilities over to private capitalists, but their efforts to have the site operated by the government had been defeated by presidential vetoes.

Roosevelt wanted to make the Tennessee Valley area a broad experiment in social planning. Besides expanding the hydroelectric plants at Muscle Shoals and developing nitrate manufacturing in order to produce cheap fertilizers, he envisioned a coordinated program of soil conservation, reforestation, and industrialization.

Over the objections of private power companies, led by Wendell L. Willkie of the Commonwealth and Southern Corporation, Congress passed the TVA Act in May 1933. This law created a board authorized to build dams, power plants, and transmission lines and to sell fertilizers and electricity to individuals and local communities. The board could undertake flood control, soil conservation, and reforestation projects and improve the navigation of the river. Although the TVA never became the comprehensive regional planning organization some of its sponsors had anticipated, it improved the standard of living of millions of inhabitants of the valley. In addition to producing electricity and fertilizers and providing a "yardstick" whereby the efficiency—and thus the rates—of private power companies could be tested, it took on other functions ranging from the eradication of malaria to the development of recreational facilities.

THE UNEMPLOYED

At least 9 million persons were still without work in 1934 and hundreds of thousands of them were in real need. Malcolm Little, later famous as the radical black leader, Malcolm X, recalled:

The Tennessee Valley Authority
Although the Tennessee Valley Authority (TVA) never fully became the regional planning organization its sponsors had anticipated, the TVA nevertheless was able to expand the hydroelectric plants at Muscle Shoals, Alabama, and build dams, power plants, and transmission lines to service the surrounding area.

By 1934, we really began to suffer. This was about the worst depression year, and no one we knew had enough to eat or live on. . . . There was a bakery where, for a nickel, a couple of us children would buy a tall flour sack of day-old bread and cookies. . . . But there were times when there wasn't even a nickel and we would be so hungry we were dizzy. My mother would boil a big pot of dandelion greens and we would eat that.

Yet the Democrats confounded the political experts, including their own, by increasing their already large majorities in both houses of Congress in the 1934 elections. All the evidence indicates that most of the jobless continued to support the administration. Their loyalty can best be explained by Roosevelt's unemployment policies.

In May 1933 Congress had established the Federal Emergency Relief Administration (FERA) and given it $500 million to be dispensed through state relief organizations. Roosevelt appointed Harry L. Hopkins, an eccentric but brilliant and dedicated social worker, to direct the FERA. Hopkins insisted that the unemployed needed jobs, not handouts. In November he persuaded Roosevelt to create the Civil Works Administration (CWA) and swiftly put 4 million people to work building and repairing roads and public buildings, teaching, decorating the walls of post offices with murals, and utilizing their special skills in dozens of other ways.

The cost of this program frightened Roosevelt—Hopkins spent about $1 billion in less than five months—and he soon abolished the CWA. But an extensive public works program was continued throughout 1934 under the FERA. Despite charges that many of the projects were "boondoggles," thousands of roads, bridges, schools, and other structures were built or refurbished.

Unemployment and Federal Action, 1929–1941
Unemployment of non-farm workers reached nearly 40 percent by early 1933. The Federal Emergency Relief Act (FERA) of May 1933 was followed by the Civil Works Administration (CWA) later that year, and then by the Works Progress Administration (WPA) in April 1935.

In May 1935 Roosevelt put Hopkins in charge of the Works Progress Administration (WPA). By the time this agency was disbanded in 1943 it had found employment for 8.5 million people. Besides building public works, the WPA made important cultural contributions. It developed the Federal Theatre Project, which put actors, directors, and stagehands to work; the Federal Writers' Project, which turned out valuable guidebooks, collected local lore, and published about 1000 books and pamphlets; and the Federal Art Project, which employed painters and sculptors. In addition, the National Youth Administration created part-time jobs for more than 2 million high school and college students.

At no time during the New Deal years did unemployment fall below 10 percent of the workforce, and in some places it was much higher. Unemployment in Boston, for instance, ranged between 20 and 30 percent throughout the 1930s. WPA did not go far enough, chiefly because Roosevelt could not escape his fear of drastically unbalancing the budget. Halfway measures did not stimulate the economy. The president also hesitated to undertake projects that might compete with private enterprises. Yet his caution did him no good politically; the business interests he sought to placate were becoming increasingly hostile to the New Deal.

LITERATURE IN THE DEPRESSION

Some American novelists found Soviet communism attractive and wrote "proletarian" novels in which ordinary workers were the heroes, and stylistic niceties gave way to the rough language of the street and the factory. Most of these books are of little artistic merit, and none achieved great commercial success. The best of the Depression writers avoided the party line, although they were critical of many aspects of American life. One was John Dos Passos, author of the trilogy *U.S.A.* (1930–1936).

Dos Passos came from a well-to-do family of Portuguese descent. He was educated at Harvard and drove an ambulance in France during the Great War. *U.S.A.* was a massive, intricately constructed work with an anticapitalist and deeply pessimistic point of view. Throughout the narrative Dos Passos scattered capsule sketches of famous people, ranging from Andrew Carnegie and William Jennings Bryan to the movie idol Rudolph Valentino and the architect Frank Lloyd Wright. Dos Passos's method was relentless, cold, and methodical—utterly realistic. He displayed no sympathy for his characters or their world. *U.S.A.* was a monument to the despair and anger of liberals confronted with the Depression. After the Depression, however, Dos Passos rapidly abandoned his radical views.

The novel that best portrayed the desperate plight of the millions impoverished by the Depression was John Steinbeck's *The Grapes of Wrath* (1939), which described the fate of the Joads, an Oklahoma farm family driven by drought and bad times to abandon their land and become migratory laborers in California. Steinbeck captured the patient bewilderment of the downtrodden, the brutality bred of fear that characterized their exploiters, and the furious resentments of the radicals of the 1930s. He depicted the parching blackness of the Oklahoma dust bowl, the grandeur of California, the backbreaking toil of the migrant fruit pickers, and the ultimate indignation of a people repeatedly degraded. "In the eyes of the hungry there is a growing wrath. In the souls of the people the grapes of wrath are filling and growing heavy, growing heavy for the vintage."

William Faulkner, among the finest of modern American novelists, responded to the era in still another way. Born in 1897, within a year of Fitzgerald and Hemingway, like Wolfe he attained literary maturity only in the 1930s. After service in the Canadian air force in the Great War, he returned to his native Mississippi, working at a series of odd jobs and publishing relatively inconsequential poetry and fiction. Suddenly, between 1929 and 1932, he burst into prominence with four major novels: *The Sound and the Fury, As I Lay Dying, Sanctuary,* and *Light in August.*

Faulkner created a local world, Yoknapatawpha County, and peopled it with some of the most remarkable characters in American fiction—the Sartoris family, typical of the old southern aristocracy worn down at the heels; the Snopes clan, shrewd, unscrupulous, boorish representatives of the new day; and many others. He pictured vividly the South's poverty and its pride, its dreadful racial problem, the guilt and obscure passions plaguing white and black alike. No contemporary excelled him as a commentator on the multiple dilemmas of modern life. His characters are possessed, driven to pursue high ideals yet weighted down with awareness of their inadequacies and their sinfulness.

THREE EXTREMISTS: LONG, COUGHLIN, AND TOWNSEND

Roosevelt's moderation and the desperation of the poor roused extremists both on the left and on the right. The most formidable was Louisiana's Senator Huey Long, the "Kingfish." Raised on a farm in northern Louisiana, Long was succes-

Although Louisiana Senator Huey Long supported FDR in 1932, "the Kingfish" had changed his mind two years later, when this picture was taken. He opposed Roosevelt's large government bureaucracies, such as the National Recovery Administration (NRA), and sought more aggressive income redistribution. Also, he wanted to be president.

sively a traveling salesman, a lawyer, state railroad commissioner, governor, and, after 1930, United States senator. By 1933 his rule in Louisiana was absolute. Long was certainly a demagogue—yet the plight of all poor people concerned him deeply. More important, he tried to do something about it.

As a reformer, Long stood in the populist tradition; he hated bankers and "the interests." He believed that poor people, regardless of color, should have a chance to earn a decent living and get an education. His arguments were simplistic, patronizing, possibly insincere, but effective. "Don't say I'm working for niggers," he told one northern journalist. "I'm for the poor man—all poor men. Black and white, they all gotta have a chance. . . . 'Every Man a King'—that's my slogan."

By 1935 Long's "Share Our Wealth" movement had a membership of over 4.6 million. His program called for the confiscation of family fortunes of more than $5 million and a tax of 100 percent on incomes over $1 million a year, the money to be used to buy every family a "homestead" (a house, a car, and other necessities) and provide an annual family income of $2000 to $3000, plus old-age pensions, educational benefits, and veterans' pensions. As the 1936 election approached, he planned to organize a third party to split the liberal vote. He assumed that the Republicans would win the election and so botch the job of fighting the Depression that he could sweep the country in 1940.

Less powerful than Long but more widely influential was Father Charles E. Coughlin, the "Radio Priest." A genial Canadian of Irish lineage, Coughlin in

Father Charles Coughlin, the "Radio Priest," whose weekly program reached 30 to 45 million listeners nationwide, photographed in Detroit as he promoted his National Union for Social Justice.

1926 began broadcasting a weekly religious message over station WJR in Detroit. His mellifluous voice and orotund rhetoric attracted a huge national audience, and the Depression gave him a secular cause. In 1933 he had been an eager New Dealer, but his dislike of New Deal financial policies—he believed that inflating the currency would end the Depression—and his need for ever more sensational ideas to hold his radio audience led him to turn against the New Deal. By 1935 he was calling Roosevelt a "great betrayer and liar."

Another rapidly growing movement alarmed the Democrats in 1934–1935: Dr. Francis E. Townsend's campaign for "old-age revolving pensions." Townsend, a retired California physician, colorless and low-keyed, had an oversimplified and therefore appealing "solution" to the nation's troubles. The pitiful state of thousands of elderly persons, whose job prospects were even dimmer than those of the mass of the unemployed, he found shocking. He advocated paying every person aged 60 years and over a pension of $200 a month, the only conditions being that the pensioners not hold jobs and that they spend the entire sum within 30 days. Their purchases, he argued, would stimulate production, thereby creating new jobs and revitalizing the economy. A stiff transactions tax, collected whenever any commodity changed hands, would pay for the program.

Economists quickly pointed out that with about 10 million persons eligible for the Townsend pensions, the cost would amount to $24 billion a year—roughly half the national income. But among the elderly the scheme proved extremely popular. Townsend Clubs, their proceedings conducted in the spirit of revivalist camp meetings, flourished everywhere, and the *Townsend National Weekly* reached a circulation of over 200,000. Although most Townsendites were anything but radical politically, their plan, like Long's Share Our Wealth scheme, would have revolutionized the distribution of wealth in the country. The movement marked the emergence of a new force in American society. With medical advances lengthening the average life span, the percentage of old people in the population was rising. The breakdown of close family ties in an increasingly mobile society now caused many of these citizens to be cast adrift to live out their last years poor, sick, idle, and alone.

With the possible exception of Long, the extremists had little understanding of practical affairs. (It could be said that Townsend knew what to do with money but not how to get it, and Coughlin knew how to get money but not what to do with it.) Collectively they represented a threat to Roosevelt; their success helped to make the president see that he must move boldly to restore good times or face serious political trouble in 1936.

Political imperatives had much to do with Roosevelt's decisions, and the influence of Supreme Court Justice Louis Brandeis and his disciples, notably Felix Frankfurter, was great. They urged Roosevelt to abandon his probusiness programs, especially the NRA, and stress restoring competition and taxing corporations more heavily. The fact that most businessmen were turning away from him encouraged the president to accept this advice; so did the Supreme Court's decision in *Schechter* v. *United States* (May 1935), which declared the National Industrial Recovery Act unconstitutional. (The case involved the provisions of the NRA Live Poultry Code; the Court voided the act on the grounds that Congress had delegated too much legislative power to the code authorities and that the defendants, four brothers engaged in slaughtering chickens in New York City, were not engaged in interstate commerce.)

THE SECOND NEW DEAL

Existing laws had failed to end the Depression. Conservatives roundly denounced Roosevelt, and extremists were luring away some of his supporters. Voters, heartened by the partial success of early New Deal measures, were clamoring for further reforms. But the Supreme Court had declared many key New Deal measures unconstitutional. For these many reasons, Roosevelt, in June 1935, launched what historians call the Second New Deal.

There followed the "Second Hundred Days," one of the most productive periods in the history of American legislation. The National Labor Relations Act—commonly known as the Wagner Act—restored the labor guarantees wiped out by the *Schecter* decision. It gave workers the right to bargain collectively and prohibited employers from interfering with union organizational activities in their factories. A National Labor Relations Board (NLRB) was established to supervise plant elections and designate successful unions as official bargaining agents when a majority of the workers approved. It was difficult to force some big corporations to bargain "in good faith," as the law required, but the NLRB could conduct investigations of employer practices and issue cease and desist orders when "unfair" activities came to light.

The Social Security Act of August 1935 set up a system of old-age insurance, financed partly by a tax on wages (paid by workers) and partly by a tax on payrolls (paid by employers). It created a state-federal system of unemployment insurance, similarly financed. Liberal critics considered this social security system

A vigorous Roosevelt has lassoed the Supreme Court, which now must gallop in tandem with his (second) New Deal. Roosevelt's image, even among critics, is that of a powerful leader; all but forgotten is the fact that Roosevelt's legs had atrophied from polio.

inadequate because it did not cover agricultural workers, domestics, self-employed persons, and some other groups particularly in need of its benefits. Health insurance was not included, and because the size of pensions depended on the amount earned, the lowest-paid workers could not count on much support after reaching 65. Yet the law was of major significance. Over the years the pension payments were increased and the classes of workers covered expanded. (The system, though substantially modified, remains in place today.)

The Rural Electrification Administration (REA), created by executive order, also began to function during this remarkable period. The REA lent money at low interest rates to utility companies and to farmer cooperatives interested in bringing electricity to rural areas. When the REA went into operation, only one farm in ten had electricity; by 1950 only one in ten did not.

Another important measure was the Wealth Tax Act of August 1935, which, while not the "soak the rich" measure both its supporters and its opponents claimed, raised taxes on large incomes considerably. Estate and gift taxes were also increased. Stiffer taxes on corporate profits reflected the Brandeis group's desire to penalize corporate giantism. Much of the opposition to other New Deal legislation arose from the fact that after these changes in the tax laws were made, the well-to-do had to bear a larger share of the cost of *all* government activities.

Whether the Second New Deal was more radical than the first depends largely on the vantage point from which it is considered. Measures like the Social Security Act had greater long-range effect on American life than the legislation of the First Hundred Days but were fundamentally less revolutionary than laws like the National Industrial Recovery Act and the Agricultural Adjustment Act, which attempted to establish a planned economy.

Herbert Hoover epitomized the attitude of conservatives when he called the New Deal "the most stupendous invasion of the whole spirit of Liberty that the nation has witnessed." Undoubtedly many opponents of the New Deal sincerely believed that it was undermining the foundations of American freedom. The cost of the New Deal also alarmed them. By 1936 some members of the administration had fallen under the influence of the British economist John Maynard Keynes, who argued that the world Depression could be conquered if governments would deliberately unbalance their budgets by reducing interest rates and taxes and by increasing expenditures to stimulate consumption and investment.

Roosevelt never accepted Keynes's theories; he conferred with the economist in 1934 but could not grasp the "rigmarole of figures" with which Keynes deluged him. Nevertheless the imperatives of the Depression forced him to spend more than the government was collecting in taxes; thus he adopted in part the Keynesian approach. Conservative businessmen considered him financially irresponsible, and the fact that deficit spending seemed to be good politics made them seethe with rage.

THE ELECTION OF 1936

The election of 1936 loomed as a showdown. "America is in peril," the Republican platform declared. The GOP candidate, Governor Alfred M. Landon of Kansas, was a former follower of Theodore Roosevelt, a foe of the Ku Klux Klan in the 1920s, and a believer in government regulation of business. But he was a poor speaker, colorless, and handicapped by the reactionary views of many of his backers. Against the charm and political astuteness of Roosevelt, Landon's arguments—chiefly that he could administer the government more efficiently than the president—made little impression. He won the support of some anti–New Deal Democrats, among them two former presidential candidates, Al Smith and John W. Davis, but this was not enough.

The radical fringe put a third candidate in the field, Congressman William Lemke of North Dakota, who ran on the Union party ticket. Father Coughlin, denouncing Roosevelt as the "dumbest man ever to occupy the White House," rallied his National Union for Social Justice behind Lemke; Dr. Townsend also supported him. However, the extremists were losing ground by 1936. Huey Long had fallen victim to an assassin in September 1935, and his organization was taken over by a blatantly demagogic rightist, Gerald L. K. Smith.

On election day the country gave the president a tremendous vote of confidence. He carried every state but Maine and Vermont. The Republicans elected only 89 members of the House of Representatives and their strength in the Senate fell to 16, an all-time low. In dozens of city and state elections, Democratic candidates also made large gains. Both Roosevelt's personality and his program had captivated the land. He seemed irresistible, the most powerfully entrenched president in the history of the United States.

Roosevelt did not win in 1936 because of the inadequacies of his foes. Having abandoned his efforts to hold the businessmen, whom he now denounced as "economic royalists," he appealed for the votes of workers and the underprivileged. The new labor unions gratefully poured thousands of dollars into the campaign to reelect him. Black voters switched to the Democrats in record numbers. Farmers liked Roosevelt because of his evident concern for their welfare. Countless elderly persons backed Roosevelt out of gratitude for the Social Security Act. Homeowners were grateful for his program guaranteeing mortgages—eventually about 20 percent of all urban private dwellings were refinanced by the Home Owners Loan Corporation—and for the Federal Housing Administration, which, beginning in 1934, made available low-cost, long-term loans for modernizing old buildings and constructing new ones.

ROOSEVELT TRIES TO UNDERMINE THE SUPREME COURT

On January 20, in his second inaugural address, Roosevelt spoke of the plight of millions of citizens "denied the greater part of what the very lowest standards of today call the necessities of life." A third of the nation, he added without exaggeration, was "ill-housed, ill-clad, ill-nourished." He interpreted his landslide victory as a mandate for further reforms, and with his prestige and his immense congressional majorities, nothing appeared to stand in his way. Nothing, that is, except the Supreme Court.

Throughout Roosevelt's first term the Court had stood almost immovable against increasing the scope of federal authority and broadening the general power of government, state as well as national, to cope with the exigencies of the Depression. Moreover, much of the early New Deal legislation, pushed through Congress at top speed during the Hundred Days, had been drafted without proper regard for the Constitution. Even liberal justices considered the National Industrial Recovery Act unconstitutional (the *Schecter* decision was unanimous).

The reactionaries on the Court seemed governed by no consistent constitutional philosophy; they tended to limit the police power of the states when wages-and-hours laws came before them and to interpret it broadly when state laws restricting civil liberties were under consideration. In 1937 all the major measures of the Second Hundred Days appeared doomed. The Wagner Act had little chance of winning approval, experts predicted. Lawyers were advising employers to ignore the Social Security Act, so confident were they that the Court would declare it unconstitutional.

Faced with this situation, Roosevelt decided to ask Congress to shift the balance on the Court by increasing the number of justices, thinly disguising the purpose of his plan by making it part of a general reorganization of the judiciary. A member of the Court who reached the age of 70 would have the option of retiring at full pay. Should such a justice choose not to retire, the president was to appoint an additional justice, up to a maximum of six, to ease the burden of work for the aged jurists who remained on the bench.

Although polls showed the public fairly evenly divided on the "Court-packing" bill, the opposition was vocal and influential. To the expected denunciations of conservatives were added the complaints of liberals fearful that the principle of court packing might in the future be used to subvert civil liberties. What, Senator Norris asked, would have been the reaction if a man like Harding had proposed such a measure? Opposition in Congress was immediate and intense; many who had cheerfully supported every New Deal bill came out against the plan. The press denounced it, and so did most local bar associations.

For months Roosevelt stubbornly refused to concede defeat, but in July 1937, he had to yield. Minor administrative reforms of the judiciary were enacted, but the size of the Court remained unchanged.

The struggle did result in saving the legislation of the Second New Deal. Alarmed by the threat to the Court, a majority of the justices upheld key New Deal measures, such as the minimum wage, the Wagner Act, and the Social Security Act.

THE NEW DEAL WINDS DOWN

The Court fight marked the beginning of the end of the New Deal. Social and economic developments contributed to its decline, and the final blow originated in the area of foreign affairs. With unemployment high, wages low, and workers relatively powerless against their employers, most Americans had liked New Deal labor legislation and sympathized with the industrial unions whose growth it stimulated. The NRA, the Wagner Act, and the CIO's organization of industries like steel and automobiles changed the power structure within the economy. What amounted to a revolution in the lives of wage earners had occurred. Aside from the obvious changes—higher wages, shorter hours, paid vacations, insurance of various kinds—unionization had meant fair methods of settling disputes about work practices and a measure of job security based on seniority for tens of thousands of workers. The CIO in particular had done much to increase the influence of labor in politics and to bring blacks and other minorities into the labor movement.

In 1937 a series of "sit-down strikes" broke out, beginning at the General Motors plant in Flint, Michigan. Striking workers barricaded themselves inside the factories; when police and strikebreakers tried to dislodge them, they drove them off with barrages of soda bottles, tools, spare parts, and crockery. The tolerant attitude of the Roosevelt administration ensured the strikers against government intervention. "It is illegal," Roosevelt said of the General Motors strike, "but shooting it out . . . [is not] the answer. . . . Why can't those fellows in General Motors meet with the committee of workers?" Fearful that all-out efforts to clear their plants would result in the destruction of expensive machinery,

DEBATING THE PAST

Did the New Deal succeed? A swimming pool such as this one in Carbon Hill, Alabama, built with federal "New Deal" funds, can be found in many cities and in most towns and villages in the United States. The New Deal visibly changed the nation; but did it succeed?

Few issues have been more controversial. At the time and for decades afterward conservative historians such as Edgar E. Robinson (1955) denounced the New Deal as an economic failure that infringed on individual rights. Most liberals—foremost among them Arthur M. Schlesinger, Jr. (1957–1960)—acknowledged that the New Deal did not end the Depression but it did restrain corporations and address the needs of most workers, farmers, and consumers. That such people benefited from its actions was proven by how many of them voted for FDR, time and again.

William Leuchtenburg (1963) approved of much of the New Deal, but claimed that it left share croppers, slum dwellers, and most blacks "outside of the new equilibrium." It was but a "halfway revolution." A few years later Barton Bernstein (1968) led the far left in a blistering attack: "The New Deal failed to solve the problem of depression, it failed to raise the impoverished, it failed to redistribute income, it failed to extend equality and generally countenanced racial discrimination and segregation." The New Deal, in short, was no revolution at all.

In subsequent decades historians were more inclined to assess the New Deal in light of what was possible at the time. David Kennedy (1999), while acknowledging the New Deal's many failures, was struck by the "the boldness of its vision." Its achievements were as tangible as the city halls and high schools it had built, the people it had put to work, and the democratic nation it had preserved in time of crisis.

Edgar E. Robinson, *The Roosevelt Leadership* (1955), Arthur M. Schlesinger, Jr., *The Age of Roosevelt*, 3 volumes (1957–1960), William Leuchtenburg, *Franklin D. Roosevelt and the New Deal, 1932–1940* (1963), Barton Bernskin, *Toward a New Past* (1968), David M. Kennedy, *Freedom from Fear* (1999).

most employers capitulated to the workers' demands. All the automobile manufacturers but Henry Ford quickly came to terms with the United Automobile Workers.

The major steel companies, led by U.S. Steel, recognized the CIO and granted higher wages and a 40-hour week. The auto and steel unions alone boasted more than 725,000 members by late 1937; other CIO units conquered the rubber industry, the electrical industry, the textile industry, and many more.

While the sit-down strikes and the Court fight were going on, the New Deal suffered another heavy blow. Business conditions had been gradually improving since 1933. Heartened by the trend, Roosevelt, who had never fully grasped the importance of government spending in stimulating recovery, cut back sharply on the relief program in June 1937, with disastrous results. Between August and October the economy slipped downward like sand through a chute. Stock prices plummeted; unemployment rose by 2 million; industrial production slumped. This "Roosevelt recession" further damaged the president's reputation, and for many months he aggravated the situation by adopting an almost Hoover-like attitude. "Everything will work out all right if we just sit tight and keep quiet," he actually said.

While the president hesitated, rival theorists within his administration warred. The Keynesians clamored for stepped-up government spending. The conservatives, led by Treasury Secretary Henry Morgenthau, Jr., advocated retrenchment. Perhaps confused by the conflict, Roosevelt seemed incapable of decisive action. When Keynes offered him "some bird's eye impressions" of the recession in February 1938, urging "large scale recourse to . . . public works and other investments aided by Government funds," Roosevelt sent him only a routine acknowledgment drafted by Morgenthau.

In April 1938 Roosevelt finally committed himself to heavy deficit spending. At his urging Congress passed a $3.75 billion public works bill. Two major pieces of legislation were also enacted at about this time. A new AAA program (February 1938) set marketing quotas and acreage limitations for growers of staples like wheat, cotton, and tobacco and authorized the Commodity Credit Corporation to lend money to farmers on their surplus crops.

The second measure, the Fair Labor Standards Act, abolished child labor and established a national minimum wage of 40 cents an hour and a maximum workweek of 40 hours, with time and a half for overtime. Although the law failed to cover many of the poorest-paid types of labor, its passage meant wage increases for 750,000 workers. In later years many more classes of workers were brought within its protection, and the minimum wage was repeatedly increased.

These measures further alienated conservatives without dramatically improving economic conditions. The resistance of many Democratic members of Congress to additional economic and social "experiments" hardened. As the 1938 elections approached, Roosevelt decided to go to the voters in an effort to strengthen party discipline and reenergize the New Deal. He singled out a number of conservative Democratic senators, notably Walter F. George of Georgia,

Millard F. Tydings of Maryland, and "Cotton Ed" Smith of South Carolina, and tried to "purge" them by backing other Democrats in the primaries.

The purge failed. Southern voters liked Roosevelt but resented his interference in local politics. In the nation at large, the Republicans made important gains for the first time since Roosevelt had taken office. The Democrats maintained nominal control of both houses of Congress, but the conservative coalition, while unable to muster the votes necessary to do away with accomplished reforms, succeeded in blocking additional legislation.

SIGNIFICANCE OF THE NEW DEAL

After World War II broke out in 1939, the Great Depression was swept away on a wave of orders from the beleaguered European democracies. For this prosperity, Roosevelt received much undeserved credit. His New Deal had not returned the country to full employment. Despite the aid given to the jobless, the generation of workers born between 1900 and 1910 who entered the 1930s as unskilled laborers had their careers permanently stunted by the Depression. Far fewer rose to middle-class status than at any time since the 1830s and 1840s.

Roosevelt's fondness for establishing new agencies to deal with specific problems vastly increased the federal bureaucracy, indirectly added to the influence of lobbyists, and made it more difficult to monitor government activities. His cavalier attitude toward constitutional limitations on executive power, which he justified as being necessary in a national emergency, set in motion trends that so increased the prestige and authority of the presidency that the balance among the executive, legislative, and judicial branches was threatened.

Yet these are criticisms after the fact; they ignore what one historian has called the "sense of urgency and haste" that made the New Deal "a mixture of accomplishment, frustration, and misdirected effort." On balance, the New Deal had a constructive impact. By 1939 the country was committed to the idea that the federal government should accept responsibility for the national welfare and act to meet specific problems in every necessary way. What was most significant was not the proliferation of new agencies or the expansion of federal power. These were continuations of trends already a century old when the New Deal began. The importance of the "Roosevelt revolution" was that it removed the issue from politics. "Never again," the Republican presidential candidate was to say in 1952, "shall we allow a depression in the United States."

Because of New Deal decisions, many formerly unregulated areas of American life became subject to federal authority: the stock exchange, agricultural prices and production, labor relations, old-age pensions, relief of the needy. If the New Deal failed to end the Depression, it effected changes that have—so far, at least—prevented later economic declines from becoming catastrophes. By encouraging the growth of unions, the New Deal probably helped workers obtain a larger share of the profits of industry. By putting a floor under the income of many farmers, it checked the decline of agricultural living standards, though

The proliferation of federal agencies during the New Deal inspired cartoonists. In this example, Swift's Gulliver—the United States—is tied down by the Lilliputian Brain Trusters.

not that of the agricultural population. The social security program, with all its inadequacies, lessened the impact of bad times on an increasingly large proportion of the population and provided immense psychological benefits to all.

WOMEN AS NEW DEALERS: THE NETWORK

Largely because of the influence of Eleanor Roosevelt and Molly Dewson, head of the Women's Division of the Democratic National Committee, the Roosevelt administration employed far more women in positions of importance than any earlier one. Secretary of Labor Frances Perkins, the first woman appointed to a Cabinet post, had been active in labor relations for more than 20 years, as secretary of the Consumers' League during the progressive period, as a factory inspector immediately after the war, and as chair of the New York State Industrial Commission. As secretary of labor she helped draft New Deal labor legislation and kept Roosevelt informed on various labor problems outside the government.

Eleanor Roosevelt dispensing soup to the needy. As a wealthy young socialite, she exhibited little interest in public matters. But after Eleanor discovered that Franklin was having an affair with her own social secretary, Lucy Mercer, Eleanor began to change. Her marriage, she confided to a friend, ceased to have any "fundamental love to draw on." Liberated and energized, she threw herself into social and political reform.

Through her newspaper column "My Day" and as a speaker on public issues, Eleanor Roosevelt became a major political force, especially in the area of civil rights, where the administration needed constant prodding.

She particularly identified with efforts to obtain better treatment for blacks, in and out of government. Her best-known action occurred in 1939 after the Daughters of the American Revolution (DAR) refused to permit the use of their Washington auditorium for a concert by the black contralto Marian Anderson. Eleanor Roosevelt resigned from the DAR in protest, and after the President arranged for Anderson to sing at the Lincoln Memorial, she persuaded a small army of dignitaries to sponsor the concert. An interracial crowd of 75,000 people attended the performance. The *Chicago Defender,* an influential black newspaper, noted that the First Lady "stood like the Rock of Gibraltar against pernicious encroachments on the rights of minorities." (A disgruntled white Southerner made the same point differently: "She goes round telling the Negroes they are as good as anyone else.")

BLACKS DURING THE NEW DEAL

The shift of black voters from the Republican to the Democratic party during the New Deal years was one of the most significant political turnarounds in American history. In 1932 when things were at their worst, fewer African Americans defected from the Republican party than the members of any other traditionally Republican group. Four years later, however, blacks voted for Roosevelt in overwhelming numbers.

Black sharecroppers evicted from their tenant farms were photographed by Arthur Rothstein along a Missouri road in 1939. Rothstein was one of a group of outstanding photographers who created a unique "sociological and economic survey" of the nation between 1936 and 1942 under the aegis of the Farm Security Administration.

Blacks supported the New Deal for the same reasons that whites did, but how the New Deal affected blacks in general and racial attitudes specifically are more complicated questions. Claiming that he dared not antagonize southern congressmen, whose votes he needed for his recovery programs, Roosevelt did nothing about civil rights before 1941 and relatively little thereafter. For the same reason, many southern white liberals hesitated to support racial integration for fear that other liberal causes could be injured as a result.

Many of the early New Deal programs treated blacks as second-class citizens. Blacks were often paid at lower rates than whites under NRA codes (and so joked that NRA stood for "Negro Run Around" and "Negroes Ruined Again"). The early farm programs shortchanged black tenants and sharecroppers. Blacks in the Civilian Conservation Corps were assigned to all-black camps. TVA developments were rigidly segregated, and almost no blacks got jobs in TVA offices. New Deal urban housing projects inadvertently but nonetheless effectively increased the concentration of blacks in particular neighborhoods. Because the Social Security Act excluded agricultural laborers and domestic servants, it did nothing for hundreds of thousands of poor black workers or for Mexican American farmhands in the Southwest. In 1939 unemployment was twice as high among blacks as among whites, and whites' wages were double the level of blacks' wages.

In the labor movement the new CIO unions accepted black members, a particularly significant move because these unions were organizing industries—steel, automobiles, and mining among others—that employed large numbers of blacks. Thus, while black Americans suffered horribly during the Depression, New Deal efforts to counteract its effects brought them some relief and a measure of hope. And this became increasingly true with the passage of time. During Roosevelt's second term, blacks found far less to criticize than had been the case earlier.

A NEW DEAL FOR INDIANS

New Deal policy toward American Indians built on earlier trends but carried them further. During the Harding and Coolidge administrations more Indian land had passed into the hands of whites, and agents of the Bureau of Indian Affairs had tried to suppress elements of Indian culture they considered "pagan" or "lascivious." In 1924 Congress finally granted citizenship to all Indians, but most whites still generally believed that Indians should be treated as wards of the state.

Government policy took a new direction in 1933 when President Roosevelt named John Collier commissioner of Indian affairs. When he was appointed commissioner, the Depression had reduced perhaps a third of all Indians living on reservations to penury.

Collier favored a pluralistic approach, seeking to help the Indians preserve their ancient cultures but also (somewhat contradictorily) to help them earn more money and make use of modern medical advances and modern techniques of soil conservation. He was particularly eager to encourage the revival of tribal governments that could represent the Indians in dealings with the U.S. government.

In part because of Collier's urging, Congress passed the Indian Reorganization Act of 1934. This law did away with the Dawes Act allotment system and enabled Indians to establish tribal governments with powers like those of cities, and it encouraged Indians to return individually owned lands to tribal control. About 4 million of the 90 million acres of land lost under the allotment system were returned to the tribes.

New Deal Indian policy was controversial—among Indians as well as among many white groups. Some critics charged Collier with trying to turn back the clock. Others attacked him as a segregationist and claimed that he was trying to restore "pagan" religious practices and convert the Indians to communism.

Collier resigned in 1945, and in the 1950s Congress "terminated" most government efforts aimed at preserving Indian cultures. Nevertheless, like so many of its programs, the New Deal's Indian policy was a bold effort to deal constructively with a long-standing national problem.

THE ROLE OF ROOSEVELT

How much of the credit for New Deal policies belongs personally to Franklin D. Roosevelt is debatable. He had little to do with many of the details and some of the broad principles behind the New Deal. His knowledge of economics was skimpy, his understanding of many social problems superficial, his political philosophy distressingly vague. The British leader Anthony Eden described him as "a conjurer, skillfully juggling with balls of dynamite, whose nature he failed to understand."

Nevertheless, every aspect of the New Deal bears the brand of Roosevelt's remarkable personality. Rexford Tugwell has left one of the best-balanced judgments of the president. "Roosevelt was not really very much at home with ideas," Tugwell explained. But he was always open to new facts, and something within him "forbade inaction when there was something to be done." Roosevelt constructed the coalition that made the program possible; his humanitarianism made it a reform movement of major significance. Although considered by many a terrible administrator because he encouraged rivalry among his subordinates, assigned different agencies overlapping responsibilities, failed to discharge many incompetents, and frequently put off making difficult decisions, he was in fact one of the most effective chief executives in the nation's history. His seemingly haphazard practice of dividing authority among competing administrators unleashed the energies and sparked the imaginations of his aides.

Like Andrew Jackson, Roosevelt maximized his role as leader of all the people. His informal biweekly press conferences kept the public in touch with developments and himself in tune with popular thinking. His "fireside chats" convinced millions that he was personally interested in each citizen's life and welfare, as in a way he was. At a time when the size and complexity of the government made it impossible for any one person to direct the nation's destiny, Roosevelt managed the minor miracle of personifying that government to 130 million people. Under Hoover, a single clerk was able to handle the routine mail that flowed into the office of the president from ordinary citizens. Under Roosevelt, the task required a staff of 50.

While the New Deal was still evolving, contemporaries recognized Roosevelt's right to a place beside Washington, Jefferson, and Lincoln among the great presidents. Yet as his second term drew toward its close, some of his most important work still lay in the future.

THE TRIUMPH OF ISOLATIONISM

The danger of another world war mounted steadily as Germany, Italy, and Japan repeatedly resorted to force to achieve their expansionist aims. In March 1935 Adolf Hitler instituted universal military training and denounced the settlement at Versailles. In May Benito Mussolini massed troops in Italian Somaliland in Africa, using a trivial border clash as a pretext for threatening the ancient kingdom of Ethiopia.

Congress responded by passing the Neutrality Act of 1935, which forbade the sale of munitions to all belligerents whenever the president should proclaim that a state of war existed. Americans who took passage on belligerent ships after such a proclamation had been issued would do so at their own risk. Roosevelt would have preferred a discretionary embargo or no new legislation at all, but he dared not rouse the ire of the isolationists by vetoing the bill.

In October 1935 Italy invaded Ethiopia and Roosevelt invoked the new neutrality law. Secretary of State Cordell Hull asked American exporters to support a "moral embargo" on the sale of oil and other products not covered by the act. His plea was ignored; oil shipments to Italy tripled between October and January. Italy quickly overran and annexed Ethiopia. In February 1936 Congress passed a second neutrality act forbidding all loans to belligerents.

Then, in the summer of 1936, civil war broke out in Spain. The rebels, led by the reactionary General Francisco Franco and strongly backed by Italy and Germany, sought to overthrow the somewhat leftist Spanish Republic. Here, clearly, was a clash between democracy and fascism, and the neutrality laws did not apply to civil wars. However, Roosevelt now became more fearful of involvement than some isolationists. The president believed that American interference might cause the conflict in Spain to become a global war, and he was wary of antagonizing the substantial number of American Catholics who were sympathetic to the Franco regime. At his urging Congress passed another neutrality act broadening the arms embargo to cover civil wars.

Isolationism now reached its peak. A public opinion poll revealed in March 1937 that 94 percent of the people thought American policy should be directed at keeping out of all foreign wars rather than trying to prevent wars from breaking out. In April Congress passed still another neutrality law. It continued the embargo on munitions and loans, forbade Americans to travel on belligerent ships, and gave the president discretionary authority to place the sale of other goods to belligerents on a cash-and-carry basis. This played into the hands of the aggressors. While German planes and cannons were turning the tide in Spain, the United States was denying the hard-pressed Spanish loyalists even a case of cartridges.

In January 1938, the House narrowly defeated the Ludlow amendment, which would have prohibited Congress from declaring war without the prior approval of the nation's voters.

"With every surrender the prospects of a European war grow darker," Claude G. Bowers, the American ambassador to Spain, warned. The *New York Herald Tribune* pointed out that the neutrality legislation was literally reactionary—designed to keep the United States out of the war of 1914–1918, not the conflict looming on the horizon. President Roosevelt, in part because of domestic problems such as the Supreme Court packing struggle and the wave of sit-down strikes, and in part because of his own vacillation, seemed to have lost control over the formulation of American foreign policy. The American people, like wild creatures before a forest fire, were rushing in blind panic from the conflagration.

WAR AGAIN IN EUROPE

There were limits beyond which Americans would not go. In July 1937 the Japanese resumed their conquest of China, pressing ahead on a broad front. Roosevelt believed that invoking the neutrality law would only help the well-armed Japanese. Taking advantage of the fact that neither side had formally declared war, he allowed the shipment of arms and supplies to both sides.

Then the president went further. Speaking in Chicago in October, he condemned nations—he mentioned none by name—who were "creating a state of international anarchy and instability from which there is no escape through mere isolation or neutrality." The way to deal with "the epidemic of world lawlessness" was to "quarantine" it. Evidently Roosevelt had no specific plan in mind; nevertheless the "quarantine speech" produced a windy burst of isolationist rhetoric that forced him to back down. "It's a terrible thing," he said, "to look over your shoulder when you are trying to lead—and to find no one there."

Roosevelt came gradually to the conclusion that resisting aggression was more important than keeping out of war, but when he did, the need to keep the country united led him at times to be less than candid in his public statements. Hitler's annexation of Austria in March 1938 caused him deep concern. The Nazis' vicious anti-Semitism had caused many of Germany's 500,000 Jewish citizens to seek refuge abroad. Now 190,000 Austrian Jews were under Nazi control. When Roosevelt learned that the Germans were burning synagogues, expelling Jewish children from schools, and otherwise mistreating innocent people, he said that he "could scarcely believe that such things could occur." But public opinion opposed changing the immigration law so that more refugees could be admitted, and the president did nothing.

In September 1938 Hitler demanded that Czechoslovakia cede the German-speaking Sudetenland to the Reich. British Prime Minister Neville Chamberlain and French Premier Edouard Daladier, in a conference with Hitler at Munich, yielded to Hitler's threats and promises and persuaded the Czechs to surrender the region. Roosevelt failed again to speak out. But when the Nazis seized the rest of Czechoslovakia in March 1939, Roosevelt called for "methods short of war" to demonstrate America's determination to check the fascists.

When Hitler threatened Poland in the spring of 1939, demanding the free city of Danzig and the Polish Corridor separating East Prussia from the rest of Germany, and when Mussolini invaded Albania, Roosevelt urged Congress to repeal the 1937 neutrality act so that the United States could sell arms to Britain and France in the event of war. Congress refused. "Captain," Vice President Garner told Roosevelt after counting noses in the Senate, "you haven't got the votes," and the president, perhaps unwisely, did not press the issue.

In August 1939 Germany and the Soviet Union signed a nonaggression pact, prelude to their joint assault on Poland. On September 1 Hitler's troops invaded Poland, at last provoking Great Britain and France to declare war. Roosevelt immediately asked Congress to repeal the arms embargo. In November, in a vote that followed party lines closely, the Democratic majority pushed through a law permitting the sale of arms and other contraband on a cash-and-carry basis. Short-term loans were authorized, but American vessels were forbidden to carry any products to the belligerents. Since the Allies controlled the seas, cash-and-carry gave them a tremendous advantage.

The German attack on Poland effected a basic change in American thinking. Keeping out of the war remained an almost universal hope, but preventing a

Hitler's troops invaded Poland with tremendous force and firepower. The Nazi occupiers rounded up the Jewish residents of the Warsaw ghetto and deported them to slave labor camps that soon became mass extermination camps.

Nazi victory became the ultimate, if not always conscious, objective of many citizens. In Roosevelt's case it was perfectly conscious, although he dared not express his feelings candidly because of isolationist strength in Congress and the country. He moved slowly, responding to rather than directing the course of events.

Cash-and-carry did not stop the Nazis. Poland fell in less than a month; then, after a winter lull that cynics called the "phony war," Hitler loosed his armored divisions. Between April 9 and June 22 he taught the world the awful meaning of *Blitzkrieg*—lightning war. Denmark, Norway, the Netherlands, Belgium, and France were successively overwhelmed. The British army, pinned against the sea at Dunkirk, saved itself from annihilation only by fleeing across the English Channel. After the French submitted to his harsh terms on June 22, Hitler controlled nearly all of western Europe.

Roosevelt responded to these disasters in a number of ways. In the fall of 1939, reacting to warnings from Albert Einstein and other scientists that the Germans were trying to develop an atomic bomb, he committed federal funds to a top-secret atomic bomb program, which came to be known as the Manhattan Project. Even as the British and French were falling back, he sold them, without legal authority, surplus government arms. When Italy entered the war against France, the president called the invasion a stab in the back. During the first five months of 1940 he asked Congress to appropriate over $4 billion for national defense. To strengthen national unity he named Henry L. Stimson secretary of war[2] and another Republican, Frank Knox, secretary of the navy.

After the fall of France, Hitler attempted to bomb and starve the British into submission. The epic air battles over England during the summer of 1940 ended in a decisive defeat for the Nazis, but the Royal Navy, which had only about 100 destroyers, could not control German submarine attacks on shipping. Far more destroyers were needed. In this desperate hour, Prime Minister Winston Churchill, who had replaced Chamberlain in May 1940, asked Roosevelt for 50 old American destroyers to fill the gap.

The navy had 240 destroyers in commission and more than 50 under construction. But direct loan or sale of the vessels would have violated both international and American laws. Any attempt to obtain new legislation would have roused fears that the United States was going down the path that had led it into World War I. Long delay if not outright defeat would have resulted. Roosevelt therefore arranged to "trade" the destroyers for six British naval bases in the Caribbean. In addition, Great Britain leased bases in Bermuda and Newfoundland to the United States.

The destroyers-for-bases deal was a masterful achievement. It helped save Great Britain, and at the same time it circumvented isolationist prejudices since the president could present it as a shrewd bargain that bolstered America's defenses. A string of island bastions in the Atlantic was more valuable than 50 old destroyers.

Lines were hardening throughout the world. In September 1940, despite last-ditch isolationist resistance, Congress enacted the first peacetime draft in American history. Some 1.2 million draftees were summoned for one year of service, and 800,000 reservists were called to active duty. That same month Japan signed a mutual-assistance pact with Germany and Italy. This Rome-Berlin-Tokyo axis fused the conflicts in Europe and Asia, turning the struggle into a global war.

A THIRD TERM FOR FDR

In the midst of these events the 1940 presidential election took place. Why Roosevelt decided to run for a third term is a much-debated question. Partisanship had something to do with it, for no other Democrat seemed so likely to carry the country. Nor would the president have been human had he not been tempted to hold on to power, especially in such critical times. His conviction that no one else could keep a rein on the isolationists was probably decisive. In any case, he was easily renominated. Vice President Garner, who had become disenchanted with Roosevelt and the New Deal, did not seek a third term; at Roosevelt's dictation, the party chose Secretary of Agriculture Henry A. Wallace to replace him.

---

[2]*Stimson had held this post from 1911 to 1913 in the Taft Cabinet!*

By using concern about the European war to justify running for a tradition-breaking third term, Roosevelt brought down on his head the hatred of conservative Republicans and the isolationists of both major parties, just when they thought they would be rid of him. The leading Republican presidential candidates were Senator Robert A. Taft of Ohio, son of the former president, and District Attorney Thomas E. Dewey of New York, who had won fame as a "racket buster" and political reformer. Taft was considered conservative and lacking in political glamour; Dewey, barely 38, seemed too young and inexperienced. Instead the Republicans nominated the darkest of dark horses, Wendell L. Willkie of Indiana, the utility magnate who had led the fight against the TVA in 1933.

Despite his political inexperience and Wall Street connections, Willkie made an appealing candidate. He was an energetic, charming, openhearted man. His rough-hewn, rural manner (one Democrat called him "a simple, barefoot Wall Street lawyer") won him wide support in farm districts. Willkie had difficulty, however, finding issues on which to oppose Roosevelt. Good times were at last returning. The New Deal reforms were too popular and too much in line with his own thinking to invite attack. He believed as strongly as the president that America could no longer ignore the Nazi threat.

In the end Willkie focused his campaign on Roosevelt's conduct of foreign relations. A preponderance of the Democrats favored all-out aid to Britain, while most Republicans still wished to avoid foreign "entanglements." But the crisis was causing many persons to shift sides. Among interventionists, organizations like the Committee to Defend America by Aiding the Allies, headed by Republican William Allen White, and the small but influential Century Group contained members of both parties. So did the isolationist America First Committee, led by Robert E. Wood of Sears Roebuck and the famous aviator Charles A. Lindbergh.

While rejecting the isolationist position, Willkie charged that Roosevelt intended to make the United States a participant in the war. "If you reelect him," he told one audience, "you may expect war in April 1941," to which Roosevelt retorted (disingenuously, since he knew he was not a free agent in the situation), "I have said this before, but I shall say it again and again and again: Your boys are not going to be sent into any foreign wars." In November Roosevelt carried the country handily, though by a smaller majority than in 1932 or 1936. The popular vote was 27 million to 22 million, the electoral count 449 to 82.

THE UNDECLARED WAR

The election encouraged Roosevelt to act more boldly. When Prime Minister Churchill informed him that the cash-and-carry system would no longer suffice because Great Britain was rapidly exhausting its financial resources, he decided at once to provide the British with whatever they needed. Instead of proposing to lend them money, a step certain to rouse memories of the vexatious war debt controversies, he devised the lend-lease program, one of his most ingenious and imaginative creations.

First he delivered a "fireside chat" that stressed the evil intentions of the Nazis and the dangers that a German victory would create for America. Aiding Britain should be looked at simply as a form of self-defense. "As planes and ships and guns and shells are produced," he said, American defense experts would decide "how much shall be sent abroad and how much shall remain at home." When the radio talk provoked a favorable public response, Roosevelt went to Congress in January 1941 with a plan calling for the expenditure of $7 billion for war materials that the president could sell, lend, lease, exchange, or transfer to any country whose defense he deemed vital to that of the United States. After two months of debate, Congress gave him what he had asked for.

Although the wording of the Lend-Lease Act obscured its immediate purpose, the saving of Great Britain, the president was frank in explaining his plan. He did not minimize the dangers involved, yet his mastery of practical politics was never more in evidence. To counter Irish-American prejudices against the English, he pointed out that the Irish Republic would surely fall under Nazi domination if Hitler won the war. He coupled his demand for heavy military expenditures with his enunciation of the idealistic "Four Freedoms"—freedom of speech, freedom of religion, freedom from want, and freedom from fear—for which, he said, the war was being fought.

After the enactment of lend-lease, aid short of war was no longer seriously debated. The American navy began to patrol the North Atlantic, shadowing German submarines and radioing their locations to British warships and planes. In April 1941 United States forces occupied Greenland; in May the president declared a state of unlimited national emergency. After Hitler invaded the Soviet Union in June, Roosevelt moved slowly, for anti-Soviet feeling in the United States was intense.[3] But it was obviously to the nation's advantage to help any country that was resisting Hitler's armies. In November, $1 billion in lend-lease aid was put at the disposal of the Soviet Union.

Meanwhile, Iceland was occupied in July 1941, and the draft law was extended in August—by the margin of a single vote in the House of Representatives. In September the German submarine *U–652* fired a torpedo at the destroyer *Greer* in the North Atlantic. The *Greer,* which had provoked the attack by tracking *U–652* and flashing its position to a British plane, avoided the torpedo and dropped 19 depth charges in an effort to sink the submarine.

Roosevelt (nothing he ever did provided more ammunition for his critics) announced that the *Greer* had been innocently "carrying mail to Iceland." He called the U-boats "the rattlesnakes of the Atlantic" and ordered the navy to "shoot on sight" any German craft in the waters south and west of Iceland and to convoy merchant vessels as far as that island. After the sinking of the destroyer *Reuben James* on October 30, Congress voted to allow the arming of American merchant ships and to permit them to carry cargoes to Allied ports. For all practical purposes, though not yet officially, the United States had gone to war.

---

[3]During the 1930s the Soviet Union took a far firmer stand against the fascists than any other power, but after joining Hitler in swallowing up Poland, it attacked and defeated Finland during the winter of 1939–1940 and annexed the Baltic states. These acts virtually destroyed the small communist movement in the United States.

MILESTONES

1933   FDR becomes president

Hitler is elected German chancellor

FDR proclaims Good Neighbor Policy

Banking Act gives FDR broad powers

Civilian Conservation Corps (CCC) employs 250,000 young men

Federal Emergency Relief Act (FERA) funds relief programs

Agricultural Adjustment Act (AAA) seeks relief for farmers

Tennessee Valley Authority (TVA) plans dams and power plants

National Industrial Recovery Act (NIRA) establishes Public Works Administration (PWA) and National Recovery Administration (NRA)

Banking Act establishes Federal Deposit Insurance Corporation (FDIC)

Civil Works Administration puts 4 million to work

Twenty-first Amendment ends Prohibition

1934   Indian Reorganization Act gives tribes more autonomy

Securities and Exchange Commission (SEC) regulates stocks and bonds

Federal Communications Commission (FCC) regulates interstate and foreign communication

Federal Housing Administration (FHA) gives housing loans

1935   Emergency Relief Appropriation Act creates Works Project Administration (WPA)

Rural Electrification Administration brings electricity to farms

Supreme Court rules NIRA unconstitutional in *Schechter* v. *United States*

National Labor Relations Act (Wagner-Connery) encourages unionization

Social Security Act guarantees pensions and other benefits

Neutrality Act forbids wartime arms sales to belligerents

Italy invades and annexes Ethiopia

Walter Millis publishes isolationist *The Road to War: America, 1914–1917*

1936   FDR is reelected in record landslide

Supreme Court declares AAA unconstitutional

1937   Roosevelt tries to pack Supreme Court

Japanese in China seize Beijing, Shanghai, Nanking

1938   Fair Labor Standards Act abolishes child labor, sets minimum wage

House of Representatives defeats Ludlow (isolationist) Amendment

Britain and France appease Hitler at Munich

1939   Germany invades Poland; World War II begins

1940   Hitler conquers Denmark, Norway, the Netherlands, Belgium, France

FDR is reelected to third term

Axis powers sign Rome-Berlin-Tokyo pact

Isolationists form America First Committee

1941   Lend-Lease Act helps Britain

28

---✦——◆——✦---

WAR AND PEACE

By December 1941 the United States was at the brink of war, but public opinion would not have supported a formal declaration had it not been for Japan. Relations between Japan and the United States had worsened steadily after Japan resumed its war on China in 1937. As they extended their control, the invaders systematically froze out American and other foreign business interests. They declared that the Open Door policy was obsolete. Roosevelt retaliated by lending money to China and asking American manufacturers not to sell airplanes to Japan. In September 1940, Congress prohibited all sales of scrap iron to Japan. Japan immediately signed a treaty of alliance with Germany and Italy, which prompted Roosevelt to extend the embargo to include machine tools and other items. Despite these economic measures, Japan pushed ahead relentlessly to expand its economic empire in the Pacific.

THE ROAD TO PEARL HARBOR

Neither the United States nor Japan wanted war. Roosevelt considered Germany by far the more dangerous enemy and was alarmed by the possibility of engaging in a two-front war. In the spring of 1941 Secretary of State Hull conferred in Washington with the Japanese ambassador, Kichisaburo Nomura, in an effort to resolve their differences. Hull showed little appreciation of the political and military situation in East Asia. He demanded that Japan withdraw from China and promise not to attack the Dutch and French colonies in Southeast Asia.

Japan might well have accepted limited annexations in the area in return for the removal of American trade restrictions, but Hull seemed bent on converting the Japanese to pacifism by exhortation. He insisted on total withdrawal, to which even the moderates in Japan would not agree. When Hitler invaded the Soviet Union, thereby removing the threat of Russian intervention in East Asia, Japan decided to occupy French Indochina even at the risk of war with the United States. Roosevelt retaliated (July 1941) by freezing Japanese assets in the United States and clamping an embargo on oil. He hoped that the Japanese war machine, deprived of American oil, would grind to a halt.

Now the ultranationalist war party in Japan assumed control. Nomura was instructed to tell Hull that Japan would refrain from further expansion if the United States and Great Britain would cut off all aid to China and lift the economic blockade. Japan promised to pull out of Indochina once "a just peace" had been established with China. When the United States rejected these demands, the Japanese prepared to assault the Dutch East Indies, British Malaya, and the Philippines. To immobilize the United States Pacific fleet, they planned a surprise aerial raid on the Hawaiian naval base at Pearl Harbor.

An American cryptanalyst, Colonel William F. Friedman, had cracked the Japanese diplomatic code: the Japanese were making plans to attack in early December. But in the hectic rush of events, both military and civilian authorities failed to make effective use of the information collected. They expected the blow to fall somewhere in East Asia, possibly the Philippines.

The garrison at Pearl Harbor was alerted against "a surprise aggressive move in any direction." The commanders there, Admiral Husband E. Kimmel and General Walter C. Short, believing an attack impossible, took precautions only against Japanese sabotage. Thus when planes from Japanese aircraft carriers swooped down upon Pearl Harbor on the morning of December 7, 1941, they found easy targets. In less than two hours they reduced the Pacific fleet to a smoking ruin: two battleships destroyed, six others heavily battered, nearly a dozen lesser vessels put out of action. More than 150 planes were wrecked; over 2300 soldiers and sailors were killed and 1100 wounded.

On December 8 Congress declared war on Japan. Formal war with Germany and Italy was still not inevitable—isolationists were far more ready to resist the "yellow peril" in Asia than to fight in Europe. The Axis powers, however, honored their treaty obligations to Japan and on December 11 declared war on the United States. America was now fully engaged in another great war, World War II. (The Great War fought by the previous generation was now identified as World War I.)

MOBILIZING THE HOME FRONT

Roosevelt was an inspiring war leader but not a very good administrator. Any honest account of the war on the home front must reveal glaring examples of confusion, inefficiency, and pointless bickering. The squabbling and waste characteristic of the early New Deal period made relatively little difference—what mattered then was raising the nation's spirits and keeping people occupied; efficiency was less than essential, however desirable. But in wartime, the nation's

Japan's surprise attack on Pearl Harbor on December 7, 1941, killed more than 2400 American servicemen and thrust the United States into World War II. President Roosevelt asked Congress for a declaration of war the next day, calling the attack "a date that will live in infamy."

fate, perhaps that of the entire free world, depended on delivering weapons and supplies to the battlefronts.

The confusion attending economic mobilization can easily be overstressed. Nearly all of Roosevelt's basic decisions were sensible and humane: to pay a large part of the cost of the war by collecting taxes rather than by borrowing and to base taxation on ability to pay; to ration scarce raw materials and consumer goods; to regulate prices and wages. If these decisions were not always translated into action with perfect effectiveness, they operated in the direction of efficiency and the public good.

Roosevelt's greatest accomplishment was his inspiring of industrialists, workers, and farmers with a sense of national purpose. In this respect his function duplicated his earlier role in fighting the Depression, and he performed it with even greater success.

The tremendous economic expansion can be seen in the official production statistics. In 1939 the United States was still mired in the Great Depression. The gross national product amounted to about $91.3 billion. In 1945, after allowing for changes in the price level, it was $166.6 billion. More specifically, manufacturing output nearly doubled and agricultural output rose 22 percent. In 1939 the United States turned out fewer than 6000 airplanes, in 1944 more than 96,000. Shipyards produced 237,000 tons of vessels in 1939, 10 million tons in 1943.

Wartime experience proved that the Keynesian economists were correct in saying that government spending would spark economic growth. About 8 million people were unemployed in June 1940. After Pearl Harbor, unemployment virtually disappeared, and by 1945 the civilian workforce had increased by nearly 7 million. Military mobilization had begun well before December 1941, by which time 1.6 million men were already under arms. Economic mobilization proceeded much more slowly, mainly because the president refused to centralize authority. For months after Pearl Harbor various civilian agencies squabbled with the military over everything from the allocation of scarce raw materials to the technical specifications of weapons. Roosevelt refused to settle these conflicts.

THE WAR ECONOMY

Yet by early 1943 the nation's economic machinery had been converted to a wartime footing and was functioning effectively. Supreme Court Justice James F. Byrnes resigned from the Court to become a sort of "economic czar." His Office of War Mobilization had complete control over priorities and prices. Rents, food prices, and wages were strictly regulated, and items in short supply were rationed to consumers. While wages and prices had soared during 1942, after April 1943 they leveled off. Thereafter the cost of living scarcely changed until controls were lifted after the war.

Expanded industrial production together with conscription caused a labor shortage that increased the bargaining power of workers. At the same time, the national emergency required some limitation on the workers' right to take advantage of this power. After Pearl Harbor Roosevelt created a National War Labor Board (NWLB) to arbitrate disputes and stabilize wage rates, and he banned all changes in wages without NWLB approval.

Prosperity and stiffer government controls added significantly to the strength of organized labor; indeed, the war had more to do with institutionalizing industrywide collective bargaining than the New Deal. As workers recognized the benefits of union membership, they flocked into the organizations. Strikes declined sharply, but some crippling work stoppages did occur. In May 1943, after John L. Lewis's United Mine Workers walked out of the pits, the government seized the coal mines. This strike led Congress to pass, over Roosevelt's veto, the Smith-Connally War Labor Disputes Act, which gave the president the power to take over any war plant threatened by a strike and outlawed strikes against seized plants.

The federal government spent twice as much money between 1941 and 1945 as in its entire previous history. This made heavy borrowing necessary. The national debt, which stood at less than $49 billion in 1941, increased by more than that amount each year between 1942 and 1945 and totaled nearly $260 billion when the war ended. However, more than 40 percent of the total was met by taxation, a far larger proportion than in any earlier war.

This policy helped to check inflation by siphoning off money that would otherwise have competed for scarce consumer goods. Heavy excise taxes on amusements and luxuries further discouraged spending, as did the government's war bond campaigns, which persuaded patriotic citizens to lend part of their income to Uncle Sam. High taxes on incomes (up to 94 percent) and on excess profits

(95 percent), together with a limit of $25,000 a year after taxes on salaries, convinced people that no one was profiting inordinately from the war effort.

The income tax, which had never before touched the mass of white-collar and industrial workers, was extended downward until nearly everyone had to pay it. To collect efficiently the relatively small sums paid by most persons, Congress adopted the payroll-deduction system proposed by Beardsley Ruml, chairman of the Federal Reserve Bank of New York. Employers withheld the taxes owed by workers from their paychecks and turned the money over to the government.

The steeply graduated tax rates, combined with a general increase in the income of workers and farmers, effected a substantial shift in the distribution of wealth in the United States. The poor became richer, while the rich, if not actually poorer, collected a smaller proportion of the national income. The wealthiest 1 percent of the population had received 13.4 percent of the national income in 1935 and 11.5 percent in 1941. In 1944 this group received 6.7 percent.

WAR AND SOCIAL CHANGE

Enormous social effects stemmed from this shift, but World War II altered the patterns of American life in so many ways that it would be wrong to ascribe the transformations to any single source. Never was the population more fluid. The millions who put on uniforms found themselves transported first to training camps in every section of the country and then to battlefields scattered from Europe and Africa to the far reaches of the Pacific. Burgeoning new defense plants, influenced by a government policy of locating them in "uncongested areas," drew other millions to places like Hanford, Washington, and Oak Ridge, Tennessee, where great atomic energy installations were constructed, and to the aircraft factories of California and other states. As in earlier periods the trend was from east to west and from the rural south to northern cities. The population of California increased by more than 50 percent in the 1940s, that of other far western states almost as much.

During the war the marriage rate rose steeply, from 75 per thousand adult women in 1939 to 118 in 1946. A kind of backlog existed because many people had been forced to put off marrying and having children for financial reasons during the Great Depression. Now wartime prosperity put an end to that problem at the same time that large numbers of young couples were feeling the need to put down roots before the husbands went off to risk death in distant lands. The population of the United States had increased by only 3 million during the Depression decade of the 1930s; during the next *five* years it rose by 6.5 million.

AFRICAN AMERICANS IN TIME OF WAR

The war affected black Americans in many ways. Several factors operated to improve their lot. One was their own growing tendency to demand fair treatment. Another was the reaction of Americans to Hitler's barbaric treatment of millions

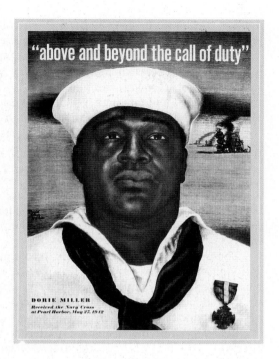

"above and beyond the call of duty"

DORIE MILLER
Received the Navy Cross
at Pearl Harbor, May 27, 1942

A poster commemorating Doris "Dorie" Miller, a mess attendant aboard the USS West Virginia at Pearl Harbor. Before the ship sank, Miller manned an antiaircraft machine gun and shot down several Japanese planes. He won the Navy Cross for courage, the first awarded to an African American.

of Jews, an outgrowth of his doctrine of "Aryan" superiority. These barbarities compelled millions of white citizens to reexamine their views about race. If the nation expected African Americans to risk their lives for the common good, how could it continue to treat them as second-class citizens? Black leaders pointed out the inconsistency between fighting for democracy abroad and ignoring it at home. "We want democracy in Alabama," the NAACP announced, and this argument too had some effect on white thinking.

Blacks in the armed forces were treated more fairly than they had been in World War I. They were enlisted for the first time in the air force and the marines, and they were given more responsible positions in the army and navy. The army commissioned its first black general. Some 600 black pilots won their wings. Altogether about a million served, about half of them overseas. The extensive and honorable performance of these units could not be ignored by the white majority.

However, segregation in the armed services was maintained. Especially in and around army camps in the southern states, rigid segregation proved shocking to many northern white soldiers. In some cases German prisoners of war were seated in front of black American soldiers at camp movies. Such practices led frequently to rioting and even to local mutinies among black recruits.

The navy continued to confine black and Hispanic sailors to demeaning, noncombat tasks, and black soldiers were often provided with inferior recreational facilities and otherwise mistreated in and around army camps, especially those in the South. In 1943 William Hastie, a former New Dealer who was serving as an adviser on racial matters to Secretary of War Stimson, resigned in protest because of the "reactionary policies and discriminatory practices of the Army and Air Forces in matters affecting Negroes." The NAACP, which increased its membership from 50,000 in 1940 to almost 405,000 in 1946, adopted a more militant stance than in World War I. Discrimination in defense plants seemed far less tolerable than it had in 1917–1918.

Prejudice and mistreatment did not cease. In areas around defense plants white resentment of the black "invasion" mounted. By 1943, 50,000 new blacks had crowded into Detroit. A wave of strikes disrupted production at U.S. Rubber and several former automobile plants where white workers laid down their tools to protest the hiring of blacks. In June a race riot marked by looting and bloody fighting raged for three days. By the time federal troops restored order, 25 blacks and 9 whites had been killed. Rioting also erupted in New York and many other cities.

The willingness of white leaders to tolerate attacks on blacks at a time when national unity was so necessary was particularly frustrating. For example, blood plasma from blacks and whites was kept separately even though the two "varieties" were indistinguishable and the process of storing plasma had been devised by a black doctor, Charles Drew.

Blacks became increasingly embittered. Roy Wilkins, head of the NAACP, put it this way in 1942: "No Negro leader with a constituency can face his members today and ask full support for the war in the light of the atmosphere the government has created." Many black newspaper editors were so critical of the administration that conservatives demanded they be indicted for sedition.

INTERNMENT OF THE JAPANESE

Although World War II affected the American people far more drastically than had World War I, it produced much less intolerance and fewer examples of the repression of individual freedom of opinion. People seemed able to distinguish between Italian fascism and Italian Americans and between the government of Nazi Germany and Americans of German descent in a way that had escaped their parents. The nation's 100,000 conscientious objectors, too, met with little hostility.

The relatively tolerant treatment accorded most people makes the nation's policies toward American citizens of Japanese extraction all the more difficult to comprehend. Generals on the west coast were understandably unnerved by the Japanese attack on Pearl Harbor and warned that people of Japanese descent might engage in sabotage or espionage for Japan. "The Japanese race is an enemy race," General John L. Dewitt claimed. The 112,000 Americans of Japanese ancestry, the majority of them native-born citizens, were "potential enemies." "The very fact that no sabotage has taken place to date," Dewitt observed, "is a disturbing and confirming indication that such action will be taken." This is like

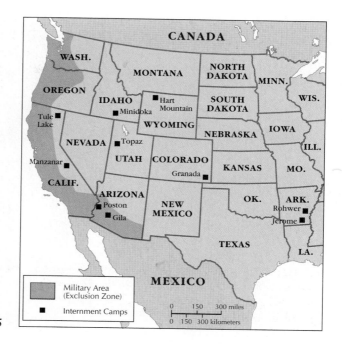

Japanese Relocation from the West Coast, 1942–1945

Military Area (Exclusion Zone)

Internment Camps

arguing that the driver with a perfect record is all the more likely to have an accident at any moment. Secretary of War Stimson proposed the relocation of the west coast people of Japanese extraction, including American citizens, to internment camps in Wyoming, Arizona, and other interior states. President Roosevelt concurred but weakly suggested: "Be as responsible as you can."

The Japanese were properly indignant but also baffled, in some cases hurt more than angry. "We didn't feel Japanese. We felt American," one woman, the mother of three small children, recalled many years later. Some Japanese Americans refused to submit to military authorities. Gordon Hirabayashi, an American citizen and senior at the University of Washington, refused to report for transportation to an internment camp. After being convicted and sentenced to prison, he decided to appeal. Previous Supreme Courts had ruled that the government could deprive Americans of their freedoms during war only when the "military necessity" was compelling. By the time the Supreme Court ruled on his and similar cases, the Japanese military had been thrown back in the Pacific; no invasion was even conceivable. Yet the justices worried that if they declared the internment policy to be unconstitutional, they would appear "out of step" with the nation, as Justice Felix Frankfurter put it. In June 1943, the Court upheld the conviction of Hirabayashi. Finally, in *Ex parte Endo,* it forbade the internment of loyal Japanese American citizens. Unfortunately the latter decision was not handed down until December 1944.

Identification tags hang from the collars of the Mochida children as they pose with their parents for photographer Dorothea Lange. The date was May 8, 1942, and the family was awaiting transportation from their home in Hayward, California, to an internment camp.

WOMEN'S CONTRIBUTION TO THE WAR EFFORT

With economic activity on the rise and millions of men going off to war, a sudden need for more women workers developed. The trends of the 1920s—more women workers and more of them married—soon accelerated. By 1944, 6.5 million additional women had entered the workforce, and at the peak of war production in 1945, more than 19 million women were employed, many of them in well-paying industrial jobs. Additional thousands were serving in the armed forces: 100,000 in the Women's Auxiliary Army Corps, others in navy, marine, and air corps auxiliaries.

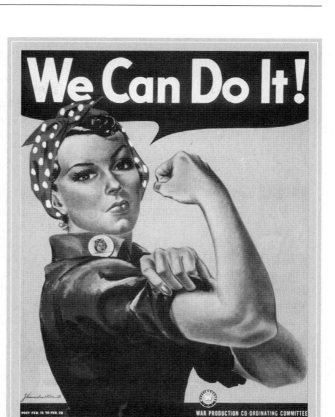

Posters such as this one helped persuade two million women to take jobs in defense plants. It suggests that although defense work required determination and strength, women who undertook such jobs would not lose their femininity (note the lipstick and mascara). In fact, most young women were given monotonous work on assembly lines; less than one in twenty were assigned to skilled jobs.

At first there was considerable resistance to what was happening. About one husband in three objected in principle to his wife taking a job. Many employers in so-called heavy industry and in other fields traditionally dominated by men doubted that women could handle such tasks.

These attitudes lost force in the face of the escalating demand for labor. That employers usually did not have to pay women as much as men made them attractive, as did the fact that they were not subject to the draft. A breakthrough occurred when the big Detroit automobile manufacturers agreed to employ women on their wartime production lines. Soon women were working not only as riveters and cab drivers but also as welders, as machine tool operators, and in dozens of other occupations formerly the exclusive domain of men.

Black women workers had a particularly difficult time, employers often hesitating to hire them because they were black, black men looking down on them because they were women. But the need for willing hands was infinite. Sybil Lewis of Sapula, Oklahoma, went to Los Angeles and found a job as a waitress in a black restaurant. Then she responded to a notice of a training program at

Lockheed Aircraft, took the course, and became a riveter making airplane gas tanks. When an unfriendly foreman gave her a less attractive assignment, she moved on to Douglas Aircraft. By 1943 she was working as a welder in a shipyard.

The war also affected the lives of women who did not take jobs. Families by the tens and hundreds of thousands pulled up stakes and moved to the centers of war production, such as Detroit and southern California. Housing was always in short supply in these areas, and while the men went off to the familiar surroundings of yard and factory, their wives had to cope with cramped quarters, ration books, the absence of friends and relatives, the problems encountered by their children in strange schools and playgrounds, in some situations even with outdoor toilets. With so many people living among strangers and in unstable circumstances it is not surprising that crime, juvenile delinquency, and prostitution increased, as indeed they did in other parts of the country too.

Housewives also had to deal with shortages, ration books, and other inconveniences during the war. In addition most took on other duties and bore other burdens, such as tending "victory gardens" and preserving their harvests, using crowded public transportation when there was no gas for the family car, mending and patching old clothes when new ones were unavailable, participating in salvage drives, and doing volunteer work for hospitals, the Red Cross, or various civil defense and servicemen's centers.

ALLIED STRATEGY: EUROPE FIRST

Only days after Pearl Harbor, British Prime Minister Churchill and his military chiefs met in Washington with Roosevelt and his advisers. In every quarter of the globe, disaster threatened. The Japanese were gobbling up East Asia. Hitler's armies, checked outside Leningrad and Moscow, were preparing for a massive attack in the direction of Stalingrad, on the Volga River. German divisions under General Erwin Rommel were beginning a drive across North Africa toward the Suez Canal. U-boats were taking a heavy toll in the North Atlantic. British and American leaders believed that eventually they could muster enough force to smash their enemies, but whether the troops already in action could hold out until this force arrived was an open question.

The decision of the strategists was to concentrate first against the Germans. Japan's conquests were in remote and, from the Allied point of view, relatively unimportant regions. If the Soviet Union surrendered, Hitler could throw all of German might against Great Britain. If it were defeated, Hitler's position in Europe might prove impregnable.

But how to strike at Hitler? American leaders wanted a second front in France, at least by 1943, and the Soviets, with their backs to the wall and bearing the full weight of the German war machine, heartily agreed. Churchill, however, was more concerned with protecting Britain's overseas possessions than with easing the pressure on the Soviet Union. He advocated instead air bombardment of German industry combined with an attempt to drive the Germans out of North Africa, and his argument carried the day.

During the summer of 1942 Allied planes began to bomb German cities. In a crescendo through 1943 and 1944, British and American bombers pulverized the centers of Nazi might. While air attacks did not destroy the German army's capacity to fight, they hampered war production, tangled communications, and brought the war home to the German people in awesome fashion.

In November 1942 an Allied army commanded by General Dwight D. Eisenhower struck at French North Africa. After the fall of France, the Nazis had set up a puppet regime in those parts of France not occupied by their troops, with headquarters at Vichy in central France. This collaborationist Vichy government controlled French North Africa. But the North African commandant, Admiral Jean Darlan, promptly switched sides when Eisenhower's forces landed. After a brief show of resistance, the French surrendered.

The Allies were willing to do business with Darlan despite his record as a collaborationist. This angered General Charles de Gaulle, who had organized a government in exile immediately after the collapse of France and who considered himself the true representative of the French people. Many Americans agreed with de Gaulle, but the arrangement with Darlan paid large dividends. Eisenhower was able to press forward quickly against the Germans. In February 1943 at Kasserine Pass in the desert south of Tunis, American tanks met Rommel's Afrika Korps. The battle ended in a standoff, but with British troops closing in from their Egyptian bases to the east, the Germans were soon trapped and crushed. In May, after Rommel had been recalled to Germany, his army surrendered.

In July 1943, while air attacks on Germany continued and the Russians slowly pushed the Germans back from the gates of Stalingrad, the Allies invaded Sicily from Africa. In September they advanced to the Italian mainland. Mussolini had already fallen from power and his successor surrendered. However, the German troops in Italy threw up an almost impregnable defense across the rugged Italian peninsula. The Anglo American army inched forward, paying heavily for every advance. Monte Cassino, halfway between Naples and Rome, did not fall until May 1944, the capital itself not until June; months of hard fighting remained before the country was cleared of Germans. The Italian campaign was an Allied disappointment even though it weakened the enemy.

GERMANY OVERWHELMED

By the time the Allies had taken Rome, the mighty army needed to invade France had been collected in England under Eisenhower's command. On D-day, June 6, 1944, the assault forces stormed ashore at five points along the coast of Normandy, supported by a great armada and thousands of planes and paratroops. Against fierce but ill-coordinated German resistance, they established a beachhead: Within a few weeks a million troops were on French soil. (See the feature essay, Re-Viewing the Past: "*Saving Private Ryan,*" pp. 786–787.)

Thereafter victory was assured, though nearly a year of hard fighting lay ahead. In August the American Third Army under General George S. Patton, an eccentric but brilliant field commander, erupted southward into Brittany and

The Liberation of Europe

then veered east toward Paris. Another Allied army invaded France from the Mediterranean in mid-August and advanced rapidly north. Free French troops were given the honor of liberating Paris on August 25. Belgium was cleared by British and Canadian units a few days later. By mid-September the Allies were fighting on the edge of Germany itself.

The front now stretched from the Netherlands along the borders of Belgium, Luxembourg, and France all the way to Switzerland. If the Allies had mounted a massive assault at any one point, as the British commander, Field Marshal Bernard Montgomery, urged, the struggle might have been brought to a quick conclusion. Although the two armies were roughly equal in size, the Allies had complete control of the air and 20 times as many tanks as the foe. The pressure of the advancing Russians on the eastern front made it difficult for the Germans to reinforce their troops in the west. But General Eisenhower believed a concentrated attack too risky. He prepared instead for a general advance.

While he was regrouping, the Germans on December 16 launched a counter-attack, planned by Hitler himself, against the Allied center in the Ardennes Forest. The Germans hoped to break through to the Belgian port of Antwerp, thereby splitting the Allied armies in two. The plan was foolhardy and therefore unexpected, and it almost succeeded. The Germans drove a salient ("the bulge") about 50 miles into Belgium. But once the element of surprise had been overcome, their chance of breaking through to the sea was lost. Eisenhower concentrated first on preventing them from broadening the break in his lines and then on blunting the point of their advance. By late January 1945 the old line had been reestablished.

The Battle of the Bulge cost the United States 77,000 casualties and delayed Eisenhower's offensive, but it exhausted the Germans' last reserves. The Allies then pressed forward to the Rhine, winning a bridgehead on the far bank of the river on March 7. Thereafter, one German city fell almost daily. With the Soviets racing westward against crumbling resistance, the end could not be long delayed. In April, American and Soviet forces made contact at the Elbe River. A few days later, with Soviet shells reducing his capital to rubble, Hitler, by then probably insane, took his own life in his Berlin air raid shelter. On May 8 Germany surrendered.

As the Americans drove swiftly forward in the late stages of the war, they began to overrun Nazi concentration camps where millions of Jews had been murdered. The Americans were horrified by what they discovered, but they should not have been surprised. Word of this holocaust, in which no less than 6 million people were slaughtered, had reached the United States much earlier. At first the news had been dismissed as propaganda, then discounted as grossly exaggerated. Hitler was known to hate Jews and to have persecuted them, but that he could order the murder of millions of innocent people, even children, seemed beyond belief. By 1943, however, the truth could not be denied.

Little could be done about those already in the camps, but there were thousands of refugees in occupied Europe who might have been spirited to safety. President Roosevelt declined to make the effort; he refused to bomb the Auschwitz death camp in Poland or the rail lines used to bring victims to its gas chambers on the grounds that the destruction of German soldiers and military equipment took precedence over any other objective. Thus, when American journalists entered the camps with the advancing troops, saw the heaps of still-unburied corpses, and talked with the emaciated survivors, their reports caused a storm of protest in America.

THE NAVAL WAR IN THE PACIFIC

Defeating Germany first had not meant abandoning the Pacific region entirely to the Japanese. While armies were being trained and matériel accumulated for the European struggle, much of the available American strength was diverted to maintaining vital communications in East Asia and preventing further Japanese expansion.

Re-Viewing the Past

Saving Private Ryan

Steven Spielberg's *Saving Private Ryan* (1998), starring Tom Hanks, has been widely praised as the most realistic combat movie ever made. This judgment is based chiefly on its re-creation of the June 6, 1944, Allied assault on Omaha Beach during the invasion of Normandy. The camera focuses on Hanks, rain dripping from helmet, huddled in a crowded landing vessel. Explosions rumble in the distance. The ship plows through heavy seas toward a blackened brow of land. Around him, men vomit. Explosions become louder and sharper. Nearby ships strike mines and blow up; others are obliterated by shellfire. Hanks's landing craft lurches to avoid the mayhem. Like hail against a tin roof, gunfire riddles the landing craft. Some of the men are hit, and the others hunch lower, still vomiting. A deafening din envelops the ship as its bow opens. A curtain of bullets instantly cuts down the men in front. Hanks and several others leap into the sea. They sink: the ship has stopped far short of the beach. As bullets tear through the water, ripping into those still submerged, Hanks struggles to the surface. He swims, weaponless, toward the beach.

He has crossed the threshold of hell, and over the next 15 minutes viewers descend with him the rest of the way.

Saving Private Ryan differs from other combat films not in the graphic horror of the bloodshed, but in its randomness. The audience expects Hanks to survive the opening scenes of the movie in which he stars, and he does. But all other bets are off: a valiant exploit, a kind gesture, a handsome face—none influences the grim lottery of battle. When huge armies converge, hurling high explosives and steel at each other, one's chances of survival are unaffected by ethics or aesthetics.

But having made this point with heart-pounding emphasis, the movie subverts it. Hanks, unnerved and dispirited, for a time hunkers down in the relative safety of the seawall. Then he begins to do his job and others rally

around him. They blast a hole through obstacles, crawl toward the concrete fortifications above, penetrate trench defenses, blow up bunkers, and seize the hill. Many perish in the effort; Hanks, an infantry captain, is among the survivors.

Then comes a new mission, which occupies the remainder of the movie. George C. Marshall, U.S. Army Chief of Staff, has learned of a Mrs. Ryan who has been notified on a single day that three of her sons were killed in action. Her fourth son, James, a private in the 101st Airborne, has just parachuted into Normandy behind German lines. Marshall orders that he be returned to safety. This mission is given to Hanks and the eight surviving members of his platoon. They march inland, encounter snipers, ambushes, and, in the final scenes, a large detachment of German armored vehicles. But they also find Private Ryan (played by Matt Damon).

Along the way, the movie asks many provocative questions, such as whether war improves those who fight. "I think this is all good for me, sir," one earnest soldier confides to Hanks. "Really," Hanks says with a faint smile, "how is that?" The soldier cites Ralph Waldo Emerson: "War educates the senses. Calls into action the will. Perfects the physical constitution." "Emerson had a way of finding the bright side," Hanks deadpans, and the movie endorses his cynicism.

Except in one sense, and that may be all that matters: Hanks and his men have repeatedly demonstrated a willingness to give up their lives for others. Indeed, the movie's central dilemma concerns the moral arithmetic of sacrifice. Is it right to risk eight men to save one? To send a thousand men to near certain death in an initial assault to improve the chances of those that follow? To make one generation endure hell so that another may have freedom? The movie provides no ready answers. But in nearly the final scene it does issue a challenge. Hanks, mortally wounded, is lying amidst the corpses of his platoon, and he beckons to Ryan, who is un-

Tom Hanks, Matt Damon, and Edward Burns in Saving Private Ryan

Actual photograph of American troops approaching code-named Omaha Beach at Normandy.

hurt. "Earn this," Hanks says, vaguely gesturing to the others.

Saving Private Ryan was part of a wave of nostalgic appreciation during the 1990s for the generation that had won World War II. A spate of books, movies, and TV documentaries were other expressions of this phenomenon. On accepting the Oscar for his film, Spielberg thanked his father, a World War II vet, "for showing me that there is honor in looking back and respecting the past."

But respect for the past entails getting it right, and the movie makes some significant errors and omissions. For one, it suggests that the men huddled at the base of the seawall blew up the concrete bunkers on their own. This was not possible. In fact, commanders of destroyers took their ships close to the beaches and fired countless heavy shells into the fortifications, allowing the infantry to move up the hills.

The movie also shows the German soldiers as uniformly expert and professional. But the German army had been decimated by losses in the Soviet Union. The army manning the Normandy defenses included many units composed mostly of old men, boys, or conscripted soldiers from Poland or the Soviet Union. Many surrendered as soon as they encountered American soldiers.

Of the movie's implausible elements, the premise that the U.S. Army high command ordered a special mission to pluck a grieving mother's son from danger was based on fact. A real Mrs. Niland received telegrams on the same day that three of her sons had been killed in action. Her fourth son, "Fritz," had parachuted into Normandy with the 101st Airborne. The army did in fact snatch him from the front line and return him to safety.

Saving Private Ryan captures the effect of war on soldiers. Many men at Omaha Beach, like those depicted in the movie, were shattered by the experience. One private, nearly hit by a shell, recalled that he burst into tears. "My buddies got me behind a burned-out craft, where I cried for what seemed like hours. I cried until tears would no longer come. To this day I've never shed another." Other men confessed that, after the terror of a firefight, they shot Germans who had raised their arms in surrender. "In my opinion any enemy shot during this intense action had waited too long to surrender," one G.I. declared.

Yet through it all, some men, like the captain portrayed by Hanks, drew heroism from some unfathomed depths of the soul. One real soldier at Omaha Beach remembered "a captain and two lieutenants who demonstrated courage beyond belief as they struggled to bring order to the chaos around them."

Saving Private Ryan is not a fully accurate representation of the attack on Omaha Beach, but it depicts—realistically and memorably— how soldiers conferred meaning on the heedless calculus of modern warfare.

On February 13 and 14, 1945, British and American incendiary bombs razed Dresden, the cultural capital of Germany. Some 35,000 perished. The purpose of the raid was to terrorize and demoralize the German people; the city's few war industries were not even targeted. This picture was taken more than a year after the bombing.

The navy's aircraft carriers had escaped destruction at Pearl Harbor, a stroke of immense good fortune because, without most tacticians realizing it, the airplane had revolutionized naval warfare. Commanders discovered that carrier-based planes were far more effective against warships than the heaviest naval artillery because of their greater range and more concentrated firepower. Battleships made excellent gun platforms from which to pound shore installations and support land operations, but against other vessels aircraft were of prime importance.

This truth was demonstrated in May 1942 in the Battle of the Coral Sea. Having captured an empire in a few months without the loss of any warship larger than a destroyer, the Japanese believed the war already won. This led them to overextend themselves.

The Coral Sea lies northeast of Australia and south of New Guinea and the Solomon Islands. Japanese mastery of these waters would cut Australia off from Hawaii and thus from American aid. Admiral Isoroku Yamamoto had dispatched a large fleet of troopships screened by many warships to attack Port Moresby, on the southern New Guinea coast. On May 7–8 planes from the American carriers *Lexington* and *Yorktown* struck the convoy's screen, sinking a small carrier and damaging a large one. Superficially, the battle seemed a victory

Once into Germany the Third Army advanced so quickly in the spring of 1945 that it came upon military installations almost without warning. The photograph here is of General Dwight D. Eisenhower inspecting the condition of the concentration camp at Gotha, Germany, where slain inmates had been left unburied by their fleeing captors.

for the Japanese, for their planes mortally wounded the *Lexington* and sank two other ships, but the troop transports had been forced to turn back—Port Moresby was saved. Although large numbers of cruisers and destroyers took part in the action, none came within sight or gun range of an enemy ship. All the destruction was wrought by carrier aircraft.

Encouraged by the Coral Sea "victory," Yamamoto decided to force the American fleet into a showdown battle by assaulting the Midway Islands, west of Hawaii. His armada never reached its destination. Between June 4 and 7 control of the central Pacific was decided entirely by airpower. American dive bombers sent four large Japanese carriers to the bottom. About 300 Japanese planes were destroyed. The United States lost only the *Yorktown* and a destroyer. Thereafter the initiative in the Pacific war shifted to the Americans, but victory came slowly and at painful cost.

American land forces were under the command of Douglas MacArthur, a brilliant but egocentric general whose judgment was sometimes distorted by his

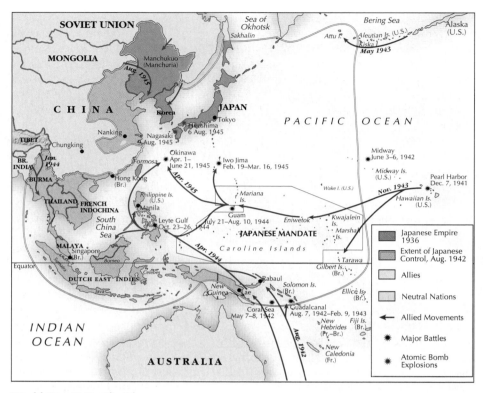

World War II, Pacific Theater

intense concern for his own reputation. MacArthur was in command of American troops in the Philippine Islands when the Japanese struck in December 1941. After his heroic but hopeless defense of Manila and the Bataan peninsula, President Roosevelt had him evacuated by PT boat to escape capture; those under MacArthur's command endured horrific conditions as prisoners of Japan.

Thereafter MacArthur was obsessed with the idea of personally leading an American army back to the Philippines. Although many strategists believed that the islands should be bypassed in the drive on the Japanese homeland, in the end MacArthur convinced the Joint Chiefs of Staff, who determined strategy. Two separate drives were undertaken, one from New Guinea toward the Philippines under MacArthur, the other through the central Pacific toward Tokyo under Admiral Chester W. Nimitz.

ISLAND HOPPING

Before commencing this two-pronged advance, the Americans had to eject the Japanese from the Solomon Islands in order to protect Australia from a flank attack. Beginning in August 1942, a series of land, sea, and air battles raged around Guadalcanal Island in this archipelago. Once again American airpower was decisive, although the bravery and skill of the ground forces that actually won the island must not be underemphasized. American pilots, better trained and with tougher planes than the Japanese, had a relatively easier task. They inflicted losses five to six times heavier on the enemy than they sustained themselves. Japanese airpower disintegrated progressively during the long battle, and this in turn helped the fleet to take a heavy toll on the Japanese navy. By February 1943 Guadalcanal had been secured.

In the autumn of 1943 the American drives toward Japan and the Philippines got under way at last. In the central Pacific campaign the Guadalcanal action was repeated on a smaller but equally bloody scale from Tarawa in the Gilbert Islands to Kwajelein and Eniwetok in the Marshalls. The Japanese soldiers on these islands fought for every foot of ground. They had to be blasted and burned from tunnels and concrete pillboxes with hand grenades, flamethrowers, and dynamite. They almost never surrendered. But Admiral Nimitz's forces were in every case victorious. By midsummer of 1944 this arm of the American advance had taken Saipan and Guam in the Marianas. Now land-based bombers were within range of Tokyo.

Meanwhile, MacArthur was leapfrogging along the New Guinea coast toward the Philippines. In October 1944 he made good his promise to return to the islands, landing on Leyte, south of Luzon. Two great naval clashes in Philippine waters, the Battle of the Philippine Sea (June 1944) and the Battle for Leyte Gulf (October 1944), completed the destruction of Japan's sea power and reduced its air force to a band of fanatical suicide pilots called *kamikazes,* who tried to crash bomb-laden planes into American warships and airstrips. The *kamikazes* caused much damage but could not turn the tide. In February 1945 MacArthur liberated Manila.

The end was now inevitable. B-29 Superfortress bombers from the Marianas rained high explosives and firebombs on Japan. The islands of Iwo Jima and Okinawa, only a few hundred miles from Tokyo, fell to the Americans in March and June 1945. But such was the tenacity of the Japanese soldiers that it seemed possible that it would take another year of fighting and a million more American casualties to subdue the main Japanese islands.

BUILDING THE ATOM BOMB

At this point came the most controversial decision of the entire war, and it was made by a newcomer on the world scene. In November 1944 Roosevelt had been elected to a fourth term, easily defeating Thomas E. Dewey. Instead of renominating Henry A. Wallace for vice president, whom conservatives considered too radical, the Democratic convention had nominated Senator Harry S Truman of Missouri, a reliable party man well liked by professional politicians. Then, in April 1945, President Roosevelt died of a cerebral hemorrhage. Thus it was Truman, a man painfully conscious of his limitations yet equally aware of the power and responsibility of his office, who had to decide what to do when, in

July 1945, American scientists placed in his hands a new and awful weapon, the atomic bomb.

After Roosevelt had responded to Albert Einstein's warning in 1939, government-sponsored atomic research had proceeded rapidly, especially after the establishment of the so-called Manhattan Project in May 1943. The manufacture of the element plutonium at Hanford, Washington, and of uranium 235 at Oak Ridge, Tennessee, continued, along with the design and construction of a transportable atomic bomb at Los Alamos, New Mexico, under the direction of J. Robert Oppenheimer. Almost $2 billion was spent before a successful bomb was exploded at Alamogordo, in the New Mexican desert, on July 16, 1945. As that first mushroom cloud formed over the desert, Oppenheimer recalled the prophetic words of the *Bhagavad Gita:* "I am become death, the shatterer of worlds."

Should a bomb with the destructive force of 20,000 tons of TNT be employed against Japan? By striking a major city, its dreadful power could be demonstrated convincingly, yet doing so would bring death to tens of thousands of Japanese civilians. Many of the scientists who had made the bomb now argued against its use. Others suggested alerting the Japanese and then staging a demonstration explosion at sea, but that idea was discarded because of concern that the bomb might fail to explode.

Truman was torn between his awareness that the bomb was "the most terrible thing ever discovered" and his hope that using it "would bring the war to an end." The bomb might cause a revolution in Japan, might lead the emperor to intervene, might even persuade the military to give up. Considering the thousands of Americans who would surely die in any conventional invasion of Japan and, on a less humane level, influenced by a desire to end the Pacific war before the Soviet Union could intervene effectively and thus claim a role in the peacemaking, the president chose to go ahead.

The moral soundness of Truman's decision has been debated ever since. There is no doubt that hatred of the Japanese had something to do with the decision. What is often forgotten by those who deplore it is the fact that while the immediate result was the death of many thousands of innocent Japanese civilians, far more Japanese would have died—many more than the Americans who would have perished—if Japan had had to be invaded.

On August 6 the Superfortress *Enola Gay* dropped an atomic bomb on Hiroshima, killing about 78,000 persons (including 20 American prisoners of war) and injuring nearly 100,000 more out of a population of 344,000. Over 96 percent of the buildings in the city were destroyed or damaged. Three days later, while the stunned Japanese still hesitated, a second atomic bomb, the only other one that had so far been assembled, blasted Nagasaki. This second drop was less defensible morally, but it had the desired result. On August 15 Japan surrendered.

Thus ended the greatest war in history. Its cost was beyond calculation. No accurate count could be made even of the dead; we know only that the total was in the neighborhood of 20 million. As in World War I, American casualties—291,000 battle deaths and 671,000 wounded—were smaller than those of the other major belligerents. About 7.5 million Soviets died in battle, 3.5 million

DEBATING THE PAST

Should the United States have used atomic bombs against Japan? Robert J. C. Butow's (1954) analysis of Japanese sources proved that the devastation of Hiroshima and Nagasaki had led to Japan's surrender. If there had been no atom bomb, the United States would probably have been forced to invade the islands. According to military estimates cited at the time, an invasion would have resulted in a half million American casualties. Biographers such as David McCullough (1992) and Alonzo L. Hamby (1995) agreed that, given public and congressional opinion, Truman had little choice but to end the war as quickly as possible and with the fewest American casualties.

But Gar Alperovitz (1965), writing when the United States was mired in a global struggle against the Soviet Union, proposed that Truman had been influenced more by a desire to intimidate Stalin than to force the surrender of Japan. This position was strengthened by subsequently declassified documents indicating that few U.S. military analysts anticipated losses as high as those reported in Butow and other sources. John Dower (1986) discovered evidence in Japanese sources that the Soviet declaration of war, which came in the wake of Hiroshima, shattered the confidence of the Japanese high command as much as the atomic bombs. Soviet entry alone might have ended the war. The American rush to use atomic weapons against Japan was due to "sheer visceral hatred" of the Japanese, Dower insisted.

The revisionist hypothesis—that Japan might have surrendered without the atomic bombs—is belied by exhaustive last-ditch Japanese preparations for defending the home islands. Whether this information justifies this first—and to date, only—use of weapons of mass destruction will forever remain a source of debate.

Robert J. C. Butow, *Japan's Decision to Surrender* (1954), Alonzo L. Hamby, *Man of the People* (1995), David McCullough, *Truman* (1992), Gar Alperovitz, *Atomic Diplomacy* (1965), and *The Decision to Use the Atomic Bomb and the Architecture of an American Myth* (1995), John W. Dower, *War Without Mercy* (1986), and Martin J. Sherwin, *A World Destroyed* (1975).

Germans, 1.2 million Japanese, and 2.2 million Chinese; Britain and France, despite much smaller populations, suffered losses almost as large as did the United States. And far more than in World War I, American resources, human and material, had made victory possible.

No one could account the war a benefit to humanity, but in the late summer of 1945 the future looked bright. Fascism was dead. The successful wartime diplomatic dealings of Roosevelt, Churchill, and the Soviet dictator, Joseph Stalin, encouraged many to hope that the communists were ready to cooperate in rebuilding Europe. In the United States isolationism had disappeared; the message of Wendell Willkie's best-selling *One World,* written after a globe-circling tour made by the 1940 Republican presidential candidate at the behest of President Roosevelt in 1942, appeared to have been absorbed by the majority of the people.

Out of the death and destruction had come technological developments that seemed to herald a better world as well as a peaceful one. Enormous advances in the design of airplanes and the development of radar (which some authorities think was more important than any weapons system in winning the war) were about to revolutionize travel and the transportation of goods. Improvements in surgery and other medical advances gave promise of saving millions of lives, and the development of penicillin and other antibiotics, which had greatly reduced the death rate among troops, would perhaps banish all infectious diseases.

Above all, there was the power of the atom. The force that seared Hiroshima and Nagasaki could be harnessed to serve peaceful needs, the scientists promised, with results that might free humanity forever from poverty and toil. The period of reconstruction would be prolonged, but with all the great powers adhering to the new United Nations charter, drafted at San Francisco in June 1945, international cooperation could be counted on to ease the burdens of the victims of war and help the poor and underdeveloped parts of the world toward economic and political independence. Such at least was the hope of millions in the victorious summer of 1945.

WARTIME DIPLOMACY

That hope was not to be realized, in large part because of a conflict that developed between the Soviet Union and the western Allies. During the war Americans with as different points of view as General Douglas MacArthur and Vice President Henry A. Wallace took strongly pro-Soviet positions, and American newspapers and magazines published many laudatory articles about Russia. These views were naive, to say the least, but the United States and the Soviet Union agreed emphatically on the need to defeat Hitler. The Soviets repeatedly expressed a willingness to cooperate with the Allies in dealing with postwar problems. The Soviet Union was one of the 26 signers of the Declaration of the United Nations (January 1942), in which the Allies promised to eschew territorial aggrandizement after the war, to respect the right of all peoples to determine their own form of government, to work for freer trade and international economic cooperation, and to force the disarmament of the aggressor nations.[1]

Between August and October 1944, Allied representatives met at Dumbarton Oaks, outside Washington, to plan a new league of nations. The chief Soviet delegate, Andrei A. Gromyko, opposed limiting the use of the veto

---

[1]*These were the principles first laid down in the so-called Atlantic Charter, drafted by Roosevelt and Churchill at a meeting on the USS* Augusta *off Newfoundland in August 1941.*

Churchill, Roosevelt, and Stalin photographed at the week-long Yalta conference in February 1945. By April 1945, Roosevelt was dead.

by the great powers on the future United Nations (UN) Security Council, but he did not take a deliberately obstructionist position. At a conference held at Yalta in the Crimea in February 1945 Stalin joined Roosevelt and Churchill in the call for a meeting in April at San Francisco to draft a charter for the UN.

The UN charter drafted at the 50-nation San Francisco Conference gave each UN member a seat in the General Assembly, a body designed for discussion rather than action. The locus of authority in the new organization resided in the Security Council, "the castle of the great powers." This consisted of five permanent members (the United States, the Soviet Union, Great Britain, France, and China) and six others elected for two-year terms.

The Security Council was charged with responsibility for maintaining world peace, but any great power could block UN action whenever it wished to do so. The United States insisted on this veto power as strongly as the Soviet Union did. In effect the charter paid lip service to the Wilsonian ideal of a powerful international police force, but it incorporated the limitations that Henry Cabot Lodge had proposed in his 1919 reservation to Article X of the League Covenant, which relieved the United States from the obligation of enforcing collective security without the approval of Congress.

ALLIED SUSPICION OF STALIN

Long before the war in Europe ended, however, the Allies had clashed over important policy matters. Since later world tensions developed from decisions made at this time, an understanding of the disagreements is essential for evaluating several decades of history.

Much depends on one's view of the postwar Soviet system. If the Soviet government under Stalin was bent on world domination, events fall readily into one pattern of interpretation. If, having at enormous cost endured an unprovoked assault by the Nazis, it was seeking only to protect itself against the possibility of another invasion, these events are best explained differently.

It is clear, however, that the Soviets resented the British-American delay in opening up a second front. They were fighting for survival against the full power of the German armies; any invasion, even an unsuccessful one, would have relieved some of the pressure. Roosevelt and Churchill would not move until they were ready, and Stalin had to accept their decision. At the same time, Stalin never concealed his determination to protect his country from future attack by extending its western frontier after the war. He warned the Allies repeatedly that he would not tolerate any unfriendly government along the western boundary of the Soviet Union.

Most Allied leaders, including Roosevelt, admitted privately during the war that the Soviet Union would annex territory and possess preponderant power in Eastern Europe after the defeat of Germany, but they never said this publicly. They believed that free governments could somehow be created in countries like Poland and Bulgaria that the Soviets would trust enough to leave to their own devices. "The Poles," Winston Churchill said early in 1945, "will have their future in their own hands, with the single limitation that they must honestly follow . . . a policy friendly to Russia. This is surely reasonable."

However reasonable, Churchill's statement was impractical. The Polish question was a terribly difficult one. The war, after all, had been triggered by the German attack on Poland; the British in particular felt a moral obligation to restore that nation to its prewar independence. During the war a Polish government in exile was set up in London, and its leaders were determined—especially after the discovery in 1943 of the murder of some 5000 Polish officers several years earlier at Katyn, in Russia, presumably by the Soviet secret police—to make no concessions to Soviet territorial demands. Public opinion in Poland (and indeed in all the states along Russia's western frontier) was not so much anti-Soviet as anti-Russian. Yet the Soviet Union's legitimate interests (to say nothing of its power in the area) could not be ignored.

YALTA AND POTSDAM

At the Yalta Conference, Roosevelt and Churchill agreed to Soviet annexation of large sections of eastern Poland. In return they demanded that free elections be held in Poland itself. "I want this election to be . . . beyond question," Roosevelt told Stalin. "It should be like Caesar's wife." In a feeble attempt at a joke he added: "I did not know her but they said she was pure." Stalin agreed, almost certainly without intending to keep his promise. The elections were never held; Poland was run by a pro-Soviet puppet regime.

Stalin apparently could not understand why the Allies were so concerned about the fate of a small country remote from their strategic spheres. That they professed to be concerned seemed to him an indication that they had some secret, devious purpose. He could see no difference (and "revisionist" American historians agree with him) between the Soviet Union's dominating Poland and maintaining a government there that did not reflect the wishes of a majority of the Polish people and the United States's dominating many Latin American nations and supporting unpopular regimes within them. Roosevelt, however, was worried about the political effects that Soviet control of Poland might have in the United States. Polish Americans would be furious if the United States allowed the Soviets to control their homeland.

But had Roosevelt described the difficulties to the Poles and the rest of the American people more frankly, their reaction might have been less angry. In any case, when he realized that Stalin was going to act as he pleased, Roosevelt was furious. "We can't do business with Stalin," he said shortly before his death in April 1945. "He has broken every one of the promises he made at Yalta." In July 1945, following the surrender of Germany, the new president, Harry Truman, met with Stalin and Churchill at Potsdam, outside Berlin.[2] They agreed to try the Nazi leaders as war criminals, made plans for exacting reparations from Germany, and confirmed the division of the country into four zones to be occupied separately by American, Soviet, British, and French troops. Berlin, deep in the Soviet zone, had itself been split into four sectors. Stalin rejected all arguments that he loosen his hold on Eastern Europe, and Truman (who received news of the successful testing of the atom bomb while at Potsdam) made no concessions. But he was impressed by Stalin. The dictator was "smart as hell," he wrote in his diary. "Stalin was an SOB," the plainspoken president explained to some officers while returning to the United States from Potsdam on the cruiser *Augusta*. Then he added: "Of course he thinks I'm one too."

On both sides suspicions were mounting, positions hardening. Yet all the advantages seemed to be with the United States. Was this not, as Henry Luce, the publisher of *Time* had declared, "the American century," an era when American power and American ideals would shape the course of events the world over? Besides its army, navy, and air force and its immense industrial potential, alone among the nations the United States possessed the atomic bomb. When Stalin's actions made it clear that he intended to control Eastern Europe and to exert influence elsewhere in the world, most Americans first reacted somewhat in the manner of a mastiff being worried by a yapping terrier: Their resentment was tempered by amazement. It took time for them to realize that the war had caus a fundamental change in international politics. The United States might b strongest country in the world, but the western European nations, vic vanquished alike, were reduced to their own and America's surprise t of second-class powers. The Soviet Union, on the other hand, ha influence than it had held under the czars and regained the terri a result of World War I and the communist revolution.

---

[2]*Clement R. Attlee replaced Churchill during the conference after his Labou*

MILESTONES

1941   Japan attacks Pearl Harbor

Roosevelt and Churchill draft Atlantic Charter

1942   Executive Order 9066 sends Japanese Americans to relocation camps

Japanese take Philippines

Carrier-based planes dominate Battle of Coral Sea

U.S. airpower takes control of central Pacific at Battle of Midway

U.S. troops invade North Africa

1943   Oppenheimer directs Manhattan Project to make atom bomb

Allies invade Italy

1944   Allies invade Normandy, France (D-Day)

Battle of the Bulge exhausts German reserves

1945   Roosevelt, Churchill, and Stalin meet at Yalta Conference

Fifty nations draft UN Charter at San Francisco

Roosevelt dies; Truman becomes president

Germany surrenders (V-E Day)

United States tests atom bomb at Alamogordo, New Mexico

Truman, Churchill, Stalin meet at Potsdam

United States drops atom bombs on Hiroshima and Nagasaki, Japan

Japan surrenders (V-J Day)

29

THE AMERICAN CENTURY

In late 1945 most Americans were probably more concerned with what was happening at home than with foreign developments, and no one was more aware of this than Harry Truman. When he received the news of Roosevelt's death, he claimed that he felt as though "the moon, the stars, and all the planets" had suddenly fallen upon him. Although he could not have been quite as surprised as he indicated (Roosevelt was known to have been in extremely poor health), he was acutely conscious of his own limitations.

Truman was born in Missouri in 1884. After his service in a World War I artillery unit, he opened a men's clothing store in Kansas City. The store failed in the postwar depression. Truman then became a minor cog in the political machine of Democratic boss Tom Pendergast. In 1934 Truman was elected to the U.S. Senate, where he proved to be a loyal but obscure New Dealer. He first attracted national attention during World War II when his "watchdog" committee on defense spending, working with devotion and efficiency, saved the government immense sums. This led to his nomination and election as vice president.

As president, Truman sought to carry on in the Roosevelt tradition. Curiously, he was at the same time humble and cocky, even brash—both idealistic and cold-bloodedly political. He adopted liberal objectives only to pursue them sometimes by rash, even repressive means. Too often he insulted opponents instead of convincing or appeasing them. Complications tended to confuse him, in which case he either dug in his heels or struck out blindly, usually with unfortunate results. On balance, however, he was a strong and in many ways a successful president.

THE POSTWAR ECONOMY

Nearly all the postwar leaders were worried by the possibility of a serious depression, and nearly all accepted the necessity of employing federal authority to stabilize the economy and speed national development. The Great Depression and the huge government expenditures made necessary by the war had proven the theories of John Maynard Keynes. Democrats and Republicans alike were convinced that it was possible to prevent sharp swings in the business cycle and therefore to do away with serious unemployment by monetary and fiscal manipulation.

When World War II ended, nearly everyone wanted to demobilize the armed forces, remove wartime controls, and reduce taxes. Yet everyone also hoped to prevent any sudden economic dislocation, to check inflation, and to make sure that goods in short supply were fairly distributed. Neither the politicians nor the public could reconcile these conflicting objectives. Labor wanted price controls retained but wage controls lifted; industrialists wished to raise prices and keep the lid on wages. Farmers wanted subsidies but opposed price controls and the extension of social security benefits to agricultural workers. In this difficult situation President Truman failed to win either the confidence of the people or the support of Congress.

Yet the country weathered the reconversion period with remarkable ease. The pent-up demand for houses, automobiles, clothing, washing machines, and countless other products, backed by the war-enforced savings of millions, kept factories operating at capacity. But when the veterans returned (more than 60,000 of them accompanied by foreign brides), few went without work for long. Because of the boom, the demand for labor was large and growing. In addition, the government made an unprecedented educational opportunity available to veterans. Instead of a general bonus, which would have stimulated consumption and inflation, in 1944 Congress passed the GI Bill of Rights, which made subsidies available to veterans so they could continue their educations, learn new trades, or start new businesses. Nearly 8 million veterans took advantage of the education and training grants, greatly to their long-term advantage, and thus to the country's.

Cutting taxes and removing price controls did cause a period of rapid inflation. Food prices rose more than 25 percent between 1945 and 1947, which led to demands for higher wages and a wave of strikes—nearly 5000 in 1946 alone. Inflation and labor unrest helped the Republicans to win control of both houses of Congress in 1946 for the first time since the 1920s.

High on the Republican agenda was the passage of a new labor relations act. Labor leaders tended to support the Democrats, for they remembered gratefully the Wagner Act and other help given to them by the Roosevelt administration during the labor-management struggles of the 1930s. In 1943 the CIO had created a Political Action Committee to mobilize the labor vote. But the strikes of 1946 had alienated many citizens because they delayed the satisfaction of the demand for consumer goods.

This was the climate when in June 1947 the new Congress passed the Taft-Hartley Act over the veto of President Truman. The measure outlawed the closed shop (a provision written into many labor contracts requiring new workers to join the union before they could be employed). Most important, it authorized the president to seek court injunctions to prevent strikes that in his opinion endangered the national interest. The injunctions would hold for 80 days—a "cooling-off" period during which a presidential fact-finding board could investigate and make recommendations. If the dispute remained unresolved after 80 days, the president was to recommend "appropriate action" to Congress.

The Taft-Hartley Act made the task of unionizing unorganized industries more difficult, but it did not seriously hamper existing unions. Although it outlawed the closed shop, it permitted union shop contracts, which forced new workers to join the union after accepting employment.

THE CONTAINMENT POLICY

Although postwar economic recovery went more smoothly than most expected, foreign policy issues vexed the Truman presidency. Repeatedly Stalin made it clear that he had no intention of even consulting with Western leaders about his domination of Eastern Europe, and he seemed intent on extending his power deep into war-devastated central Europe. The Soviet Union also controlled Outer Mongolia, parts of Manchuria, and northern Korea, and it had annexed the Kurile Islands and regained the southern half of Sakhalin Island from Japan. It was fomenting trouble in Iran. By January 1946 Truman had decided to stop "babying" the Russians. "Only one language do they understand," he noted in a memorandum. "How many divisions have you?"

Truman's problem—and it would bedevil American policymakers for years—was that Stalin had far more divisions than anyone else. Truman, a seasoned politician, had swiftly responded to the postwar clamor to "bring the boys home." In the two years following the surrender of Japan, the armed forces of the United States had dwindled from 6 million to 1.5 million. Stalin, who kept domestic foes out of office by having them shot, ignored domestic pressure to demobilize the Red Army, estimated by U.S. intelligence at twice the size of the American army.

Stalin and the Red Army evoked the image of Hitler's troops pouring across the north European plains. Like Hitler, Stalin was a cruel dictator who championed an ideology of world conquest. Averill Harriman, American ambassador to the Soviet Union, warned that communist ideology exerted an "outward thrust" more dangerous than Nazism. George Kennan, a scholarly foreign officer who also had served in Moscow, called for a policy of "long-term, patient but firm and vigilant containment" of the Soviet Union.

A TURNING POINT IN GREECE

The strategy of containment began to take shape early in 1947 as a result of a crisis in Greece. Greek communists, waging a guerrilla war against the monarchy, were receiving aid from communist Yugoslavia and Bulgaria. Great Britain had been assisting the monarchists but could no longer afford this drain on its re-sources. In February 1947 the British informed President Truman that they would cut off aid to Greece.

The British predicament forced American policymakers to confront the fact that their European allies had not been able to rebuild their war-weakened economies. The communist "Iron Curtain" (a phrase coined by Winston Churchill) seemed about to close down on another nation. Policymakers ignored the fact that the Soviet Union was actually discouraging the rebels out of fear of American intervention in the area. As Undersecretary of State Dean Acheson put it, the "corruption" of Greece might "infect" the entire Middle East and then spread through Asia Minor and Egypt and to Italy and France.

Truman therefore asked Congress to approve what became known as the Truman Doctrine. If Greece or Turkey fell to the communists, he said, all of the Middle East might be lost. To prevent this "unspeakable tragedy," he asked for $400 million in military and economic aid to Greece and Turkey. "It must be the policy of the United States to support free peoples who are resisting attempted subjugation by armed minorities or by outside pressures," he said.

By exaggerating the consequences of inaction and by justifying his request on ideological grounds, Truman obtained his objective. The result was the establish-ment of a right-wing, military-dominated government in Greece. In addition, by not limiting his request to the specific problem posed by the situation in Greece, Truman caused considerable concern in many countries.

The threat to Western Europe certainly loomed large in 1947. With the re-gion, in the words of Winston Churchill (the great phrase-maker of the era), "a rubble-heap, a charnel house, a breeding-ground of pestilence and hate," the en-tire continent seemed in danger of falling into communist hands without the Soviet Union raising a finger.

THE MARSHALL PLAN AND THE LESSON OF HISTORY

In a 1946 speech entitled "The Lesson of History," George C. Marshall, army chief of staff during World War II, reminded Americans that their isolationism had contributed to Hitler's unchecked early aggression. This time, Marshall noted, the people of the United States must be prepared to act against foreign ag-gressors. In 1947 Marshall was named secretary of state. He outlined an extraor-dinary plan by which the United States would finance the reconstruction of the European economy. "Hunger, poverty, desperation, and chaos" were the real en-emies of freedom and democracy, Marshall said. The need was to restore "the confidence of the European people in the economic future of their own coun-tries." Even the Soviet Union and Soviet-bloc nations would be eligible for American aid.

The European powers eagerly seized upon Marshall's suggestion. They set up a 16-nation Committee for European Economic Cooperation, which soon sub-mitted plans calling for up to $22.4 billion in American assistance.

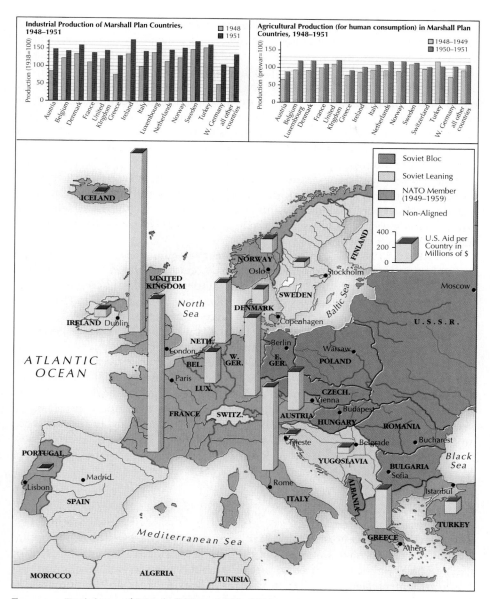

European Recipients of Marshall Plan, 1948–1952

The Soviet Union and its European satellites were tempted by the offer of aid and sent representatives to the initial planning meetings. But Stalin grew anxious that his satellite states, attracted by American money, would be drawn into the American orbit. He recalled his delegates and demanded that Eastern European nations do likewise. Those who hesitated were ordered to report to the Kremlin. "I went to Moscow as the Foreign Minister of an independent sovereign state," Jan Masaryk of Czechoslovakia commented bitterly. "I returned as a lackey of the Soviet government."

In February 1948 a communist coup took over the Czechoslovak government; Masaryk fell (or more likely was pushed) out a window to his death. These strong-arm tactics brought to mind the Nazi takeover of Czechoslovakia a decade earlier and helped persuade Congress to appropriate over $13 billion for the Marshall aid program. Results exceeded all expectations. By 1951 Western Europe was booming.

But Europe was now divided in two. In the West, where American-influenced governments were elected, private property was respected if often taxed heavily, and corporations gained influence and power. In the East, where the Soviet Union imposed its will and political system on client states, deep-seated resentment festered among subject peoples.

In March 1948 Great Britain, France, Belgium, the Netherlands, and Luxembourg signed an alliance aimed at social, cultural, and economic collaboration. The Western nations abandoned their understandable but counterproductive policy of crushing Germany economically. They announced plans for creating a single West German Republic with a large degree of autonomy.

In June 1948 the Soviet Union retaliated by closing off surface access to Berlin from the west. For a time it seemed that the Allies must either fight their way into the city or abandon it to the communists. Unwilling to adopt either alternative, Truman decided to fly supplies to the capital from Frankfurt, Hanover, and Hamburg. American C-47 and C-54 transports shuttled back and forth in fair weather and foul, carrying enough food, fuel, and other goods necessary to maintain more than 2 million West Berliners. The Berlin airlift put the Soviets in an uncomfortable position; if they were determined to keep supplies from West Berlin, they would have to start the fighting. They were not prepared to do so. In May 1949 they lifted the blockade.

THE ELECTION OF 1948

In the spring of 1948 President Truman's fortunes were at low ebb. Public opinion polls suggested that a majority of the people considered him incompetent or worse. The Republicans seemed so sure to win the 1948 presidential election that many prominent Democrats began to talk of denying Truman the nomination. Two of FDR's sons came out for General Eisenhower as the Democratic candidate. Governor Dewey, who again won the Republican nomination, ran confidently (even complacently), certain that he would carry the country.

Truman's position seemed hopeless because he had alienated both southern conservatives and northern liberals. The Southerners were particularly distressed because in 1946 the president had established a Committee on Civil Rights, which had recommended antilynching and anti–poll tax legislation and the creation of a permanent Fair Employment Practices Commission. When the

Air Relief to Berlin

Democratic convention adopted a strong civil rights plank, the southern delegates walked out. Southern conservatives then founded the States' Rights ("Dixiecrat") party and nominated J. Strom Thurmond of South Carolina for president.

As for the liberals, in 1947 a group that believed Truman's containment policy a threat to world peace organized a new Progressive party and nominated former Vice President Henry A. Wallace. With two minor candidates sure to cut into the Democratic vote, the president's chances seemed minuscule.

Promising to "give 'em hell," Truman launched an aggressive whistle-stop campaign. Traveling by rail, he made several hundred informal but hard-hitting speeches. He excoriated the "do-nothing" Republican Congress, which had rejected his program and passed the Taft-Hartley Act, and he warned labor, farmers, and consumers that if Dewey won, Republican "gluttons of privilege" would do away with all the gains of the New Deal years.

In June 1948 the Soviet Union cut off all water and road traffic into West Berlin. Truman's plan to airlift food and fuel to provision 2.5 million people seemed impossible, but during the fifteen months of the Berlin crisis, planes such as this one, landing every four minutes, delivered nearly 2.5 million tons of supplies.

Millions were moved by Truman's arguments and by his courageous fight against great odds. The success of the Berlin airlift during the presidential campaign helped him considerably, as did disaffection among normally Republican midwestern farmers. The Progressive party fell increasingly into the hands of communist sympathizers, driving away many liberals who might otherwise have supported Wallace.

Dewey's smug, lackluster speeches failed to attract independents. One party satirized his campaign by boiling it down to four platitudes: "Agriculture is important." "Our rivers are full of fish." "You cannot have freedom without liberty." "The future lies ahead." The president reinvigorated the New Deal coalition and won an amazing upset victory on election day. He collected 24.1 million votes to Dewey's 21.9 million, the two minor candidates being held to about 2.3 million. In the Electoral College his margin was a thumping 303 to 189.

Truman's victory encouraged him to press forward with what he called his Fair Deal program. He urged Congress to raise the minimum wage, fund an ambitious public housing program, develop a national health insurance system, and repeal the Taft-Hartley Act. However, relatively little of Truman's Fair Deal was enacted into law. Congress approved a federal housing program and measures increasing the minimum wage and social security benefits, but these were merely extensions of New Deal legislation.

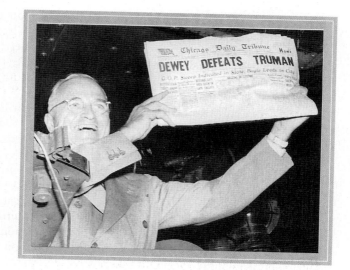

In 1948 the strongly Republican Chicago Daily Tribune guessed its postelection editions before all the returns were in. For Truman, it was the perfect climax to his hard-won victory.

CONTAINING COMMUNISM ABROAD

During Truman's second term the confrontation between the United States and the Soviet Union dominated the headlines. To strengthen ties with the European democracies, in April 1949 the North Atlantic Treaty was signed in Washington. The United States, Great Britain, France, Italy, Belgium, the Netherlands, Luxembourg, Denmark, Norway, Portugal, Iceland, and Canada[1] agreed "that an armed attack against one or more of them in Europe or North America shall be considered an attack against them all" and that in the event of such an attack each would take "individually and in concert with the other Parties, such action as it deems necessary, including the use of armed force." The pact established the North Atlantic Treaty Organization (NATO).

In September 1949 the Soviet Union detonated an atomic bomb. Truman had expressed doubts that the Soviets could build such sophisticated weapons. But when the explosion was confirmed, he called for rapid expansion of the American nuclear arsenal. He also asked his advisers to determine whether the United States should develop a new weapon thousands of times more destructive than atomic bombs. The "super" or hydrogen bomb would replicate the fusion process on the surface of the sun. The Atomic Energy Commission argued that there was no military use for hydrogen bombs, which would destroy hundreds of square miles as well as precipitate a dangerous arms race with the Soviet Union. The Joint Chiefs of Staff disagreed. Even if the hydrogen bomb could not be used

---

[1]*In 1952, Greece and Turkey joined the alliance, and in 1954, West Germany.*

in battle, they argued, its mere existence would intimidate enemies; and, the military men added, the Soviets would themselves build a hydrogen bomb whether or not the United States did so. (Unbeknownst to American leaders, Stalin was already developing a hydrogen bomb.) On January 31, 1950, Truman publicly announced that "though none wants to use it" he had no choice but to proceed with a hydrogen bomb.

In Asia the effort to contain communism in China failed utterly. Civil war erupted following Japan's surrender. By the end of 1949 the communists under Mao Zedong had crushed the Nationalists under Chiang-Kai shek (sometimes spelled Jiang Jieshi). The remnants of Chiang Kai-shek's forces fled to the island of Formosa, now called Taiwan. The "loss" of China to communism strengthened right-wing elements in the Republican party. They charged that Truman had not backed the Nationalists strongly enough and that he had stupidly underestimated Mao's dedication to the cause of world revolution.

Despite a superficial plausibility, neither charge made much sense. American opinion would not have supported military intervention, and such intervention unquestionably would have alienated the Chinese people. That *any* American action could have changed the outcome in China is unlikely. The United States probably gave the Nationalists too much aid rather than too little.

Containment had relied on American money, materials, and know-how, but not on American soldiers. In early 1950, Truman proposed to pare the budget by further reducing the nation's armed forces. Truman also called for a thorough review of the concept of containment. Dean Acheson, who recently had succeeded George Marshall as secretary of state, supervised the study. In March, it was submitted to the National Security Council, assigned a numerical designation (NSC-68), classified top secret, and sent to the nation's military and diplomatic leaders for review.

NSC-68 called for an enormous military expansion. The Soviet Union, it declared, was engaged in a worldwide assault on freedom. "A defeat of free institutions anywhere is a defeat everywhere." Instead of relying on other nations, the United States itself must develop sufficient military forces to stop communism from spreading *anywhere in the world.* Military spending therefore had to be increased by a staggering 350 percent to nearly $50 billion. If the Soviet Union failed to keep up with the American armed forces, it would no longer pose a threat, and if it attempted to match the high levels of American military spending, its less efficient economic system would collapse from the strain.

The document was submitted to Truman on April 7, 1950. He was initially cool to the idea and appalled by its cost. He had planned to cut $1 billion from the $14 billion military budget. Within a few months, however, events in Korea changed his mind.

HOT WAR IN KOREA

After the Second World War the province of Korea was taken from Japan and divided at 38° north latitude into the Democratic People's Republic in the north, backed by the Soviet Union, and the Republic of Korea in the south, backed by the United States and the UN. Both powers withdrew their troops from the

DEBATING THE PAST

Did Truman needlessly exacerbate relations with the Soviet Union? Here Stalin applauds Soviet military might. Historian Thomas A. Bailey (1950), like most Americans at the time, blamed Stalin's takeover of Eastern Europe and his threats elsewhere for the onset of the Cold War. In his view, Truman was right to contain Stalin.

But as the Cold War intensified and its costs mounted, historians looked more critically at Truman's actions. William Appleman Williams (1959) proposed that Truman, like American policymakers before him, had promoted worldwide containment of the Soviet Union chiefly to advance American economic interests abroad. Michael Hogan (1987) more subtly argued that the Marshall Plan put corporations at the center of the reconstruction of Europe. Walter La Feber (1967) and other revisionists found Truman's actions and rhetoric needlessly provocative.

John Lewis Gaddis (1972, 1982) rejected the contention that Truman was motivated by economic considerations. Truman's goal, rather, was to cobble together a military coalition of independent allies capable of containing the Soviet Union militarily.

Historians focused on Truman because little was known of Stalin's thinking. But as Soviet archives opened up following the collapse of the Soviet Union, Gaddis revised his views. In *Now We Know* (1997), he emphasized Stalin's commitment to communist ideology. Truman had not goaded him into these beliefs. Thomas Mastny (1996) attributed the despot's behavior to his insecurity rather than his belief in communist ideology.

Thomas A. Bailey, *America Faces Russia* (1950), William Appleman Williams, *The Tragedy of American Diplomacy* (1959), Walter La Feber, *America, Russia and the Cold War* (1967), Michael Hogan, *Marshall Plan* (1987), John Lewis Gaddis, *The United States and the Origins of the Cold War* (1972), *Strategies of Containment* (1982), and *Now We Know* (1997), and Thomas Mastny, *The Cold War and Soviet Insecurity* (1996).

peninsula. The Soviets left behind a well-armed local force, but the Republic of Korea's army was small and ill trained. In June 1950, when North Korean armored divisions, led by 150 Soviet-made tanks, rumbled across the 38th parallel, the South Koreans were unable to stop them.

Truman was at his family home in Independence, Missouri, when Acheson telephoned with the news of the North Korean attack. "Dean," Truman explained, "we've got to stop the sons of bitches no matter what." Truman hastened to Washington. On the flight, he recalled how the communists in Korea were acting "just as Hitler, Mussolini, and the Japanese had acted ten, fifteen, and twenty years earlier." "If this were allowed to go unchallenged," he concluded, "it would mean a third world war, just as similar incidents had brought on the Second World War." With the backing of the UN Security Council (but without asking Congress to declare war), he sent American planes into battle.[2] Ground troops soon followed. Truman also ordered the adoption of NSC-68 "as soon as feasible."

Nominally the Korean War was a struggle between the invaders and the United Nations. General MacArthur, placed in command, flew the blue UN flag over his headquarters, and 16 nations supplied troops for his army. However, more than 90 percent of the forces were American. At first the North Koreans pushed them back rapidly, but in September a front was stabilized around the port of Pusan, at the southern tip of Korea. Then MacArthur executed a brilliant amphibious maneuver, striking at the west coast city of Inchon, about 50 miles south of the 38th parallel. Outflanked, the North Koreans retreated in disorder. By October the battlefront had moved north of the 1945 boundary.

General MacArthur now proposed the conquest of North Korea, even if it meant bombing "privileged sanctuaries" on the Chinese side of the Korean border. Less sanguine military officials balked at taking on China but urged occupying North Korea to protect the future security of the south. A few of Truman's civilian advisers, the most important being George Kennan, opposed advancing beyond the 38th parallel, fearing intervention not only by the Red Chinese but also by the Soviets. "When we start walking inland from the tip of Korea, we have about a 10,000 mile walk if we keep going," Kennan pointed out. "We are going to have to stop somewhere."

Truman authorized MacArthur to advance as far as the Yalu River, the boundary between North Korea and China. It was an unfortunate decision, an example of how power, once unleashed, so often gets out of hand. As the advance progressed, ominous reports came from north of the Yalu. Foreign Minister Chou En-lai warned that the Chinese would not "supinely" tolerate seeing their neighbors being "savagely invaded by imperialists." Chinese "volunteers" began to turn up among the captives taken by UN units.

Alarmed, Truman flew to Wake Island, in the Pacific, to confer with MacArthur, but the general, who had a low opinion of Asian soldiers, assured him that the Chinese would not dare to intervene. If they did, he added, his army would crush them easily; the war would be over by Christmas.

Seldom has a general miscalculated so badly. Ignoring intelligence reports and dividing his advancing units recklessly, he drove toward the Yalu. Suddenly, on November 26, 33 Chinese divisions, hidden in the interior mountains of

---

[2]*The Soviet Union, which could have vetoed this action, was at the moment boycotting the Security Council because the UN had refused to give the Mao Zedong regime China's seat on that body.*

North Korean Offensive, June–August 1950

Korea, smashed through the center of MacArthur's lines. Overnight a triumphant advance became a bloody, disorganized retreat. MacArthur now spoke of the "bottomless well of Chinese manpower" and justified his earlier confidence by claiming that he was fighting "an entirely new war."

The Chinese counteroffensive of November 1950 caught the Americans by surprise and cut off many units. Here, U.S. Marines retreat southward, harassed by communist Chinese soldiers in the hills. American bombers blast a way through communist defenses to help the Americans escape.

The UN army rallied south of the 38th parallel, and MacArthur then urged that he be permitted to bomb Chinese installations north of the Yalu. He also suggested a naval blockade of the coast of China and the use of Chinese Nationalist troops. When Truman rejected these proposals on the ground that they would lead to a third world war, MacArthur, who tended to ignore the larger political aspects of the conflict, attempted to rouse Congress and the public against the president by openly criticizing administration policy. Truman ordered him to be silent, and when the general persisted, he removed him from command.

At first the Korean "police action" had been popular in the United States, but as the months passed and the casualties mounted, many citizens became disillusioned and angry. To Americans accustomed to triumph and fond of oversimplifying complex questions, containment seemed, as its costs in blood and dollars mounted, a monumentally frustrating policy. Military men backed the president almost unanimously. General Omar N. Bradley, chairman of the Joint Chiefs of Staff, said that a showdown with communist China "would involve us in the wrong war, at the wrong place, at the wrong time and with the wrong enemy." In

June 1951 the communists agreed to discuss an armistice in Korea, although the negotiations dragged on interminably. The war was unresolved when Truman left office: by the time it was over, it had produced 157,000 American casualties, including 54,200 dead.

If the Korean War persuaded Truman to adopt NSC-68, it also exposed the failings of the policy. By conceiving of communism as a monolithic force it tended to make it so, driving Red China and the Soviet Union into each other's arms. By committing American military forces to potential trouble spots throughout the world, it increased the likelihood they would prevail in none.

THE COMMUNIST ISSUE AT HOME

The Korean War highlighted the paradox that, at the pinnacle of its power, the influence of the United States in world affairs was declining. Its monopoly on nuclear weapons had been lost. China had passed into the communist orbit. Elsewhere in Asia and throughout Africa, new nations, formerly colonial possessions of the Western powers, were adopting a "neutralist" position in the Cold War. Despite the billions poured into armaments and foreign aid, national security seemed far from ensured.

Internal as well as external dangers loomed. Alarming examples of communist espionage in Canada, in Great Britain, and in the United States itself convinced many citizens that clever conspirators were everywhere at work undermining American security. Both the Republicans and conservative Democratic critics of Truman's domestic policies were charging that he was "soft" on communists.

There were never more than 100,000 communists in the United States, and party membership plummeted after the start of the Cold War. However, the possibility that a handful of spies could do enormous damage fueled a kind of panic that could be used for partisan purposes. In 1947, hoping to defuse the communists-in-government issue by being more zealous in pursuit of spies than his critics, Truman established a Loyalty Review Board to check up on government employees. The program made even sympathy for a long list of vaguely defined "totalitarian" or "subversive" organizations grounds for dismissal. During the following 10 years about 2700 government workers were discharged, only a relative handful of them for legitimate reasons. A much larger number resigned.

In 1948 Whittaker Chambers, an editor of *Time* who had formerly been a communist, charged that Alger Hiss, president of the Carnegie Endowment for International Peace and a former State Department official, had been a communist in the 1930s. Hiss denied the charge and sued Chambers for libel. Chambers then produced microfilms purporting to show that Hiss had copied classified documents for dispatch to Moscow. Hiss could not be indicted for espionage because of the statute of limitations; instead he was charged with perjury. His first trial resulted in a hung jury; his second, ending in January 1950, in conviction and a five-year jail term.

If a distinguished official such as Hiss had been disloyal, anything seemed possible. The case fed the fears of those who believed in the existence of a powerful communist underground in the United States. The disclosure in February 1950 that a British scientist, Klaus Fuchs, had betrayed atomic secrets to the Soviets heightened these fears, as did the arrest and conviction of his American associate, Harry Gold, and two other Americans, Julius and Ethel Rosenberg, on the same charge.

Although they were not major spies and the information they revealed was not important, the Rosenbergs were executed, to the consternation of many liberals in the United States and elsewhere. However, information gathered by other spies had speeded the Soviet development of nuclear weapons. This fact encouraged some Republicans to press the communists-in-government issue hard.

McCarthyism

In February 1950 an obscure senator, Joseph R. McCarthy of Wisconsin, introduced this theme in a speech to the even less well-known Ohio County Republican Women's Club of Wheeling, West Virginia. "The reason we find ourselves in a position of impotency," he stated, "is not because our only powerful potential enemy has sent men to invade our shores, but rather because of the traitorous actions of those who have been treated so well by this nation." The State Department, he added, was "infested" with communists. "I have here in my hand a list of 205—a list of names that were known to the Secretary of State as being members of the Communist Party and who nevertheless are still working and shaping . . . policy."[3]

McCarthy was totally unscrupulous. The "big lie" was his most effective weapon: The enormity of his charges and the status of his targets convinced thousands that there must be some truth in what he was saying. Nevertheless, his crude tactics would have failed if the public had not been so worried about communism. The worries were caused by the reality of Soviet military power, the attack on Korea, the loss of the nuclear monopoly, and the stories about spies, some of them true.

⑥. Dwight D. Eisenhower

As the 1952 presidential election approached, Truman's popularity was again at low ebb. Senator McCarthy attacked him relentlessly for his handling of the Korean conflict and his "mistreatment" of General MacArthur. In choosing their candidate, the Republicans passed over the twice-defeated Dewey and their most prominent leader, Senator Robert A. Taft of Ohio, an outspoken conservative, and nominated General Dwight D. Eisenhower.

Eisenhower's popularity did not grow merely out of his achievements in World War II. Although a West Pointer (class of 1915), he struck most persons as

---

[3]*McCarthy was speaking from rough notes, and no one made an accurate record of his words. The exact number mentioned has long been in dispute. On other occasions he said there were 57 and 81 "card-carrying" communists in the State Department.*

anything but warlike. After the bristly, combative Truman, his genial personality and evident desire to avoid controversy proved widely appealing. In his reluctance to seek political office, Eisenhower reminded the country of George Washington, whereas his seeming ignorance of current political issues was no more a handicap to his campaign than the similar ignorance of Jackson and Grant in their times. People "liked Ike" because his management of the Allied armies suggested that he would be equally competent as head of the complex federal government. His promise during the campaign to go to Korea if elected to try to bring the war to an end was a political masterstroke.

The Democrats nominated Governor Adlai E. Stevenson of Illinois, whose grandfather had been vice president under Grover Cleveland. Stevenson's unpretentiousness was appealing, and his witty, urbane speeches captivated intellectuals. In retrospect, however, it is clear that he had not the remotest chance of defeating the popular Eisenhower. Eisenhower received almost 34 million votes to Stevenson's 27 million, and in the Electoral College his margin was 442 to 89.

Eisenhower was unwilling to do away with existing social and economic legislation or to cut back on military expendi-

Many critics lampooned Eisenhower for his banal amusements. A popular bumper sticker read: "BEN HOGAN [a famous golfer] FOR PRESIDENT. IF WE'RE GOING TO HAVE A GOLFER FOR PRESIDENT, LET'S HAVE A GOOD ONE." Others have viewed Eisenhower's passion for golf as characteristic of his presidential style: methodical, prudent, and, when in the rough, disarmingly shrewd.

tures. Some economists claimed that he reacted too slowly in dealing with business recessions and that he showed insufficient concern for speeding the rate of national economic growth. Yet he adopted an almost Keynesian approach to economic problems; that is, he tried to check downturns in the business cycle by stimulating the economy.

Eisenhower approved the extension of social security to an additional 10 million persons; created a new Department of Health, Education, and Welfare; began the St. Lawrence Seaway project; and in 1955 came out for federal support of education and a highway construction act that eventually produced a 40,000-mile network of superhighways covering every state in the Union. His somewhat doctrinaire belief in decentralization and private enterprise reduced the effectiveness of his social welfare measures, but on balance, he proved to be an excellent politician. He knew how to be flexible without compromising his basic values.

THE EISENHOWER-DULLES FOREIGN POLICY

The American people, troubled and uncertain over the stalemate in Korea, counted on Eisenhower to find a way to employ the nation's immense strength constructively. The new president shared the general feeling that a change of tactics in foreign affairs was needed. He counted on his secretary of state to solve the practical problems.

His choice, John Foster Dulles, was a lawyer with considerable diplomatic experience. He had been an outspoken critic of Truman's foreign policy. In a May 1952 article in *Life* entitled "A Policy of Boldness," he argued that global military containment was both expensive and ineffective: "We cannot build a 20,000-mile Maginot Line or match the Red armies man for man, gun for gun, and tank for tank at any particular time or place their general staff selects." Instead of waiting for the communist powers to make a move and then "containing" them, the United States should put more emphasis on nuclear bombs and less on conventional weapons. Such a "new look" military would be cheaper to maintain than a force of conventional weapons and a large standing army, and it would prevent the United States from being caught up in "local" conflicts like the Korean War. The nation's military forces, spearheaded by its formidable nuclear arsenal, would serve as "a deterrent of war instead of a mere means of waging war after we got into it."

Korea offered the first test of his views. After Eisenhower's postelection trip to Korea failed to bring an end to the war, Dulles signaled his willingness to use tactical nuclear weapons in Korea by showily transferring nuclear warheads from the United States mainland to bomber units stationed in East Asia. He also issued a calculatedly vague warning about tough new measures. Several weeks later, in July 1953, the Chinese signed an armistice that ended hostilities but left Korea divided. The administration interpreted the softening of the Chinese position as proof that the nuclear threat had worked. (Dulles was apparently mistaken about the effectiveness of his Korean gambit. In recent years, Chinese officials have said that they were unaware at the time of the American nuclear threats.)

Emboldened by his evident triumph, Dulles again brandished the nuclear threat. Chiang Kai-shek had stationed 90,000 soldiers—one-third of his army—in Quemoy and Matsu, two small islands located a few miles from mainland China. In 1954 the Chinese communists began shelling the islands, presumably in preparation to invade them. Chiang appealed for American protection, warning that loss of the islands would bring about the collapse of Nationalist China. Dulles concurred that the consequences throughout East Asia would be "catastrophic." At a press conference in 1955 Eisenhower announced his willingness to use nuclear weapons to defend the islands, "just exactly as you would use a bullet or anything else." The Chinese communists backed down.

Massive retaliation succeeded, further, in reducing the defense budget. The reliance on a nuclear threat allowed Eisenhower to pare another half million men from the armed forces, saving $4 billion annually. On balance, however, Dulles's strategy was flawed, and many of his schemes were preposterous. Above all, massive retaliation made little sense when the Soviet Union possessed nuclear weapons as powerful as those of the United States.

MCCARTHY SELF-DESTRUCTS

Although the State Department was now controlled by Dulles, a hard-line anti-communist, Senator McCarthy continued his attacks on the department. Finally, he overreached himself. Early in 1954 he turned his guns on the army, accusing Pentagon officials of trying to blackmail his committee. The resulting Army-McCarthy hearings, televised before the country, proved the senator's undoing. For weeks his dark scowl, his blind combativeness, and his disregard for every human value stood exposed for millions to see. When the hearings ended in June 1954 after some million words of testimony, his spell had been broken.

The Senate, with President Eisenhower, who despised McCarthy but considered it beneath his dignity as president to "get into the gutter with that guy," applying pressure behind the scenes, at last moved to censure the senator in December 1954. This reproof completed the destruction of his influence. Although he continued to issue statements and wild charges, the country no longer listened. In 1957 he died of cirrhosis of the liver.

17 ASIAN POLICY AFTER KOREA

Shortly after an armistice was finally arranged in Korea in July 1953, new trouble erupted far to the south in the former French colony of Indochina. Nationalist rebels led by the communist Ho Chi Minh had been harassing the French in

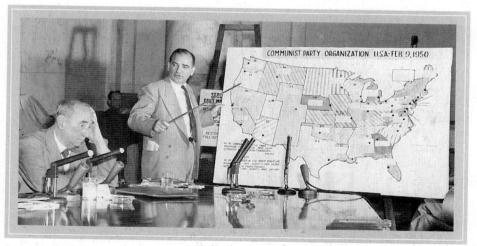

Senator Joseph McCarthy's unsubstantiated charges of communist infiltration of the army led finally to his downfall.

Vietnam, one of the three puppet kingdoms (the others were Laos and Cambodia) fashioned by France in Indochina after the defeat of the Japanese. When China recognized the rebels, who were known as the Vietminh, and supplied them with arms, President Truman countered with economic and military assistance to the French, and President Eisenhower continued and expanded this assistance.

Early in 1954 Ho Chi Minh's troops trapped and besieged a French army in the remote stronghold of Dien Bien Phu. In May the 20,000-man garrison surrendered. In July France, Great Britain, the Soviet Union, and China signed an agreement dividing Vietnam along the 17th parallel. France withdrew from the area. The northern sector became the Democratic Republic of Vietnam, controlled by Ho Chi Minh; the southern remained in the hands of the emperor, Bao Dai. An election to settle the future of all Vietnam was scheduled for 1956.

When it seemed likely that the communists would win that election, Ngo Dinh Diem, a conservative anticommunist, overthrew Bao Dai and became president of South Vietnam. The United States supplied his government liberally with aid. The planned election was never held, and Vietnam remained divided.

Dulles responded to the diplomatic setback in Vietnam by establishing the Southeast Asia Treaty Organization (SEATO), but only three Asian nations—the Philippine Republic, which was granted independence in 1947, Thailand, and Pakistan—joined this alliance.[4]

ISRAEL AND THE MIDDLE EAST

The extermination of six million European Jews by the Nazis strengthened Jewish claims to a homeland and intensified pressure to allow hundreds of thousands of Jewish refugees to immigrate to Palestine, which was governed by Great Britain according to a League of Nations mandate. But the influx of Jewish settlers, and their calls for creation of a Jewish state (Israel), provoked Palestinian and Arab leaders. Fighting broke out. President Truman angered Arab leaders by endorsing the partition of the region into Israel and a Palestinian state. In 1947, the United Nations voted for partition and on May 14, 1948, the State of Israel was established. Within hours, Truman recognized its sovereignty.

Then Arab armies from Egypt, Jordan, Iraq, Syria, and Lebanon attacked Israel. Although badly outnumbered, the Israelis were better organized and better armed than the Arabs and drove them off with relative ease. With them departed nearly a million local Arabs, thereby creating a desperate refugee problem in nearby countries.

President Truman had consistently placed support for Israel before other considerations in the Middle East, partly because of the conviction that survivors of the Nazi holocaust were entitled to a country of their own and partly because of the political importance of the Jewish vote in the United States. Dulles and Eisenhower tried to restore balance by deemphasizing American support of

---

[4]*The other signatories were Great Britain, France, the United States, Australia, and New Zealand.*

Israel. They hoped to mollify the Arabs. Of increasing importance to the United States were the seas of oil that lay beneath the Middle East's deserts. Iran, Iraq, Kuwait, and Saudi Arabia sat upon nearly 60 percent of the world's known reserves. Gas-hungry Americans could ill-afford to alienate the Arab world.

In 1952 a revolution in Egypt had overthrown the dissolute King Farouk. Colonel Gamal Abdel Nasser emerged as the strongman of Egypt. When Eisenhower refused to sell Egypt arms, Nasser drifted toward the communist orbit and nationalized the Suez Canal. The British, in conjunction with the French and without consulting the French, decided to take back the canal by force. The Israelis, alarmed by repeated Arab hit-and-run raids, also attacked Egypt.

Events moved swiftly. Israeli armored columns crushed the Egyptian army in the Sinai Peninsula in a matter of days. Then Nikita Khrushchev, who had become First Secretary of the Communist party of the Soviet Union following Stalin's death in 1953, threatened to send "volunteers" to Egypt and launch atomic missiles against France and Great Britain if they did not withdraw. Eisenhower also demanded that the invaders pull out of Egypt. In London large crowds demonstrated against their own government. On November 6, only nine days after the first Israeli units invaded Egypt, Prime Minister Anthony Eden, haggard and shaken, announced a cease-fire. Israel withdrew its troops. The crisis subsided as rapidly as it had arisen.

The United States had won a measure of respect in the Arab countries, but at what cost? Its major allies had been humiliated. Their ill-timed attack had enabled the Soviet Union to recover much of the prestige it had lost as a result of its brutal suppression of a Hungarian revolt that had broken out a week before the Suez fiasco.

EISENHOWER AND KHRUSHCHEV

In 1956 Eisenhower was reelected, defeating Adlai Stevenson even more decisively than he had in 1952. Despite evident satisfaction with their leader, however, the American people were in a sober mood. Hopes of pushing back the Soviet Union with clever stratagems and moral fervor were fading. Although the United States detonated the first hydrogen bomb in November 1952, the Soviets followed suit within six months. The Cold War between the superpowers had become yet more chilling.

The United States had far more air force bases, bombers, and radar installations than the Soviet Union. But this advantage disappeared in the exhaust cloud of a Soviet rocket, launched on October 4, 1957, that carried a 184-pound capsule named *Sputnik* far above the atmosphere into earth orbit. Soon, American policymakers knew, Soviet missiles capable of reaching American soil would be tipped with nuclear warheads. The nation's far-flung network of bomber defenses had become obsolete, and with it the strategy of massive retaliation.

Several weeks later Khrushchev rubbed hard at the rawest sore in the American psyche: the anguished memory of Pearl Harbor. In an interview with publisher William Randolph Hearst, Jr., Khrushchev blustered that the Soviet

Vice President Richard M. Nixon and Soviet leader Nikita Khrushchev engaged in their "kitchen debate" over the future of capitalism at a Moscow trade fair in 1959. Although this encounter did little to advance United States–Soviet relations, it established Nixon's credentials as a tough negotiator.

Union could launch 10 or 20 intercontinental missiles with nuclear warheads "tomorrow." He boasted that the American military was no match for the Soviet military behemoth. This was nonsense and Eisenhower knew it. Yet to point out the weaknesses of the Soviet military—to call Khrushchev's bluff—was potentially to goad the unstable Soviet leader to rash action. While critics at home flayed Eisenhower for allowing a "missile gap" with the Soviet Union, the president testily reassured the American people that they had little to fear, but otherwise remained silent. In September 1960, however, Khrushchev told the United Nations that the Soviet Union was turning out nuclear missiles "like sausages from an automatic machine."

LATIN AMERICA AROUSED

Events in Latin America compounded Eisenhower's difficulties. During World War II the United States, needing Latin American raw materials, had supplied its southern neighbors liberally with economic aid. In the period following victory a hemispheric mutual defense pact was signed at Rio de Janeiro in September 1947, and the following year the Organization of American States (OAS) came into being. In the OAS, decisions were reached by a two-thirds vote; the United States had neither a veto nor any special position.

But as the Cold War progressed, the United States neglected Latin American questions. Economic problems plagued the region, and in most nations reactionary governments reigned. Radical Latin Americans accused the United States of supporting cliques of wealthy tyrants, whereas conservatives blamed insufficient American economic aid for the plight of the poor.

Eisenhower, eager to improve relations, stepped up economic assistance. Resistance to communism nonetheless continued to receive first priority. In 1954 the government of Jacobo Arbenz Guzman in Guatemala began to import Soviet weapons. The United States promptly dispatched arms to neighboring Honduras. Within a month an army led by an exiled Guatemalan officer marched into the country from Honduras and overthrew Arbenz. Elsewhere in Latin America, Eisenhower, as Truman had before him, continued to support regimes that were kept in power by the local military.

The depth of Latin American resentment of the United States became clear in the spring of 1958, when Vice President Nixon made what was supposed to be a goodwill tour of South America. Everywhere he was met with hostility. In Lima, Peru, he was mobbed; in Caracas, Venezuela, students pelted him with eggs and stones. He had to abandon the remainder of his trip. For the first time the American people gained some inkling of Latin American opinion and the social and economic troubles that lay behind it.

Events in Cuba demonstrated that there was no easy solution to Latin American problems. In 1959 a revolutionary movement headed by Fidel Castro overthrew Fulgencio Batista, one of the most noxious of the Latin American dictators. Eisenhower recognized the Castro government at once, but the Cuban leader soon began to criticize the United States in highly colored speeches. Castro confiscated American property without providing adequate compensation, suppressed civil liberties, and entered into close relations with the Soviet Union. After he negotiated a trade agreement with the Soviet Union in February 1960, which enabled the Russians to obtain Cuban sugar at bargain rates, the United States retaliated by prohibiting the importation of Cuban sugar into America.

Khrushchev then announced that if the United States intervened in Cuba, he would defend the country with atomic weapons. "The Monroe Doctrine has outlived its time," Khrushchev warned. Shortly before the end of his second term, Eisenhower broke off diplomatic relations with Cuba.

THE POLITICS OF CIVIL RIGHTS

During Eisenhower's presidency a major change occurred in the legal status of American blacks. Eisenhower had relatively little to do with this change, which was part of a broad shift in attitudes toward the rights of minorities in democracies. After 1945 the question of racial equality took on special importance because of the ideological competition with communism. Evidence of color prejudice in the United States damaged the nation's image, particularly in Asia and Africa, where the United States and the Soviet Union were competing for influence. An awareness of foreign criticism of American racial attitudes, along with resentment that almost a century after the Emancipation Proclamation they were still second-class citizens, produced a growing militancy among American blacks. At the same time, fears of communist subversion in the United States led to the repression of the rights of many white citizens. Even before McCarthy's fateful Wheeling speech, Congress contemplated a crackdown on suspected communists. In 1950, over Truman's veto, it passed an Internal Security Act (better known as the McCarran Act), which required every "communist-front organization" to register with the attorney general. Members of such organizations were barred from defense work and from traveling abroad. The law even provided for construction of internment camps in the event of a national emergency.

Under Eisenhower, while the McCarthy hysteria reached its peak and declined, the government compiled a spotty record on civil rights. The search for subversive federal employees continued. The refusal to grant security clearance to Oppenheimer, one of the fathers of the atomic bomb, on the grounds that he had associated with communists and communist sympathizers, was the most glaring instance of the administration's catering to anticommunist extremists, for it was based on the supposition that Oppenheimer could be denied access to discoveries he had helped to make possible. Eisenhower completed the integration of the armed forces begun by Truman, but he was temperamentally incapable of a frontal assault on the racial problem. This was done by the Supreme Court, which interjected itself into the civil rights controversy in dramatic fashion in 1954.

Under pressure of litigation sponsored by the NAACP, the Court had been gradually undermining the "separate but equal" principle laid down in *Plessy* v. *Ferguson* in 1896, at least insofar as it applied to higher education. In 1938 it ordered the University of Missouri law school to admit a black student because no law school for blacks existed in the state. This decision gradually forced some southern states to admit blacks to advanced programs. "You can't build a cyclotron for one student," the president of the University of Oklahoma confessed when the Court, in 1948, ordered Oklahoma to provide equal facilities. Two years later, when Texas actually attempted to create a separate law school for a single black applicant, the Court ruled that truly equal education could not be provided under such circumstances.

In 1953 President Eisenhower appointed California's Governor Earl Warren chief justice of the United States Supreme Court. Convinced that the Court must take the offensive in the cause of civil rights, Warren succeeded in welding his associates into a unit on this question. In 1954 an NAACP-sponsored case, *Brown* v. *Board of Education of Topeka,* came up for decision. The NAACP lawyer, Thurgood Marshall, challenging the "separate but equal" doctrine, submitted a mass of sociological evidence to show that the mere fact of segregation made equal education impossible and did serious psychological damage to both black and white children. Speaking for a unanimous Court, Warren reversed the *Plessy* decision. "In the field of public education, the doctrine of 'separate but equal' has no place," he declared. "Separate educational facilities are inherently unequal." The next year the Court ordered the states to end segregation "with all deliberate speed."

Despite these decisions, few districts in the southern and border states tried to integrate their schools. Many white Southerners who deplored the way blacks were treated in the region nonetheless opposed integrating the schools. As late as September 1956, barely 700 of the South's 10,000 school districts had been desegregated. The region became more alienated from the rest of the nation than at any time since Reconstruction.

White citizens' councils dedicated to all-out opposition sprang up throughout the South. When the school board of Clinton, Tennessee, integrated the local high school in September 1956, a mob rioted in protest, shouting "Kill the niggers!" and destroying the property of blacks. The school was kept open with the help of the National Guard until segregationists blew up the building with dynamite. In Virginia the governor announced a plan for "massive resistance" to integration that denied state aid to local school systems that wished to desegregate. When the University of Alabama admitted a single black woman in 1956, riots broke out. University officials forced the student to withdraw temporarily and then expelled her when she complained more forcefully than they deemed proper.

President Eisenhower thought equality for blacks could not be obtained by government edict. He said that the Court's ruling must be obeyed, but he did little to discourage southern resistance to desegregation. "I am convinced that the Supreme Court decision set back progress in the South at least fifteen years," he remarked to one of his advisers. "The fellow who tries to tell me you can do these things by force is just plain nuts."

5. However, in 1957 events compelled him to act. When the school board of Little Rock, Arkansas, opened Central High School to a handful of black students, the governor of the state, Orval M. Faubus, called out the National Guard to prevent them from attending. Unruly crowds taunted the students and their parents. Eisenhower could not ignore the direct flouting of federal authority. After the mayor of Little Rock sent him a telegram saying, in part, "situation is out of control and police cannot disperse the mob," he dispatched 1000

Angry jeers from whites rain down on Elizabeth Eckford, one of the first black students to arrive for registration at Little Rock's Central High School in 1957. State troops turned black students away from the school until President Eisenhower overruled the state decision and called in the National Guard to enforce integration.

paratroopers to Little Rock and summoned 10,000 National Guardsmen to federal duty, thus removing them from Faubus's control. The black students then began to attend class. A token force of soldiers was stationed at Central High for the entire school year to protect them.

32. THE ELECTION OF 1960

As the end of his second term approached, Eisenhower somewhat reluctantly endorsed Vice President Richard Nixon as the Republican candidate to succeed him. Nixon had originally skyrocketed to national prominence by exploiting the public fear of communist subversion. "Traitors in the high councils of our government," he charged in 1950, "have made sure that the deck is stacked on the Soviet side of the diplomatic tables." In 1947 he was an obscure young congressman from California; in 1950 he won a seat in the Senate; two years later Eisenhower chose him as his running mate.

The Democrats nominated Senator John F. Kennedy of Massachusetts. His chief rival for the nomination, Lyndon B. Johnson of Texas, the Senate majority leader, became his running mate. Kennedy was the son of Joseph P. Kennedy, a wealthy businessman who had served as ambassador to Great Britain under Franklin Roosevelt. An indifferent student at Harvard, Kennedy in his junior year—1939—traveled with his father to Europe. When Hitler attacked Poland a few months later, Kennedy had the topic for his senior thesis: "Appeasement at Munich," in which he chastised British and American leaders in the 1920s and 1930s for a lack of foresight and resolve. Published in 1940 as *Why England Slept,* the book received favorable reviews and was briefly a best seller. During World War II, Kennedy served in the Pacific, captaining a torpedo boat. When the boat was sliced in two by a Japanese destroyer, Kennedy showed personal courage in rescuing his men. Besides wealth, intelligence, good looks, and charm, Kennedy had the advantage of his Irish-Catholic ancestry, a particularly valuable asset in heavily Catholic Massachusetts. After three terms in the House, he moved on to the Senate in 1952.

After his landslide reelection in 1958, only Kennedy's religion seemed to limit his political future. No Catholic had ever been elected president, and the defeat of Alfred E. Smith in 1928 had convinced most students of politics (including Smith) that none ever would be elected. Nevertheless, influenced by Kennedy's victories in the Wisconsin and West Virginia primaries—the latter establishing him as an effective campaigner in a predominantly Protestant region—the Democratic convention nominated him.

Kennedy had not been a particularly liberal congressman. He was not involved in the civil rights movement (which was not a major issue in the presidential campaign). He enthusiastically endorsed the Cold War and indicted the Eisenhower administration for falling behind the Soviet Union in the race to build missiles. He admitted frankly that he liked Senator Joseph McCarthy and thought that "he may have something" in his campaign against supposed communists in government. However, as a presidential candidate, he sought to appear more forward-looking. He stressed his youth and "vigor" (a favorite word) and promised to open a "New Frontier" for the country. Nixon ran on the Eisenhower record, which he promised to extend in liberal directions.

A series of television debates between the candidates helped Kennedy by enabling him to demonstrate his maturity and mastery of the issues. Although both candidates laudably avoided it, the religious issue was important. His Catholicism helped Kennedy in eastern urban areas but injured him in many farm districts and throughout the West. Kennedy's victory, 303 to 219 in the Electoral College, was paper-thin in the popular vote, 34,227,000 to 34,109,000.

MILESTONES

1944	Congress provides subsidies to veterans in GI Bill of Rights
1947	Taft-Hartley Act regulates unions and labor disputes
	Truman announces Truman Doctrine to stop communism's spread
1948	Marshall Plan provides funds to rebuild Europe
	Harry S Truman is elected president
	State of Israel is created as Jewish homeland; Arabs declare war
1948–1949	United States supplies West Berlin during Berlin airlift
1949	North Atlantic Treaty Organization (NATO) formed
	USSR explodes atom bomb
1950	North Korea invades South Korea
	NSC-68 calls for massive military buildup
	Alger Hiss is convicted of perjury
	McCarran Act restricts "subversive" activity
	Senator Joseph McCarthy charges that the State Department is riddled with communists
	UN counterattack in Korea is driven back by Red Chinese army
1952	Dwight D. Eisenhower is elected president
1953	John Foster Dulles institutes nuclear-based foreign policy
	Korean War ends with armistice
1954	Senate holds Army-McCarthy hearings
	United States helps overthrow Arbenz in Guatemala
	French are defeated after siege of Dien Bien Phu
	Supreme Court orders school desegregation in *Brown* v. *Board of Education of Topeka*
1956	Egypt nationalizes Suez Canal in Suez Crisis
	Eisenhower is reelected president
1957	National Guard enforces desegregation of Central High School in Little Rock, Arkansas
1959	Fidel Castro overthrows Fulgencio Batista, takes power in Cuba
1960	John F. Kennedy is first Roman Catholic to be elected president

30

❧ ⟶ ——— ⟵ ❧

FROM CAMELOT TO WATERGATE

Having lampooned the Eisenhower administration as stodgy and unimaginative, President Kennedy made a show of his style and wit. He flouted convention by naming his younger brother Robert attorney general. "I can't see that it's wrong to give him a little legal experience before he goes out to practice law," the president quipped. Kennedy also prided himself on being a man of letters, winner of a Pulitzer Prize for *Profiles in Courage*. He quoted Robert Frost and Dante. He played and replayed recordings of Winston Churchill, hoping to imprint the great orator's sonorous cadences on his own flat Bostonian vowels. At the instigation of his elegant wife, Jacqueline, Kennedy surrounded himself with the finest intellects at glittering White House galas to honor Nobel Prize winners and celebrated artists.

Kennedy's youthful senior staff boasted impressive scholarly credentials. His national security adviser, McGeorge Bundy, had been dean of the faculty at Harvard (and the first undergraduate at Yale to receive perfect scores in three college entrance examinations). Secretary of Defense Robert McNamara also had taught at Harvard before becoming the first non–family member to head the Ford Motor Company. The administration constituted, as journalist David Halberstam observed later, and somewhat ruefully, "the best and the brightest."

THE CUBAN CRISES

"The torch has been passed to a new generation of Americans," Kennedy declared in his inaugural address. Their chief task was to stop the spread of communism. Whereas Eisenhower had relied on the nation's nuclear arsenal to intim-

Fidel Castro celebrates in Havana on May 1, 1961, several weeks after the debacle at the Bay of Pigs. Stung by this humiliating defeat, President Kennedy resolved to destroy Castro by other means. "My idea," Robert Kennedy said privately in November, "is to stir things up on the island with espionage, sabotage, general disorder." This CIA program, code-named MONGOOSE, included dozens of schemes to assassinate Castro. Pop-art then imitated life, as weekly television shows such as I Spy *and* Mission: Impossible *featured daffy escapades much like those hatched by MONGOOSE.*

idate the Kremlin, Kennedy proposed to challenge communist aggression whenever and wherever it occurred. "We shall pay any price, bear any burden, meet any hardship, support any friend, oppose any foe to assure the survival and the success of liberty," Kennedy intoned. A new breed of cold warrior, Kennedy called on young men and women to serve in the Peace Corps, an organization that he created to mobilize American idealism and technical skills to help developing nations. His was a call for commitment—and action.

Perhaps seduced by his own rhetoric, Kennedy blundered almost immediately. Anti-Castro exiles were eager to organize an invasion of their homeland, reasoning that the Cuban people would rise up against Castro and communism as soon as "democratic" forces provided the necessary leadership. Under Eisenhower the CIA had begun training some 2000 Cuban exiles in Nicaragua. Kennedy was of two minds about the proposed invasion. Some in his administration opposed it strongly, but his closest advisers, including his brother Robert, urged him to give his approval. In the end he did.

The invaders, 1400 strong, struck in April 1961. They landed at the Bay of Pigs, on Cuba's southern coast. But the Cuban people failed to flock to their lines, and soon Castro's army pinned the invaders down and forced them to surrender. Because American involvement could not be disguised, the affair exposed the United States to all the criticism that a straightforward assault would have produced, without accomplishing the overthrow of Castro. Worse, it made Kennedy appear impulsive as well as unprincipled. Castro tightened his connections with the Soviet Union.

In June, Kennedy met with Soviet Premier Khrushchev in Vienna. Furious over the invasion of Cuba, Khrushchev blustered about grabbing West Berlin. In

August, he abruptly closed the border between East and West Berlin and erected a wall of concrete blocks and barbed wire across the city to stop the flow of East Germans into the noncommunist zone. At the same time, the Soviets resumed nuclear testing. Khrushchev ordered detonation of a series of gigantic hydrogen bombs, including one with a power 3000 times that of the bomb that had devastated Hiroshima.

Kennedy followed suit: He announced plans to build thousands of nuclear missiles, known as Minutemen, capable of hitting targets on the other side of the world. He expanded the American space program, vowing that an American would land on the moon within ten years. The president called on Congress to pass a large increase in military spending.

In 1962 Khrushchev precipitated the most dangerous confrontation of the Cold War. To forestall the anticipated American invasion of Cuba, he moved tanks, heavy bombers, and 42,000 Soviet troops and technicians to the island. But his most fateful step was to sneak several dozen guided nuclear missiles into the country and begin constructing launching pads for them. Although the range of these missiles was far less than that of the American Minutemen, if fired from Cuba the Soviet missiles could have delivered nuclear warheads to most of the eastern United States.

On October 14 American spy planes spotted the launching pads and missiles. The president faced a dreadful decision. After the Bay of Pigs fiasco, he could not again appear to back down to the communists. But if he invaded Cuba or bombed the Soviet bases and missile sites, Khrushchev would likely seize West Berlin or bomb United States missile sites in Turkey. Either action might lead to a full-scale nuclear war and millions of deaths.

On October 22 Kennedy went on television to address the nation. The Soviet buildup was "a deliberately provocative and unjustified change in the status quo." He ordered the American navy to stop and search all vessels headed for Cuba and to turn back any containing "offensive" weapons. Kennedy called on Khrushchev to dismantle the missile bases and remove from the island all weapons capable of striking the United States. Any Cuban-based nuclear attack would result, he warned, in "a full retaliatory response upon the Soviet Union."

For days, while the world held its breath, Soviet ships steamed toward Cuba and work on the missile bases continued. Then Khrushchev backed down. He recalled the ships, withdrew the missiles, and reduced his military establishment in Cuba to modest proportions. Kennedy then lifted the blockade. He also promised not to invade Cuba, thus ensuring Castro's survival; Kennedy also agreed to withdraw U.S. missiles from Turkey, though this latter concession was not made public at the time.

Immediately the president was hailed for his steady nerve and consummate statesmanship; the Cuban missile crisis was widely regarded as his finest hour. Yet in retrospect it appears that he may have overreacted to the missiles in Cuba. The Soviet nuclear threat had been exaggerated. After *Sputnik,* the Soviet long-range missile program flopped, though this was not known at the time. By the summer of 1962 a "missile gap" existed, but it was overwhelmingly in favor of the United States, whose nuclear missiles outnumbered those of the Soviet Union

This photograph, taken by an American U–2 spy plane and released during the Cuban missile crisis, shows the installation of liquid-fueled Soviet missiles. Khrushchev had assumed that the missiles could be kept secret. "Our military specialists informed us that strategic missiles can be reliably concealed in the palm forests of Cuba," one of Khrushchev's advisers recalled. Khrushchev, who assumed that the missiles would be harder to spot if they were in a horizontal position, ordered that the missiles be placed in an upright position only at night. This was a mistake: The U–2's easily detected the missiles in their horizontal position.

by a ratio of 17 to 1. Khrushchev's decision to put medium-range missiles in Cuba signified Soviet weakness rather than impending aggression.

Both Kennedy and Khrushchev were sobered by the missile crisis; afterward neither spoke so glibly about superpower confrontation. They agreed to the installation of a telephone "hot line" between the White House and the Kremlin, so that in any future crisis leaders of the two nations could communicate instantly. They also signed a treaty outlawing nuclear testing in the atmosphere. But Khrushchev's bluff had been called—a public humiliation from which he would never recover. Within two years, hard-liners in the Kremlin forced him out of office. His successor, Leonid Brezhnev, was an old-style Stalinist who inaugurated an intensive program of long-range missile development. The nuclear arms race moved to new terrain, uncertain and unimaginably dangerous.

THE VIETNAM WAR

After the French withdrew from Vietnam in 1954, the Vietnamese people were supposed to determine their own future. But Ngo Dinh Diem, the U.S.-backed leader in the south, feared that he would be defeated by Ho Chi Minh, a well-known nationalist and leader of the communist Viet Minh. Diem canceled the election scheduled for 1956. With Eisenhower's help, he attempted to build a new nation in the south. The United States sent weapons and a handful of American military "advisers" to help Diem equip and train a South Vietnamese army. Ho decided to ignore Diem and consolidate his rule in the north. Those Viet Minh units that remained in the south—they soon came to be known as Vietcong—were instructed to form secret cells and bide their time. During the late 1950s they gained in strength and militancy.

In May 1959 Ho decided that the time had come to overthrow Diem. Vietcong guerrillas infiltrated thousands of villages, ambushed South Vietnamese convoys, and assassinated government officials. Soon the Vietcong controlled large sections of the countryside, some almost within sight of the capital city of Saigon.

By the time Kennedy took office, Diem's government was tottering. As a senator, Kennedy had endorsed Diem and the attempt to build a noncommunist South Vietnam. He called it the "cornerstone of the Free World in Southeast Asia, the keystone in the arch, the finger in the dike." After the Bay of Pigs debacle, furthermore, Kennedy worried that his credibility with Khrushchev had been damaged. "If he thinks I'm inexperienced and have no guts," he told an aide, "we won't get anywhere with him. So we have to act." Vietnam, he added, "looks like the place."

Kennedy sharply increased the American military and economic commitment to South Vietnam. At the end of 1961 there were 3200 American military personnel in the country; within two years, there were more than 16,000, and 120 American soldiers had been killed. Despite the expanded effort, by the summer of 1963 Diem's regime was in ruins. An ardent Catholic, he cracked down on the Buddhists, who, joined by students, protested his repression. Thousands were arrested, and some were shot. In protest, several Buddhist monks became martyrs by setting themselves on fire in public.

Unable to persuade Diem to moderate his policies, Kennedy sent word to dissident Vietnamese generals of his willingness to support them if they ousted Diem. On November 1 several of these generals surrounded the presidential palace with troops and tanks, seized Diem, and killed him. Kennedy, though appalled by Diem's death, recognized the new junta.

"WE SHALL OVERCOME": THE CIVIL RIGHTS MOVEMENT

Kennedy initially approached the race question with exceeding caution. His razor-thin victory had depended on the votes both of African Americans in northern cities and white Democrats in the Deep South. As president, his visible support for one group would alienate the other. So Kennedy temporized, urging leaders on both sides to show restraint. This proved impossible.

During and after World War II, like a glacier, slowly but with massive force, a demand for change had developed in the South. Its roots lay in southern industrialization; in the shift from small sharecropping holdings to large commercial farms; in the vast wartime expenditures of the federal government on aircraft factories and army bases in the region; in the impact of the GI Bill on southern colleges and universities; and in the gradual development of a southern black middle class.

This change first came to national attention during the Eisenhower administration in the rigidly segregated city of Montgomery, Alabama. On Friday, December 1, 1955, Rosa Parks, a seamstress at the Montgomery Fair department store, boarded a bus on her way home from her job. She dutifully took a seat toward the rear as custom and law required. As white workers and shoppers filled the forward section, the driver ordered her to give up her place to a white passenger. Parks, who was also secretary of the Montgomery NAACP chapter, refused. She had decided, she later recalled, that "I would have to know once and for all what rights I had as a human being and a citizen."

She was arrested. Over the weekend, Montgomery's black leaders organized a boycott. "Don't ride the bus . . . Monday," their mimeographed notice ran. "If you work, take a cab, or share a ride, or walk." Monday dawned bitterly cold, but the boycott was a total success.

Most Montgomery blacks could not afford to miss a single day's wages, so the protracted struggle to get to work was difficult to maintain. Black-owned taxis reduced their rates sharply, and when the city declared this illegal, car pools were quickly organized. Few African Americans owned cars. Although nearly everyone who did volunteered, there were never more than 350 cars available to the more than 10,000 people who needed rides to their jobs and back every day. Nevertheless, the boycott went on.

Late in February the Montgomery authorities obtained indictments of 115 leaders of the boycott, but this move backfired because it focused national attention on the situation. A young clergyman, the Rev. Dr. Martin Luther King, Jr., was emerging as the leader of the boycott. A gifted speaker, he became an overnight celebrity. Money poured in from all over the country to support the movement. The boycott lasted for over a year. Finally the Supreme Court declared the local law enforcing racial separation unconstitutional: Montgomery had to desegregate its public transportation system.

This success encouraged blacks elsewhere in the South to band together against segregation. A new organization founded in 1957, the Southern Christian Leadership Conference (SCLC), headed by King, moved to the forefront of the civil rights movement. Other organizations joined the struggle, notably the Congress of Racial Equality (CORE), which had been founded in 1942.

In February 1960 four African American college students in Greensboro, North Carolina, sat down at a lunch counter at a Woolworth's store. "We do not serve Negroes," they were told. They returned with more and more demonstrators. By the end of the week over a thousand protesters descended on Woolworth's

This "sit-in" tactic was not new. CORE had staged sit-ins in Chicago restaurants back in 1943. But the Greensboro students sparked a national movement; students in dozens of other southern towns and cities copied their example.

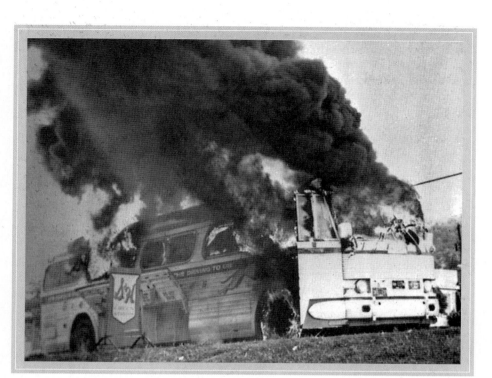

This Greyhound bus carried Freedom Riders—whites and blacks who fought segregation by intentionally violating segregation policies. When a mob of whites from Anniston, Alabama, learned of this, they descended on the bus, slashed its tires, and piled into dozens of cars to chase it as it pulled away. As the bus was racing along Highway 78, the tires went flat. After the bus stopped, someone tossed a firebomb through the back window. As the riders got out of the bus, they were beaten. This photograph was shown that evening on wire services throughout the world.

Within a fortnight more than 50 sit-ins were in progress in southern cities. By the end of 1961 over 70,000 people had participated in such demonstrations. Still another new organization, the Student Nonviolent Coordinating Committee (SNCC), was founded by black college students in 1960 to provide a focus for the sit-in movement and to conduct voter registration drives in the South, actions that more than any other roused the fury of southern segregationists.

In May 1961 black and white foes of segregation organized a "freedom ride" to test the effectiveness of federal regulations prohibiting discrimination in interstate transportation. Boarding two buses in Washington, an integrated group of 13 volunteers took off across the South toward New Orleans. In Alabama they ran into trouble. At Anniston racists set fire to one of the buses, and in Birmingham they were assaulted by a mob. But violence did not stop the freedom riders. Other groups followed, many deliberately seeking arrest to test local segregation ordinances. The resultant court cases repeatedly broke down legal racial barriers throughout the South.

This protracted struggle eventually yielded practical and moral benefits for southern whites as well as blacks. Gradually all but the most unwavering defenders of segregation changed their attitudes. But this took time, and many blacks were unwilling to wait.

Some blacks, contemptuous of white prejudices, were urging their fellows to reject "American" society and all it stood for. In the North, black nationalism became a potent force. Elijah Muhammad, leader of the Black Muslim movement, loathed whites so intensely that he demanded that a part of the United States be set aside exclusively for blacks. He urged his followers to be industrious, thrifty, and abstemious—and to view all whites with suspicion and hatred.

"This white government has ruled us and given us plenty hell, but the time has arrived that you taste a little of your own hell," Muhammad said. "There are many of my poor black ignorant brothers . . . preaching the ignorant and lying stuff that you should love your enemy. What fool can love his enemy?" Another important Black Muslim, Malcolm X, put it this way in a 1960 speech: "For the white man to ask the black man if he hates him is just like the rapist asking the raped, or the wolf asking the sheep, 'Do you hate me?'" "If someone puts a hand on you," he advised blacks on another occasion, "send him to the cemetery."

President Kennedy reluctantly began to give his support to a modest civil rights bill. When this measure ran into stiff opposition in Congress, blacks organized a demonstration in Washington, attended by 200,000 people. At this gathering, King delivered his "I Have a Dream" address, looking forward to a time when racial prejudice no longer existed and people of all religions and colors could join hands and say, "Free at last! Free at last!" Kennedy sympathized with the Washington gathering but feared it would make passage of the civil rights bill more difficult rather than easier. As in other areas, he was not a forceful advocate of his own proposals.

TRAGEDY IN DALLAS: JFK ASSASSINATED

Through it all, Kennedy retained his hold on public opinion. In the fall of 1963 most observers believed he easily would win a second term. Then, while visiting Dallas, Texas, on November 22, he was shot in the head by an assassin, Lee Harvey Oswald, and died almost instantly. One measure of Kennedy's hold on the public imagination was the outpouring of grief that attended his death. Kennedy had given hope to people who had none.

Kennedy's assassination precipitated an extraordinary series of events. Oswald had fired on the president with a rifle from an upper story of a warehouse. No one saw him pull the trigger. He was apprehended largely because he panicked and killed a policeman across town later in the day. He denied his guilt, but a mass of evidence connected him with the assassination of the president. Before he could be brought to trial, however, he was himself murdered by Jack Ruby, the owner of a Dallas nightclub. The incident took place in full view of

JFK and Jacqueline Kennedy in a motorcade in Dallas, November 22, 1963. Several minutes later, he was shot and killed.

television cameras, while Oswald was being transferred from one place of detention to another.

Each day brought new revelations. Oswald had defected briefly to the Soviet Union in 1959, then had returned to the United States and formed a pro-Castro organization in New Orleans. Many concluded that some nefarious conspiracy lay at the root of the tragedy. Oswald, the argument ran, was a pawn—either of communists or anticommunists (the conspiracy theories lost none of their appeal for being contradictory)—whose murder was designed to shield from exposure the masterminds who had engineered the assassination. A special commission headed by Chief Justice Earl Warren was convened to analyze the evidence. After a lengthy investigation, it concluded that Oswald had acted alone.

Instead of dampening charges of conspiracy, the report of the Warren Commission provoked new doubts. As word leaked out about earlier CIA assassination attempts against Castro, the failure of the Warren Report even to mention them made the commission suspect. In fact, there is little solid evidence to suggest that Oswald was part of a wider conspiracy. But the decision of Dulles and other commissioners to protect CIA secrets engendered skepticism toward the Warren Commission—and the United States government.

LYNDON BAINES JOHNSON

John F. Kennedy's death made Lyndon B. Johnson president. From 1949 until his election as vice president Johnson had been a senator from Texas and, for most of that time, Senate Democratic leader. He could be heavy-handed or subtle, and also devious, domineering, persistent, and obliging. Many people swore by him; few had the fortitude to swear at him.

Johnson, who had consciously modeled his career after that of Franklin D. Roosevelt, considered social welfare legislation his specialty. The contrast with Kennedy could not have been sharper. In his inaugural address, Kennedy had made no mention of domestic issues. Kennedy's plans for federal aid for education, urban renewal, a higher minimum wage, and medical care for the aged were blocked in Congress by Republicans and southern Democrats. The same coalition also defeated his chief economic initiative—a broad tax cut to stimulate the economy. But Kennedy had reacted to these defeats mildly, almost wistfully. He thought the machinery of the federal government was cumbersome and ineffective.

Johnson knew how to make it work. On becoming president, he pushed hard for Kennedy's programs. "Civil righters are going to have to wear sneakers to keep up with me," he boasted. Bills long buried in committee sailed through Congress. Early in 1964 Kennedy's tax cut was passed. A few months later, an expanded version of another Kennedy proposal became law as the Civil Rights Act of 1964.

14.9   THE GREAT SOCIETY

The much-strengthened Civil Rights Act outlawed discrimination by employers against blacks and also against women. It broke down legal barriers to black voting in the southern states and outlawed racial segregation of all sorts in places of public accommodation, such as movie theaters, hotels, and restaurants. In addition, unlike presidents Eisenhower and Kennedy, Johnson made sure that the government enforced civil rights legislation.

Johnson's success in steering the Civil Rights Act through Congress confirmed his belief that he could be a reformer in the tradition of Franklin Roosevelt. He declared war on poverty and set out to create a "great society" in which poverty no longer would exist. The primary objective of Johnson's war on poverty was to give poor people the opportunity to improve themselves.

The Economic Opportunity Act of 1964 created a mixture of programs, among them a Job Corps similar to the New Deal Civilian Conservation Corps; a community action program to finance local antipoverty efforts; and a system for training the unskilled unemployed and for lending money to small businesses in poor areas. The programs combined the progressive concept of government aid for those in need with the conservative idea of individual responsibility.

Buttressed by his legislative triumphs, Johnson sought election as president in his own right in 1964. He achieved this ambition in unparalleled fashion. His

LBJ as a Texas cowboy, a masculine image he assiduously cultivated. Biographers have suggested that Johnson was torn between the expectations of his father, a crude local politician who flouted polite society, and those of his mother, a refined woman who insisted that her son read poetry and practice the violin. Johnson later told biographer Doris Kearns Goodwin that he persisted in Vietnam because he worried that critics would accuse him of being "an unmanly man. A man without a spine."

championing of civil rights won him the almost unanimous support of blacks; his tax policy attracted the well-to-do and the business interests; his war on poverty held the allegiance of labor and other traditionally Democratic groups. His down-home southern antecedents counterbalanced his liberalism on the race question in the eyes of many white Southerners.

The Republicans played into his hands by nominating the conservative Senator Barry M. Goldwater of Arizona, whose objective in Congress had been "not to pass laws but to repeal them." As a presidential candidate he favored such laissez-faire policies as cutting back on the social security system and doing away with the Tennessee Valley Authority. A large majority of voters found Goldwater out-of-date on economic questions and dangerously aggressive on foreign affairs.

In November, Johnson won a sweeping victory, collecting over 61 percent of the popular vote and carrying the whole country except Goldwater's Arizona and five states in the Deep South, where many conservatives were voting more against Johnson's civil rights policies than in favor of Goldwater.

Quickly Johnson pressed ahead with his Great Society program. In January 1965 he proposed a compulsory hospital insurance system, known as Medicare, for all persons over the age of 65. As amended by Congress, the Medicare Act consisted of Part A, hospital insurance for the retired (funded by increased Social Security taxes), and a voluntary plan, Part B, covering doctors' bills (paid for in part by the government). The law also provided for grants to the states to help pay the medical expenses of poor people, even those below the retirement age of 65. This part of the system was called Medicaid. Before the passage of the Medicare Act, about half of Americans over 65 years old had had no medical insurance.

Next, Congress passed the Elementary and Secondary Education Act in 1965, which supplied federal funds to school districts. Head Start, a program for poor preschoolers, was designed to prepare them for elementary school. It also incidentally improved the children's health by providing medical examinations and nutritious meals.

16   Still another important reform was the Voting Rights Act of 1965, pressed through Congress by President Johnson after more brutal repressions of civil rights demonstrators in the South. This law provided for federal intervention to protect black registration and voting in six southern states. It applied to state and local as well as federal elections.

On balance, the achievements of the Great Society were far below what President Johnson had promised and his supporters had envisioned. The same, of course, can be said of most ambitious reform programs—of Reconstruction; of the Progressive movement; certainly of the New Deal, to which Johnson had contributed as a young man. Despite his long political experience, Johnson tried to accomplish too many things too quickly. He relied too heavily on the techniques of political manipulation. Perhaps he was carried away by his good fortune— that he would ever become president must have seemed to a man of his political acumen most unlikely after he failed to win the nomination in 1960. He seized too avidly this unexpected opportunity to make history. Without the crisis atmosphere that had appeared to justify hasty experimentation during the New Deal years, the public judged the results of the Great Society and the president who had shaped it skeptically.

22. JOHNSON ESCALATES THE WAR

After Diem's assassination, the situation in South Vietnam continued to deteriorate. One military coup followed another, and political instability aggravated military incapacity. President Johnson nevertheless felt that he had no choice but to prop up the South Vietnamese regime. "If I don't go in now," he told an adviser, "they'll be all over me in Congress. They won't be talking about my civil rights bill, or education, or beautification. No sir, they'll push Vietnam up my ass every time."

Johnson decided to punish North Vietnam directly for prosecuting the war in the south. In early 1964 he secretly ordered American warships to escort the South Vietnamese navy on missions far into the Gulf of Tonkin; the South Vietnamese attacked North Vietnamese ships and port facilities and landed commandos in North Vietnam. After one such mission, American destroyers were fired on by North Vietnamese gunboats. Several nights later during a heavy storm, American ships reported that they were being fired on, though the enemy was never spotted. Using this Tonkin "incident" as pretext, Johnson demanded, and in an air of crisis obtained, an authorization from Congress to "repel any

25.

armed attack against the forces of the United States and to prevent further aggression." With this blank check, known as the Gulf of Tonkin Resolution, and
buttressed by his sweeping defeat of Goldwater in the 1964 presidential election,
Johnson authorized air attacks in North Vietnam. By the summer of 1965,
American bombers were conducting some 5000 raids each month.

But the hail of bombs on North Vietnam had little effect on the struggle in
the south. If the war was to be won, American soldiers—lots of them—would
have to do much of the fighting themselves.

In July 1965 Johnson ordered the first of several huge increases in American
ground forces in Vietnam. By the end of 1965, 184,000 Americans were in the
field; a year later, 385,000; after another year, 485,000. By the middle of 1968
the number exceeded 538,000. Each increase was met by corresponding increases from the other side. The Soviet Union and China sent no combat troops,
but stepped up their aid, and thousands of North Vietnamese regulars filtered
across the 17th parallel to fight with the Vietcong guerrillas.

24. The new American strategy was not to seize any particular battlefield or terrain as in all previous wars, but to kill as many of the enemy as possible through
bloody "search and destroy" operations. As the scope of the action broadened,
the number of American casualties rose. The United States was engaged in a full-
scale war, one that Congress never declared.

OPPOSITION TO THE WAR

Some Americans claimed that the struggle between the South Vietnamese government and the Vietcong was a civil war in which the United States should not
meddle. They stressed the repressive character of the South Vietnamese government as proof that the war was not a contest between democracy and communism. They objected to the massive aerial bombings (more explosives were
dropped on Vietnam between 1964 and 1968 than on Germany and Japan combined in World War II), to the use of napalm and defoliants such as Agent
Orange that were sprayed on forests and crops and that wreaked havoc among
noncombatants, and to the killing of civilians by American troops. Above all, opponents of the war deplored the heavy loss of life—over 40,000 American dead
by 1970, and hundreds of thousands of Vietnamese.

The cost of the war came to exceed $20 billion a year. But in large part be-
cause so many people objected to the war, Johnson refused to ask Congress to
raise taxes to pay for it. The resulting deficits forced the government to borrow
huge sums, caused interest rates to soar, and pushed prices higher.

THE ELECTION OF 1968

Gradually the opponents of the war gained numbers and strength. They began to
include some of the president's advisers. By late 1967 McNamara, who had me-
thodically tracked kill ratios, troop replacement rates, and nearly every other
conceivable statistic, concluded that "the figures didn't add up" and the war
could not be won. Deeply despondent, he resigned.

Southeast Asia, 1954–1975

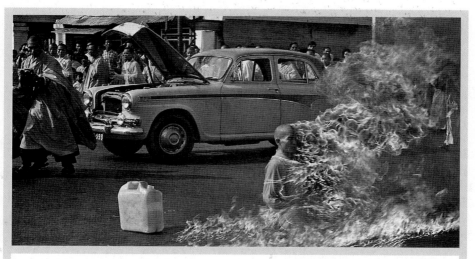

DEBATING THE PAST

Would JFK have sent a half-million American troops to Vietnam? In the summer of 1963, Buddhist monks immolated themselves to protest Diem's repression. Several months later, Diem was ousted in a coup and JFK was assassinated. Within two years, President Johnson raised American troop levels in Vietnam to 300,000 and, by 1967, to half a million.

Many historians believe that if Kennedy had lived, he, too, would have sent more troops to Vietnam. Journalist David Halberstam (1969) emphasized that the same foreign policy advisers who guided Kennedy did so for Johnson, too. These men—Robert McNamara, McGeorge Bundy, and others—were, in Halberstam's mordantly ironic phrase, "the best and the brightest." Larry Berman (1982, 1989) showed that because Johnson was inexperienced in foreign policy, he had little choice but to listen to JFK's team. Lloyd C. Gardner (1995) and Brian Van De Mark (1991) emphasized the continuity—or rigidity—of American policymaking throughout the period. David Barrett (1993) described how Johnson wanted a way out of "that bitch of a war" but could not find one.

Those who have championed Kennedy's reputation insisted that JFK would have left Vietnam earlier. Arthur M. Schlesinger, Jr. (1978) explained that while Kennedy publicly endorsed the war, he was "secretly wondering how to get out." Schlesinger's thesis received unwanted support from filmmaker Oliver Stone's movie, *JFK* (1991). The movie hypothesized that Kennedy was assassinated by pro-war hawks in the military who feared the president would pull American troops out of Vietnam. The following year John M. Newman (1992) provided a historical brief for the movie.

But if Kennedy was looking for an excuse to get out of the war, why didn't he withdraw in response to Diem's persecution of the Buddhists? His decision to support a coup to replace Diem seemingly committed the United States to helping Diem's successors.

David Halberstam, *The Best and the Brightest* (1969), Larry Berman, *Planning a Tragedy* (1982) and *Lyndon Johnson's War* (1989), Brian Van De Mark, *Into the Quagmire* (1991), Lloyd C. Gardner, *Pay Any Price* (1995), David Barrett, *Uncertain Warriors* (1993), Arthur M. Schlesinger, Jr., *Robert Kennedy and His Times* (1978), John M. Newman, *JFK and Vietnam* (1992).

Opposition to the war was especially vehement on college campuses, some students objecting because they thought the United States had no business intervening in the Vietnam conflict, others because they feared being drafted, still others because so many students obtained educational deferments, while young men who were unable to attend college were conscripted.

26. Then, in November 1967, Eugene McCarthy, a low-keyed, introspective senator from Minnesota, announced his candidacy for the 1968 Democratic presidential nomination. Opposition to the war was his issue.

Suddenly, early in 1968, on the heels of this announcement, North Vietnamese and Vietcong forces launched a general offensive to correspond with their Lunar New Year (called Tet). Striking 39 of the 44 provincial capitals, many other towns and cities, and every American base, they caused chaos throughout South Vietnam. They held Hué, the old capital of the country, for weeks. To root them out of Saigon the Americans had to level large sections of the city. Elsewhere the destruction was total, an irony highlighted by the remark of an American officer after the recapture of the village of Ben Tre: "It became necessary to destroy the town to save it."

The Tet offensive was essentially a series of raids; the communists did not expect to hold the cities indefinitely, and they did not. Their losses were enormous. Nevertheless the psychological impact in South Vietnam and in the United States made Tet a clear victory for the North. American pollsters reported an enormous shift of public opinion against further escalation of the fighting. When Westmoreland described Tet as a communist defeat and yet requested an additional 206,000 troops, McCarthy, who was campaigning in the New Hampshire primary, suddenly became a formidable figure. Thousands of students and other volunteers flocked to the state to ring doorbells on his behalf. On primary election day he polled 42 percent of the Democratic vote.

The political situation was confused. Before the primary, former attorney general Robert F. Kennedy, brother of the slain president, had refused either to seek the Democratic nomination or to support McCarthy, although he disliked Johnson intensely and was opposed to his policy in Vietnam. After McCarthy's success, he announced his candidacy.

Confronting this division in the ranks, President Johnson realized he could no longer hope to be an effective president. In a surprising televised announcement, he withdrew from the race. Vice President Hubert H. Humphrey then announced his candidacy, and Johnson threw the weight of his administration behind him.

Kennedy carried the primaries in Indiana and Nebraska. McCarthy won in Wisconsin and Oregon. In the climactic contest in California, Kennedy won by a small margin. However, immediately after his victory speech in a Los Angeles hotel, he was assassinated by Sirhan Sirhan, an Arab nationalist who had been incensed by Kennedy's support of Israel. In effect, Kennedy's death ensured the nomination of Humphrey.

The contest for the Republican nomination was far less dramatic, although its outcome, the nomination of Richard M. Nixon, would have been hard to predict a few years earlier. After his loss to Kennedy in 1960, Nixon ran unsuccessfully for governor of California in 1962, then moved to New York City and joined a prominent law firm. But he remained active in Republican affairs. In 1964 he had campaigned hard for Goldwater. When no other Republican developed extensive support as the 1968 election approached, Nixon entered the race, swept the primaries, and won an easy first-ballot victory at the Republican convention.

Nixon then astounded the country and dismayed liberals by choosing Governor Spiro T. Agnew of Maryland as his running mate. Agnew was a political unknown. ("Spiro who?" jokesters asked.) Nixon chose him primarily to attract southern votes.

Placating the South seemed necessary because Governor George C. Wallace of Alabama was making a determined bid to win enough electoral votes for his American Independent party to prevent any candidate from obtaining a majority. Wallace was flagrantly antiblack and anti-intellectual. Nixon's choice of Agnew appeared to be an effort to contend with Wallace for conservative voters in the South.

This Republican strategy heightened the tension surrounding the Democratic convention, which met in Chicago in late August. Humphrey delegates controlled the convention. The vice president had a solid liberal record on domestic issues, but he had supported Johnson's Vietnam policy with equal solidity. Those who could not stomach the Nixon-Agnew ticket and who opposed the war faced a difficult choice. Several thousand activists, representing a dozen groups and advocating tactics ranging from orderly demonstrations to civil disobedience to indiscriminate violence, descended on Chicago to put pressure on the delegates to repudiate the Johnson Vietnam policy.

In the tense atmosphere that resulted, the party hierarchy overreacted. The mayor of Chicago, Richard J. Daley, whose ability to "influence" election results in a manner favorable to Democrats had often been demonstrated, ringed the convention with policemen to protect it from disruption. This was a reasonable precaution in itself. Inside the building the delegates nominated Humphrey and adopted a war plank satisfactory to Johnson. Outside, however, provoked by the abusive language and violent behavior of radical demonstrators, the police tore into the protesters, in Norman Mailer's graphic phrase, "like a chain saw cutting into wood," while millions watched on television in fascinated horror.

At first the mayhem in Chicago seemed to benefit Nixon by strengthening the convictions of many voters that the tougher treatment of criminals and dissenters that he and Agnew were calling for was necessary. Those who were critical of the Chicago police tended to blame Humphrey, whom Mayor Daley supported.

Nixon campaigned at a deliberate, dignified pace. He made relatively few public appearances, relying instead on carefully arranged television interviews and taped commercials. He stressed firm enforcement of the law and his desire "to bring us together." As for Vietnam, he would "end the war and win the peace," by just what means he did not say.

The Democratic campaign was badly organized. Humphrey was subjected to merciless heckling from antiwar audiences. He seemed far behind in the early stages. Black voters and the urban poor had no practical choice but to vote

Alarmed by antiwar demonstrators at the 1968 Democratic national convention, Chicago Mayor Richard Daley ordered barbed wire fences erected in an attempt to control access to the convention hall. Protest demonstrations at the convention and Mayor Daley's heavy-handed response persuaded many voters that the fate of the republic would be safer in Republican hands.

Democratic. Gradually Humphrey gained ground, and on election day the popular vote was close: Nixon slightly less than 31.8 million, Humphrey nearly 31.3 million. Nixon's Electoral College margin, however, was substantial—301 to 191. The remaining 46 electoral votes went to Wallace, whose 9.9 million votes came to 13.5 percent of the total. Together, Nixon and Wallace received 57 percent of the popular vote. Nevertheless, the Democrats retained control of both houses of Congress.

NIXON AS PRESIDENT: "VIETNAMIZING" THE WAR

In office, Nixon first proposed a phased withdrawal of all non–South Vietnamese troops, to be followed by an internationally supervised election in South Vietnam. The North Vietnamese rejected this scheme and insisted that the United States withdraw its forces unconditionally. If the United States could not prevail with a half million American troops, how, the North Vietnamese negotiator asked Henry Kissinger, the American negotiator, "can you succeed when you let your puppet troops do the fighting?" That question, Kissinger later admitted, "tormented" him.

The intransigence of the North Vietnamese left the president in a difficult position. Nixon could not compel the foe to end a war it had begun against the French nearly a quarter of a century earlier, and every passing day added to the strength of antiwar sentiment, which, as it expressed itself in ever more emphatic terms, in turn led to deeper divisions in the country. Yet Nixon could not face up to the consequences of ending the war on the communists' terms.

The president responded to the dilemma by trying to build up the South Vietnamese armed forces so that American troops could pull out without South Vietnam being overrun by the communists. He shipped so many planes to the Vietnamese that they came to have the fourth-largest air force in the world. The trouble with this strategy, called Vietnamization, was that for 15 years the United States had been trying without success to make the South Vietnamese capable of defending themselves.

For a while, events appeared to vindicate Nixon's position. A gradual slowing of military activity in Vietnam had reduced American casualties. Troop withdrawals continued in an orderly fashion. A new lottery system for drafting men for military duty eliminated some of the inequities in the selective service law.

But the war continued. Early in 1970 reports that an American unit had massacred civilians, including dozens of women and children, in a Vietnamese hamlet known as My Lai revived the controversy over the purposes of the war and its corrosive effects on those who were fighting it. The American people, it seemed, were being torn apart by the war: one from another according to each one's interpretation of events; many within themselves as they tried to balance the war's horrors against their pride, their abhorrence of communism, and their unwillingness to turn their backs on their elected leader.

THE CAMBODIAN "INCURSION"

Late in April 1970 Nixon announced that Vietnamization was proceeding more rapidly than he had hoped, that communist power was weakening, and that within a year another 150,000 American soldiers would be extracted from Vietnam. A week later he announced that military intelligence had indicated that the enemy was consolidating its "sanctuaries" in neutral Cambodia and that he was therefore dispatching thousands of American troops to destroy these bases. (American planes had been bombing enemy sites in Cambodia for some time, although this fact was not revealed to the public until 1973.) Nixon even resumed bombing targets in North Vietnam. "You've got to electrify people with bold decisions," he told the Joint Chiefs of Staff. "Let's go blow the hell out of them."

Nixon's shocking announcement triggered many campus demonstrations. One college where feeling ran high was Kent State University in Ohio. For several days students there clashed with local police; they broke windows and caused other damage to property. When the governor of Ohio called out the National Guard, angry students showered the soldiers with stones. During a

The Viet Cong were initially terrified of what they called "angleworms," helicopters that swooped from the sky belching fire and rockets. The Viet Cong soon learned to aim two-thirds the distance of the fuselage ahead, so that the helicopter would fly into their bullets. Hundreds of helicopters were shot down by small arms fire.

noontime protest on May 4 the guardsmen, who were poorly trained in crowd control, suddenly opened fire. Four students were killed, two of them women who were merely passing by on their way to class.

While the nation reeled from this shock, two students at Jackson State University were killed by Mississippi state policemen. A wave of student strikes followed, closing down hundreds of colleges, including many that had seen no previous unrest. Moderate students by the tens of thousands had joined with the radicals.

The almost universal condemnation of the invasion and of the way it had been planned shook Nixon hard. He backtracked, pulling American ground troops out of Cambodia quickly. But he did not change his Vietnam policy, and in fact Cambodia apparently stiffened his determination. As American ground troops were withdrawn, he stepped up air attacks.

The balance of forces remained in uneasy equilibrium through 1971. But late in March 1972 the North Vietnamese again mounted a series of assaults throughout South Vietnam. The president responded with heavier bombing, and he ordered the approaches to Haiphong and other North Vietnamese ports sown with mines to cut off the communists' supplies.

DÉTENTE WITH COMMUNISM

But in the midst of these aggressive actions, Nixon and his National Security Adviser, Henry Kissinger, devised a bold and ingenious diplomatic offensive, executed in nearly complete secrecy—from even the State and Defense departments! Nixon and Kissinger made an effective though not always harmonious team.

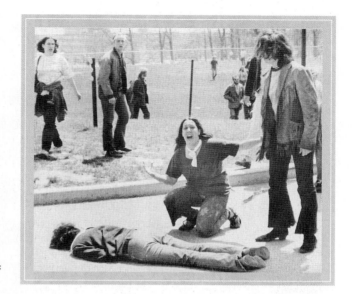

National Guardsmen firing into a crowd of antiwar protesters at Kent State University killed 4 students and injured 11 others. The shootings triggered massive demonstrations and protests across the nation.

Abandoning a lifetime of treating communism as a single worldwide conspiracy that had to be contained at all costs, Nixon decided to deal with China and the Soviet Union as separate powers and, as he put it, to "live together and work together" with both. Nixon and Kissinger called the new policy *détente,* a French term meaning "the relaxation of tensions between governments." But *détente* was not an expression of friendship so much as an acknowledgment that for decades the policy of containment had driven China and the Soviet Union closer together.

First Nixon sent Kissinger secretly to China and the Soviet Union to prepare the way for summit meetings with the communist leaders. Both the Chinese and the Soviets agreed to the meetings. Then, in February 1972, Nixon and Kissinger, accompanied by a small army of reporters and television crews, flew to Beijing. After much dining, sightseeing, posing for photographers, and consultation with Chinese officials, Nixon agreed to promote economic and cultural exchanges and supported the admission of communist China to the United Nations. (Since the founding of the United Nations, the United States had recognized only the Republic of China—Taiwan.) As a result, exports to communist China increased substantially, reaching $4 billion in 1980. Among other American products, the Chinese were introduced to Coca-Cola, marketed under a name meaning "tasty happiness," and other American products. Nixon's visit, ending more than 20 years of adamant American refusal to accept the reality of the Chinese revolution, marked a dramatic reversal; as such it was hailed throughout the world.

By the summer of 1972, with the presidential election looming in the fall, Kissinger redoubled his efforts to negotiate an end to the Vietnam war. By October he and the North Vietnamese had hammered out a settlement calling for

President and Mrs. Nixon dining with Chinese communist officials in Beijing in February 1972. Even Nixon's harshest critics conceded that his initiative in reopening United States–China relations was a diplomatic master stroke.

a cease-fire, the return of American prisoners of war, and the withdrawal of United States forces from Vietnam. Shortly before the presidential election Kissinger announced that peace was "at hand."

NIXON IN TRIUMPH

A few days later President Nixon was reelected, defeating the Democratic candidate, Senator George McGovern of South Dakota, in a landslide—521 electoral votes to 17. McGovern carried only Massachusetts and the District of Columbia. McGovern's campaign had been hampered by his tendency to advance poorly thought-out proposals, such as his scheme for funneling money directly to the poor, and by his rather bumbling, low-key oratorical style. The campaign marked the historical breakdown of the coalition that Franklin Roosevelt had fashioned and on which he and his Democratic successors, particularly Truman and Johnson, had ridden to power. Of that coalition, only African Americans voted solidly for McGovern.

Suddenly Nixon loomed as one of the most powerful and successful presidents in American history. His tough-minded but flexible handling of foreign policy questions, even his harsh Vietnamese policy, suggested decisiveness and self-confidence, qualities he had often seemed to lack in his earlier career. His willingness, despite his long history as a militant cold warrior, to negotiate with the communist nations indicated a new flexibility and creativity. His landslide victory appeared to demonstrate that a large majority of the people approved of his way of tackling the major problems of the times.

But Kissinger's agreement with the North Vietnamese came apart when Nguyen Van Thieu, the South Vietnamese president, refused to sign it. He claimed that the agreement, by permitting communist troops to remain in the south, would ensure his ultimate defeat. To Kissinger's chagrin, Nixon sided with Thieu and resumed the bombing of North Vietnam in December 1972, this time sending the mighty B-52s directly over Hanoi and other cities. The destruction they caused was great, but their effectiveness as a means of forcing concessions from the North Vietnamese was at best debatable, and in these strikes for the first time the United States lost large numbers of the big strategic bombers.

In January 1973 a settlement was finally reached. As with the October "agreement," the North Vietnamese retained control of large sections of the south, and they promised to release American prisoners of war within 60 days. Thieu assented this time, largely because Nixon secretly pledged that the United States would "respond with full force" if North Vietnam resumed its offensive. Within several months most prisoners of war were released, and the last American troops were pulled out of Vietnam. More than 57,000 Americans had died in the long war, and over 300,000 more had been wounded. The cost had reached a staggering $150 billion. Nearly a million communist soldiers and 185,000 South Vietnamese soldiers were reported killed.

DOMESTIC POLICY UNDER NIXON

When Nixon became president in 1969, the major economic problem he faced was inflation. This was caused primarily by the heavy military expenditures and easy-money policies of the Johnson administration. Nixon cut federal spending and balanced the 1969 budget, while the Federal Reserve Board forced up interest rates to slow the expansion of the money supply. When prices continued to rise, uneasiness mounted and labor unions demanded large wage increases.

In 1970 Congress passed a law giving the president power to regulate prices and wages. Nixon originally opposed this legislation, but in the summer of 1971 he changed his mind and announced a 90-day price and wage freeze. Then he set up a pay board and a price commission with authority to limit wage and price increases when the freeze ended. These controls did not check inflation completely—and they angered union leaders, who felt that labor was being short-changed—but they did slow the upward spiral.

In handling other domestic issues, the president was less firm. Like President Kennedy he was primarily interested in foreign affairs. He supported a bold plan for a "minimum income" for poor families, but dropped it when it alarmed his conservative supporters and got nowhere in Congress. But when a groundswell of public support for conserving natural resources and checking pollution led Congress to pass bills creating the Environmental Protection Agency (EPA) and the Clean Air Act of 1970, he signed them cheerfully.

Primarily he was concerned with his own political standing. Hoping to strengthen the Republican party in the South, he checked further federal efforts to force school desegregation on reluctant local districts, and he set out to add what he called "strict constructionists" to the Supreme Court, which he believed had swung too far to the left in such areas as race relations and the rights of persons accused of committing crimes. He also proposed mostly conservatives to fill vacancies in the Supreme Court.

After his triumphant reelection and the withdrawal of the last American troops from Vietnam, Nixon resolved to change the direction in which the nation had been moving for decades. He sought, on the one hand, to strengthen the power of the presidency vis-à-vis Congress and, on the other, to decentralize the administration by encouraging state and local management of government programs. He announced that he intended to reduce the interference of the federal government in the affairs of individuals. People should be more self-reliant, he said, and he denounced what he called "permissiveness." Overconcern for the interests of blacks and other minorities must end. Criminals should be punished "without pity." No person or group should be coddled by the state.

THE WATERGATE BREAK-IN

On March 19, 1973, James McCord, a former agent of the Federal Bureau of Investigation accused of burglary, wrote a letter to the judge presiding at his trial. His act precipitated a series of disclosures that first disrupted and then destroyed the Nixon administration.

McCord had been employed during the 1972 presidential campaign as a security officer of the Committee to Re-elect the President (CREEP). At about 1 A.M. on June 17, 1972, he and four other men had broken into Democratic party headquarters at the Watergate, a complex of apartments and offices in Washington. The burglars were members of an unofficial CREEP surveillance group known as "the plumbers." Nixon, who was obsessed by a need to conceal information about his administration, had formed the group after the Pentagon Papers, a confidential report on government policy in Vietnam, had been leaked to the press. The "plumbers" had been caught rifling files and installing electronic eavesdropping devices.

Two other Republican campaign officials were soon implicated in the affair. Their arrest aroused suspicions that the Republican party was behind the break-in. Nixon denied it. "I can say categorically," he announced on June 22, "that no one on the White House staff, no one in this Administration presently employed, was involved in this very bizarre incident."

Most people evidently took the president at his word despite his well-known deviousness. (He had won the nickname "Tricky Dick" when he first ran for Congress in 1946.) He was far ahead in the polls and seemed so sure to win reelection that it was hard to believe he would stoop to burglary to discover what the Democrats were up to. In any case, the affair did not materially affect the election. When brought to trial early in 1973, most of the Watergate burglars pleaded guilty.

McCord, who did not, was convicted by the jury. Before Judge John J. Sirica imposed sentences on the culprits, however, McCord wrote his letter. High Republican officials had known about the burglary in advance and had paid the defendants "hush money" to keep their connection secret, McCord claimed. Perjury had been committed during the trial.

The truth of McCord's charges swiftly became apparent. The head of CREEP, Jeb Stuart Magruder, and President Nixon's lawyer, John W. Dean III, admitted their involvement. Most of Nixon's closest advisers were implicated and forced to resign. This raised the question of the president's personal connection with the scandals. This he steadfastly denied. He insisted that he would investigate the Watergate affair thoroughly and see that the guilty were punished. He refused, however, to allow investigators to examine White House documents, again on grounds of executive privilege, which he continued to assert in very broad terms.

In the teeth of Nixon's denials, John Dean, testifying under oath, stated flatly and in circumstantial detail that the president had been closely involved in the Watergate cover-up. Dean had been a persuasive witness, but many people were reluctant to believe that a president could lie so cold-bloodedly to the entire country. Therefore, when it came out during later hearings of the Senate committee investigating the Watergate scandal that the president had systematically made secret tape recordings of White House conversations and telephone calls, the disclosure caused a sensation. It seemed obvious that these tapes would settle the question of Nixon's involvement once and for all. Again Nixon refused to allow access to the evidence.

One result of the scandals and of Nixon's attitude was a precipitous decline in his standing in public opinion polls. Calls for his resignation, even for impeachment, began to be heard. Yielding to pressure, he agreed to the appointment of an "independent" special prosecutor to investigate the Watergate affair, and he promised the appointee, Professor Archibald Cox of Harvard Law School, full cooperation.

Cox swiftly aroused the president's ire by seeking access to White House records, including the tapes. When Nixon refused to turn over the tapes, Cox obtained a subpoena from Judge Sirica ordering him to do so. The administration appealed this decision and lost in the appellate court. Then, while the case was headed for the Supreme Court, Nixon ordered the new attorney general, Elliot Richardson, to dismiss Cox. Both Richardson, who had promised the Senate during his confirmation hearings that the special prosecutor would have a free hand, and his chief assistant resigned rather than do as the president directed. The third-ranking officer of the Justice Department carried out Nixon's order.

These events of Saturday, October 20, promptly dubbed the Saturday Night Massacre, caused an outburst of public indignation. Congress was bombarded

Garry Trudeau and his politically biting cartoon strip "Doonesbury" enlivened the Vietnam and Watergate years. "Doonesbury" became the first cartoon strip to win a Pulitzer Prize. (Ron Ziegler was President Nixon's press secretary.)

by thousands of letters and telegrams demanding the president's impeachment. The House Judiciary Committee began an investigation to see if enough evidence for impeachment existed. (The House of Representatives must vote to indict federal officials for impeachment; the actual impeachment trial is conducted by the Senate.)

MORE TROUBLES FOR NIXON

The nation had never before experienced such a series of morale-shattering crises. While the seemingly unending complications of Watergate were unfolding during 1973, a number of unrelated disasters struck. First, pushed by a shortage of grain resulting from massive Soviet purchases authorized by détente policy, food prices shot up—wheat from $1.45 a bushel to over $5.00.

Then Vice President Agnew (defender of law and order, foe of permissiveness) was accused of income tax fraud and of having accepted bribes while serving as Baltimore county executive and governor of Maryland. To escape a jail term Agnew admitted in October that he had been guilty of tax evasion and resigned as vice president.

Acting according to the procedures for presidential and vice-presidential succession of the Twenty-fifth Amendment, adopted in 1967, President Nixon nominated Representative Gerald R. Ford of Michigan as vice president, and he was confirmed by Congress. Ford had served continuously in Congress since 1949 and as minority leader since 1964. His positions on public issues were close to Nixon's; he was an internationalist in foreign affairs and a conservative and convinced Republican partisan on domestic issues.

Not long after the Agnew fiasco, Nixon, responding to charges that he had paid almost no income taxes during his presidency, published his 1969 to 1972 returns. They showed that he had paid only about $1600 in two years during which his income had exceeded half a million dollars. Although Nixon claimed that his returns were perfectly legal—he had taken huge deductions for the gift of some of his vice presidential papers to the National Archives—the legality, to say nothing of the propriety, of his actions was questionable. Combined with charges that millions of dollars of public funds had been spent on improvements for his private residences in California and Florida, the tax issue further eroded his reputation, so much so that he felt obliged during a televised press conference to assure the audience: "I am not a crook."

The Judgment on Watergate: "Expletive Deleted"

In March 1974 a grand jury indicted Haldeman; Ehrlichman; former attorney general John Mitchell, who had been head of CREEP at the time of the break-in; and four other White House aides for conspiring to block the Watergate investigation. The jurors also named Nixon an "unindicted co-conspirator." Judge Sirica thereupon turned over the jury's evidence against Nixon to the House Judiciary Committee. Then both the Internal Revenue Service (IRS) and a joint congressional committee, announced that most of his deductions had been unjustified. The IRS assessed him nearly half a million dollars in taxes and interest, which he agreed to pay.

In an effort to check the mounting criticism, late in April Nixon released edited transcripts of the tapes he had turned over to the court the previous November. In addition to much incriminating evidence, the transcripts provided the public with a fascinating and shocking view of how the president conducted himself in private. In conversations he seemed confused, indecisive, and lacking in any concern for the public interest. His repeated use of foul language, so out of keeping with his public image, offended millions. The phrase "expletive deleted," inserted in place of words considered too vulgar for publication in family newspapers, overnight became a catchword.

The publication of the transcripts led even some of Nixon's strongest supporters to demand that he resign. And once the Judiciary Committee obtained the actual tapes, it became clear that the White House transcripts were in crucial respects inaccurate. Much material prejudicial to the president's case had been suppressed. Yet impeaching a president seemed so drastic a step that many people felt more direct proof of Nixon's involvement in the cover-up was necessary.

In the summer of 1974—after so many months of alarms and crises—the Watergate drama reached its climax. The Judiciary Committee, following months of study of the evidence behind closed doors, decided to conduct its deliberations in open session. While millions watched on television, 38 members of the House of Representatives debated the charges. The discussions revealed both the thoroughness of the investigation and the soul-searching efforts of the representatives to render an impartial judgment. Three articles of impeachment were adopted. They charged the president with obstructing justice, misusing the powers of his office, and failing to obey the committee's subpoenas. Except in the case of the last article, many of the Republicans on the committee joined with the Democrats in voting aye, a clear indication that the full House would vote to impeach.

On the eve of the debates, the Supreme Court had ruled unanimously that the president must turn over the 64 subpoenaed tapes to the special prosecutor. Executive privilege had its place, the Court stated, but no person, not even a president, could "withhold evidence that is demonstrably relevant in a criminal trial." For reasons that soon became obvious, Nixon seriously considered defying the Court. Only when convinced that to do so would make his impeachment and conviction certain did he agree to comply.

He would not, however, resign. Even if the House impeached him, he was counting on his ability to hold the support of at least 34 senators (one-third plus one of the full Senate) to escape conviction. But events were passing beyond his control. The 64 subpoenaed tapes had to be transcribed and analyzed. When they were, Nixon's fate was sealed. Three recorded conversations between the president and H. R. Haldeman on June 23, 1972 (less than a week after the break-in and only one day after Nixon had assured the nation that no one in the White House had been involved in the affair), proved conclusively that Nixon had tried to obstruct justice by engaging the CIA in an effort to persuade the FBI not to follow up leads in the case on the spurious grounds that national security was involved.

When the House Judiciary Committee members read the new transcripts, all the Republican members who had voted against the impeachment articles reversed themselves. Republican leaders told the president categorically that the House would impeach him and that no more than a handful of senators would vote for acquittal.

On August 8 Nixon announced his resignation. "Dear Mr. Secretary," his terse official letter to Secretary of State Kissinger ran, "I hereby resign the Office of President of the United States. Sincerely, Richard Nixon." The resignation took effect at noon on August 9, when Gerald Ford was sworn in as president. "Our long national nightmare is over," Ford declared.

Within weeks of taking office, Ford pardoned Nixon for whatever crimes he had committed in office, even any, if such existed, as had yet to come to light. Not many Americans wanted to see the ex-president lodged in jail, but pardoning him seemed both illogical and incomprehensible when Nixon had admitted no guilt and had not yet been officially charged with any crime. (Nixon's instant acceptance of the pardon while claiming to have done no wrong was also illogical but not incomprehensible.)

MILESTONES

1942	Pacifists found Congress of Racial Equality (CORE)
1955–1956	Martin Luther King, Jr. leads Montgomery, Alabama, bus boycott
1957	Southern Christian Leadership Conference (SCLC) is founded in Atlanta
1960	Black college students found Student Nonviolent Coordinating Committee (SNCC)
1961	CIA-trained Cuban exiles launch disastrous Bay of Pigs invasion
	John F. Kennedy founds Peace Corps
	Freedom riders integrate buses in South
1962	Soviet Premier Khrushchev precipitates Cuban Missile Crisis
1963	United States supports coup to oust President Ngo Dinh Diem of South Vietnam
	Martin Luther King, Jr. leads March on Washington
	Lee Harvey Oswald assassinates President Kennedy; Lyndon Johnson becomes president
1964	Congress endorses Vietnam escalation in Gulf of Tonkin Resolution
	Lyndon Johnson is elected president, begins Great Society program
	Congress passes historic Civil Rights Act
1965	Congress's Medicare Act pays some medical costs for senior citizens and the poor
	Congress funds education with Elementary and Secondary Education Act
1968	Communists strike all over South Vietnam in Tet Offensive
	Lyndon Johnson withdraws as candidate for reelection
	Richard Nixon is elected president
1969	Nixon announces "Vietnamization" of war
1970	Nixon announces "incursion" into Cambodia

Antiwar student protesters are killed at Kent State and Jackson State universities

Congress passes Clean Air Act and creates Environmental Protection Agency (EPA)

1972 Nixon's "plumbers" burglarize Democratic national headquarters at Watergate complex

Nixon and Kissinger visit China and Soviet Union

Nixon is reelected in landslide

1973 House Judiciary Committee begins impeachment hearings against Nixon

Vice President Spiro Agnew resigns; Gerald Ford is appointed vice president

Last American troops leave Vietnam

Nixon fires Watergate special prosecutor Archibald Cox (Saturday Night Massacre)

1974 Supreme Court orders release of Nixon's White House tapes

Nixon resigns; Gerald Ford becomes president and pardons Nixon

31

SOCIETY IN FLUX

In their inaugural addresses, the presidents of the postwar decades seemed preoccupied with change. In 1949 Truman described the nation as being at a "major turning point in the long history of the human race." Eight years later Eisenhower spoke of the need to lead the nation through "this tempest of change and turmoil." In 1961 Kennedy declared that the "torch had been passed to a new generation." In 1965 Lyndon Baines Johnson maintained that "ours is a time of change—rapid and fantastic change." Four years later Richard M. Nixon commented on the "spiralling pace of change."

This widespread perception of the decades after World War II as a time of change was everywhere apparent. The population was growing rapidly. People were on the move. And after the doom and gloom of the Great Depression and World War II, Americans were ready to relax and take advantage of all the goods and services that peace and prosperity made possible.

Yet the prosperity cast into sharper relief those excluded by race and gender from equal access to good education and jobs. Technological change also accelerated social change. By miniaturizing transistors, for example, the space program made it possible for teenagers to remain in continuous contact with popular music on their radios. The interpenetration of technology and popular culture was pervasive. In 1946, four days after an atomic bomb had been exploded on the Bikini atoll, a French fashion designer decided to call his skimpy bathing suit by the same name. During the 1960s wits observed that hemlines were going up faster than Saturn rockets.

A SOCIETY ON THE MOVE

One reason why Americans seemed constantly on the move was their devotion to automobiles. In the postwar decades the automobile entered its golden age. During the booming 1920s, when the car became an instrument of mass transportation, about 31 million autos were produced by American factories. During the 1950s, 58 million rolled off the assembly lines; during the 1960s, 77 million.

More people drove farther in more reliable and more comfortable vehicles over smoother if not always less congested highways. And the new cars were heavier and more powerful than their predecessors. Gasoline consumption first touched 15 billion gallons in 1931; it soared to 35 billion gallons in 1950 and to 92 billion in 1970. A new business, the motel industry (the word, typically American, was a combination of *motor* and *hotel*) developed to service the millions of tourists and business travelers who burned all this fuel.

The development of the interstate highway system, begun under Eisenhower in 1956, was a major cause of increased mobility. The new roads did far more than facilitate long-distance travel; they accelerated the shift of population to the suburbs and the consequent decline of inner-city districts.

Despite the speeds that cars maintained on them, the new highways were much safer than the old roads. The traffic death rate per mile driven fell steadily, almost entirely because of new interstates. On the other hand, the tremendous increase in automobiles led to an upsurge in traffic fatalities. In 1945, 27,000 people died in automobile accidents; in 1970, the number of fatalities approached 54,000, far more American deaths than in the Korean War. The environmental impact of the highway system was also severe. Elevated roads cut ugly swaths through cities, and the cars they carried released tons of noxious exhaust fumes into urban air. Hillsides were gashed, marshes filled in, forests felled—all in the name of speed and efficiency.

Although commercial air travel had existed in the 1930s and had profited from wartime technical advances in military aircraft, it truly came of age when the first jetliner—the Boeing 707, built in Seattle, Washington—went into service in 1958. Almost immediately jets came to dominate long-distance travel, while railroad passenger service and transatlantic liners declined in importance.

THE ADVENT OF TELEVISION

Another important postwar change was the advent of television as a means of mass communication. By 1961 there were 55 million sets in operation, and by the mid-1960s orbiting government and commercial satellites were relaying pictures from one continent to another instantly.

Television combined the immediacy of radio with the visual impact of films, and it displayed most of the strengths and weaknesses of both in exaggerated form. It swiftly became indispensable to the political system, both for its coverage of public events and as a vehicle for political advertising. Its handling of the events following President Kennedy's assassination and of other news developments made history come alive for tens of millions of viewers.

Television also brought sports events before the viewer vividly, attracting enormous audiences and producing so much money in advertising revenue that the economics of professional sports was revolutionized. Team franchises were bought and sold for huge sums, and ordinary players commanded salaries in the hundreds of thousands, stars in the millions.

Some excellent drama was presented, especially on the National Educational Television network, along with many filmed documentaries. However, Newton Minow of the Federal Communications Commission (FCC) called the programming offered by most television stations a "vast wasteland." The lion's share of television time was devoted to uninspired and vulgar serials, routine variety shows, giveaway and quiz programs designed to reveal and revel in the ignorance of the average citizen, and reruns of old movies cut to fit rigid time periods and repeatedly interrupted at climactic points by commercials. Most sets had poor acoustic qualities, which made them inferior instruments for listening to music. Yet children found television fascinating, remaining transfixed before the screen when—their elders said—they should have been out of doors or curled up with a book.

AT HOME AND WORK

Family life was changing in complicated ways. Sometimes men and women devised entirely new ways of raising families and reconciling the demands of work and marriage; at other times, they looked resolutely to the past for guidance as to their own lives.

In 1946, more than 10 percent of all single females over the age of 14 in the country got married. Government policies buttressed the inclinations of the people: to encourage taxpayers to have children, the federal government granted income tax deductions for dependents. The birthrate soared.

The period was marked by a cultural reaffirmation of domesticity. A 1947 survey by the *Woman's Home Companion* found that among possible careers, its readers favored nursing, clerical work, retailing, and teaching because these jobs offered the best preparation for women's "prime objective": marriage. Popular magazines like the *Ladies' Home Journal,* full of articles such as "Keep Those Home Fires Burning—With Hobbies" and "See How to Knit a Baby Blanket," showed college-educated women how to make a "career" of home management and child development.

Scholars mostly agreed that women belonged at home. In 1947 psychoanalyst Marynia Farnham explained that the female reproductive organs predisposed women to the protective and nurturing tasks of child rearing; women who pursued careers in the competitive world of business would forever be at odds with their bodies. Dr. Benjamin Spock, whose *Common Sense Guide to Baby and Child Care* first appeared in 1946 and sold 24 million copies during the next

Art historian Karal Ann Marling observed in As Seen on TV *(1994) that the TV set originally functioned as a kind of picture, such as would be hung over the mantelpiece. This 1950s American living room illustrates the point, which has arranged pictures above the television. But the family is looking at the TV, riveted by the antics of a clown.*

quarter century, insisted that a mother's most important job was to shore up her children's sense of self by providing continuous support and affection. Women who worked outside the home necessarily "neglected" their children. The child who was "mildly neglected," Spock added, was apt to grow up "mildly disturbed."

Although men assumed prominent roles in some domestic rituals, such as presiding over the backyard barbecue or carving the holiday turkey, their chief responsibility was to earn enough money to sustain the family. This was considerably easier than in the past. From 1949 through 1975, unemployment never exceeded 7 percent, and during the mid-1960s it fell well below 4 percent. For those who had lived during the Depression the dominant social fact of the postwar era was the availability of work. As early as 1948, half the United Auto Workers questioned by Columbia sociologist C. Wright Mills told him that they "hardly ever" worried about losing their jobs.

But the *character* of work was changing in unsettling ways. The Second World War accelerated the growth of giant corporations, whose complex, global operations were built on mountains of paper. Regiments of managers ran the systems, and vast armies of clerical workers processed the expanded flow of information. In 1870, 1 in 160 workers was employed in clerical work; by 1950, that figure was 1 in 8. One-fifth of all employees of manufacturing firms worked in offices.

The growth of suburbs gave a geographic dimension to the changing roles of husbands and wives. In the postwar years the federal government encouraged single-family home construction by allowing homeowners to deduct mortgage interest from their income taxes and by making low-cost mortgages available through the Federal Housing Administration.

New suburbs appeared almost like mushrooms after a spring rain. With their streets named after flowers or pleasant emotional states (the large postwar suburb of Levittown, near Philadelphia, featured Friendly Lane, Graceful Lane, Good Lane, and Shelter Lane), the suburbs were to function as havens for work-weary men.

This image, powerfully reiterated in television shows and films, sacrificed none of its allure for being unrealistic. Impressed as a child with the prim family life depicted in *Leave It to Beaver*, the poet Gary Soto, who grew up in the Mexican American barrio in Fresno, California, tried without success to persuade his family to dress for dinner.

In fact, the suburban world was unreal even for many of the women who inhabited it. More women were leaving the home during the day to find work in the burgeoning clerical and service sector. In 1940, only 1 in 4 civilian employees was female, one-third of them married. Three decades later, 4 in 10 paid employees were women, two-thirds of them married. Perhaps 20 million women—after returning home from work, fixing dinner, putting the children to bed, and doing a load of laundry—collapsed in front of the television set and watched domestic heroines such as Donna Reed vacuuming the house in high heels and pearls, making clothes and cakes from scratch, soothing the fragile psyches of her husband and children, and otherwise living a fantasy that accorded with the idealized image of female domesticity.

THE GROWING MIDDLE CLASS

Another postwar change was the marked broadening of the middle class. In 1947 only 5.7 million American families had what might be considered middle-class incomes—enough to provide something for leisure, entertainment, and cultural activities as well as for life's necessities. By the early 1960s more than 12 million families, about a third of the population, had such incomes.

As blue-collar workers invaded the middle class by the tens of thousands, they moved to suburbs previously reserved for junior executives, shopkeepers, and the like. They shed their work clothes for business suits. They took up golf. In sum, they adopted values and attitudes commensurate with their new status— which helps explain the growing conservatism of labor unions. During the Great

Depression, when they were underdogs of sorts, the unions fought for social justice. In the 1960s many union workers seemed more interested in preserving their gains against the ravages of inflation and taxation than in reforming society.

RELIGION IN CHANGING TIMES

Sociologists and other commentators on contemporary affairs found in the expansion of the middle class another explanation of the tendency of the country to glorify the conformist. They attributed to this expansion the blurring of party lines in politics, the national obsession with moderation and consensus, the complacency of so many Americans, and their tendency, for example, to be more interested in the social aspects of churchgoing than in the moral and philosophical aspects of religion.

Organized religion traditionally deals with eternal values, but it is always influenced by social, cultural, and economic developments. Never had this been truer in America than in the decades after World War II. All the major faiths, despite their differences, were affected. Immediately after the war the prosperity and buoyant optimism of the period led to an expansion of religious activity. The Catholic Church alone built over a thousand new schools and more than a hundred hospitals along with countless new churches. By 1950 the Southern Baptists had enrolled nearly 300,000 new members and built some 500 churches.

But while most faiths prospered materially, the faithful tended to accept the world as it was. In *Catholic, Protestant, Jew* (1955), Will Herberg argued that ethnic differences between people of different backgrounds were becoming less important, and as a result, religious toleration was becoming routine. President Eisenhower lent authority to this argument when he said: "Our government makes no sense unless it is founded on a deeply felt religious faith—and I don't care what it is." According to a Gallup poll taken shortly after the war, 97 percent of Americans believed in God. However, another poll revealed that many people were woefully ignorant of religious history and doctrine. Large numbers of Christians, for example, were unable to tell pollsters the name of any of the four gospels.

Church and state were by law and the Constitution separate institutions, but on Flag Day in 1954 Eisenhower signed a law that added the phrase "one nation under God" to the Pledge of Allegiance. The next year, Congress added "In God We Trust" to the nation's currency. New Deal welfare legislation took on a large part of a burden previously borne by church groups.

The civil rights movement and the war in Vietnam had important religious implications. Many militant blacks (Malcolm X is an early example) converted to the Muslim faith because of its lack of racial bias. Among those in the public eye who became Muslims were the heavyweight champion boxer Cassius Clay, who changed his name to Muhammad Ali, and Lew Alcindor, a basketball star who became Kareem Abdul Jabbar.

As a student at Crozer Theological Seminary, Martin Luther King, Jr. excelled at homiletics—the art of preaching. His deep, booming voice and pronounced gestures helped inspire the civil rights movement. "He's damn good," President Kennedy remarked after seeing him on television. King's powerful persona helped bring religion directly into public life.

Nearly all religious groups played significant roles in the fight for racial justice that erupted after the Supreme Court outlawed segregation. Priests, ministers, and rabbis joined in antiwar demonstrations. The Reverend Martin Luther King, Jr.'s nonviolent approach was essentially religious, his oratory deeply felt, passionate, but always dignified and controlled.

The enormous outpouring produced by King's March on Washington in 1963 was swelled by many prominent religious leaders, and their example put pressure on both church hierarchies and ordinary members to become civil rights activists. Shocking photographs of police dogs being used to "subdue" demonstrating Catholic nuns in the Deep South converted uncounted thousands to the struggle.

All the social changes of the period had religious ramifications. Feminists objected to male domination of most Christian churches and called for the ordination of female ministers and priests; some religious leaders supported the feminists, but conservatives rejected their ideas out of hand. Every aspect of the sexual revolution, from the practice of couples living together openly outside of marriage to the tolerance of homosexuality and pornography to the legalization of contraception and abortion, caused shock waves in the religious community. The Roman Catholic insistence that the clergy remain celibate resulted in a decline in the number of young Catholics becoming priests and nuns. This dealt a crippling blow to the parochial school system, which depended heavily on the clergy for teachers.

Radio and television had more direct effects on organized religion. The "Radio Priest" of the New Deal era, Father Charles Coughlin, was the prototype of a new kind of clergyman that flourished in the postwar period. The airwaves enabled rhetorically skilled preachers to reach millions with emotionally charged messages on religious topics and also on political and social questions. The most successful in the postwar years were the leaders of evangelical Protestant sects, and by the 1960s they had mastered television. Whereas most postwar revivalists, the most famous being Billy Graham, stressed interdenominational cooperation, in the 1970s a more militant, fundamentalist type emerged.

THE PERILS OF PROGRESS

The many changes of the era help explain why President Johnson warned in his inaugural address, "We have no promise from God that our greatness will endure." Looking at American society more broadly, two dilemmas seem to have emerged. One was that progress was often self-defeating. Reforms and innovations instituted with the best of motives often made things worse rather than better. Instances of this dilemma, large and small, are so numerous as to defy summary. DDT, a powerful chemical developed to kill insects that were spreading disease and destroying valuable food crops, proved to have lethal effects on birds and fish—and perhaps indirectly on human beings. Goods manufactured to make life fuller and happier (automobiles, detergents, electric power) produced waste products that disfigured the land and polluted air and water. Cities built to bring culture and employment to millions became pestholes of poverty and depravity.

The second dilemma was that modern industrial society placed an enormous premium on social cooperation, at the same time undermining the individual citizen's sense of being essential to the proper functioning of society. The economy was as complicated as a fine watch; a breakdown in any one sector swiftly spread to other sectors. Yet specialization had progressed so far that individual workers had little sense of the importance of their personal contributions and thus felt little responsibility for the smooth functioning of the whole. Effective democratic government required that all voters be knowledgeable and concerned, but few could feel that their individual voices had any effect on elections or public policies. The exhaust fumes of millions of automobiles poisoned the air, but it was difficult to expect the single motorist to inconvenience himself by leaving his car in the garage when his restraint would have no measurable effect on total pollution. "One person just can't feel that she's doing anything," a frustrated teenager wrote. "I can use soap instead of detergent . . . but what good do I feel I'm doing when there are people next door having a party with plastic spoons and paper plates?"

These dilemmas produced a paradox. The United States was the most powerful nation in the world, its people the best educated, the richest, and probably the most energetic. American society was technologically advanced and dynamic; American traditional values were idealistic, humane, democratic. Yet the nation seemed incapable of mobilizing its resources intelligently to confront the most obvious challenges, its citizens unable to achieve much personal happiness or identification with their fellows, the society helpless in trying to live up to its most universally accepted ideals.

THE COSTS OF PROSPERITY

The vexing character of modern conditions could be seen in every aspect of life. The gross national product approached and then swiftly passed a trillion dollars, but inflation was becoming increasingly serious. Workers constantly demanded raises—which only served to drive prices still higher.

Economic expansion resulted in large measure from technological advances, and these too proved to be mixed blessings. World War II stimulated the development of plastics, synthetic rubber, radar, television, and other electronic devices. After the war plastics invaded field after field—automobile parts, building materials, adhesives, packaging materials. In the 1950s public utility companies began to manufacture electricity from nuclear fuels because it was cheaper than that produced in coal- or oil-fired plants. But the possibility of catastrophic accidents and the problem of disposing of lethal radioactive waste products soon dampened public enthusiasm for nuclear power. Scientists insisted that the danger from radiation was insignificant, but the possibility of accidents could not be eliminated entirely.

Equally significant was the invention of the electronic computer, which revolutionized the collection and storage of records, solved mathematical problems beyond the scope of the most brilliant human minds, and speeded the work of bank tellers, librarians, billing clerks, statisticians—and income tax collectors. Computers lay at the heart of industrial automation, for they could control the integration and adjustment of the most complex machines. In automobile factories they made it possible to produce entire engine blocks automatically. In steel mills molten metal could be poured into molds, cooled, rolled, and cut into slabs without the intervention of a human hand, the computers locating defects and adjusting the machinery to correct them far more accurately than the most skilled steel worker, and in a matter of seconds. But the computerization of record-keeping and manufacturing raised the problem of how displaced clerks and automobile and steel workers were to find new jobs.

The vast outpouring of flimsy plastic products and the increased use of paper, metal foil, and other "disposable" packaging materials seemed about to bury the country beneath mountains of trash. Even an apparently ideal form of scientific advance, the use of commercial fertilizers to boost food output, had unfortunate side effects: phosphates washed from farmlands into streams sometimes upset the ecological balance and turned the streams into malodorous death traps for aquatic life. Above all, technology increased the capacity of the earth to support people. But as population increased, production and consumption increased, exhausting supplies of raw materials and speeding the pollution of air and water resources. And where would the process end? Viewed from a world perspective, it was obvious that the population explosion must be checked or it would check itself by pestilence, war, starvation, or some combination of these scourges. Yet how to check it?

NEW RACIAL TURMOIL

President Johnson and most of those who supported his policies expected that the 1964 Civil Rights Act, the Economic Opportunity Act, Medicare and Medicaid, and the other elements in the war on poverty would produce an era of racial peace and genuine social harmony—the Great Society that everyone wanted. The change that occurred in the thinking of the black radical Malcolm X seemed a straw in the wind. In 1964 Malcolm left the Muslims and founded his own Organization of Afro-American Unity. While continuing to stress black self-help and the militant defense of black rights, he now saw the fight for racial equality as part of a larger struggle for all human rights. "What we do . . . helps all people everywhere who are fighting against oppression," he said. Yet as in so many other aspects of modern life, progress itself created new difficulties. Early in 1965 Black Muslim fanatics, furious at his defection, assassinated Malcolm X while he was making a speech in favor of racial harmony.

The assassination was an act of vengeance, not of social protest. More significant was the fact that official white recognition of past injustices was making blacks more insistent that all discrimination end. The very process of righting some past wrongs gave them the strength to fight more vigorously. Black militancy, building steadily during the war and the postwar years, had long been ignored by the white majority; in the mid-1960s it burst forth so powerfully that the most smug and obtuse white citizens had to accept its existence.

Even Martin Luther King, Jr., the herald of nonviolent resistance, became more aggressive. "We are not asking, we are demanding the ballot," he said in January 1965. A few weeks after Malcolm's death, King led a march from Selma, Alabama, to Montgomery as part of a campaign to force Alabama authorities to allow blacks to register to vote. King chose Selma because the county in which it was located had a black majority but only 325 registered black voters. He expected the authorities to react brutally, thus attracting public sympathy for the marchers, and he was not disappointed. His marchers were assaulted by state policemen who wielded clubs and tossed canisters of tear gas. Liberal opinion was shocked as never before. Thousands of people descended on Selma to demonstrate their support for the black cause.

The Student Nonviolent Coordinating Committee (SNCC), which had been born out of the struggle for racial integration, had become by the mid-1960s a radical organization openly scornful of integration and interracial cooperation. Many students had been radicalized by the threats and open violence they had experienced while trying to register rural blacks and organize schools for black children and by the foot-dragging of the Kennedy administration in working for racial justice. The slogan of the radicals was "Black Power," an expression that was given national currency by Stokely Carmichael, chairman of SNCC. Carmichael, a West Indian by birth, had grown up in Harlem. He had worked ceaselessly for black rights in the South, and as a result he had spent considerable time in southern jails, often on such trumped-up charges as pitching a tent on the grounds of a black school. Although willing to work with black moderates such as King, he was adamantly opposed to cooperating with whites of any stripe. "The time for white involvement in the fight for equality has ended," Carmichael announced in 1966. "If we are to proceed toward true liberation, we must set ourselves off from white people." "Integration is a subterfuge for the maintenance of white supremacy," Carmichael said on another occasion. Blacks should have their own schools, their own businesses, their own political parties, their own (African) culture.

Black Power caught on swiftly among militants. This troubled white liberals, who feared that Black Power would antagonize white conservatives. They argued that since blacks made up only about 11 percent of the population, any attempt to obtain racial justice through the use of naked power was sure to fail.

Meanwhile, black anger erupted in a series of destructive urban riots. The most important occurred in Watts, a ghetto of Los Angeles, in August 1965. A trivial incident brought thousands into the streets. The neighborhood almost literally exploded: For six days Watts was swept by fire, looting, and bloody fighting between local residents and nearly 15,000 National Guardsmen, called up to assist the police. The following two summers saw similar outbursts in scores of cities.

Then, in April 1968, Martin Luther King, Jr., was murdered in Memphis, Tennessee, by a white man, James Earl Ray. Blacks in more than a hundred cities unleashed their anger in outbursts of burning and looting. Whites were shocked and profoundly depressed. The death of King appeared to destroy the hope that his peaceful appeal to reason and right could solve the problems of racism.

Public fear and puzzlement led to many investigations of the causes of the riots, the most important being that of the commission headed by Governor Otto Kerner of Illinois, which President Johnson had appointed after the 1967 riots. The conclusions of most of the studies were complex but fairly clear. Race riots had a long history in the United States, but earlier troubles usually began with attacks by whites that led to black counterattacks. Riots of the Watts type were begun by blacks. Although much white-owned property was destroyed, the fighting was mostly between blacks and law enforcement officers trying to control them.

The rioters were expressing frustration and despair; their resentment was directed more at the social system than at individuals. As the Kerner Commission put it, the basic cause was the "white racism" that deprived blacks of access to good jobs, crowded them into slums, and eroded all hope of escape from such misery. Ghettoes bred crime and depravity—as slums always have—and the complacent refusal of whites to invest enough money and energy to help ghetto residents, or even to acknowledge that the black poor deserved help, made the modern slum unbearable. While the ghettoes expanded, middle-class whites tended more and more to flee to the suburbs or to call on the police "to maintain law and order," a euphemism for cracking down hard on deviant black behavior no matter how obvious the connection between that behavior and the slum environment.

The victims of racism employed violence not so much to force change as to obtain psychic release; it was a way of getting rid of what they could not stomach, a kind of vomiting. Thus the riots concentrated in the ghettoes themselves, smashing, Samson-like, the source of degradation even when this meant self-destruction. When fires broke out in black districts, the firefighters who tried to extinguish them were often showered with bottles and bricks and sometimes shot at, while above the roar of the flames and the hiss of steam rose the apocalyptic chant, "Burn, baby, burn!"

Middle-class city residents often resented what seemed the "favoritism" of the federal government and state and local administrations, which sought through affirmative action to provide blacks with economic opportunities and social benefits. Efforts to desegregate ghetto schools by busing children out of their local neighborhoods were a particularly bitter cause of conflict. These developments caused a powerful white backlash. People already subjected to the pressures caused by inflation, specialization, and rapid change, and worried by rising urban crime rates and welfare costs, found black radicalism infuriating.

NATIVE-BORN ETHNICS

The struggles of blacks for equality went hand in hand with the struggles of those of Mexican descent, principally in the Southwest. After World War I, thousands of immigrants from Mexico flocked into that part of the country, mingling with the far larger native-born Hispanic population. They could do so legally because the restrictive immigration legislation of the 1920s did not apply to Western Hemisphere nations. When the Great Depression struck, Mexican Americans were the first to suffer—about half a million Hispanics who were not citizens were either deported or "persuaded" to return to Mexico. But during World War II and again between 1948 and 1965, federal legislation encouraged the importation of *braceros* (temporary farm workers). Many other Mexicans entered the country illegally. The latter were known as *mojados*, or "wetbacks," because they often slipped over the border by swimming across the Rio Grande.

Many of these Mexicans and other Spanish-speaking people, including the thousands from the territory of Puerto Rico who could immigrate to the mainland legally in unlimited numbers, settled in the big cities, where low-paying but usually steady work was available. They lived in slums called *barrios*, as segregated, crowded, and crime-ridden as the ghettoes of the blacks.

Spanish-speaking residents of the Southwest, native- and foreign-born, and to a lesser degree those in the big eastern cities, were for a time largely apolitical; they tended to remain close-knit and insular. But in the 1960s a new spirit of resistance arose. Leaders of the new movement called themselves Chicanos. The Chicanos demanded better schools for their children and easier access to higher education. They urged friends and relatives to take pride in their traditions and

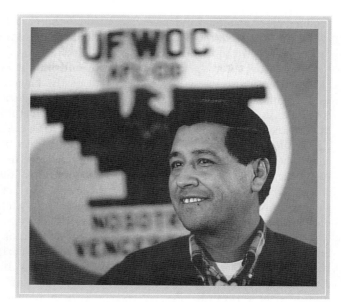

The Mexican American founder of the National Farm Workers Association and later head of the United Farm Workers Organizing Committee, César Chávez successfully organized migrant workers throughout California in the early 1960s and later led a nationwide boycott against California grape producers.

culture, to demand their rights, and to organize themselves politically. One Chicano nationalist group tried to secede from New Mexico, an act that brought it into confrontation with the army.

The Chicano leader with the widest influence was César Chávez, who concentrated on what superficially was a more limited goal—organizing migrant farm workers into unions. Chávez grew up in migrant camps in California; he had no schooling beyond the seventh grade. After serving in the navy during World War II, he went to work for the Community Service Organization (CSO), a group seeking to raise the political consciousness of the poor and to develop self-help programs for them. Chávez became general director of the CSO but resigned in 1962 because he felt it was not devoting enough attention to the plight of migrant workers. He then founded the National Farm Workers' Association, later known as the United Farm Workers' Organizing Committee.

The struggles of black people for equal treatment in the 1950s and 1960s radicalized many Indians. These militants referred to themselves as Native Americans, not Indians. They used the term *Red Power* as blacks spoke of Black Power and called their more conservative colleagues "Uncle Tomahawks." The National Indian Youth Council and later the American Indian Movement (AIM) demanded the return of lands taken illegally from their ancestors. They called for self-determination and a concerted effort to revive tribal cultures, even the use of the mind-altering controlled substance peyote in religious ceremonies,[1] and they

---

[1]*The California Supreme Court upheld the right to use peyote in this way in* People v. Woody *(1964).*

organized a Pan-Indian movement to advance the cause. Paradoxically, this policy brought them into conflict with traditionalist Indians devoted to local autonomy. (At least 40 Indian languages are still spoken.)

Some AIM leaders sought total separation from the United States; they envisaged setting up states within states, such as the Cherokees had established in Georgia in Jacksonian days. In 1973 radicals occupied the town of Wounded Knee, South Dakota (site of one of the most disgraceful massacres of Indians in the nineteenth century), and held it at gunpoint for weeks.

While traditionalists resisted the militants, liberal white opinion proved to be generally sympathetic. In 1975 Congress passed the Indian Self-Determination Act, which gave individual tribes much greater control over such matters as education, welfare programs, and law enforcement. The act specifically recognized the government's obligation to ensure "maximum Indian participation" in the management of federal policy in these areas.

Militant ethnic pride characterized the behavior of other racial minorities and of many white Americans too. Blacks donned dashikis and other African garments and wore their hair in natural "Afro" styles. Italian Americans, Polish Americans, and descendants of other "new immigrant" groups eagerly studied their history in order to preserve their culture and where necessary revive dying traditions. The American "melting pot," some historians now argued, had not amalgamated the immigrant strains as completely as had been thought. Ethnic diversity became for some an end to be desired, despite the possibility that differences might as easily inspire conflict as harmonious adjustment.

The color line was broken in major league baseball in 1947, and soon all professional sports were open to black athletes. Whereas the reign of black heavyweight boxing champion Jack Johnson (1908–1915) had inspired an open search for a "white hope" to depose him, and whereas the next black champion, Joe Louis (1937–1949), had been accepted by whites because he "knew his place" and was "well behaved," champion Muhammad Ali was a hero to both white and black boxing fans despite his often bizarre behavior, his militant advocacy of racial equality, and his adoption of the Muslim religion.

Their achievements and advances aside, African Americans had found real self-awareness. The attitude of mind that ran from the lonely Denmark Vesey to Frederick Douglass and to W. E. B. Du Bois had become the black consensus.

RETHINKING PUBLIC EDUCATION

Young people were in the forefront of the fight for the rights of minorities. In a time of uncertainty and discontent, full of conflict and dilemma, youth was affected more strongly than the older generations, and it reacted more forcefully. No institution escaped its criticisms, not even the vaunted educational system, which many students claimed poorly suited their needs. This was still another paradox of modern life, for American public education was probably the most comprehensive in the world.

After World War I, under the impact of Freudian psychology, the emphasis in elementary education shifted from using the schools as instruments of social change, as John Dewey had recommended, to using them to promote the emotional development of the students. "Child-centered" educators played down academic achievement in favor of "adjustment." The change probably stimulated the students' imaginations and may possibly have improved their psychological well-being, but observers soon noted that the system produced poor work habits and fuzzy thinking and fostered plain ignorance. Although "educationists" insisted that they were not abandoning traditional academic subjects, they surely de-emphasized them.

The demands of society for rigorous intellectual achievement made this distortion of progressive education increasingly less satisfactory. Following World War II, critics began a concerted assault on the system. The leader of the attack was James B. Conant, former president of Harvard. His book *The American High School Today* (1959) sold nearly half a million copies, and his later studies of teacher education and the special problems of urban schools also attracted wide attention.

Conant flayed the schools for their failure to teach English grammar and composition effectively, for neglecting foreign languages, and for ignoring the needs of both the brightest and the dullest students. He insisted that teachers' colleges should place subject matter above educational methodology in their curricula.

The success of the Soviet Union in launching the first *Sputnik* in 1957 increased the influence of critics like Conant because it dealt a healthy blow to American overconfidence. To match the Soviet achievement, the United States needed thousands of engineers and scientists, and the schools were not turning out enough graduates prepared to study science and engineering at the college level. Suddenly the schools were under enormous pressure, for with more and more young people desiring to go to college, the colleges were raising their admission standards. The traditionalists thus gained the initiative, academic subjects a revived prestige. The National Defense Education Act of 1958 supplied a powerful stimulus by allocating funds for upgrading work in the sciences, foreign languages, and other subjects and for expanding guidance services and experimenting with television and other new teaching devices. States encouraged small schools to consolidate into larger units; high schools became larger, as Conant proposed, allowing greater specialization among faculty and more college-level classes. Not until the large high schools were built did administrators perceive that many students, especially from disadvantaged minority groups, felt lost in them.

The post-*Sputnik* stress on academic achievement profoundly affected higher education too. Critics demanded that secondary schools and colleges raise their standards and place more stress on the sciences. Prestige institutions such as Harvard, Yale, Columbia, Stanford, and a dozen other colleges and universities, raised their entrance requirements. By the mid-1960s, the children of the baby boom generation were flocking to the nation's high schools and colleges. Population growth and the demands of society for specialized intellectual skills

High School and College Graduates, 1870–1983
Lyndon Johnson's Elementary and Secondary Education Act, passed in 1965, was a landmark in the century-long expansion of high school education and directly influenced college education in the United States. The most rapid increase in high school graduates occurred between 1920 and 1940, but the number of graduates as a percentage of all people aged 17 was greatest in 1967. The peak period for college graduates, 1945 to 1950, reflects the GI Bill after World War II.

were causing educational institutions to burst at the seams. Enrollments had risen rapidly after World War II, mostly because of the GI Bill; by 1950 there were 2.6 million students in American colleges and universities. Thirty years later there were about 12 million. To bridge the gap between high school and college, two-year community colleges proliferated. Almost unknown before 1920, there were about 1300 two-year colleges by 1980, nearly all of them publicly financed. Enrollment in these institutions rose from 1.3 million in the mid-1960s to 6.4 million in the early 1990s.

STUDENTS IN REVOLT

For a time after World War II, the expansion of higher education took place with remarkable smoothness. The veterans, more mature and eager to make up for lost time, concentrated on their studies, and younger students tended to follow their lead. But in the 1960s the mood changed. The members of this college generation had grown up during the postwar prosperity and had been trained by teachers who were, by and large, New Deal liberals. They had been told that government was supposed to regulate the economy in the general interest, help the weak against the strong, and protect the liberties of all. It seemed to many students not to be performing these functions.

Modern industrial society, with its "soul-less" corporations, its computers, and its almost equally unfeeling human bureaucracies, provided these young people with material comforts and social advantages, but it made them feel insignificant and powerless. Their advantages also made them feel guilty when they thought about the millions of Americans who did not have them. The existence of poverty in a country as rich as the United States seemed intolerable, racial prejudice both stupid and evil. Yet the government seemed incapable of attacking these disgraceful conditions head-on. Still worse in their eyes, the response of their elders to McCarthyism appeared contemptible—craven cowardice of the worst sort—and dangerous. In the age of the atom, rabid anticommunism might end in nuclear war.

All these influences were encapsulated in a manifesto put forth by a small group of students at a meeting of Students for a Democratic Society (SDS), held at Port Huron, Michigan, in 1962. "We are the people of this generation . . . looking uncomfortably to the world we inherit," the Port Huron Statement began. Their main concerns were racial bigotry, the bomb, and the "disturbing paradoxes" associated with these concerns. How could an American reconcile the contradictions between the idea that "all men are created equal" with "the facts of Negro life in the South and the big cities of the North" and between the declared peaceful intentions of the government and its huge "economic and military investments in the Cold War?" Too many people and too many institutions, concentrating on preserving what they own and can command, "have closed their minds to the future."

SDS grew rapidly, powered by rising college enrollments, protest against the escalation of the war in Vietnam, and a seemingly unending list of local campus issues. Radical students generally had little tolerance for injustice, and their dissatisfaction often found expression in public protests. The first great student outburst convulsed the University of California at Berkeley in the fall of 1964. Angry students, many veterans of the 1964 fight for black rights in the South, staged sit-down strikes in university buildings to protest the prohibition of political canvassing on the campus. This Free Speech Movement disrupted the institution over a period of weeks. Hundreds were arrested; the state legislature threatened reprisals; the faculty became involved in the controversy; and the crisis led to the resignation of the president of the University of California, Clark Kerr.

On campus after campus in the late 1960s students organized sit-ins and employed other disruptive tactics. Frequently professors and administrators played into the radicals' hands, being so offended by their methods and manners that they refused to recognize the legitimacy of some of their demands.

Equally significant in altering the students' mood was the frustration that so many of them felt with traditional aspects of college life. Regulations that students had formerly merely grumbled about evoked determined, even violent opposition. Dissidents denounced rules that restricted their personal lives, such as

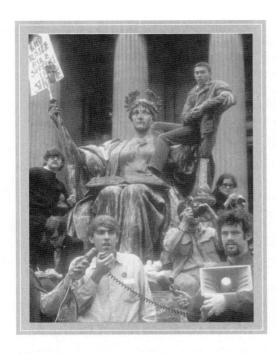

"Alma mater," outside Low Memorial Hall of Columbia University, looks on sedately as SDS leader Mark Rudd denounces the school. Later, Rudd and other radicals climbed these stairs and ordered administrators to vacate the building. The students then occupied the buildings. New York City police subsequently threw the students out.

prohibitions on the use of alcohol and the banning of members of the opposite sex from dormitories. They complained that required courses inhibited their intellectual development. They demanded a share in the government of their institutions, long the private preserve of administrators and professors.

Beyond their specific complaints, the radicals refused to put up with anything they considered wrong. The knotty social problems that made their elders gravitate toward moderation led these students to become intransigent absolutists. The line between right and wrong became as sharply defined as the edge of a ruler. Racial prejudice was evil: it must be eradicated. War in a nuclear age was insane: armies must be disbanded. Poverty amid plenty was an abomination: end poverty now. To the counsel that evil can be eliminated only gradually, that misguided persons must be persuaded to mend their ways, that compromise was the path to true progress, they responded with scorn. Extremists among them, observing the weaknesses of American civilization, adopted a nihilistic position—the only way to deal with a "rotten" society was to destroy it.

THE COUNTERCULTURE

Some young people, known generally as hippies, were so "turned off" by the modern world that they retreated from it, finding refuge in communes, drugs, and mystical religions, often wandering aimlessly from place to place. During the 1960s and 1970s groups of them could be found in every big city in the United States and Europe. Some hippies, like the poet Allen Ginsberg, one of their elder statesmen, and the novelist Ken Kesey, were genuinely creative people. Ginsberg's dark, desperate masterpiece "Howl," written apparently while under the influence of drugs in 1955, was perhaps the most widely read poem of the postwar era, certainly a work of major literary significance. "Howl" begins: "I saw the best minds of my generation destroyed by madness, starving hysterical naked," and goes on to describe the wanderings and searchings of these "angelheaded hipsters," a "lost battalion of platonic conversationalists . . . seeking jazz or sex or soup" in Houston, "whoring in Colorado," and "investigating the F.B.I. in beards and shorts" in California, all the while denouncing "the narcotic tobacco haze of Capitalism." "Howl" ends with Ginsberg's indignant, almost frantic assault on that "sphinx of cement and aluminum," the fire god Moloch, the devourer of children.

Most hippies resembled the radicals in their political and social opinions. They were disgusted by the dishonesty and sordid antics of so many of the politicians, horrified by the brutality of Vietnam, appalled by racism, contemptuous of the smugness they encountered in colleges and universities. They believed in conservation, freedom of expression, tolerance, and peace.

But they rejected activism, being almost totally apolitical. Theirs was a world of folk songs and blaring acid rock music, of "be-ins," casual sex, and drugs. Their slogan, "Make love, not war" was more a general pacifist pronouncement than a specific criticism of events in Vietnam, although Vietnam surely had a great deal to do with their underlying pessimism. Indeed, with them passivity was a philosophy, almost a principle. At rock concerts they listened where earlier generations had danced. Hallucinogenic drugs heightened users' "experiences" while they were in fact in a stupor; a Harvard psychologist advised them to "Tune in, turn on, drop out." Another hippie slogan, "Do your own thing," will work in social situations only if no one does anything. Their communes were a far cry from the busy centers of social experimentation of the pre–Civil War Age of Reform.

THE SEXUAL REVOLUTION

Young people made the most striking contribution to the revolution that took place in the late 1960s in public attitudes toward sexual relationships. Here change came with startling swiftness. Almost overnight (it seemed in retrospect) conventional ideas about premarital sex, contraception and abortion, homosexuality, pornography, and a host of related matters were openly challenged. Probably the behavior of the majority of Americans did not alter radically, but the majority's beliefs and practices were no longer automatically acknowledged as the only valid ones. It became possible for individuals to espouse different values and to behave differently with at least relative impunity. Actions that in one decade would have led to social ostracism or even to imprisonment were in the next decade accepted almost as a matter of course.

The causes of this revolution were complex and interrelated; one change led to others. More efficient methods of contraception, especially the birth control pill, and antibiotics that cured venereal disease removed the two principal practical arguments against sex outside of marriage; with these barriers down, many

Debating the Past

Did mass culture make life shallow? At the 1969 Woodstock festival in New York, a half million young people came together to commune with each other through the medium of rock music. Did mass-produced culture—pop music, movies, TV, consumer products—render life superficial or did it deepen life by allowing many to share similar experiences?

For much of the twentieth century, intellectuals had sniffed at the low-brow cultural products of the mass media: Elvis Presley and rap, western films and fast-food restaurants, television sit-coms and Disneyland. A group of European Marxists known as the "Frankfurt school," many of whom had fled to the United States to escape Nazi persecution, maintained that when popular culture was transformed into a mass-marketed consumer item, it became debased. Worse, mass culture was a form of mindless escapism that distracted people from meaningful political action.

But during the 1960s and 1970s, historians began to look at mass culture and consumption in a different way. Historians of women, minorities, workers, and other marginalized groups decided that it was not enough to recount such peoples' struggles against oppression: it was equally important to explain how they lived and what they thought. Warren Susman (1984), Robin D. Kelley (1994), Kathy Peiss (1998), and others embraced popular culture—even mass culture—because the people they studied did so, too. Lizabeth Cohen (2003) added that the triumph of mass culture did not mean that Americans had abandoned politics. On the contrary, the United States became a "Consumer Republic" ruled by "citizen consumers."

Warren Susman, *Culture as History* (1984), Robin D. Kelley, *Race Rebels* (1994), Kathy Peiss, *Hope in a Jar* (1998), Lizabeth Cohen, *A Consumers' Republic* (2003). For the Frankfurt school, see Theodor Adorno, *Culture Industry* (1991) and Christopher Lasch, *The Culture of Narcissism* (1979). Walter Benjamin, *Complete Correspondence* (1999), argued in this correspondence with Adorno that mass-produced culture could free culture from the snob fetishism of high culture.

One of the major changes to occur in the 1970s and 1980s was the willingness of homosexuals to make public their sexual preference in the course of demanding full legal standing and equal rights.

people found their moral attitudes changing. Almost concurrently, Alfred C. Kinsey's *Sexual Behavior in the Human Male* (1948), based on thousands of confidential interviews with persons from many walks of life, claimed that half of American men engaged in homosexual activities before adolescence; that 90 percent had masturbated; that between 30 and 45 percent had adulterous sexual relations; that 70 percent had patronized prostitutes; and that 17 percent of farm boys had had sexual relations with animals. Kinsey's data emphasized the diversity of sexual urges, and the foolishness of societal attempts to prescribe narrow standards of morality.

Sexual Behavior in the Human Male shocked many people, and many social scientists pointed out that a large sample was not necessarily representative. When he published *Sexual Behavior in the Human Female* in 1958, a book that demonstrated that the sexual practices of women were as varied as those of men, Kinsey was subjected to a storm of abuse and deprived of the foundation support that had financed his research. (In 1997 historian James H. Jones challenged Kinsey's claims to scientific objectivity. Jones found that Kinsey and some of his researchers organized, participated in, and even filmed all manner of sexual activities involving interview subjects, prostitutes, colleagues, and spouses.)

That the sexual revolution in its many aspects served useful functions was beyond dispute. Reducing irrational fears and inhibitions was liberating for many persons of both sexes, and it tended to help young people form permanent associations on the basis of deeper feelings than their sexual drives. Women surely profited from the new freedom, just as a greater sharing of family duties by husbands and fathers opened men's lives to many new satisfactions.

But like other changes, the revolution produced new problems, and some of its results were at best ambiguous. For young people, sexual freedom could be very unsettling; sometimes it generated social pressures that propelled them into relationships they were not yet prepared to handle, with grave psychological results. Equally perplexing was the rise in the number of illegitimate births. Easy cures did not eliminate venereal disease; on the contrary, the relaxation of sexual taboos produced what public health officials called a veritable epidemic of gonorrhea, a frightening increase in the incidence of syphilis, and the emergence of the new disease, acquired immune deficiency syndrome (AIDS).

Exercising the right to advocate and practice previously forbidden activities involved subjecting people who found those activities offensive—still a large proportion of the population—to embarrassment and even to acute emotional distress. To some people pornography seemed ethically wrong, and to most feminists it seemed degrading to women. Abortion raised difficult legal and moral questions, which exacerbated already serious social conflicts. Clearly, however, the sexual revolution was not about to end, nor the direction of change to be reversed.

WOMEN'S LIBERATION

Sexual freedom also contributed to the revival of the women's rights movement. For one thing, freedom involved a more drastic revolution for women than for men. Effective methods of contraception obviously affected women more directly than men, and the new attitudes heightened women's awareness of the way the old sexual standards and patterns of family living had restricted their entire existence. In fact the two movements interacted with each other in innumerable ways, some clear, others obscure. Concern for better job opportunities and for equal pay for equal work, for example, fed the demand for day-care centers for children.

Still another cause of the new drive for women's rights was concern for improving the treatment of minorities. Participation in and the mere observation of the civil rights movement encouraged American women—as it frequently had in earlier times—to speak out more forcefully for their own rights. Just as white people had callously demeaned and dominated black people until forced to desist by the victims of their prejudice, so, feminists argued, they were being demeaned and dominated by a male-oriented society and must fight back.

One of the leaders of the new women's movement was Betty Friedan. In *The Feminine Mystique* (1963), Friedan argued that advertisers, popular magazines, and other opinion-shaping forces were undermining the capacity of women to use their intelligence and their talents creatively by a pervasive and not very subtle form of brainwashing designed to convince them of the virtues of domesticity. This Friedan deplored. She argued that without understanding why, thousands of women living supposedly happy lives were experiencing vague but persistent feelings of anger and discomfort. "The only way for a woman . . . to know herself as a person is by creative work of her own," she wrote. A "problem that had no name" was stifling women's potential.

The Feminine Mystique was what later came to be known as "consciousness raising" for thousands of women. Over a million copies were quickly sold. Back

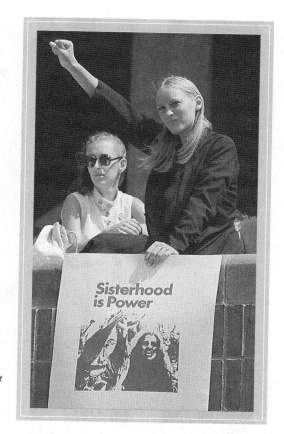

"Sisterhood is Power" proclaimed feminist groups as women sought ways to overcome discrimination leveled against them simply because of their gender.

in 1922 a committee of physicians and social scientists had queried a thousand middle-class women about their personal lives. To the question: "Is your married life a happy one?" only 116 had answered no. But after her book came out, Friedan was deluged by hundreds of letters from women who had thought that their unease and depression despite their "happy" family life were both unique and unreasonable. Many now determined to expand their horizons by taking jobs or resuming their education.

Friedan had assumed that if able women acted with determination, employers would recognize their abilities and stop discriminating against them. This did not happen. In 1966 she and other feminists founded the National Organization for Women (NOW). Copying the tactics of black activists, NOW called for equal employment opportunities and equal pay as civil rights. "The time has come for a new movement toward true equality for all women in America and toward a fully equal partnership of the sexes," the leaders announced. "The silken curtain of prejudice and discrimination against women" in government, industry, the professions, religion, education, "and every other field of importance" must be

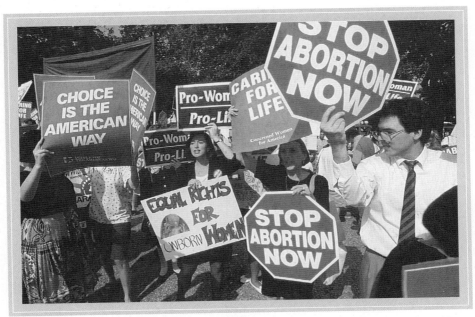

The issue of abortion continues to generate deep feelings among those on both sides of the 1973 Supreme Court Roe v. Wade *decision. In this July 1992 photo, pro-choice adherents, who support the ruling declaring a woman's constitutional right to an abortion, clash with pro-lifers, who seek to overturn the decision, outside the U.S. Supreme Court building.*

drawn back. In 1967 NOW came out for an equal rights amendment to the Constitution, for changes in the divorce laws, and for the legalization of abortion, the right of "control of one's body."

Some radical feminists advocated raising children in communal centers and doing away with marriage as a legal institution. Others described marriage as "legalized rape." Some rejected heterosexuality as a matter of principle.

The militants attacked all aspects of the standard image of the female sex. Avoiding the error of the progressive era reformers, who had fought for the vote by stressing the supposed purity and high moral character of women, they insisted on total equality. Clichés such as "the fair sex" and "the weaker sex" made them see red. They demanded that men bear as much of the burden of caring for their children, cooking, and housework as women traditionally did. They took courses in self-defense to be able to protect themselves from muggers, rapists, and casual mashers. They denounced the use of masculine words like *chairman* (favoring *chairperson*) and of such terms as *mankind* and *men* to designate people in general. They substituted *Ms.* for both *Miss* and *Mrs.* on the grounds that the language drew no such distinction between unmarried and married men.

Few people escaped being affected by the women's movement. The presence of women in new roles—as television commentators, airline pilots, police officers—did not prove that a large-scale shift in employment patterns had taken place. Yet even the most unregenerate male seemed to recognize that the balance of power and influence between the sexes had been altered. The sexual revolution was not about to end, the direction of change in gender relationships not to be reversed.

Many people in the vanguard of change thought they could catch a glimpse, in the not too distant future, of an egalitarian, tolerant, and fulfilling world. But it is hard to see clearly when one is moving, and American society in the 1960s was in flux. Many soon learned that change begets change, and not always what one expects.

MILESTONES

1946	Dr. Benjamin Spock publishes *Common Sense Guide to Baby and Child Care*
1948	Alfred C. Kinsey publishes *Sexual Behavior in the Human Male*
1955	Allen Ginsberg publishes *Howl*
1956	Federal Highway Act plans superhighway network
1957	Soviets launch *Sputnik*
1958	Congress passes National Defense Education Act
	Alfred C. Kinsey publishes *Sexual Behavior in the Human Female*
1959	James B. Conant attacks American education system in *The American High School*
1962	Students for a Democratic Society (SDS) issues Port Huron Statement
1963	Betty Friedan publishes *The Feminine Mystique*
1964	Free Speech Movement disrupts University of California at Berkeley
1965	Black Muslim fanatics assassinate Malcolm X
	César Chávez organizes boycott to support grape pickers
1965–1968	Riots rock black ghettoes
1966	National Organization for Women (NOW) is founded
1969	A half million attend Woodstock Festival in New York
1973	Supreme Court legalizes abortion in *Roe* v. *Wade*
1975	Congress gives tribes more autonomy in Indian Self-Determination Act

32

RUNNING ON EMPTY:
THE NATION TRANSFORMED

While most Americans watched, transfixed, as the events of Watergate interred the Nixon presidency, few were aware that a battle on the other side of the world was about to transform their lives. On October 6, 1973, the eve of Yom Kippur, the Jewish Day of Atonement, Egypt and Syria attacked the state of Israel. Six years earlier Israel had trounced the Egyptians with humiliating ease and taken possession of the Sinai peninsula, but now Egypt's armored divisions roared into the Sinai and threatened to slice Israel in half; Syrian troops advanced against Israel father north. Israeli Prime Minister Golda Meir pleaded with President Nixon for additional arms and aircraft. He ordered "every last goddamn airplane" be sent to Israel. "We are going to be condemned by the Arabs one way or the other," Nixon concluded. The United States immediately airlifted scores of fighter planes and other desperately needed matériel to Israel. The Israelis recrossed the Suez Canal, cut Egyptian supply lines, and forced Egypt's president, Anwar Sadat, to capitulate. But the Arab world aimed its biggest weapon and aimed it squarely at the United States: It cut off oil shipments to the West.

THE OIL CRISIS

Deprived of Middle Eastern oil, the American economy sputtered. The price of oil rose to $12 a barrel, up from $3. This sent prices soaring for nearly everything else. Homes were heated with oil, factories were powered by it, utility

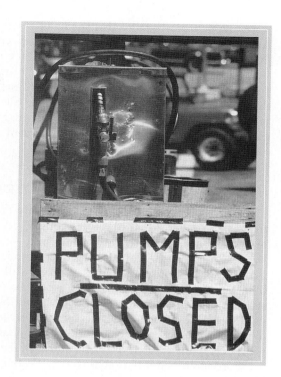

Gas stations all over the country began running dry in 1973; the shortage worsened through the winter and into 1974.

plants used it to generate electricity, and farm produce was shipped to markets on gas-fueled trucks. Nylon and other synthetic fibers as well as paints, insecticides, fertilizers, and many plastic products were based on petrochemicals. Above all else, oil was refined into gasoline. By the time of the Yom Kippur War, American car owners were driving more than a trillion miles a year, the major reason why the United States, formerly a major oil exporter, imported one-third of its oil. The Arab oil embargo pushed up gas prices; service stations intermittently ran out of gasoline; long lines formed at those that remained open.

In the spring of 1974, Henry Kissinger negotiated an agreement that required Israel's withdrawal from some territory occupied since the 1967 war; the Arab nations then lifted the oil embargo. But the principal oil exporting nations—Venezuela, Saudi Arabia, Kuwait, Iraq, and Iran—had learned a valuable lesson: if they limited production, they could drive up the price of oil. After the embargo had ended, their cartel, the Organization of Petroleum Exporting Countries (OPEC), announced another price increase. Gasoline prices doubled overnight.

American automakers who had scoffed at bulbous Volkswagen "bugs" and tiny Japanese "boxes" now winced as these foreign competitors claimed the new market for small, fuel-efficient, front-wheel-drive cars. American auto companies were unable to respond to this challenge because their contracts with the United Automobile Workers (UAW) linked wages to consumer prices, which had floated upward with the price of oil. As production costs rose, manufacturers needed to sell more of their behemoth models, loaded with expensive options such as air conditioning, power windows, and stereo systems. They could not profitably sell the small cars the public craved. (In 1982, when Ford belatedly entered the front-wheel drive market, it lost $40 on each car sold.) By the end of the 1970s, Japanese automakers had captured 30 percent of the entire American automobile market.

FORD AS PRESIDENT

The country greeted the accession of Gerald Ford to the presidency with a collective sigh of relief. Most observers considered Ford unimaginative, certainly not brilliant. But he was hardworking, and—most important under the circumstances—his record was untouched by scandal. Although he was an almost automaton-like Republican partisan, nearly all the Democrats in Congress liked him. He was Nixon's opposite as a person, being gregarious and open, and he stated repeatedly that he took a dim view of Nixon's high-handed way of dealing with Congress. A most ordinary person, earnest but limited, Ford appeared unlikely to venture beyond conventional boundaries or to act rashly. This was what nearly everyone wanted of the president in the wake of Nixon.

Ford identified inflation as the chief economic culprit and asked patriotic citizens to signify their willingness to fight it by wearing WIN (Whip Inflation Now) buttons. Almost immediately the economy entered a precipitous slump.

"My fellow Americans," Gerald Ford announced as he succeeded Richard Nixon in August, 1974, "our long national nightmare is over."

Production fell and the unemployment rate rose to above 9 percent, about twice the postwar average. The president was forced to ask for tax cuts and other measures aimed at stimulating business activity. This made inflation worse and did little to promote employment. The economic problems were difficult, and Ford was handicapped by the fact that the Democrats had solid control of Congress, but his performance was at best inept.

THE FALL OF SOUTH VIETNAM

Depressing news about the economy was compounded by unsettling events in Vietnam. In January 1975, after two years of a bloody "cease fire" (Hanoi charged Saigon with 301,000 violations; and Saigon charged its adversary with 35,673), North Vietnam initiated a two-year plan to conquer South Vietnam by striking just south of the 17th parallel. Dispirited and incompetently led, the South Vietnamese fell back, then fled headlong, and finally dissolved with a rapidity that astonished their attackers.

Ford had always supported the Vietnam war. As the military situation deteriorated, he urged Congress to pour more arms into the South to stem the North Vietnamese advance. The legislators flatly refused to do so, and on May 1, 1975 the Viet Cong and North Vietnamese entered Saigon, which they renamed Ho Chi Minh City. The long Vietnam war was finally over.

FORD VERSUS CARTER

Ford's uninspiring record on the economy and foreign policy suggested that he would be vulnerable in 1976. That year the Democrats chose James Earl Carter, a former governor of Georgia, as their candidate. Carter's rise from almost total obscurity was even more spectacular than that of George McGovern in 1972 and was made possible by the same forces: television, the democratization of the delegate-selection process, and the absence of a dominant leader among the Democrats.

Carter had been a naval officer and a substantial peanut farmer and warehouse owner before entering politics. He was elected governor of Georgia in 1970. While governor he won something of a reputation as a southern public official who treated black citizens fairly. (He hung a portrait of Martin Luther King, Jr., in his office.) Carter's political style was informal—he preferred to be called Jimmy. During the campaign for delegates he turned his inexperience in national politics to advantage, emphasizing his lack of connection with the Washington establishment rather than apologizing for it. He repeatedly called attention to his integrity and deep religious faith. "I'll never lie to you," he promised voters, a pledge that no candidate would have bothered to make before Nixon's disgrace. He won the Democratic nomination easily.

Carter sought to make the election a referendum on morality. After Watergate, an atmosphere of scandal permeated Washington, and aspiring journalists and congressmen trained their sights on Kissinger, who remained secretary of state after Nixon's resignation. The most significant of the allegations was his meddling in the affairs of Chile, which in 1970 was on the verge of electing Salvadore Allende, a Marxist, as president. "I don't see why we need to stand by and watch a country go communist due to the irresponsibility of its people," Kissinger had quipped. After Allende's election, Kissinger called on the CIA to "destabilize" Allende's regime. In 1973, Allende was murdered in a military coup and his government toppled. Carter promised an administration of "constant decency" in contrast to Kissinger's penchant for secret diplomacy and Machiavellian skullduggery.

Ford was opposed in the Republican campaign by ex-governor Ronald Reagan of California, a movie actor turned politician who was the darling of the Republican right wing. Reagan was an excellent speaker, whereas Ford proved somewhat bumbling on the stump. Reagan, too, hammered away at Kissinger, citing his "immoral" détente with Communist China. At Reagan's insistence, the Republican platform denounced "secret agreements, hidden from our people"— another jab at Kissinger.

Both Republican candidates gathered substantial blocs of delegates, but Ford staved off the Reagan challenge. That he did not win easily, possessed as he was of the advantage of incumbency, made his chances of election in November appear slim.

When the final contest began, both candidates were vague with respect to issues, a situation that hurt Carter particularly because he had made so much of honesty and straight talk. Ford stressed the need to control inflation, Carter to attack high unemployment. The election was memorable chiefly for its gaffes: Carter's admission to *Playboy* that he had "lusted after women in my heart" and Ford's declaration in a televised debate, "There is no Soviet domination in Eastern Europe." Voters were left to choose between Carter's seeming ignorance of human frailty and Ford's human frailty of seeming ignorant.

With both candidates stumbling toward the finish line, pundits predicted an extremely close contest, and they were right: Carter won, 297 electoral votes to 241, having carried most of the South, including Texas, and a few large industrial states. A key element in his victory was the fact that he got an overwhelming majority of the black vote (partly on his record in Georgia, partly because Ford had been unsympathetic toward the demands of the urban poor). He also ran well in districts dominated by labor union members. The wish of the public to punish the party of Richard Nixon probably was a further reason for his victory.

THE CARTER PRESIDENCY

Carter shone brightly in comparison with Nixon, and he seemed more forward-looking and imaginative than Ford. He tried to give a tone of democratic simplicity and moral fervor to his administration. After delivering his inaugural address he walked with his wife Rosalynn and their small daughter Amy in the parade from the Capitol to the White House instead of riding in a limousine. He enrolled Amy, a fourth-grader, in a largely black Washington public school. Soon after taking office he held a "call-in"; for two hours he answered questions phoned in by people from all over the country.

A NATIONAL MALAISE

In a heralded television speech Carter complained that "a moral and spiritual crisis" had sapped people's energies and undermined civic pride: "We've learned that piling up material goods cannot fill the emptiness of lives which have no confidence or purpose." Critics responded that the nation needed a president rather than a preacher, and that sermons on the emptiness of consumption rang hollow to those who had lost their jobs or whose paychecks had been shrunk by inflation.

The economic downturn, though triggered by the energy shortage, had more fundamental causes. In the prosperous postwar decades, many companies had become too big and complacent, more attuned to the demands of the corporate bureaucracy than the needs of customers. Workers' boredom lowered productivity. Absenteeism at General Motors and Ford doubled during the 1960s. On an average day in 1970, 5 percent of GM's workforce was missing without explanation, and on Mondays and Fridays ten percent failed to show up. That year Lee Iacocca, the president of Ford, was unnerved by employee attitudes during his visit to a plant at Wixcom, Indiana: "I see some young guy who's going full-time to school at Wayne State, his mind is elsewhere, and he doesn't give a shit what he builds, he doesn't care and he isn't involved in his job. We can't change a man like that anymore." Incapable of eliminating slipshod work in Ford plants, Iacocca recommended that dealers improve their repair shops.

Younger workers were growing impatient too with aging union leaders and a system that welded salary increases to seniority. Increasingly the young rejected the postwar accord in which organized labor essentially ceded control of the workplace in return for cost-of-living increases and job security.

Union membership slipped badly from the high point of the mid-1950s, when over one in three nonagricultural workers belonged to unions; by 1978, the proportion had declined to one in four, and by 1990, one in six. During the 1940s and 1950s, most workers voted to join a union, pay dues, and have the organization bargain for them. By 1978, however, union organizers were losing three-fourths of their campaigns to represent workers; and many workers who belonged to unions were opting to get out. Every year, 800 more union shops voted to rescind their affiliation.

STAGFLATION: THE WEIRD ECONOMY

Recessions are part of the natural business cycle: when economies overheat, they eventually cool down. But the economic crisis after 1973 was unsettling because, for the first time in the nation's history, the rising tide of unemployment had failed to extinguish inflation. Millions of workers lost their jobs, yet wages and prices continued to rise. The term "stagflation" (a combination of stagnation and inflation) was coined to describe this anomaly. In 1971 an inflation rate of 5 percent had so alarmed President Nixon that he had imposed a price freeze. By 1975 inflation had soared to 11 percent and by 1979, it peaked at a whopping 13 percent; unemployment ranged from 6 to 10 percent, nearly twice the usual postwar level.

Congress raised the minimum wage to help low-paid workers cope with inflation. It pegged social security payments to the cost of living index in an effort to protect retirees. Thereafter, when prices rose, social security payments went up automatically. The poor and the pensioners got some immediate relief, but the laws made balancing the federal budget more difficult and the increased spending power of the recipients caused further upward pressure on prices. During the decade, social welfare spending more than doubled. The federal deficit soared from $8.7 billion in 1970 to $72.7 billion in 1980. The price spiral seemed unstoppable.

The federal government made matters worse in several ways. Wages and salaries rose in response to inflation, but taxes went up more rapidly because larger dollar incomes put people in higher tax brackets. This "bracket creep" caused resentment and frustration among middle-class families. There were "taxpayer revolts" as many people turned against long-accepted but expensive government programs for aiding the poor. Federal borrowing to cover the deficit pushed up interest rates and increased the costs of all businesses that had to borrow.

Soaring mortgage rates made it more difficult to sell homes. The housing slump meant unemployment for thousands of carpenters, bricklayers, and other construction workers and bankruptcy for many builders. Double-digit interest rates also hurt small businesses seeking to expand. Savings and loan institutions were especially hard-hit because they were saddled with countless mortgages made when rates were as low as 4 and 5 percent. Now they had to pay much more than that to hold deposits and offer even higher rates to attract new money.

FAMILIES UNDER STRESS

Bad as inflation was in the mid-1970s, it got worse in 1979 when further instability in the Middle East nearly tripled the price of oil, which now reached $34 a barrel. This sent gasoline far over the $1 a gallon price barrier many had thought inconceivable. Within months Ford stock, at 32 in 1978, plummeted to 16; its credit rating with Standard and Poor's fell from AAA to an ignominious BBB. Chrysler, the third largest automaker, tottered near bankruptcy and then fell over the edge, saved in mid-fall only by a $1.2 billion federal loan guarantee. From 1978 to 1982, the jobs of one in three autoworkers were eliminated.

For the millions of young women whose gender consciousness had been shaped by Betty Friedan and other feminists, the recession struck at the worst possible time. Those who had anticipated a scamper up the corporate ladder dis-

An abandoned steel mill at Youngstown, Ohio, in 1986. The sign (right) *reads: "Free Wood at Your Own Risk." The backbone of American industry throughout the twentieth century, midwestern steel sharply declined in the 1970s and all but collapsed during the 1980s.*

covered that the lower rungs were the first to be cut during recession. Many abandoned the idea of a career and settled for low-paying, dead-end jobs in the clerical or service sector. Yet some women, especially those who were well-educated, achieved strong gains during the 1970s: female lawyers jumped from 5 to 12 percent of the profession; and accountants, from 25 to 33 percent.

Just when the feminist movement required a united fight to gain legal parity with men, women increasingly were divided: into an intellectual and professional elite, eager to prove their merits on the job in fair competition with men; and an underpaid and ill-used underclass, vulnerable to the vagaries of a recessionary economy and to the dictates of (mostly male) bosses.

One casualty was the Equal Rights Amendment (ERA), which would make it unconstitutional to deny equal rights "on account of sex." First proposed by the National Woman's party in 1923, the ERA got nowhere. The National Organization for Women (NOW) revived the measure in the 1960s. The House of Representatives approved the ERA in 1971 and the Senate in 1972. By the end of 1972, 22 states had ratified the amendment, 16 short of the three-fourths needed for the ERA to become part of the constitution.

In 1973 Phyllis Schlafly, a former vice president of the National Federation of Republican Women and publisher of a conservative newsletter, spearheaded a nationwide campaign against the ERA. She argued that it would subject young women to the military draft, deprive divorced women of alimony and child custody, and make married women legally responsible for providing 50 percent of

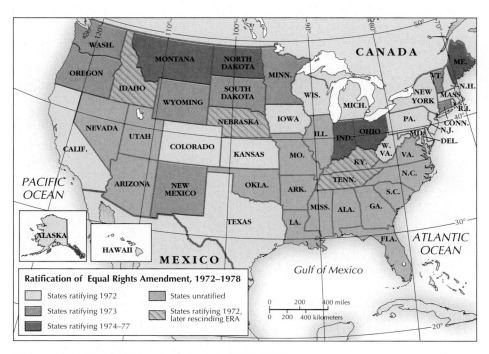

Failure of the Equal Rights Amendment, 1972–1982
In 1972, Congress approved the Equal Rights Amendment. For it to become part of the Constitution, three-fourths of the states—38—had to ratify it. By the end of the year, 32 states had ratified. But then Phyllis Schlafly's campaign against ERA began to take hold. Only 8 ratified in 1973, and 3 in 1974. By the fall of 1978, only 35 states had ratified. Congress voted to extend the ratification deadline for four years, but failed to win enough states; in the meantime, some states that had ratified rescinded their vote, an action of uncertain legality. Opposition to ERA was focused in the South and in the Rocky Mountain states.

household income. Although most polls indicated that a majority of voters supported the ERA, Schlafly's words struck a responsive chord among anxious housewives and low-wage-earning women who doubted they could survive the recessionary economy on their own. The ratification campaign lost momentum and stalled, falling just three states short.

COLD WAR OR DÉTENTE?

"It is a new world," Carter declared in his first speech on foreign affairs. In contrast to the shadowy dealings and sly gambits of the Nixon-Kissinger years, he based his foreign policy on "constant decency." He announced that he would deal with other nations in a fair and humane way, putting the defense of "basic human rights" before all other concerns. He then cut off aid to Chile and Argentina because of human rights violations. He also negotiated treaties with

Panama that provided for the gradual transfer of the Panama Canal to that nation and guaranteed the canal's neutrality. But he said little about what was going on in a long list of other nations whose citizens' rights were being repressed.

In 1979 another Strategic Arms Limitation Treaty (SALT II) was signed with the Soviet Union, but the following winter the Soviet Union sent troops into Afghanistan to overthrow the government there. Carter denounced the invasion and warned the Soviets that he would use force if they invaded any of the countries bordering the Persian Gulf. He withdrew the SALT treaty, which he had sent to the Senate for ratification. He also refused to allow American athletes to compete in the 1980 Olympic games, which were held in Moscow, and he began a new nuclear arms buildup.

Carter's one striking diplomatic achievement was the so-called Camp David Accords negotiated by Israel and Egypt. In September 1978 President Anwar Sadat of Egypt and Prime Minister Menachem Begin of Israel came to the United States at Carter's invitation to seek a peace treaty ending the state of war that had existed between their two countries for many years.

For two weeks they conferred at Camp David, the presidential retreat outside the capital, and Carter's mediation had much to do with their successful negotiations. In the treaty Israel promised to withdraw from territory captured from Egypt during the 1967 Israeli-Egypt war. Egypt in turn recognized Israel as a nation, the first Arab country to do so. Peace ensured an uninterrupted supply of Arab oil to the United States. The Camp David Accords were the first and, as it turned out, the last significant agreement of the twentieth century between Israel and a major Arab state.

THE IRAN CRISIS: ORIGINS

At this point a dramatic shift in the Middle East thrust Carter into the spotlight as never before. On November 4, 1979, about 400 armed Muslim militants broke into the American embassy compound in Tehran, Iran, and took everyone within the walls captive.

The seizure had roots that ran far back in Iranian history. During World War II, Great Britain, the Soviet Union, and later the United States occupied Iran and forced its pro-German shah into exile, replacing him with his 22-year-old son, Muhammad Reza Pahlavi. But in the early 1950s power shifted to prime minister Muhammad Mossadegh, a leftist who sought to finance social reform by nationalizing the mostly American-owned Anglo-Iranian Oil Company.

In 1953, the Iranian army, backed by the CIA, arrested Mossadegh and put the young Pahlavi in power. The fall of Mossadegh ensured a steady flow of cheap oil, but it turned most Iranians against the United States and Shah Pahlavi. Because his American-supplied army and his American-trained secret police kept the shah in power, his opponents hated the United States almost as much as they hated their autocratic ruler.

Throughout 1977, riots and demonstrations convulsed Iran. When soldiers fired on protesters, the bloodshed caused more unrest, and that unrest, more bloodshed. Over 10,000 civilians were killed; many times that number were wounded. In 1978 the whole country seemed to rise against the shah. Finally, in January 1979, he was forced to flee. A revolutionary government headed by a religious leader, the Ayatollah Ruhollah Khomeini, assumed power.

Khomeini denounced the United States, the "Great Satan," whose support of the shah, he said, had caused the Iranian people untold suffering. When President Carter allowed the shah to come to the United States for medical treatment for cancer, militants in Tehran seized the American embassy.

THE IRAN CRISIS: CARTER'S DILEMMA

The militants announced that the Americans at the embassy would be held hostage until the United States returned the shah to Iran for trial as a traitor. They also demanded that the shah's vast wealth be confiscated and surrendered to the Iranian government. President Carter rejected these demands. Instead Carter froze Iranian assets in the United States and banned trade with Iran until the hostages were freed.

A stalemate developed. Months passed. Even after the shah, who was terminally ill, left the United States for Panama, the Iranians remained adamant. The crisis produced a remarkable emotional response in the United States. For the first time since the Vietnam war the entire country agreed on something.

Nevertheless the hostages languished in Iran. In April 1980 Carter finally ordered a team of marine commandos flown into Iran in Sea Stallion helicopters in a desperate attempt to free the hostages. The raid was a fiasco. Several helicopters broke down when their rotors sucked sand into the engines. While the other helicopters were gathered at a desert rendezvous south of Tehran, Carter called off the attempt. In the confusion of a night departure there was a crash and eight commandos were killed. The Iranians made political capital of the incident, gleefully displaying on television the wrecked aircraft and captured American equipment. The stalemate continued. When the shah died in exile in Egypt in July 1980, the Iranians made no move to release the hostages.

THE ELECTION OF 1980

Despite the failure of the raid and the persistence of stagflation, Carter had more than enough delegates at the Democratic convention to win nomination on the first ballot. His Republican opponent in the campaign that followed was Ronald Reagan. At age 69, Reagan was the oldest person ever nominated for president by a major party. However, his age was not a serious handicap in the campaign; he was physically trim and vigorous and seemed no older than most other prominent politicians.

Reagan had grown up a New Deal Democrat, but during and immediately after World War II he became disillusioned with liberalism. As president of the Screen Actors' Guild he attacked the influence of communists in the movie industry. After his movie career ended (he always insisted that he had not been typed

Iranian militants in Tehran burning the American flag. Such demonstrations attracted millions and helped establish the revolutionary regime's legitimacy among its own people. The alternative means of creating legitimacy, by holding elections, was often rejected on theological (and pragmatic) grounds by rulers in the Middle East.

as "the nice guy who didn't get the girl"), Reagan did publicity for General Electric until 1960, then worked for various conservative causes. Reagan won the undying loyalty of supporters of the Vietnam war, as well as the permanent enmity of the left, by proposing that the United States "level North Vietnam, pave it, paint stripes on it, and make a parking lot out of it." In 1966 he ran for governor of California. "Hippies," he quipped, "act like Tarzan, look like Jane, and smell like Cheetah." He won the election.

The 1980 presidential campaign ranks among the most curious in American history. One of Reagan's opponents at the Republican convention, Congressman John Anderson of Illinois, refused to accept defeat and ran for president as an independent because he thought both Carter and Reagan had little genuine popular support. But Anderson, too, inspired little enthusiasm.

Both Carter and Reagan spent much time explaining why the other was unsuited to be president. Carter defended his record, though without much conviction. Reagan denounced criminals, drug addicts, and all varieties of immorality and spoke in support of patriotism, religion, family life, and other "old-fashioned" virtues. This won him the enthusiastic backing of fundamentalist religious sects and other conservative groups. He also called for increased spending

Ronald Reagan astride a horse—a familiar photo-opportunity for presidents. (Recall the similar picture of LBJ, p. 837). But Reagan was an amiable cowboy; his smile and sense of humor were his most disarming weapons. In 1966 just after the election, when reporters asked him what sort of governor he would be, Reagan, a former actor, answered, "I don't know. I've never played a governor." Three months into his presidency, moments after he was seriously wounded in an assassination attempt, he took his wife's hand. "Honey," he said, "I forgot to duck." While being wheeled into the operating room, he quipped to the surgeons, "I hope you are all Republicans."

on defense, and he promised to transfer some functions of the federal government to the states and to cut taxes. He insisted at the same time that the budget could be balanced and inflation sharply reduced.

Reagan's tendency to depend on popular magazine articles, half-remembered conversations, and other informal sources for his economic "facts" reflected a mental imprecision that alarmed his critics, but his sunny disposition and his easygoing style compared favorably with Carter, who seemed tight-lipped and tense even when flashing his habitual toothy smile. A television debate between Carter and Reagan pointed up their personal differences, but Reagan's question to the audience: "Are you better off now than you were four years ago?" had more effect on the election than any policy he said he would pursue.

On election day the voting was light, but those who cast ballots gave Reagan over 43 million votes to Carter's 35 million and Anderson's 5.6 million. Dissatisfaction with the economy and the unresolved hostage crisis seem to have determined the result. The Republicans also gained control of the Senate and cut deeply into the Democratic majority in the House of Representatives.

Carter devoted his last weeks in office to the continuing hostage crisis. War had broken out between Iran and Iraq in September. The Iraqi president, Saddam

Hussein, had hoped to exploit the chaos following the downfall of the shah to seize oil-rich territory in Iran. Early Iraqi victories prompted the Iranians to free the hostages in return for the release of Iranian assets that had been frozen in the United States. After 444 days in captivity, the 52 hostages were set free on January 20, the day Reagan was inaugurated.

REAGAN AS PRESIDENT

Reagan hoped to change the direction in which the country was moving. He demanded steep reductions in federal spending and the deficit, to be accomplished by cutting social welfare expenditures, such as welfare, food stamps and student loans, and by turning many functions of the federal government over to the states. The marketplace, not federal bureaucratic regulations, should govern most economic decisions.

He asked Congress to lower income taxes by 30 percent. When critics objected that this would increase the deficit, the president and his advisers reasoned that the tax cut would leave people with more money, which they would invest in productive ways. The new investment would generate more goods and jobs—and, ultimately, taxes for the federal government. This scheme became known as Reaganomics.

Helped by the votes of conservative Democrats, Reagan won congressional approval of the Budget Reconciliation Act, which reduced government expenditures on domestic programs by $39 billion. But Congress resisted reducing the politically popular "entitlement" programs, such as Social Security and Medicare, which accounted for about half of the budget.

Reagan also eliminated many government regulations affecting businesses. Long and complicated antitrust suits against International Business Machines and American Telephone and Telegraph, two of the largest corporations in the country, were dropped.

Many of Reagan's advisers urged him to reduce the military budget to bring the government's income more nearly in line with its outlays. Instead, reviving the containment policy wholeheartedly, the president insisted that the military buildup was necessary because of the threat posed by the Soviet Union, which he called an "evil empire." In particular, he sought to expand and improve the nation's nuclear arsenal. He made no secret of his wish to create so formidable a nuclear force that the Soviets would have to back down in any confrontation.

In Central America he sought the overthrow of the left-wing government of Nicaragua and the defeat of communist rebels in El Salvador. He even used American troops to overthrow a Cuban-backed regime on the tiny Caribbean island of Grenada. When criticized for opposing leftist regimes while backing rightist dictators, Jeane Kirkpatrick, U.S. ambassador to the United Nations, explained "rightist authoritarian regimes can be transformed peacefully into democracies, but totalitarian Marxist ones cannot."

FOUR MORE YEARS

Being a sitting president with an extraordinarily high standing in public opinion polls, Reagan was nominated for a second term at the 1984 Republican convention without opposition. The Democratic nomination went to Walter Mondale of Minnesota, who had been vice president under Carter. Mondale electrified the country by choosing Representative Geraldine Ferraro of New York as his running mate. An Italian American and a Catholic, Ferraro was expected to appeal to conservative Democrats who had supported Reagan in 1980 and to win the votes of many Republican women.

Reagan began the campaign with several important advantages. He was especially popular among religious fundamentalists and other social conservatives, and these groups were increasingly vocal. President Nixon had spoken of a "silent majority." By 1980 the kind of people he was referring to were no longer silent. Fundamentalist television preachers were almost all fervent Reaganites and the most successful of them were collecting tens of millions of dollars annually in contributions from viewers. One of these, the Reverend Jerry Falwell, founded the Moral Majority and set out to create a new political movement. "Americans are sick and tired of the way the amoral liberals are trying to corrupt our nation," Falwell announced in 1979.

During the first Reagan administration, the Moral Majority had become a powerful political force. Falwell was against drugs, the "coddling" of criminals, homosexuality, communism, and abortion, all things that Reagan also disliked. While not openly antiblack, Falwell disapproved of forced busing to integrate schools and a number of other government policies designed to help blacks and other minorities. Of course, Walter Mondale was also against many of the things that Falwell and his followers denounced, but Reagan was against them all. In addition, Reagan was in favor of government aid to private schools run by church groups, something dear to the Moral Majority despite the constitutional principle of separation of church and state.

But the Moral Majority, despite its name, was far from being an actual majority. Reagan's support was much more broadly based. Thousands of working people and an enormous percentage of white Southerners, types that had been solidly Democratic during the New Deal and beyond, now voted Republican. The president's personality was another important plus—voters continued to admire his informal yet firm style and his stress on patriotism and other "old-fashioned" virtues.

The tendency of voters to support a sitting president when the economy was on the rise was still another advantage. Unemployment fell to 7 percent, investment finally picked up, and inflation remained low. Interest rates were moving down slowly but steadily.

From the start Mondale emphasized the difficulties that he saw ahead for the nation. The president's economic policies, he said, hurt the poor, women, and minorities. Mondale also tried to focus attention on the huge increase in the federal deficit that Reagan's policies had produced. These were conventional campaign tactics. But Mondale, in a daring move, announced that he would *raise* taxes if elected. This promise, most unusual for a person running for office, was an attempt to counter his reputation for political caution.

Most polls showed Reagan far in the lead when the campaign began, and this remained true throughout the contest. Nothing Mondale or Ferraro did or said affected the president's popularity. Bad news, even his own mistakes, had so little effect on Reagan's standing that people began to call him "the Teflon president." On election day he got nearly 60 percent of the popular vote and lost only in Minnesota, Mondale's home state, and in the District of Columbia. Reagan's Electoral College margin was overwhelming, 525 to 13.

Of all the elements in the Democratic New Deal coalition, only African Americans, who voted solidly for Mondale, remained loyal. The Democratic strategy of nominating a woman for vice president was a failure; far more women voted for Reagan than for the Mondale-Ferraro ticket.

Reagan's triumph, like the two landslide victories of Dwight Eisenhower in the 1950s, was a personal one. The Republicans made only minor gains in the House of Representatives and actually lost two seats in the Senate.

"THE REAGAN REVOLUTION"

Reagan's agenda for his second term closely resembled that of his first. In foreign affairs, he ran into continuing congressional resistance to his requests for military support for his anticommunist crusade. This was particularly true after Mikhail S. Gorbachev became the Soviet premier in March 1985. Gorbachev seemed far more moderate and flexible than his predecessors. He began to encourage political debate and criticism in the Soviet Union—the policy known as *glasnost* (openness)—and he sought to stimulate the stagnant Soviet economy by decentralizing administration and rewarding individual enterprise *(perestroika)*.

Gorbachev also announced that he would continue to honor the unratified SALT II agreement, whereas Reagan, arguing that the Soviet Union had not respected the limits laid down in the pact, seemed bent on pushing ahead with the expansion and modernization of America's nuclear arsenal. Reagan sought funds to develop an elaborate system of missile defenses. He referred to it as the strategic defense initiative (SDI), although it was popularly known as Star Wars, a reference to the 1977 George Lucas film. SDI would consist of a network of computer-controlled space stations that would supposedly detect oncoming enemy missiles and destroy them.

When the president realized that the Soviets were eager for an agreement to limit nuclear weapons, he gradually abandoned his talk about Russia being an "evil empire." In October 1986 he met with Gorbachev in Iceland in search of an agreement on arms control. This summit went nowhere. The chief sticking point was SDI, which Gorbachev denounced as "space strike" weaponry that might be used to wipe out Soviet cities. Gorbachev proposed instead the elimination of all nuclear weapons. Reagan was determined to push Star Wars, partly because he apparently did not understand that the Europeans, fearing a conventional Soviet assault, were unsettled by the thought of *total* nuclear disarmament. The Iceland setback, however, proved to be temporary, and in 1988 at a second summit, Reagan and Gorbachev signed a treaty eliminating medium-range nuclear missiles.

Reagan nevertheless persisted in pressing for the Star Wars defense-in-space system. Congress, however, balked at the enormous cost of Star Wars. Costs aside, the idea of relying for national defense on the complex technology involved in controlling machines in outer space suffered a further setback in 1986, when the space shuttle *Challenger* exploded shortly after takeoff, killing its seven-member crew. This disaster put a stop to the program until the cause had been discovered. In 1989 the shuttles began to fly again.

Reagan's basic domestic objectives—to reduce the scope of federal activity, particularly in the social welfare area; to lower income taxes; and to increase the strength of the armed forces—remained constant. Despite the tax cuts already made, congressional leaders of both parties agreed to the Income Tax Act of 1986, which reduced the top levy on personal incomes from 50 percent to 28 percent and the tax on corporate profits from 46 percent to 34 percent.

Liberal members of Congress, remembering how the voters had reacted to Mondale's talk about increasing taxes, found it politically difficult to oppose the measure. But the existing tax system was extremely complicated and full of loopholes benefiting particular interests. The new law did away with most of the tax shelters and special credits that corporations and well-to-do individuals had used to reduce their tax bills. The law also relieved 6 million low-income people from paying any federal income tax at all.

Reagan advanced another of his objectives more gradually. This was his appointment of conservatives to federal judgeships, including Sandra Day O'Connor, the first woman named to the Supreme Court. By 1988 Reagan had appointed three Supreme Court justices and well over half the members of the federal judiciary.

CHANGE AND UNCERTAINTY

But if the "Reagan revolution" seemed to have triumphed, powerful countering forces were at work that no individual or party could effectively control. For one thing, the makeup of the American people, always in a state of flux, was changing at a rate approaching that of the early 1900s when the "new" immigration had been at its peak. In the 1970s, after the Immigration Act of 1965 had put an end to the national-origins concept, more than 4 million immigrants entered the country, and the vast majority of these newcomers came from Asia and Latin America. This trend continued; of the 643,000 who arrived in 1988, more than 550,000 were from these two regions. More than 111,000 of the immigrants came from the Philippines, Korea, Vietnam, and other parts of the Pacific rim and East Asia. In addition, uncounted thousands entered the United States illegally, most crossing the long, sparsely settled border with Mexico. The nation's Hispanic population increased by 53 percent during the 1980s.

DEBATING THE PAST

Did Reagan end the Cold War? In 1983 President Ronald Reagan denounced the Soviet Union as an "evil empire." In that same speech he made a prophecy that few took seriously at the time: The "last pages" in the history of communism "even now are being written." Six years later, when the Berlin wall came down (shown here), the Soviet empire was over. Within a few years, the Soviet Union itself had disintegrated.

Many credited Reagan with having won the Cold War. Caspar Weinberger, secretary of defense, explained that the Reagan administration had had a "secret campaign" to undermine the Soviet economy. Others credited Reagan's massive arms buildup with causing the Soviet economy to collapse from exhaustion. On the other hand, historian William Pemberton (1997) doubted whether Reagan had any coherent foreign policy at the outset; his chief contribution to winning the Cold War was resisting the advice of skeptical hardliners and accepting the conciliatory overtures of Mikhail Gorbachev, the Soviet premier.

Arthur M. Schlesinger, Jr. and John Lewis Gaddis (1992) saw the victory as a long-term and largely bipartisan team effort dating from the Truman presidency. Robert M. Gates (1996), Director of Central Intelligence under George H. W. Bush, said that Bush and his four predecessors in the presidency had ground down the Soviet opposition.

On the left, some scholars insisted that there had been no winner in a protracted dispute that had led to such chaos throughout the Third World. The United States, burdened with massive deficits, was not in much better shape. Others maintained that Reagan was fortunate to be the American president when a new generation of leaders, foremost among them Gorbachev, came to power in the Soviet Union.

For now, perhaps the last word can be that of George Smiley, the anti-Soviet spymaster created by novelist John le Carré (1991): "We won. Not that the victory matters a damn. And perhaps we didn't win anyway. Perhaps they just lost."

Peter Schweizer, *Victory* (1994), William E. Pemberton, *Exit with Honor* (1997), Robert M. Gates, *From the Shadows* (1996), Dana Allin, *Cold War Illusions* (1998); Schlesinger and Gaddis are cited in Michael J. Hogan, ed., *The End of the Cold War* (1992), and John le Carré, *The Secret Pilgrim* (1991).

Some of the new immigrants were refugees from repressive regimes in Vietnam, Cuba, Haiti, and Central America, and nearly all were poor. Most tended, like their predecessors, to crowd together in ethnic neighborhoods. Spanish could be heard more often than English in large sections of Los Angeles, New York, Miami, and many other cities.

No strong demand for immigration restriction developed, perhaps because so many Americans were descendents of immigrants, and because the immigrants did work that needed to be done. However, conservatives found it appalling that so many people could enter the country illegally, and even Americans sympathetic to the so-called undocumented aliens agreed that control was desirable. Finally, in 1986, Congress passed a law offering amnesty to illegal immigrants long resident in the country and penalizing employers who hired illegal immigrants in the future. Many persons legalized their status under the new law, but the influx of illegal immigrants continued. Problems developed because some employers refused to hire anyone with a foreign accent on the grounds that they might be "illegals" bearing false papers.

AIDS

During the 1980s, the nation confronted its most serious health crisis in decades. In the late 1970s, world health officials had spotted the outbreak of yet another viral epidemic in central Africa; but no one noticed that this virus had mutated into a more lethal strain and was spreading to Europe and North America. On June 5, 1981, the Centers for Disease Control (CDC) alerted American health officials to an outbreak of a rare bacterial infection in Los Angeles. What made the outbreak distinctive was that this particular infection, usually found in infants or older people with fragile immune systems, had struck five healthy young men. All were homosexuals. Within months, all died.

By 1982 the CDC decided to call this new disease acquired immunodeficiency syndrome (AIDS). They learned that AIDS was caused by the human immunodeficiency virus (HIV), a lethal retro virus that destroys the body's defenses against infection, making victims susceptible to many diseases. HIV spreads when an infected person's body fluids come in contact with someone else's. By the end of 1982, the CDC had documented 900 cases of AIDS; the disease was increasing exponentially. Soon HIV contaminated some of the nation's blood banks, and some recipients of transfusions came down with AIDS. In June 1983, when the federal budget approached $1 trillion, Congress finally voted $12 million for AIDS research and treatment.

Not until 1985, when the square-jawed romantic actor Rock Hudson confirmed that he was dying of AIDS, did the subject command widespread public attention. President Reagan, an old friend of Hudson's, publicly acknowledged that the disease constituted a grave health crisis. Congress approved Reagan's call for a substantial increase in AIDS funding. But Reagan's appeal was belated and insufficient. By then, nearly 21,000 Americans had died; by 1999, the total number of AIDS-related deaths approached 400,000.

In this electron microscope image, the Human Immunodeficiency Virus (HIV)—the smaller cells—gloms onto a T-cell. The T-cell is a type of white blood cell that quarterbacks the body's defenses against infection. Many researchers looking for a cure for AIDS seeks to prevent the HIV from glomming onto the T-cells.

The AIDS epidemic affected public policy and private behavior. A nationwide educational campaign urged "safe" sex, especially the use of condoms, which by 1990 were distributed free in many high schools. Fear of the disease, and of those who suffered from it, exacerbated many people's homophobia. But the AIDS epidemic also forced most people to confront homosexuality directly and perhaps for the first time, and thus contributed to a deeper understanding of the complexity of human nature. After Hudson's revelation, for example, the *New York Times* commenced using "gay" and "lesbian," the terms then preferred by the people so identified, instead of "homosexual." Gay and lesbian organizations, the vanguard in the initial war against AIDS, continued to fight for social acceptance and legal rights.

THE NEW MERGER MOVEMENT

The Reagan years witnessed a mad frenzy of corporate mergers. The person most responsible was Michael Milken, a shrewd stockbroker of the firm of Drexel Burnham Lambert. Milken specialized in selling "junk bonds," the debt offerings of companies whose existing debts were already high. He persuaded hundreds of savings and loan associations, insurance companies, pension funds, and other big investors to buy these junk bonds, which, though risky, offered unusually high interest rates. The success of his initial ventures prompted Milken to approach smaller companies, invite them to issue huge numbers of junk bonds, and use the proceeds to acquire larger firms.

In 1985 Ronald Perelman, an aggressive entrepreneur, employed this strategy to perfection. He had recently obtained control of Pantry Pride, a small supermarket chain with a net worth of about $145 million, and sought to acquire Revlon, a $2 billion cosmetics and health care conglomerate. With Milken's help, he sold $1.5 billion in Pantry Pride bonds ("junk," because the debt so greatly exceeded the company's worth) and used that capital to buy Revlon. He then paid off the Pantry Pride bonds by selling huge chunks of Revlon and amalgamated the remainder of the company into Pantry Pride. The bond purchasers profited handsomely from the high return on the junk bonds, and Perelman made a fortune on the acquisition and reorganization of Revlon. That same year the R. J. Reynolds Tobacco Company purchased the food conglomerate Nabisco for $4.9 billion. Three years later this new giant, RJR Nabisco, was itself taken over by Kohlberg, Kravis, Roberts and Company for $24.9 billion.

During the frenzied decade of the 1980s, one-fifth of the Fortune 500 companies were taken over, merged, or forced to go private; in all, some 25,000 mergers and acquisitions were successfully undertaken; their total value was nearly a half-trillion dollars. To make their companies less tempting to cash-hungry raiders, many corporations took on whopping debts or acquired unprofitable companies. By the late 1980s, many American corporations were wallowing in red ink. Debt payments were gobbling up 50 percent of the nation's corporate pretax earnings.

"A Job for Life": Layoffs Hit Home

Most corporations coped with the debt in two ways: they sold assets, such as factories, offices, and warehouses; or they cut costs through layoffs. U.S. Steel, whose rusting mills desperately needed an infusion of capital, instead spent $5 billion to acquire Marathon Oil of Ohio; that decision meant that nearly 100,000 steelworkers lost their jobs. No firm was immune, nor any worker secure. "A job for life" had long been IBM's unofficial but endlessly repeated slogan. As late as 1985, it ran an advertisement to reassure employees: "Jobs may come and go—But people shouldn't." Yet during the next nine years a crippled IBM eliminated 80,000 jobs and more than a third of its workforce. During the 1980s, the total number of employees who worked for the Fortune 500 companies declined by three million; nearly one-third of all positions in middle management were eliminated. Millions of "organization men" (about one-third of whom now were women) were laid off as the organizations themselves "downsized," the corporate euphemism for wholesale firings.

Many of the jobs went abroad, where labor costs were lower and unions nonexistent. In 1980 Xerox of America, realizing that it could no longer compete with its more efficient Japanese subsidiary, transferred contracts to Japan and laid off tens of thousands of American workers. In 1984 Nike moved sewing operations to Indonesia, where it could hire female workers for a mere 14 cents an hour. In 1986 the chassis for the Mustang, the symbol of American automotive style, was built by Mazda in Hiroshima, Japan.

Towering mountains of private corporate debt nearly were overshadowed by the Everest of public debt held by the federal government itself. Reagan's insistence on a sharp cut in personal taxes and a substantial increase in military expenditures produced huge—and growing—annual federal deficits. When Reagan took office, the total federal debt was $900 million; eight years later, it exceeded $2.5 *trillion.* "No one imagined how bad the outcome would be," explained David Stockman, Reagan's budget director. "It got away from us."

A "BIPOLAR" ECONOMY, A FRACTURED SOCIETY

Although weighed down by debt, the economy did not crash through the floor, as many expected. In 1982 it began to gain strength and by the late 1980s it was growing at a rate unparalleled since the halcyon days of the 1960s. Despite the ominous, persistent increase in corporate layoffs, the stock market soared. Prices were coming down—traditionally evidence of slackening demand—yet the volume of business was growing!

Many economists and pundits warned that the run-up in stock prices was excessive; the bubble would surely burst. These misgivings were seemingly confirmed in 1987, when on a single day, the Dow-Jones industrial average fell 508 points to 1738. But stock prices quickly recovered and embarked on yet another long period of growth.

Although few perceived it at the time, the economy was undergoing a transformation of historic dimensions. Much as the depression after 1893 had strengthened the nation's economy by wiping out thousands of inefficient steel and machinery firms in New England and the Northeast, the seismic economic upheavals of the 20 years after 1973 toppled many of those same industries but thrust up new ones. As weeds grew in the parking lots of the factories of the "Rust Belt" of the Midwest, new companies and new technology industries sprouted in the "Silicon Valley" of California, along Route 128 outside of Boston, and in booming cities such as Seattle, Washington, and Austin, Texas.

By the end of the Reagan era, the economy consisted of two separate and increasingly unequal components: a battered sector of traditional heavy industry, characterized by declining wages and diminishing job opportunities; and an advancing high-tech and service sector dominated by aggressive, innovative, and individualistic entrepreneurs. The older corporations that survived the shakeout of the 1980s were leaner and better equipped to compete in expanding global markets.

Yet American society was becoming as fractured as the "bipolar" economy from which it drew sustenance. The Reagan tax cuts had disproportionately benefited the wealthy, as had the extraordinary rise of the stock market. Conversely, the economic transformation struck low- or semiskilled wage earners hardest; at the same time, the Reagan administration's shifting of much of the burden of social welfare onto state and local governments reduced benefits to those who lost jobs or could not find work in the strange new economy dominated by information services and bewildering new technologies. At the end of Reagan's second term the standard of living of the poorest fifth of the population (40 million people) was 9 percent lower than it had been in 1979, while that of the wealthiest fifth had risen about 20 percent.

THE IRAN-CONTRA ARMS DEAL

The Reagan administration was generally credited with the nation's successes, and absolved of its failures. The effectiveness of the administration was finally compromised by two self-inflicted wounds involving American policy in Central America and the Middle East.

The Central American problem resulted from a revolution in Nicaragua, where in 1979 leftist rebels had overthrown the dictatorial regime of Anastasio Somoza. Because the victorious Sandinista government was supported by both Cuba and the Soviet Union, President Reagan was determined to force it from power. He backed anti-Sandinista elements in Nicaragua known as the Contras and in 1981 persuaded Congress to provide these "freedom fighters" with arms.

But the Contras made little progress, and many Americans feared that aiding them would lead, as it had in Vietnam, to the use of American troops in the fighting. In October 1984 Congress banned further military aid to the rebels. The President then sought to persuade other countries and private American groups to help the Contras (as he put it) keep "body and soul together."

In the Middle East, the war between Iran and Iraq continued to rage. If either won decisively, it could control the flow of Middle Eastern oil. The United States therefore preferred a stalemate. Thus when Iran gained the advantage, Reagan provided $500 million a year in credits to Iraq. In early 1986, however, Reagan authorized the secret sale of American weapons directly to the Iranians in return for their help in releasing Americans held hostage to Islamic fundamentalists elsewhere in the Middle East.

The arms sale was arranged by Marine Colonel Oliver North, an aide of Reagan's national security adviser. North, who was already in charge of the administration's effort to supply the Nicaraguan Contras indirectly, used $12 million of the profit from the Iranian sales to provide weapons for the Contras, in plain violation of the Congressional ban on such aid.

News of the sales to Iran and of the use of the profits to supply the Contras came to light in November 1986 and of course caused a sensation. Colonel North was fired from his job with the security council, a special prosecutor was appointed to investigate the affair, and both a presidential committee and a joint congressional committee also began investigations. Reagan insisted that he knew nothing about the aid to the Contras. Critics pointed out that if he was telling the truth it was almost as bad since that meant that he had not been able to control his own administration.

Although he remained personally popular, President Reagan's influence with Congress and his reputation as a political leader plummeted. Comments by

"*Mistakes were made," a cartoon in the* Washington Post, 1986, *which pointedly contrasts President Reagan with Teddy Roosevelt, Franklin D. Roosevelt, and Harry S Truman.*

reporters ranged from "disengaged" and "gravely uninformed" to "out to lunch." Even earlier Martin Anderson, Reagan's chief economic adviser, had admitted that the president "made decisions like an ancient king or a Turkish pasha, passively letting his subjects serve him."

Reagan was not an able administrator; the Iran-Contra and financial scandals of his administration did not stick to him because he was seldom close enough to the action to get splattered by it. Reagan articulated, simply and persuasively, a handful of concepts—the "evil" character of Soviet communism, the need to get government off people's backs—and in so doing created a political climate conducive to change. Reagan was directly responsible for neither of the great transformations of the late twentieth century—the collapse of the Soviet Union and the restructuring of American corporations. Yet his actions and, indeed, his failures to act indisputably influenced them. His decision to increase military spending and undertake the fantastically expensive SDI ("Star Wars") forced Gorbachev to seek an accommodation with the United States. Reagan's tax cuts precipitated unimaginably large federal deficits, and deregulation unloosed a sordid pack of predators who preyed on the economy.)Yet the ensuing Darwinian chaos strengthened those corporations that survived and gave them the muscle to prevail in emerging global markets. "We are the change," Reagan declared in his farewell address. What he had done, exactly, he did not say. Yet the statement, however roseate, vague, and self-congratulatory, was not untrue.

During the preceding 15 years, the American nation, like the automobiles that stretched for blocks in line to buy gasoline during the oil embargo, had been running on empty. The federal government was deeply in debt. Corporations had exhausted their cash reserves. Workers lived in fear of the layoff or bank foreclosure notice. Gone were the fanciful expressions of an earlier era—long and wide-bodied chassis, roaring V–8 engines, sweeping tail fins, chromium grills like the jaws of a barracuda. Most cars had become simple boxes, trimmed with plastic, whose efficient four-cylinder engines thrummed steadily.

The nation's aspirations, like its cars, had become smaller, more sensible. Politicians muted their rhetoric, rarely issuing grandiose declarations of war against some intractable foe of humanity. Corporate executives spoke of "downsizing" firms rather than building them into empires. And the American people increasingly hunkered down in their own private spaces, which they locked up and wired with alarms.

MILESTONES

1973	Israel, aided by United States, defeats Egypt and Syria
1973–1974	Arabs impose oil embargo
1974–1976	Gerald Ford serves as president after Nixon's resignation
1975	Vietnam War ends when South Vietnam falls
1976	Jimmy Carter is elected president
1978	Egypt and Israel sign Camp David Accords
1979	Jerry Falwell founds the Moral Majority
	Muslim militants seize U.S. Embassy in Tehran, Iran
1980	Soviet troops invade Afghanistan
	U.S. rescue mission in Iran fails
	Ronald Reagan is elected president
1980s	Enterpreneurs' merger movement leads to huge corporate debt
1981	Iran releases U.S. hostages
	Reagan appoints Sandra Day O'Connor to Supreme Court
1981–1988	War persists between Iran and Iraq
1982	Centers for Disease Control (CDC) identify new disease, AIDS
1984	Reagan is reelected president
1985	Mikhail Gorbachev becomes premier of the Soviet Union
	Reagan secretly sells arms to Iran to finance Nicaraguan Contras
1986	Space shuttle *Challenger* explosion kills crew of seven

33

MISDEMEANORS AND HIGH CRIMES

D uring the final decade of the twentieth century and the opening years of the twenty-first, America was not so much stained by crime as saturated in it. Violent criminals and lesser miscreants held the spotlight partly because the dominant issues of the past were slipping from view. The Soviet Union was collapsing, burying communism in the rubble; and the American economy, after initial hesitation, was gaining momentum and surging forward at breakneck pace. Yet by the early years of the twenty-first century, victory on both fronts seemed hollow. The lifting of the iron curtain of Soviet domination allowed smoldering ethnic and religious tensions to flare up in former satellite states. And the superheated "new economy" of the 1990s bubbled with an insubstantial frothiness, as if its gains might evaporate at any moment. Through it all, the American people were so absorbed in their own affairs—gruesome crimes and lurid scandals amid an exuberant and gaudy materialism—that they failed to perceive the new threat, from abroad and above, that was about to crash into their lives.

THE ELECTION OF 1988

In the absence of the issues of recent decades—the Soviet threat, the energy crisis, stagflation—the presidential election of 1988 might have easily been dominated by a compelling personality. But the candidates were anything but compelling. The selection of Vice President George H. W. Bush for the Republican nomination was a foregone conclusion. Bush, the son of a Connecticut senator, had attended an elite private school and Yale. He served as a pilot during World War II and then settled in Texas, where he worked in the family's oil business and became active in Republican politics. From 1971 to 1973 he served as ambassador to the UN and from 1976 to 1977 as director of the CIA. As Republican presidential hopeful, he trumpeted his experience as vice president; but when the Reagan administration was tarnished by the Iran-Contra scandal, Bush claimed that he had been "out of the loop" and thus free of the scandal. When testimony proved otherwise, he dithered.

The Democratic race was far more complicated but scarcely more inspiring. So many lackluster candidates entered the field that wits called them "the seven dwarfs." Governor Michael Dukakis of Massachusetts, stressing his record as an efficient manager, accumulated delegates steadily. During one debate, however, another Democratic hopeful, Senator Albert Gore of Tennessee, accused Dukakis of handing out "weekend passes for convicted criminals." This referred to a policy, adopted by Massachusetts and many other states, of granting brief furloughs to convicts with satisfactory prison records. Dukakis brushed aside the accusation and went on to win the nomination.

But Lee Atwater, campaign manager for Bush, discovered that during one such furlough Willie Horton, an African American who was serving time in a Massachusetts prison for rape and assault, had stabbed and raped a Maryland woman. "If I can make Willie Horton a household name," Atwater predicted, "we'll win the election." Atwater produced and aired a television advertisement showing prisoners, many of them black, streaming through a revolving door. After describing Horton's record, a voice intoned: "Dukakis wants to do for America what he's done for Massachusetts." The ad struck a responsive chord among white voters. Dukakis's attempts to shift the focus away from race and crime failed.

The presidential campaign became, in effect, a referendum on violent crime in which Dukakis failed the toughness test. Bush won 54 percent of the vote and carried the Electoral College, 426 to 112.

CRIME AND PUNISHMENT

The "law and order" movement had been initiated by Nixon in the late 1960s, but many of its goals were achieved during the next two decades. Responding to widespread calls for a crackdown on crime, elected officials hired more police, passed tougher laws, and built additional prisons.

The shift toward capital punishment was symptomatic. During the 1960s only a handful of criminals were executed. When the Supreme Court ruled in 1972 in the *Furman* decision that jury-imposed capital punishment was racially biased and thus unconstitutional, the matter seemed moot: no criminal had been executed since 1967. But many states, responding to a public demand for a crackdown on crime, rewrote capital punishment statutes in light of the *Furman* decision, depriving juries of discretion in sentencing. The Supreme Court upheld these laws and capital punishment resumed in 1976. Since then, nearly a thousand convicts have been executed.

State legislatures also imposed tougher sentences and made it more difficult for prisoners to obtain parole. In 1973 New York State passed laws that mandated harsh sentences for repeat drug offenders. In 1977 California replaced its parole system with mandatory sentencing, which denied convicts the prospect of early release. Ten other states adopted similar parole restrictions. Nationwide, the proportion of convicts serving long, mandatory sentences increased sharply.

Another manifestation of the crackdown on crime was the increase in the nation's prison population. From 1973 to 1980 the number of convicts tripled, and during the 1980s it doubled again. The growth in the nation's prison population during the early 1990s required the construction of a new 1000-bed prison every week. In 1995 California spent twice as much on prisons as on its huge university system. Human Rights Watch reported that the United States incarcerated more people than any country in the world, except perhaps Communist China, which did not disclose such information.

"CRACK" AND URBAN GANGS

Several factors intensified the problem of violent crime, especially in the inner cities. One was a shift in drug use. During the 1960s marijuana had become commonly available, especially on college campuses; this was followed by cocaine, which was far more powerful and addictive but so expensive that few could afford it.

During the 1980s growers of coca leaves in Peru and Bolivia greatly expanded production. Drug traffickers in Colombia devised sophisticated systems to transport cocaine to the United States. The price of cocaine dropped from $120 an ounce in 1981 to $50 in 1988.

Still more important was the proliferation of a cocaine-based compound called "crack" because it crackled when smoked. Crack was sold in $10 vials. Many users found that it gave an intense spasm of pleasure that overrode all other desires.

The lucrative crack trade led to bitter turf wars in the inner cities; dealers hired neighborhood youths, organized them into gangs, armed them with automatic weapons, and told them to drive competitors away. The term "drive-by shooting" entered the vocabulary. A survey of Los Angeles County in the early 1990s found that more than 150,000 young people belonged to 1000 gangs. Violence had become a fact of life. In 1985, before crack had seized hold of the inner city, there were 147 murders in Washington, D.C.; in 1991, the figure skyrocketed to 482.

Black on black murder had become an important cause of death for African Americans in their twenties. In 1988 Monsta' Kody Scott, who at age 11 pumped shotgun blasts into rival gang members, returned after prison to his Los Angeles neighborhood. He was horrified: gangs no longer merely shot their rivals but "sprayed" them with automatic weapons, 75 rounds to a clip, or blew

A teenage boy in a Texas jail; most prisons did not allow shoes or belts, which might be fashioned into weapons. During the 1990s, about 19 of 20 prison inmates were male. The great majority had been first arrested during their late teens and early twenties. In 1990 six in ten federal inmates had been convicted of drug charges.

them away with small rockets. In 1995, 30 percent of African American men in their twenties were in prison, or on probation or parole. The recurrent refrain of rap performers—that America was a prison—had become, for many, an everyday reality.

GEORGE H. W. BUSH AS PRESIDENT

In 1989 President Bush, having attacked Dukakis for being soft on crime, named a "drug czar" to coordinate various bureaucracies, increased federal funding of local police, and spent $2.5 billion to stop the flow of illegal drugs into the nation. Although the campaign generated plenty of arrests, drugs continued to pour in: as one dealer or trafficker was arrested, another took his place.

Bush also worked to shed the tough image he had cultivated during the campaign. In his inaugural address he said that he hoped to "make kinder the face of the nation and gentler the face of the world." He also displayed a more traditional command of the workings of government and the details of current events than his predecessor. At the same time he pleased right-wing Reagan loyalists by his opposition to abortion and gun control, and by calling for a constitutional amendment prohibiting the burning of the American flag. His standing in the polls soared.

THE COLLAPSE OF COMMUNISM IN EASTERN EUROPE

One important reason for this was the flood of good news from abroad. The reforms instituted in the Soviet Union by Gorbachev led to demands from its Eastern European satellites for similar liberalization. Gorbachev responded by announcing that the Soviet Union would not use force to keep communist governments in power in these nations. Swiftly the people of Poland, Hungary, Czechoslovakia, Bulgaria, Romania, East Germany, and the Baltics did away with the repressive regimes that had ruled them throughout the postwar era. Except in Romania, where the dictator Nicolae Ceausescu was executed, all these fundamental changes were carried out peacefully.

Almost overnight the international political climate changed. Soviet-style communism had been discredited. The Warsaw Pact was no longer a significant force. A Soviet attack anywhere was almost unthinkable. The Cold War was over at last.

President Bush profited from these developments immensely. He expressed moral support for the new governments (and in some cases provided modest financial assistance) but he refrained from embarrassing the Soviets. At a summit meeting in Washington in June 1990 Bush and Gorbachev signed agreements reducing American and Russian stockpiles of long-range nuclear missiles by 30 percent and eliminating chemical weapons.

In 1989 President Bush sent troops to Panama to overthrow General Manuel Noriega, who had refused to yield power when his figurehead presidential candi-

The Collapse of Communism in Eastern Europe

date lost a national election. Noriega was under indictment in the United States for drug trafficking. After temporarily seeking refuge in the Vatican embassy in Panama, he surrendered to the American forces and was taken to the United States, where he was tried, convicted, and imprisoned.

Bush thus accomplished the objective of the invasion. Latin Americans, however, were alarmed by the way the United States had used force in the region, and the fact that far more Panamanian civilians were killed and wounded in the affair than armed supporters of Noriega.

Meanwhile, in the summer of 1991, civil war broke out in Yugoslavia as Croatia and Slovenia sought independence from the Serbian-dominated central government. This conflict soon became a religious war, pitting Serb and Croatian Christians against Bosnian Muslims. In the Soviet Union, nationalist and anticommunist groups demanded more local control of their affairs. President Gorbachev, who opposed this breakup, sought compromise, backing a draft treaty that would increase local autonomy and further privatize the Soviet economy.

In August, however, before this treaty could be ratified, hard-line communists attempted a coup. They arrested Gorbachev, who was vacationing in the Crimea, and ordered tanks into Moscow. But Boris Yeltsin, the anticommunist president of the Russian Republic, defied the rebels and roused the people of Moscow. The coup swiftly collapsed. Its leaders were arrested, the Communist party was officially disbanded, and the Soviet Union itself was replaced by a federation of states, of which Russia, led by Yeltsin, was the most important. Gorbachev, who had begun the process of liberation, found himself without a job.

THE WAR IN THE PERSIAN GULF

Although Reagan had provided economic assistance to Saddam Hussein of Iraq to prevent Iran from winning the Iran-Iraq war, few in the administration were enthusiastic about the Iraqi dictator. For years Saddam had been crushing the Kurds, an ethnic minority in northern Iraq that sought independence. In 1987 the U.S. State Department reported on his "widespread destruction and bulldozing of Kurdish villages." In March 1988, after Kurdish rebels had supported an Iranian advance into Iraq near Halabja, a mostly Kurdish city, Saddam's troops dropped mustard gas, sarin, and other chemical weapons on the city. Some 5000 civilians died. More chemical attacks followed. The United States protested the use of chemical weapons but said little about Saddam's relentless assault on the Kurds.

Worse was to come. In 1988, after the Iran-Iraq war had ended in a stalemate, Saddam intensified his war on the Kurds. Then, in August 1990, he launched an all-out attack on Iraq's tiny neighbor to the south, the oil-rich sheikdom of Kuwait. Saddam hoped to swallow up Kuwait, thus increasing Iraq's already large oil reserves to about 25 percent of the world's total. His soldiers overran Kuwait swiftly, then systematically carried off everything of value they

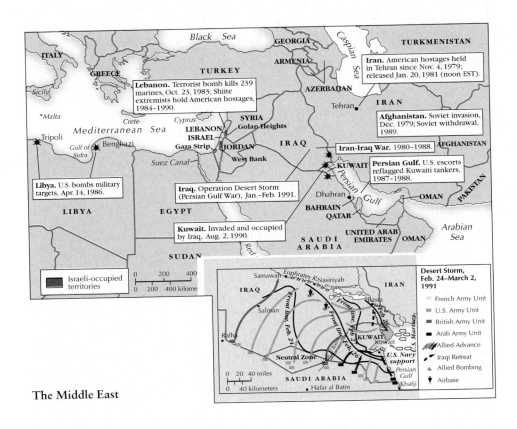

The Middle East

could bring back to Iraq. Within a week Saddam annexed Kuwait and massed troops along the border of neighboring Saudi Arabia.

The Saudis and the Kuwaitis turned to the United States and other nations for help, and it was quickly given. In a matter of days the UN applied trade sanctions against Iraq, and at the invitation of Saudi Arabia, the United States (along with Great Britain, France, Italy, Egypt, and Syria) moved troops to Saudi bases.

By November, Bush had increased the American troops in the area from 180,000 to more than 500,000. In late November the UN took the fateful step of authorizing the use of this force if Saddam did not withdraw from Kuwait by January 15, 1991. He flatly refused to do so.

Congress voted to use force to dislodge Saddam and on January 17, the Americans unleashed an enormous air attack, directed by General Norman Schwarzkopf. This air assault went on for nearly a month, and it reduced much of Iraq to rubble. The Iraqi forces, aside from firing a number of Scud missiles at Israel and Saudi Arabia and setting fire to hundreds of Kuwaiti oil wells, simply endured the rain of destruction that fell on them daily.

As the routed Iraqi army fled Kuwait, it ignited (literally) an ecological disaster by setting fire to the Kuwaiti oil fields. Here American soldiers advance past a burning oil well; it took many months before all the wells could be extinguished.

On February 23 Bush issued an ultimatum to Saddam: Pull out of Kuwait or face an invasion. When Saddam ignored the deadline, UN troops, more than 200,000 strong, struck. Bush called the assault "Desert Storm." Between February 24 and February 27 they retook Kuwait, killing tens of thousands of Iraqis in the process and capturing still larger numbers. Some 4000 Iraqi tanks and enormous quantities of other military equipment were destroyed.

Bush then stopped the attack, and Saddam agreed to UN terms that included paying reparations to Kuwait, allowing UN inspectors to determine whether Iraq was developing atomic and biological weapons, and agreeing to keep its airplanes out of "no-fly" zones over Kurdish territory and other strategic areas.

President Bush and indeed most observers expected Saddam to be driven from power in disgrace by his own people. Indeed, Bush publicly urged the Iraqis to do so. The Kurds in northern Iraq and pro-Iranian Muslims in the south then took up arms, but Saddam used the remnants of his army to crush them. He also refused repeatedly to carry out the terms of the peace agreement, chiefly by hindering the UN inspections for weapons of mass destruction. This led critics to argue that Bush should not have stopped the fighting until Baghdad, the Iraqi capital, had been captured and Saddam's army destroyed.

THE DEFICIT WORSENS

The huge cost of the Persian Gulf War exacerbated the federal deficit. Candidate Bush had promised not to raise taxes, saying in a phrase he would later regret: "Read my lips: No new taxes." As President he recommitted himself to that objective; in fact he even proposed reducing the tax on capital gains. But like his conservative predecessor, Bush could not control the deficit. Congress obstinately resisted closing local military bases or cutting funding for favored defense contractors. Reducing nonmilitary expenditures, especially popular entitlement programs such as Medicare and Social Security, also proved nearly impossible.

The deficit for 1992 hit $290 billion. Bush had no choice but to join with Congress in raising the top income tax rate from 28 percent to 31 percent and levying higher taxes on gasoline, liquor, expensive automobiles, and certain other luxuries. This damaged his credibility and angered conservative Republicans. "Read my lips," critics muttered: "No more Bush."

ENTER BILL CLINTON

William (Bill) Clinton was born William Jefferson Blythe IV, but his father died in a car accident before he was born. Though his stepfather was abusive and an alcoholic, at age 15 Bill legally took his stepfather's name. He graduated from Georgetown, won a Rhodes scholarship to study at Oxford University, and graduated from Yale Law school. He returned to Arkansas and was soon elected state attorney general.

In 1977 Clinton and his wife, Hillary Rodham, joined with James McDougal, a banker, to secure a loan to build vacation homes in the Ozarks. But the development, which they named Whitewater, eventually became insolvent. McDougal covered the debts with a loan from a savings and loan company he had acquired. In 1989 the savings and loan failed, costing the federal government $60 million to reimburse depositors. In 1992 federal investigators claimed that the Clintons had been "potential beneficiaries" of McDougal's illegal activities.

By this time Clinton, now governor of Arkansas, was campaigning in the New Hampshire primary for the Democratic nomination for president. Few voters could make much sense of this tangled web of fiduciary finagling, nor did they have much opportunity to do so: another, far more explosive story threatened to sink the Clinton campaign. It came out that Clinton had for many years engaged in an extramarital affair with one Gennifer Flowers; Clinton's standing in the polls tumbled.

Hillary Rodham Clinton appeared with her husband on CBS's *60 Minutes* to address the allegations. Bill Clinton indignantly denied Flowers's statements but then issued an earnest if ambiguous appeal for forgiveness. "I have acknowledged causing pain in my marriage," he said. "I think most Americans will know what we're saying; they'll get it." Clinton was right, early evidence of his ability to address the American people directly, but on his own—carefully worded— terms. He finished second in New Hampshire, captured most of the remaining primaries, and won the Democratic nomination with ease. His choice of running mate—Senator Al Gore of Tennessee, a Vietnam veteran, family man, and environmentalist—helped the ticket considerably.

THE ELECTION OF 1992

While Clinton tiptoed through a minefield of personal scandal, President Bush rested secure in the belief that, after crushing Saddam's forces in the Gulf War, the 1992 election campaign would be little more than a victory lap. But he encountered unexpectedly stiff opposition within the Republican party. Patrick Buchanan, an outspoken conservative, did well enough to alarm White House strategists. Then Ross Perot, a billionaire Texan, announced his independent candidacy. Perot charged that both major parties were out of touch with "the people." He promised to spend $100 million of his own money on his campaign. Perot's platform had both conservative and liberal planks. He would "take the shackles off of American business," avoid raising taxes, and cut government spending by "getting rid of waste." He also supported gun control, backed a woman's right to have an abortion, promised to get rid of political action committees, and called for an all-out effort to "restructure" the health care system.

Polls quickly revealed that Perot was popular in California, Texas, and other key states that Bush was counting on winning easily. For a time it seemed possible that in a three-way race no one would win a majority of the Electoral College and the election would be thrown into the House of Representatives for the first time since 1824. At the Republican convention in August, Bush was nominated without opposition.

Clinton accused Bush of failing to deal effectively with the lingering economic recession, which had worsened during the summer. He promised to undertake public works projects, to encourage private investment, and to improve the nation's education and health insurance systems. Bush played down the seriousness of the recession, but his jaunty comments offended those who had lost their jobs.

On election day, more than 100 million citizens voted, a record. About 44 million voted for Clinton, 38 million for Bush, and 20 million for Perot. Clinton was elected with 370 electoral votes to Bush's 168. Perot did not win any electoral votes.

A NEW START: CLINTON

One reason for Clinton's success was his expressed intention to change health insurance and the welfare system, and to bring the budget deficit under control. His solid knowledge of public issues was impressive, and he created a general impression of mastery and self-confidence.

Another reason for Clinton's success was his willingness to reconcile differences. "Cooperation is better than conflict," he said on more than one occasion. But however valuable during a campaign, this reasonableness was sometimes a

Young Bill Clinton (left) *shakes hands with President John F. Kennedy. "The torch has been passed to a new generation of Americans," Kennedy had declared in his inaugural. "Ask not what your country can do for you—ask what you can do for your country," JFK added. Thirty years later, Clinton's inaugural echoed Kennedy's: "Today, a generation raised in the shadows of the Cold War assumes new responsibilities," Clinton declared. "I challenge a new generation of young Americans to a season of service."*

disadvantage once the power of the presidency was at Clinton's command. He set out to reverse many of the policies of the Reagan-Bush era, but when opposition developed, circumstances often persuaded him to retreat.

In July 1993 Clinton used his executive authority to strengthen the Supreme Court majority in favor of upholding the landmark case of *Roe* v. *Wade*. The majority included three conservative justices who had been appointed by Reagan and Bush. Clinton appointed Ruth Bader Ginsberg, a judge known to believe that abortion was constitutional. Clinton also indicated that he would veto any bill limiting abortion rights. He also reversed important Bush policies by signing a revived family leave bill into law and by authorizing the use of fetal tissue for research purposes.

The first major test of the president's will came when he submitted his first budget to Congress. He hoped to reduce the deficit by roughly $500 billion in five years, half by spending cuts, half by new taxes. The proposal for a tax increase roused a storm of protest. A number of congressional Democrats refused to go along with Clinton's budget, and since the Republicans in Congress voted solidly against any increase in taxes, the president was forced to accept major changes. Even so, the final bill passed by the narrowest of margins. Clinton rightly claimed a victory.

He then turned to his long-awaited proposal to reform the nation's expensive and incomplete health insurance system. A committee headed by his wife had been working for months with no indication that a plan acceptable to the medical profession, the health insurance industry, and ordinary citizens was likely to come from its deliberations. The plan that finally emerged seemed even more complicated and quite possibly more costly than the existing system. It never came to a vote in Congress.

EMERGENCE OF THE REPUBLICAN MAJORITY

The Whitewater scandal, which Clinton had managed to brush aside during the campaign, gnawed at his presidency. Public pressure forced Attorney General Janet Reno to appoint a special prosecutor. She named Kenneth W. Starr, a Republican lawyer, to investigate Whitewater and other alleged misdeeds of the Clintons.

More troubles followed. Paula Corbin Jones, a State of Arkansas employee, charged that Clinton, while governor, had invited her to his hotel room and asked her to engage in oral sex. Clinton's attorney denied the accusation and sought to have the case dismissed on the grounds that a president could not be sued while in office. The case commenced a torturous route through the courts.

Eager to take advantage of Clinton's troubles, Republicans looked to the 1994 congressional elections. Led by congressman Newt Gingrich of Georgia, they offered voters an ambitious program to stimulate the economy by reducing both the federal debt and the federal income tax. This would turn many of the functions of the federal government over to the states or to private enterprise. Federally administered welfare programs were to be replaced by block grants to the states. Many measures protecting the environment, such as those making businesses responsible for cleaning up their waste, were to be repealed.

On election day, the Republicans gained control of both houses of Congress. Under the firm direction of Gingrich, now Speaker, the House approved nearly all of the provisions of this "contract with America." This appalled Clinton, who vetoed the 1995 budget drafted by the Republicans. When neither side agreed to a compromise, the government for a time ran out of money and shut down all but essential services.

THE ELECTION OF 1996

The public tended to blame Congress, and particularly Speaker Gingrich, for the shutdown. The president's approval rating rose. But the main issue of the day was the economy, and the upturn during and after 1991 benefited Clinton enormously. By the fall of 1996, unemployment had fallen well below 6 percent, and inflation below 3 percent. The Dow Jones industrial stock average of leading stocks soared past 6000, more than triple the average in 1987. Clinton was renominated for a second term without opposition.

A number of Republicans competed in their primaries, but after a slow start Bob Dole of Kansas, the Senate majority leader, won the nomination. Dole had been a senator for more than 30 years, but despite his experience he was a poor campaigner, stiff and monotone. His main proposal was a steep reduction of the deficit and a 15 percent income tax cut. Pressed to explain how this could be done without drastic cuts in popular social programs, especially Social Security and Medicare, he gave a distressingly vague reply. He captured headlines by criticizing popular music as "the leading edge of a culture becoming dangerously coarse" and denouncing Hollywood for making films that "revel in mindless violence and loveless sex."

Clinton, a charismatic campaigner, also promised to reduce the deficit, but by a lesser amount, so as to be able to spend more on education, the environment, and social welfare needs. He stressed preparing for the twenty-first century and took, in general, an optimistic view of the economy.

On election day Clinton won an impressive victory, sweeping the Northeast, all the Midwest except Indiana, the upper Mississippi Valley, and the Far West. He divided the South with Dole, who carried a band of states running north from Texas. Clinton's Electoral College margin was substantial, 379 to 159. The Republicans, however, retained control of both houses of Congress. Many retained, as well, an unquenchable hatred of Clinton.

A RACIAL DIVIDE

The decade of the 1990s had a hard edge, as political rhetoric was saturated by allegations of crimes and misdemeanors. Contributing to the harsh tone of the era was the arrest and spectacular murder trial of O. J. Simpson, a former star football running back for the University of Southern California and the Buffalo Bills. Simpson, who was black, was accused of stabbing his estranged wife and another man. Both of them were white. After a tempestuous nine-month trial, Simpson was acquitted.

To many whites, Simpson was another violent black male, while to many African Americans, he was another innocent black abused by a prejudiced criminal justice system. According to polls, 85 percent of blacks agreed with the "not guilty" verdict of the first Simpson trial, while only 34 percent of whites did. For the most part, neither race could understand the other's reasoning.

Many concluded that the cultural chasm between whites and blacks was widening. In 1992 Supreme Court justice Thurgood Marshall observed that educated Americans of each race appeared to have "given up on integration." After the Simpson trial Louis Farrakhan, leader of the black separatist Nation of Islam, called on African American men to express their solidarity by participating in a "Million Man March" on Washington, D.C. Many black leaders, including Jesse Jackson, embraced it. On October 16, 1995, the demonstration attracted perhaps a half million marchers, far more than had participated in Martin Luther King, Jr.'s "March on Washington" in 1963. But where King welcomed the whites in the audience and declared, "We cannot walk alone," Farrakhan called for "a more perfect union" of the multitude of black men gathered before him.

The persistence of inequality was one reason for the new separatism. In 1972 the incomes of black families were one-third less than those of white families; this was virtually unchanged 20 years later. The leading sectors of the post–1973 economy—technology and information services—placed a premium on education, and here, too, the record in the late 1990s was unsettling. The math and reading scores of 17-year-old African American students rose relative to those of white students in the 1980s. But after 1988 black test scores fell sharply. The extent of the decline—it affected the children of the rich and poor alike, and the students of both public and parochial schools—suggests the importance of broader cultural factors.

A significant casualty of the changing tone of race relations was "affirmative action," which gave minorities preference in hiring and college admissions. Initially justified on the grounds that the legacy of slavery and the persistence of racism put blacks at an unfair disadvantage in finding jobs or gaining admission to college, affirmative action programs spread during the 1970s and 1980s. But in July 1995 the Regents of the University of California ordered an end to affirmative action. This decision touched off protests throughout the university system. The protests, however, drew attention to the issue and the following year California voters approved Proposition 209, which abolished racial and gender preferences in all government hiring and education. The U.S. Supreme Court let the law stand. Other states enacted similar laws.

The overt racism of an earlier era, enforced by custom and law, had become socially unacceptable and often explicitly illegal. But as the British writer Godfrey Hodgson observed, Americans in the 1990s appeared to be moving toward "a kind of voluntary apartheid" in which blacks and whites preferred to keep their distance. In 1997, when President Clinton went to Little Rock to celebrate the fortieth anniversary of the desegregation of Central High School, he commented on the deterioration in race relations. The formerly all-white school was now mostly black, as were all public schools in Little Rock. "For the first time since the 1950s, our schools in America are resegregating," he noted.

VIOLENCE AND POPULAR CULTURE

Popular culture, like athletics, often bridged the racial divide. But some observers took little solace in the broad appeal of youth-focused movies, pop songs, video and computer games, and TV shows. Such entertainment, they contended, romanticized an increasingly bloody culture of crime and violence. They cited as proof the intense violence of the movie industry, pointing out that in *Public Enemy,* reputedly the most violent film of the 1930s, and *Death Wish,* a controversial vigilante fantasy of 1974, the body count reached eight. But three movies released during the late 1980s—*Robocop, Die Hard,* and *Rambo III*—each produced a death tally of 60 or more, nearly one every two minutes. The trend culminated in *Natural Born Killers* (1994), director Oliver Stone's unimaginably violent "spoof" of media violence. Television imitated the movies as the networks crammed violent crime shows into prime time. In 1991 an exhaustive survey found that by the age of 18, the average viewer had witnessed some 40,000 murders on TV.

Popular music also acquired a new edge. In 1981 Warner Brothers launched a television channel featuring pop songs set to video. Music TV (MTV) was an instant success; within three years, some 24 million tuned in every day. Michael Jackson's video extravaganza, *Thriller* (1984), transformed the genre. Its surreal images, disjointed editing, and frenzied music set a new standard. Pop music acquired a harder beat and more explicit lyrics. In 1988 the American Academy of Pediatrics expressed concern that teenagers on the average spent two hours a day watching rock videos. Over half featured violence and three-fourths contained sexually suggestive material.

A new sound called "rap" then emerged from the ghetto and spread by means of radio, cassettes, and CDs. Rap consisted of unpredictably metered lyrics set against an exaggeratedly heavy downbeat. Rap performers did not play musical instruments or sing songs so much as convey, in words and gestures, an attitude of defiant, raw rage against whatever challenged their sense of manhood: other young males; women, whom they derided in coarse sexual epithets; and the police. Predictably, raps such as "Cop Killer" and "Illegal Search" contributed to the charge that rap condoned violence and crime.

The appeal of rap quickly spread beyond black audiences. When Dr. Dre (Andrew Young), founder of a gangsta rap group and head of a record firm, discovered that whites bought more rap CDs than blacks, he promoted the career of a young white rapper, Eminem. Born Marshall Bruce Mathers III, Eminem attracted attention with songs such as "Murder, Murder," "Kill You," "Drug Ballad," and "Criminal." He bashed women, gays, his wife, and nearly everyone else. His lyrics were of such surpassing offensiveness that he became an overnight celebrity and instant millionaire. His fans, whom he treated with scorn, were delighted by the universality of his contempt. The list of those suing him included his mother.

Most consumers of pop violence in the 1990s and early years of the 2000s had little difficulty distinguishing between cultural fantasies and everyday life. But for those who had grown up in ghettoes where gangs ruled the streets and where friends and relatives were commonly swallowed up by the criminal justice system, the culture of violence seemed to legitimate the meanness of everyday life. Moreover, violence and criminality were becoming so much a part of popular culture, and popular culture of adolescent life, that some retreated wholly to imaginative worlds conjured by movies, video and computer games, TV, and pop music. To them, the world of parents and teachers seemed duller and less responsive—less *real*—than the one inside their heads.

A few went so far as to act out destructive fantasies. On October 1, 1997, a 16-year-old boy stabbed his mother, shot and killed two students, and wounded seven others at his high school in Pearl, Mississippi. Over the next 18 months similar shootings in West Paducah, Kentucky; Jonesboro, Arkansas; and Springfield, Oregon, left 5 more students dead and 23 wounded. On April 20,

1999, two teenagers, wearing trench coats and armed with automatic weapons, went on a rampage at Columbine High School in Littleton, Colorado. Before shooting themselves to death, they killed 12 students and a teacher and wounded more than 30. Their crime, previewed in a video prepared as a class project, turned out to be a replay of a 1995 movie, *The Basketball Diaries,* in which Leonardo DiCaprio, wearing a long, black coat and carrying a shotgun, bursts into school and shoots his classmates and teachers.

CLINTON IMPEACHED

Although President Clinton steadfastly denied allegations of womanizing, in January 1998 a judge ordered Clinton to testify in the lawsuit Paula Corbin Jones had filed against him. Jones, who sought to strengthen her suit by showing that Clinton had a history of propositioning women, also subpoenaed a former White House intern. Her name was Monica Lewinsky.

Lewinsky and Clinton were separately asked if they had had an affair, and each denied the charge. When word of their alleged relationship was leaked to the press, Clinton declared in a TV news conference: "I did not have sexual relations with that woman, Miss Lewinsky." Hillary Clinton denounced the allegations as part of a "vast right-wing conspiracy" against her husband.

Unbeknown to the Clintons, however, Lewinsky had been confiding to Linda Tripp, a former White House employee. Tripp had secretly tape-recorded some 20 hours of their conversations. She turned these tapes over to special prosecutor Starr, whose investigations of the Clintons' roles in the Whitewater scandal had broadened into a more general inquiry. In the Tripp tapes Lewinsky provided intimate details of repeated sexual encounters with the president. Clinton and Lewinsky appeared to have lied under oath. Starr threatened to indict Lewinsky for perjury. In return for immunity from prosecution, she repudiated her earlier testimony and admitted that she had engaged in sexual relations with the president and that he and his aides had encouraged her to give misleading testimony in the Jones case.

When called in August to testify on videotape before the Starr grand jury, Clinton conceded that he had engaged in "inappropriate intimate contact" with Lewinsky. But he insisted, "I have not had sex with her as I defined it." When pressed to supply his own definition, he responded with legalistic obfuscation: "My understanding of this definition is it covers contact by the person being deposed with the enumerated areas, if the contact is done with an intent to arouse or gratify." Because Clinton had not intended to arouse or gratify Lewinsky, he had not "had sex" with her. He allowed that this definition was "rather strange."

More legalisms followed. When asked if he had ever been alone with her, he responded, "It depends on how you define alone." When asked if his lawyer had been correct when he had assured the judge in January that "there is absolutely no sex of any kind," Clinton said that the statement was not untrue because "it depends on what the meaning of the word 'is' is."

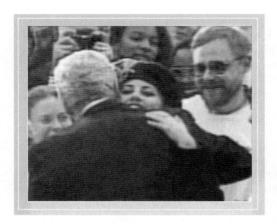

A seemingly anonymous well-wisher from the crowd greets President Bill Clinton. When Clinton was later investigated for having an affair with Monica Lewinsky, a former White House intern, this photograph of the two surfaced. Clinton's lack of discretion struck many as self-destructive.

Clinton's testimony infuriated Starr, who made public Lewinsky's humiliatingly detailed testimony and announced that Clinton's deceptive testimony warranted consideration by the House of Representatives for impeachment.

But throughout Clinton's legal battles, opinion polls suggested that two in three Americans approved of his performance as president. Buoyed by the vibrant economy, most Americans blamed the scandal on the intrusive Starr nearly as much as the evasive Clinton. The November election proved disastrous for the Republicans, who nearly lost their majority in the House.

Clinton's troubles, however, were by no means over. Republican leaders in the House impeached Clinton on the grounds that he had committed perjury and had obstructed justice by inducing Lewinsky and others to give false testimony in the Jones case. The vote closely followed party lines.

The impeachment trial in the Senate began in January 1999. Chief Justice William Rehnquist presided. The Republicans numbered 55, enough to control the proceedings but twelve short of the two-thirds necessary to convict the president and remove him from office. Democrats, while publicly critical of Clinton's behavior, maintained that his indiscretions did not constitute "high crimes and misdemeanors" as specified in the Constitution for removal from office. They prevailed. The article accusing Clinton of perjury was defeated by a vote of 55 to 45; on the article alleging obstruction of justice, the vote was 50 to 50. Clinton remained president.

CLINTON'S LEGACY

One reason why Clinton survived was the health of the economy. Few wanted to rock the ship of state when it was stuffed with cash. Until the final months, the Clinton years coincided with the longest economic boom in the nation's history. Clinton deserves considerable credit for the remarkable prosperity of the era. By reducing the federal deficit, interest rates came down, spurring investment and economic growth. By August 1998 unemployment had fallen to 4.5 percent, the lowest level since the 1960s; inflation had eased to a miniscule 1 percent, the lowest level since the 1950s. In 1998 the federal government operated at its first surplus since 1969. Then, as the economy soared during the next two years, so did government income. In the 2000 fiscal year, the surplus hit $237 billion.

Clinton also promoted globalization of the economy. He successfully promoted the North American Free Trade Agreement to reduce restrictions on trade. During the last half of the 1990s, the United States led all industrial nations in the rate of growth of its real gross domestic product. But the new global economy harmed many. Some union leaders bitterly asked how their members could compete against convict labor in China or sweatshop workers in Indonesia or Malaysia. Others complained that the emphasis on worldwide economic growth was generating an environmental calamity. International protests against the World Trade Organization culminated in the disruption of its 2000 meeting in Seattle, when thousands of protesters went on a rampage, setting fires and looting stores.

Clinton's record in foreign affairs was mixed. In 1993 he failed in an effort to assemble an international force to prevent "ethnic cleansing" by Serbian troops against Muslims in Bosnia, formerly part of Yugoslavia. That same year a U.S. initiative to Somalia, an African nation wracked by civil war and famine, ended in failure when a Somali warlord ambushed and killed 15 American commandos. "Operation Restore Hope," as it was called, did not. In 1999 critics predicted another debacle when Clinton proposed a NATO effort to prevent General Slobodan Milosevic of Yugoslavia from crushing the predominantly Muslim province of Kosovo, which was attempting to secede. But after several months of intense NATO bombing of Serbia, Milosevic withdrew from Kosovo. Within a year, he was forced out of office and into prison, awaiting trial for war crimes before a UN tribunal.

Clinton labored, as had his predecessors in the White House, to broker peace between Israel and the Palestinians. Like his predecessors, he failed. In 1993 Yitzhak Rabin, Israeli Prime Minister, and Yassir Arafat, leader of the Palestine Liberation Organization, signed an agreement preparing the groundwork for a Palestinian state. But extremists on both sides shattered the fragile accord. In 1995 Rabin was assassinated by a Jewish zealot. Palestinians, enraged by the construction of Israeli settlements in Palestinian territory, stepped up their campaign of suicide bombings. Israel retaliated with tank and helicopter attacks on suspected terrorist strongholds. In the fall of 2000, Clinton pressured the Israeli prime minister and Arafat to reach an accord. Despite some concessions on both sides, the talks collapsed. Arafat unleashed a new wave of uprisings, and hardliners, headed by Ariel Sharon, took charge of Israel. Violence intensified on both sides.

Whatever the successes and shortcomings of his administration, the Clinton presidency will always be linked to his relationship with a White House intern and the impeachment proceedings that ensued. Though by no means the first president to stray from matrimonial propriety, Clinton's behavior, in an era when the media thrived on scandal and crime, was symptomatic of an almost willful self-destructiveness.

THE ECONOMIC BOOM AND THE INTERNET

A significant part of the prosperity of the 1990s came from new technologies such as cellular phones and genetic engineering. But the most important was the development of a revolutionary form of communication: the Internet. Developed in the 1970s by U.S. military and academic institutions to coordinate research, the Internet initially proved an awkward means of linking information. Data in one computer did not readily relate to that elsewhere. The Internet was a communication system that lacked a common language.

That was remedied in the early 1990s by Tim Berners-Lee, a British physicist working at a research institute in Switzerland. He devised the software that became the grammar—the "protocols"—of the Internet "language." With this language, the internet became the World Wide Web (WWW), a conduit for a stream of electronic impulses flowing among hundreds of millions of computers.

The number of Websites increased exponentially. In 1995 Bill Gates's Microsoft entered the picture with its Windows operating system, which made the computer easy to use. Rather than drown in the coming deluge, Microsoft seized control of it. It competed with Netscape by creating a Web browser—Microsoft Internet Explorer—and embedded its software in the Windows 95 bundle. This provoked howls of protest from Netscape as well as from other service providers: America Online, CompuServe, and Prodigy. Microsoft, they complained, was threatening to monopolize access to and use of the Internet. (A federal judge concurred, ordering that Microsoft be broken up; his ruling was overturned on appeal in 2001.)

In the meantime, Jeff Bezos dreamed of using the Internet to sell books. In 1995 his company, Amazon.com, sold its first book. Within six years, its annual sales approached $3 billion and its stock soared. Bezos became one of the richest men in the nation.

If Bezos could use the Web for selling books, others imagined they could sell everything from pet food to pornography. (eBay, an Internet auction house, had an online catalog consisting of three million items). Many start-up companies (dot-coms, in the argot of the day) consisted of little more than the hopes of the founders. "Venture capitalists," independent investors seeking to fund emerging "tech" companies, sensed a glittering new economic frontier somewhere down the Internet superhighway, and they poured billions into start-up dot-coms. In 1999 some 200 Internet companies "went public," selling shares in the major stock exchanges. They raised $20 billion easily. NASDAQ, the exchange that specialized in tech companies, saw the value of its stocks skyrocket, its index more than doubling between October 1999 and March 2000. The prices of dot-com stocks kept on climbing though few generated profits; some lacked any revenue whatsoever.

In the spring of 2000, with the stock market still surging, a selling wave hit the tech stocks and spilled over to other companies. Stock prices plummeted. Within six months NASDAQ lost nearly half its value. In all, some $2 trillion in stocks and stock funds disappeared. As the 2000 election approached, many feared that the economy was nearing a recession.

THE 2000 ELECTION: GEORGE W. BUSH WINS BY ONE VOTE

During the 2000 campaign, Vice President Al Gore sought to prove his indispensability to President Clinton, whose administration was credited for the economic growth of the 1990s, as well as his distance from Bill Clinton, whose personal life was discredited by scandal. Gore showed his loyalty by raising money for the Democratic party, and his independence, by avoiding mention of Clinton. The strategy failed. Gore ran afoul of election laws when he solicited contributions too energetically and in inappropriate places, ranging from a Buddhist temple to the White House itself. And the president, irritated by Gore's refusal to champion the Clinton record, devoted his energies to his wife's successful campaign to represent New York in the Senate. Gore nevertheless secured the Democratic nomination and chose as running mate Senator Joseph Lieberman of Connecticut, an orthodox Jew and outspoken critic of Clinton during the impeachment proceedings.

The leading contender was George W. Bush, son of former President Bush. Like his father, Bush graduated from Yale and worked in the family oil business. He headed a group that bought the Texas Rangers baseball team. Although some doubted Bush's abilities, his visible success with the Rangers catapulted him into Texas politics. An effective and personable campaigner, he was elected governor in 1994. Six years later he defeated Senator John McCain of Arizona in a battle for the Republican nomination for president. Bush selected as running mate Richard Cheney, who had served as defense secretary in his father's administration.

Consumer activist and environmentalist Ralph Nader also entered the presidential race, running on the Green party ticket. This worried Gore, author of *Earth in the Balance;* he had hoped to carry the environmentalist vote.

The main issue was what to do with the federal surplus, which by some projections would reach over $1 trillion within five years. Bush called for a substantial tax cut; Gore wanted to increase spending on education and shore up the social security system.

Gore, though knowledgeable, seemed stiff, and he occasionally indulged in self-serving bombast, as when he claimed to have "invented" the Internet. Bush's principal offense was against the English language. "Rarely is the question asked," he once declaimed, "Is our children learning?" His poetic flights of fancy did not stay long aloft, as when he evoked American aspirations for "wings to take dream" and endorsed economic growth to "make the pie higher." However exaggerated or garbled their message, the candidates spent a record $1 billion in getting it to the voters.

Having been inundated with advertisements, many on election night breathed a sigh of relief that the election was finally over. They were wrong. By midnight it appeared that Bush had 246 electoral votes, and Gore, 267, with 270 necessary to win; but Florida, with 25 electoral votes, had not been decided. As returns trickled in, the television networks reversed themselves and declared Florida—and the election—"too close to call." Bush's lead there was 1784 out of nearly 6 million cast.

After a machine recount, Bush's margin in Florida was reduced to several hundred votes, with Democrats complaining that a punch-card ballot used in some communities was confusing, depriving Gore of thousands of votes; worse, the machines routinely failed to count incompletely punched ballots. Gore's lawyers demanded that the ballots in several predominantly Democratic counties be counted by hand. Republicans countered that Democrats had no right to change voting procedures after the election. They demanded that the hand recounts cease.

But when overseas absentee ballots began pouring in, many of them from military personnel, Republicans demanded that technical rules, such as those requiring that ballots be postmarked on or before the election, be waived. Gore objected.

The entire election ended up in the courts. On December 12, more than a month after the election, the Supreme Court ruled by a 5 to 4 vote that the selective hand recounts violated the Constitution's guarantee of equal protection. Bush's margin would stand.

Nationwide, Gore received 51 million votes, Bush, 50.5 million. Nader, who did not win any electoral votes, received nearly 3 million.

TERRORISM INTENSIFIES

After the fall of the Soviet Union, American military might seemed unassailable. Many foreign leaders, once valuable allies in the Cold War between the superpowers, bristled that that lucrative game had ended. Military dictators who been kept afloat by the Soviets or the Americans—and often from both simultaneously—now were obliged to seek the support of the people they had long ruled. This often proved to be destabilizing.

In many Arab nations, for example, rulers cultivated popular support by denouncing Israel, which refused to return Palestinian land seized in the 1967 war. The United States encouraged Israel to trade that land for peace. But few Israelis believed the promises of Arab leaders who had steadfastly called for the annihilation of Israel and had trained and funded terrorism. American diplomats called on Arab leaders to demonstrate their good faith by putting an end to terrorism;

Israel would then return some of the Palestinian land. But Arab leaders, whose nations were often mired in poverty, knew that whenever their popularity waned, they could win the approval of the Arab multitude with a rousing denunciation of Israel. And insofar as Israel relied ultimately on American support, the Arab rage was increasingly directed at the United States and American soldiers stationed abroad.

During these years, several dozen separate terrorist organizations were behind the attacks on American targets. But in 1998 a new figure surfaced among the ranks of Islamist terrorists: Osama bin Laden, the son of a Saudi oil billionaire. In 1998, bin Laden published a *fatwa*—a religious edict—to Islamic peoples throughout the world: "To kill Americans and their allies, both civil and military, is an individual duty of every Muslim who is able . . ." By now, bin Laden was protected by an extremist Islamic group, the Taliban, which ruled Afghanistan. Six months later, bin Laden's terrorist organization—al-Qaeda—had perpetrated the bombings of the U.S. embassies in Nairobi and Dar es-Salaam in Africa. Worse was to follow.

September 11, 2001

At 8:40 on the morning of September 11, 2001, Madeline Amy Sweeney, an attendant on American Airlines Flight 11, placed a cell phone call from the galley of the plane to her supervisor in Boston. In a whisper, she said that four Arab men had slashed the throats of two attendants, forced their way into the cockpit, and taken over the plane. She gave him their seat numbers so that their identities could be determined from the passenger log. The supervisor asked if she knew where the plane was headed. She looked out the window and noted that it was descending rapidly. "I see water and buildings." Then she paused: "Oh my God." The water was the Hudson River, and the buildings were the skyscrapers of lower Manhattan, foremost among them the 110-story twin towers of the World Trade Center.

The hijackers pushed the throttle to full, and the Boeing 767 was traveling at 500 miles per hour at 8:46 when it slammed into the 96th floor of the north tower. A fireball, fed by 10,000 gallons of jet fuel, instantly engulfed eight or nine stories.

Fifteen minutes later a second airliner came into view over Manhattan harbor, banked sharply, and plowed into the 80th floor of the south tower. New York mayor Rudolph Giuliani, who had raced to the scene, asked Fire Chief Peter Ganci, "What should I communicate to people?" "Tell them to get in the stairways," Ganci replied. "I think we can save everyone below the fire." The World Trade Center employed 50,000. As thousands fled the buildings, hundreds of firefighters, Ganci among them, charged up the stairs to rescue those who were trapped.

At 9:30 the White House received word that another hijacked airliner was barreling toward Washington, D.C. Secret Service agents rushed Vice President Richard Cheney to an emergency command bunker far below the White House.

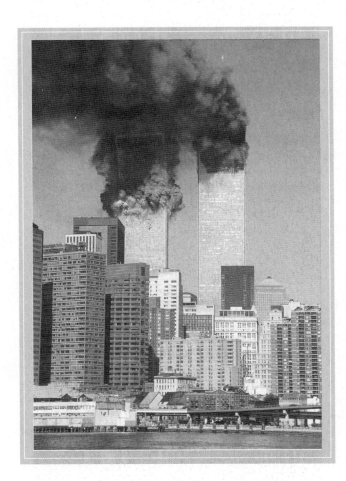

The smoldering twin towers of the World Trade Center after they had been hit by airplanes on September 11, 2001. The jet fuel burned at nearly 2000°F, which caused the steel casing of the towers to expand. The upper floors of the South Tower (left) can be seen pushing outward and twisting. This separated the concrete floors from their steel supports, causing the floors to fall and collapsing the stories below.

At 9:35 the airliner plunged into the Pentagon and burst into flames. Cheney telephoned President Bush, who was in Sarasota, Florida. The nation was under attack. Bush authorized the Air Force to shoot down any other hijacked airliners. A few minutes later a fourth hijacked airliner crashed into a field in Pennsylvania after passengers had declared their intention—again by cell phone—to retake the plane.

While television viewers absorbed these shocks, they watched as the upper floors of the World Trade Center towers blackened, like charred matches. At 9:59, the south tower collapsed, followed by the north tower a half hour later, pulverizing millions of tons of concrete and glass and enveloping lower Manhattan in choking dust. Nearly three thousand lay dead in the mountain of rubble, including Chief Ganci and 350 firemen; several hundred more perished at the Pentagon and in the crash of the airliner in Pennsylvania.

Teams of four or five Arabic-speaking men had hijacked each of the planes. Several of the hijackers were quickly linked to the al-Qaeda terrorist network run by Osama bin Laden, who had previously been indicted (but not captured) for the 1998 bombing of U.S. embassies in East Africa and the 2000 attack on the USS *Cole*. Bin Laden operated with impunity in Afghanistan, a nation governed by the Taliban, an extremist Islamic group.

That evening President Bush addressed the nation. He spoke simply and with force. "We will find these people," he said of the terrorists. "They will pay." Any government harboring the terrorists—an obvious reference to the Taliban—would be held equally responsible for the attack. Bin Laden, in a video recorded from an undisclosed location, denied involvement in the attack but praised those who carried it out.

Several weeks later, Bush declared that bin Laden would be taken "dead or alive." The president also offered a $25 million reward for his death or capture, an evocation of swift frontier justice that suited the national mood. Within the United States, thousands of Arabs were rounded up and detained; those with visa and immigration violations were imprisoned.

Then more trouble arrived at the capital, this time in the mail. Several letters addressed to government officials included threatening messages and a white powder consisting of billions of anthrax spores, which could prove fatal if touched or inhaled. Thousands of government employees took antibiotics as a precaution, but some spores had seeped out of the envelopes and killed a half dozen postal workers and mail recipients.

Bush responded to these multiple threats by creating a Cabinet position, the Office of Homeland Security, and naming Pennsylvania governor Tom Ridge to direct it. Repeatedly Ridge issued vague warnings of imminent terrorist attacks. How exactly Americans were to protect themselves, he did not say.

AMERICA FIGHTS BACK: WAR IN AFGHANISTAN

Bush had declared "war on terror," but it was to be a battle unlike any the nation had ever fought. Al-Qaeda had secret terrorist cells in many countries. Bin Laden was ensconced in remote Afghanistan, protected by thousands of Taliban soldiers who had inflicted heavy losses on Soviet invaders in the 1980s. (At the time, the United States had provided bin Laden and the Taliban with money and weapons.) The source of the anthrax letters proved even more problematic, because the spores resembled a strain developed in American military laboratories.

Bush's challenge was all the greater because of his own stated opposition to ill-defined and far-flung military operations. He had chastised the Clinton-Gore administration for "extending our troops all around the world." He underscored his reticence for such ventures by naming Colin Powell secretary of state. Powell, who had been sobered by his experiences in Vietnam, maintained that U.S. troops should only be deployed when their political objective was clear, military advantage overwhelming, and means of disengaging secure. This became known as the Powell doctrine, and Bush had endorsed it during the campaign. But the proposed war against terror adhered to none of its precepts. Now such scruples did not matter; the president had little choice but to fight.

Powell urged many European, Asian, and even Islamic states to crack down on terrorist cells in their countries and to provide assistance in the U.S. military campaign against the Taliban; he also persuaded anti-Taliban factions within Afghanistan to join forces to topple the regime. On September 20 Bush ordered the Taliban to surrender bin Laden and top al-Qaeda leaders; when the Taliban refused, Bush unloosed missiles and warplanes against Taliban installations and defenses, much like the campaign that had ended Serbian aggression against ethnic Muslims in Kosovo.

For several weeks, Taliban soldiers cowered in bunkers as bombs thudded nearby; but they defended their positions when anti-Taliban forces attacked. Then small teams of elite American soldiers, armed with hand-held computers and satellite-linked navigational devices, joined with anti-Taliban contingents, marking Taliban positions with laser spotters and communicating with high-altitude bombers. These planes, circling at 30,000 feet, dropped electronically guided bombs on Taliban troops with uncanny (but not infallible) accuracy. Now the Taliban soldiers fled; some switched allegiance and joined the anti-Taliban coalition. Within weeks the Taliban were driven from power. Only one American soldier was killed by hostile fire. (A few American soldiers and hundreds of noncombatants were killed by errant bombs.) The United States had won the first battles in the war against terror. But more were to come.

THE SECOND IRAQ WAR

In January 2002, after the Taliban had been crushed, President Bush declared that he would not "wait on events while dangers gather." The United States would take "preemptive actions"—war—against regimes that threatened it. Bush identified Iran, North Korea, and Iraq as an "axis of evil" that warranted special scrutiny. Immediately after the terrorist attacks on September 11, 2001, he secretly initiated plans to attack Iraq, ruled by Saddam Hussein.

Secretary of State Colin Powell advised Bush not to attack Iraq. If Saddam were driven from power, Powell warned, Bush would become "the proud owner of 25 million people—you'll own it all." Vice President Dick Cheney, Defense Secretary Donald Rumsfeld, and others in the administration insisted that the Iraqis would welcome liberation and embrace democracy. A free Iraq, they added, would stimulate democratic reforms throughout the Middle East, as had happened in eastern Europe following the collapse of the Soviet Union. Bush agreed.

The Joint Chiefs of Staff proposed an invasion force numbering a half-million troops, as had been hurled against Saddam in 1991. Rumsfeld insisted on a smaller, faster, and cheaper force of 125,000. In the spring of 2002 CIA agents were spirited into Iraq and airplanes and soldiers were deployed to Kuwait.

When reporters asked Bush if he were planning for war with Iraq, the famously tidy president replied, "I have no plans to attack on my desk."

In September, Bush sought congressional support. "The Iraqi regime possesses chemical and biological weapons," he declared, adding that Saddam also sought nuclear weapons. Congress voted overwhelmingly for the war appropriation.

Bush then called on the United Nations to join in the attack on Saddam. That Saddam had used chemical weapons during the Iran-Iraq war and also against the Kurds was beyond dispute; but following Saddam's defeat in 1991, UN inspectors had destroyed thousands of tons of chemical weapons. In recent years these inspectors had found little evidence of Iraqi chemical weapons, and none of a nuclear program. Bush saw this as proof that Saddam had hoodwinked the inspectors. Then Powell, like Adlai Stevenson during the Cuban missile crisis in 1962, presented classified U.S. intelligence to the United Nations. Saddam, he said, had indeed been building and stockpiling weapons of mass destruction. The UN Security Council ordered Saddam to cooperate with UN inspectors and warned of "serious consequences" if he refused to do so.

After several months Bush grew impatient with the slow pace of the inspections. When the Security Council refused to take action against Saddam, Bush decided to form a coalition on his own to oust the Iraqi leader. He was joined by Great Britain, Italy, Spain and a few other countries.

On March 20, 2003, American missiles and bombs pounded Saddam's defenses. The "Shock and Awe" campaign to liberate Iraq had begun. Two immense armored columns roared across the Kuwaiti border into Iraq, passing burned-out Iraqi tanks from the first Gulf War. British forces moved along the coast toward the oil port of Basra. Television reporters, perched atop Humvees and armored personnel carriers, provided live coverage. Iraqi resistance was ineffective. The first night, American units advanced deep into Iraq, halfway to Baghdad, Saddam's capital.

On April 4, the U.S. army seized the Baghdad International Airport, twelve miles from the city. That day, television footage aired on Al Jezeera, an Arab television network, showed a man—apparently Saddam—walking through Baghdad and exhorting the Iraqis: "Resist them, O courageous citizens of Baghdad. Our martyrs will go to paradise, and their dead will go to hell." The next morning, some 800 American soldiers in tanks and armored vehicles raced down Highway 8 and blasted their way into downtown Baghdad. Some Iraqis poured into the streets to celebrate; others looted government buildings, museums, stores, and hospitals. Within several days Saddam's government had evaporated and he had disappeared. By mid-April, the Pentagon declared that major combat operations had come to an end. United States casualties were 138 dead and over 500 wounded.

But Iraq was in chaos. There were too few U.S. troops to preserve order and install a new government. Islamist radicals, enraged by the American occupation of Iraq, increasingly joined with Saddam's supporters in attacking American soldiers as well as those who worked for the occupation forces. The insurgents

President George W. Bush aboard the USS Abraham Lincoln on May 1, 2004. "Major combat operations in Iraq have ended," he declared. But in the months to come, American casualties mounted as some Iraqis resisted occupation by the United States. By that fall, more than 1000 United States servicemen had been killed in the Second Iraq War.

rammed trucks filled with explosives into police stations, wired cell phones to artillery shells and detonated them as Americans approached, and sabotaged oil pipelines and power generators.

THE ELECTION OF 2004

By autumn of 2003, the war in Iraq had become the main issue of the presidential campaign. Among Democratic candidates, Howard Dean, former governor of Vermont, zoomed ahead in the polls by denouncing the war. He also proved adept at using the Internet to raise funds and recruit supporters—"Deaniacs," as they were called. He endorsed national health insurance and same-sex civil unions—legal recognition of marriage for gay and lesbian couples. In December the campaign shifted when American soldiers captured Saddam in an underground bunker. Bush's approval rating soared.

Many Democratic voters, worried that Bush would win in a landslide, looked for an alternative to the liberal Dean. By January Senator John Kerry of Massachusetts was gaining in the polls. The son of a diplomat and a graduate of Yale, Kerry, though stentorian, appeared accomplished and steady. He won the Iowa caucuses and upset Dean in the New Hampshire primary. After the New

A U.S. soldier taunting an Iraqi prisoner at Abu Ghraib prison. U.S. Major General Antonio M. Taguba reported on many such instances of "sadistic, blatant, and wanton criminal abuses." At least one prisoner died while being interrogated. The commander of the prison was dismissed and criminal charges were filed against some of the soldiers.

Hampshire primary, Dean gave an over-the-top exhortation that culminated in a roar—"the scream," as pundits called it—that caused many to doubt his suitability for high office. By April, Kerry had won the nomination. He chose Senator John Edwards of North Carolina, a wealthy trial lawyer, as his running mate.

In Iraq, the situation had deteriorated further. In April the *60 Minutes* news program revealed that American captors had tortured Iraqi captives in the Abu Ghraib prison. Photographs of American soldiers, including women, taunting naked Muslim men fueled the insurgency. Casualties mounted. The cost of the occupation was spiraling upward. Bush, committed to lowering taxes, could do little as the deficit approached $250 billion. More damaging politically was the failure to find any Iraqi weapons of mass destruction. Saddam had posed no immediate danger to the United States. At the Democratic convention in July, Kerry emphasized his military background. "I am John Kerry, and I am reporting for duty," he said in his acceptance speech. This was followed by footage of his service as commander of a patrol boat in Vietnam, where he was twice wounded and awarded the Bronze Star for courage under enemy fire.

"As president," Kerry declared, "I will fight a smarter, more effective war on terror." He criticized Bush for attacking Iraq before capturing Osama bin Laden, who remained at large. He also criticized Bush for not sending enough troops to preserve order and rebuild Iraq, and for initiating war with insufficient international support.

Republicans pounced on Kerry's war record. Vietnam veterans challenged his heroism, others his leadership. Many seized on the fact that in 1971 Kerry had told a congressional committee that the Vietnam war was wrong and immoral. How, they asked, could an antiwar activist lead the nation in time of war?

Republicans also portrayed Kerry as opportunistic. If Kerry and Edwards thought the war was a mistake, why did they vote for the original war resolution in the Senate? Kerry became entangled in long-winded explanations. "I actually voted for the $87 billion before I voted against it," he said on one occasion. Bush gleefully seized on this "flip-flop" and dubbed Kerry "Flipper." During a debate with Bush, Kerry conceded that he had "made a mistake" in explaining his position on Iraq. "But the president made a mistake in invading Iraq. Which is worse?"

Bush also attacked Kerry for his liberal voting record and insisted that the Democrat would likely raise taxes. "There's a mainstream in American politics," Bush told Kerry, "and you sit on the far left bank." Kerry, citing the huge federal deficit, replied: "Being lectured by the president on fiscal responsibility is a little bit like Tony Soprano talking to me about law and order."

Bush mobilized conservatives and religious fundamentalists by proposing a constitutional amendment that would define marriage as the union between a man and a woman only; this would prevent states from sanctioning same-sex marriages, as Massachusetts had already done. In over a dozen states, anti-gay marriage referenda were placed on the ballot. Kerry endorsed gay rights but endlessly qualified earlier statements in support of same-sex marriage.

The election, one of the most divisive in recent decades, brought twelve million more voters to the polls than in 2000. Kerry received 57 million votes, three million more than Ronald Reagan in his 1984 landslide. But Bush got over 60 million, a record. He also prevailed in the Electoral College, 286 to 252. Exit polls indicated that "moral issues" figured prominently among one-fourth of the voters. In every referendum, gay marriage was defeated.

THE IMPONDERABLE FUTURE

No wartime president had ever lost a reelection campaign, and the pattern held true in 2004. As the situation in Iraq deteriorated, moreover, Bush's standing in the polls improved. Many voters preferred Bush's simple nostrums, even if flawed, to Kerry's complicated (and sometimes contradictory) approach. They wanted a leader who would lead; they had little patience with one who puzzled too long over the maps and the ultimate destination. "You know where I stand," Bush had declared at nearly every campaign stop, and in the end a majority of voters stood with him. But few took much solace from the view. In Iraq, bombings rocked police stations and public squares, and smoldering tensions between rival Muslim sects threatened to ignite a civil war. By early 2005, over 1400 American soldiers had been killed, ten times more than had died in the fighting that toppled Saddam. The federal deficit approached a half trillion dollars. Would the defeat of Saddam discourage terrorists elsewhere and discourage rogue states such as Iran and North Korea from seeking nuclear weapons? Would a protracted U.S. military presence promote Iraqi democracy or generate resentment throughout the Arab world? If the situation worsened, would the United States be able to find a way out?

If the specter of Vietnam haunted the 2004 election, it was because these questions echoed those that had been asked forty years earlier. Historians are probably better than most other people at explaining how things got to be the way they are at any present moment. This is because events have causes and results, and these

DEBATING THE PAST

Do historians ever get it right? The Debating the Past essays in previous chapters have offered hundreds of interpretations, many of them contradictory. Why, if historians are looking at the same past, do they see it so differently?

Consider the photograph (*left*). It shows a cityscape as reflected on the many windows of a new skyscraper. Each pane of glass has its own angle of reflection, imposing unique distortions on the scene; note that one window—all black— is open, about to receive a pipe. Historians, too, look at the past from different perspectives, and sometimes crucial pieces of evidence are missing.

Well into the twentieth century, most historians believed that their collective labors—more research, more books— were leading to a composite picture that provided a fuller and clearer rendering of the past. But some recent historians have doubted whether their profession can sharpen the picture's focus, or whether a coherent vista of "the past" even existed. If our own lives are a jumble of motivations and confusions, how can one think it possible to paint a portrait of an entire people?

In an exhaustive study of the American Historical Association, Peter Novick (1988) further demonstrated that while historians have long championed objectivity in principle, their research has been riddled with bias. Ignorant of their cultural blinders, historians grope for historical truths they can never see.

By undercutting their profession's claims of "truth," Novick's book made historians more susceptible to an idea that was sweeping through literature departments. Known as "deconstruction" or "textualism" and derived from French philosopher Jacques Derrida, it held that "there is nothing outside the text." (Or, to use the metaphor of the photograph, there is nothing beyond the reflections.) No one could reasonably claim to know what a novelist meant by any novel, or what any statesman or historical figure meant by the words he or she spoke or wrote. By extension, no historian can explain what any historical record meant to the people of the times it reflected. Inspired by such observations, Robert F. Berkhofer (1995) repudiated the very idea of a grand historical narrative, partly because readers would interpret that narrative in their own ways.

Raising Berkhofer's contention at the end of a book that purports to provide just such a narrative may seem perverse. But his point contains an obvious truth: Readers of any work of history, this one included, will make of it what they will.

Peter Novick, *That Noble Dream* (1988), Robert F. Berkhofer, Jr., *Beyond the Great Story* (1995), Jacques Derrida, *Deconstruction in a Nutshell* (1997).

are things that historians are trained to study and understand. But historians are no better than anyone else at predicting the future. In the modern world just about everything that happens is in some way related to everything else that is going on. Far too many things are happening for anyone to sort out which is going to have what effect on tomorrow's events, let alone those that occur a year from now. "Then" (whether tomorrow or the next year) historians will be able to study those particular events and puzzle out their chief causes—but not "now." Yet "now" is where we happen to be, and thus this book, so full of events and their causes and results, must end inconclusively. No one knows what will happen next. But not knowing what will happen is one reason why life is so interesting.

MILESTONES

1988   Republican George H. W. Bush elected president.

1989   Gorbachev allows Eastern European nations to establish independent democratic governments.

1990   Iraq invades Kuwait.

Germany is reunited.

1991   UN forces, led by the United States, drive Iraqi forces from Kuwait.

Soviet Union is dissolved; Boris Yeltsin becomes president of Russia.

1992   Democrat Bill Clinton elected president.

1993   Ruth Bader Ginsberg becomes second woman associate justice of the Supreme Court.

Bomb explodes in parking garage of World Trade Center in New York, killing 6 and injuring 1000.

1994   Republicans win control of both houses of Congress.

Congress defeats Clinton's health care reform plan.

1995   Terrorist bomb destroys Alfred P. Murrah Federal Building in Oklahoma City, killing 169.

1996   Democrat Bill Clinton is reelected president; Republicans retain control of Congress.

Measure revamping federal welfare system is passed by Congress and signed by President Clinton.

1998   Clinton is impeached by House of Representatives.

1999   Clinton is acquitted by Senate and remains president.

NATO troops, including Americans, are sent to Kosovo to stop Serbian "ethnic cleansing."

Gun violence in schools escalates; 12 die at Columbine High School in Colorado

2000   Republican George W. Bush becomes president when Supreme Court halts Florida recounts.

2001   Terrorists airliners fly airliners into World Trade Center in New York and into Pentagon in Washington, D.C.; third hijacked airliner crashes in Pennsylvania when passengers storm hijackers.

United States attacks and defeats Taliban in Afghanistan.

2002   President Bush prepares for war as he accuses Saddam Hussein of Iraq of developing weapons of mass destruction.

2003   U. S. and United Kingdom attack and defeat Iraq and capture Saddam Hussein.

Hostilities persist in Iraq.

2004   George W. Bush is reelected president.

2005   Bush appoints Condoleeza Rice Secretary of State, the first African American woman in that position.

APPENDIX

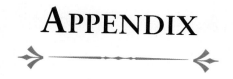

The Declaration of Independence

The Constitution of the United States of America

Amendments to the Constitution

Supplementary Reading

Suggested Websites

Present-day United States

Present-day World

The Declaration of Independence

In Congress, July 4, 1776

The Unanimous Declaration
of the Thirteen United States of America,

When, in the course of human events, it becomes necessary for one people to dissolve the political bonds which have connected them with another, and to assume, among the powers of the earth, the separate and equal station to which the laws of nature and of nature's God entitle them, a decent respect to the opinions of mankind requires that they should declare the causes which impel them to the separation.

We hold these truths to be self-evident: That all men are created equal; that they are endowed by their Creator with certain unalienable rights; that among these are life, liberty, and the pursuit of happiness; that, to secure these rights, governments are instituted among men, deriving their just powers from the consent of the governed; that whenever any form of government becomes destructive of these ends, it is the right of the people to alter or to abolish it, and to institute new government, laying its foundation on such principles, and organizing its powers in such form, as to them shall seem most likely to effect their safety and happiness. Prudence, indeed, will dictate that governments long established should not be changed for light and transient causes; and accordingly all experience hath shown that mankind are more disposed to suffer, while evils are sufferable, than to right themselves by abolishing the forms to which they are accustomed. But when a long train of abuses and usurpations, pursuing invariably the same object, evinces a design to reduce them under absolute despotism, it is their right, it is their duty, to throw off such government, and to provide new guards for their future security. Such has been the patient sufferance of these colonies; and such is now the necessity which constrains them to alter their former systems of government. The history of the present King of Great Britain is a history of repeated injuries and usurpations, all having in direct object the establishment of an absolute tyranny over these states. To prove this, let facts be submitted to a candid world.

He has refused his assent to laws, the most wholesome and necessary for the public good.

He has forbidden his governors to pass laws of immediate and pressing importance, unless suspended in their operation till his assent should be obtained; and, when so suspended, he has utterly neglected to attend to them.

He has refused to pass other laws for the accommodation of large districts of people, unless those people would relinquish the right of representation in the legislature, a right inestimable to them, and formidable to tyrants only.

He has called together legislative bodies at places unusual, uncomfortable, and distant from the depository of their public records, for the sole purpose of fatiguing them into compliance with his measures.

He has dissolved representative houses repeatedly, for opposing, with manly firmness, his invasions on the rights of the people.

He has refused for a long time, after such dissolutions, to cause others to be elected; whereby the legislative powers, incapable of annihilation, have returned to the people at large for their exercise; the state remaining, in the mean time, exposed to all the dangers of invasions from without and convulsions within.

He has endeavored to prevent the population of these states; for that purpose obstructing the laws for naturalization of foreigners; refusing to pass others to encourage their migration hither, and raising the conditions of new appropriations of lands.

He has obstructed the administration of justice, by refusing his assent to laws for establishing judiciary powers.

He has made judges dependent on his will alone, for the tenure of their offices, and the amount and payment of their salaries.

He has erected a multitude of new offices, and sent hither swarms of officers to harass our people and eat out their substance.

He has kept among us, in times of peace, standing armies, without the consent of our legislatures.

He has affected to render the military independent of, and superior to, the civil power.

He has combined with others to subject us to a jurisdiction foreign to our constitution, and unacknowledged by our laws, giving his assent to their acts of pretended legislation:

For quartering large bodies of armed troops among us;

For protecting them, by a mock trial, from punishment for any murder which they should commit on the inhabitants of these states;

For cutting off our trade with all parts of the world;

For imposing taxes on us without our consent;

For depriving us, in many cases, of the benefits of trial by jury;

For transporting us beyond seas, to be tried for pretended offenses;

For abolishing the free system of English laws in a neighboring province, establishing therein an arbitrary government, and enlarging its boundaries, so as to render it at once an example and fit instrument for introducing the same absolute rule into these colonies;

For taking away our charters, abolishing our most valuable laws, and altering fundamentally the forms of our governments;

For suspending our own legislatures, and declaring themselves invested with power to legislate for us in all cases whatsoever.

He has abdicated government here, by declaring us out of his protection and waging war against us.

He has plundered our seas, ravaged our coasts, burned our towns, and destroyed the lives of our people.

He is at this time transporting large armies of foreign mercenaries to complete the works of death, desolation, and tyranny already begun with circumstances of cruelty and perfidy scarcely paralleled in the most barbarous ages, and totally unworthy the head of a civilized nation.

He has constrained our fellow-citizens, taken captive on the high seas, to bear arms against their country, to become the executioners of their friends and brethren, or to fall themselves by their hands.

He has excited domestic insurrection among us, and has endeavored to bring on the inhabitants of our frontiers the merciless Indian savages, whose known rule of warfare is an undistinguished destruction of all ages, sexes, and conditions.

In every stage of these oppressions we have petitioned for redress in the most humble terms; our repeated petitions have been answered only by repeated injury. A prince, whose character is thus marked by every act which may define a tyrant, is unfit to be the ruler of a free people.

Nor have we been wanting in our attentions to our British brethren. We have warned them, from time to time, of attempts by their legislature to extend an unwarrantable jurisdiction over us. We have reminded them of the circumstances of our emigration and settlement here. We have appealed to their native justice and magnanimity; and we have conjured them, by the ties of our common kindred, to disavow these usurpations, which would inevitably interrupt our connections and correspondence. They, too, have been deaf to the voice of justice and of consanguinity. We must, therefore, acquiesce in the necessity which denounces our separation, and hold them, as we hold the rest of mankind, enemies in war, in peace friends.

We, therefore, the representatives of the United States of America, in General Congress assembled, appealing to the Supreme Judge of the world for the rectitude of our intentions, do, in the name and by the authority of the good people of these colonies, solemnly publish and declare, that these United Colonies are, and of right ought to be, FREE AND INDEPENDENT STATES; that they are absolved from all allegiance to the British crown, and that all political connection between them and the state of Great Britain is, and ought to be, totally dissolved; and that, as free and independent states, they have full power to levy war, conclude peace, contract alliances, establish commerce, and do all other acts and things which independent states may of right do. And for the support of this declaration, with a firm reliance on the protection of Divine Providence, we mutually pledge to each other our lives, our fortunes, and our sacred honor.

JOHN HANCOCK

Button Gwinnett
Lyman Hall
Geo. Walton
Wm. Hooper
Joseph Hewes
John Penn
Edward Rutledge
Thos. Heyward, Junr.
Thomas Lynch, Junr.
Arthur Middleton
Samuel Chase
Wm. Paca
Thos. Stone
Charles Carroll of
  Carrollton
George Wythe
Richard Henry Lee
Th. Jefferson
Benj. Harrison

Thos. Nelson, Jr
Francis Lightfoot Lee
Carter Braxton
Robt. Morris
Benjamin Rush
Benja. Franklin
John Morton
Geo. Clymer
Jas. Smith
Geo. Taylor
James Wilson
Geo. Ross
Caesar Rodney
Geo. Read
Tho. M'Kean
Wm. Floyd
Phil. Livingston
Frans. Lewis
Lewis Morris

Richd. Stockton
Jno. Witherspoon
Fras. Hopkinson
John Hart
Abra. Clark
Josiah Bartlett
Wm. Whipple
Saml. Adams
John Adams
Robt. Treat Paine
Eldbridge Gerry
Step. Hopkins
William Ellery
Roger Sherman
Sam'el Huntington
Wm. Williams
Oliver Wolcott
Matthew Thornton

The Constitution of the United States of America

PREAMBLE

We the People of the United States, in Order to form a more perfect Union, establish Justice, insure domestic Tranquility, provide for the common defence, promote the general Welfare, and secure the Blessings of Liberty to ourselves and our Posterity, do ordain and establish this Constitution for the United States of America.

ARTICLE 1

Section 1

All legislative Powers herein granted shall be vested in a Congress of the United States, which shall consist of a Senate and House of Representatives.

Section 2

The House of Representatives shall be composed of Members chosen every second Year by the People of the several States, and the Electors in each State shall have the Qualifications requisite for Electors of the most numerous Branch of the State Legislature.

No Person shall be a Representative who shall not have attained to the Age of twenty five Years, and been seven Years a Citizen of the United States, and who shall not, when elected, be an inhabitant of that State in which he shall be chosen.

Representatives and direct Taxes shall be apportioned among the several States which may be included within this Union, according to their respective Numbers, *which shall be determined by adding to the whole Number of free Persons, including those bound to Service for a Term of Years, and excluding Indians not taxed, three fifths of all other Persons.** The actual Enumeration shall be made within three Years after the first Meeting of the Congress of the United States, and within every subsequent Term of ten Years, in such Manner as they shall by Law direct. The Number of Representatives shall not exceed one for every thirty Thousand, but each State shall have at Least one Representative; *and until such enumeration shall be made, the State of New Hampshire shall be entitled to chuse three, Massachusetts eight, Rhode-Island and Providence Plantations one, Connecticut five, New York six, New Jersey four, Pennsylvania eight, Delaware one, Maryland six, Virginia ten, North Carolina five, South Carolina five, and Georgia three.*

When vacancies happen in the Representation from any State, the Executive Authority thereof shall issue Writs of Election to fill such Vacancies.

The House of Representatives shall chuse their Speaker and other Officers; and shall have the sole Power of Impeachment.

Section 3

The Senate of the United States shall be composed of two Senators from each State, *chosen by the Legislature thereof,* for six Years; and each Senator shall have one Vote.

Immediately after they shall be assembled in Consequence of the first Election, they shall be divided as equally as may be into three Classes. The Seats of the Senators of the first Class shall be vacated at the Expiration of the second Year, of the second Class at the Expiration of the fourth Year, and of the third Class at the Expiration of the sixth Year so that one third may be chosen every sec-

---

*Passages no longer in effect are printed in italic type.

ond Year; *and if Vacancies happen by Resignation, or otherwise, during the Recess of the Legislature of any state, the Executive thereof may make temporary Appointments until the next Meeting of the Legislature, which shall then fill such Vacancies.*

No Person shall be a Senator who shall not have attained to the Age of thirty Years, and been nine Years a Citizen of the United States, and who shall not, when elected, be an Inhabitant of that State for which he shall be chosen.

The Vice President of the United States shall be President of the Senate, but shall have no Vote, unless they be equally divided.

The Senate shall chuse their other Officers, and also a President *pro tempore,* in the Absence of the Vice President, or when he shall exercise the Office of President of the United States.

The Senate shall have the sole Power to try all Impeachments. When sitting for that Purpose, they shall be on Oath or Affirmation. When the President of the United States is tried the Chief Justice shall preside: And no Person shall be convicted without the Concurrence of two thirds of the Members present.

Judgment in Cases of Impeachment shall not extend further than to removal from Office, and disqualification to hold and enjoy any Office of honor, Trust or Profit under the United States: but the Party convicted shall nevertheless be liable and subject to Indictment, Trial, Judgment and Punishment, according to Law.

Section 4

The Times, Places and Manner of holding Elections for Senators and Representatives, shall be prescribed in each State by the Legislature thereof; but the Congress may at any time by Law make or alter such Regulations, except as to the Places of chusing Senators.

The Congress shall assemble at least once in every Year, *and such Meeting shall be on the first Monday in December, unless they shall by Law appoint a different Day.*

Section 5

Each House shall be the Judge of the Elections, Returns and Qualifications of its own Members, and a Majority of each shall constitute a Quorum to do Business; but a smaller Number may adjourn from day to day, and may be authorized to compel the Attendance of absent Members, in such Manner, and under such Penalties as each House may provide.

Each House may determine the Rules of its Proceedings, punish its Members for disorderly Behaviour, and, with the Concurrence of two thirds, expel a Member.

Each House shall keep a Journal of its Proceedings, and from time to time publish the same, excepting such Parts as may in their Judgment require Secrecy; and the Yeas and Nays of the Members of either House on any question shall, at the Desire of one fifth of those Present, be entered on the Journal.

Neither House, during the Session of Congress, shall, without the Consent of the other, adjourn for more than three days, nor to any other Place than that in which the two Houses shall be sitting.

Section 6

The Senators and Representatives shall receive a Compensation for their Services, to be ascertained by Law, and paid out of the Treasury of the United States. They shall in all Cases, except Treason, Felony and Breach of the Peace, be privileged from Arrest during their Attendance at the Session of their respective Houses, and in going to and returning from the same; and for any Speech or Debate in either House, they shall not be questioned in any other Place.

No Senator or Representative shall, during the Time for which he was elected, be appointed to any civil Office under the Authority of the United States, which shall have been created, or the Emoluments whereof shall have been encreased during such time, and no Person holding any Office under the United States, shall be a Member of either House during his Continuance in Office.

Section 7

All Bills for raising Revenue shall originate in the House of Representatives; but the Senate may propose or concur with Amendments as on other Bills.

Every Bill which shall have passed the House of Representatives and the Senate, shall, before it become a Law, be presented to the President of the United States; If he approve he shall sign it, but if not he shall return it, with his Objections to the House in which it shall have originated, who shall enter the Objections at large on their Journal, and proceed to reconsider it. If after such Reconsideration two thirds of that House shall agree to pass the Bill, it shall be sent, together with the Objections, to the other House, by which it shall likewise be reconsidered, and if approved by two thirds of that House, it shall become a Law. But in all such Cases the Votes of both Houses shall be determined by Yeas and Nays, and the Names of the Persons voting for and against the Bill shall be entered on the Journal of each House respectively. If any Bill shall not be returned by the President within ten Days (Sundays excepted) after it shall have been presented to him, the Same shall be a Law, in like Manner as if he had signed it, unless the Congress by their Adjournment prevent its Return, in which Case it shall not be a Law.

Every Order, Resolution, or Vote to which the Concurrence of the Senate and House of Representatives may be necessary (except on a question of Adjournment) shall be presented to the President of the United States; and before the Same shall take Effect, shall be approved by him, or being disapproved by him, shall be repassed by two thirds of the Senate and House of Representatives, according to the Rules and Limitations prescribed in the Case of a Bill.

Section 8

The Congress shall have Power To lay and collect Taxes, Duties, Imposts and Excises, to pay the Debts and provide for the common Defence and general Welfare of the United States; but all Duties, Imposts and Excises shall be uniform throughout the United States;

To borrow Money on the credit of the United States;

To regulate Commerce with foreign Nations, and among the several States, and with the Indian Tribes;

To establish an uniform Rule of Naturalization, and uniform Laws on the subject of Bankruptcies throughout the United States;

To coin Money, regulate the Value thereof, and of foreign Coin, and fix the Standard of Weights and Measures;

To provide for the Punishment of counterfeiting the Securities and current Coin of the United States;

To establish Post Offices and post Roads;

To promote the Progress of Science and useful Arts, by securing for limited Times to Authors and Inventors the exclusive Right to their respective Writings and Discoveries;

To constitute Tribunals inferior to the supreme Court;

To define and punish Piracies and Felonies committed on the high Seas, and Offences against the Law of Nations;

To declare War, grant Letters of Marque and Reprisal, and make Rules concerning Captures on Land and Water;

To raise and support Armies, but no Appropriation of Money to that Use shall be for a longer Term than two Years;

To provide and maintain a Navy;

To make Rules for the Government and Regulation of the land and naval Forces;

To provide for calling forth the Militia to execute the Laws of the Union, suppress Insurrections and repel Invasions;

To provide for organizing, arming, and disciplining, the Militia, and for governing such Part of them as may be employed in the Service of the United States, reserving to the States respectively, the Appointment of the Officers, and the Authority of training the Militia according to the discipline prescribed by Congress;

To exercise exclusive Legislation in all Cases whatsoever, over such District (not exceeding ten Miles square) as may, by Cession of particular States, and the Acceptance of Congress, become the Seat of the Government of the United States, and to exercise like Authority over all Places purchased by the Consent of the Legislature of the State in which the Same shall be, for the Erection of Forts, Magazines, Arsenals, dock-Yards, and other needful Buildings;—And

To make all Laws which shall be necessary and proper for carrying into Execution the foregoing Powers, and all other Powers vested by this Constitution in the Government of the United States, or in any Department or Officer thereof.

Section 9

The Migration or Importation of such Persons as any of the States now existing shall think proper to admit, shall not be prohibited by the Congress prior to the Year one thousand eight hundred and eight, but a Tax or duty may be imposed on such Importation, not exceeding ten dollars for each Person.

The Privilege of the Writ of Habeas Corpus shall not be suspended, unless when in Cases of Rebellion or Invasion the public Safety may require it.

No Bill of Attainder or ex post facto Law shall be passed.

No Capitation, or other direct, Tax shall be laid, unless in Proportion to the Census or Enumeration herein before directed to be taken.

No Tax or Duty shall be laid on Articles exported from any State.

No Preference shall be given by any Regulation of Commerce or Revenue to the Ports of one State over those of another: nor shall Vessels bound to, or from, one State, be obliged to enter, clear, or pay Duties in another.

No Money shall be drawn from the Treasury, but in Consequence of Appropriations made by Law; and a regular Statement and Account of the Receipts and Expenditures of all public Money shall be published from time to time.

No Title of Nobility shall be granted by the United States: And no Person holding any Office of Profit or Trust under them, shall, without the Consent of the Congress, accept of any present, Emolument, Office, or Title, of any kind whatever, from any King, Prince, or foreign State.

Section 10

No State shall enter into any Treaty, Alliance, or Confederation; grant Letters of Marque and Reprisal; coin Money; emit Bills of Credit; make any Thing but gold and silver Coin a Tender in Payment of Debts; pass any Bill of Attainder, ex post facto Law, or Law impairing the obligation of Contracts, or grant any Title of Nobility.

No State shall, without the Consent of the Congress, lay any Imposts or Duties on Imports or Exports, except what may be absolutely necessary for executing its inspection Laws: and the net Produce of all Duties and Imposts, laid by any State on Imports or Exports, shall be for the Use of the Treasury of the United States; and all such Laws shall be subject to the Revision and Controul of the Congress.

No State shall, without the Consent of Congress, lay any Duty of Tonnage, keep Troops, or Ships of War in time of Peace, enter into any Agreement or Compact with another State, or with a foreign Power, or engage in War, unless actually invaded, or in such imminent Danger as will not admit of delay.

ARTICLE II

Section 1

The executive Power shall be vested in a President of the United States of America. He shall hold his Office during the Term of four Years, and, together with the Vice President, chosen for the same Term, be elected, as follows:

Each State shall appoint, in such Manner as the Legislature thereof may direct, a Number of Electors, equal to the whole Number of Senators and Representatives to which the State may be entitled in the Congress: but no Senator or Representative, or Person holding an Office of Trust or Profit under the United States, shall be appointed an Elector.

The Electors shall meet in their respective States, and vote by Ballot for two Persons, of whom one at least shall not be an Inhabitant of the same State with themselves. And they shall make a List of all the Persons voted for, and of the Number of Votes for each; which List they shall sign and certify, and transmit sealed to the Seat of the Government of the United States, directed to the President of the Senate. The President of the Senate shall, in the Presence of the Senate and House of Representatives, open all the Certificates, and the Votes shall then be counted. The Person having the greatest Number of Votes shall be the President, if such Number be a Majority of the whole number of Electors appointed; and if there be more than one who have such Majority, and have an equal Number of Votes, then the House of Representatives shall immediately chuse by Ballot one of them for President; and if no Person have a Majority, then from the five highest on the List the said House shall in like Manner chuse the President. But in chusing the President, the Votes shall be taken by States, the Representation from each State having one Vote; A quorum for this Purpose shall consist of a Member or Members from two thirds of the States, and a Majority of all the States shall be necessary to a Choice. In every Case, after the Choice of the President, the Person having the greatest Number of Votes of the Electors shall be the Vice President. But if there should remain two or more who have equal Votes, the Senate shall chuse from them by Ballot the Vice President.

The Congress may determine the time of chusing the Electors, and the Day on which they shall give their Votes; which Day shall be the same throughout the United States.

No person except a natural born Citizen, *or a Citizen of the United States, at the time of the Adoption of this Constitution,* shall be eligible to the Office of President; neither shall any Person be eligible to that Office who shall not have attained to the Age of thirty five Years, and been fourteen Years a Resident within the United States.

In Case of the Removal of the President from Office, or of his Death, Resignation, or Inability to discharge the Powers and Duties of the said Office, the Same shall devolve on the Vice President, and the Congress may by Law provide for the Case of Removal, Death, Resignation or Inability, both of the President and Vice President, declaring what Officer shall then act as President, and such Officer shall act accordingly, until the Disability be removed, or a President shall be elected.

The President shall, at stated Times, receive for his Services, a Compensation, which shall neither be encreased nor diminished during the Period for which he shall have been elected, and he shall not receive within that period any other Emolument from the United States, or any of them.

Before he enter on the Execution of his Office, he shall take the following Oath or Affirmation:—"I do solemnly swear (or affirm) that I will faithfully execute the Office of President of the United States, and will to the best of my Ability, preserve, protect and defend the Constitution of the United States."

Section 2

The President shall be Commander in Chief of the Army and Navy of the United States, and of the Militia of the several States, when called into the actual Service of the United States; he may require the Opinion, in writing, of the principal Officer in each of the executive Departments, upon any Subject relating to the Duties of their respective Offices, and he shall have Power to grant Reprieves and Pardons for Offences against the United States, except in Cases of Impeachment.

He shall have Power, by and with the Advice and Consent of the Senate, to make Treaties, provided two thirds of the Senators present concur; and he shall nominate, and by and with the Advice and Consent of the Senate, shall appoint Ambassadors, other public Ministers and Consuls, Judges of the supreme Court, and all other Officers of the United States, whose Appointments are not herein otherwise provided for, and which shall be established by Law: but the Congress may by Law vest the Appointment of such inferior Officers, as they think proper in the President alone, in the Courts of Law, or in the Heads of Departments.

The President shall have Power to fill up all Vacancies that may happen during the Recess of the Senate, by granting Commissions which shall expire at the End of their next Session.

Section 3

He shall from time to time give to the Congress Information of the State of the Union, and recommend to their Consideration such Measures as he shall judge necessary and expedient; he may, on extraordinary Occasions, convene both Houses, or either of them, and in Case of disagreement between them, with Respect to the Time of Adjournment, he may adjourn them to such Time as he shall think proper; he shall receive Ambassadors and other public Ministers; he shall take Care that the Laws be faithfully executed, and shall Commission all the officers of the United States.

Section 4

The President, Vice President and all civil Officers of the United States, shall be removed from Office on Impeachment for, and Conviction of, Treason, Bribery or other high Crimes and Misdemeanors.

ARTICLE III

Section 1

The judicial Power of the United States, shall be vested in one supreme Court, and in such inferior Courts as the Congress may from time to time ordain and establish. The Judges, both of the supreme and inferior Courts, shall hold their offices during good Behaviour, and shall, at stated Times, receive for their Services, a Compensation, which shall not be diminished during their Continuance in Office.

Section 2

The judicial Power shall extend to all Cases, in Law and Equity, arising under this Constitution, the Laws of the United States, and Treaties made, or which shall be made, under their Authority;—to all Cases affecting Ambassadors, other public Ministers and Consuls;—to all Cases of admiralty and maritime Jurisdiction;—to Controversies to which the United States shall be a Party;—to Controversies between two or more States;—*between a State and Citizens of another State;*—between Citizens of different States;—between Citizens of the same State claiming Lands under Grants of different States, and between a State, or the Citizens thereof, and foreign States, Citizens or Subjects.

In all Cases affecting Ambassadors, other public Ministers and Consuls, and those in which a State shall be Party, the supreme Court shall have original Jurisdiction. In all the other Cases before mentioned, the supreme Court shall have appellate Jurisdiction, both as to Law and Fact, with such Exceptions, and under such Regulations as the Congress shall make.

The Trial of all Crimes, except in Cases of Impeachment, shall be by Jury; and such Trial shall be held in the State where the said Crimes shall have been committed, but when not committed within any State, the Trial shall be at such Place or Places as the Congress may by Law have directed.

Section 3

Treason against the United States, shall consist only in levying War against them, or in adhering to their Enemies, giving them Aid and Comfort. No person shall be convicted of Treason unless on the Testimony of two Witnesses to the same overt Act, or on Confession in open Court.

The Congress shall have Power to declare the Punishment of Treason, but no Attainder of Treason shall work Corruption of Blood, or Forfeiture except during the Life of the Person attainted.

ARTICLE IV

Section 1

Full Faith and Credit shall be given in each State to the public Acts, Records, and judicial Proceedings of every other State. And the Congress may by general Laws prescribe the Manner in which such Acts, Records and Proceedings shall be proved, and the Effect thereof.

Section 2

The Citizens of each State shall be entitled to all Privileges and Immunities of Citizens in the several States.

A Person charged in any State with Treason, Felony, or other Crime, who shall flee from Justice, and be found in another State, shall on Demand of the executive Authority of the State from which he fled, be delivered up, to be removed to the State having Jurisdiction of the Crime.

No Person held to Service or Labour in one State, under the Laws thereof, escaping into another, shall, in Consequence of any Law or Regulation therein, be discharged from such Service or Labour, but shall be delivered up on Claim of the Party to whom such Service or Labour may be due.

Section 3

New States may be admitted by the Congress into this Union; but no new State shall be formed or erected within the Jurisdiction of any other State; nor any State be formed by the Junction of two or more States, or Parts of States, without the Consent of the Legislatures of the States concerned as well as of the Congress.

The Congress shall have Power to dispose of and make all needful Rules and Regulations respecting the Territory or other Property belonging to the United States; and nothing in this Constitution shall be so construed as to Prejudice any Claims of the United States, or of any particular States.

Section 4

The United States shall guarantee to every State in this Union a Republican Form of Government, and shall protect each of them against Invasion; and on Application of the Legislature, or of the Executive (when the Legislature cannot be convened) against domestic violence.

ARTICLE V

The Congress, whenever two thirds of both Houses shall deem it necessary, shall propose Amendments to this Constitution, or, on the Application of the Legislatures of two thirds of the several States, shall call a Convention for proposing Amendments, which, in either Case, shall be valid to all Intents and Purposes, as Part of this Constitution, when ratified by the Legislatures of three fourths of the several States, or by Conventions in three fourths thereof, as the one or the other Mode of Ratification may be proposed by the Congress; Provided *that no Amendment which may be made prior to the Year One thousand eight hundred and eight shall in any Manner affect the first and fourth Clauses in the Ninth Section of the first Article;* and that no State, without its Consent, shall be deprived of its equal Suffrage in the Senate.

ARTICLE VI

All Debts contracted and Engagements entered into, before the Adoption of this Constitution, shall be as valid against the United States under this Constitution, as under the Confederation.

This Constitution, and Laws of the United States which shall be made in Pursuance thereof; and all Treaties made, or which shall be made, under the Authority of the United States, shall be the supreme Law of the Land; and the Judges in every State shall be bound thereby, any Thing in the Constitution or Laws of any State to the Contrary notwithstanding.

The Senators and Representatives before mentioned, and the Members of the several State Legislatures, and all executive and Judicial Officers, both of the United States and of the several States, shall be bound by Oath or Affirmation, to support this Constitution; but no religious Test shall ever be required as a Qualification to any Office of public Trust under the United States.

ARTICLE VII

The Ratification of the Conventions of nine States, shall be sufficient for the Establishment of this Constitution between the States so ratifying the Same.

Done in Convention by the Unanimous Consent of the States present the Seventeenth Day of September in the Year of our Lord one thousand seven hundred and Eighty seven and of the Independence of the United States of America the Twelfth.* IN WITNESS whereof We have hereunto subscribed our Names,

GEORGE WASHINGTON
President and Deputy from Virginia

Delaware
GEORGE READ
GUNNING BEDFORD, JR.
JOHN DICKINSON
RICHARD BASSETT
JACOB BROOM

Maryland
JAMES MCHENRY
DANIEL OF ST. THOMAS JENIFER
DANIEL CARROLL

Virginia
JOHN BLAIR
JAMES MADISON, JR.

North Carolina
WILLIAM BLOUNT
RICHARD DOBBS SPRAIGHT
HUGH WILLIAMSON

South Carolina
JOHN RUTLEDGE
CHARLES COTESWORTH PINCKNEY
CHARLES PINCKNEY
PIERCE BUTLER

Georgia
WILLIAM FEW
ABRAHAM BALDWIN

New Hampshire
JOHN LANGDON
NICHOLAS GILMAN

Massachusetts
NATHANIEL GORHAM
RUFUS KING

Connecticut
WILLIAM SAMUEL JOHNSON
ROGER SHERMAN

New York
ALEXANDER HAMILTON

New Jersey
WILLIAM LIVINGSTON
DAVID BREARLEY
WILLIAM PATERSON
JONATHAN DAYTON

Pennsylvania
BENJAMIN FRANKLIN
THOMAS MIFFLIN
ROBERT MORRIS
GEORGE CLYMER
THOMAS FITZSIMONS
JARED INGERSOLL
JAMES WILSON
GOUVERNEUR MORRIS

The Constitution was submitted on September 17, 1787, by the Constitutional Convention, was ratified by the Convention of several states at various dates up to May 29, 1790, and became effective on March 4, 1789.

Amendments to the Constitution

AMENDMENT I

Congress shall make no law respecting an establishment of religion, or prohibiting the free exercise thereof; or abridging the freedom of speech, or of the press; or the right of the people peaceably to assemble, and to petition the Government for a redress of grievances.

AMENDMENT II

A well regulated Militia being necessary to the security of a free State, the right of the people to keep and bear Arms, shall not be infringed.

AMENDMENT III

No Soldier shall, in time of peace be quartered in any house, without the consent of the Owner, nor in time of war, but in a manner to be prescribed by law.

AMENDMENT IV

The right of the people to be secure in their persons, houses, papers, and effects, against unreasonable searches and seizures, shall not be violated, and no Warrants shall issue, but upon probable cause, supported by Oath or affirmation, and particularly describing the place to be searched, and the persons or things to be seized.

AMENDMENT V

No person shall be held to answer for a capital, or otherwise infamous crime, unless on a presentment or indictment of a Grand Jury, except in cases arising in the land or naval forces, or in the Militia, when in actual service in time of War or public danger; nor shall any person be subject for the same offense to be twice put in jeopardy of life or limb; nor shall be compelled in any criminal case to be a witness against himself, nor be deprived of life, liberty, or property, without due process of law; nor shall private property be taken for public use, without just compensation.

AMENDMENT VI

In all criminal prosecutions, the accused shall enjoy the right to a speedy and public trial, by an impartial jury of the State and district wherein the crime shall have been committed, which district shall have been previously ascertained by law, and to be informed of the nature and cause of the accusation; to be confronted with the witnesses against him; to have compulsory process for obtaining witnesses in his favor, and to have the Assistance of Counsel for his defence.

AMENDMENT VII

In Suits at common law, where the value in controversy shall exceed twenty dollars, the right of trial by jury shall be preserved, and no fact tried by a jury, shall be otherwise re-examined in any Court of the United States, than according to the rules of the common law.

AMENDMENT VIII

Excessive bail shall not be required, nor excessive fines imposed, nor cruel and unusual punishments inflicted.

AMENDMENT IX

The enumeration in the Constitution, of certain rights, shall not be construed to deny or disparage others retained by the people.

AMENDMENT X*

The powers not delegated to the United States by the Constitution, nor prohibited by it to the States, are reserved to the States respectively, or to the people.

AMENDMENT XI
[ADOPTED 1798]

The Judicial power of the United States shall not be construed to extend to any suit in law or equity, commenced or prosecuted against one of the United States by Citizens of another State, or by Citizens or Subjects of any Foreign State.

AMENDMENT XII
[ADOPTED 1804]

The Electors shall meet in their respective states, and vote by ballot for President and Vice President, one of whom, at least, shall not be an inhabitant of the same state with themselves; they shall name in their ballots the person voted for as President, and in distinct ballots the person voted for as Vice President, and they shall make distinct lists of all persons voted for as President, and of all persons voted for as Vice President, and of the number of votes for each, which lists they shall sign and certify, and transmit sealed to the seat of the government of the United States, directed to the President of the Senate;—The President of the Senate shall, in the presence of the Senate and House of Representatives, open all the certificates and the votes shall then be counted;—The person having the greatest number of votes for President, shall be the President, if such number be a majority of the whole number of Electors appointed; and if no person have such majority, then from the persons having the highest numbers not exceeding three on the list of those voted for as President, the House of Representatives shall choose immediately, by ballot, the President. But in choosing the President, the votes shall be taken by states, the representation from each state having one vote; a quorum for this purpose shall consist of a member or members from two-thirds of the states, and a majority of all the states shall be necessary to a choice. And if the House of Representatives shall not choose a President whenever the right of choice shall devolve upon them, before *the fourth day of March* next following, then the Vice President shall act as President, as in the case of the death or other constitutional disability of the President.—The person having the greatest number of votes as Vice President, shall be the Vice President, if such number be a majority of the whole number of Electors appointed, and if no person have a majority, then from the two highest numbers on the list, the Senate shall choose the Vice President; a quorum for the purpose shall consist of two-thirds of the whole number of Senators, and a majority of the whole number shall be necessary to a choice. But no person constitutionally ineligible to the office of President shall be eligible to that of Vice President of the United States.

AMENDMENT XIII
[ADOPTED 1865]

Section 1

Neither slavery nor involuntary servitude, except as a punishment for crime whereof the party shall have been duly convicted, shall exist within the United States, or any place subject to their jurisdiction.

---

*The first ten amendments (the Bill of Rights) were ratified, and their adoption was certified, on December 15, 1791.

Section 2

Congress shall have power to enforce this article by appropriate legislation.

AMENDMENT XIV
[ADOPTED 1868]

Section 1

All persons born or naturalized in the United States, and subject to the jurisdiction thereof, are citizens of the United States and of the State wherein they reside. No State shall make or enforce any law which shall abridge the privileges or immunities of citizens of the United States; nor shall any State deprive any person of life, liberty, or property, without due process of law; nor deny to any person within its jurisdiction the equal protection of the laws.

Section 2

Representatives shall be apportioned among the several States according to their respective numbers, counting the whole number of persons in each State, excluding Indians not taxed. But when the right to vote at any election for the choice of electors for President and Vice President of the United States, Representatives in Congress, the Executive and Judicial officers of a State, or the members of the Legislature thereof, is denied to any of the male inhabitants of such State, being twenty-one years of age, and citizens of the United States, or in any way abridged, except for participation in rebellion, or other crime, the basis of representation therein shall be reduced in the proportion which the number of such male citizens shall bear to the whole number of male citizens twenty-one years of age in such State.

Section 3

No person shall be a Senator or Representative in Congress, or elector of President and Vice President, or hold any office, civil or military, under the United States, or under any State, who, having previously taken an oath, as a member of Congress, or as an officer of the United States, or as a member of any State legislature, or as an executive or judicial officer of any State, to support the Constitution of the United States, shall have engaged in insurrection or rebellion against the same, or given aid or comfort to the enemies thereof. But Congress may by a vote of two-thirds of each House, remove such disability.

Section 4

The validity of the public debt of the United States, authorized by law, including debts incurred for payment of pensions and bounties for services in suppressing insurrection or rebellion, shall not be questioned. But neither the United States nor any State shall assume or pay any debt or obligation incurred in aid of insurrection or rebellion against the United States, or any claim for the loss or emancipation of any slave; but all such debts, obligations and claims shall be held illegal and void.

Section 5

The Congress shall have power to enforce, by appropriate legislation, the provisions of this article.

AMENDMENT XV
[ADOPTED 1870]

Section 1

The right of citizens of the United States to vote shall not be denied or abridged by the United States or by any State on account of race, color, or previous condition of servitude.

Section 2

The Congress shall have power to enforce this article by appropriate legislation.

AMENDMENT XVI
[ADOPTED 1913]

The Congress shall have power to lay and collect taxes on incomes, from whatever source derived, without apportionment among the several States, and without regard to any census or enumeration.

AMENDMENT XVII
[ADOPTED 1913]

The Senate of the United States shall be composed of two Senators from each State, elected by the people thereof, for six years; and each Senator shall have one vote. The electors in each State shall have the qualifications requisite for electors of the most numerous branch of the State legislatures.

When vacancies happen in the representation of any State in the Senate, the executive authority of such State shall issue writs of election to fill such vacancies: *Provided,* That the legislature of any State may empower the executive thereof to make temporary appointments until the people fill the vacancies by election as the legislature may direct.

This amendment shall not be so construed as to affect the election or term of any Senator chosen before it becomes valid as part of the Constitution.

AMENDMENT XVIII
[ADOPTED 1919, REPEALED 1933]

Section 1

After one year from the ratification of this article the manufacture, sale, or transportation of intoxicating liquors within, the importation thereof into, or the exportation thereof from the United States and all territory subject to the jurisdiction thereof for beverage purposes is hereby prohibited.

Section 2

The Congress and the several States shall have concurrent power to enforce this article by appropriate legislation.

Section 3

This article shall be inoperative unless it shall have been ratified as an amendment to the Constitution by the legislatures of the several States, as provided in the Constitution, within seven years from the date of the submission hereof to the States by the Congress.

AMENDMENT XIX
[ADOPTED 1920]

The right of citizens of the United States to vote shall not be denied or abridged by the United States or by any State on account of sex.

Congress shall have power to enforce this article by appropriate legislation.

AMENDMENT XX
[ADOPTED 1933]

Section 1

The terms of the President and Vice President shall end at noon on the 20th day of January, and the terms of Senators and Representatives at noon on the 3d day of January, of the years in which such terms would have ended if this article had not been ratified and the terms of their successors shall then begin.

Section 2

The Congress shall assemble at least once in every year, and such meeting shall begin at noon on the 3d day of January, unless they shall by law appoint a different day.

Section 3

If, at the time fixed for the beginning of the term of the President, the President elect shall have died, the Vice President elect shall become President. If a President shall not have been chosen before the time fixed for the beginning of his term, or if the President elect shall have failed to qualify, then the Vice President elect shall act as President until a President shall have qualified; and the Congress may by law provide for the case wherein neither a President elect nor a Vice President elect shall have qualified, declaring who shall then act as President, or the manner in which one who is to act shall be selected, and such person shall act accordingly until a President or Vice President shall have qualified.

Section 4

The Congress may by law provide for the case of the death of any of the persons from whom the House of Representatives may choose a President whenever the right of choice shall have devolved upon them, and for the case of the death of any of the persons from whom the Senate may choose a Vice President whenever the right of choice shall have devolved upon them.

Section 5

Sections 1 and 2 shall take effect on the 15th day of October following the ratification of this article.

Section 6

This article shall be inoperative unless it shall have been ratified as an amendment to the Constitution by the legislatures of three fourths of the several States within seven years from the date of its submission.

AMENDMENT XXI
[ADOPTED 1933]

Section 1

The eighteenth article of amendment to the Constitution of the United States is hereby repealed.

Section 2

The transportation or importation into any State, Territory, or possession of the United States for delivery or use therein of intoxicating liquors in violation of the laws thereof, is hereby prohibited.

Section 3

This article shall be inoperative unless it shall have been ratified as an amendment to the Constitution by conventions in the several States, as provided in the Constitution, within seven years from the date of the submission hereof to the States by the Congress.

AMENDMENT XXII
[ADOPTED 1951]

Section 1

No person shall be elected to the office of the President more than twice, and no person who has held the office of President, or acted as President, for more than two years of a term to which some other person was elected President shall be elected to the office of the President more than once. But this Article shall not apply to any person holding the office of President when this Article was proposed by the Congress, and shall not prevent any person who may be holding the office of President, or acting as

President, during the term within which this Article becomes operative from holding the office of President or acting as President during the remainder of such term.

Section 2

This article shall be inoperative unless it shall have been ratified as an amendment to the Constitution by the legislatures of three-fourths of the several States within seven years from the date of its submission to the States by the Congress.

AMENDMENT XXIII
[ADOPTED 1961]

Section 1

The District constituting the seat of Government of the United States shall appoint in such manner as the Congress shall direct:

A number of electors of President and Vice President equal to the whole number of Senators and Representatives in Congress to which the District would be entitled if it were a State, but in no event more than the least populous State; they shall be in addition to those appointed by the States, but they shall be considered, for the purposes of the election of President and Vice President, to be electors appointed by a State; and they shall meet in the District and perform such duties as provided by the twelfth article of amendment.

Section 2

The Congress shall have power to enforce this article by appropriate legislation.

AMENDMENT XXIV
[ADOPTED 1964]

Section 1

The right of citizens of the United States to vote in any primary or other election for President or Vice President, for electors for President or Vice President, or for Senator or Representative in Congress, shall not be denied or abridged by the United States or any state by reason of failure to pay any poll tax or other tax.

Section 2

The Congress shall have the power to enforce this article by appropriate legislation.

AMENDMENT XXV
[ADOPTED 1967]

Section 1

In case of the removal of the President from office or his death or resignation, the Vice President shall become President.

Section 2

Whenever there is a vacancy in the office of the Vice President, the President shall nominate a Vice President who shall take the office upon confirmation by a majority vote of both houses of Congress.

Section 3

Whenever the President transmits to the President pro tempore of the Senate and the Speaker of the House of Representatives his written declaration that he is unable to discharge the powers and duties of his office, and until he transmits to them a written declaration to the contrary, such powers and duties shall be discharged by the Vice President as Acting President.

Section 4

Whenever the Vice President and a majority of either the principal officers of the executive departments or of such other body as Congress may by law provide, transmit to the President pro tempore of the Senate and the Speaker of the House of Representatives their written declaration that the President is unable to discharge the powers and duties of his office, the Vice President shall immediately assume the powers and duties of the office as Acting President.

Thereafter, when the President transmits to the President pro tempore of the Senate and the Speaker of the House of Representatives his written declaration that no inability exists, he shall resume the powers and duties of his office unless the Vice President and a majority of either the principal officers of the executive department or of such other body as Congress may by law provide, transmit within four days to the President pro tempore of the Senate and the Speaker of the House of Representatives their written declaration that the President is unable to discharge the powers and duties of his office. Thereupon Congress shall decide the issue, assembling within 48 hours for that purpose if not in session. If the Congress, within 21 days after receipt of the latter written declaration, or, if Congress is not in session, within 21 days after Congress is required to assemble, determines by two-thirds vote of both houses that the President is unable to discharge the powers and duties of his office, the Vice President shall continue to discharge the same as Acting President; otherwise, the President shall resume the powers and duties of his office.

AMENDMENT XXVI
[ADOPTED 1971]

Section 1

The right of citizens of the United States, who are 18 years of age or older, to vote shall not be denied or abridged by the United States or any state on account of age.

Section 2

The Congress shall have the power to enforce this article by appropriate legislation.

AMENDMENT XXVII
[ADOPTED 1992]

No law, varying the compensation for the services of the Senators and Representatives shall take effect, until an election of Representatives shall have intervened.

Supplementary Reading

PROLOGUE | BEGINNINGS

During the 1990s the prehistoric era in North America witnessed an explosion of interest, especially among archaeologists. A global perspective, focusing on geography as a causal force, is outlined in Jared Diamond, *Guns, Germs, and Steel* (1997). David Hurst Thomas, *Exploring Native North America* (2000), provides detailed analyses of representative archaeological sites.

A good survey of the first peoples of North America is David J. Meltzer, *Search for the First Americans* (1993). The "overkill hypothesis" is developed in Paul Martin and Richard Klein, eds., *Quaternary Extinctions* (1984). The best survey on the southwestern peoples is Linda S. Cordell, *Prehistory of the Southwest* (1997). See also J. J. Brody, *The Anasazi* (1990), David Roberts, *In Search of the Old Ones: Exploring the Anasazi World of the Southwest* (1995), R. Gwinn Vivian, *The Chacoan Prehistory of the San Juan Basin* (1990), John P. Andrews and Todd W. Bostwick, *Desert Farmers at the River's Edge: The Hohokam and Pueblo Grande* (1997), and, on early agriculture, R. G. Matson, *The Origins of Southwestern Agriculture* (1991). For a study of Hopewell peoples, see Bruce D. Smith, *Rivers of Change* (1992).

On the Mississippian societies, see Thomas E. Emerson, *Cahokia and the Archaeology of Power* (1997), Thomas E. Emerson and R. Barry Lewis, eds., *Cahokia and the Hinterlands: Middle Mississippian Cultures of the Midwest* (1991), Biloine W. Young and Robert Fowler, *Cahokia, The Great Native American Metropolis* (2000), Timothy Pauketat, *The Ascent of Chiefs: Cahokia and Mississippian Politics in Native North America* (1994), and Robert A. Birmingham and Leslie Eisenberg, *Indian Mounds of Wisconsin* (2000). For early peoples elsewhere, see Vance T. Holliday, *Paleoindian Geoarchaeology of the Southern High Plains* (1997) and Ruth Kirk and Richard D. Daugherty, *Hunters of the Whale* (1974), for the Makah of the Northwest.

For an overview of political structures, see Robert D. Drennan, *Chiefdoms in the Americas* (1987). That warfare was a product of gender tensions is explored in Bruce G. Trigger, *Natives and Newcomers* (1985). The contention that the early peoples of North America lived in perfect harmony with nature is rebutted in Shepard Krech, *The Ecological Indian* (1999). Another common assumption, based on Native American folklore, of the essentially peaceful character of Southwestern peoples has been challenged by recent studies such as Glen E. Rice and Steven A. Leblanc, eds., *Deadly Landscapes: Case Studies in Prehistoric Southwestern Warfare* (2001), and Tim D. White, *Prehistoric Cannibalism at Mancos* (1992). In *Eve's Seed: Biology, the Sexes and the Course of History* (2001), Robert S. McElvaine argues that men enshrined raids and warfare in response to women's increasingly important economic role in farming activities.

CHAPTER 1 | ALIEN ENCOUNTERS: EUROPE IN THE AMERICAS

On the explorers and the world they opened up, see Samuel E. Morison, *The European Discovery of America* (1971–1974). Morison's biography of Columbus, *Admiral of the Ocean Sea* (1942), is a classic; for a recent study see Miles Davidson, *Columbus Then and Now* (1997). David Stannard, *American Holocaust* (1992), and Kirkpatrick Sale, *The Conquest of Paradise* (1990), are highly critical of Columbus. The history of Spanish colonization in the Southwest is treated in David J. Weber, *The Spanish Frontier in North America* (1992) and, in the Southeast, in Paul E. Hoffman, *A New Andalucia and a Way to the Orient* (1991) and *Florida's Frontiers* (2002). The classic study is Charles Gibson, *Spain in America* (1966). For an imaginative attempt to reconstruct the Native American response, see Ramon Guitierrez, *When Jesus Came, The Corn Mothers Went Away* (1991).

Accounts of the English background of colonization can be found in Nicholas Canny, ed., *The Oxford History of the British Empire: The Origins of Empire* (1998). On French colonization, see William J. Eccles, *The French in North America, 1500–1765* (1998), Carl J. Ekberg, *French Roots in the Illinois Country* (1998), and Carole Blackburn, *Harvest of Souls* (2000), which focuses on the Jesuit Missionaries.

Contemporary scholarship on Indian-colonist relations focuses on their interactions. Important studies in that vein include Richard White, *Indians, Empires and Republics in the Great Lakes Region, 1650–1815* (1991), James Merrell, *Into the American Woods: Negotiators on the Pennsylvania Frontier* (1999), Jill Lepore, *Name of War: King Philip's War and the Origins of American Identity* (1999), and Karen Kupperman, *Indians and English: Facing Off in Early America* (2000).

The impact of the Europeans is discussed in the Debating the Past (p. 25). See also Alfred W. Crosby, *Ecological Imperialism: The Biological Expansion of Europe, 900–1900* (1993) and, though it deals with a later period, Robert Boyd, *The Coming of the Spirit of Pestilence: Introduced Infectious Diseases and Population Decline among Northwest Coast Indians* (1999). Joyce E. Chaplin, *Subject Matter: Technology, the Body, and Science on the Anglo-American Frontier, 1500–1676* (2001) argues that Europeans did not assume that they were racially superior until they saw how readily native peoples died of diseases.

For a general study of American slave trade, see David Eltis, *The Rise of African Slavery in the Americas* (2000). General surveys of slavery include Ira Berlin, *Many Thousands Gone* (1998), and Peter Kolchin, *American Slavery, 1619–1877* (1993).

On Virginia, see David H. Fischer and James C. Kelly, *Bound Away: Virginia and the Westward Movement* (2000), and Edmund S. Morgan, *American Slavery, American Freedom* (1975). Jack P. Greene, *Pursuits of Happiness* (1988), argues for the centrality of the Chesapeake in the formation of American identity. On Roanoke, see Ivor Noel Hume, *The Virginia Adventure* (1994). See also Everett Emerson, *Captain John Smith* (1993). For Maryland, consult Gloria T. Main, *Tobacco Colony* (1982), and A. C. Land, *Colonial Maryland* (1981); for Carolina, see Roger Ekirch, *Poor Carolina* (1981).

For the middle colonies, see Michael Kammen, *Colonial New York* (1975) and Donna Merwick, *Possessing Albany, 1630–1710: The Dutch and English Experiences* (1990). In addition to Merrell, see Mary Geiter, *William Penn* (2000).

On New England, Edmund Morgan's *The Puritan Dilemma: The Story of John Winthrop* (1958), long a classic, has been superseded by Francis J. Bremer, *John Winthrop: America's Forgotten Founding Father* (2003). The dispute over Anne Hutchinson has been enlivened by Michael P. Winship, *Making Heretics: Militant Protestantism and Free Grace in Massachusetts, 1636–1641* (2002), who notes that few at the time accused Hutchinson of antinomianism. Louise A. Breen, *Transgressing the Bounds: Subversive Enterprises among the Puritan Elite in Massachusetts, 1630–1692* (2001) draws a connection between religious dissenters such as Hutchinson and economic entrepreneurship. Selma R. Williams, *Divine Rebel* (1981) focuses on Hutchinson as a persecuted woman. For Rhode Island, see Edwin S. Gaustad, *Liberty of Conscience: Roger Williams in America* (1991). William Bradford's classic, *Of Plymouth Plantation*, is also well worth sampling.

CHAPTER 2 | AMERICAN SOCIETY IN THE MAKING

Among general interpretations, D. J. Boorstin's *The Americans: The Colonial Experience* (1958), emphasizes the modern aspects of colonial society; Jon Butler's *Becoming America: The Revolution Before 1776* (2000) similarly and more broadly emphasizes the rapid evolution of colonial society. Alan Kulikoff, *From British Peasants to Colonial American Farmers* (2000) underscores the importance of land in defining American life. Alan Taylor, *American Colonies* (2001) emphasizes the links between European and American societies.

On economic conditions, see John J. McCusker and Russell R. Menard, eds., *The Economy of British America, 1607–1789* (1991). For the economic growth of colonial New England, see Margaret Ellen Newell, *From Dependency to Independence* (1998). On the chronologically and geographically uneven development of slavery in America, consult Ira Berlin, *Generations of Captivity: A History of African-American Slaves* (2003) and *Many Thousands Gone* (1998). See also Philip D. Morgan, *Slave Counterpoint* (1998) and P. D. Curtin, *The Rise and Fall of the Plantation Complex* (1990). Alan Gallay, *The Indian Slave Trade* (2002) uncovers an issue that has long been overlooked.

On life in the colonial South, see T. W. Tate and David Ammerman, eds., *The Chesapeake in the Seventeenth Century* (1979), Allan Kulikoff, *Tobacco and Slaves* (1986), D. B. and A. H. Rutman, *A Place in Time* (1984), and Timothy H. Breen and Stephen Innes, *"Myne Owne Ground": Race and Freedom on Virginia's Eastern Shore* (1980).

Family and community life are surveyed in D. F. Hawke, *Everyday Life in Early America* (1988), and Edmund S. Morgan, *The Puritan Family* (1966). The places of women and children are effectively presented in Laurel T. Ulrich, *Good Wives: Image and Reality in the Lives of Women in Northern New England* (1982), and Philip Greven, *The Protestant Temperament: Patterns of Child-Rearing, Religious Experience, and the Self in Early America* (1980). Richard Godbeer, *Sexual Revolution in Early America* (2002) corrects the stereotype of the puritans as sexually repressive.

The works of Perry Miller remain the starting point for any serious study of the cultural life of colonial New England. Among them, *Errand into the Wilderness* (1956) provides a good introduction. More recent studies, most of which modify Miller's judgments, include D. D. Hall, *Worlds of Wonder, Days of Judgment* (1989), and Patricia U. Bonomi, *Under the Cope of Heaven* (1986). Some recent scholarship contends that puritan practices complemented economic development: for example, John Frederick Martin, *Profits in the Wilderness* (1991), Stephen Innes, *Creating the Commonwealth* (1995), and Mark A. Peterson, *The Price of Redemption* (1997).

Larry D. Gragg, *The Salem Witch Crisis* (1992) provides a narrative account. Paul Boyer and Stephen Nissenbaum, *Salem Possessed* (1974), argue that the episode grew out of tensions between different factions within the community. Mary Beth Norton, *In the Devil's Snare: The Salem Witchcraft Crisis of 1692* (2002), views the crisis as a response to fear of Indians. The subject is considered more generally in John Demos, *Entertaining Satan: Witchcraft and the Culture of Early New England* (1982). On women and witchcraft, see Elizabeth Reis, *Damned Women* (1997), Elaine G. Breslaw, *Tituba, Reluctant Witch of Salem* (1996), and Carol F. Karlsen, *The Devil in the Shape of a Woman* (1987).

For an engaging overview of the ideology of gender authority in the seventeenth century, see Mary Beth Norton, *Founding Mothers and Fathers* (1996). On women and religion in New England, see also Susan Juster, *Disorderly Women* (1994). Karin Wolf, *Not All Wives* (2000), describes the range of women's activities in Philadelphia. For the role of women in Virginia, see Kathleen M. Brown, *Good Wives, Nasty Wenches and Anxious Patriarchs* (1996).

Educational and intellectual developments are treated in Bernard Bailyn, *Education in the Forming of American Society* (1960), and L. A. Cremin, *American Education: The Colonial Experience* (1970).

In the past decade there has been a profusion of studies on the interrelationship between settlers and Indians: Jane T. Merritt, *At the Crossroads: Indians and Empire on a Mid-Atlantic Frontier* (2003), Richard White, *The Middle Ground* (1991), Daniel K. Richter, *Ordeal of the Longhouse* (1992), Daniel H. Usner, *Indians, Settlers, and Slaves in a Frontier Exchange Economy* (1992), Colin G. Calloway, *New Worlds for All: Indians, Europeans, and the Remaking of Early America* (1997), Karen O. Kupperman, *Indians and English* (2001) and James F. Brooks, *Captives and Cousins* (2002).

CHAPTER 3 | AMERICA IN THE BRITISH EMPIRE

A full analysis of the British imperial system can be found in the early volumes of L. H. Gipson's *British Empire Before the American Revolution* (1936–1968). See also James A. Henretta, *The Evolution of American Society* (1973), and Michael Kammen, *Empire and Interest* (1974). Jack P. Greene, *Peripheries and Center* (1989), describes how the colonists extended their control of political affairs. On colonial trade and the mercantilist system, see J. J. McCusker and R. R. Menard, *The Economy of British America* (1985), and P. J. Marshall, ed., *The Oxford History of the British Empire: The Eighteenth Century* (1998).

On the Great Awakening, Richard Bushman, *From Puritan to Yankee* (1967) emphasizes psychosocial factors while Frank Lambert, *Inventing the "Great Awakening"* (1999) focuses on the intersection of religion and economics. Catherine A. Brekus, *Strangers and Pilgrims: Female Preaching in America* (1998) addresses a long-neglected subject. See also P. U. Bonami, *Under the Cope of Heaven: Religion, Society, and Politics in Colonial America* (1986). For the Enlightenment, see H. F.

May, *The Enlightenment in America* (1976). Fred Anderson, *The Crucible of War* (2000) is a readable and thorough narrative of the Great War for the Empire; see also his *A People's Army: Massachusetts Soldiers and Society in the Seven Years' War* (1984).

On the causes of the Revolution, see Pauline Maier, *From Resistance to Revolution* (1972), Edmund S. Morgan, *The Birth of the Republic* (1977), and Edward Countryman, *The American Revolution* (1985). Valuable local studies include T. H. Breen, *Tobacco Culture* (1985), on Virginia; Countryman's *A People in Revolution* (1989), on New York; and T. M. Doerflinger, *A Vigorous Spirit of Enterprise* (1986), on Philadelphia. Specific issues during the period are treated in E. S. and H. M. Morgan, *The Stamp Act Crisis* (1953), John Shy, *Toward Lexington* (1965), and Alfred F. Young, *The Shoemaker and the Tea Party* (1999).

Bernard Bailyn's *The Ideological Origins of the American Revolution* (1967) and *The Origins of American Politics* (1968) are brilliant analyses of the political thinking and political structure of eighteenth-century America. Other seminal works include Gordon S. Wood, *The Radicalism of the American Revolution* (1992), and Edmund S. Morgan, *Inventing the People: The Rise of Popular Sovereignty in England and America* (1988). See also Pauline Maier, *The Old Revolutionaries* (1980). On Benjamin Franklin, see two good recent biographies, by Edmund Morgan (2002) and Walter Isaacson (2003).

CHAPTER 4 | THE AMERICAN REVOLUTION

Good brief surveys of the Revolutionary years are Edward Countryman, *The American Revolution* (1985) and E. S. Morgan, *The Birth of the Republic* (1977). The best one-volume account of the war is Piers Mackesey, *The War for America, 1775–1783* (1964). See also Jack Greene, *Understanding the American Revolution* (1995). David Hackett Fischer's account of the battle of Lexington and Concord in *Paul Revere's Ride* (1994) shows why the colonists won the war; his *Washington's Crossing* (2004) outlines the importance of the New Jersey campaign. See also John W. Shy, *A People Numerous and Armed* (1990).

For a short biography of Washington, see James MacGregor Burns and Susan Dunn, *George Washington* (2004). Longer biographies include Richard Norton Smith, *Patriarch: George Washington and the New American Nation* (1993), and Henry Wiencek, *Imperfect God: George Washington, His Slaves, and the Creator of America* (2003). John E. Ferling, *Setting the World Ablaze* (2000) and his *A Leap in the Dark* (2003) provide a good overview of how Washington, Jefferson, and John Adams interacted. See also Joseph Ellis, *Founding Brothers: The Revolutionary Generation* (2000), and David McCullough *John Adams* (2001).

On the broader context of the Revolution, see Lester Langley, *The Americas in the Age of Revolution, 1750–1850* (1996); Eliga Gould emphasizes the continuity in America of British political culture, *The Persistence of Empire* (2000).

On the Continental Congress and the Articles of Confederation, see Jackson T. Main, *The Sovereign States* (1973) and Jack N. Rakove, *The Beginnings of National Politics* (1979). P. S. Onuf, *Statehood and Union* (1987), deals with the Northwest Ordinance. Eric Foner, *Tom Paine and Revolutionary America* (1976), is an excellent brief biography. James K. Martin makes a case for his subject in *Benedict Arnold, Revolutionary Hero* (1997).

The classic study of the Declaration of Independence is C. L. Becker, *The Declaration of Independence* (1922); for contemporary analysis see Pauline Maier, *American Scripture* (1997), and Jay Fliegelman, *Declaring Independence* (1993).

The early history of the state governments is covered in W. P. Adams, *The First American Constitutions* (1980). Edward Countryman, *A People in Revolution* (1982), deals with conditions in New York; for Maryland, see Jean B. Lee, *The Price of Nationhood* (1994). The development of political and social ideas, before, during, and after the Revolution, is admirably described and analyzed in G. S. Wood, *The Creation of the American Republic* (1969) and *The Radicalism of the American Revolution* (1992).

The effects of the Revolution on slavery are treated in W. D. Jordan, *White over Black* (1968), and on the Indians, in Colin G. Calloway, *The American Revolution in Indian Country* (1995). For an account of Indians, debtors, and slaves in Virginia, see Woody Holton, *Forced Founders* (1999).

L. K. Kerber, *Women of the Republic* (1980), M. B. Norton, *Liberty's Daughters* (1980), and Joy Day Buel and Richard Buel, *The Way of Duty* (1984) discuss the effects of the Revolution on women and the family.

CHAPTER 5 | THE FEDERALIST ERA: NATIONALISM TRIUMPHANT

On the Constitution, in addition to the works cited in the Debating the Past (p. 165), see Reginald Horsman, *The New Republic* (2000), a good brief survey. Bernard Bailyn, *To Begin the World Anew* (2003) shows how the Founders embraced ambiguity. For Madison's role, see Lance Banning, *The Sacred Fire of Liberty* (1995), Drew R. McCoy, *The Last of the Fathers* (1989), and Gary Rosen, *American Compact* (1999). On Hamilton, Ronald Chernow, *Alexander Hamilton* (2004) offers a balanced account while Richard Brookhiser's brief *Alexander Hamilton, American* (1999) is more partisan. See also Karl-Friedrich Walling, *Republican Empire: Alexander Hamilton on War and Free Government* (1999). The *Federalist Papers* of Hamilton, Madison, and Jay, available in many editions, are essential for the arguments of the supporters of the new government. For the Bill of Rights, consult Bernard Schwartz, *The Great Rights of Mankind* (1977).

For Washington, in addition to the works cited in the previous chapter, see Alexander De Conde, *Entangling Alliance: Politics and Diplomacy Under George Washington* (1958), Harry Ammon, *The Genet Mission* (1973), two volumes by S. F. Bemis, *Jay's Treaty* (1923) and *Pinckney's Treaty* (1926), Alexander De Conde, *The Quasi-War* (1966), and William Stinchcombe, *The XYZ Affair* (1980). On economic development, see E. J. Ferguson, *The Power of the Purse* (1968), and C. P. Nettels, *The Emergence of a National Economy* (1962), which puts this subject in the broader perspective of the period 1775–1815. On the radical western movements, see D. P. Szatmary, *Shays' Rebellion* (1980) and Thomas P. Slaughter, *The Whiskey Rebellion* (1986).

John Patrick Diggins, *John Adams* (2003) is a useful brief biography. Excellent full-length biographies include Joseph J. Ellis, *Passionate Sage* (1993), and David McCullough, *John Adams* (2001). Stanley Elkins and Eric McKitrick, *The Age of Federalism* (1993), and James Roger Sharp, *American Politics in the Early Republic* (1993) provide detailed accounts of the politics of this period. For the Alien and Sedition Acts, see J. M. Smith, *Freedom's Fetters* (1956), and L. W. Levy, *Freedom of Speech and Press in Early American History* (1963). Paul Nagel's collective biography, *The Adams Women* (1987), provides a superb account of a remarkable family.

CHAPTER 6 | JEFFERSONIAN DEMOCRACY

No student interested in Jefferson's political and social philosophy should miss sampling his writings. A useful compilation is Merrill D. Peterson, ed., *Thomas Jefferson* (1984). Lance Banning, *The Jeffersonian Persuasion* (1978), is valuable, as are the books on Jefferson mentioned in Debating the Past (p. 194).

For the election of 1800, see Bernard A. Weisberger, *America Afire* (2000). Arnold Rogow, *Fatal Friendship* (1998), describes the relationship of Hamilton and Burr; see also Joanne B. Freeman, *Affairs of Honor* (2001) on politics and dueling more generally.

For a general treatment of the Jeffersonian era, consult Marshall Smelser, *The Democratic Republic* (1968). On the parties of the era, see James Roger Sharp, *American Politics in the Early Republic* (1993) and N. E. Cunningham, Jr., *The Jeffersonian Republicans in Power* (1963); a useful monograph is Anthony F. C. Wallace, *Jefferson and the Indians* (1999).

Jefferson's battle with the judges can be followed in R. E. Ellis, *The Jeffersonian Crisis* (1971). For *Marbury* v. *Madison,* see J. A. Garraty, ed., *Quarrels That Have Shaped the Constitution* (1964), and D. O. Dewey's more detailed *Marshall Versus Jefferson* (1970) as well as R. Kent Newmeyer, *John Marshall and the Heroic Age of the Supreme Court* (2001).

Thomas Fleming, *The Louisiana Purchase* (2003) is a brief, clear account; Jon Kukla, *A Wilderness So Immense: The Louisiana Purchase and the Destiny of America* (2003) argues that the region was acquired chiefly as a place for resettling Indians.

An excellent general treatment of western exploration is contained in R. A. Billington, *Westward Expansion* (1967). On Lewis and Clark, see Stephen E. Ambrose, *Undaunted Courage* (1996).

Thomas P. Slaughter, *Exploring Lewis and Clark* (2003) is a scholarly examination of the explorers' writings.

The best account of the neutral rights question is Bradford Perkins, *Prologue to War* (1961).

CHAPTER 7 | NATIONAL GROWING PAINS

On Madison, see Lance Banning, *Sacred Fire of Liberty* (1995), and Jack N. Rakove, *James Madison and the Creation of the American Republic* (1999). The best modern account of the causes and course of the War of 1812 is J. C. A. Stagg, *Mr. Madison's War* (1983). Irving Brant, *James Madison: Commander-in-Chief* (1961), vigorously defends Madison's handling of the war. Jackson's part in the conflict is described in R. V. Remini, *Andrew Jackson and the Course of American Empire* (1977). Richard Barbuto, *Niagara 1814: America Invades Canada* (2000), and David Curtis Skaggs and Larry L. Nelson, *The Sixty Years' War for the Great Lakes* (2001), provide accounts of the war in the North.

On the Treaty of Ghent, see F. L. Engelman, *The Peace of Christmas Eve* (1962), and Bradford Perkins, *Castlereagh and Adams* (1964). For the decline of the Federalist party and the Hartford Convention, consult D. H. Fischer, *The Revolution of American Conservatism* (1965), and J. M. Banner, *To the Hartford Convention* (1981).

For the postwar diplomatic settlements and the Era of Good Feelings, see James Lewis, *The American Union and the Problem of Neighborhood: The United States and the Collapse of the Spanish Empire, 1783–1829* (1998), George Dangerfield, *The Era of Good Feelings* (1952), and Harry Ammon, *James Monroe: The Quest for National Identity* (1971), and on his famous doctrine, Ernest May, *The Making of the Monroe Doctrine* (1976).

Merrill D. Peterson, *The Great Triumvirate* (1987), is an interesting study of Clay, Calhoun, and Webster. Other biographies of statesmen of the period include Paul C. Nagel, *John Quincy Adams* (1997), Robert Remini, *Daniel Webster* (1997), Irving Bartlett, *John C. Calhoun* (1993), Maurice Baxter, *Henry Clay and the American System* (1995), and C. C. Mooney, *William H. Crawford* (1974). On the Missouri Compromise, see Glover Moore, *The Missouri Controversy* (1953). See also P. C. Nagel, *One Nation Indivisible* (1965).

On Indians, in addition to the works cited in Debating the Past (p. 220), see John Sugden, *Tecumseh* (1998), R. David Edmonds, *The Potawatomis* (1978), and Michael N. McConnell, *A Country Between: The Upper Ohio Valley and Its Peoples* (1992).

CHAPTER 8 | TOWARD A NATIONAL ECONOMY

On the consumer revolution, see especially Richard Bushman, *The Refinement of America* (1992). In addition to the works cited in Debating the Past (p. 265) on the market revolution, see Melvyn Stokes and Stephen Conway, eds., *The Market Revolution in America* (1996), and Christopher Clark, *The Roots of Rural Capitalism: Western Massachusetts, 1780–1860* (1991). See also Laurel Thatcher Ulrich, *The Age of Homespun* (2001).

On the industrial revolution in America, see A. D. Chandler, Jr., *The Visible Hand: The Managerial Revolution in American Business* (1977). On the role of inventors, see Carroll Pursell, *The Machine in America* (1995), and B. M. Tucker, *Samuel Slater and the Origins of the American Textile Industry* (1984).

The growth of cities in the Jacksonian era can be traced in Richard C. Wade, *The Urban Frontier* (1957), and Howard Chudacoff, *The Evolution of American Urban Society* (1981). Allen F. Davis and Mark Halle, eds., *The Peoples of Philadelphia* (1973), Oscar Handlin, *Boston's Immigrants* (1968 ed.), and P. R. Knights, *The Plain People of Boston* (1971), deal with individual cities.

On immigration and ethnicity, see P. T. Knoble, *Paddy and the Republic* (1986), J. P. Dolan, *Immigrant Church: New York's Irish and German Catholics* (1982), and, generally, Philip Taylor, *The Distant Mirror: European Migration to the United States* (1971), and Stephan Thernstrom, ed., *Harvard Encyclopedia of American Ethnic Groups* (1980).

On changes in the nature of work, consult Paul Johnson, *A Shopkeeper's Millennium* (1978), Sean Wilentz, *Chants Democratic* (1984), Bruce Laurie, *Artisans into Workers* (1989), Norman Ware, *The Industrial Worker* (1990), and Anthony F. C. Wallace, *Rockdale* (1978); on women in the early factories, see Mary Blewett, *Men, Women, and Work* (1988), and Thomas Dublin, *Women at Work* (1979). On the lengthening commute to work, see Sam Bass Warner, *The Private City: Philadelphia in Three Periods of Its Growth* (1968).

Evan Cornog describes the origins and impact of the Erie Canal in *The Birth of Empire* (1998). On canal building, consult R. E. Shaw, *Canals for a Nation* (1990). Two works by Carter Goodrich, *Government Promotion of American Canals and Railroads* (1960) and *Canals and American Economic Development* (1961), describe the role of government aid in canal construction authoritatively. John Lauritz Larson, *Internal Improvement: National Public Works and the Promise of Popular Government in the Early United States* (2001), blames Andrew Jackson for the abandonment of public support for transportation infrastructure.

R. Kent Newmyer, *John Marshall and the Heroic Age of the Supreme Court* (2001) is strongly supportive of Marshall's actions; see also G. Edward White, *The Marshall Court and Cultural Change* (1991), as well as the sources cited in previous chapters.

CHAPTER 9 | JACKSONIAN DEMOCRACY

The nature of Jacksonian democracy was analyzed brilliantly by Alexis de Tocqueville, *Democracy in America* (1835–1840). Other commentaries by foreigners throw much light on Jacksonian democracy. See especially, in addition to Tocqueville, Frances Trollope, *Domestic Manners of the Americans* (1832), Michel Chevalier, *Society, Manners and Politics in the United States* (1961), Harriet Martineau, *Retrospect of Western Travel* (1838) and *Society in America* (1837), and F. J. Grund, *Aristocracy in America* (1859).

In addition to the works on Jackson cited in Debating the Past (p. 292), see Bray Hammond, *Banks and Politics in America from the Revolution to the Civil War* (1957), and J. M. McFaul, *The Politics of Jacksonian Finance* (1972). Peter Temin, *The Jacksonian Economy* (1969), minimizes the effects of Jackson's policies on economic conditions. Jill Norgren, *The Cherokee Cases* (1996) is critical of Jackson's policies toward Indians; Robert Remini is more supportive in *Andrew Jackson and His Indian Wars* (2001).

On the transformation of political parties, see Richard P. McCormick, *The Second American Party System* (1966), and Michael Holt, *The Rise and Fall of the American Whig Party* (1999), which focuses on variations at the state level. Gerald Leonard, *The Invention of Party Politics* (2002) provides a detailed study of Illinois.

On the nullification controversy, see R. E. Ellis, *The Union at Risk* (1987), and William W. Freehling, *The Road to Disunion* (1990), which stresses the close relationship between the nullifiers and the slavery issue.

For the Van Buren administration, see John Niven, *Martin Van Buren* (1983), and M. L. Wilson, *The Presidency of Martin Van Buren* (1984). The election of 1840 is treated in R. G. Gunderson, *The Log-Cabin Campaign* (1957).

Louis Masur's *1831, Year of Eclipse* (2001), provides an interesting perspective on that pivotal year.

CHAPTER 10 | THE MAKING OF MIDDLE-CLASS AMERICA

On Tocqueville and his views of America, see Alexis de Tocqueville, *Democracy in America*, J. P. Mayer, ed. (1966 edition); also Andre Jardin, *Alexis de Tocqueville* (1988). For an analysis of the middle class, see Stuart M. Blumin, *The Emergence of the Middle Class* (1989).

On the changing place of the family and the changes within it, see Mary P. Ryan, *Cradle of the Middle Class: The Family in Oneida, New York* (1981), Catherine E. Kelly, *In the New England Fashion: Reshaping Women's Lives in the Nineteenth Century* (1999), Nancy Cott, *The Bonds of Womanhood* (1977), and Carl Degler, *At Odds: Women and Family in America from the Revolution to the Present* (1980).

The Second Great Awakening has been examined both as a religious and as a social phenomenon. Still useful is Whitney Cross, *The Burned-Over District* (1950), but see also Paul E. Johnson, *A Shopkeeper's Millennium* (1978). Mark A. Noll, *America's God: From Jonathan Edwards to Abraham Lincoln* (2002) provides a broader study of the religious dimension of reform movements.

For the Shakers, see Stephen J. Stein, *The Shaker Experience in America* (1992). Richard Bushman, *Joseph Smith and the Beginnings of Mormonism* (1984), provides a good introduction to the subject. For a broader study see Leonard J. Arrington, *The Mormon Experience* (1992).

For the origins of feminism, see Nancy Cott, *The Grounding of Modern Feminism* (1987), Ellen C. DuBois, *Feminism and Suffrage: The Emergence of an Independent Women's Movement in America, 1848–1869* (1978), and Linda K. Kerber, *No Constitutional Right to Be Ladies* (1998). Bruce Dorsey, *Reforming Men and Women* (2002) shows how men often initiated reforms but women took control of them.

On utopianism generally, see Ronald G. Walters, *American Reformers, 1815–1860* (1978). Accounts of the temperance movement include Barbara L. Epstein, *The Politics of Domesticity* (1981), and W. J. Rorabaugh, *The Alcoholic Republic* (1979).

For a general study of the context of abolitionism, see Richard S. Newman, *The Transformation of American Abolitionism* (2002). For sharply contrasting views of the abolitionist movement, see Stanley Elkins, *Slavery* (1975), and Lewis Perry and Michael Fellman, eds., *Anti-Slavery Reconsidered* (1979). Women's role in the movement is discussed in Julie Roy Jeffrey, *The Great Silent Army of Abolitionism* (1998). The persistence of slavery in the North, a topic that is often overlooked, is examined in Joanne P. Melish, *Disowning Slavery* (1998). Biographical accounts include John L. Thomas, *The Liberator: William Lloyd Garrison* (1963), Gerda Lerner, *The Grimké Sisters from South Carolina* (1967), and Nathan Huggins, *Slave and Citizen: The Life of Frederick Douglass* (1980).

Carolyn L. Karcher, *The First Woman in the Republic: A Cultural Biography of Lydia Maria Child* (1994), Charles Capper, *Margaret Fuller* (1992), Elizabeth Griffith, *In Her Own Rights: The Life of Elizabeth Cady Stanton* (1984), and Kathryn K. Sklar, *Catharine Beecher* (1973), are solid biographies of important women in the era.

On Sojourner Truth, see Nell Irvin Painter, *Sojourner Truth* (1996) and, for her time with Mathias, Paul F. Johnson and Sean Wilentz, *Kingdom of Mathias* (1994).

CHAPTER 11 | AN AMERICAN CULTURE

Useful surveys of cultural and intellectual currents in this period are Daniel Boorstin, *The Americans: The National Experience* (1967), and Rush Welter, *The Mind of America, 1820–1860* (1975). See also Richard Hofstadter, *Anti-intellectualism in American Life* (1963), and Stow Persons, *The Decline of American Gentility* (1975), for a more critical assessment.

For Emerson and Thoreau, see the biographies by Robert D. Richardson, *Emerson: The Mind on Fire* (1995), and *Henry Thoreau: The Life of the Mind* (1986). For Poe, the biography by Kenneth Silverman (1991) is excellent. David S. Reynold's *Walt Whitman's America* (1995) examines the poet's relation to other trends in American life. See also Hershel Parker, *Herman Melville: 1819–1851* (1996) and *Herman Melville: 1851–1891* (2002).

On the cultural life of the South, see Bertram Wyatt-Brown, *Hearts of Darkness* (2003), and Drew Faust, *A Sacred Circle* (1977).

On education, in addition to works cited in the previous chapter, see Lawrence A. Cremin, *American Education: The National Experience* (1980), and C. F. Kaestle, *Pillars of the Republic* (1983). Jill Lepore, *A Is For American* (2002) is also useful.

Scholars have recently been interested in the proliferation of unconventional popular ideas during these years. See David S. Reynolds, *Beneath the American Renaissance* (1988), and John M. Brooke, *The Refiner's Fire* (1994). In *Carnival on the Page: Popular Print Media in Antebellum America* (2000), Isabelle Lehuu argues that a rowdy and "subversive" popular press was another manifestation of this subversive culture.

CHAPTER 12 | WESTWARD EXPANSION

For John Tyler, perhaps the least examined of the presidents, see Dan Monroe, *The Republican Vision of John Tyler* (2003); on the Whigs more generally, see Michael F. Holt, *The Rise and Fall of the American Whig Party* (1999), and Daniel Walker Howe, *The Political Culture of the American Whigs* (1979).

On diplomatic affairs, see P. A. Varg, *United States Foreign Relations: 1820–1860* (1979), and D. M. Pletcher, *The Diplomacy of Annexation: Texas, Oregon, and the Mexican War* (1973).

The new expansionism is discussed in Frederick Merk, *Manifest Destiny and Mission in American History* (1963) and *The Monroe Doctrine and American Expansionism* (1966). H. N. Smith, *Virgin Land* (1950), is also important for an understanding of this subject. The course of western development is treated in R. A. Billington and Martin Ridge, *The Far Western Frontier* (1982). Important recent studies of the California gold rush include Malcolm J. Rohrbough, *Days of Gold* (1997), and Susan Lee Johnson, *Roaring Camp: The Social World of the California Gold Rush* (2000). On the effects of the settling of the Great Plains, see Elliott West, *The Contested Plains: Indians, Goldseekers and the Rush to Colorado* (1998) and J. D. Unruh, *The Plains Across* (1979). Francis Parkman's classic account, *The Oregon Trail* (1849) is absorbing.

For the election of 1844, see J. C. N. Paul, *Rift in the Democracy* (1961). Two recent, brief biographies of Polk are John Seigenthaler, *James K. Polk* (2004), and Thomas M. Leonard, *James K. Polk: A Clear and Unquestionable Destiny* (2001). The standard biography of Polk is Charles G. Sellers's *James K. Polk* (1957–1966). William Dusinberre, *Slavemaster President: The Double Career of James Polk* (2003) is sharply critical.

On the Mexican War, see Richard Bruce Winders, *Mr. Polk's Army* (1997), R. W. Johannsen, *To the Halls of the Montezumas* (1987), and K. J. Bauer, *The Mexican War* (1974). J. H. Schroeder, *Mr. Polk's War* (1973), discusses American opposition to the conflict. See also Marshall De Bruhl, *Sword of San Jacinto* (1993), a biography of Sam Houston. Randy Roberts and James S. Olson, *A Line in the Sand: The Alamo in Blood and Memory* (2001) is an accessible account.

For the Compromise of 1850, see David M. Potter, *The Impending Crisis, 1848–1861* (1976), and Holman Hamilton, *Prologue to Conflict* (1964). See also Robert Remini, *Daniel Webster: The Man and His Time* (1997), and Irving H. Bartlett, *John C. Calhoun* (1993).

CHAPTER 13 | THE SECTIONS GO THEIR WAYS

Most of the volumes dealing with economic developments mentioned in earlier chapters continue to be useful for this period. On the Panic of 1857, see J. L. Huston, *The Panic of 1857 and the Coming of the Civil War* (1987). For a useful comparative study, see John Majewski, *A House Dividing: Economic Development in Pennsylvania and Virginia before the Civil War* (2000). On the economy of the South, see Gavin Wright, *The Political Economy of the Cotton South* (1978), and Michael Tadman, *Speculators and Slaves* (1989).

On slavery, in addition to the essential works listed in Debating the Past (p. 367), see Brenda Stevenson, *Life in Black and White* (1996), and Walter Johnson, *Soul by Soul: Life Inside the Antebellum Slave Market* (1999), which focuses on New Orleans. Recent evidence of slave resistance is documented in John Hope Franklin and Loren Schweninger, *Runaway Slaves* (1999), David Robertson, *Denmark Vesey* (1999), and Douglas R. Egerton, *Gabriel's Rebellion* (1993). An earlier study is Eugene D. Genovese, *From Rebellion to Revolution* (1979).

Excellent regional studies include Peter Coclanis, *The Shadow of a Dream* (1989), for South Carolina, as well as Charles E. Joyner, *Down by the Riverside: A South Carolina Slave Community* (1984), and Ann Patton Malone, *Sweet Chariot: Slave Family and Household Structure in Nineteenth-Century Louisiana* (1992).

Among specialized volumes, Bertram Wyatt-Brown, *Southern Honor* (1982), and Ira Berlin, *Slaves Without Masters* (1975), are important. Richard C. Wade, *Slavery in the Cities* (1964), contends that urban life eroded slavery, while Robert Starobin, *Industrial Slavery in the Old South* (1970), found that the institution could be adapted to industrial purposes. Most local studies take an intermediate position; see, for example, Midori Takagi, *"Rearing Wolves to Our Own Destruction": Slavery in Richmond, Virginia, 1782–1865* (1999).

On industrial developments, see H. J. Habbakuk, *American and British Technology in the Nineteenth Century* (1962), and Nathan Rosenberg, *Technology and American Economic Growth* (1972). John F. Stover, *American Railroads* (1997), is a good survey. Among the specialized studies of railroad development see Sarah Gordon, *Passage to Union* (1997), which considers the political implications of railroad development, as well as T. C. Cochran, *Railroad Leaders* (1953).

On labor history, many of the books cited in the three previous chapters apply to this one as well. On the New England shoe industry and labor organization, see Mary Blewett, *Men, Women and Work* (1988); for a more general study see her *Constant Turmoil: The Politics of Industrial Life in Nineteenth Century New England* (2000). For workingmen's political activities, Edward Pessen's *Most Uncommon Jacksonians* (1967) remains valuable.

CHAPTER 14 | THE COMING OF THE CIVIL WAR

On the origins of the Civil War, in addition to the Debating the Past (p. 391), see David M. Potter, *The Impending Crisis* (1976), Don E. Fehrenbacher, *Sectional Crisis and Southern Constitutionalism* (1995), and Marshall De Rosa, *The Politics of Dissolution* (1998). In *States' Rights and the Union* (2000), as in his other works, Forrest McDonald affirms the South's right to secede. William A. Link, *Roots of Secession: Slavery and Politics in Antebellum Virginia* (2003) is a useful state study.

On slave resistance, see especially John Hope Franklin and Loren Schweninger, *Runaway Slaves* (1999), William Dusinberre, *Them Dark Days: Slavery in the American Rice Swamps* (1996), and Steven Weisenburger, *Modern Medea: A Family Story of Slavery and Child-Murder from the Old South* (1998).

On the enforcement of the Fugitive Slave Act, see S. W. Campbell, *The Slave Catchers* (1970), and T. D. Morris, *Free Men All: The Personal Liberty Laws* (1974). Everyone should read Harriet Beecher Stowe's *Uncle Tom's Cabin*. Joan Hedrick's *Harriet Beecher Stowe* (1994) is excellent.

For the foreign policy of the 1850s, see C. H. Brown, *Agents of Manifest Destiny* (1980), and P. B. Wiley and Korogi Ichiro, *Yankees in the Land of the Gods* (1990).

On Stephen A. Douglas, see Robert W. Johannsen, *Stephen A. Douglas* (1973). Sumner's role in the deepening crisis is brilliantly discussed in David H. Donald, *Charles Sumner and the Coming of the Civil War* (1960) and *Charles Sumner and the Rights of Man* (1970); a more recent, brief study is Frederick J. Blue, *Charles Sumner and the Conscience of the North* (1994). Jean Baker, *James Buchanan* (2004) is solid and concise. On Dred Scott, see Paul Finkelman, *Dred Scott v. Sandford* (1997).

For Lincoln's own well-crafted words, see Abraham Lincoln, *Selections* (2 vols., 1989). The best modern biographies of Lincoln are David H. Donald, *Lincoln* (1995), and Mark Neely, *The Last Best Hope on Earth* (1993). Lincoln's early struggles are thoughtfully examined in Douglas L. Wilson, *Honor's Voice: The Transformation of Abraham Lincoln* (1998). W. E. Gienapp, *The Origins of the Republican Party* (1987), and Eric Foner, *Free Soil, Free Labor, Free Men* (1970), are excellent analyses of Republican ideas and policies. Allen Guelzo, *Lincoln's Emancipation Proclamation* (2004) is also useful.

John Stauffer, *Black Hearts of Men* (2001) examines John Brown and other radical abolitionists. See also Stephen B. Oates, *To Purge This Land with Blood* (1984).

CHAPTER 15 | THE WAR TO SAVE THE UNION

The best survey of the Civil War period is James M. McPherson, *Battle Cry of Freedom* (1988), but see also Russell F. Weigley, *A Great Civil War* (2000).

On the precipitating events of the war, see Maury Klein, *Days of Defiance: Sumter, Secession and the Coming of the Civil War* (1997), and Wallace Hettle, *The Peculiar Democracy: Southern Democrats in Peace and Civil War* (2001).

For Lincoln, in addition to books mentioned in previous chapters, see Philip Paludan, *The Presidency of Abraham Lincoln* (1994). Lincoln's dealings with the Radicals have been extensively investigated. H. L. Trefousse, *The Radical Republicans: Lincoln's Vanguard for Racial Justice* (1969), which praises Lincoln's management of the Radicals and minimizes his differences with them, is a good summary, but see also Richard Franklin Bensel, *Yankee Leviathan: The Origins of Central State Authority in America* (1990). Mark E. Neely, *The Fate of Liberty* (1991) examines Lincoln's position on civil liberties. Frank Klement, *The Limits of Dissent* (1998) focuses on Clement Vallandigham. For the movement to make abolition a war aim and the reaction to it, see Michael Vorenberg, *Final Freedom* (2001).

On economic issues, see Heather Cox Richardson, *The Greatest Nation on Earth: Republican Economy Policies During the Civil War* (1997), and Bray Hammond, *Sovereignty and an Empty Purse: Banks and Politics in the Civil War* (1970).

On African Americans in the Union army, see Joseph T. Glatthaar, *Forged in Battle: The Civil War Alliance of Black Soldiers and White Officers* (1990); Peter Burchard, *One Gallant Rush* (1965), recounts the story of Robert Gould Shaw and the Massachusetts 54th. See also Martin H. Blatt, *Hope & Glory: Essays on the Legacy of the 54th Massachusetts Regiment* (2001).

For aspects of economic and social history, see Philip S. Paludan, *"A People's Contest": The Union at War* (1988). Edward L. Ayers, *In the Presence of Mine Enemies* (2003) examines the effect of the war on various communities. For women and the war, see Drew Gilpin Faust, *Mothers of Invention* (1997), Judith Ann Giesberg, *Civil War Sisterhood: The U.S. Sanitary Commission and Women's Politics in Transition* (2000), and Laura Edwards, *Scarlett Doesn't Live Here Anymore* (2000). Elizabeth Young considers the literary heritage of women and the war in *Disarming the Nation: Women's Writing and the American Civil War* (1999). See also Iver Bernstein, *The New York City Draft Riots* (1990).

For the Confederacy, see Gary W. Gallagher, *The Confederate War* (1997). See also his edited collection, *Lee the Soldier* (1996). On divisions within the Confederacy, see William W. Freehling, *The South vs. The South: How Anti-Confederate Southerners Shaped the Course of the Civil War* (2001). Important biographies include William Cooper, *Jefferson Davis, American* (2000). See also Mark Grimsley and Brooks D. Simpson, eds., *Collapse of the Confederacy* (2001), and Steven V. Ash, *When the Yankees Came: Conflict and Chaos in the Occupied South* (1995).

Gerald F. Linderman, *Embattled Courage* (1988) argues that the soldiers on both sides grew disillusioned with the fighting; the persistence of the initial ideals is a theme in James McPherson, *What They Fought For, 1861–1865* (1994), and Reid Mitchell, *The Vacant Chair* (1993). Bertram Wyatt-Brown, *The Shaping of Southern Culture: Honor, Grace and War, 1760s–1880s* (2001) contends that while soldiers on both sides used the same rhetoric to defend their cause, they had different notions of what terms such as "honor" meant.

Among the biographies of Civil War generals, northern and southern, the following are especially noteworthy: Brooks D. Simpson, *Ulysses S. Grant: Triumph over Adversity, 1822–1865* (2000), Jean E. Smith, *Grant* (2001), William S. McFeely, *Grant* (1981), Michael Fellman, *The Making of Robert E. Lee* (2000), Douglass S. Freeman, *R. E. Lee* (1934–1935), James I. Robertson, *Stonewall Jackson* (1997), Stephen W. Sears, *George B. McClellan* (1988), Stanley P. Hirshson, *The White Tecumseh: A Biography of William T. Sherman* (1997), and Chester G. Hearn, *Admiral David Glasgow Farragut* (1998).

The diplomacy of the Civil War period is covered in two works by Howard Jones, *Union in Peril* (1992), on British intervention, and *Abraham Lincoln and a New Birth of Freedom* (1999), on issues of slavery. See also John Taylor, *William Henry Seward* (1991).

John C. Waugh, *Reelecting Lincoln* (1997) considers the election of 1864. The assassination of Lincoln and its aftermath is the subject of Jay Winik, *April 1865: The Month That Saved America* (2001).

The legacy of the Civil War is thoughtfully examined in David W. Blight, *Race and Reunion: The Civil War in American Memory* (2001), and Tony Horwitz, *Confederates in the Attic: Dispatches from the Unfinished Civil War* (1998).

CHAPTER 16 | RECONSTRUCTION AND THE SOUTH

Lincoln's ideas about Reconstruction are analyzed in William C. Harris, *With Charity for All* (1997) and in many of the Lincoln volumes mentioned in earlier chapters. Hans Trefousse, *Andrew Johnson: A Biography* (1989) is a balanced account. See also Brooks D. Simpson, *The Reconstruction Presidents* (2001), Eric L. McKitrick, *Andrew Johnson and Reconstruction* (1960), and M. L. Benedict, *The Impeachment and Trial of Andrew Johnson* (1973).

A number of biographies provide information helpful in understanding the Radicals. The most important are Hans Trefousse, *Thaddeus Stevens* (1997), and David Donald, *Charles Sumner and the Rights of Man* (1970). J. M. McPherson, *The Struggle for Equality: Abolitionists and the Negro in* the Civil War and Reconstruction (1964) is also valuable. On the Fourteenth Amendment, see W. E. Nelson, *The Fourteenth Amendment* (1988); on the Fifteenth Amendment, see William Gillette, *The Right to Vote* (1965).

Conditions in the South during Reconstruction are discussed in Edward Ayers, *The Promise of the New South* (1992). The Freedmen's Bureau is examined in Paul Cimbala, *Under the Guardianship of the Nation* (1997). See also R. H. Abbott, *The Republican Party and the South* (1986), Michael Perman, *Reunion Without Compromise* (1973), H. N. Rabinowitz, *Race Relations in the Urban South* (1978), J. L. Roark, *Masters Without Slaves* (1977), and Leon Litwack, *Been in the Storm Too Long* (1979). Daniel Stowell's *Rebuilding Zion* (1998) explores the religious dimensions of Reconstruction.

Of state studies see, for Virginia, Jane E. Dailey, *Before Jim Crow* (2000); for South Carolina, Julie Saville, *The Work of Reconstruction* (1994), W. L. Rose, *Rehearsal for Reconstruction* (1964), Thomas Holt, *Black over White: Negro Political Leadership in South Carolina* (1977); for Texas, Randolph B. Campbell, *Grass-Roots Reconstruction in Texas* (1997). Much recent work on the Ku Klux Klan similarly focuses on particular states: see Lou F. Williams, *The Great South Carolina Ku Klux Klan Trials* (1996), Glenn Feldman, *Politics, Society and the Klan in Alabama* (1999), and Noel Fisher, *War at Every Door* (1997), which examines East Tennessee.

On the economic and social effects of Reconstruction, see G. D. Jaynes, *Branches Without Roots: Genesis of the Black Working Class* (1986), R. L. Ransom and Richard Sutch, *One Kind of Freedom: The Economic Consequences of Emancipation* (1977), Robert Higgs, *Competition and Coercion* (1977), and C. F. Oubre, *Forty Acres and a Mule* (1978). The ambiguities of dependence and independence as they relate to racial and gender issues are explored in Laura F. Edwards, *Gendered Strife and Confusion* (1997), and Amy Dru Stanley, *From Bondage to Contract* (1998).

On Grant's presidency, see Jean Edwards Smith, *Grant* (2001), Geoffrey Perret, *Ulysses S. Grant* (1997) and W. S. McFeely, *Grant* (1981). On the Republican reform movement, see J. G. Sproat, *"The Best Men": Liberal Reformers in the Gilded Age* (1968). For the disputed election of 1876 and the compromise following it, consult C. V. Woodward, *Reunion and Reaction* (1951), and William Gillette, *Retreat from Reconstruction* (1980).

David W. Blight, *Race and Reunion* (2001) considers the Civil War and Reconstruction in a deeper historical perspective.

Chapter 17 | In the Wake of War

Recent historians of the West do not regard it as a frontier to be settled, but as a region where white settlers and Native American peoples converged, to the destruction of the latter's way of life. For the older view, see Frederick Jackson Turner's *The Frontier in American History* (1920), which has been updated in R. A. Billington and Martin Ridge, *Westward Expansion* (1982). For a summary of the newer interpretation, see Gregory H. Nobles, *American Frontiers* (1997). See also Patricia Nelson Limerick, *The Legacy of Conquest* (1987), Richard White, *"It's Your Misfortune and None of My Own"* (1991), and Elliott West, *Contested Plains: Indians, Goldseekers, and the Rush to Colorado* (1998).

The economic, political, and legal ideas current in this period are covered in David M. Wrobel, *Promised Lands* (2002), Sidney Fine, *Laissez Faire and the General Welfare State* (1956), and James W. Hurst, *Law and the Conditions of Freedom in the Nineteenth Century United States* (1956).

On government policy and white attitudes toward Indians, see Robert F. Berkhofer, Jr., *The White Man's Indian* (1978), Robert Wooster, *The Military and U.S. Indian Policy* (1988), and Andrew C. Isenberg, *The Destruction of the Bison* (2000).

On race relations in the South, see Michael Perman, *Struggle for Mastery: Disfranchisement in the South, 1888–1908* (2001), Leon Litwack, *Trouble in Mind* (1998), Glenda E. Gilmore, *Gender and Jim Crow* (1996), Joel Williamson, *The Crucible of Race* (1984), C. Vann Woodward, *The Strange Career of Jim Crow* (1966), and Samuel Spencer, *Booker T. Washington* (1967). For a thoughtful study of the persistence of the black elite in Washington, D.C., see Jacqueline M. Moore, *Leading the Race* (1999). On immigration, see Ronald Takaki, *Strangers from a Different Shore: A History of Asian Americans* (1989), and John Higham, *Strangers in the Land* (1955).

Two superb recent studies, in addition to Elliott West, cited above, have transformed our understanding of the California gold rush: Susan Lee Johnson, *Roaring Camp: The Social World of the*

California Gold Rush (2000), and Malcolm J. Rohrbough, *Days of Gold: The California Gold Rush and the American Nation* (1997). Bonanza farming is described in H. M. Drache, *The Day of the Bonanza* (1964). For women on the frontier, see also Julie R. Jeffrey, *Frontier Women* (1979), John Mack Faragher, *Women and Men on the Overland Trail* (1979), Sandra L. Myres, *Westering Women and the Frontier Experience* (1982), and Paula Petric, *No Step Backward: Women and Family on the Rocky Mountain Frontier* (1987).

For a compelling account of the development of transcontinental railroads see David Haward Bain, *Empire Express: Building the First Transcontinental Railroad* (1999). See also David Lavender, *The Great Persuader* (1970), Albro Martin, *James J. Hill* (1976), and Robert G. Athearn, *Union Pacific Country* (1971).

On cattle ranching on the Plains, a good account is Lewis Atherton, *The Cattle Kings* (1961), but see also Don Worcester, *The Chisholm Trail* (1980). For the cowboy and his life, see Joe B. Frantz and Julian E. Choate, *The American Cowboy* (1955), and Robert R. Dykstra, *The Cattle Towns* (1968).

CHAPTER 18 | AN INDUSTRIAL GIANT

In addition to the works cited in Debating the Past (p. 519), see John A. Garraty, *The New Commonwealth* (1968), Alfred D. Chandler, Jr., *Railroads: The Nation's First Big Business* (1965), and Thomas Cochran, *Railroad Leaders* (1953). On the ways that technology transformed the way people understood daily life, see David E. Nye, *Electrifying America* (1990), and Jill Jonnes, *Empires of Light* (2003). Sven Beckert, *The Monied Metropolis: New York City and the Consolidation of the American Bourgeoisie, 1850–1896* (2001) outlines the special significance of that city in the nation's economic development and cultural mores.

The nation's expansive economy in the 1990s sparked interest in the leading businessmen and inventors a century earlier. For a detailed study of the key investment figure, see Jean Strouse, *Morgan: American Financier* (1999). Other examples include Harold C. Livesay, *Andrew Carnegie and the Rise of Big Business* (2000); Michael P. Malone, *James J. Hill* (1996); Ron Chernow, *Titan* (1998), on John D. Rockefeller and the oil industry; James A. Mackey, *Alexander Graham Bell: A Life* (1997); and Neil Baldwin, *Edison: Inventing the Century* (2001).

For the radical critics, see John L. Thomas, *Alternative Americas: Henry George, Edward Bellamy, Henry Demarest Lloyd* (1983), Howard H. Quint, *The Forging of American Socialism* (1964), L. Glen Seretan, *Daniel De Leon: The Odyssey of an American Marxist* (1979), and also the radicals' own writings.

On the growth of unions see David Montgomery, *Beyond Equality* (1967), Leon Fink, *Workingmen's Democracy: The Knights of Labor and American Politics* (1983), and Nick Salvatore, *Eugene V. Debs* (1982). Jo Ann Argersinger, *Making the Amalgamated* (1999) describes the relation of gender and ethnicity in the rise of the clothing workers' union in Baltimore. Robert E. Weird, *Knights Unhorsed* (2000) blames internal dissension for the Knights' rapid decline. Lawrence Blickman, *A Living Wage* (1997) insists that labor radicalism persisted even after unionized workers won steady wages. The important strikes and labor violence of the period are covered in David O. Stowell, *Streets, Railroads, and the Great Strike of 1877* (1999), R. V. Bruce, *1877: Year of Violence* (1959), Paul Avrich, *The Haymarket Tragedy* (1984), Carl S. Smith, *Urban Disorder and the Shape of Belief* (1995), and Richard Schneirov, ed., *The Pullman Strike and the Crisis of the 1890s* (1999). On working-class culture, see Herbert G. Gutman, *Work, Culture, and Society in Industrializing America* (1976), and Roy Rosenzweig, *Eight Hours for What We Will* (1983). On the challenge confronting the unions, see David Montgomery, *The Fall of the House of Labor* (1987).

CHAPTER 19 | AMERICAN SOCIETY IN THE INDUSTRIAL AGE

Henry Adams, *The Education of Henry Adams* (1918), is a fascinating if highly personal view of the period, and James Bryce, *The American Commonwealth* (1888), while primarily a political analysis, contains a great deal of information about social conditions. For two classic accounts of the settlement house movement, see Jane Addams, *Twenty Years at Hull House* (1910), and Lillian Wald, *The House on Henry Street* (1915). Addams's own life is the subject of two recent biographies: Jean

Bethke Elshtain, *Jane Addams and the Dream of American Democracy* (2002), and Victoria Bissel Brown, *The Education of Jane Addams* (2004).

An enormous number of books deal with the social history of late nineteenth-century America. John A. Garraty, *The New Commonwealth* (1968), treats most of the subjects covered in this chapter; Arthur M. Schlesinger's classic study, *The Rise of the City* (1933), provides a wealth of information about social trends. Robert Wiebe's *The Search for Order* (1967) shows how corporate and administrative bureaucracies overspread the nation, while Alan Trachtenberg, *The Incorporation of America* (1982), considers the cultural implications of Wiebe's insight. See also Gunther Barth, *City People* (1980).

On middle-class life and culture, see John Kasson, *Rudeness and Civility* (1990), Karen Halttunen, *Confidence Men and Painted Women* (1982), Burton Bledstein, *The Culture of Professionalism* (1976), and Mark C. Carnes, *Secret Ritual and Manhood in Victorian America* (1989). Karen Lystra, *Searching the Heart* (1989), emphasizes the close character of marriage, and Peter Gay, *The Bourgeois Experience* (1984–1997), argues that the middle classes throughout the Western world were not prudes; the repressive hypothesis is outlined in Ronald Walter, *Primers for Prudery* (1974). On contraception see Janet F. Brodie, *Contraception and Abortion in Nineteenth-Century America* (1994). On the family generally, see Colleen McDannell, *The Christian Home in Victorian America* (1986), and Carl Degler, *At Odds* (1980). On prostitution, Marilyn Wood Hill, *Their Sisters' Keepers* (1993), and Timothy Gilfoyle, *City of Eros* (1992). On issues of consumption see Daniel Horowitz, *The Morality of Spending* (1985), William Leach, *Land of Desire: Merchants, Power, and the Rise of a New American Culture* (1993), and Elaine S. Abelson, *When Ladies' Go A-Thieving* (1989).

A broad survey on issues of disease is Gerald N. Grob, *The Deadly Truth: A History of Disease in America* (2002).

On working-class culture, Keith Peiss, *Cheap Amusements: Working Women and Leisure in Turn-of-the-Century New York* (1986), and Roy Rosenzweig, *Eight Hours for What We Will* (1983) are excellent. Roy Rosenzweig and Elizabeth Blackmar provide an interesting account of cultural tensions between middle and working classes in *The Park and the People: A History of Central Park* (1992).

A brief interpretive history of urban development is Charles N. Glaab and A. Theodore Brown, *A History of Urban America* (1967). Kenneth T. Jackson, *Crabgrass Frontier* (1985), is a pioneering history of suburban development, and Jon C. Teaford, *The Unheralded Triumph* (1984), gives weight to the accomplishments of the cities as well as to their inadequacies. For the growing pains of American cities, consult Jacob Riis, *How the Other Half Lives* (1890). S. B. Warner, Jr., *Streetcar Suburbs* (1962) is an interesting study of Boston's development that is full of suggestive ideas about late nineteenth-century growth. See also Paul Boyer, *Urban Masses and Moral Order in America* (1978).

On the early development of intercollegiate sports, see Ronald A. Smith, *Sports and Freedom: The Rise of Big-Time College Athletics* (1988); on sports and modernization, see Melvin L. Adelman, *A Sporting Time* (1986), and Allen Guttmann, *From Ritual to Record* (1978). The response of religion to industrialism is discussed in Henry F. May, *Protestant Churches and Industrial America* (1949).

CHAPTER 20 | INTELLECTUAL AND CULTURAL TRENDS

All the surveys of American intellectual history deal extensively with this period. The modern classics include Louis Hartz, *The Liberal Tradition in America* (1955), Clinton Rossiter, *Conservatism in America* (1962), and Henry S. Commager, *The American Mind* (1950). Louis Menand, *The Metaphysical Club* (2001), John Patrick Diggins, *The Promise of Pragmatism* (1994), Jackson Lears, *No Place for Grace: Antimodernism and the Transformation of American Culture, 1880–1920* (1981), and Gail Bederman, *Manliness and Civilization* (1995) are also stimulating.

On the impact of Darwin on late nineteenth-century America, see Richard Hofstadter's *Social Darwinism in American Thought* (1955), though his view has been substantially modified by Robert C. Bannister, *Social Darwinism* (1979). See also Carl Degler, *In Search of Human Nature: The Decline and Revival of Darwinism in American Social Thought* (1991), and Paul Crook, *Darwinism, War and History* (1994). James Turner, *Without God Without Creed: The Origins of Unbelief in America* (1996), contends that Darwinism promoted skepticism.

A recent interpretation of the Chautauqua movement is John E. Tapia, *Circuit Chautauqua* (1997). On journalism, see especially David Nasaw, *The Chief: The Life of William Randolph Hearst* (2000), and George Juergens, *Joseph Pulitzer and the New York World* (1966).

On higher education, see George Marsden, *The Soul of the American University* (1994), and Laurence R. Veysey, *The Emergence of the American University* (1965). Kim Townsend, *Manhood at Harvard* (1996), William McNeill, *Hutchins' University* (1992), on the University of Chicago, and Robert McCaughey, *Stand, Columbia* (2004) are especially stimulating. Thorstein Veblen, *The Higher Learning in America* (1918) is full of provocative opinions.

Good introductions to law and the social sciences during this period include, respectively, Morton Horwitz, *The Transformation of American Law, 1870–1960* (1992), and Dorothy Ross, *The Origins of American Social Science* (1991). See also Linda Simon, *Genuine Reality: A Life of William James* (1998). For trends in educational theory, see Lawrence A. Cremin, *American Education: The Metropolitan Experience* (1988).

On women, see Rosalind Rosenberg, *Beyond Separate Spheres: Intellectual Roots of Modern Feminism* (1982), and Regina Morantz-Sanchez, *Sympathy and Science: Women Physicians in American Medicine* (1985). See also Jane Hunter, *How Young Ladies Became Girls: The Victorian Origins of American Girlhood* (2003).

On Twain, see Everett Emerson, *Mark Twain: A Literary Life* (1999); on Henry Adams during this period, Edward Chalfant, *Better in Darkness* (1994); on Henry James, Leon Edel, *Henry James* (1953–1962). Interesting studies of art and society include Kathleen Pyne, *Art and the Higher Life: Painting and Evolutionary Thought in Late Nineteenth-Century America* (1996), and Barbara Novak, *Nature and Culture* (1995).

CHAPTER 21 | POLITICS: LOCAL, STATE, AND NATIONAL

There are several superb analyses of the political system of the period written by men who studied it firsthand: James Bryce, *The American Commonwealth* (1888), and Woodrow Wilson, *Congressional Government* (1886). On the evolution of political parties, see Paul Kleppner, *The Third Electoral System, 1853–1892* (1979), and Michael E. McGerr, *The Decline of Popular Politics* (1986).

C. Vann Woodward, *Origins of the New South* (1951) is an important regional study. Following in Woodward's path are Heather Cox Richardson, *The Death of Reconstruction* (2001), and Michael Perman, *Struggle for Mastery: Disfranchisement in the South, 1888–1908* (2001), who focus on the 1890s as the pivotal decade for the defeat of Reconstruction. Samuel C. Hyde, Jr., examines the tension between the old planting elite of the South and plain folk in *Pistols and Politics* (1996). Suzanne Lebsock, *A Murder in Virginia* (2003), provides a fascinating account of the intersection of race, politics, and economic factors in a murder trial. On lynching, see Christopher Waldrep, *The Many Faces of Judge Lynch: Extralegal Violence and Punishment in America* (2002).

See also Gretchen Ritter, *Goldbugs and Greenbacks* (1997), Ross Evans Paulson, *Liberty, Equality and Justice: Civil Rights, Women's Rights and the Regulation of Business, 1865–1932* (1997), Irwin Unger, *The Greenback Era* (1964), Walter T. K. Nugent, *Money and American Society* (1968), Geoffrey Blodgett, *The Gentle Reformers* (1966), and Ari Hoogenboom, *Outlawing the Spoils* (1961).

Among biographies of political leaders, the following are especially worth consulting: Ari Hoogenboom, *Rutherford B. Hayes* (1995), Allan Peskin, *Garfield* (1999), Thomas C. Reeves, *Gentleman Boss: Chester A. Arthur* (1975), H. Paul Jeffers, *An Honest President* (2000); on Cleveland, Allan Nevins, *Grover Cleveland* (1932), Homer E. Socolovsky and Allan B. Spetter, *The Presidency of Benjamin Harrison* (1987), H. Wayne Morgan, *William McKinley and His America* (1963), and Stephen D. Kantrowitz, *Ben Tillman and the Reconstruction of White Supremacy* (2000).

Populism has been the subject of intensive study. Richard Hofstadter, *The Age of Reform* (1955), takes a dim view of populism as a reform movement; Lawrence Goodwyn, *Democratic Promise: The Populist Movement in America* (1976), calls it "a people's movement of mass democratic aspiration." Elizabeth Sanders, *Roots of Reform* (1999), champions the farmers' political efforts, a position amplified by Gene Clanton, *Congressional Populism and the Crisis of the 1890s* (1998). Peter Argersinger, *The Limits of Agrarian Radicalism: Western Populism and American Politics* (1995),

Sheldon Hackney, *Populism to Progressivism in Alabama* (1969), and Steven Hahn, *The Roots of Southern Populism* (1983), are more than local studies. Michael Kazin, *The Populist Persuasion* (1994), insists on the enduring legacy of the movement.

On the depression of the 1890s, consult Charles Hoffman, *The Depression of the Nineties* (1970), Carlos Schwantes, *Coxey's Army* (1985), Stanley Buder, *Pullman* (1967), and Nick Salvatore, *Eugene V. Debs* (1982). On Bryan and the election of 1896, see Paul E. Glad, *The Trumpet Soundeth* (1960), Robert W. Cherny, *A Righteous Cause: William Jennings Bryan* (1985), Stanley L. Jones, *The Presidential Election of 1896* (1964), and Robert F. Durden, *The Climax of Populism* (1965).

Chapter 22 | The Age of Reform

The Progressive Era is surveyed in A. S. Link, *Woodrow Wilson and the Progressive Era* (1954), Steven J. Diner, *A Very Different Age* (1997), and Michael McGerr, *A Fierce Discontent: The Rise and Fall of the Progressive Movement in America, 1870–1920* (2003). Two recent scholars examine American progressivism in the context of reform movements elsewhere: Daniel T. Rodgers, *Atlantic Crossings: Social Politics in a Progressive Age* (1998) and Alan Dawley, *Changing the World: American Progressives in War and Revolution* (2003). The works cited in Debating the Past (p. 614) are also essential.

The role of muckraking journalism is explored in David Nasaw, *The Chief: The Life of William Randolph Hearst* (2000). See also D. M. Chalmers, *The Social and Political Ideas of the Muckrakers* (1964), and Peter Lyon, *Success Story: The Life and Times of S. S. McClure* (1963).

On workers and the radical intellectuals, see Leon Fink, *Progressive Intellectuals and the Dilemmas of Democratic Commitment* (1997), Leslie Fishbein, *Rebels in Bohemia* (1982), Thomas Bender, *New York Intellectuals* (1987), Henry F. May, *The End of American Innocence* (1964), and Nathan G. Hale, *Freud and the Americans* (1971).

Studies of the South include Dewey W. Grantham, *The South in Modern America* (1994), and George B. Tindall, *The Emergence of the New South* (1967). For particular states, consult, for Wisconsin, Nancy Unger, *Fighting Bob La Follette* (2000) and Bernard A. Weisberger, *The La Follettes of Wisconsin* (1994); also Hoyt L. Warner, *Progressivism in Ohio* (1964), Sheldon Hackney, *Populism to Progressivism in Alabama* (1969), and Zane L. Miller, *Boss Cox's Cincinnati* (1968). See also John D. Buenker, *Urban Liberalism and Progressive Reform* (1973). Kenneth Finegold, *Experts and Politicians* (1995) compares the struggles between urban machines and reformers in New York, Cleveland, and Chicago. James J. Connolly, *The Triumph of Ethnic Progressivism* (1998) examines the political dynamics in Boston. J. Anthony Lukas, *Big Trouble* (1997), provides a detailed account of labor strife in Idaho and Colorado.

On the woman suffrage campaign, see Ellen Carol DuBois, *Harriot Stanton Blanch and the Winning of Woman Suffrage* (1997), and Gayle Gullett, *Becoming Citizens: The Emergence and Development of the California Women's Movement, 1880–1911* (2000). Other useful works include Lynn D. Gordon, *Gender and Higher Education in the Progressive Era* (1990), Robyn Muncy, *Creating a Female Dominion in American Reform, 1890–1935* (1991), and Paula Baker, *The Moral Frameworks of Public Life: Gender, Politics and the State in Rural New York, 1870–1930* (1991). On the plight of orphans, see Linda Gordon, *The Great Arizona Orphan Abduction* (1999).

Books treating special aspects of progressivism include Edward A. Purcell, *Brandeis and the Progressive Constitution* (2000), and Samuel Haber, *Efficiency and Uplift* (1964). On the regulation of business, see Tony Freyer, *Regulating Big Business: Antitrust in Great Britain and America, 1880–1990* (1992), James Weinstein, *The Corporate Ideal and the Liberal State* (1981), Albro Martin, *Enterprise Denied: Origins of the Decline of American Railroads* (1971), and Naomi Lamoreaux, *The Great Merger Movement in American Business, 1895–1940* (1985).

On African Americans, see David Levering Lewis, *W. E. B. DuBois: Biography of a Race, 1868–1919* (1993), and W. E. B. DuBois, *The Fight for Equality, 1919–1963* (2000), Charles F. Kellogg, *NAACP: A History of the National Association for the Advancement of Colored People* (1970). On the treatment of Indians, consult Frederick E. Hoxie, *A Final Promise: The Campaign to Assimilate the Indians* (1984).

H. W. Brands, *TR* (1997), and William H. Harbaugh, *Power and Responsibility* (1961) provide sound, scholarly treatments of Roosevelt's career. Edmund Morris's *Theodore Rex* (2001) is engaging. An interesting critique of Roosevelt's environmental policies can be found in Karl Jacoby, *Crimes Against Nature* (2001).

On Taft, see Donald F. Anderson, *William Howard Taft: A Conservative's Conception of the Presidency* (1973), and Paolo E. Coletta, *The Presidency of William Howard Taft* (1973). The Republican party breakup and the history of the Progressive party are discussed in John. A. Garraty, *Right-hand Man: The Life of George W. Perkins* (1960).

The standard multi-volume biography of Wilson is Arthur S. Link, *Wilson* (1947–1965). See also August Heckscher, *Woodrow Wilson* (1991), and John A. Garraty, *Woodrow Wilson* (1956).

CHAPTER 23 | FROM ISOLATION TO EMPIRE

Contemporary attitudes are reflected in Josiah Strong, *Our Country* (1885), and Alfred T. Mahan, *The Influence of Sea Power Upon History* (1890), which provides the clearest presentation of Mahan's thesis.

For post–Civil War diplomatic history the works cited in Debating the Past (p. 634) are essential. See also Milton Plesur, *America's Outward Thrust* (1971), John A. S. Grenville and George B. Young, *Politics, Strategy, and American Diplomacy: Studies in Foreign Policy* (1966), Thomas D. Schoonover, *The United States in Central America* (1991), and David Healy, *U.S. Expansionism: The Imperialist Urge in the 1890's* (1970). Emily S. Rosenberg, *Financial Missionaries to the World: The Politics and Culture of Dollar Diplomacy, 1900–1930* (1999) shows how cultural and economic forces intersected to promote expansionism.

On Hawaiian annexation, see Merze Tate, *The United States and the Hawaiian Kingdom* (1965). On the Spanish-American War, see John L. Offner, *An Unwanted War: The Diplomacy of the United States and Spain over Cuba, 1895–1898* (1992).

On the consequences of imperialism Robert L. Beisner, *Twelve Against Empire: The Anti-imperialists* (1968) contains lively and thoughtful sketches of leading foes of expansion. See also E. Berkeley Tompkins, *Anti-imperialism in the United States* (1970). For colonial problems in the Philippines, see Stuart Creighton Miller, *"Benevolent Assimilation": The American Conquest of the Philippines, 1899–1903* (1982), and H. W. Brands, *Bound to Empire: The United States and the Philippines* (1992). On the Caribbean, see Thomas O'Brien, *The Revolutionary Mission: American Enterprise in Latin America, 1900–1945* (1996). David McCullough, *The Path Between the Seas* (1977), is excellent on the history of the Panama Canal.

CHAPTER 24 | WOODROW WILSON AND THE GREAT WAR

The war on the home front is covered in David M. Kennedy, *Over Here: The First World War and American Society* (1980). Paul A. C. Koistinen, *Mobilizing for Modern War* (1997) examines the emergence of business and military ties during the war. Other useful volumes include Robert D. Cuff, *The War Industries Board* (1973), Stephen L. Vaughn, *Holding Fast the Inner Lines* (1980), which deals with the Committee on Public Information, Donald Johnson, *The Challenge to American Freedoms* (1963), and David Brody, *Steelworkers in America* (1960).

On American military participation, see Mark Meigs, *Optimism at Armageddon* (1997), and Frank E. Vandiver, *Black Jack: The Life and Times of John J. Pershing* (1977). On blacks in the army, see Arthur E. Barbeau and Florette Henri, *The Unknown Soldiers* (1974). Women's role with the AEF is examined in Susan Zeiger, *In Uncle Sam's Service* (1999).

On the peace settlement, in addition to the biographies of Wilson, consult Thomas J. Knock, *The War to End All Wars: Woodrow Wilson and the Quest for a New World Order* (1992), A. J. Mayer, *Politics and Diplomacy of Peacemaking* (1967), John M. Cooper, *Breaking the Heart of the World* (2001), focusing on Wilson, John A. Garraty, *Henry Cabot Lodge* (1953), and Ralph Stone, *The Irreconcilables* (1970).

On labor, see David Montgomery, *The Fall of the House of Labor: The Workplace, the State, and American Labor Activism, 1865–1921* (1987). For a detailed study of organized labor in the South, see Bryant Simon, *A Fabric of Defeat* (1998). Kathleen Kennedy, *Disloyal Mothers and Scurrilous Citizens* (1999), examines the intersection of war, gender, and free speech. On radicalism and the red scare, see R. K. Murray, *The Red Scare* (1955), Stanley Coben, *A. Mitchell Palmer* (1963), David

Brody, *The Steel Strike of 1919* (1965), and E. Anthony Lukas, *Big Trouble* (1997), on labor disturbances in the Far West. On the election of 1920, see Wesley Bagby, *The Road to Normalcy* (1962), Burl Noggle, *Into the Twenties* (1974), and Robert K. Murray, *The Harding Era* (1969). On the Spanish influenza epidemic see John Barry, *The Great Influenza* (2004), and Gina Kolata, *Flu: The Story of the Great Influenza Pandemic of 1918 and the Search for the Virus That Caused It* (1999).

Wilson's handling of foreign relations is discussed in several volumes by Arthur S. Link: *Woodrow Wilson and the Progressive Era* (1954), and *Wilson the Diplomatist* (1957). See also N. Gordon Levin, Jr., *Woodrow Wilson and World Politics* (1968), Lloyd Ambrosius, *Woodrow Wilson and the American Diplomatic Tradition* (1987), and Manfred Jonas, *The United States and Germany* (1984). Latin American affairs under Wilson are treated in Dana G. Munro, *Intervention and Dollar Diplomacy in the Caribbean* (1964).

CHAPTER 25 | POSTWAR SOCIETY AND CULTURE: CHANGE AND ADJUSTMENT

In addition to the summaries outlined in Debating the Past (p. 694), Ann Douglas, *Terrible Honesty: Mongrel Manhattan in the 1920s* (1995), emphasizes the positive aspects of urban life, and Stanley Coben, *Rebellion Against Victorianism* (1991), emphasizes its elements of change. David Goldberg's survey, *Discontented America* (1999), focuses on divisions of race, ethnicity, and class. See also the volumes mentioned in previous chapters.

Nativism and immigration restriction are covered in Desmond King, *Making Americans* (2000), and John Higham, *Strangers in the Land* (1955). On changes in the family, see Steven Mintz and Susan Kellogg, *Domestic Revolutions* (1988); on other social trends, John D'Emilio and Estelle Freedman, *Intimate Matters* (1988), and Paula Fass, *The Damned and the Beautiful* (1977).

The "new" woman is discussed in Nancy F. Cott, *The Grounding of Modern Feminism* (1987), William Chafe, *The American Woman* (1972), Ellen Chesler, *Woman of Valor* (1992) (on Margaret Sanger and the birth control movement), Dorothy M. Brown, *Setting a Course: American Women in the 1920s* (1987), and Nancy Woloch, *Women and the American Experience* (1971). Women workers are dealt with in Winifred D. Wandersee, *Women's Work and Family Values* (1981). Peter N. Stearns, *Anxious Parents* (2003) is a survey of childrearing advice, with special emphasis on the early twentieth century.

On the evolution of celebrity in popular culture, see Charles L. Ponce de Leon, *Self-Exposure: Human-Interest Journalism and the Emergence of Celebrity in America, 1890–1940* (2002). On Hollywood, see Steven J. Ross, *Working-Class Hollywood: Silent Film and the Shaping of Class in America* (1998), and Robert Sklar, *Movie-Made America* (1976). On radio, see Susan J. Douglas, *Inventing American Broadcasting* (1987), Philip T. Rosen, *The Modern Stentors: Radio Broadcasting and the Federal Government* (1980), and Hugh R. Slotten, *Radio and Television Regulation: Broadcast Technology in the United States* (2000). Tona J. Hangen, *Redeeming the Dial: Radio, Religion, and Popular Culture in America* (2002), examines the intersection of popular culture and religion. On the rise of consumer credit, see Lendol Calder, *Financing the American Dream* (1999).

Fundamentalism is treated in Joel A. Carpenter, *Revive Us Again: The Reawakening of American Fundamentalism* (1997); the Scopes trial in Edward J. Larson, *Summer for the Gods: The Scopes Trial and America's Continuing Debate over Science and Religion* (1997), and Paul Conkin, *When All the Gods Trembled* (1998). On prohibition see Andrew Sinclair, *Prohibition: The Era of Excess* (1962), and Stanley Walker, *The Night Club Era* (1999), which focuses on New York. On the Klan, consult Nancy MacLean, *Behind the Mask of Chivalry: The Making of the Second Ku Klux Klan* (1994), Jim Ruiz, *The Black Hood of the Ku Klux Klan* (1998), Kathleen Blee, *Women of the Klan* (1991), and Richard K. Tucker, *The Dragon and the Cross: The Rise and Fall of the Ku Klux Klan in Middle America* (1991).

Francis Russell, *Tragedy in Dedham* (1962), casts doubt on the innocence of Sacco and Vanzetti; see also Paul Avrich, *Sacco and Vanzetti: The Anarchist Background* (1991).

Milton C. Sernet, *Bound for the Promised Land* (1997), emphasizes the religious dimensions of the black migration to the North. Alfred L. Brophy, *Reconstructing the Dreamland: The Tulsa Riot of 1921* (2002) is useful on that important episode. On blacks in Harlem, see Gilbert Osofsky,

Harlem: The Making of a Ghetto (1965). The Harlem Renaissance is the subject of Steven Watson, *The Harlem Renaissance* (1995), and J. Martin Favor, *Authentic Blackness* (1999). Eric Porter, *What Is This Thing Called Jazz?* (2002) explores the connections between music and intellectual life.

The literature of the period is analyzed in Alfred Kazin, *On Native Grounds* (1942), Malcolm Cowley, *Exiles Return* (1934), and Edmund Wilson, *The Twenties* (1975). *See* Jeffrey Meyers, *Scott Fitzgerald: A Biography* (1994) and also his *Hemingway: A Biography* (1999); also Carlos H. Baker, *Hemingway* (1956); on Mencken, William R. Manchester, *Disturber of the Peace* (1951); on Lewis, Mark Schorer, *Sinclair Lewis* (1961); on Wharton, R. W. B. Lewis, *Edith Wharton* (1975), and Shari Benstock, *No Gifts from Chance* (1994). On the popularization of literature, see Joan Shelley Rubin, *The Making of Middlebrow Culture* (1992).

On Henry Ford, see Douglas Brinkley, *Wheels for the World* (2004); Clarence Hooker, *Life in the Shadows of the Crystal Palace 1910–1927* (1997), illuminates the role of labor at Ford. On the early history of General Motors, see David Farber, *Sloan Rules: Alfred P. Sloan and the Triumph of General Motors* (2002). On women and cars, see Virginia Scharff, *Taking the Wheel* (1991). Beth Bailey, *From Front Porch to Back Seat* (1988), considers the ramifications of the automobile on courtship.

CHAPTER 26 | THE NEW ERA: 1921–1933

The political history of the 1920s is surveyed in Robert K. Murray, *The Politics of Normalcy* (1973), Ellis W. Hawley, *The Great War and the Search for a Modern Order* (1979), Michael Parrish, *Anxious Decades: America in Prosperity and Depression, 1920–1941* (1992) and Geoffrey Parret, *America in the Twenties* (1982).

On the labor history of the postwar decade, see Robert H. Zieger, *Republicans and Labor* (1969). The best brief biography of Harding is Andrew Sinclair, *The Available Man* (1965). Robert Ferrell, *The Presidency of Calvin Coolidge* (1998), is the best study of Coolidge in the White House. On Hoover, see Martin L. Fausold, *The Presidency of Herbert Hoover* (1985), and a narrower monograph, Kendrick A. Clements, *Hoover, Conservatives and Consumerism* (2000).

David Burner, *The Politics of Provincialism* (1968), deals with the Democratic party in the 1920s. On the trade association movement, see Robert F. Himmelberg, *The Origins of the National Recovery Act* (1976).

Diplomatic developments are summarized in Selig Adler, *The Uncertain Giant* (1965), Akira Iriye, *After Imperialism* (1965), and *Across the Pacific* (1967), Stephen Kneeshaw, *The Pursuit of Peace* (1991), on the Kellogg-Briand pact, Thomas H. Buckley, *The United States and the Washington Conference* (1970), Charles De Benedetti, *Origins of the Modern Peace Movement* (1978), and John H. Wilson, *American Business and Foreign Policy* (1971).

On farm problems, see John D. Hicks, *Twentieth-Century Populism* (1951), and Gilbert C. Fite, *George N. Peek and the Fight for Farm Parity* (1954). On the election of 1928, see Oscar Handlin, *Al Smith and His America* (1958).

On isolationism, see Robert A. Divine, *The Reluctant Belligerent* (1965), and *The Illusion of Neutrality* (1962). On Latin American relations, see Irwin F. Gellman, *Good Neighbor Diplomacy* (1979).

CHAPTER 27 | THE NEW DEAL: 1933–1941

The most important surveys of the New Deal are listed in the Debating the Past (p. 756). Analytical studies include Maxwell Bloomfield, *Peaceful Revolution* (2000), Ronald Edsforth, *The New Deal* (2000), Alan Brinkley, *Liberalism and Its Discontents* (1998), and Mark Leff, *The Limits of Symbolic Reform* (1984).

Of the many biographies of Roosevelt, see especially Frank Freidel, *Franklin D. Roosevelt* (1952–1973), James M. Burns, *Roosevelt: The Lion and the Fox* (1956), Geoffrey Ward, *Before the Trumpet: Young Franklin Roosevelt* (1985), and *A First-Class Temperament: The Emergence of Franklin Roosevelt* (1989). On Eleanor Roosevelt, see Blanche W. Cook, *Eleanor Roosevelt* (1992–1999), and Lois Scharf, *Eleanor Roosevelt: First Lady of American Liberalism* (1987). On Roosevelt's team of advisers, see Elliot A. Rosen, *Hoover, Roosevelt, and the Brains Trust* (1977).

For regional studies, see Bruce Shulman, *From Cotton Belt to Sunbelt* (1991), Charles H. Trout, *Boston, the Great Depression, and the New Deal* (1977), and Richard Lowitt, *The New Deal in the West* (1984).

On the New Deal and agriculture, see David E. Hamilton, *From New Day to New Deal: American Farm Policy from Hoover to Roosevelt, 1928–1933* (1991); on the problems of the Dust Bowl, see James N. Gregory, *American Exodus: The Dust Bowl Migration and Okie Culture in California* (1989).

On the New Deal and business, see Ellis W. Hawley, *The New Deal and the Problem of Monopoly* (1966), Morton Keller, *Regulating the New Economy: Public Policy and Economic Change in America* (1990) and *Regulating a New Society: Public Policy and Social Change in America, 1900–1933* (1994).

On workers and the New Deal, see Edwin Amenta, *Bold Relief: Institutional Politics and the Origins of Modern Social Policy* (1998), Gery Gerstle, *Working-Class Americanism: The Politics of Labor in a Textile City 1914–1960* (1989), Vicki Ruiz, *Cannery Women, Cannery Lives: Mexican Women, Unionization, and the California Food Processing Industry, 1930–1950* (1987), Lizabeth Cohen, *Making a New Deal: Industrial Workers in Chicago, 1919–1939* (1990), and Melvyn Dubofsky, *The State and Labor in Modern America* (1994). Bruce Nelson, *Divided We Stand: American Workers and the Struggle for Black Equality* (2001), describes a cleavage within the labor movement over racial issues. On the relation of private pensions and social security, see Jennifer Klein, *For All These Rights: Business, Labor, and the Shaping of America's Public-Private Welfare State* (2003).

On constitutional questions, see William E. Leuchtenburg, *The Supreme Court Reborn: The Constitutional Revolution in the Age of Roosevelt* (1995), and Paul L. Murphy, *The Constitution in Crisis Times* (1972).

For the activities of the radical fringe, consult Michael Denning, *The Cultural Front: The Laboring of American Culture in the Twentieth Century* (1996), Donald R. McCoy, *Angry Voices: Left-of-Center Politics in the New Deal Era* (1958), and D. H. Bennett, *Demagogues in the Depression* (1969). On blacks during the 1930s, see Raymond Wolters, *Negroes and the Great Depression* (1970), Nancy J. Weiss, *Farewell to the Party of Lincoln* (1983), and Harvard Sitkoff, *A New Deal for Blacks* (1978).

On women and gender, apart from the works cited above, see Suzanne Mettler, *Dividing Citizens* (1998), Landon Storrs, *Civilizing Capitalism* (2000), Susan Ware, *Beyond Suffrage: Women in the New Deal* (1981), and *Partner and I* (1987), a life of Molly Dewson. Also Linda Gordon, *Pitied But Not Entitled: Single Mothers and the History of Welfare* (1994), and Susan Ware, *Holding Their Own: American Women in the 1930s* (1982). On New Deal Indian policy, see Kenneth R. Philip, *John Collier's Crusade for Indian Reform* (1977). A chronologically broader but perceptive study is Kenneth R. Philp, *Termination Revisited: American Indians on the Trail to Self-Determination, 1933–1953* (1999).

A provocative analysis of modern art and the New Deal appears in Michael Szalay, *New Deal Modernism* (2000).

On isolationism and the events leading to Pearl Harbor, see Justus D. Doenecke, *Storm on the Horizon: The Challenge to American Intervention, 1939–1941* (2000), and David Reynolds, *From Munich to Pearl Harbor: Roosevelt's America and the Origins of the Second World War* (2001).

CHAPTER 28 | WAR AND PEACE

On prewar relations between the United States and Japan, see Akira Iriye, *After Imperialism* (1965). The best history of the worldwide events leading to the Japanese attack on Pearl Harbor is Waldo Heinrichs, *Threshold of War* (1988), but for more detail see Gordon W. Prange, *At Dawn We Slept* (1981), and Michael S. Stackman, *Target: Pearl Harbor* (1990). Charles C. Tansill, *Back Door to War* (1952), and Charles A. Beard, *President Roosevelt and the Coming of the War* (1948), are interesting interpretations by isolationists. Useful overviews include David M. Kennedy, *Freedom from Fear: The American People in Depression and War* (1999), Murray Williamson and Allan R. Millett, *A War to Be Won* (2000), and Warren F. Kimball, *Forged in War: Roosevelt, Churchill and the Second World War* (1997). Mark A. Stoler, *Allies and Adversaries* (2000) focuses on the Joint Chiefs of Staff. Thomas S. Fleming, *The New Dealers' War* (2001) is critical of Roosevelt. See also Michael S. Sherry, *The Rise of American Airpower* (1987).

A recent, sober assessment of Pearl Harbor is Akira Iriye, *Pearl Harbor and the Coming of the Pacific War* (1999). On aerial warfare, see Williamson Murray, *War in the Air, 1914–1945* (1999) and Geoffrey Peret, *Winged Victory* (1993). Paul Fussell, *Wartime: Understanding and Behavior in the Second World War* (1989), provides a realistic rendering of the carnage and chaos of modern warfare; Gerald F. Linderman, *The World Within War: America's Combat Experience in World War II* (1997), contends that the spectacle of war offers little sustenance to soldiers. The term "the greatest generation" is from Tom Brokaw's 1998 book by that title.

For a general, brief overview of the home front, see Lewis A. Erenberg and Susan E. Hirsch, *The War in American Culture: Society and Consciousness During World War II* (1996), John Morton Blum, *V Was for Victory* (1976), Doris Kearns Goodwin, *No Ordinary Time* (1995), and Steven Mintz and Susan Kellogg, *Domestic Revolutions* (1988). The effects of the war on women are described in D'Ann Campbell, *Women at War with America* (1984), Karen Anderson, *Wartime Women* (1981), and Susan M. Hartmann, *The Home Front and Beyond* (1982). William M. Tuttle, Jr., *"Daddy's Gone To War": The Second World War in the Lives of America's Children* (1993) offers an interesting perspective. The impact of the war on radical politics is examined in Bill V. Mullen, *Popular Fronts: Chicago and African-American Cultural Politics, 1935–46* (1999).

African American participation is the subject of Nat Brandt, *Harlem at War* (1996), Neil A. Wynn, *The Afro-American and the Second World War* (1993), Dominic J. Capeci, Jr., *Race Relations in Wartime Detroit* (1984), and A. Russell Buchanan, *Black Americans in World War II* (1977). On the Japanese internment, see Greg Robinson, *By Order of the President: FDR and the Internment of Japanese Americans* (2001), and Roger Daniels, *Concentration Camps USA: Japanese Americans and World War II* (1971), and Peter Irons, *Justice at War* (1984).

Major biographies include Geoffrey Perret, *Eisenhower* (1999), Stephen Ambrose, *Eisenhower* (1983), and Ed Cray, *General of the Army: George C. Marshall* (1990).

Richard Rhodes, *The Making of the Atom Bomb* (1986), is superb. On Leslie Groves, see Robert S. Norris, *Racing for the Bomb* (2002). For the relationship of the key scientists, see Gregg Herken, *Brotherhood of the Bomb* (2002).

CHAPTER 29 | THE AMERICAN CENTURY

General surveys include William Chafe, *The Unfinished Journey* (1986), James T. Patterson, *Grand Expectations: Postwar America, 1945–1974* (1996), David Halberstam, *The Fifties* (1993), H. W. Brands, *The Devil We Knew: Americans and the Cold War* (1993), John Patrick Diggins, *The Proud Decades, 1941–1960* (1989), and Michael S. Sherry, *In the Shadow of War* (1995). Older but influential interpretive works include Arthur M. Schlesinger Jr., *The Vital Center* (1949), Richard E. Neustadt, *Presidential Power* (1960), and James M. Burns, *The Deadlock of Democracy* (1964).

The evolution of American policy toward nuclear weapons is debated in Gar Alperovitz, *Atomic Diplomacy: Hiroshima and Potsdam* (1985), Gregg Herken, *The Winning Weapon: The Atomic Bomb in the Cold War* (1982), and Melvyn P. Leffler, *A Preponderance of Power: National Security, the Truman Administration, and the Cold War* (1992). An accessible overview is Richard Rhodes, *Dark Sun: The Making of the Hydrogen Bomb* (1995).

The 1948 election is described in Gary Donaldson, *Truman Defeats Dewey* (1999). On the origins of the shift of the South away from the Democrats, see Kari Frederickson, *The Dixiecrat Revolt and the End of the Solid South, 1932–1968* (2001). Postwar domestic politics are also treated in William L. O'Neill, *Riding High* (1986), and Alonzo L. Hamby, *The Imperial Years* (1976). On the cultural effects of the Cold War, see Elaine Tyler May, *Homeward Bound: American Families in the Cold War* (1988), and Paul Boyer, *By the Bomb's Early Light* (1986).

In addition to works cited in the previous chapter, see Donald R. McCoy, *The Presidency of Harry S Truman* (1984). David McCullough's, *Truman* (1992), is accessible and sympathetic; Alonzo L. Hamby's *Man of the People: A Life of Harry S Truman* (1995) is scholarly and analytical.

Among many analyses and evaluations of American foreign policy, George F. Kennan's writings stand out, both as primary sources and as interpretations. See his *Memoirs* (1969, 1972), *Realities of American Foreign Policy* (1954), and *Russia and the West Under Lenin and Stalin* (1961).

On Truman's foreign policy, see Paul G. Pierpaoli, Jr., *Truman and Korea* (1999), and Michael J. Hogan, *The Marshall Plan* (1987). Roger C. Miller, *To Save a City: The Berlin Airlift* (2000) is a succinct account.

The origins of the Korean War are now becoming clearer. In two volumes Bruce Cummings, *The Origins of the Korean War* (1981, 1990) emphasizes that the struggle was, at the outset, a civil war; William Stueck, *The Korean War: An International History* (1995) focuses on miscalculations by Stalin and Mao Zedong. On the war itself, see Stanley Sandler, *The Korean War* (1999). On MacArthur, see Geoffrey Perret, *Old Soldiers Never Die* (1996).

On McCarthyism, Ellen Schrecker, *Many Are the Crimes: McCarthyism in America* (1998) argues that the phenomenon was broader than McCarthy and became institutionalized in the FBI under J. Edgar Hoover. David Caute, *The Great Fear* (1978) is sharply critical. For different views of McCarthy himself, see Thomas C. Reeves, *Life and Times of Joe McCarthy* (1997), and Arthur Herman, *Joseph McCarthy* (2000). On the Hiss case see Allen Weinstein, *Perjury: The Hiss-Chambers Case* (1978), and Sam Tanenhaus, *Whittaker Chambers* (1997).

On the early history of the Civil Rights movement, see Mark Tushnet, *Making Civil Rights Law* (1994), and *Making Constitutional Law: Thurgood Marshall and the Supreme Court* (1997). See also Richard Kluger, *Simple Justice* (1976), and Harvard Sitkoff, *The Struggle for Black Equality* (1993). The writings of Martin Luther King, Jr., especially *Stride Toward Freedom* (1958) are also useful. The first volume of Taylor Branch's superb biography of Martin Luther King, Jr., *Parting the Waters* (1988), covers 1959 through 1963. Thomas Borstelmann, *The Cold War and the Color Line* (2001), and Mary Dudziak, *Cold War Civil Rights* (2000), show how the civil rights movement became embroiled in foreign policy issues, especially with respect to African nations.

Eisenhower's own view of his presidency can be found in Dwight D. Eisenhower, *Mandate for Change* (1963) and *Waging Peace* (1965). Recent (and increasingly positive) assessments include Robert Bowie and Richard Immerman, *Waging Peace: How Eisenhower Shaped an Enduring Cold War Strategy* (1998), Craig Campbell, *Destroying the Village: Eisenhower and Thermonuclear War* (1998), and Ray Takeyh, *The Origins of the Eisenhower Doctrine* (2000) on Suez.

Biographies on the central figures, in addition to those cited in the previous chapter, include James Chace, *Acheson* (1998), and Richard H. Immerman, *John Foster Dulles* (1999).

CHAPTER 30 | FROM CAMELOT TO WATERGATE

On Kennedy, consult Robert Dallek, *Unfinished Life: John F. Kennedy, 1917–1963* (2003), W. J. Rorabaugh, *Kennedy and the Promise of the Sixties* (2002), Richard Reeves, *President Kennedy* (1992), Herbert S. Parmet, *JFK: The Presidency of John F. Kennedy* (1983), and James Giglio, *The Presidency of John F. Kennedy* (1991). Arthur M. Schlesinger, Jr., *A Thousand Days* (1965) and Theodore Sorensen, *Kennedy* (1965) are rich in eyewitness detail but extremely pro-Kennedy. On Kennedy's foreign policy, see Lawrence Freedman, *Kennedy's Wars* (2000), and William Taubman, *Khrushchev* (2003). The Kennedy style can be "heard" in Ernest R. May and Philip D. Zelikow, eds., *The Kennedy Tapes: Inside the White House During the Cuban Missile Crisis* (1997). Also on the Cuban missile crisis, see Sheldon M. Stern, *Averting "The Final Failure": John F. Kennedy and the Secret Cuban Missile Crisis Meetings* (2003), Robert Weisbrot, *Maximum Danger* (2001), and Mark J. White, *The Cuban Missile Crisis* (1996). Gerald Posner, *Case Closed: Lee Harvey Oswald and the Assassination of JFK* (1994) debunks the conspriracy theorists.

Robert Caro, *The Years of Lyndon B. Johnson: The Path to Power* (1982) and *Means of Ascent* (1990) are extremely critical; Robert Dallek, *Lone Star Rising: Lyndon Johnson and His Times, 1908–1960* (1991) and *Flawed Giant: Lyndon B. Johnson, 1960–1973* (1998) are more balanced. Recent works include Irwin Unger, *LBJ: A Life* (1999), and H. W. Brands, *The Wages of Globalism: Lyndon Johnson and the Limits of American Power* (1995). See also Doris Kearns Goodwin, *Lyndon Johnson and the American Dream* (1976). Michael Beschloss, ed., *Taking Charge: The Johnson White House Tapes, 1963–1969* (1997) provides a verbatim, previously secret, account.

On Goldwater, see Robert A. Goldberg, *Barry Goldwater* (1995); Lisa McGirr, *Suburban Warriors: The Origins of the New American Right* (2001) examines the 1960s origins of a grassroots conservative movement.

For civil rights, in addition to works cited in the previous chapter, consult Taylor Branch's second volume in his biography of Martin Luther King, Jr., *Pillar of Fire* (1998). Diane McWhorter, *Carry Me Home* (2001) provides a gripping account of the civil rights struggle in Birmingham, Alabama. Nicholas Lemann, *The Promised Land: The Great Black Migration and How It Changed America* (1991) is also indispensable. Malcolm X, *Autobiography*, is a classic account of black alienation. See also Karl Evanzz, *The Messenger: The Rise and Fall of Elijah Muhammed* (1999) provides a detailed account of the founder of the Black Muslims; Michael E. Dyson's *Making Malcolm* (1995) is also solid. James T. Patterson, *Brown v. Board of Education* (2001) has provided a thorough account of that Supreme Court decision.

On the election of 1968, Theodore H. White's *The Making of the President, 1968* (1969), is lively and entertaining. The best biography of Nixon is Stephen Ambrose, *Nixon* (1987–1991), but see also Richard Reeves, *Richard Nixon: Alone in the White House* (2001), Joan Hoff, *Nixon Reconsidered* (1994), and Herbert S. Parmet, *Richard Nixon and His America* (1990). Allen J. Matusow, *Nixon's Economy* (1998) is excellent. Dean J. Kotlowski, *Nixon's Civil Rights* (2001) argues that Nixon's actions—if not his rhetoric—were mostly supportive; J. Brooks Flippen, *Nixon and the Environment* (2000) makes a similar point about Nixon and environmental issues.

Henry Kissinger's memoirs, *White House Years* (1979) and *Years of Upheaval* (1982), are important though, like most such works, self-serving. Walter Isaacson's *Kissinger* (1992) is more balanced. See also Christopher Hitchens *The Trial of Henry Kissinger* (2001).

The literature on the war in Vietnam is enormous. Recent interpretations include David E. Kaiser, *American Tragedy: Kennedy, Johnson and the Origins of the Vietnam War* (2000), Lawrence Freedman, *Kennedy's Wars: Berlin, Cuba, Laos, and Vietnam* (2000), A. J. Langguth, *Our Vietnam: The War: 1954–1975* (2000), and Robert D. Schulzinger, *A Time for War* (1997). Neil Sheehan, *A Bright and Shining Lie* (1988), an account of the war from one American adviser's perspective, provides the best explanation of why the war could not be won. See also Lloyd C. Gardner, *Pay Any Price: Lyndon Johnson and the Wars for Vietnam* (1995). John Laurence, *The Cat from Hue: A Vietnam War Story* (2002) approaches the subject from a journalistic perspective.

For the antiwar movement, see Robert Buzzanco, *Masters of War: Military Dissent and Politics in the Vietnam Era* (1996), Rhodri Jeffreys-Jones, *Peace Now!* (1999), and Mary Hershberger, *Traveling to Vietnam: American Peace Activists and the War* (1998) on the ending of the war. See also Michael S. Foley, *Confronting the War Machine: Draft Resistance during the Vietnam War* (2003).

The best analysis of the Watergate affair is Stanley I. Kutler, *The Wars of Watergate* (1990) and *Abuse of Power* (1997), but see also Carl Bernstein and Robert Woodward, *All the President's Men* (1974) and *Final Days* (1976), John W. Dean, *Blind Ambition* (1976), and Leon Jaworski, *The Right and the Power* (1976). On Ford's elevation to the presidency, see James Cannon, *Time and Chance* (2001).

CHAPTER 31 | SOCIETY IN FLUX

Kenneth T. Jackson, *Crabgrass Frontier* (1985) is indispensable on the evolution of the suburbs. On Jackson's argument that home ownership contributed to political conservativism, see Becky M. Nicolaides, *My Blue Heaven: Life and Politics in the Working-Class Suburbs of Los Angeles, 1920–1965* (2002). Elaine Tyler May, *Homeward Bound: American Families in the Cold War* (1988), locates the rise of a conservative ideological mindset within the home. The environmental consequences of suburbanization are the subject of Adam Rome, *The Bulldozer in the Countryside* (2001). For the cities, see Robert M. Fogelson, *Downtown: Its Rise and Fall, 1880–1950* (2001).

On the effects of the automobile, see Jane H. Kay's history/manifesto, *Asphalt Nation* (1997), and Virginia Scharff's *Taking the Wheel: Women and the Coming of the Motor Age* (1992).

For a favorable account of the New Left of the 1960s, by a former leader of the SDS, see Todd Gitlin, *The Sixties: Years of Hope, Days of Rage* (1987). Maurice Isserman and Michael Kazin, *America Divided: The Civil War of the 1960s* (2000), though sympathetic to the New Left, note that conservatives emerged from the decade victorious. David Burner, *Making Peace with the Sixties* (1996) argues that the New Left unwisely abandoned its Old Left origins, and thus slipped into self-destructive hedonism. Peter Collier and David Horowitz, *Destructive Generation: Second Thoughts about the '60s* (1989) contend that the decade's "hedonism" and "revolutionary passion" culminated in "tragic consequences." See also Roger Kimball, *The Long March: How the Cultural Revolution of the 1960s Changed America* (2000), Dominick Cavallo, *A Faction of the Past: The Sixties in American History* (1999), and David Farber, *Chicago 68* (1988). Ellen Fitzpatrick, *History's Memory: Writing America's Past, 1880–1980* (2002) is especially critical of historians of this period for neglecting their scholarly forebears.

For television, see Mary Ann Watson, *The Expanding Vista: American Television in the Kennedy Years* (1994), James L. Baughman, *The Republic of Mass Culture: Journalism, Filmmaking, and Broadcasting in America Since 1941* (1991), Karal Ann Marling, *As Seen on TV: The Visual Culture of Everyday Life in the 1950s* (1994), and Josh Ozersky, *Archie Bunker's America: TV in an Era of Change* (2003). See also Glenn C. Altschuler, *All Shook Up: How Rock 'n' Roll Changed America* (2003).

On black radicalism, in addition to works cited in the previous chapter, see the first person accounts by Malcolm X, *Autobiography* (1966), Stokely Carmichael and C. V. Hamilton, *Black Power* (1967), and Eldridge Cleaver, *Soul on Ice* (1967). Other important books on race relations include Taylor Branch's multi-volume biography of Martin Luther King, Jr.: *Parting the Waters: 1954–1963* (1988), and *Pillar of Fire: America in the King Years, 1963–1965* (1998). On SNCC, see John Lewis's memoir, *Walking with the Wind* (1998), as well as Clayborne Carson, *In Struggle: SNCC and the Black Awakening of the 1960s* (1981). The neglected role of women in the movement is addressed in Chana Kai Lee, *For Freedom's Sake: The Life of Fannie Lou Hamer* (1999), and Carolyn Wedin, *Inheritors of the Spirit: Mary White Ovington and the Founding of NAACP* (1998).

Ronald Takaki, *A Different Mirror: A History of Multicultural History* (1993), provides an overview of the contemporary immigrant experience. Rodolfo Acuna, *Occupied America: A History of Chicanos* (2000), Manuel Gonzales, *Mexicanos: A History of Mexicans in the United States* (1999), and Ernesto Vigil, *The Crusade for Justice* (1999) provide surveys of broad trends of Chicano history in the United States. Biographies of César Chávez include, Richard Griswold del Castillo and Richard A. Garcia, *A Triumph of the Spirit* (1998), and Joan London and Henry Anderson, *So Shall Ye Reap: The Story of César Chávez and the Farm Workers Movement* (1970). James S. Olson and Raymond Wilson, *Native Americans in the Twentieth Century* (1984), is a good survey.

The literature on the women's movement is voluminous. Betty Friedan's *The Feminine Mystique* (1963), is essential, though her account must be modified in light of Daniel Horowitz, *Betty Friedan and the Making of The Feminine Mystique* (1998). Rosalind Rosenberg, *Divided Lives: American Women in the Twentieth Century* (1992) is a good introduction to women's history. See also Jo Freeman, *The Politics of Women's Liberation* (1975), and Susan M. Hartmann, *From Margin to Mainstream: Women and American Politics Since 1960* (1989). Narrower monographs include Dennis A. Deslippe, *"Rights, Not Roses": Unions and the Rise of Working-Class Feminism* (2000).

On abortion, Rickie Solinger, *Wake Up Little Suzie: Single Pregnancy and Race before Roe v. Wade* (1992), considers the situation before 1973. On the *Roe v. Wade* decision itself, see Laurence H. Tribe, *Abortion: The Clash of Absolutes* (1990), and Linda Gordon, *Moral Property of Women: A History of Birth Control Politics in America* (2002). Andrea Tone, *Devices and Desires: A History of Contraceptives in America* (2001) is useful on contraception more generally.

James H. Jones, *Alfred C. Kinsey: A Public/Private Life* (1997), finds that Kinsey's odd behavior discredits his scholarship; Jonathan Gathorne-Hardy, *Alfred C. Kinsey: Sex the Measure of All Things* (1998) is less critical. On sexual trends more generally, see Beth Bailey, *Sex in the Heartland* (1999) on Kansas in the 1960s and 1970s.

The early history of the AIDS crisis is movingly told in Randy Shilts, *And the Band Played On* (1987). See also Elizabeth Fee and Daniel M. Fox, eds., *AIDS: The Making of a Chronic Disease* (1992).

CHAPTER 32 | RUNNING ON EMPTY: THE NATION TRANSFORMED

Bruce J. Schulman, *The Seventies* (2001), surveys that decade, as Haynes Johnson, *Sleepwalking Through History* (1992) does for the 1980s. On Gerald Ford, see James M. Cannon, *Time and*

Chance: Gerald Ford's Appointment with History (1994), and John R. Greene, *The Presidency of Gerald R. Ford* (1995).

Peter G. Bourne, *Jimmy Carter* (1997), relates his subject's life and policies. Donald Spencer, *The Carter Implosion: Jimmy Carter and the Amateur Style of Diplomacy* (1988) contains its thesis in the title; Robert A. Strong, *Working the World: Jimmy Carter and the Making of American Foreign Policy* (2000), defends Carter's record.

On Reagan, in addition to the works cited in Debating the Past (p. 899), see Lou Cannon, *President Reagan* (1991) and *Governor Reagan* (2003), and Michael Schaller, *Reckoning with Reagan* (1992). Although Edmund Morris's *Dutch: A Memoir* (1999), which includes fictional characters and footnotes, is not what it purports to be, it nevertheless offers interesting observations. David A. Stockman, *The Triumph of Politics* (1986), contains a frank discussion of administration fiscal policies. Reagan's foreign policy remains controversial. Especially useful is Jack F. Matlock, *Reagan and Gorbachev* (2004). Peter Schweizer, *Victory: The Reagan Administration's Secret Strategy That Hastened the Collapse of the Soviet Union* (1994) summarizes its achievements; Frances FitzGerald, *Way Out There in the Blue: Reagan, Star Wars and the End of the Cold War* (2000), is sharply critical. See also Jay Winik, *On the Brink* (1996).

The early history of the AIDS crisis is movingly told in Randy Shilts, *And the Band Played On* (1987); see also Elizabeth Fee and Daniel M. Fox, eds., *AIDS: The Making of a Chronic Disease* (1992). John-Manual Andriote examines its impact on gays themselves in *Victory Deferred: How AIDS Changed Gay Life in America* (1999).

On the transformation of the economy, see Robert M. Collins, *More: The Politics of Economic Growth in Postwar America* (2000), Daniel Yergin, *The Prize: The Epic Quest for Oil, Money and Power* (1991), and Barry Bluestone and Bennett Harrison, *The Deindustrializing of America* (1982). On Michael Milken and junk bonds, see Harlan Platt, *The Predators Ball* (1988); also James B. Stewart, *Den of Thieves* (1991). On the United States and the global economy, see Robert Kuttner, *The End of Laissez Faire: National Purpose and the Global Economy After the Cold War* (1991), and Henry R. Nau, *The Myth of America's Decline: Leading the World Economy in the 1990s* (1990).

CHAPTER 33 | MISDEMEANORS AND HIGH CRIMES

Haynes Johnson, *Divided We Fall: Gambling with History in the Nineties* (1994), notwithstanding its expansive title, discusses the first few years of the 1990s; for the end of the Cold War see Michael R. Beschloss and Strobe Talbot, *At the Highest Levels: The Inside Story of the End of the Cold War*, and John Lewis Gaddis, *The United States and the End of the Cold War* (1992).

Many scholars have attempted to fit the political developments of the era into a traditional framework: see Mary Jo Bane and David Ellwood, *Welfare Realities: From Rhetoric to Reform* (1994), Theodore J. Lowi, *The End of the Republican Era* (1995), and Robert S. McElvaine, *The End of the Conservative Era: Liberalism After Reagan* (1987).

For accounts of the George H. W. Bush administration, see Herbert Parmet, *George Bush: The Life of a Lone Star Yankee* (1997), and John R. Greene, *The Presidency of George Bush* (2000). Gary R. Hess provides a thoughtful comparison on war-making processes in *Presidential Decisions for War: Korea, Vietnam and the Persian Gulf* (2001). The Panama invasion is discussed in David Harris, *Shooting the Moon* (2001).

On Clinton prior to his move to the White House, see David Maranis, *First in His Class: A Biography of Bill Clinton* (1995). The *Starr Report* (1998), though hastily released and published, constituted the evidentiary base and set the tone for the subsequent impeachment debate. See also Richard A. Posner, *An Affair of State: The Investigation, Impeachment, and Trial of President Clinton* (1999). On foreign policy, see David Halberstam, *War in a Time of Peace: Bush, Clinton and the Generals* (2001).

On the advance of conservatism, see Godfrey Hodgson, *The World Turned Rightside Up: A History of the Conservative Ascendancy in America* (1996). On the defeat of the ERA, see Mary Francis Berry, *Why ERA Failed* (1986), and Donald G. Mathews and Jane Sherron De Hart, *Sex, Gender, and the Politics of E.R.A.* (1990).

David Courtwright, *Violent Land: Single Men and Social Disorder from the Frontier to the Inner City* (1996) argues that much of the nation's crime has come from single males; for a cultural analysis of the infatuation with aggression, see Richard Slotkin, *Gunfighter Nation: The Myth of the Frontier in Twentieth-Century America* (1992). Bruce Jacobs, *Dealing Crack* (1999), provides a case study of the drug problem.

On race and ethnicity, see David A. Hollinger, *Postethnic America: Beyond Multiculturalism* (1995), Andrew Hacker, *Two Nations: Black and White, Separate, Hostile, Unequal* (1992), and Stephen Thernstrom and Abigail Thernstrom, *America in Black and White: One Nation, Indivisible* (1997).

John Cassidy, *Dot.con* (2002) surveys the Internet economy. For a history of the Internet, see Janet Abbate, *Inventing the Internet* (1999).

On the 2000 election, see David A. Kaplan, *The Accidental President* (2001), and Richard Posner, *Breaking the Deadlock* (2001).

The literature on terrorism is expanding rapidly. *The 9/11 Commission* Report (2004) is a detailed assessment of multiple failures in intelligence and security. Douglas Little, *American Orientalism: The United States and the Middle East Since 1945* (2002) provides a useful overview of American policies, while Thomas L. Friedman, *From Beirut to Jerusalem* (1989) offers a thoughtful analysis of the complex problems of the region.

Bob Woodward's two books provide the best account of George W. Bush after the terrorist attack of September 11, 2001. *Bush at War* (2002) chronicles his leadership immediately after 9/11; *Plan of Attack* (2004), more critical, details Bush's campaign to oust Saddam Hussein of Iraq. Douglas Brinkley, *Tour of Duty: John Kerry and the Vietnam War* (2004) is a solid narrative.

Suggested Websites

PROLOGUE | BEGINNINGS

Pre-Contact and Colonial Maps
http://www.lib.utexas.edu/maps/americas/
This University of Texas site contains numerous maps from the pre-contact and colonial periods.

Ancient Mesoamerican Civilization
http://www.angelfire.com/ca/humanorigins/index.html
Kevin L. Callahan of the University of Minnesota Department of Anthropology maintains this page that supplies information regarding Mesoamerican civilizations with well-organized essays and photos.

National Museum of the American Indian
http://www.si.edu/nmai
The Smithsonian Institution museum is dedicated to the Native American experience.

Cahokia Mounds
http://medicine.wust/edu/~mckinney/cahokia/cahokia.html
The Cahokia Mounds State Historical site gives information about this fascinating pre-Columbian North American culture.

CHAPTER 1 | ALIEN ENCOUNTERS: EUROPE IN THE AMERICAS

Vikings in the New World
http://www.anthro.mankato.msus.edu/prehistory/vikings/vikhome.html
This site explores the history of some of the earliest European visitors to the Americas.

The Columbus Doors
http://xroads.virginia.edu/~cap/columbus/col1.html
On this University of Virginia Website, historians discuss the Columbus myth and how it has changed over time.

1492: An Ongoing Voyage
http://www.ibiblio.org/expo/1492.exhibit/Intro.html
An exhibit of the Library of Congress, Washington, D.C., that includes brief essays and images about early civilizations and contact in the Americas.

The Computerized Information Retrieval System on Columbus and the Age of Discovery
http://www.millersv.edu/~columbus/
The History Department and Academic Computing Services of Millersville University, Pennsylvania, provide this text retrieval system containing more than 1000 articles from various magazines, journals, newspapers, speeches, official calendars, and other sources relating to various encounter themes.

Interacting with Native Americans in New Hampshire
http://seacoastnh.com/history/contact/index.html
This brief history of contact era New Hampshire has interesting links and gives a good picture of the earliest contacts.

The Discoverers' Web
http://www.win.tue.nl/cs/fm/engels/discovery/
Andre Engels offers information on the various exploration efforts.

The Plymouth Colony Archives Project at the University of Virginia
http://www.people.virginia.edu/~jfd3a/
This site contains extensive information about late seventeenth-century Plymouth colony.

Jamestown Rediscovery
http://www.apva.org/
This site, mounted by the Association for the Preservation of Virginia Antiquity, has excellent material on archaeological excavations at Jamestown.

Jamestown
http://www.nps.gov/colo/
This National Park Service site has information on Jamestown and other important colonial historical sites.

Williamsburg
http://www.history.org/
This commercial site explores colonial Williamsburg, Virginia.

William Penn, Visionary Proprietor
http://xroads.virginia.edu/~CAP/PENN/pnhome.html
William Penn had an interesting life, and this University site is a good introduction to the man and some of his achievements.

CHAPTER 2 | AMERICAN SOCIETY IN THE MAKING

LVA Colonial Records Project—Index of Digital Facsimiles of Documents on Early Virginia
http://eagle.vsla.edu/colonial/
This site contains reproductions of numerous documents.

Anglicans, Puritans, and Quakers in Colonial America
http://www.mun.ca/rels/ang/texts/
This site provides information on the major religious movements in colonial America.

DSL Archives: Slave Movement During the Eighteenth and Nineteenth Centuries (Wisconsin)
http://dpls.dacc.wisc.edu/slavedata/index.html
This site explores the slave ships and the slave trade that carried thousands of Africans to the New World.

Witchcraft in Salem Village
http://etext.virginia.edu/salem/witchcraft/
This University of Virginia site offers an extensive archive of the 1692 trials as well as life in late seventeenth-century Massachusetts.

Salem Witchcraft Trials (1692)
http://www.law.umkc.edu/faculty/projects/ftrials/salem/salem.htm
Images, chronology, court and officials documents by Dr. Doug Linder of the University of Missouri–Kansas City Law School.

Benjamin Franklin
http://sln.fi.edu/franklin/rotten.html
This Benjamin Franklin Institute site contains information and sources treating one of early America's most well-known figures.

Religion and the Founding of the American Republic
http://lcweb.loc.gov/exhibits/religion/religion.html
This Library of Congress site is an online exhibit about religion and the formation of the United States.

DoHistory, Harvard University Film Center
http://www.dohistory.org/
Focusing on the life of Martha Ballard, a late eighteenth-century New England woman, this site employs selections from her diary, excerpts from a book and film about her life, and other primary documents that enable students to conduct their own historical investigation.

CHAPTER 3 | AMERICA IN THE BRITISH EMPIRE

Colonial Era Timeline
www.historyplace.com/unitedstates/revolution/re-col.htm
This site provides information about colonial-era issues.

Colonial Documents
http://www.yale.edu/lawweb/avalon/18th.htm
The key documents are reproduced on this Yale University site, as are some important documents from other periods of U.S. history.

Jonathan Edwards
http://www.jonathanedwards.com/
This site includes the text of speeches delivered by Preacher Jonathan Edwards.

The French and Indian War
http://web.syr.edu/~laroux/
This site, treating the French and Indian War, includes chronologies and documents, as well as materials dealing with the French soldiers who fought in the conflict.

The Early America Review
http://earlyamerica.com/
This site explores the colonies through the colonial media.

White Oak Fur Post
http://www.whiteoak.org/
This site documents an eighteenth-century fur trading post among the Indians in the region that would become Minnesota.

CHAPTER 4 | THE AMERICAN REVOLUTION

Revolutionary War Songs
http://www.mcneilmusic.com/rev.html
This site contains colonial and revolutionary era songs.

Maryland Loyalists and the American Revolution
http://users.erols.com/candidus/index.htm
This examination of Maryland's Loyalists promotes the author's book on that subject. Nonetheless, the site has good information about an underappreciated phenomenon, including Loyalist songs and poems.

Canada History
http://www.civilization.ca
Canada and the United States shared a colonial past, but developed along different lines. This site is part of the virtual museum of the Canadian Museum of Civilization Corporation.

Georgia's Rare Map Collection
http://scarlett.libs.uga.edu/darchive/hargrett/maps/colamer.html
http://scarlett.libs.uga.edu/darchive/hargrett/maps/revamer.html
These two University of Georgia sites contain maps of colonial and revolutionary America.

The American Revolution
http://revolution.h-net.msu.edu/
This site accompanies the PBS series *Revolution* with essays and resource links.

CHAPTER 5 | THE FEDERALIST ERA: NATIONALISM TRIUMPHANT

George Washington at Home
http://www.mountvernon.org/
Pictures and documents from Mount Vernon, the home of the first president, George Washington.

George Washington
http://memory.loc.gov/ammem/gwhtml/gwhome.html
This Library of Congress site contains information on Washington and his papers.

Biographies of the Founders
http://www.colonialhall.com/
This site provides interesting information about the men who signed the Declaration of Independence and includes a trivia section.

The Federalist Papers
http://www.law.emory.edu/FEDERAL/federalist/
This Emory University site is a collection of the most important *Federalist Papers,* a series of documents designed to convince people to support the new Constitution and the Federalist Party.

The Continental Congress and the Constitutional Convention, 1774–1798
http://memory.loc.gov/ammem/bdsds/bdsdhome.html
The Continental Congress Broadside Collection (253 titles) and the Constitutional Convention Broadside Collection (21 titles) contain 274 documents relating to the work of Congress and the drafting and ratification of the Constitution.

The Constitution and the Amendments
http://www.law.emory.edu/FEDERAL/usconst.html
A searchable Constitution site, especially useful for its information on the Bill of Rights and other constitutional amendments.

The George Washington Papers
http://www.virginia.edu/gwpapers/
This site provides information on the University of Virginia publishing project, with selected documents, essays, and an index to the published volumes.

Archiving Early America
http://earlyamerica.com
Old newspapers provide a window into issues of the past. This site includes the Keigwin and Matthews collection of historic newspapers.

Alexander Hamilton
http://odur.let.rug.nl/~usa/B/hamilton/hamilxx.htm
This site from *A Hypertext of American History* examines Hamilton's life and influence in the United States during the early national period.

The XYZ Affair
http://ap.grolier.com/article?assetid=0425920-00&templatename=/article/article.html
This site examines the XYZ affair, the first major crisis of U.S. foreign policy.

CHAPTER 6 | JEFFERSONIAN DEMOCRACY

Thomas Jefferson
http://www.pbs.org/jefferson/
This site, the companion to the PBS series on Jefferson, includes material on how people understand Jefferson today.

Thomas Jefferson Resources Online
http://etext.virginia.edu/jefferson/
"Mr. Jefferson's University," The University of Virginia, provides resources about Jefferson and his times.

The Jefferson Home
http://www.monticello.org/
This site explores Jefferson's gifted mind through an examination of Monticello, Jefferson's unique home.

Lewis and Clark—The PBS Website
http://www.pbs.org/lewisandclark
This is a companion site to Ken Burns's film, containing a timeline of the expedition, a collection of related links, a bibliography, and more than 800 minutes of unedited, full-length Real Player interviews with seven experts featured in the film.

CHAPTER 7 | NATIONAL GROWING PAINS

Documents from the War of 1812
http://www.yale.edu/lawweb/avalon/diplomacy/britian/brtreaty.htm
This site includes the important documents from the War of 1812.

The War of 1812
http://members.tripod.com/~war1812/index.html
This site provides in-depth information about the War of 1812.

The Monroe Doctrine
http://www.yale.edu/lawweb/avalon/monroe.htm
Read the Monroe Doctrine, an important early articulation of U.S. foreign policy, online.

The Seminole Indians of Florida
http://www.seminoletribe.com/
Before becoming president, Andrew Jackson began a war against the Seminole Indians.

CHAPTER 8 | TOWARD A NATIONAL ECONOMY

The Era of the Mountain Men
http://www.xmission.com/~drudy/amm.html
Private letters help students learn about the concerns and environment of the writers and recipients. This site has correspondence from early settlers west of the Mississippi River.

The Marshall Cases
http://odur.let.rug.nl/~usa/D/1801-1825/marshallcases/marxx.htm
John Marshall, and the cases he heard, shaped the form and function of the judicial system in the United States.

Whole Cloth: Discovering Science and Technology Through American Textile History
http://www.si.edu/lemelson/centerpieces/whole_cloth/
The Jerome and Dorothy Lemelson Center for the Study of Invention and Innovation/Society for the History of Technology put together this site, which includes activities and sources about early-American manufacturing and industry.

Erie Canal Online
http://www.syracuse.com/features/eriecanal
This site, built around the diary of a 14-year-old girl who traveled from Amsterdam to Syracuse, New York, in the early nineteenth century, explores the construction and importance of the Erie Canal.

CHAPTER 9 | JACKSONIAN DEMOCRACY

Indian Affairs: Laws and Treaties, Compiled and Edited by Charles J. Kappler (1904)
http://digital.library.okstate.edu/kappler/
This digitized text at Oklahoma State University includes preremoval treaties with the Five Civilized Tribes and other tribes.

Andrew Jackson and Indian Removal
http://www.iwchildren.org/genocide/murderer1.htm
This site offers a critical appraisal of Jackson's Indian removal policy.

The Second Bank of the United States, 1816–1836
http://odur.let.rug.nl/~usa/E/usbank/bank04.htm
The political fighting surrounding the Second Bank of the United States occupied the United States during the Jackson era, and led to the rise of the Whig party.

Daniel Webster
http://www.dartmouth.edu/~dwebster
Background information and selected writings from one of the nineteenth century's most noted orators.

The American Whig Party, 1834–1856
http://odur.let.rug.nl/~usa/E/uswhig/whigsxx.htm
This site treats the rise and fall of an important nineteenth-century political movement.

National Museum of the American Indian
http://www.si.edu/nmai
The Smithsonian Institution maintains this site, providing information about the museum that is dedicated to everything about Native Americans.

CHAPTER 10 | THE MAKING OF MIDDLE-CLASS AMERICA

The Alexis de Tocqueville Tour: Exploring Democracy in America
http://www.tocqueville.org/

Text, images, and teaching suggestions are all part of this companion site to C-SPAN's recent programming on de Tocqueville.

Votes for Women: Selections from the National Women Suffrage Association Collection, 1848–1921
http://memory.loc.gov/ammem/naw/nawshome.html

This Library of Congress site contains books, pamphlets, and other artifacts that document the suffrage campaign.

By Popular Demand: "Votes for Women" Suffrage Pictures, 1850–1922
http://memory.loc.gov/ammem/vfwhtml/vfwhome.html

Portraits, suffrage parades, picketing suffragists, an anti-suffrage display, and cartoons commenting on the movement are all part of this Library of Congress site.

Important Black Abolitionists
http://www.loc.gov/exhibits/african/afam006.html

An exhibit from the Library of Congress, with pictures and text, that discuss some of the key African American abolitionists and their efforts to end slavery.

Pioneering the Upper Midwest: Books from Michigan, Minnesota, and Wisconsin, ca. 1820–1910
http://memory.loc.gov/ammem/umhtml/umhome.html

This Library of Congress site looks at first-person accounts, biographies, promotional literature, ethnographic and antiquarian texts, colonial archival documents, and other works from the seventeenth to early twentieth century. It covers many topics and issues that affected Americans in the settlement and development of the upper Midwest.

History of the Suffrage Movement
http://www.rochester.edu/SBA

This site includes a chronology, important texts relating to women's suffrage, and bibliographical information about Susan B. Anthony and Elizabeth Cady Stanton.

CHAPTER 11 | AN AMERICAN CULTURE

America's First Look into the Camera: Daguerreotype Portraits and Views, 1839–1862
http://memory.loc.gov/ammem/daghtml/daghome.html

The Library of Congress's daguerreotype collection consists of more than 650 photographs from the 1839–1864 period. Portraits, architectural views, and some street scenes make up most of the collection.

The Era of the Mountain Men
http://www.xmission.com/~drudy/amm.html

Private letters help students of the past learn about the concerns and environment of the writers and recipients. This site has correspondence from early settlers in the area west of the Mississippi River.

Edgar Allan Poe
http://www.eapoe.org/index.html

The Edgar Allan Poe Society of Baltimore provides the original works, history, criticism, images and more about the writer.

Eastern State Penitentiary Official Homepage
http://www.easternstate.com/index.html
This is the official Website for America's most historic prison; the model for 300 prisons worldwide. Eastern State Penitentiary is now open to the public as an historic site.

CHAPTER 12 | WESTWARD EXPANSION

From Slave to Master
http://moa.umdl.umich.edu/cgi/sgml/moa-idx?notisid=ABT6752
This site contains an autobiography of a slave who became a master, with strong comments on the place of blacks in pre-Civil War America.

Sam Houston and the Texas Revolution, 1825–1836
http://www.lnstar.com/mall/texasinfo/shouston.htm
This site provides information on the revolution, including the dynamic Sam Houston.

On the Trail in Kansas
http://www.ukans.edu/heritage/owk/128/trails.htm/#oregon
This Kansas Collection site provides good primary sources and images relating to the Oregon Trial and America's early movement westward.

"Been Here So Long": Selections from the WPA American Slave Narratives
http://newdeal.feri.org/asn/index.htm
Slave narratives are some of the most interesting primary sources about slavery.

Slave Narratives
http://docsouth.unc.edu/neh/texts.html
This site presents narratives of several slaves housed at the Documents of the American South collection and the University of North Carolina.

The Settlement of African Americans in Liberia
http://www.loc.gov/exhibits/african/afam003.html
This site contains images and text relating to the colonization movement to return African Americans to Africa.

Images of African Americans from the Nineteenth Century
http://digital.nypl.org/schomburg/images_aa19/
The New York Public Library–Schomburg Center for Research in Black Culture site contains numerous visuals of nineteenth-century African Americans.

The Compromise of 1850 and the Fugitive Slave Act
http://www.pbs.org/wgbh/aia/part4
From the series on Africans in America, an analysis of the Compromise of 1850 and the effect of the Fugitive Slave Act on black Americans.

Words and Deeds in American History
http://lcweb2.loc.gov/ammem/mcchtml/corhome.html
A Library of Congress site containing links to Frederick Douglas, the Compromise of 1850, as well as speeches by John C. Calhoun, Daniel Webster, and Henry Clay; and other topics from the Civil War era.

CHAPTER 13 | THE SECTIONS GO THEIR WAYS

"Been Here So Long": Selections from the WPA American Slave Narratives
http://newdeal.feri.org/asn/index.htm
Slave narratives are some of the most interesting primary sources about slavery.

The Settlement of African Americans in Liberia
http://www.loc.gov/exhibits/african/afam003.html
This site contains images and text relating to the colonization movement to return African Americans to Africa.

Images of African Americans from the Nineteenth Century
http://digital.nypl.org/schomburg/images_aa19/
The New York Public Library Schomburg Center for Research in Black Culture site contains numerous visuals of nineteenth-century African Americans.

CHAPTER 14 | THE COMING OF THE CIVIL WAR

Secession Era Editorial Project
http://history.furman.edu/~benson/docs/
Furman University is digitizing editorials about the secession crisis and already includes scores of them on this site.

John Brown Trial Links
http://www.law.umkc/edu/faculty/projects/ftrials/Brown.html
For information about the John Brown trial, this site provides a list of excellent links.

Harriett Beecher Stowe and Uncle Tom's Cabin
http://xroads.virginia.edu/~HYPER/STOWE/stowe.html
This site provides both text and description of Stowe's important books, as well as information about the author's life.

Abraham Lincoln
http://showcase.netins.net/web/creative/lincoln.html
This site both contains useful information about President Lincoln and links to other web destinations.

Abraham Lincoln Association
http://www.alincolnassoc.com/
This site allows the search of digital versions of Lincoln's papers.

CHAPTER 15 | THE WAR TO SAVE THE UNION

The American Civil War Homepage
http://sunsite.utk.edu/civil-war/warweb.html
This site has a great collection of hypertext links to the most useful identified electronic files about the American Civil War.

Abraham Lincoln
http://showcase.netins.net/web/creative/lincoln.html
This site both contains useful information about President Lincoln and links to other web destinations.

Abraham Lincoln Association
http://www.alincolnassoc.com/
This site allows searches of Lincoln's papers.

Assassination of President Abraham Lincoln
http://memory.loc.gov/ammem/alhtml/alrintr.html
Part of the American memory series with introduction, timeline, and gallery.

U.S. Civil War Center
http://www.cwc.lsu.edu/
The mission of this site is to "locate, index and/or make available all appropriate private and public data regarding the Civil War and to promote the study of the Civil War from the perspective of all professional, occupations, and academic disciplines."

Selected Civil War Photographs
http://memory.loc.gov/ammem/cwphtml/cwphome.html
Library of Congress site has more than one thousand photographs, many from Mathew Brady.

A Timeline of the Civil War
http://www.historyplace.com/civilwar/index.html
This site offers a comprehensive Civil War timeline that includes photographs.

National Civil War Association
http://www.ncwa.org/
This site documents one of the many Civil War reenactment organizations in the United States.

CHAPTER 16 | RECONSTRUCTION AND THE SOUTH

The Impeachment of Andrew Johnson
http://www.impeach-andrewjohnson.com/
This HarpWeek site about the impeachment includes images and text from the Reconstruction period.

Diary and Letters of Rutherford B. Hayes
http://www.ohiohistory.org/onlinedoc/hayes/index.cfm
The Rutherford B. Hayes Presidential Center in Fremont, Ohio, maintains this searchable database of Hayes's writings.

Rutherford B. Hayes
http://www.ipl.org/ref/POTUS/rbhayes.html
This site contains information relating to Hayes and his presidency.

Images of African Americans from the Nineteenth Century
http://digital.nypl.org/schomburg/images_aa19/
The New York Public Library–Schomburg Center for Research in Black Culture site contains numerous visuals.

Freedman and Southern Society Project (University of Maryland, College Park)
http://www.inform.umd.edu/ARHU/Depts/History/Freedman/home.html
This site contains a chronology and sample documents from several collections or primary sources about emancipation and freedom in the 1860s.

CHAPTER 17 | IN THE WAKE OF WAR

Indian Affairs: Laws and Treaties, Compiled and Edited by Charles J. Kappler (1904)
http://www.digital.library.okstate.edu/kappler/
This digitized text at Oklahoma State University includes pre-removal treaties with the five Civilized Tribes and other tribes.

Geronimo
http://odur.let.rug.nl/~usa/B/geronimo/geronixx.htm
This site contains biographical and autobiographical information about the famous Native American who resisted European American domination.

National Museum of the American Indian
http://www.si.edu/
The Smithsonian Institution maintains this site, providing information about the museum. The museum is dedicated to everything about Native Americans.

The Northern Great Plains, 1880–1920: Photographs from the Fred Hulstrand and F. A. Pazandak Photograph Collections
http://memory.loc.gov/ammem/award97/ndfahtml/ngphome.html
This American Memory site from the Library of Congress contains "two collections from the Institute for Regional Studies at North Dakota State University" with "900 photographs of rural and small-town life at the turn of the century." Included are "images of sod homes and the people who built them; images of farms and the machinery that made them prosper; and images of one-room schools and the children who were educated in them."

The Transcontinental Railroad
http://www.sfmuseum.org/hist1/rail.html
The Museum of the City of San Francisco site has excellent information on the Transcontinental Railroad.

African American Perspectives: Pamphlets from the Daniel A. P. Murry Collections, 1818–1907
http://memory.loc.gov/ammem/aap/aaphome.html
This collection includes writings of famous African Americans, including Frederick Douglass, Booker T. Washington, Ida B. Wells-Barnett, Benjamin W. Arnett, Alexander Crummel, and Emanuel Love.

CHAPTER 18 | AN INDUSTRIAL GIANT

Alexander Graham Bell Family Papers at the Library of Congress
http://memory.loc.gov/ammem/bellhtml/bellhome.html
This site contains papers from 1862 to 1939, as well as a chronology, images, selected, selected documents, and interpretive essays about Bell.

Alexander Graham Bell Telephone Sketch
http://lcweb2.loc.gov/cgi-bin/query/D?mcc:1:./temp/~ammem_gqbY::
This Library of Congress site has the sketch Bell made of his invention, the telephone.

Anarchist Archives at Pitzer University
http://dwardmac.pitzer.edu/Anarchist_Archives/archivehome.html
This archive includes classic anarchist texts, especially information about and graphics of the Haymarket Riot.

John D. Rockefeller and the Standard Oil Company
http://www.micheloud.com/FXM/SO/
This study with accompanying images by François Micheloud tells of the rise of Rockefeller and his mammoth company.

National Refinery Company
http://www.enarco.com/
This positive history of the company reflects industrial changes of late-nineteenth-century America.

Labor–Management Conflict in American History
http://history.osu.edu/Projects/LaborConflict/Default.htm
This Ohio State University site includes primary accounts of some of the major events in the history of the labor–management conflict in the late-nineteenth and early-twentieth centuries.

Samuel Gompers Papers at the University of Maryland
http://www.history.umd.edu/Gompers/index.html
This site includes information about the papers project. It also has a photo gallery, selected documents, and a brief history of the first president of the American Federation of Labor.

CHAPTER 19 | AMERICAN SOCIETY IN THE INDUSTRIAL AGE

Coal Mining During the Gilded Age and Progressive Era
http://history.osu.edu/Projects/Gilded_Age/default.htm
This Ohio State University site examines the development of the coal industry, including the sometimes violent labor-management conflict.

Touring Turn-of-the-Century America: Photographs from the Detroit Publishing Company, 1880–1920
http://memory.loc.gov/ammem/detroit/dethome.html
This Library of Congress collection has thousands of photographs from turn-of-the-century America.

Inside an American Factory: The Westinghouse Works, 1904
http://lcweb2.loc.gov/ammem/papr/west/westhome.html
Part of the American Memory Project at the Library of Congress, this site provides a glimpse inside a turn-of-the-century factory.

Thorsten Veblen's The Theory of the Leisure Class
http://xroads.virginia.edu/~HYPER/VEBLEN/veb_toc.html
This University of Virginia site includes a picture of Veblen as well as the text of his influential book.

CHAPTER 20 | INTELLECTUAL AND CULTURAL TRENDS

Touring Turn-of-the-Century America: Photographs from the Detroit Publishing Company, 1880–1920
http://memory.loc.gov/ammem/detroit/dethome.html
This Library of Congress collection has thousands of photographs from turn-of-the-century America.

American Authors
http://xroads.virginia.edu/~HYPER/hypertex.html
This University of Virginia site contains hypertexts of the works of many prominent American authors, including Mark Twain, Stephen Crane, and Theodore Dreiser.

I Hear America Singing
http://www.thirteen.org/cgi-bin/ihas.cgi
American music came into its own at the turn of the century, as this fascinating site demonstrates.

National Geographic and the Titanic
http://www.nationalgeographic.com/society/ngo/explorer/titanic/movie.html
This National Geographic site offers historical perspective and balanced coverage of the *Titanic* tragedy.

CHAPTER 21 | POLITICS: LOCAL, STATE, AND NATIONAL

James Garfield
http://www.ipl.org/ref/POTUS/jagarfield.html
This site contains basic factual data about Garfield's election and presidency, speeches, and online bibliography.

Benjamin Harrison
http://www.ipl.org/ref/POTUS/bharrison.html
This site contains basic factual data about Harrison's election and presidency, speeches, and online bibliography.

Chester Arthur
http://www.ipl.org/ref/POTUS/caarthur.html
This site contains basic factual data about Arthur's election and presidency, speeches, and online bibliography.

William Jennings Bryan
http://ap.grolier.com/article?assetid=0064310-00&templatename=/article/article.htm/
This site treats the career and ideas of the three-time presidential candidate.

William McKinley
http://www.ipl.org/ref/POTUS/wmckinley.html
This site contains basic factual data about McKinley's election and presidency, speeches, and online bibliography.

The Era of William McKinley
http://history.osu.edu/projects/mckinley/
This site contains numerous images from various stages of William McKinley's career along with a brief bibliographical essay. This Ohio State University site also has a section with an excellent collection of McKinley-era cartoons.

CHAPTER 22 | THE AGE OF REFORM

History of the Suffrage Movement
http://www.rochester.edu/SBA
This site includes a chronology, important texts relating to woman suffrage, and bibliographical information about Susan B. Anthony and Elizabeth Cady Stanton.

The Conservation Movement, 1850–1920
http://memory.loc.gov/ammem/amrvhtml/conshome.html
This American Memory site brings together scores of primary sources and photographs about "the historical formation and cultural foundations of the movement to conserve and protect America's natural heritage."

African American Perspectives: Pamphlets from the Daniel A. P. Murry Collections, 1818–1907
http://memory.loc.gov/ammem/aap/aaphome.html
This collection includes writings of famous African Americans, including Frederick Douglass, Booker T. Washington, Ida B. Wells-Barnett, Benjamin W. Arnett, Alexander Crummel, and Emanuel Love.

Coal Mining During the Gilded Age and Progressive Era
http://www.history.osu.edu/Projects/Gilded_Age/default.htm
This Ohio State University site examines the development of the coal industry, including the sometimes violent labor–management conflict.

Theodore Roosevelt Association
http://www.theodoreroosevelt.org/
This site contains much bibliographical and research information about Theodore Roosevelt.

NAACP On-line
http://www.naacp.org/past_future/index.html
The National Association for the Advancement of Colored People's official website explains its mission and includes a primary document explaining the start of the NAACP.

The Triangle Shirtwaist Factory Fire, March 25, 1911
http://www.ilr.cornell.edu/trianglefire/
The Kheel Center for Labor–Management Documentation and Cornell University Archives put together this excellent site of oral histories, images, and essays.

Labor–Management Conflict in American History
http://www.history.osu.edu/Projects/Laborconflict/default.htm
This Ohio State University site includes primary accounts of some of the major events in the history of the labor–management conflict.

Bill Haywood Trial (1907)
http://www.law.umkc.edu/faculty/projects/ftrials/haywood/haywood.htm
This site contains images, chronology, court, and official documents maintained by Dr. Doug Linder at the University of Missouri—Kansas City Law School.

Theodore Roosevelt
http://www.ipl.org/dir/POTUS/troosevelt.html
This site contains basic factual data about Roosevelt's election and presidency, speeches, and online bibliography.

The 1906 San Francisco Earthquake
http://www-socal.wr.usgs.gov/wald/1906/1906.html
This site contains scholarly articles dealing with the earthquake, its source and history.

Federal Reserve Act of 1913
http://odur.let.rug.nl/~usa/E/usbank/bank13.htm
The federal government's role in U.S. banking was finally resolved in 1913.

William Howard Taft
http://www.ipl.org/dir/POTUS/whtaft.html
This site contains basic factual data about Taft's election and presidency, speeches, and online bibliography.

CHAPTER 23 | FROM ISOLATION TO EMPIRE

William McKinley
http://www.ipl.org/div/POTUS/wmckinley.html
This site contains basic factual data about McKinley's election and presidency, speeches, and online bibliography.

The Era of William McKinley
http://www.history.osu.edu/Projects/Mckinley/default.htm
This site contains numerous images from various stages of William McKinley's career along with a brief bibliographical essay. This Ohio State University site also has a section with an excellent collection of McKinley-era cartoons.

William McKinley and the Spanish-American War
http://www.history.osu.edu/Projects/Mckinley/SpanAmWar.html
Part of the Ohio State University site about William McKinley. This section highlights the Spanish-American War with an essay and photographs.

Sentenaryo/Centennial: The Philippine Revolution and the Philippine-American War
http://www.boondocksnet.com/centennial/index.html
Jim Zwick organizes primary documents, images, and essays focusing on U.S. involvement in the Philippines.

Selected Naval Documents: The Spanish-American War
http://www.history.navy.mil/wars/spanam/sn98-1.htm
The primary documents speak volumes to the activity of the U.S. Navy during the conflict with Spain.

The Spanish-American War
http://lcweb.loc.gov/rr/hispanic/1898/trask.html
This article by historian David Trask includes links to other related sites. The article is provided by the Library of Congress.

The First Open Door Note
http://odur.let.rug.nl/~usa/D/1876-1900/foreignpolicy/opendr.htm
The Open Door note played an important ideological role in U.S. foreign policy at the end of the nineteenth century. Read the text of that document on this site.

Imperialism Web Page
http://www.smplanet.com/imperialism/toc.html
Focusing on the period around 1900, this site puts much information about American imperialism in one place.

Theodore Roosevelt Association
http://www.theodoreroosevelt.org/
This site contains much bibliographical and research information about Theodore Roosevelt.

CHAPTER 24 | WOODROW WILSON AND THE GREAT WAR

Woodrow Wilson
http://www.ipl.org/div/POTUS/wwilson.html
This site contains basic factual data about Wilson's election and presidency, speeches, and online bibliography.

World War 1 Document Archives
http://www.lib.byu.edu/~rdh/wwi/
This archive contains sources about World War I in general, not just America's involvement.

World War 1: Trenches on the Web
http://www.worldwar1.com
This site provides a mass of data concerning the prosecution of the world's first global war.

American Leaders Speak: Recordings from World War 1 and the 1920 Election
http://memory.loc.gov/ammem/nfhtml/
This Library of Congress site contains fifty-nine recordings from American leaders at the turn of the century.

The Great Migration in Chicago
http://lcweb.loc.gov/exhibits/african/afam011.html
This site looks at the black experience in the great migration to one prominent destination.

The Flu Epidemic of 1918
http://www.pbs.org/wgbh/amex/influenza/
Today, the flu is an annoyance for most people. Yet in 1918, a major flu epidemic swept the United States, killing 600,000 people.

CHAPTER 25 | POSTWAR SOCIETY AND CULTURE: CHANGE AND ADJUSTMENT

Margaret Sanger Papers Projects
http://www.nyu.edu/projects/sanger/
This site at New York University contains information about Margaret Sanger and digital versions of several of her works.

Harlem: The Mecca of the New Negro
http://etext.lib.virginia.edu/harlem/
This site is the online text of the March 1925 Survey Graphic Harlem Number; the journal was the premier social work journal of the decade.

Harlem 1900–1940: An African American Community
http://www.si.umich.edu/CHICO/Harlem/
The New York Public Library's Schomburg Center for Research in Black Culture hosts this site that includes a database, a timeline, and an exhibit.

William P. Gottlieb Photographs of the Golden Age of Jazz
http://memory.loc.gov/ammem/wghtml/wghome.html
The Music Division of the Library of Congress has numerous images, audio, and scanned articles from the 1940s.

The Scopes Trial
http://xroads.virginia.edu/~UG97/inherit/1925home.html
This site gives general descriptions of the trial and the issues surrounding the landmark case.

Temperance and Prohibition
http://prohibition.osu.edu/
This site looks at the temperance movement over time and contains many informative links.

National Arts and Crafts Archives
http://arts-crafts.com/index.html
This site serves as a guide to materials on the Arts and Crafts movement, which lasted roughly from 1890 to 1929.

CHAPTER 26 | THE NEW ERA: 1921–1933

America from the Great Depression to World War II: Photographs from the FSA and OWI, c. 1935–1945
http://memory.loc.gov/ammem/fsowhome.html
These images in the Farm Security Administration and Office of War Information Collection show Americans from all over the nation experiencing everything from despair to triumph in the 1930s and 1940s.

CHAPTER 27 | THE NEW DEAL: 1933–1941

Voices from the Dust Bowl: The Charles L. Todd and Robert Sonkin Migrant Worker Collection, 1940–1941
http://memory.loc.gov/ammem/afctshtml/tshome.html
Farm Security Administration (FSA) studies of migrant work camps in central California in 1940 and 1941 are the bulk of this site. The collections include audio recordings, photographs, manuscript material, and publications.

The New Deal Network
http://newdeal.feri.org
This database includes photographs, political cartoons, and texts—including speeches, letters, and other historic documents—from the New Deal period.

Franklin Delano Roosevelt
http://www.ipl.org/div/POTUS/fdroosevelt.html
This site provides information about Roosevelt, the only president to serve more than two terms.

A New Deal for the Arts
http://www.archives.gov/exhibit_hall/new_deal_for_the_arts/work_pays_america.html
Artwork, documents, and photographs recount the federal government's efforts to fund artists in the 1930s in the National Archives site.

Eleanor Roosevelt
http://ap.grolier.com/assetid=0336050-00&template=/article/article.html
This site provides both information about the first lady and links to other relevant sites.

America from the Great Depression to World War II: Photographs from the FSA and OWI, c. 1935–1945
http://memory.loc.gov/ammem/fsowhome.html
These images in the Farm Security Administration—Office of War Information Collection show Americas from all over the nation experiencing everything from despair to triumph in the 1930s and 1940s.

American Life Histories: Manuscripts from the Federal Writers Project, 1936–1940
http://memory.loc.gov/ammem/wpaintro/wpahome.html
The staff of the Folklore Project of the Federal Writers Project wrote these histories. Typically between 2000–15,000 words, the manuscripts provide a wonderful glimpse into American life.

CHAPTER 28 | WAR AND PEACE

Franklin Delano Roosevelt
http://www.ipl.org/ref/POTUS/fdroosevelt.html
This site provides information about Roosevelt, the only president to serve more than two terms.

America from the Great Depression to World War II: Photographs from the FSA and OWI, c. 1935–1945
http://memory.loc.gov/ammem/fsowhome.html
These images in the Farm Security Administration—Office of War Information Collection show Americans from all over the nation experiencing everything from despair to triumph in the 1930s and 1940s.

A People at War
http://www.archives.gov/exhibit_hall/a_people_at_war/a_people_at_war.html
This National Archives exhibit takes a close look at the contributions millions of Americans made to the war effort.

Powers of Persuasion—Poster Art of World War II
http://www.archives.gov/publications/posters/original_posters.html
These powerful posters at the National Archives were part of the battle for the hearts and minds of the American people.

A-Bomb WWW Museum
http://www.csi.ad.jp/ABOMB/
This site offers information about the impact of the first atomic bomb as well as the background and context of weapons of total destruction.

The United States Holocaust Memorial Museum
http://www.ushmm.org/
This is the official Website of the Holocaust Museum in Washington, D.C.

The Seabees During World War II
http://www.seabeecook.com/history/
The Seabees are a U.S. Navy support unit best known for their construction projects. This site provides articles, pictures, and reminiscences of Seabees during the war. This site looks at the war behind the lines.

Tuskegee Airmen
http://www.wpafb.af.mil/museum/history/prewwii/ta.htm
The Air Force Museum at Wright-Patterson Air Force Base maintains this site about the African American pilots of World War II.

George C. Marshall
http://www.marshallfoundation.org/
This site, maintained by the George C. Marshall Foundation at the Virginia Military Institute, Lexington, Virginia, provides information on the values and career of U.S. Army Chief of Staff George C. Marshall.

Chapter 29 | The American Century

Harry S Truman
http://www.ipl.org/dir/POTUS/hstruman.html
This site contains basic factual data about Truman's election, presidency, and speeches.

Cold War
http://cnn.com/SPECIALS/cold.war/
This is the companion site to the CNN Perspectives series on the Cold War. It contains information including interactive timelines and a quiz.

The Marshall Plan
http://www.archives.gov/exhibit_hall/featured_documents/marshall_plan/
The National Archives site contains useful information on the Marshall Plan.

Korean War Project
http://www.koreanwar.org/
This site has information about the Korean War and is a guide to resources on that conflict.

NATO at 50
http://www.cnn.com/SPECIALS/1999/nato/
This CNN site has an excellent timeline and images that tell the history of the North Atlantic Treaty Organization.

Senator Joe McCarthy—A Multimedia Celebration
http://webcorp.com/mccarthy/
This Webcorp site includes audio and visual excerpts of McCarthy's speeches.

Harry S Truman Library and Museum
http://www.trumanlibrary.org
This presidential library site has numerous photos and important documents relating to Truman.

Dwight David Eisenhower
http://www.ipl.org/dir/POTUS/ddeisenhower.html
This site contains an online bibliography covering Eisenhower's election, presidency, and speeches.

1950s America
http://www.writing.upenn.edu/~afilreis/50s/home.html
This site by University of Pennsylvania Professor Al Filreis contains a large array of 1950s literature and images in an alphabetical index.

Hollywood and the Movies During the 1950s
http://lib.berkeley.edu/MRC/50sbib.html
This site proves information on cinema and film during the 1950s.

The Dwight D. Eisenhower Library and Museum
http://www.eisenhower.utexas.edu/
This site contains mainly photographs of the presidents.

CHAPTER 30 | FROM CAMELOT TO WATERGATE

Presidents Kennedy, Johnson, Nixon, and Ford
http://www.ipl.org/dir/POTUS/jfkennedy.html
http://www.ipl.org/dir/POTUS/lbjohnson.html
http://www.ipl.org/dir/POTUS/rmnixon.html
http://www.ipl.org/dir/POTUS/grford/html
These sites contain basic data about each president's election, presidency, and speeches.

Vietnam Online
http://www.pbs.org/wgbh/pages/amex/vietnam/
From PBS and the American Experience, this site contains a detailed, interactive timeline of the war, interpretive essays, and autobiographical reflections.

My Lai Court Martial (1970)
http://www.law.umkc.edu/faculty/projects/ftrials/mylai/mylai.htm
This site contains images, chronology, court and officials documents maintained by Dr. Douglas Linder at University of Missouri–Kansas City Law School.

Civil Rights Oral History Bibliography
http://www.usm.edu/crdp/html/dah.shtml/
This University of Southern Mississippi site includes complete transcripts of the selected oral resources.

United States v. Cecil Price et al. (The "Mississippi Burning" Trial), 1967
http://www.law.umkc.edu/faculty/projects/ftrials/price&bowers.html
This site contains images, chronology, and court and officials documents maintained by Dr. Doug Linder at the University of Missouri–Kansas City Law School.

Watergate
http://www.journale.com/watergate.html
This site contains primary and secondary sources relating to the event that forced Nixon's resignation.

CHAPTER 31 | SOCIETY IN FLUX

1950s America
http://www.writing.upenn.edu/~afilreis/50s/home.html
This site by University of Pennsylvania Professor Al Filreis contains a large array of 1950s literature and images in an alphabetical index.

Hollywood and the Movies During the 1950s
http://lib.berkeley.edu/MRC/50sbib.html
This site proves information on cinema and film during the 1950s.

Rock and Roll
http://www.rockhall.com/
By the late-1950s, rock and roll had become the music of the new generation.

Martin Luther King, Jr.
http://www.seattletimes.com/mlk/
This *Seattle Times* site has several articles about King and the Civil Rights Movement.

Martin Luther King, Jr. Papers Project
http://www.stanford.edu/group/King/
This Stanford University site has links and selected documents by and concerning Martin Luther King, Jr.

National Civil Rights Museum
http://www.civilrightsmuseum.org
This site allows a virtual tour of the museum with its interpretive exhibits.

The Diggers Archives
http://www.diggers.org/
This site provides information about The San Francisco Diggers, one of the legendary groups in the Haight-Ashbury from 1966–1968.

The Sixties Project
http://lists.village.virginia.edu/sixties/
This University of Virginia site has extensive exhibits, documents, and personal narratives from the 1960s.

Civil Rights Oral History Bibliography
http://www.dept.usm.edu/crdp/html/dah.shtml
This University of Southern Mississippi site includes complete transcripts of the selected oral resources.

1969 Woodstock Festival and Concert
http://www.woodstock69.com
This site provides pictures and lists of songs from the famous rock festival.

Virtual Museum of Computing
http://vmoc.museophile.sbu.ac.uk
This site relates history of computing through a series of online exhibits.

The Computer Museum History Center
http://www.computerhistory.org
This site for the Computer Museum History Center features online archives and exhibits tracing decades of computer history.

CHAPTER 32 | RUNNING ON EMPTY: THE NATION TRANSFORMED

Gerald Rudolph Ford
http://www.ipl.org/div/POTUS/grford.html
This site contains basic factual data about Ford's elections and presidency, speeches, and online bibliography.

James Earl Carter, Jr.
http://www.ipl.org/div/POTUS/jecarter.html
This site contains basic factual data about Carter's elections and presidency, speeches, and online bibliography.

The 80s Server
http://www.80s.com
Although the best parts of this site are restricted to members, it nonetheless has some great information about the 1980s.

Ronald Wilson Reagan
http://www.ipl.org/div/POTUS/rwreagan.html
This site contains basic factual data about Reagan's elections and presidency, speeches, and online biography.

CHAPTER 33 | MISDEMEANORS AND HIGH CRIMES

Desert Storm
http://www.desert-storm.com/
This site shows U.S. involvement in the Persian Gulf conflict.

Presidents George H. W. Bush and Bill Clinton
http://www.ipl.org/ref/POTUS/ghwbush.html
http://www.ipl.org/ref/POTUS/wjclinton.html
These sites contain basic data about each president's election, presidency, and speeches as well as an online biography of each.

Investigating the President: The Trial
http://www.cnn.com/ALLPOLITICS/resources/1998/lewinsky/
This CNN site provides information and documents about the scandals surrounding President Clinton and his impeachment.

Kosovo
http://www.cnn.com/SPECIALS/1998/10/kosovo/
This in-depth CNN Interactive site looks at the development and current resolution to the turmoil in Kosovo.

Oklahoma City Bombing
http://www.cnn.com/US/9703/okc.trial/
This CNN Interactive site has information about this terrorist act.

9/11 Attacks
http://911digitalarchives.org
This site preserves information about the terror attacks.

130° W   125° W   120° W   115° W   110° W   105° W   100° W

CANADA

Cape Flattery
Puget Sound
Tacoma
Olympia ★ Seattle
WASHINGTON
Mt. St. Helens
8,366 ft.
(2,550 m) ▲ Mt. Rainier
14,410 ft.
(4,300 m)
Portland
Columbia River
Salem ★
Eugene

Columbia River
Spokane

ROCKY

MOUNTAINS

Great Falls   Missouri River

Helena ●   MONTANA

Billings ●

NORTH DAKOT

Bismarck ●   ★

Grand F

45° N

CAPE Blanco

OREGON
IDAHO
★ Boise
Idaho Falls ●
Snake River
Pocatello ●

WYOMING

SOUTH DAKOT

Rapid City ●

BLACK
HILLS

Pierre ●   ★

Sio

COAST   RANGES

Cape Mendocino

40° N

CASCADE

COLUMBIA PLATEAU

GREAT

Reno ●
Carson City ★
Lake Tahoe
Sacramento ★

SIERRA

NEVADA
BASIN

Great
Salt
Lake
Ogden ●
Salt Lake City ●
Provo ●

UTAH

Casper ●

ROCKY

Laramie ●   Cheyenne ★
Longs Peak
14,256 ft.
(4,344 m) ▲

NEBRASKA

Grand Island ●
Platte River

GREAT

PLAINS

San Francisco Bay
San Francisco
San Jose ●   Oakland ●

CENTRAL   Sacramento River

VALLEY   San Joaquin River

35° N

COAST

NEVADA

RANGES

Fresno ●   ▲ Mt. Whitney
14,500 ft.
(4,400 m)
DEATH
VALLEY

CALIFORNIA
Bakersfield ●

Las
Vegas ●

MOJAVE DESERT

Green River

Colorado River

COLORADO
PLATEAU

Denver ★
COLORADO
Mt. Elbert
14,433 ft.
(4,400 m) ▲   ▲ Colorado Springs
Pikes Peak   ●
14,110 ft.
(4,300 m)   Pueblo ●

South Platte River
North Platte River

Arkansas River

KANS

Los Angeles ●
Long Beach ●   ● Anaheim
Santa Ana ●
San Diego ●

ARIZONA

Salton
Sea
Colorado River

Phoenix ●
Mesa ●

Santa Fe ★

Albuquerque ●

NEW MEXICO

Rio Grande

OKLA

Oklaho

Lawto

Brazos River

Red

Fort

PACIFIC
OCEAN

Tucson ●

Las Cruces ●
El Paso ●

LLANO
ESTACADO

TEXAS

San Antor

30° N

MEXICO

25° N

Rio Grande

Corpu

A-68

Kauai   Oahu
Honolulu ★   Molokai
Lanai   Maui
HAWAII
PACIFIC OCEAN
0   50 miles
0   50 kilometers
Hilo ●
Hawaii
22° N
19° N
160° W   155° W

ARCTIC OCEAN

RUSSIA

BROOKS   RANGE

Nome ●   ALASKA   Arctic Circle   CANADA

Bering Strait
Yukon River   Fairbanks ●
RANGE   ▲ Mt. McKinley
20,320 ft.
(6,194 m)
● Anchorage
ALASKA
KENAI
PENINSULA

Bering Sea

PACIFIC
OCEAN

ALEUTIAN   ISLANDS

Kodiak Is.
Gulf of Alaska

Juneau ★

0   250 miles
0   250 kilometers

Tropic of Cancer

70° W   160° W   150° W   140° W   130° W   60° N

50° N

170° E   180°

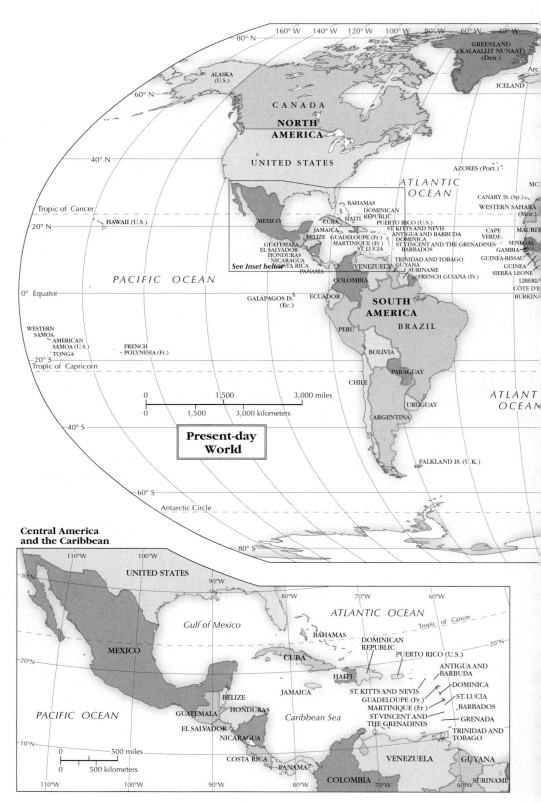

Present-day World

Central America and the Caribbean

CREDITS

CHAPTER 16 449 Picture History **458** The Granger Collection, New York **460** Library of Congress **462** Culver Pictures, Inc. **467** Library of Congress

CHAPTER 17 477 The Granger Collection, New York **479** Library of Congress **483** Sterling Memorial Library, Manuscripts & Archives/Yale University **487** Burton Historical Collection, Detroit Public Library **490** © Bettmann/CORBIS **495** Courtesy of the Bancroft Library, University of California, Berkeley **499** Solomon D. Butcher Collection, Nebraska State Historical Society

CHAPTER 18 506 © Tony Arruza/CORBIS **508** Library of Congress **515** © Collection of The New-York Historical Society **519, left** Used with permission from The Biltmore Company, Asheville, North Carolina **519, right** Picture History **524** © Bettmann/CORBIS **525** © CORBIS

CHAPTER 19 533 © Bettmann/CORBIS **535** Fred Hulstrand History in Pictures Collection, NDIRS-NDSU, Fargo, ND **541** The Granger Collection, New York **543** National Park Service, Statue of Liberty Monument **544** Library of Congress **547** Culver Pictures, Inc. **549** © Bettmann/CORBIS **553** Alice Kellogg Tyler, *Portrait of Jane Addams*, 1893. Chicago Historical Society, (P&S-1971.0140)

CHAPTER 20 557 © Bettman/CORBIS **558** Private Collection, Photograph by David Gulick **560** © Bettmann/CORBIS **561** Smith College Archives, Smith College Northampton, MA **566** Nebraska State Historical Society, Solomon D. Butcher Collection **571, left** Photofest **571, right** Brown Brothers, Inc. **573** © Bettmann/CORBIS

CHAPTER 21 579 © CORBIS **580** Brown Brothers, Inc. **582** Culver Pictures, Inc. **584** National Museum of American History, Smithsonian Institution **588** Kansas State Historical Society, Topeka **589** The Granger Collection, New York **590** Kansas State Historical Society, Topeka **593** Culver Pictures, Inc.

CHAPTER 22 600 Culver Pictures, Inc. **601** © Bettmann/CORBIS **606** Courtesy of the Fogg Art Museum, Harvard University Art Museums, on deposit from the Carpenter Center for the Visual Arts **608** Culver Pictures, Inc. **612** National Museum of American History, Smithsonian Institution **614** Library of Congress **622** Brown Brothers, Inc. **625** Library of Congress **627** National Portrait Gallery, Smithsonian Institution/Art Resource, NY, (detail)

CHAPTER 23 634, top Private Collection/Bridgeman Art Library 634, bottom Killie Family Papers/Presbyterian Historical Society, Presbyterian Church U.S.A. 635 Hawaii State Archives/Historical Records Branch 639 The Granger Collection, New York 640 Chicago Historical Society, (ICHi-08428) 642 Vermont State House 647 © Bettmann/CORBIS 654 Library of Congress

CHAPTER 24 661 Imperial War Museum, London 663 Brown Brothers, Inc. 670 Photoworld/FPG International/Getty Images 672 Courtesy of the Hagley Museum and Library 673 © Bettmann/CORBIS 675 Library of Congress 684, left Library of Congress 684, right Library of Congress 686 Chicago Historical Society

CHAPTER 25 690 Culver Pictures, Inc. 694 Getty Images 695 © Bettmann/CORBIS 696 The Kobal Collection 697, left DN-0076751, *Chicago Daily News* negatives collection, Chicago Historical Society 697, right DN-0076798, *Chicago Daily News* negatives collection, Chicago Historical Society 700 Culver Pictures, Inc. 702 © Bettmann/CORBIS 704 © Bettmann/CORBIS 705 © Bettmann/CORBIS 706 Kansas State Historical Society, Topeka 711 Hulton Archive/Getty Images 713 Culver Pictures, Inc.

CHAPTER 26 718 Culver Pictures, Inc. 721 Culver Pictures, Inc. 725 AP/Wide World Photos 726 Getty Images 728 © Bettmann/CORBIS 734 University of Washington Libraries, Special Collections, Lee 20102 735 Library of Congress 737 Library of Congress 738 Franklin D. Roosevelt Library 739 © Bettmann/CORBIS

CHAPTER 27 742 © Bettmann/CORBIS 749 AP/Wide World Photos 750 © Bettman/CORBIS 752 The Granger Collection, New York 756 William C. Pryor/National Archives, Still Pictures Branch 759 © William Gropper/Vanity Fair, Condé Nast Publications, Inc. 760 © Bettmann/CORBIS 761 Library of Congress 766 © Roger-Viollet/Getty Images

CHAPTER 28 774 SuperStock, New York 777 Library of Congress 780 National Archives 781 National Archives 787, right © Bettmann/CORBIS 787, left Photofest 788 © Bettmann/CORBIS 789 Culver Pictures, Inc. 793 © CORBIS 795 The Granger Collection, New York

CHAPTER 29 806 AP/Wide World Photos 807 © Bettmann/CORBIS 809 Sovfoto/Eastfoto 812 National Archives 815 © Bettmann/CORBIS 817 © Bettmann/CORBIS 820 © Elliot Erwitt/Magnum Photos, Inc. (detail) 823 © Bettmann/CORBIS

CHAPTER 30 828 Hulton Archive/Getty Images 830 © Bettmann/CORBIS 833 AP/Wide World Photos 835 © Bettmann/CORBIS 837 © Bettmann/CORBIS 841 AP/Wide World Photos 844 © Bettmann/CORBIS 846 Time Life Pictures/Getty Images 847 Getty Images 848 Magnum Photos, Inc. (detail) 852 ©1997 G. P. Trudeau. Reprinted with permission of Universal Press Syndicate. All rights reserved.

CHAPTER 31 860 © Harold M. Lambert/SuperStock 869 Time Life Pictures/Getty Images 869 © Robert D./Black Star/Stock Photo 874 Getty Images News Services 876 ©

H. Diltz/CORBIS SYGMA **877** © J. L. Atlan/CORBIS SYGMA **879** © Owen Franken/Stock Boston, Inc. **880** Time Life Pictures/Getty Images

CHAPTER 32 **883** © S. Seitz/Woodfin Camp & Associates **884** © Bettman/CORBIS **889** Liaison/Getty Images **893** © Sipa Press **894** Ronald Reagan Library **899** AP/Wide World Photos **901** SPL/Photo Researchers, Inc. **905** Library of Congress/© 1986 by Herblock in *The Washington Post*

CHAPTER 33 **911** © Bob Daemmrich/The Image Works **915** AP/Wide World Photos **918** Arnie Sachs/Consolidated News Pictures/Liaison/Getty Images **924** Getty Images **930** AP/Wide World Photos **934** AP/Wide World Photos **935** AFP/Getty Images **937** Photodisc/Getty Images

INDEX

Note: Italicized letters *f* and *m* following page numbers indicate figures (photos, illustrations, and graphs) and maps respectively.

A & P food chain, 729
AAA. *See* Agricultural Adjustment Administration
Abilene, Kansas, 490*f*, 497
Abolitionist movement, antislavery societies in, 456
Abortion, 876, 880*f*, 918
Abraham Lincoln (ship), 934*f*
Abu Ghraib prison, 935*f*
Accidents, on-the-job, 606
Acheson, Dean, 808
Acquired immunodeficiency syndrome (AIDS), 878, 900–901, 901*f*
Adams, Charles Francis, Jr., 517
Adams, Henry, 473, 518, 554, 565, 611
Addams, Jane: as anti-imperialist, 645; and NAACP, 627; and settlement house movement, 552–554, 553–554, 553*f*; on women, 609; and World War I, 669
Adkins v. *Children's Hospital,* 695
Advertising: newspaper publishing and, 557; in post–World War I period, 700, 700*f*, 713*f*; on television, 858–859
AEF. *See* American Expeditionary Force
Affirmative action, 868, 921
Afghanistan, 931–932; bin Laden in, 929; in late 20th-century, 914*m*; Soviet invasion of, 891; Taliban in, 929; U.S. retaliation against, 931–932
AFL. *See* American Federation of Labor
Africa: colonization by freed slaves in, 478; embassy bombings in, 931; in World War II, 783, 784*m*
African Americans. *See* Black Americans
Afro-American League, 478
Age (newspaper), 478

The Age of Innocence (Wharton), 708
Agnew, Spiro T., 843, 852
Agricultural Adjustment Act (1933), 744–745, 753
Agricultural Adjustment Administration (AAA), 744–745, 753
Agricultural Marketing Act (1929), 732
Agriculture: in 19th-century, 503; Farm Loan Act and, 664; in Great Depression, 731, 732, 733; New Deal policies for, 744–745; in post–Civil War South, 461–463, 462*f*, 463*f*; post–World War I, 729–730; railroads and, 492; in South, 461–463, 462*f*, 463*f*; in West, 492–493; in World War I, 668, 678
Aguinaldo, Emilio, 641, 646, 647*f*
Aid. *See* Foreign aid
AIDS. *See* Acquired immunodeficiency syndrome
AIM. *See* American Indian Movement
Airplane(s): early development of, 714–715; industry, 714–715; terrorism and, 929–931; in World War I, 714–715; in World War II, 788, 789
Air travel, 714–715, 858
Alabama: bus boycott in, 832–833; civil rights movement in, 832–833, 833, 866; iron industry in, 507
Alaska, purchase of, 630
Albania, 765
Alcindor, Lew (Abdul-Jabbar, Kareem), 862
Alcohol consumption: 19th-century, 548; post–World War I, 704–705. *See also* Prohibition; Temperance movement
Alcorn, John L., 456
Alcorn University, 458*f*
Aldrich, Nelson, 473
Ali, Muhammad, 862, 870
Allen, Frederick Lewis, 694*f*

Allende, Salvadore, 886–887
Alliance movement, 586–589
Allied Powers (World War I), 660, 725–727
Allied Powers (World War II): in European theater, 782–785, 784m; trade with, 768–769
Alperovitz, Gar, 793f
al-Qaeda terrorist network, 931, 932
Amalgamated Association of Iron and Steel Workers, 527, 540
Amalgamated Copper, 599
Amazon.com, 926
Amendments, constitutional. See specific amendments
America First Committee, 768
American Academy of Arts and Sciences, 572
American Academy of Pediatrics, 922
American Airlines Flight 11, 929
American Anti-Slavery Society, 456
American Birth Control League, 693
American Civil Liberties Union (ACLU), and Scopes trial, 703
The American Commonwealth (Bryce), 630
American Economic Association, 518
American Expeditionary Force (AEF), 674
American Federation of Labor (AFL), 525; CIO and, 744; in early 20th-century, 602; and unskilled workers, 744; women and, 698
The American High School Today (Conant), 871
American Historical Association, 937f
American Independent party, 843
American Indian(s). See Indian Americans
American Indian Movement (AIM), 869–870
American League, 549
American Legion, 719
American Museum of Natural History, 547
American Political Economy (Bowen), 516
American Railway Union, 527
American Steel and Wire Company, 512
American Sugar Refining Company, 522
American Telephone and Telegraph (AT&T), 507, 895
American Tin Plate Company, 512

American Tobacco Company, 613
American Woman's Suffrage Association, 607
America Online (AOL), 926
Amusement parks, 549f
Anaconda Mining, 491
Anarchists: and Haymarket Square bombing, 524, 525f; post–World War I persecution of, 685–686, 707
Anderson, John, 893
Anderson, Martin, 905
Andersonville prison, 448
Angell, James B., 561
Angleworms, 846f
Anglo-American relations: in late 19th-century, 630–632, 636–637; Latin American diplomacy and, 636–637; in World War I, 660–661
Anglo-Iranian Oil Company, 891
Annan, Beulah, 696f, 697f
Anthony, Susan B., 607
Anthrax letters (2001), 931
Anti-imperialists, 645–646
Anti-Semitism: in Nazi Germany, 765; in post–World War I period, 691
Antislavery societies, 456
Antitrust Division, of Justice Department, 729
Antitrust legislation: Supreme Court on, 522–523, 591, 613; Wilson and, 623
Antitrust legislation, Roosevelt (Theodore) and, 612–613
AOL. See America Online
Apache Indians, 486
Applied Christianity (Gladden), 551
Arafat, Yassir, 925
Arapaho Indians, 483
Arbenz Guzman, Jacobo, 821
Argentina, 890
Arizona, territorial organization of, 491
Arkansas: desegregation in, 823; progressive reform in, 604; readmission to Union, 454
Army: blacks in, 673–674, 776–778, 777f; late 19th-century, 632; McCarthy and, 817; in Spanish-American War, 641–643; women in, 780; in World War I, 668, 673–674, 674–675; in World War II, 776–778, 777f, 780, 790m

Army-McCarthy hearings, 817
Arthur, Chester A., 476, 581
Asia. *See* Far East
As I Lay Dying (Faulkner), 748
As Seen On TV (Marling), 860f
Assembly line, 714
Astor, John Jacob, 570f
Astor, Mrs. John Jacob, 571f
Atchison, Topeka, and Santa Fe Railroad, 493, 496m
Athletics. *See* Sports
Atkins, John, 488
Atlanta Compromise (1895), 480
Atlantic and Pacific Railroad, 496m
Atlantic Coast Line, 505
Atlantic Monthly (magazine), 558, 565, 568, 601
Atomic bomb: Soviet development of, 807; United Nations on, 807; U.S. development of, 766–767; in World War II, 766–767, 791–794, 793f. *See also* Nuclear weapons
Atomic Energy Commission, 807
AT&T. *See* American Telephone and Telegraph
Atwater, Lee, 909
Augusta (ship), 797
Auschwitz death camp, 785
Australia, in World War II, 788
Austria-Hungary, after World War I, 676
Automobile, impact of, 712–714, 713f, 858
Automobile industry: Ford and, 713–714; in Great Depression, 731; in New Deal period, 755; in oil crisis, 883–884, 888; post–World War I, 712–714, 729; post–World War II, 858, 887; strikes in, 755; unionization of, 755
Awakening. *See* Great Awakening
"Axis of evil," 932
Axis Powers (World War II), 772–773, 784m

Babbitt (Lewis), 709
Babcock, Orville E., 465
Baer, George F., 613
Baghdad International Airport, capture of, 933
Bailey, Thomas A., 809f

Baker, John "Home Run," 701
Baker, Newton D., 671
Ballinger, Richard A., 618
Baltimore, Maryland, infrastructure of, 542
Baltimore and Ohio Railroad, 526, 559
Baltimore Evening Sun (newspaper), 703
Baltimore Sun (newspaper), 558, 593
Bank(s) and banking: Federal Reserve system of, 622–623; Great Depression and, 731–733, 741–742; investment banking, 743; in post–World War I period, 729; under Wilson, 622–623
Bank notes. *See* Currency
Bao Dai, 818
Baptists, fundamentalism and, 702
Barbed wire, 498–500, 499f
Barnard, Henry, 537
Barnard College, 561, 571f
Barnstorming, 715
Barrett, David, 841f
Barrios, 868
Barton, Bruce, 712
Baseball: integration of, 870; in late 19th-century, 549; in post–World War I period, 701
Bases-for-destroyers deal, 767
Basketball, 549
The Basketball Diaries (film), 923
Batista, Fulgencio, 821
Batteries, 508
Bayard, Thomas, daughter of, 609
Bay of Pigs invasion, 828
Beard, Frank, 541f
Begin, Manachem, 891
Beijing, China, 634f
Belgian Relief Commission, 667
Belgium, in World War II, 784
Belknap, William W., 465–466
Bell, Alexander Graham, 507, 582f
Bellamy, Edward, 518–520, 551
Ben Hur (Wallace), 567
Berkhofer, Robert E., 937f
Berkman, Alexander, 527
Berlin, Germany: in Cuban missile crisis, 828–829; division into east and west, 804, 805m, 828–829; in Potsdam agreement, 797; reunification of, 899f
Berlin airlift, 803f, 804, 806

Berlin Wall, 805m; destruction of, 899f
Berman, Larry, 841f
Berners-Lee, Tim, 926
Bernstein, Barton, 756f
Bessemer, Henry, 506
Bessemer process, 506, 512
Bezos, Jeff, 926
Bible, Darwin's theory of evolution and, 572
Bicycling, 548, 550
Big Bonanza, 489
Biltmore Estate, 519f
bin Laden, Osama, 929, 931, 932
Birmingham, Alabama: in Great Depression, 733; iron industry in, 507
Birth control: in post–World War I period, 693–698; and sexual revolution, 875
The Birth of a Nation (movie), 457f, 699
Birthrate: in 19th-century, 531; in Great Depression, 736
Bison. See Buffalo
Black Americans: affirmative action and, 868, 921; and African colonization plans, 478; as campus radicals, 873; crime and, 910–911; in Democratic Party, 754, 760–762; Du Bois and, 626–628; in early 20th-century, 626–628; education for, 448, 457f, 459, 460f, 478, 479f, 626, 822–823, 868, 921; in government, 456–459; Klan persecution of, 464, 706–707; in late 19th-century, 476–481; in late 20th-century, 920–921; literature of, 710–711; Long and, 749; lynchings of, 480, 625, 625f, 674; migration of, 671–674, 709–711; in military, 673–674, 776–778, 777f, 822; New Deal and, 754, 760–762; in North, 671–674; in Populist party, 588; in post–World War II period, 821–824; in post–World War I period, 709–711; prejudice against, 625–628, 776–778; in 1868 presidential election, 455; progressivism and, 625; racial pride among, 870; rap music by, 922; after Reconstruction, 476–478; as Reconstruction-era legislators, 456–459, 458f; in Republican party, 456–459, 474, 754, 760–762; Roosevelt (Franklin) and, 754; Simpson trial and, 920; white violence against, 464, 480–481; women, 461, 481; in World War I, 675f; World War I and, 671–674, 673f; in World War II, 776–778. See also Black suffrage; Civil rights movement; Segregation; Slavery
Black Codes, 451, 452
Blackfoot Indians, 482
Black Hand, 660
Black Hills Indian reservation, 484, 485, 489
Black militancy, 626–628; in 1960s, 866–867; and racial pride, 870; after World War I, 709–711
Black Muslims, 834, 862, 866
Black nationalism, 478, 709–711, 834
Black Power, 866–867, 867
Black separatism, 478, 709–711, 834, 866–867, 867
Black Star Line Steamship Company, 710
Black suffrage: civil rights movement and, 866; Fifteenth Amendment and, 456; Fourteenth Amendment and, 452; under Johnson (Lyndon), 836, 838; in mid-1960s, 866; Populist party and, 588; and 1848 presidential election, 455; resistance to, 463–464, 476–478
Blaine, James G.: in 1876 presidential election, 466; in 1884 presidential election, 583–584
Bliss, William D. P., 551
Blitzkrieg, 766
Bloody shirt issue, 474–475
Blount, James H., 635
Board of Indian Commissioners, 485
Bodnar, John, 543f
Boeing, William E., 715
Boeing Air Transport, 715
Bok, Edward W., 723
Bonsack cigarette-rolling machine, 503
"Bonus Army," 734, 735f
Book(s). See Publishing
Book-of-the-Month Club, 709
Booth, John Wilkes, 447
Bootleggers, 705
Borah, William E., 682

Border issues, with Indians, 484–486
Bosnia, 925
"Boss Tweed," 579*f*
Boston (ship), 633
Boston, Massachusetts: civic culture of, 547; in Great Depression, 732, 747; 1919 steel strike in, 685; settlement houses in, 552, 553
Boston Guardian (newspaper), 628
Boston Herald (newspaper), 593
Boston Symphony, 547
Boundary disputes, with Indians, 484–486
Bowen, Francis, 516
Bowers, Claude G., 764
Boxer Rebellion, 651
Boxing, 548–549, 870
Bozeman Trail, 484
Braceros, 868
Bracket creep, 888
Bradley, Joseph P., 468
Bradley, Omar N., 812
Brandegee, Frank, 713*f*
Brandeis, Louis D.: appointment to Supreme Court, 664; influence on Roosevelt (Franklin), 751; on working hour legislation, 606
Brezhnev, Leonid, 830
Briand, Aristide, 723
Britain. *See* Anglo-American relations; Great Britain
British Guiana, 637
Brooks, N. C., 631
Brown, Joseph E., 456
Brown v. *Board of Education of Topeka,* 822
Bruce, Blanche K., 458*f*
Bryan, William Jennings, 748; in fundamentalist movement, 703; and Philippines, annexation of, 646; in 1896 presidential election, 592, 593*f,* 595*m*; in 1900 presidential election, 646; in 1908 presidential election, 617; and Scopes trial, 703
Bryan-Chamorro Treaty (1914), 659
Bryce, James, 579*f,* 600, 630
Bryn Mawr College, 561
Buck, Pearl, 709
Buddhists, in Vietnam, 831
Budget, federal, balancing of: and Carter, 888; and Clinton, 918; and Hoover, 732

Budget deficit: under Bush (George H. W.), 916; under Bush (George W.), 936; under Carter, 888; under Clinton, 917, 925; under Reagan, 895, 903
Budget Reconciliation Act (1981), 895
Buenker, John, 579*f*
Buffalo, 487*f*; destruction of, 486, 487*f*; Plains Indians and, 482
Buffalo Bill, 487*f*
Bulgaria: and Greek civil war, 801–802; liberalization of, 912
Bulge, Battle of the, 785
Bunau-Varilla, Philippe, 652
Bundy, McGeorge, 841*f*
Bunyan, John, 601
Bureaucracy, federal, New Deal and, 758, 759*f. See also* Civil service
Bureau of Corporations, 613, 623
Burlingame Treaty (1868), 482
Burnett, Frances Hodgson, 567
Burns, Edward, 787*f*
Bush, George H. W., 908–909; Cold War and, 899*f*; deficit under, 916; foreign policy of, 912–915; Iran-Contra arms deal and, 909; and Persian Gulf War, 915; presidency of, 911; in 1988 presidential election, 908–909; in 1992 presidential election, 917
Bush, George W. (Jr.): in 2000 presidential election, 927–928; in 2004 presidential election, 934–936; and Second Iraq War, 931–934, 934*f*; 2001 terrorist attacks and, 930–931
Business: big, ambivalence toward, 516–518; and military, alliance between, 667; in political campaigns, 594; after Reconstruction, 465; after World War I, 712–713, 729–730. *See also* Commerce; Corporations; Monopolies
Business codes, in New Deal, 743, 751
Business regulation, 521–522; under Coolidge, 720, 721, 729; under Harding, 719–720, 730; in New Deal, 743–744, 751; progressivism and, 599, 600–601; under Reagan, 895; under Roosevelt (Theodore), 612–613, 615–616; under Wilson, 621–622, 667; in World War I, 667; in World War II, 775–776

Butcher, S. D., 499*f*
Butow, Robert J. C., 793*f*
Byrnes, James F., 775

Cables, transoceanic, 557
Calamity Jane, 491
Caldwell, as cattle town, 490*f*
California: affirmative action in, 921; Chinese immigration and, 481, 482; immigrants in, post–Civil War, 481–482; prisons in, 910; Reagan governorship in, 893, 894*f*; women's suffrage in, 609
California Jack, 491
Cambodia, in Vietnam war, 840*m*, 845–846
Cameron, James, 570*f*
Camp, Walter, 700
Campaigns. *See* Political campaigns
Camp David Accords, 891
Canal Zone. *See* Panama Canal
Canning, 503
Capitalism: churches and, 551; Marxist critics of, 520–521; progressivism and, 602
Capital punishment, 909–910
Capone, Alphonse "Scarface Al," 705, 705*f*
Car. *See* Automobile
Carbon Hill, Alabama, 756*f*
Caribbean: post–World War I relations with, 724; U.S. expansionism in, 647–649, 650*m*
Carmichael, Stokely, 867
Carnegie, Andrew, 511–512, 519*f*, 622*f*, 748; as anti-imperialist, 646; as businessman, 511–512; defense of big business by, 517; as example of social mobility, 532; philanthropy of, 512, 517, 556; on Sherman Act, 523; and unions, 526
Carnegie Endowment for International Peace, 723, 813
Carnegie Steel Company, 512
Carolinas. *See* North Carolina; South Carolina
Carpetbaggers, 456
Carranza, Venustiano, 659
Carter, Amy, 886–887
Carter, Jimmy: foreign policy of, 890–891; hostage crisis and, 891, 892, 894–895; presidency of, 886–887; in

1976 presidential election, 885–886; in 1980 presidential election, 892–895
Carter, Rosalynn, 886
Cash-and-carry system, 766
Castro, Fidel, 821, 828–829, 828*f*, 835
Catholics and Catholic Church: in cities, late 19th-century, 550–552; in civil rights movement, 862–863; and Coughlin, 750, 753; immigrants, 540; Ku Klux Klan and, 706–707, 707; in mid-20th century, 862–863, 863; nativists against, 540; in 1928 presidential election, 707, 727; in 1960 presidential election, 824–825; and Spanish civil war, 764; in Vietnam, 831
Catholic University, 540
Catt, Carrie Chapman, 698
Cattle drives, 497
Cattle ranching, 496–500
Cattle towns, in West, 490*f*
CDC. *See* Centers for Disease Control
Ceausescu, Nicolae, 912
"The Celebrated Jumping Frog of Calaveras County" (Twain), 567
Centers for Disease Control (CDC), 900
Central America. *See* Latin America
Central Intelligence Agency (CIA): agents, in Second Iraq War, 932–933; Allende regime and, 887; in Cuban missile crisis, 828*f*; in Iran, 891; and Warren Report, 835; and Watergate scandal, 854
Central Pacific Railroad, 473, 493, 495*f*, 496*m*; and Union Pacific, competition between, 494–495
Central Powers (World War I), 660
The Century (magazine), 478, 558–559
Century Group, 768
Cervera, Pascual, 642
Challenger (space shuttle), 898
Chamberlain, John, 614*f*
Chamberlain, Neville, 765
Chambers, Whittaker, 813–814
Chandler, Jr., Alfred, D., 519*f*
Charity, by churches, 550–552
Chase, Salmon P., 455
Chauncy, George, 694*f*
Chávez, César, 869, 869*f*
Chemical weapons, U.S.–Soviet ban on, 912

Cheney, Dick, 927, 929–930, 932
Chesapeake and Ohio Railroad, 504
Chesapeake colonies. *See* Virginia
Cheyenne Indians, 482, 483, 484
Chiang Kai-shek, 724, 808, 816
Chicago (film), 696–697*f*
Chicago, Illinois: blacks in, 672; in Great
    Depression, 732; Haymarket Square
    bombing, 524, 525*f*; infrastructure of,
    542; meat industry in, 616; 1968
    Democratic convention in, 843, 844*f*;
    Pullman strike in, 527–528; settlement
    houses in, 552, 553
Chicago Chronicle (newspaper), 593
Chicago Daily Tribune (newspaper), 807*f*
Chicago Defender (newspaper), 760
Chicago River, 542
Chicago Tribune (newspaper), 738
Chicano movement, 868–869
Child labor: in early 20th-century, 599;
    legislation on, 605; progressivism and,
    599, 605; Wilson and, 664; World War
    I and, 671
Children: Great Depression and, 736; in
    late 19th-century, 531; in post–World
    War I period, 692; television and, 859.
    See also Education
Chile, 890
China: communism in, rise of, 808;
    détente and, 846–848, 848*f*; immigra-
    tion from, 481, 482, 538; Japan and,
    650, 659, 722–723, 724–725, 725*f*,
    764–765; and Korean War, 810–811,
    812*f*, 816; 19th-century relations with,
    633; Open Door policy and, 650–652,
    722–723; post–World War I, 722–723;
    post–World War II, 808
Chinese Americans, in American West,
    481, 482, 494, 495*f*
Chisholm Trail, 497
Chivington, J. M., 484
Chivington massacre, 484
Chou En-lai, 810
Christianity: expansionism and, 632; in
    mid-20th century, 862–864
Christian Socialists, 551–552
Chrysler Corporation: in late 20th-century,
    888; in post–World War I period, 729
Church(es): and big business, 551; in civil
    rights movement, 863; in mid-20th

century, 862–864; and urban prob-
    lems, 550–552; women in, 863. *See
    also* Religion(s)
Churchill, Winston: on Iron Curtain, 802;
    post–World War II diplomacy of, 795,
    795*f*, 796; in World War II, 767, 782
CIA. *See* Central Intelligence Agency
Cigarettes, 463, 503, 729
Cincinnati Red Stockings, 549
CIO. *See* Congress of Industrial
    Organizations
Cities: automobiles and, 712–713; black
    migration to, 671–674, 709–711; city
    manager system in, 603–604; corrup-
    tion in, 576–578, 603–604; entertain-
    ment in, 547–550; geographic mobility
    in, 536; housing in, late 19th-century,
    542–545; immigrants in, 536–537,
    541, 542–545; infrastructure of,
    542–545; modernization of, 545–547;
    political bosses in, 576–578; popula-
    tion growth in, 691–692; in
    post–World War I period, 691–692;
    progressive reforms in, 603–604; and
    rural areas, conflicts between,
    704–705; in West, 481. *See also*
    Ghettos; Slums
Citizenship: Fourteenth Amendment defi-
    nition of, 452; for immigrants, 542
City manager system, 603–604
Civilian Conservation Corps, 743, 761
Civilization, concept of, 500
Civil liberties: in post–World War I red
    scare, 685–686; in World War I,
    669–670
Civil rights: Eisenhower and, 821–824;
    Johnson (Lyndon) and, 836, 866;
    Kennedy and, 831–834; progressivism
    and, 624–626; Truman and, 804
Civil Rights Act(s): of 1866, 451; of 1964,
    836
Civil rights movement, 831–834; mili-
    tancy in, 866–867; religious impacts
    of, 862–863; and women's rights
    movement, 878–881
Civil service: corruption in, 457*f*; under
    Grant, 465–466; under Harrison
    (Benjamin), 585*f*; late 19th-century re-
    form of, 475–476, 583–584; in
    post–Reconstruction South, 458–459

Civil Service Act (1883), 582, 594
Civil Service Commission, 582, 585
Civil War, materialism and, 472
Civil Works Administration (CWA), 746, 747f
Clark, J. Reuben, 724
Clark, Jonas, 560
Clarke, Edward Y., 706
Clark Memorandum (1930), 724
Clark University, 560
Class structure: in 1896 presidential election, 596. *See also* Middle class; Working class
Clay, Cassius (Ali, Muhammad), 862, 870
Clayton Antitrust Act (1914), 623
Clayton-Bulwer Treaty (1850), 636, 652
Clean Air Act, 850
"Clear and present danger" doctrine, 670
Clemenceau, Georges, 679
Clemens, Samuel L. *See* Twain, Mark
Cleveland, Frances Folsom, 584f
Cleveland, Grover, 584–585, 584f; on blacks, 476–477; and Cuban revolution, 638; first term of, 584; foreign policy of, 637; and Hawaii, 635; and immigration, 540–541; presidency of, 584–585; in 1884 presidential election, 583–584; in 1888 presidential election, 585; in 1892 presidential election, 589; on 1896 presidential election, 593–595; and silver coinage controversy, 591, 592; and strikes, 527–528
Cleveland, Ohio: oil industry in, 512; progressivism in, 603
Clews, Elsie, 571f
Clinton, Bill, 916–917, 918f; economy under, 919, 924–925; foreign policy of, 925; Gore and, 927; impeachment of, 923–924, 924f; legacy of, 924–926; presidency of, 917–918, 924–926; in 1992 presidential election, 917; in 1996 presidential election, 919–920; on race relations, 921; Whitewater and, 916, 919
Clinton, Hillary Rodham, 916, 918–919, 923
Coal: post–Civil War extraction of, 463, 507; post–World War I decline, 729; strike of 1902, 615
Coca-Cola, 847

Cocaine, 910–911
Cochran, Thomas C., 519f
Cody, William F. (Buffalo Bill), 487f
Coeur d'Alene, Idaho, 527
Cohen, Lizabeth, 876f
Coit, Stanton, 552
Cold War: containment policy and, 801, 807–808, 819–820; Cuban missile crisis in, 827–830; domestic repercussions of, 813–814; end of, 899f, 912–913, 912m; Far East conflicts in, 817–818; Latin American conflicts in, 820–821; Middle East conflicts in, 818–819; nuclear weapons in, 807–808, 816–817, 819–820; Reagan and, 899f; U.S.-Soviet relations during, 819–820
Cole (ship), bombing of, 931
College of New Jersey. *See* Princeton University
Colleges and universities: affirmative action at, 921; expansion of, 559–562, 871–872, 872f; football in, 550; integration of, 822; Jews at, 691; in late 19th-century, 559–562; post–World War II reforms at, 871–872; sports at, 550; student radicals at, 872–874; and Vietnam war protests, 839, 845–846; women in, 561, 561f
Collier, John, 762
Collins, Ellen, 547
Colombia: drug trade in, 910; loss of Panama, 653–654
Colonialism. *See* Expansionism
Colonization, by freed slaves, 478
Colorado: gold rush in, 489; Indian Wars in, 484; progressive reform in, 604; territorial organization of, 491; women's suffrage in, 609
Colored Alliance, 588
"Colored Rule in a Reconstructed (?) State" (Nast), 457f
Columbia School of Journalism, 558f
Columbia University: quotas on Jews at, 691; student radicals at, 874f
Columbine High School (Colorado), 923
Columbus, Christopher, 496
Commager, Henry Steele, 694f
Commerce. *See* Business; Corporations; Monopolies; Trade

Commerce and Labor, Department of, 612

Commerce Court, 617

Commercial and Financial Chronicle (newspaper), 574

Committee for European Economic Cooperation, 802

Committee for Industrial Organization (CIO), 744. *See also* Congress of Industrial Organizations

Committee on Civil Rights, 804

Committee on Public Information (CPI), 669

Committee to Defend America by Aiding the Allies, 768

Committee to Re-elect the President (CREEP), 850–851, 851

Commodity Credit Corporation, 757

Common Sense Guide to Baby and Child Care (Spock), 859

Commonwealth and Southern Corporation, 745

Communist Manifesto (Marx), 735f

Communists and communism: Cold War domestic fears of, 813–814; collapse of, in Eastern Europe, 912–913, 912m; détente and, 846–848; in Great Depression, 735; and red scare, 685; after World War I, 676, 685. *See also* Containment policy

Community colleges, 871–872

Community Service Organization (CSO), 869

Compromise of 1877, 469–470, 469f, 580

Compuserve, 926

Computers, 865

Comstock Act (1873), 693

Comstock Lode, 489

Conant, James B., 871

Concentration camps, in World War II, 785

"Concentration" policy, Plains Indians and, 483, 484

Coney Island, 549f

Congress, U.S.: blacks in, 456–459, 458f; in late 19th-century, 473–474, 585; post–Civil War debates in, 448–452; progressive reforms of, 609–611; and Reconstruction, 449, 450–451, 454–455. *See also* Congressional elections; House of Representatives; Senate

Congressional elections: of 1866, 453; of 1874, 466; of 1890, 585; of 1892, 588; of 1894, 592; of 1934, 751; of 1936, 753; of 1994, 919

Congressional Government (Wilson), 621

Congressional Medal of Honor, to black soldiers, 673

Congressional Union, 609

Congress of Industrial Organizations (CIO): blacks in, 761–762; contributions to labor movement, 755; formation of, 744

Congress of Racial Equality (CORE), 832

Connecticut, in presidential politics, 578

A Connecticut Yankee in King Arthur's Court (Twain), 568

Conscription. *See* Draft

Conservation: under Nixon, 850; under Roosevelt (Theodore), 617; under Taft, 618

Constitution(s), state, in post-Reconstruction era, 449, 453–454

Consumerism: drop in, and Great Depression, 731; in post–World War I period, 712–713

Consumers' League, 606, 759

Containment policy, 801, 807–808, 819–820, 895

Contraception. *See* Birth control

Contract with America, 919

Contras, 904–905

Coolidge, Calvin, 717, 721f; Boston steel strike and, 685; economic policies of, 720, 721, 729; foreign policy of, 722–727; on Hoover, 728f; presidency of, 721–722; in 1924 presidential election, 721–722; in 1928 presidential election, 727–728; on war, 723

Cooper, Peter, 475

Cooper, William, 449f

The Cooperative Commonwealth (Gronlund), 520

Copperheads, 450

Coral Sea, Battle of, 788

CORE. *See* Congress of Racial Equality

Cornell University, 560f, 572, 579f

Corporations: effect on culture, 530; mergers of, 599–600, 901–902; vs. trusts, 515. *See also* Business; Commerce

Corruption: in city government, 576–578, 603–604; in civil service, post-Reconstruction, 457f, 476; in Grant administration, 465–466, 467f; in Harding administration, 720; progressive reforms and, 603–604; in Reconstruction governments, 457f

Cosmetics, advertising, in post–World War I period, 700f

Cotton: in late 19th-century, 585; in post–Civil War South, 462, 462f, 463, 463f; in South, 462, 462f, 463, 463f

Cotton States International Exposition, 479

Coughlin, Charles E., 749–750, 750f, 751, 753

Counterculture, 874–875

Courtship, in 1920s, 692–693

Cowboys, 490f

Cox, Archibald, 851

Cox, James M., 686–687

Coxey, Jacob S., 591

CPI. See Committee on Public Information

Crack cocaine, 910–911

Crane, Stephen, 569, 708

Crazy Horse, 486

Creel, George, 669

CREEP. See Committee to Re-elect the President

Crime: under Bush (George H. W.), 909–910; drug use and, 910–911; in late 19th-century, 544–545; in late 20th-century, 908, 909–910, 911f, 922–923; in 1988 presidential election, 909; in prohibition era, 705, 705f

The Crisis (journal), 628, 674, 710

Croatia, 913

Crocker, Charles, 494, 495

Croker, Richard, 577

Crop-lien system, 461–463, 462f

Croquet, 550

Crude oil, 507

CSO. See Community Service Organization

Cuba, 634f; Bay of Pigs invasion of, 829; as colony, 655; 1868 revolt in, 638–641; Guantanamo Bay sold by, 654; missile crisis in, 827–830, 933; and Nicaraguan Sandinistas, 904; 19th-century expansionism and, 631; 1959 revolution in, 821; protectorate relations with, 647–649, 724; slavery in, 638; Spanish-American war and, 641–643; struggle for independence from Spain, 638–641; U.S. interests in, 638–641, 654

Culture(s): in 19th-century cities, 547–550; gay, post–World War I, 692; Works Progress Administration and, 747. See also Intellectual life; Literature; Popular culture

Currency: late 19th-century reform of, 475; silver vs. gold, 589–591, 596

Currier and Ives, 689f

Custer, George A., 485–486

Custer County, Nebraska, 566f

CWA. See Civil Works Administration

Czechoslovakia: communist coup in, 804; creation of, 679; German aggression in, 765; liberalization of, 912; Marshall plan and, 804

Czolgosz, Leon, 611

Dakotas: Alliance movement in, 586, 587; population in late 19th-century, 585

Daley, Richard J., 843, 844f

Dalrymple, Louis, 639f

Damon, Matt, 786f, 787f

DAR. See Daughters of the American Revolution

Dar Es Salaam, Tanzania, 929

Darlan, Jean, 783

Darrow, Clarence, 703

Darwin, Charles, 516

Darwinism, 556; academic theories of, 562–563; and feminism, 609; and immigration, 540; and intellectual life, late 19th-century, 562–563, 572; religious fundamentalism and, 703

Das Kapital (Marx), 520, 528

Dating, in post–World War I period, 692–693

Daugherty, Harry M., 718

Daughters of the American Revolution (DAR), 760

Davis, Jefferson, after Civil War, 448

Davis, John W., 721, 753

Dawes, Henry L., 487

Dawes Act (1887), 762

Dawes Plan (1924), 727
Dawes Severalty Act (1887), 487–488
The Dawn (journal), 552
D-day, 783, 784*f*
DDT, 864
Dead Indian Land Act (1902), 624
Deadwood Dick, 491
Dean, Howard, 934–935
Dean, John W., III, 851
Death penalty, 909–910
Death Wish (film), 921
Debs, Eugene V., 527–528; imprisonment of, 669; Margaret Sanger and, 693; in 1900 presidential election, 602; in 1904 presidential election, 602; in 1912 presidential election, 621
Debt, corporate, 903
Debt, national: under Reagan, 903; in World War I, 668–669
Declaration of Independence, and racial equality, 450
Deficit. *See* Budget deficit
Deflation: in late 19th-century, 475, 509, 589–591
de Gaulle, Charles, 783
Deladier, Edouard, 765
De Leon, Daniel, 602
De Lesseps, Ferdinand, 636
de Lôme, Dupuy, 639
De Mille, Cecil B., 697*f*
Democracy: frontier and, 565, 566*f*; intrafamily, 691–692; late 19th-century academic studies of, 565; monopolies and, 528
Democracy (Adams), 473
Democratic National Convention: of 1868, 455; of 1896, 592; of 1916, 665; of 1968, 843, 844*f*
Democratic party: in 1868 election, 455; in 1872 election, 466; in 1874 congressional election, 466; in 1876 election, 466–468; in 1896 election, 592, 594, 595*m*; in 1912 election, 621*m*; in 1916 election, 665; in 1920 election, 698; in 1924 election, 721–722; in 1928 election, 727–728; in 1934 congressional election, 751; Alliance movement and, 586; blacks in, 754, 760–762; extremists' threat to, 749; in late 19th-century, 474, 475, 578–580; and League

of Nations, 681, 682; in post–Civil War North, 464–465; prohibition and, 705
Dempsey, Jack, 701
Denby, Edwin, 720
Denmark, in World War II, 766
Department stores, 482, 516, 533, 533*f*, 546
Depression(s), economic: of 1890s, 509, 510–511, 591–592. *See also* Great Depression
Derrida, Jacques, 937*f*
Desert Land Act (1877), 498
Desert Storm, 914*m*
Détente: Carter and, 890–891; Nixon and, 846–848, 848*f*
Detroit, Michigan: blacks in, 672; progressivism in, 603
Dewey, George, 641, 642*f*, 647*f*
Dewey, John, 566*f*; and educational reform, 564, 871; and NAACP, 627; pragmatism and, 573
Dewey, Thomas E.: in 1940 presidential election, 768; in 1944 presidential election, 791; in 1948 presidential election, 806, 807*f*
Dewitt, John, 778
Dewson, Molly, 759
Díaz, Adolfo, 659
DiCaprio, Leonardo, 570*f*, 571*f*, 922–923
Die Hard (film), 921
Dien Bien Phu, 818
Diplomacy: Indian nations and, 483; in World War II, 794–795. *See also* Foreign policy
Direct primary system, 604
Discounts, railroads and, 510
Disease(s): in Great Depression, 738*f*; sexually transmitted, 878
District of Columbia. *See* Washington, D.C.
Divorce, 692
Dixiecrats, 805
Dodd, C. T., 514
Dodge City, as cattle town, 490*f*
Doheny, Edward L., 720
Dole, Bob, 919–920
Dollar diplomacy, 654, 658; in Latin America, 656
Dominican Republic: attempt to annex, 631; dollar diplomacy in, 654; as U.S. protectorate, 649, 724

Donnelly, Ignatius, 588
Doonesbury (comic strip), 852*f*
Dos Passos, John, 747–748
Dostoevsky, Fyodor, 569
Dot-coms, 926–927
Douglass, Frederick, 870; on Hayes, 476
Dower, John, 793*f*
Downsizing, 902–903
Dr. Dre (Andrew Young), 922
Draft: in Civil War, 544; in World War I, 667, 669, 673; in World War II, 767
Drake, Edwin L., 507
Dreiser, Theodore, 569
Dresden, Germany, 788*f*
Drew, Charles, 778
Drexel Burnham Lambert, 901
Drought, cattle ranching and, 499–500
Drugs: in counterculture, 875; and crime, 910–911
Du Bois, W. E. B., 457*f*, 626–628, 627*f*, 870; *The Crisis*, 627, 674, 710; on integration vs. separatism, 710; on Washington (Booker T.), 626, 627; on Wilson, 627, 674; on World War I, 674
Dukakis, Michael, 909
Dulles, Allen, 835
Dulles, John Foster, 816–817; McCarthyism and, 817
Dumbarton Oaks, 794
Dunning, William A., on Reconstruction, 457*f*

Earth in the Balance (Gore), 927
Eastern Europe: communism in, fall of, 912–913, 912*m*; immigrants from, 539, 540, 691; Marshall plan and, 804; post–World War II, 796; Soviet domination of, 801, 804
Eastern Trunk Line Association, 505
East Germany, 805*m*, 912
Eastman, George B., 503
East Saint Louis, Illinois, 1917 riot in, 672, 673*f*
eBay, 926
Eckford, Elizabeth, 823*f*
Economic aid. *See* Foreign aid
Economic mobility, late 19th-century, 536–537
Economic Opportunity Act (1964), 836

Economics: classical school of, 563; government regulation of, 516–518; institutionalist school of, 563; Keynesian, 753, 800; progressive reform of, 606, 607; study of, late 19th-century, 562–563, 563
Economy: Carter and, 887–888; Clinton and, 919, 920, 924–925; expansionism and, 654; Ford and, 884–885; globalization of, 924–925; government regulation of, 516–518, 521–522; in Great Depression, 731–736; in late 19th-century, 502–503, 509–511; New Deal and, 743–744, 753, 758–759; Nixon and, 849–850; oil crisis and, 882–884; post–Civil War, 459–461, 465; post–World War I, 712–713, 729–730; post–World War II, 800–801; railroads and, 503–505; Reagan and, 895, 896, 901–904; southern, 459–461; technology and, 865–866; in World War I, 666–668; in World War II, 775–776
Economy Act (1933), 742
Eden, Anthony, 819
Ederle, Gertrude, 701
Edison, Thomas A., 507–508, 508*f*
Edison Illuminating Company, 509
Education: for blacks, 448, 457*f*, 459, 460*f*, 478, 479*f*, 626, 822–823, 868, 921; desegregation of, 822–823; Great Society programs for, 838; for Indians, 624; for Japanese Americans, 651; in late 19th-century, 537, 559–562; and mobility, 537; post–World War I, 703, 870–872; post–World War II, 870–872; progressive, 563–564; religious fundamentalism and, 703; 20th-century expansion of, 871–872, 872*f*; for women, 561; for World War II veterans, 800, 871–872, 872*f*. *See also* Colleges and universities; Teachers
Edwards, John, 935
Egypt: Camp David Accords and, 891; Suez Canal crisis and, 819; in Yom Kippur War, 882
Ehrlichman, John, 853
Eighteenth Amendment, 671, 704
Eight-hour work day, 525
Einstein, Albert, 766, 792

Eisenhower, Dwight D., 815*f*; and civil rights, 821–824; and Cuba, 821; foreign policy of, 816–821; Khrushchev and, 819–820; and Latin America, 821; presidency of, 814–815; in 1952 presidential election, 814–815; and Vietnam, 818; in World War II, 783–785, 789*f*

Elderly: insurance for, 750; Townsend's campaign for, 750

Elections. *See* Congressional elections; Presidential election(s)

Elective system, in higher education, 559–560, 562

Electoral college: constitutional provisions for, 468; in 1876 presidential election, 467–468, 469*f*; in 2000 presidential election, 928; in 2004 presidential election, 936

Electricity: development of, 507–509; New Deal and, 745, 746*m*, 752; from nuclear fuels, 865; in post–World War I period, 711; in rural areas, 752

Elementary and Secondary Education Act (1965), 838, 872*f*

Eliot, Charles W., 559, 645

Elk Hills oil reserve, 720

Elkhorn Ranch, 498, 500

Elkins Railroad Act (1903), 612

Elliot, Robert Brown, 458*f*

El Salvador, 895

Ely, Richard T., 563

Emancipation. *See* Abolitionist movement

Embassy bombings, in Africa, 929.931, 931

Emerson, Ralph Waldo: on Lincoln, 530; on war, 786*f*

Eminem (Marshall Mathers III), 922

Engels, Friedrich, 735*f*

England. *See* Anglo-American relations; Great Britain

English Channel, 701

Enola Gay (plane), 792

Entertainment, in late 19th-century, 547–550

Environmental protection. *See* Conservation

Environmental Protection Agency (EPA), 850

E pluribus unum, 691

Equality: social, 451; and women's suffrage, 609, 698. *See also* Racial equality

Equal rights. *See* Women's rights movement

Equal rights amendment (ERA), 698, 879–880, 889–890; failure of, 890*m*

Equitable Life Company, 516

ERA. *See* Equal rights amendment

Erie Canal, and petroleum industry, 512

Erie Railroad, 512

Espionage Act (1917), 670

Ethiopia, Italian invasion of, 763

Ethnic cleansing, in Bosnia, 925

Ethnic diversity, desirability of, 870

Ethnic pride, 870

Eugenicists, 693

Europe: in late 19th-century foreign policy, 630–633; Marshall plan and, 802–804; post–World War I, 676–679, 679*m*, 680*m*; post–World War II, 805*m*; pre–World War I, 679, 678*m*; in World War II, 764–767, 782–785, 784*m*. *See also* Eastern Europe

"Evil empire," 899*f*

Evolution, theory of, 572, 703. *See also* Darwinism

Exclusion Act (1882), 540

Expansionism, 655–656

Expansionism, Soviet Union, 796–797, 801

Expansionism, U.S., 643–645, 654; in Caribbean, 647–649, 650*m*; in Cuba, 638–641, 647–649; domestic opposition to, 645–646; late 19th-century, 630–633, 643–645; in Latin America, 631, 636–637, 652–655; and Open Door policy, 650–652; origins of, 630–633; in Pacific region, 633–636, 643–645; and Panama Canal, 636, 652–655

Ex parte Endo (1944), 779

Exports. *See* Trade

Extremists, in Great Depression years, 748–751, 753

Factories, post–World War I, 712–713

Fair, James G. "Bonanza," 473

Fair Employment Practices Commission, 804

Fair Labor Standards Act, 757
Fall, Albert B., 719, 720
Falwell, Jerry, 896
Family life: in 1940s, 859; of freedmen, 461; in Great Depression, 736; in late 19th-century, 531; post–World War I, 691–692; working-class, 691–692; in World War II, 776, 780–782
Far East, policy toward: late 19th–early 20th-century, 633–636, 650–652; post-Korean War, 817–818; post–World War I, 722–723
A Farewell to Arms (Hemingway), 708
Farm bloc, 730
Farmers, 534–535; in late 19th-century, 492–493; in politics, 586–589. *See also* Agriculture
Farmers Alliance, 586
Farm Loan Act (1916), 664
Farm Security Administration, 761*f*
Farnham, Marynia, 859
Farouk (King of Egypt), 819
Farrakhan, Louis, 920
Fatwa, 929
Faubus, Orval M., 823
Faulkner, William, 709, 748
FCC. *See* Federal Communications Commission
FDIC. *See* Federal Deposit Insurance Corporation
Federal Art Project, 747
Federal Communications Commission (FCC), 522, 700, 859
Federal Deposit Insurance Corporation (FDIC), 743
Federal Emergency Relief Act (FERA), 746, 747*f*
Federal Farm Board, 732
Federal Housing Administration (FHA), 754, 861
Federal Reserve Act (1913), 622
Federal Reserve Board: creation of, 622; New Deal and, 743; in post–World War I period, 711, 720
Federal Steel Company, 512
Federal Theatre Project, 747
Federal Trade Commission (FTC): creation of, 623; in post–World War I period, 720
Federal Writers' Project, 747

The Feminine Mystique (Friedan), 878
Feminism. *See* Women's rights movement
FERA. *See* Federal Emergency Relief Act
Ferber, Edna, 709
Ferraro, Geraldine, 896, 897
Fertility, geographic gradient of. *See* Birthrate
Fetterman, W. J., 484
FHA. *See* Federal Housing Administration
Fiction. *See* Literature
Field, Marshall, 516
Fifteenth Amendment, 455–456, 477
Films, 698–700, 921
Fireside chats, Roosevelt's, 742, 763, 769
Fiske, John, 631
Fitzgerald, F. Scott, 708, 709, 748
Fitzpatrick, Thomas, 483
Five-Power Treaty (1921), 723
Florida, in 2000 presidential election, 928
Flowers, Gennifer, 916
Foner, Eric, on Reconstruction, 457*f*
Food: canning factories and, 503; in Great Depression, 732, 733; in late 19th-century, 503; safety legislation for, 616; in World War I, 668, 717; in World War II, 776
Food chains, 729
Football, 550; college, 550; in post–World War I period, 700–701
Foraker Act (1900), 648
Foran Act (1885), 538
Forbes, Charles R., 719
Force Acts (1870–1871), 464
Ford, Gerald R., 884*f*; Nixon's resignation and, 854; presidency of, 884–885; in 1976 presidential election, 885–886; as vice president, 853
Ford, Henry, 713–714
Ford Motor Company: assembly lines at, 714; in early 20th-century, 713–714; in late 20th-century, 884, 888; in post–World War I period, 729
Foreign aid: from 1945 to 1984, 803*f*; to Latin America, 820–821, 890–891; Marshall plan and, 802–804; Truman Doctrine and, 802
Foreign Debt Commission, 725–727
Foreign policy: under Bush (George H. W.), 912–915; under Carter, 891;

under Cleveland, 637; under Clinton, 925; under Coolidge, 722–727; dollar diplomacy in, 654, 658; under Eisenhower, 816–821; Good Neighbor policy, 724; under Grant, 631, 636; under Harding, 722–727; under Hoover, 724; under Kennedy, 827–831; "large," 632; late 19th-century, 630–633; under McKinley, 633, 638–639, 643–645, 647, 652; missionary diplomacy in, 659; neutrality in, 660–661, 665–666, 763–764; under Nixon, 844–848; Open Door policy, 650–652, 722–723, 772; under Reagan, 895, 897–898; under Roosevelt (Franklin), 764–767; under Roosevelt (Theodore), 649–650, 651–652; under Taft, 654; under Truman, 801, 807–808, 818; under Wilson, 658–660. *See also* Diplomacy; Expansionism; Isolationism
Formosa. *See* Taiwan
Fort Laramie, Wyoming, 483, 484
Fortune, T. Thomas, 478
Fosse, Bob, 697*f*
Foster, William Z., 685
Four-Power Treaty, 723
Fourteen Points, plan of Woodrow Wilson, 680–681
Fourteenth Amendment, 452–453, 454
France: in Indochina, 817–818; and Mexico, 630; in Paris Peace Conference, 679; Suez Canal crisis and, 819; and World War I, 662, 674–675; in World War II, 765, 766, 783, 784
Franco, Francisco, 764
Frankfurter, Felix, 668, 734, 751, 779
Franz Ferdinand (Archduke of Austria), 660
Frasch, Herman, 507
Fraser River, Canada, 489
Freedmen: economic hardships of, 459–463; education for, 457*f*, 459, 460*f*, 478; family life of, 461; in post-Reconstruction South, 457*f*; Radical Republicans and, 451–452; southern mistreatment of, 451, 453, 480–481; white backlash against, 463–464. *See also* Reconstruction

Freedmen's Bureau, 451, 459, 460*f*
Freedom of speech, suppression in World War I, 669
Freedom Riders, 833*f*
Freedom rides, 832
Free Speech Movement, 873
Freudian psychology, 871
Frick, Henry Clay, 527
Friedan, Betty, 878, 888
Friedman, William F., 773
Frontier: concept of, 500; and democracy, 565, 566*f*. *See also* West
Front-porch campaigns, 594
FTC. *See* Federal Trade Commission
Fuchs, Klaus, 814
Fundamentalism: in 1980s politics, 896; in post–World War I period, 702–704, 704*f*
Furman decision, 909

Gaddis, John Lewis, 809*f*, 899*f*
Gaertner, Belva, 696*f*, 697*f*
Galbraith, John K., 735*f*
Galveston, Texas, 603
Ganci, Peter, 929, 930
Gangs: late 19th-century, 545; late 20th-century, 910; in prohibition era, 705, 705*f*
Gangsta rap, 922
GAR. *See* Grand Army of the Republic
Gardner, Lloyd C., 841*f*
Garfield, James A., 453, 456, 581; assassination of, 581, 582*f*; in Compromise of 1877, 469; on Fifteenth Amendment, 456; on Indian Bureau, 485; policies for freedmen, 476; on post–Civil War South, 453; in 1880 presidential election, 581
Garland, Hamlin, 569
Garner, John N., 738, 739*f*, 765, 767
Garraty, John, 735*f*
Garvey, Marcus, 710, 711*f*
Gary, Elbert H., 613
"Gas and water" socialism, 603
Gasoline, 507, 858, 882–884, 883*f*, 888
Gates, Robert M., 899*f*
Geddes, Eric, 677
General Intelligence Division, of Justice Department, 685

General Motors (GM): 1937 strike at, 755; post–World War II malaise at, 887; in post–World War I period, 729; vs. Ford, 714

Gentlemen's Agreement (1907), 624, 651

Geographic mobility: in late 19th-century, 536–537. *See also* Migration

George, Henry, 518, 563

George, Walter F., 757

Georgia: Alliance movement in, 587; progressive reform in, 604; readmission to Union, 454

Gere, Richard, 696*f*

German Americans, 539, 540; World War I and, 662, 669

Germany: division into East and West, 805*m*; under Hitler, 764–767; immigration from, 539, 539*f*; post–World War I debts and aid to, 726–727; post–World War II treatment of, 796; reunification of, 899*f*; universities in, 559; in World War I, 662–664, 665, 674–675; in World War II, 764–767, 782–785, 788*f*, 789*f*; World War I peace settlement and, 677, 678, 679–680

Geronimo, 486

Ghettos: compensating advantages of, 710; formation after World War I, 709. *See also* Slums

GI Bill of Rights, 800, 872, 872*f*

Gilded Age, 472, 565

Gilman, Daniel Coit, 559

Gingrich, Newt, 919

Ginsberg, Allen, 874

Ginsberg, Ruth Bader, 918

Giuliani, Rudolph, 929

Gladden, Washington, 551

Glasnost, 897

Glidden, Joseph F., 499

Globalization: of economy, 924–925; economy and, 925

GM. *See* General Motors

GNP. *See* Gross national product

Gold, as currency, 475

Gold, Harry, 814

The Golden Battle (Donnelly), 588

Goldman, Emma, 693

Gold rush: effect on Indians, 482–483, 485; in post-Reconstruction era, 488–492

Gold standard, 589–591, 596; withdrawal from, 742

Goldwater, Barry M., 837

Golf, 548

Gompers, Samuel, 525, 645

Good Housekeeping (magazine), 503

Good Neighbor policy, 724

Goodnight, Charles, 497

Goodwin, Doris Kearns, 837*f*

Gorbachev, Mikhail S., 897–898, 899*f*, 912, 913

Gore, Al: in 1988 presidential election, 909; in 1992 presidential election, 917; in 2000 presidential election, 927–928

Gould, Jay, 504, 524, 557, 614*f*

Government(s): economic regulation by, 516–518, 521–522; post–Civil War, 476; progressivism and, 598–601, 601; Reconstruction and, 454–455; state, 449, 455–456. *See also* Business regulation; Civil service

Graham, Billy, 864

Grand Army of the Republic, 474–475

Grange, Harold "Red," 701

Granger laws, 521

Granger movement, 521, 534

Grant, Ulysses S.: on Fifteenth Amendment, 456; foreign policy of, 631, 636; presidency of, 465–466, 467*f*, 485; in 1868 presidential election, 455; in 1872 presidential election, 466

The Grapes of Wrath (Steinbeck), 748

Great Awakening, 551

Great Barbecue, Parrington on, 472

Great Britain: Greek crisis of 1947 and, 801–802; immigration from, 539; Latin America and, 636–637; and Panama Canal, 636, 652; Suez Canal crisis and, 819; and Venezuela, 637; World War I and, 661–664, 679; World War II and, 766–767, 768–769, 782–783, 783–785. *See also* Anglo-American relations

Great Depression, 730–736; and blacks, 760–762; causes of, 735*f*; Hoover's policies for, 731–736; literature in, 747–748; origins of, 730; psychological effects of, 736; stock market crash of 1929 and, 730–731; World War II and, 775. *See also* New Deal

Great Eastern (ship), 537

The Great Gatsby (Fitzgerald), 708

"Great Men and Their Environment" (James), 573

Great migration, of blacks to North, 671–674, 709–711

Great Northern Railroad, 495, 496m

The Great Plains (Webb), 500

Great Society, 836–838

The Great Train Robbery (film), 698

Greece: civil war in, 801–802; immigrants from, 542; Truman Doctrine and, 802

Greeley, Horace: and *New York Tribune,* 466; in 1872 presidential election, 466

Greenback Labor party, 475

Greenbacks, 475, 591–592

Greenland, in World War II, 769

Green party, 927

Greensboro, North Carolina, Woolworth's sit-in, 832

Greer (ship), 769

Grenada, 895

Griffith, D. W., 457f

Griffith, David W., 699

Griffith, Ernest S., 579f

Grocery stores, 729

Gromyko, Andrei A., 794

Gronlund, Laurence, 520–521

Gross national product (GNP): in late 19th-century, 502; World War II and, 775

Guadalcanal Island, battles around, 791

Guam, 643; as colony, 655

Guangzhou, China, 634f

Guantanamo base, as colony, 655

Guantanamo Bay, 654

Guatemala, 821

Guerrilla warfare, 484–485

Guiteau, Charles J., 581

Gulf of Tonkin Resolution, 839

Gulf War, Persian, 913–915, 914m, 915f

Haiti: dollar diplomacy in, 654; 1930s withdrawal from, 724

Halberstam, David, 841f

Haldeman, H. R., 853

Hamby, Alonzo L., 793f

Hampton, Wade, 476

Handlin, Oscar, 543f

Hanks, Tom, 786–787f, 787f

Hanna, Marcus Alonzo, 594, 596

Harding, Warren, 721f

Harding, Warren G., 713f, 717; agricultural policies of, 730; and business, 719–720, 730; death of, 720; foreign policy of, 722–727; presidency of, 718–720; in 1920 presidential election, 687; scandals under, 720

Harlan, John Marshall, 478

Harlem, 711

Harlem Renaissance, 710–711

Harper, William Rainey, 560

Harper's Weekly (magazine), 457f, 478, 558, 568

Harriman, Averill, 801

Harrison, Benjamin, 584; on foreign affairs, 630; presidency of, 585; in 1888 presidential election, 585; in 1892 presidential election, 589

Harvard Encyclopedia of American Ethnic Groups (Handlin, Schlesinger), 543f

Harvard University: in 19th-century, 559, 562; elective system at, 559, 562; football at, 550; James (William) at, 572; quotas on Jews at, 691; reform of, late 19th-century, 559, 562; and Washington (Booker T.), 479

Hastie, William, 778

Havemeyer, Henry O., 516

Hawaii, as colony, 655

Hawaiian Islands: annexation of, 636; attempts to annex, 633–635

Hawaiian Islands, 19th-century expansionism and, 633–635

Hawthorn, Nathaniel, 565

Hay, John, 650, 652

Hayes, Rutherford B., 580–585, 580f; presidency of, 580–585; in 1876 presidential election, 466–468, 469f, 580; and railroad strike, 527; and southern blacks, 476, 580

Haymarket Square bombing, 525, 525f, 540

Haywood, "Big Bill," 602, 693
A Hazard of New Fortunes (Howells), 568
Head Start program, 838
Health, Education, and Welfare, Department of, 815
Health insurance, 671, 837, 838, 918–919, 934
Hearst, George, 557
Hearst, William Randolph, 558, 638, 639
Helicopters, in Vietnam war, 846*f*
Hemingway, Ernest, 708, 709, 748
Henry Street Settlement (New York), 552
Hepburn Act (1906), 616
Herbart, Johann Friedrich, 563
Herrán, Tomás, 653
Hewitt, Abram S., 520
Hickok, Wild Bill, 491
Higham, John, 694*f*
The Higher Learning in America (Veblen), 562
Highway system, interstate, 858
Hijacking. *See* Terrorism
Hill, David B., 593
Hill, James J., 495, 496*m*, 504, 614*f*
Hippies, 874–875
Hirabayashi, Gordon, 779
Hiroshima, 792, 793*f*
Hispanic Americans, civil rights for, 868–870
Hiss, Alger, 813–814
History, late 19th-century study of, 562, 564–565
History of the United States During the Administrations of Jefferson and Madison (Adams), 565
Hitler, Adolf: aggression in Europe, 764–767, 769; Japanese invasion of China and, 725; pre-war actions of, 763, 765; in World War II, 783, 785
HIV. *See* Human immunodeficiency virus
Hoar, George Frisbie, 522, 645
Ho Chi Minh, 817–818, 830
Ho Chi Minh City, 885
Hodgson, Godfrey, 921
Hofstader, Richard, 614*f*, 694*f*
Hogan, Michael, 809*f*
HOLC. *See* Home Owners Loan Corporation
Hollywood, California, 699

Holmes, Oliver Wendell, Jr., 670, 685, 742*f*
Holocaust, 785, 789*f*
Home(s). *See* Housing
Home Buildings, 546
Homeland Security, Office of, 931
Home Owners Loan Corporation (HOLC), 743, 754
Homestake Mining, 491
Homestead Act (1862), 460, 492
Homestead steel plant, 527
Homestead steel strike (1892), 527
Homicides, in cattle towns, 490*f*
Homosexuals: AIDS and, 900–901; and gay culture, in post–World War I period, 692, 694*f*; same-sex marriage and, 934; sexual revolution and, 877*f*, 878
Honduras, 821
Hookworm, 738*f*
Hoover, Herbert, 717, 728*f*; economic policies of, 724–725, 727; as food administrator in World War I, 667, 717; foreign policy of, 725; in Harding administration, 719, 730; 1929 stock market crash and, 730–731; in 1928 presidential election, 727–728; in 1932 presidential election, 737, 738; on prohibition, 704; on Roosevelt (Franklin), 738
Hoover, J. Edgar, 685
"Hoovervilles," 733
Hopkins, Harry L., 746
Hopkins, Johns, 559
Hopkins, Mark, 494
Horse(s), and Plains Indians, 483*f*
Horsecars, 546
Horse Creek, 483
Horse dance, of Plains Indians, 483*f*
Horse racing, 548
Horton, Willie, 909
Hose, Sam, 480
House of Representatives, U.S., in late 19th-century, 473
Housing: in late 19th-century cities, 542–545; in late 20th-century, 888; New Deal and, 754, 761
Howells, William Dean, 568–569, 627, 645

"Howl" (Ginsberg), 874–875
"How to Make Our Ideas Clear" (Peirce), 572
Huckleberry Finn (Twain), 567–568
Hudson, Rock, 900
Huerta, Victoriano, 659
Hughes, Charles Evans: in Harding administration, 718, 722; in 1916 presidential election, 665
Hughes, Langston, 710–711
Hull, Cordell, 764, 772
Hull House (Chicago), 552, 553
Human immunodeficiency virus (HIV), 900–901, 901*f*
Human Rights Watch, 910
Humphrey, Hubert H., 842
Hundred Days, 741–743; Second, 751–753, 754–758
Hungary: liberalization of, 912; 1956 revolt in, 819
Huntington, Collis P., 494
Hussein, Saddam, 894–895, 913–915; in Second Iraq War, 932–933
Hyde, Henry B., 516
Hydroelectric plants, 745
Hydrogen bomb, 807–808, 819

Iacocca, Lee, 887
IBM. *See* International Business Machines
Ibsen, Henrik, 569
ICC. *See* Interstate Commerce Commission
Iceland: Reagan-Gorbachev summit in, 897–898; in World War II, 769
Idaho: gold rush in, 489; silver miners' strike in, 527; territorial organization of, 491; women's suffrage in, 609
"I Have a Dream" (King), 834
Illinois: colleges in, 560; Granger movement in, 521; in presidential politics, 578
Illinois Central Railroad, 492, 493
Immigrants: assimilation of, 543*f*; in cities, 536–537, 540, 542–545; ethnic pride among, 870; in Great Depression, 734; illegal, 898, 900; Ku Klux Klan and, 706–707; old vs. new, 539–541; in post–World War I period, 686, 686*f*, 689–691, 690*f*; prejudice by

and against, 706–707; progressivism and, 602, 603, 624–626; railroads and, 494, 505; transatlantic travel by, 537–539; World War I and, 660; World War II and, 778–779
Immigration: in 19th-century, 481–482, 503, 537–539, 539*f*; in 20th-century, 537–539, 539*f*, 689–691, 861, 898, 900; National Origins Act and, 691; post–World War I, 689–691; pre–World War II, 765; quota system for, 689–691; restrictions on, 482, 538, 540, 542, 651, 689–691; to West, 481–482
Immigration Act (1965), 898
Impeachment: Clinton and, 923–924, 924*f*; Johnson and, 455; Nixon and, 854–855
Imperialism. *See* Expansionism
Import(s). *See* Trade
Import duties. *See* Tariff(s)
Income tax: under Carter, 888; in Civil War, 591; and Nixon administration, 852–853; under Reagan, 895, 898; Supreme Court on, 591; in World War I, 669; in World War II, 776
Income Tax Act (1986), 898
Incorporation laws. *See* Corporations
Indiana: Ku Klux Klan in, 706, 706*f*; in presidential politics, 578
Indian Americans: destruction of tribal life of, 486–488; gold rush and, 482–483, 485; land loss by, 488*m*; militant movements by, mid-20th century, 869–870; New Deal and, 762; progressivism and, 624; reservations of, 484, 485; wars with, late 19th-century, 484–486
Indian Bureau, 485
Indian lands, loss of, 488*m*
Indian Reorganization Act (1934), 762
Indian Ring, 485
Indian Self-Determination Act (1975), 870
Indian Territory (Oklahoma), 482, 485
Individualism, 566*f*; frontier and, 565, 566*f*
Indochina: post-Korean War, 817–818; in World War II, 773
Industrial combinations. *See* Monopolies

Industrial-military complex, development of, in World War I, 667
Industrial Workers of the World (IWW), 602, 685
Industry and industrialization: computers in, 865; consolidation of, 599, 600, 730; discontent with, 554; in early 20th-century, 729–730; and education, 537; and immigrants, 537–539; in late 19th-century, 502–503; New Deal and, 743–744, 751; in post–World War I period, 712–713, 729–730; in Progressive Era, 599, 600; and workers, 531–532; in World War I, 666–668; in World War II, 773–775. *See also* Manufacturing
Inflation: Carter and, 887–888; Ford and, 884; in late 19th-century, 475; Nixon and, 849, 888
The Influence of Sea Power Upon History (Mahan), 632
The Influence of Sea Power Upon the French Revolution and Empire (Mahan), 632
The Innocents Abroad (Twain), 567
Insurance: health, 671, 837, 838, 918–919, 934; life, 516, 606; old-age, 750, 752; unemployment, 752
Intellectual life: late 19th-century, 559–562. *See also* Culture(s); Literature
Intellectuals: alienation of, post–World War I, 707–709; and Communist party, in Great Depression, 735
Interior, Department of the, 485
International Business Machines (IBM), 895, 902
International Harvester Company, 599
Internet, 926–927; political fundraising and, 934
Internment, of Japanese Americans, 779m, 780f
Interstate Commerce Act (1887), 521–522, 599
Interstate Commerce Commission (ICC): under Coolidge, 720; establishment of, 521; under Harding, 720; under Roosevelt (Theodore), 612, 615; under Taft, 617
Interstate highway system, 858. *See also* Road(s)

Investment banking, 743
Iowa, progressive reform in, 604
Iran, 893f; hostage crisis in, 891, 892, 894–895; in late 20th-century, 914m; post–World War II, 891–892; Soviet Union and, 801
Iran-Contra arms deal, 904–906, 909
Iran-Iraq War, 913–914
Iraq: Carter and, 894–895; in late 20th-century, 914m; in Persian Gulf War, 913–915, 915f; in Second Iraq War, 931–934
Irish Americans, 540; in American West, 494; World War II and, 769
Iron Curtain, 802, 805m
Iron industry: after Civil War, 463; in late 19th-century, 506–507, 506–509; monopoly in, 511–512
Islam, *fatwa* and, 929
Isolationism: under Harding and Coolidge, 722, 724–725; late 19th-century, 630–633; and League of Nations ratification debate, 682; pre–World War II, 768; Wilson's attempt to break with, 678
Israel: Camp David Accords and, 891; Clinton and, 925; Reagan and, 895; Suez canal crisis and, 819; terrorism and, 928–929; in Yom Kippur War, 882, 883
Italian Americans, 539, 542
Italy: in Paris Peace Conference, 679; pre–World War II aggression of, 763–764, 765; after World War I, 679; in World War II, 766, 767, 782
Iwo Jima, 790m, 791
IWW. *See* Industrial Workers of the World

J. Edgar Thomson Steel Works, 512
J. P. Morgan and Company, 528
J. Walter Thompson advertising agency, 700f
Jabbar, Kareem Al, 862
Jackson, Michael, 922
Jackson State University, 846
James, Henry, 569–572, 573f
James, William, 572, 573f
Japan: atomic bomb and, 791–794, 793f; and China, 650, 659, 722–723, 725,

725f, 764–765; early 20th-century relations with, 650–652, 659; Pearl Harbor attack by, 772–773, 774f; Perry's expedition to, 633; post–World War I relations with, 722–723; in World War II, 767, 772–773, 785–790

Japanese Americans: exclusion of, 624, 651; internment of, 778–779, 779m, 780f; segregation of, 651

Jazz, 710

Jazz Age, 692–693

The Jazz Singer (film), 699

Jews: Holocaust and, 785, 789f; immigration of, 539, 542, 691, 765; in Israel, 818–819; Ku Klux Klan and, 706–707; in Nazi Europe, 765, 766f, 785; in post–World War I period, 691; prejudice against, 691, 765; as Supreme Court justices, 664

JFK (film), 841f

Jiang Jieshi. *See* Chiang Kai-shek

Job Corps, 836

Johns Hopkins University, 559, 563, 565

Johnson, Andrew, 449–450, 449f; Fourteenth Amendment and, 453; impeachment of, 455; and Reconstruction, 450–452, 454–455

Johnson, Hiram, 665

Johnson, Jack, 870

Johnson, Lyndon Baines, 836, 837f; on change, 857; civil rights under, 836, 866; Great Society program of, 836–838; presidency of, 836; in 1960 presidential election, 824; in 1964 presidential election, 836; in 1968 presidential election, 839–844; on society, 857, 864; Vietnam war under, 838–839, 839, 840m

Johnson, Tom L., 603

Jones, James H., 877

Jones, Mary Harris "Mother," 602

Jones, Paula Corbin, 919, 922–923

Jones, Robert T. "Bobby," 701

Jordan, David Starr, 645

Joseph (Indian Chief), 486

Josephson, Matthew, 519f

Journalism: and Cuban revolution, 638; early 20th-century, 601; and Harlem Renaissance, 710–711; late 19th-century, 558–560; and political campaigns, 593–595; in Progressive Era, 601; racism in, 478

Joy, James F., 510

Judiciary. *See* Supreme Court

The Jungle (Sinclair), 616

Junk bonds, 901–902

Justice Department: General Intelligence Division of, 686; and red scare, 686

Justice Department, Antitrust Division of, 729

Kalakaua (King of Hawaii), 633

Kalstedt, Harry, 696f

Kamikazes, 791

Kansas: Alliance movement in, 586, 587; population in late 19th-century, 585; Populists in, 588; progressive reform in, 604

Kansas Indians, 484

Kansas Pacific Railroad, 497, 504

Keating-Owen Child Labor Act (1916), 665

Kelley, Oliver H., 521

Kelley, Robin D., 876f

Kellogg, Frank B., 723

Kellogg-Briand Pact (1928), 723, 725

Kelly, William, 506

Kenna, "Hinky Dink," 577

Kennan, George, 684f, 801, 810

Kennan, George F., 634f

Kennedy, David, 756f

Kennedy, Jacqueline, 827, 835f

Kennedy, John F., 824–825, 918f; assassination of, 834–835, 859; and civil rights movement, 831–834; in Cuban missile crisis, 827–830; presidency of, 827; in 1960 presidential election, 824–825; in Vietnam, 830–831; in World War II, 824–825

Kennedy, Robert, 835f; assassination of, 842; as attorney general, 827; in Cuban missile crisis, 828f, 829; in 1968 presidential election, 842

Kent State University, 846, 847f

Keppler, Joseph, 477f

Kerner, Otto, 867

Kerner Commission, 867

Kerosene, 507

Kerr, Clark, 873
Kerry, John, in 2004 presidential election, 934–936
Kesey, Ken, 874
Key, David M., 470
Keynes, John Maynard, 753, 757, 800
Khomeini, Ayatollah Ruhollah, 892
Khrushchev, Nikita, 819–820, 820f; in Cuban missile crisis, 829; Cuban revolution and, 821; Eisenhower and, 819–820; Kennedy and, 829, 830; rise of, 819–820; Suez Canal crisis and, 819
Kills Two (Oglala Sioux Indian), 483f
Kimmel, Husband E., 773
Kinetoscope, 508f
King, Martin Luther, Jr.: approach to civil rights, 834, 863, 866, 920; assassination of, 867; in Montgomery bus boycott, 832; in SCLC, 832; writings and speeches of, 834
Kinsey, Alfred C., 877
Kissinger, Henry, 886–887; and détente, 846–848; and Nixon's resignation, 854; and Vietnam, 846, 849; and Yom Kippur War, 883
Kitchen Debate, 819, 820f
Klan. See Ku Klux Klan
Knights of Labor, 523–524, 540, 587
Knights of Reliance, 586
Knights of the White Camelia, 464
Knox, Henry, 767
Knox, Philander C., 613
Kodak camera, 503
Kohlberg, Kravis, Roberts and Company, 902
Kolko, Gabriel, 614f
Korea: division into North and South, 808–813, 811m; Soviet control of, 801; war between Japan and China over, 650
Korean War, 808–813, 811m, 812f, 816–817
Kosovo, 925
Ku Klux Klan, 463–464; in Birth of a Nation, 699; post–World War I revival of, 706–707, 706f
Kurds: in late 20th-century, 913, 915; in Second Iraq War, 933
Kurile Islands, 801

Kuwait, 913–915, 915f; in late 20th-century, 914m; in Second Iraq War, 932, 933

Labor. See Work
Labor legislation: in New Deal, 743–744, 751; post–World War II, 800–801; in World War II, 775–776
Labor unions: blacks and, 673f, 761–762; in early 20th-century, 602–603; growth in 1930s, 755–756; in late 19th-century, 523–528; in mid-20th century, 861, 887; migrant workers in, 869; militancy of, late 19th-century, 526–528; New Deal and, 743–744, 751, 755–756; Nixon and, 849; post–World War I, 686; post–World War II, 800, 887; and 1896 presidential election, 596; progressivism and, 602; radicalism in, 602–603; red scare and, 684; Roosevelt (Franklin) and, 754, 755; Roosevelt (Theodore) and, 615; socialism and, 602–603; in World War I, 668, 673f; in World War II, 775–776. See also Strikes
Ladies' Home Journal, 723, 859
La Feber, Walter, 809f
La Follette, Robert M., 604; in 1924 presidential election, 721; reforms of, 604
Laissez faire: challenges to, 520; in post–World War I period, 721; progressive denunciation of, 600
Lake Shore and Michigan Southern Railroad, 504
Land: access to water and, 498, 499, 499f; classification of, 498; Indian, loss of, 488m; late 19th-century, 492–493, 497–500; for railroads, 493–495, 494, 505; in Reconstruction South, 459–463; in West, 492–493, 497–500, 498. See also Border issues
Land-grant system, railroads and, 494, 505
Land-grant universities, 561
Landon, Alfred M., 753
Lange, Dorothea, 737f, 780f
Laos, in Vietnam war, 840m
Large policy, 632

Latin America: Cold War conflicts in, 820–821; dollar diplomacy in, 654, 656; early 20th-century policy toward, 652–655, 658–660; Good Neighbor policy toward, 724; Iran-Contra arms deal and, 904–905; late 19th-century policy toward, 631, 636–637, 639*f,* 647–649; post–World War I policy toward, 724

Latinos. *See* Hispanic Americans

Law(s). *See* Labor legislation; *specific laws*

Law, Walter, 696*f*

Layoffs, 902–903

Lazarus, Emma, 690*f,* 691

League of Nations, 680; and Japanese invasion of China, 725; U.S. refusal to ratify, 681–683; vs. United Nations, 795

Lease, Mary Elizabeth, 588*f*

Leave It To Beaver, 861

Lebanon, in late 20th-century, 914*m*

le Carré, John, 899*f*

Lee, Robert E., daughter of, 625

Legislation. *See* Labor legislation; *specific laws*

Legislature. *See* Congress

Leisure activities. *See* Entertainment; Sports

Lemke, William, 753

Lend-Lease Act (1941), 769

"The Lesson of History" (Marshall), 802

Leuchtenburg, William, 694*f,* 756*f*

Lever Act (1917), 667

Lewinsky, Monica, 923–924, 924*f*

Lewis, John L., 744

Lewis, Sinclair, 709

Lexington (ship), 788

Leyte Gulf, Battle for, 791

Liberal Republican party, 466, 598

Liberties. *See* Civil liberties

Liberty and Victory Loan drives, 668–669

Libraries, 556

Libya, in late 20th-century, 914*m*

Lieberman, Joseph, 927

Life (magazine), 816

Life insurance business, 516, 606

Life on the Mississippi (Twain), 568

Light bulb, invention of, 508–509

Light in August (Faulkner), 748

Liliuokalani (Queen of Hawaii), 633–635, 635*f*

Lincoln, Abraham: assassination of, 447; and Reconstruction, 447, 448–450

Lindbergh, Charles A., 715, 768

Link, Arthur, 684*f*

Linotype, 557

Lippmann, Walter, 717, 738

Literacy: and black suffrage, 477; and immigrants, 542

Literature: in 1920s, 707–709; black, 710–711; of counterculture, 874–875; in the Depression, 747–748; late 19th-century, 565–572; naturalism in, 569; realism in, 565–567, 568, 569; of West, 567

Little, Malcolm. *See* Malcolm X

Little Bighorn, 486

Little Lord Fauntleroy (Burnett), 567

Little Rock, Arkansas, desegregation in, 823, 823*f*

Little Rock and Fort Smith Railroad, 583

Littleton, Colorado, school shooting at, 923

Lloyd, Henry Demarest, 514, 520, 601

Lloyd George, David, 679–680

Lockheed, Haimes, 715

Lockheed, Malcolm, 715

Locomotives, 505

Lodge, Henry Cabot, 684*f*; and Harding, 718; and navy, 632; opposition to League of Nations, 681–683, 795; on Philippines, 644; reservations of, 684*f*; and Taft-Roosevelt dispute, 618

Lodge Reservations, 682, 683, 684*f*

Long, Huey, 748–751, 749*f,* 753

Longfellow, Henry Wadsworth, 565

Longstreet, James, 456, 529

Looking Backward 2000–1887 (Bellamy), 518, 528, 551, 620

Los Angeles, California: gangs in, 910; progressivism in, 602; socialism in, 602; Watts riots in (1965), 867

Louis, Joe, 870

Louisiana, Long in, 748–751

Louisville and Nashville Railroad, 505

Loving, Oliver, 497

Low, Seth, 603

Lowden, Frank, 718

Loyalty Review Board, 813
Luce, Henry, 797
Luce, Stephen B., 632
Luna Park, 549*f*
Lusitania (ship), 663*f*, 664
Lynchings, 480, 625, 625*f*, 674

MacArthur, Douglas: in Korean War, 810–811; in World War II, 789–790, 791
Magazines, 478, 558–559, 601. *See also individual magazines by name*
Maggie, A Girl of the Streets (Crane), 569
Magón, Ricardo Flores, 669
Magruder, Jeb Stuart, 851
Mahan, Alfred Thayer, 632
Mailer, Norman, 843
Maine (ship), 639–640, 640F
Main Street (Lewis), 709
Malcolm X, 745, 834, 862, 866
Mammoth Oil Company, 720
Manchuria, Japan and, 651, 722, 725, 725*f*
Manchuria, Soviet control of, 801
Manhattan Island, 545
Manhattan Project, 792
Manifest destiny, 631
Mann, Horace, 537
Mann-Elkins Act (1910), 617
The Man Nobody Knows (Barton), 712
Manufacturing: assembly line impact on, 714; in Great Depression, 732; innovations in, 712–714; in late 19th-century, 502–503, 506–509, 631; in post–Civil War South, 463; post–World War I, 712–714, 729; southern, 463; in World War I, 667; in World War II, 773–775
Mao Zedong, 808
Marathon Oil, 902
Marchand, Roland, 694*f*
Marijuana, 910
Marion Star (newspaper), 717
Marling, Karal Ann, 860*f*
Marriage: in 19th-century, 531; companionate, 691–692; post–World War I, 691–692, 693; same-sex, 934; in World War II, 776, 782
Marshall, George C., 786*f*, 802
Marshall, Thurgood, 822, 920

Marshall Plan, 802–804, 809*f*
Marx, Karl, 450, 520, 528, 735*f*
Marxism, 520–521
Marxist Socialist Labor party, 520
Masaryk, Jan, 804
Massachusetts, mobility in, 536
The Masses (magazine), 669
Mastny, Thomas, 809*f*
Materialism: Civil War and, 472; late 19th-century, 554
Mathers, Marshall Bruce, III, 922
Maximilian (Archduke of Austria), 630
Mazda, 902
McAdoo, William G., 667, 721
McCain, John, 927
McCarthy, Eugene, 842
McCarthy, Joseph R., 814, 817, 817*f*, 824
McCarthyism, 814
McClure, S. S., 601
McClure's (magazine), 601, 601*f*
McCord, James, 851
McCormick Harvesting Machine Company, 524
McCoy, Joseph G., 497
McCullough, David, 793*f*
McDougal, James, 916
McGovern, George, 848
McKinley, William, 475, 596; assassination of, 611; and Cuba, 638–639, 647; and expansionism, 643–645, 647; foreign policy of, 633, 638–639, 643–645, 647, 653; in 1896 presidential election, 592, 593–595, 595*f*, 595*m*; in 1900 presidential election, 647
McKinley Tariff Act (1890), 633
McNamara, Robert, 841*f*
McTeague (Norris), 569
Meat packing industry, 616
Medicaid, 837, 838
Medicare, 837, 838, 895
Medicare Act (1965), 837
Medicine Lodge Creek, 484
Mellon, Andrew: in Coolidge administration, 721; on Great Depression, 731; in Harding administration, 719–720; taxation program of, 719–720, 731; on World War I debts, 725
Melville, Herman, 581

Mencken, H. L., 542, 703
Menlo Park, New Jersey, 508
Mercer, Lucy, 760*f*
Mergenthaler, Ottmar, 557
Mergers, 599, 600, 901–902
Mesabi region, 507
Methodists, fundamentalism and, 702
Metropolitan Health Board (New York City), 544
Metropolitan Museum of Art, 547
Metropolitan Opera, 547
Mexican Americans: civil rights for, 868–870; deportation in Great Depression, 734, 869
Mexico: cattle in, 496; dollar diplomacy in, 654; expansionism and, 630; French protectorate over, 630; missionary diplomacy in, 659; post–World War I relations with, 724
Michigan: banks in, 741; colleges in, 561
Michigan Central Railroad, 504
Michigan State University, 561
Microsoft Internet Explorer, 926
Middle class: in 19th-century, 530–531; in mid-20th century, 861–862; in post–World War I period, 691–692; and prohibition, 704
Middle East: Camp David Accords and, 891; Cold War conflicts in, 818–819; hostages in, Iran-Contra arms deal and, 904; Israel and, 818–819; in late 20th-century, 914*m*; Truman on, 802
Midway, Battle at, 789
Midway Islands: acquisition of, 631; in World War II, 789
Migrant families, 737*f*
Migrant labor system, reform of, 869
Migration: by blacks, 671–674, 709; World War I and, 671–674; World War II and, 776. *See also* Geographic mobility
Militant movements, by minorities, 626–628, 709–711, 866–867
Military: in Afghanistan, 932; blacks in, 673–674, 776–778, 777*f*; Cold War expansion of, 808–809; under Eisenhower, 816–817; post–World War II demobilization of, 801; under Reagan, 895; in Second Iraq War,

933–934; women in, 780; World War II mobilization, 773–775. *See also* Army; Navy
Military bases: bases-for-destroyers deal, 767; overseas, importance of, 632
Milken, Michael, 901
Miller, Doris "Dorie," 777*f*
Miller, William, 519*f*
Million Man March, 920
Mills, C. Wright, 860
Milosevic, Slobodan, 925
Mimeograph, 508
Minimum wage, New Deal legislation on, 743
Mining industry: late 19th-century boom in, 488–492; 1902 coal strike and, 615; strikes against, 527–528
Mining towns, 489, 491
Minnesota: Alliance movement in, 587; Populist party in, 588; progressive reform in, 604
Minorities: rights for, progressivism and, 624–628; in World War II, 776–779
Minow, Newton, 859
Minutemen missiles, 829
Missionary diplomacy, 659
Mississippi: Black Code in, 451; black suffrage in, 464, 477; progressive reform in, 604
Missouri Pacific Railroad, 497, 504, 524
Mitchell, John, 853
Mitchell, John P., 603
Mobility: late 19th-century, 536–537. *See also* Migration
Mobilization: in World War I, 666–668; in World War II, 773–775
Model A Ford, 714
Model G airplane, 715
Model T Ford, 714, 715
Moderate Republicans, after Civil War, 450
Mojados, 868
Moley, Raymond, 739
Mondale, Walter, 896
Monetary policy: gold vs. silver in, 589; New Deal and, 743. *See also* Currency
Money Trust, 528
Mongolia, Outer, 801
Monkey Trial, 703

Monopolies, 503, 509–516; attacks on, 516–523, 601; and democracy, 528; and economic system of 1920s, 730; progressive attacks on, 601, 607; Roosevelt's (Theodore) attacks on, 612–613. *See also* Trust(s)

Monroe Doctrine, 637; Khrushchev on, 821; Roosevelt Corollary to, 649–650, 724; Venezuela crisis and, 637

Montana: gold rush in, 489; territorial organization of, 491

Monte Cassino, 783

Montgomery, Alabama, 506*f*; civil rights movement in, 832–833, 866

Montojo, Admiral, 641

Moody, Dwight L., 551

Moral Majority, 896

Moran, George "Bugs," 705*f*

Morgan, J. Pierpont, 511, 512, 528, 592, 614*f*, 615

Morganizations, 511

Morgenthau, Jr., Henry, 757

Morison, Samuel Eliot, 694*f*

Morrill Land Grant Act (1862), 559, 561

Morrow, Dwight W., 724

Motel industry, 858

Motion picture industry, 508*f*

Motion-picture projector, 508

Motion pictures, 698–700

Mount Holyoke College, 561

Movies, 698–700, 921; first, 508*f*

Moving assembly line, 714

MTV, 922

Muckrakers, 601

Mugwumps, 598

Muhammad, Elijah, 834

Muller v. *Oregon,* 606

Mulligan letters, 583

Municipal socialism, 602

Munn v. *Illinois,* 521

Munsey, Frank, 619

Musaddig, Muhammad, 891

Muscle Shoals, Alabama, 745, 746*m*

Museum of Fine Arts (Boston), 547

Music: in 1920s, 710; in 1990s, 922; MTV and, 922; popular, 922; rap, 922

Muslims, Black, 834, 862, 866

Mussolini, Benito, 763, 783

Mutual Life, 516

My Lai massacre, 845

NAACP. *See* National Association for the Advancement of Colored People

Nabisco, 902

Nader, Ralph, 927

Nagasaki, 792, 793*f*

Nairobi, Kenya, 929

Naismith, James, 550

Nashville (ship), 653

Nasser, Gamal Abdel, 819

Nast, Thomas, 457*f*

The Nation (magazine), 568, 708

National American Women's Suffrage Association (NAWSA), 609

National Association for the Advancement of Colored People (NAACP): civil rights litigation by, 822; founding of, 627

National Broadcasting Company, 699

National Child Labor Committee, 605

National debt. *See* Debt, national

National Defense Education Act (1958), 871

National Democrats, 593

National Educational Television, 859

National Farm Workers' Association, 869, 869*f*

National Federation of Republican Women, 889

National Football League, 701

National Grange of the Patrons of Husbandry, 521

National Greenback party, 475

National Indian Youth Council, 869

National Industrial Recovery Act (NIRA), 743–744, 751, 753

Nationalism: black, 478, 709–711, 834; after Civil War, 465; New, 620; after World War I, 679

National Labor Relations (Wagner) Act (1935), 751

National Labor Relations Board (NLRB), 751

National Labor Union, 523

National League, 549

National Organization for Women (NOW), 879–880, 889

National Origins Act (1921), 691

National Recovery Administration (NRA), 744–745, 751
National Security Council (NSC), 808
National Tube Company, 512
National Union for Social Justice, 753
National War Labor Board (NWLB), 775
National Women's Party, 889
National Youth Administration (NYA), 747
Native Americans. *See* Indian Americans
Nativism, 542, 641*f*, 651f
NATO. *See* North Atlantic Treaty Organization
Natural Born Killers (film), 921
Naturalism, in literature, 569
Naval Affairs Committee, 632
Naval War College, 632
Naval War of 1812 (Roosevelt), 611
Navigation. *See* Navy
Navy: bases-for-destroyers deal, 767; blacks in, 777; buildup in 1920s, 722–723; in Cuban missile crisis, 829; in late 19th-century, 632; in Spanish-American War, 641, 642, 751*m*; in World War I, 674; before World War II, 767, 769; in World War II, 785–790
Nazi Germany. *See* Germany; Hitler
Nebraska: Alliance movement in, 587; population in late 19th-century, 585; progressive reform in, 604
Nebraska Land and Cattle Company, 498
Neighborhood Guild, 552
Netherlands, in World War II, 766
Netscape, 926
Neutrality, in foreign policy: in World War I, 661–664, 665–666; in World War II, 763–764
Neutrality Act (1935), 763
Nevada: gold rush in, 489; territorial organization of, 491
Newburyport, Massachusetts, 536
New Deal, 739, 752*f*; agricultural policies of, 744–745, 753; and blacks, 754, 760–762; critique of, 758–759; extremists and, 748–751; and Indians, 762; industrial policies of, 743–744, 751; influences on, 751; Keynesian economics and, 753; labor unions and, 743–744, 751, 755–756; monetary policies of, 742–743; opposition to, 748–751, 753; Roosevelt's role in, 762–763; Second, 751–753; significance of, 758–759; slowing down of, 755–756; social insurance program of, 752; success of, 756*f*; and Supreme Court, 751, 754–758; unemployment policies of, 745–747, 747*f*, 752; utility policies of, 745, 752; and women, 759–760
"New era," 711, 727
New Freedom policy, 621–624, 667
New Jersey: in presidential politics, 578; progressive reform in, 604
Newlands Act (1902), 612
Newman, John M., 841*f*
New Nationalism policy, 620
"New Negro," 709–711
New Orleans, Louisiana, jazz in, 710
New Panama Canal Company, 652, 653
Newspapers: on blacks after Reconstruction, 478; late 19th-century, 558–559; and political campaigns, 593; printing press and, 557–558
New York (state): in presidential politics, 578; progressivism in, 604; Roosevelt (Franklin) and, 737
New York, Port of, 581
New York Associated Press, 557
New York Central Railroad, 504, 510, 512, 536
New York City: blacks in, 671, 672, 709–710; civic culture in, 547; draft riots in, 544; Harlem Renaissance in, 710–711; immigrants in, 536, 538, 542; infrastructure of, 544–545; mobility in, 536; politics in, early 20th-century, 577, 578; progressivism in, 603, 604; settlement houses in, 552; transportation in, 546; Triangle shirtwaist factory fire in, 606; Tweed Ring in, 466, 577–578; 2001 World Trade Center attacks in, 929–931; women's suffrage in, 609; World Trade Center attacks in, 930*f*
New York Custom House, 476
New York Herald (newspaper), 558
New York Journal (newspaper), 558, 638, 639

New York Life, 516

New York Sun (newspaper), 558, 615

New York Times (newspaper), 509, 901

New York Tribune (newspaper), 466, 558

New York World (newspaper), 558, 593, 638

New York Yankees, 701, 702*f*

Nez Percé Indians, 486

Ngo Dinh Diem, 818, 830–831

Nguyen Van Thieu, 849

Niagara movement, 627

Nicaragua: dollar diplomacy in, 654; in Iran-Contra arms deal, 904; as possible canal zone, 653; Reagan and, 895; U.S. protectorate over, 654, 659, 724

Nickelodeons, 699

Niebuhr, Reinhold, 734

Nike, 902

Nimitz, Chester W., 790, 791

Nine-Power Treaty, 723, 725

Nineteenth Amendment, 698; effects of passage, 698; ratification of, 609; and women's equality, 671

NIRA. *See* National Industrial Recovery Act

Nixon, Pat, 848*f*

Nixon, Richard M., 824; and détente, 846–848, 848*f*; domestic policy of, 849–850; economic policy of, 849–850; Khrushchev and, 820*f*; in Latin America, 821; in 1960 presidential election, 824–825; in 1968 presidential election, 842–844; in 1972 presidential election, 848, 849; resignation of, 854; as vice president, 820*f*, 821; Vietnam war under, 844–848, 848; Watergate and, 850–852, 853–855; and Yom Kippur War, 882

NLRB. *See* National Labor Relations Board

Nomura, Kichisaburo, 772

Noriega, Manuel, 912–913

Normalcy, 718

Normandy beach, 783, 784*f*

Norris, Frank, 569

Norris, George W., 745

North: black migration to, 671–674, 709–710. *See also* Union

North, Oliver, 904

North Africa, in World War II, 783, 784*m*

North Atlantic, in World War II, 767, 769

North Atlantic Treaty, 807

North Atlantic Treaty Organization (NATO), 807, 925

North Carolina, civil rights movement in, 832

North Dakota: Alliance movement in, 586; population in late 19th-century, 585

Northern Pacific Railroad, 485, 493, 496*m,* 504

Northern Securities Company, 615

North Korea, 808–813, 811*m*

Norway, in World War II, 766

Novick, Peter, 937*f*

NOW. *See* National Organization for Women

Now We Know (Gaddis), 809*f*

NRA. *See* National Recovery Administration

NSC. *See* National Security Council

NSC-68 (classified document), 808, 810

Nuclear power, 865–866

Nuclear weapons: in Cold War, 807–808, 816–817, 819–820; in Cuban missile crisis, 829; as deterrent, 808, 816–817, 819; in Iran and North Korea, 936; reduction of, 846–848, 897–898, 912; Soviet development of, 807–808; in World War II, 791–794

Nursing, 533, 561

NWLB. *See* National War Labor Board

NYA. *See* National Youth Administration

OAS. *See* Organization of American States

O'Connor, Sandra Day, 898

Office of Homeland Security, 931

Office of War Mobilization, 775

"Of Mr. Booker T. Washington and Others" (Du Bois), 626

Ogden, Utah, 495, 496*m*

Oglala Sioux Indians, 483*f,* 484

Ohio: colleges in, 561; in presidential politics, 578

"Ohio Gang," 719, 720

Ohio State Journal (newspaper), 568

Ohio State University, 561

Oil: crisis of 1973, 882–884; industry, 507, 512–516, 517; in Middle East,

818–819, 904; in Persian Gulf War, 913–915, 915*f*; scandal under Harding, 720; in World War II, 773
Okinawa, 790*m,* 791
Oklahoma: desegregation in, 822; Indians in, 482, 484, 485
Old-age insurance, 895; Social Security, 752; Townsend's campaign for, 750
Old Guard, of Republican party, 619
Olds, Ransom E., 713
Olney, Richard, 637
Olympic games, 891
Omaha beach, 784*f*
One World (Willkie), 794
Only Yesterday (Allen), 694*f*
OPEC. *See* Organization of Petroleum Exporting Countries
Open Door policy, 634*f,* 650–652, 722–723, 772
Open-range ranching, 497–498; end of, 500
Operation Mongoose, 828*f*
Operation Restore Hope, 925
Oppenheimer, J. Robert, 792
Oregon: initiative system in, 604; progressive reform in, 604, 606
Oregon (ship), 652
Organization of Afro-American Unity, 866
Organization of American States (OAS), 820
Organization of Petroleum Exporting Countries (OPEC), 883
Orient. *See* Far East
The Origin of Species (Darwin), 516
Orlando, Vittorio, 679
Orphans, in early 20th-century, 606*f*
Oswald, Lee Harvey, 834, 835
Our American Cousin (play), 447
Our Country (Strong), 631
Outer Mongolia, 801

Pacific Coast, San Francisco and, 481
Pacific Railway Act (1862), 493–494
Pacific region: American expansionism in, 633–636, 643–645; in World War II, 785–790, 790*m*
Padrone system, 539
Pahlavi, Muhammad Reza (Shah of Iran), 891

Palace Car factory, 527
Pale Faces, 464
Palestine, Clinton and, 925
Palestine Liberation Organization (PLO), 925
Palestinian Arabs, 818–819
Palmer, A. Mitchell, 685
Pan African Conferences, 710
Panama: independence from Colombia for, 653–654; Noriega in, 912–913
Panama Canal, 636, 652–655; transfer to Panama, 891; Zone, 650*m,* 653, 654*m*
Panama Canal Zone, as colony, 655
Pan-American Petroleum Company, 720
Panic(s): of 1873, 465; of 1933, 741
Pan-Indian movement, 869–870
Pantry Pride, 902
Paris, liberation of, 784
Paris Peace Conference (1919), 679–681
Park(s), amusement, 549*f*
Parker, Alton B., 615
Parker, Dorothy, 721*f*
Parks, Rosa, 832
Parrington, Vernon, 472
The Path I Trod (Powderly), 523
Patronage, 476. *See also* Civil service
Patrons of Husbandry, 521
Patton, George S., 783
Paturage land, 498
Paul, Alice, 609, 698
Pauncefote, Lord, 652
Peace Corps, 828
Peace movement(s), in post–World War I period, 723–724
Pearl, Mississippi, school shooting in, 922
Pearl Harbor, 633, 772–773, 774*f,* 777*f,* 819
Peirce, Charles S., 572
Peiss, Kathy, 694*f,* 876*f*
Pemberton, William, 899*f*
Pendergast, Tom, 799
Pendleton Civil Service Act (1883), 582, 594
Pennsylvania, hijacked plane crash in, 930
Pennsylvania Railroad, 504, 512
Pensions, Social Security, 752
Pensions, Townsend, 750
Pentagon, 2001 terrorist attack on, 930
Pentagon Papers, 850

People's party. See Populist party
Perelman, Ronald, 902
Perestroika, 897
Perkins, Frances, 759
Perkins, George W., 619
Perot, Ross, 917
Perry, Matthew C., 633
Pershing, John J., 660, 674
Persian Gulf War, 913–915, 914m, 915f
Peru, Nixon's visit to, 821
Petroleum industry, 507, 512–516, 517.
    See also Oil
Philadelphia, Pennsylvania: in Great
    Depression, 733; immigrants in, 542
Philadelphia Public Ledger (newspaper), 558
Philippine Commission, 617
Philippine Islands: annexation by U.S.,
    643–645; as colony, 655; insurrection
    against U.S., 646–647; Roosevelt
    (Theodore) on, 652; Spanish-American
    War and, 641, 643, 645; Taft as governor
    of, 617; in World War II, 773, 790, 791
Philippine Sea, Battle of, 791
Philosophy, pragmatic school, 572–574
Phonograph, 508
Pierrepont, Edwards, 465
Pikes Peak, 489
Pilgrim's Progress (Bunyan), 601
Pinchot, Gifford, 618
Pinkerton detectives, 527, 587
Pittsburgh, Pennsylvania, as iron and steel
    capital, 507
Plains Indians, 482–483; culture of, 482;
    horse dance of, 483f; wars with,
    484–486
Plantations, 459–460
Plastics, 865
Platt Amendment (1900), 648
Playboy (magazine), 886
Plessy v. Ferguson, 477–478, 822
PLO. See Palestine Liberation
    Organization
Poe, Edgar Allen, 565
Poetry. See Literature
Poker Alice, 491
Poland: creation of, 679; immigrants
    from, 542; liberalization of, 912;
    post–World War II, 796–797; in World
    War II, 765, 766, 766f

"A Policy of Boldness" (Dulles), 816
Political campaigns: business involvement
    in, 594; changing nature of, 593–595;
    in late 19th-century, 578–580; televi-
    sion and, 858–859
Political parties: and blacks, affiliation of,
    474, 760–762; early 20th-century,
    474–475, 728; late 19th-century,
    474–475, 575–576, 578–580
Politics: city, 576–578; farmers in,
    586–589; late 19th-century, 474–476,
    575–576; progressive reforms of,
    603–604
Pollock v. Farmers' Loan and Trust Company,
    591
Poll taxes, 477
Pond's Company, 700f
Pop music, 922
Popular culture: early 20th-century,
    698–700; violence and, 921–923
Popular Science Monthly (magazine), 563
Population density, in urban vs. rural ar-
    eas, 542
Population growth: 20th-century, 776,
    865; urban, 691–692; in World War II,
    776
Populist party, 588–589, 588f; formation
    of, 587; in 1896 presidential election,
    592, 595, 596
Port Huron Statement, 873
Port of New York, 581
Potsdam conference, 797
Pound, Ezra, 708
Poverty: in 19th-century, 536; in 20th-
    century, 836; Johnson's war on, 836;
    Long on, 748–751; in Progressive Era,
    599, 600; and race riots, 867–868; ur-
    ban, 550–552, 599
Powderly, Terence V., 523, 536
Powell, Colin, 931–932
Powell, John Wesley, 498
Powell doctrine, 932
Pragmatism, 572–574, 573f
Precious metals, search for. See Gold rush
Prejudice. See Racial prejudice
Presidency: late 19th-century, 580–585;
    Reconstruction and, 455
Presidential election(s): of 1868, 455; of
    1872, 466; of 1876, 466–468, 475,

580; of 1880, 581; of 1884, 474,
583–584; of 1888, 585; of 1892, 474,
589; of 1896, 592, 595*m*, 638; of
1900, 602, 646, 647; of 1904, 602; of
1908, 617; of 1912, 620–621, 621*m*,
628; of 1916, 664–665; of 1920,
686–687, 718; of 1924, 721–722; of
1928, 707, 727–728, 824; of 1932,
736–740; of 1936, 753–754; of 1940,
767–768; of 1944, 791; of 1948,
804–806; of 1952, 814–815; of 1960,
824–825; of 1964, 836, 838; of 1968,
839–844; of 1972, 848; of 1976,
885–886; of 1980, 892–895; of 1984,
896–897; of 1988, 908–909; of 1992,
917; of 1996, 919–920; of 2000,
927–928; of 2004, 934–936
Presley, Elvis, 876*f*
Primary system, direct, 604
Princeton University: football at, 550;
   Wilson at, 621, 622*f*
Princip, Gavrilo, 660
Principles of Psychology (James), 572
Printing press, 557–558
Prisons: Civil War, 448; in Iraq, 935, 935*f*;
   late 20th-century, 909, 910, 911*f*
Prize fighting. *See* Boxing
Prodigy, 926
Profiles in Courage (Kennedy), 827
Progress, perils of, 864–865
Progress and Poverty (George), 518
Progressive education, 563–564,
   870–872
Progressive party: in 1912 presidential
   election, 620, 621*m*; in 1916 presiden-
   tial election, 664; in 1924 presidential
   election, 721; in 1948 presidential
   election, 806
Progressivism: meaning of term, 598; in
   Mexico, 659; minority rights and,
   624–628; muckraking journalists and,
   601; 1912 presidential election and,
   620–621; political reforms, 603–611;
   prohibition and, 704; radical, 602;
   Roosevelt (Theodore) and, 615,
   616–617, 618; roots of, 598–601; social reforms, 605–606; in states, 604;
   Taft and, 617–618, 618; urban reforms, 603–604; vs. socialism, 602;

Wilson and, 624; women's suffrage
   and, 607–609; World War I and, 660,
   671
Prohibition, 704–705; end of, 741; during
   World War I, 671, 704
Promontory, Utah, 495, 496*m*
Propaganda, in World War I, 669–670
Property, private, tax on, 518
Proposition 209, 921
Prosperity, 865–866
Prostitution, World War I and, 671
Protectionism, under Adams (John
   Quincy) administration. *See* Tariff(s)
Protestants, in cities, 551
Psychology, 572; Freudian, 871
Public Enemy (film), 921
Public utilities. *See* Utilities
Public Works Administration, 743
Publishing, 556–559; 19th-century,
   558–560; printing press and, 557–558.
   See also Journalism
Puerto Rico, 643, 647, 650*m*; as colony,
   655
Pulitzer, Joseph, 558, 558*f*, 638
Pulitzer Prize, 558*f*
Pullman, George, 505, 527
Pullman strike, 527–528, 591, 596
Pure Food and Drug Act (1906), 616

Quota system: in education, 691; in immigration, 689–691

R. J. Reynolds Tobacco Company, 902
Rabin, Yitzhak, 925
Race relations, new separatism in,
   920–921
Race riots, 778; of 1877, 482; of 1960s,
   867; reasons for, 867–868
Racial equality: black militants and,
   866–867; churches in fight for,
   862–864; Declaration of Independence
   and, 450; Reconstruction-era debates
   on, 450–452; status of, in late 20th-
   century, 920–921; Supreme Court on,
   477–478; Washington (Booker T.) and,
   479–480; after World War II, 821–824
Racial prejudice: against American
   Indians, 624; among progressives,
   624–626; in biology textbooks, 704; in

Racial prejudice (continued)
early 20th-century, 625–628; against
Japanese, 624; against Jews, 691, 765;
1960s student revolts and, 872–874; in
post–World War I period, 704; in
World War II, 776–779. See also Ku
Klux Klan
Racial pride, 870
Racial segregation. See Segregation
Radical(s), post–World War I persecution
of, 683–686
Radical feminism, 698, 880
Radical progressivism, 602–603
Radical Republicans: and black rights,
450–452, 455–456; and Fifteenth
Amendment, 455–456; and Johnson
impeachment, 454–455; and southern
readmission, 449, 450, 451–452
Radical students, in 1960s, 872–874
Radio: and religion, 863; rise of,
698–700; sports on, 700
Radio Corporation of America, 730
Railroad(s): and agriculture, 492; as big
business, 503–505; cattle and, 497;
Chinese labor and, 482, 495f; competition between, 494–495; discounts and
rebates given by, 510; and economy,
503–505; and Indians, 485, 486; integrated system for, 504; land-grant sys-
tem and, 494; monopoly in, 509–511;
regulation of, 521–522, 617; in South,
459; strikes against, 524, 527–528; un-
der Taft, 617; in West, 493–495, 496m;
in World War I, 667. See also
Transcontinental railroads
Railroad Administration, 667
Rain-in-the-Face, 486
Rambo III (film), 921
Ranching, 496–500; barbed wire and,
498–500, 499f; open-range, 497–498,
500
Rap music, 922
Raulston, John, 703
Ray, James Earl, 867
REA. See Rural Electrification
Administration
Reading Railroad, 613
Reagan, Ronald, 894f, 895; on AIDS, 900;
assignation attempt on, 894f; Cold War

and, 899f; economy under, 895, 896,
901–904; first term of, 895; foreign
policy of, 895, 897–898; Iran-Contra
and, 904–905; presidency of, 905–906,
906f; in 1976 presidential election,
886; in 1980 presidential election,
892–895; in 1984 presidential election,
896–897; second term of, 897–898
Realism, late 19th-century, in literature,
565–567, 568, 569
Rebates, railroads and, 510
Recession, economic: under Carter,
887–888. See also Inflation
Reconstruction: black legislators in,
456–459, 458f; economic conditions
of, 459–463; end of, 470, 472;
Fifteenth Amendment in, 455–456;
Fourteenth Amendment in, 452–453,
454; historians on, 457f; Johnson and,
450–452; Lincoln and, 447, 448–450;
Radical Republicans and, 448–452;
white backlash against, 463–465
Reconstruction Acts, 453–454
Recreation. See Entertainment
Red Army, 801
The Red Badge of Courage (Crane), 569
Red Cloud (Indian chief), 484
Red Power, 869
Red scare, 683–686, 686f
Referendums, 604
Reform: of civil service, 475–476,
583–584; Civil War and, 530; eco-
nomic, 518–521; of education,
563–564; financial, 475; pragmatism
and, 572; through education, 563–564;
in World War I, 671. See also New Deal
Reiss, Winold, 627f
Relativism, pragmatism and, 572–574
Religion(s): in early 20th-century,
702–704; and evolution, theory of,
572; fundamentalism in, 702–704,
896; Great Awakening, 551; in mid-
20th century, 862–864; television and,
863, 896. See also Church(es)
Remington company, 503
Remington typewriter, 557f
Reno, Janet, 919
Report on the Lands of the Arid Region of the
United States (Powell), 498

Representation: post–Civil War, 450–451; Thirteenth Amendment and, 450
Republican National Convention: of 1868, 455; of 1880, 581; of 1912, 620
Republican party (GOP): in 1866 congressional election, 453; in 1868 election, 455; in 1874 congressional election, 466; in 1876 election, 466–468, 580; in 1880 election, 581; in 1884 election, 583–584; in 1890 congressional election, 585; in 1896 election, 592, 595–596, 595*m*; in 1912 election, 620, 621*m*; in 1920 election, 686–687, 718; in 1924 election, 721–722; in 1928 election, 727–728; in 1936 election, 753–754; in 1940 election, 767–768; in 1994 congressional election, 919; Alliance movement and, 586, 587; blacks in, 456–459, 474, 754, 760–762; and black suffrage, 455–456; and communists-in-government issue, 814; under Grant, 465–466; in late 19th-century, 474–475, 474–476, 578–580; and League of Nations, 681, 682; Old Guard-progressive split under Taft, 620; Reconstruction and, 449, 450–452, 454–455; in South, 466
Reuben James (ship), 769
Revels, Hiram, 458*f*
Revlon, 902
Condoleeza Rice, 939
Richardson, Henry Hobson, 506*f*
Richmond, Virginia, trolley line in, 546
Richmond and West Point Terminal Company, 505
Richmond Times (newspaper), 593
Ridge, Tom, 931
Rights. *See* Civil rights
Riis, Jacob, 544*f*
Rike's Department Store, 533*f*
Riots: draft, 544. *See also* Race riots
The Rise of Silas Lapham (Howells), 568
RJR Nabisco, 902
Road(s): interstate highway system of, 858; in post–World War I period, 712
Roaring Twenties, 694*f*, 696*f*
Robber Barons, 503
Robinson, Edgar E., 756*f*

Robocop (film), 921
Rockefeller, John D., 512–514, 514, 515*f*, 517, 520, 560, 615*f*, 685
Rockefeller Foundation, 738*f*
Rockefeller National City Bank, 528
Rocky Mountain Fur Company, 483
Rocky Mountain Husbandman, 500
Rocky Mountains: gold rush in, 488–492; states, ERA failure in, 890*m*
Rodgers, Daniel, 614*f*
Roe v. *Wade*, 880*f*, 918
Rogers, Will, 735
Roman Catholicism. *See* Catholics and Catholic Church
Romania, 912
Romanticism, 565
Rome, in World War II, 783
Rommel, Erwin, 783
Roosevelt, Eleanor, 759–760, 760*f*
Roosevelt, Franklin Delano, 736–740, 742*f*, 752*f*; assessment of, 762–763; and blacks, 760–762; conservative opposition to, 753; critique of policies, 758–759; death of, 794, 799; extremist opposition to, 748–751, 753–754; foreign policy of, 764–767; inaugural addresses of, 642, 754; and labor unions, 754, 755; as New York governor, 737; philosophy of, 739; in 1932 presidential election, 736–740, 739*f*; in 1936 presidential election, 753–754; in 1940 presidential election, 767–768; in 1944 presidential election, 791; Reagan compared with, 906*f*; vs. Supreme Court, 754–758; women in administration of, 759–760; and World War II, before U.S. entry, 764–767; in World War II, 773–775, 785; at Yalta, 795*f*, 796. *See also* New Deal
Roosevelt, Theodore, 498, 611–617; on 1896 presidential campaign, 595; and blacks, 627, 628; at Civil Service Commission, 585; conservation efforts of, 617; at Elkhorn Ranch, 500; foreign policy of, 649–650, 651–652; on Harrison (Benjamin), 585; on Indians, 624; leftward shift of, 616–617; in McKinley administration, 632; and Monroe Doctrine, 649–650; on

Roosevelt, Theodore *(continued)*
  muckrakers, 601; and navy, 632;
  New Nationalism policy of, 620; 1902
  coal strike and, 615; and Panama
  Canal, 653–654, 655*f*; on patronage,
  476; on politics, 578; presidency of,
  615–616; in 1912 presidential election,
  619, 621*m*, 628; in 1916 presidential
  election, 664, 665; Reagan compared
  with, 906*f*; and Rough Riders, 642;
  in Spanish-American War, 641;
  and Taft, 619; trustbusting by,
  612–613
Roosevelt Corollary, 649–650, 725
Root, Elihu, 649, 653
Rosenberg, Ethel, 814
Rosenberg, Julius, 814
Rothstein, Arthur, 761*f*
Rough Riders, 642
Ruby, Jack, 834
Rudd, Mark, 874*f*
Rugby, 550
Ruml, Beardsley, 776
Rumsfeld, Donald, 932
Rural areas: and cities, conflicts between,
  702–705; electricity brought to, 752
Rural Electrification Administration
  (REA), 752
Russia: Alaska sold by, 631; Germany and,
  nonaggression pact between, 765; im-
  migrants from, 539, 542; and
  Manchuria, 651. *See also* Soviet Union
Russian Revolution (1917), 666
Rutgers University, 550
Ruth, Babe, 702*f*
Ryan, Paddy, 548

Sacco, Nicola, 707
Sacco-Vanzetti case, 707
Sadat, Anwar, 891
Saigon, fall of, 885
Sakhalin Islands, 801
Saloons, 548, 705
Salvation Army, 551
Samoan Islands, 633
Sampson, William T., 643
Sanctuary (Faulkner), 748
Sand Creek, Colorado, 484
Sandinistas, 904

San Francisco, California: commercial im-
  portance of, 481; immigrants in, 481,
  651; in late 19th-century, 481
San Francisco Conference, 795
Sanger, Margaret, 693–698, 695*f*
Sargent, John Singer, 558*f*
Saturday Night Massacre, 851
Saudi Arabia, and Persian Gulf War,
  913–915
Saving Private Ryan (film), 786–787*f,* 787*f*
Sawyer, Philetus, 473
Scalawags, 456
Schecter v. *United States,* 751, 755
Schenck v. *United States,* 670
Schlafly, Phyllis, 889–890, 890*m*
Schlesinger, Arthur M., Jr., 543*f,* 756*f,* 899*f*
Schley, Winfield Scott, 643
School(s). *See* Colleges and universities;
  Education
The School and Society (Dewey), 564
School shootings, 922–923
Schwarzkopf, Norman, 914
Science: in public education, 537; and re-
  ligion, 572–573
Scientific method, 562
Scientific shop management, 713
SCLC. *See* Southern Christian Leadership
  Conference
Scobey, "Ed," 719
Scopes, John T., 703
Scopes trial, 703
Scott, Emmett J., 674
Scott, Monsta' Kody, 910
Scott, Thomas A., 504
Scribner's (magazine), 478
Scripps, Edward W., 557
SDI. *See* Strategic defense initiative
SDS. *See* Students for a Democratic
  Society
Sea power, importance of, 632
SEATO. *See* Southeast Asia Treaty
  Organization
Seattle, Washington, during Great
  Depression, 734*f*
Secession, readmission after, 448–450,
  453–454, 454*m*
Second Hundred Days, 751–753
Second Iraq War, 931–934; casualties in,
  933, 934*f*

Second New Deal, 751–753
Sedition Act (1918), 669
Segregation, 822–823; in education, end of, 822–823, 867; of Japanese Americans, 651; in military, 674, 776–778; in post–World War I period, 709–711; in Progressive Era, 625; psychological effects of, 822–823; and race riots, 867; in sports, end of, 870; Supreme Court on, 477–478, 822, 832; voluntary, 921; Washington (Booker T.) on, 479; under Wilson, 628. *See also* Civil rights
Selma, Alabama, 866
Senate, U.S.: in late 19th-century, 473–474, 477*f*; opposition to League of Nations by, 681–683
Separate but equal doctrine, 822
Separatism, black, 478, 710, 834, 866–867, 867, 920–921
September 11, 2001, 929–931
Settlement houses, 552–554, 563–564, 599
Severalty Act (1887), 487–488
Sewall, Arthur, 592
Seward, William H., 631
Sexual behavior: in 19th-century, 531; AIDS and, 901; in post–World War I period, 692–693, 693–698; sexual revolution and, 875–878
Sexual Behavior in the Human Female (Kinsey), 877
Sexual Behavior in the Human Male (Kinsey), 877
Sexually transmitted diseases (STDs), 877, 878
Seymour, Horatio, 455
Shafter, William, 643
The Shame of the Cities (Steffens), 579*f*
Sharecropping: in Great Depression, 745, 761*f*; in post-Reconstruction South, 461–463, 462*f*
Share Our Wealth movement, 749
Share tenancy, 461
Sheridan, Philip, 485, 580*f*
Sherman, William Tecumseh, 485
Sherman Antitrust Act (1890), 522–523; failure of, 599; Roosevelt (Theodore) administration and, 615; Supreme

Court on, 522, 591; Taft's use of, 617; unions and, 528
Sherman Silver Purchase Act (1890), 590, 591
"Shock and Awe" campaign, in Second Iraq War, 933
Sholes, Christopher, 557*f*
Shop management, scientific, 711
"The Significance of the Frontier in American History" (Turner), 565
Silver: as currency, 475, 589–591; in West, 488–492
Silver Purchase Act (1890), 590, 591
Simmons, William J., 706
Simpson, Nicole Brown, 920
Simpson, O. J., 920
Sinclair, Harry F., 720
Sinclair, Upton, 616
Single tax, 518
Sioux Indians, 482, 483, 483*f,* 484, 486
Sirhan Sirhan, 842
Sirica, John J., 851
Sit-in protests, 832
Sitting Bull, 486
60 Minutes (television show), 916, 935
Slavery: in Cuba, 638. *See also* Abolitionist movement
Slovenia, 913
Slums: in 19th-century, 542–545; in 20th-century, 599; churches and, 550–552; and race riots, 867–868; schools in, 564; settlement houses in, 552–554, 564
Smiley, George (fictional spymaster), 899*f*
Smith, Adam, 517
Smith, Alfred E.: Ku Klux Klan and, 707; New Deal and, 753; in 1924 presidential election, 722; in 1928 presidential election, 707, 727, 824
Smith, "Cotton Ed," 758
Smith College, 561, 561*f*
Smoot-Hawley tariff, 735*f*
Snake River Valley, gold rush in, 489
SNCC. *See* Student Nonviolent Coordinating Committee
Sobel, Robert, 735*f*
Social change, in World War II, 776
Social Darwinism, 517. *See also* Darwinism

Social equality, 451
Social feminism, 698
Social Gospel, 551, 600
Socialism: in early 20th-century, 602–603; "gas and water," 603; and labor movement, 520–521, 602–603, 685; in late 19th-century, 520–521, 551–552; municipal, 602; and progressivism, 602; World War I and, 669–670
Socialist Labor party, 520–521
Socialist party: in 1912 presidential election, 621m; in Progressive Era, 602
Social mobility, 531, 536–537
Social reforms. See Progressivism; Reform
Social science, 562–563
Social Security, 752, 895
Social Security Act (1935), 752, 754
Social workers: and progressivism, 599; women as, 561
Society of Christian Socialists, 551–552
Society of St. Vincent de Paul, 551
Sociology, 563
Sod house, 535f
Solomon Islands, 789
Somalia, 925
Somoza, Anastasio, 904
The Sound and the Fury (Faulkner), 748
South: agriculture in, 461–463, 462f, 463f; blacks in, 476–478, 480–481; civil rights movement in, 831–834; cotton in, 462, 462f, 463, 463f; desegregation in, 822–823; economy after Civil War, 459–461; ERA failure in, 890m; railroads in, 459; readmission to Union, 448–450, 453–454, 454m; segregation in, 476–478, 822–823; troop withdrawal from, 470; and Truman, 804. See also Reconstruction; Slavery
South America. See Latin America
South Carolina: Alliance movement in, 587; black politicians in, 458–459
South Dakota: Alliance movement in, 586, 587; population in late 19th-century, 585
Southeast Asia Treaty Organization (SEATO), 818
South End House (Boston), 553
Southern Alliance, 586

Southern Christian Leadership Conference (SCLC), 832
Southern Pacific Railroad, 493, 496m
South Korea, 808–813, 811m
Sovereignty, of Indian nations, 483
Soviet Union: atomic bomb developed by, 807–808; and Berlin blockade, 803f; breakup of, 908, 913; Carter and, 891; containment policy and, 801, 807–808; Cuba and, relations between, 821, 829; in Cuban missile crisis, 829; détente and, 846–848; disintegration of, 899f; expansionism of, 796–797, 801; Greek crisis of 1947 and, 802; under Khrushchev, 819–820; Marshall plan and, 802–804; post–World War II, 794–797; Reagan and, 895, 897–898; and Sandinista government, 904; spies working for, 813–814; Suez Canal crisis and, 819; in World War II, 765, 769, 773, 782, 794–797, 796. See also Russia
Space program, 829, 898
Spain: civil war in, 764; Cuban struggle for independence from, 638–641
Spanish-American War, 641–643
Speakeasies, 705
Speech, freedom of, suppression in World War I, 669–670
Spencer, Herbert, 563, 573
Spielberg, Steven, 786f
Spirit of St. Louis (airplane), 715
Spock, Benjamin, 859, 860
Spoils system. See Civil service; Patronage
Sports, 870; college, 550; in early 20th-century, 700–701; in late 19th-century, 548–550; on television, 859; women in, 550
Sprague, Frank J., 546
Springer v. United States, 591
Sputnik, 819, 871
St. Lawrence Seaway project, 815
St. Louis Post-Dispatch (newspaper), 558
Stagflation, 887–888
Stalin, Joseph: Marshall plan and, 803; post–World War II expansion by, 796–797, 801; support for, in United States, 795; in World War II, 795–797, 796–797; at Yalta, 795f, 796, 797
Stampp, Kenneth, on Reconstruction, 457f

Standard of living, under Reagan, 903–904

Standard Oil Company, 512–516, 515*f*, 601*f*, 615*f*; attacks on, 520, 601, 601*f*

Stanford, Leland, 473, 494, 495*f*

Stanford, Mrs. Leland, 562

Stanford University, 562

Stanton, Edwin M., 454

Stanton, Elizabeth Cady, 455, 607

Starr, Kenneth W., 923–924

Star Wars (strategic defense initiative), 897–898

State(s): constitutions of, 453–454; direct primary system in, 604; ERA failure in, 890*m*; progressive political reforms in, 604; progressive social reforms in, 605–606; "ten percent," 447–448; women's suffrage in, 609, 610*m*. *See also individual states by name*

The State (Wilson), 621

State Department: communists in, 813–814, 817; Open Door policy and, 722–723, 723; under Taft, 654

States' Rights party, 805

Status revolution, 600

STDs. *See* Sexually transmitted diseases

Steam, replacement by electricity, 509

Steel industry: labor organization in, 685; in late 19th-century, 506–507, 631; in late 20th-century, 889*f*; monopoly in, 511–512; railroads and, 506–507; strikes against, 527–528, 685; in World War I, 669

Steffens, Lincoln, 579*f*, 601, 603, 645, 736

Stein, Gertrude, 708, 709

Steinbeck, John, 748

Stephens, Alexander H., 451

Stephens, Uriah S., 523–524

Stephenson, David C., 707

Stevens, Thaddeus, 448, 450, 455, 460

Stevenson, Adlai E., 815, 819, 933

Stewart, Alexander T., 516, 533

Stimson, Henry L., 778

Stockman, David, 903

Stock market: in 1980s, 903–904; Internet companies in, 926–927; New Deal controls over, 743. *See also* Panic(s)

Stone, Oliver, 841*f*, 921

Strasser, Adolph, 525

Strategic Arms Limitation Treaty (SALT), SALT II, 891, 897

Strategic defense initiative (SDI), 897–898

Stratification, social. *See* Class structure

Strauss, Levi, 482

Streetcars, 546, 547

Strikes: in coal industry, 615; government reaction to, 591–592; IWW and, 602–603; by migrant workers, 869; in New Deal period, 755–756; in post–World War I period, 683; in steel industry, 527–528; unions and, 524, 526–528

Strong, Josiah, 631

Strowd, Rebecca, 481

Student Nonviolent Coordinating Committee (SNCC), 866

Student radicals, in 1960s, 872–874

Students for a Democratic Society (SDS), 873

Submarine warfare: in World War I, 662–664, 663*f*, 665–666, 674; in World War II, 769

Suburbs: late 19th-century migration to, 546, 547*f*; post–World War II growth of, 861–862; trolley cars and, 546, 547*f*

Sudetenland crisis, 765

Suez Canal crisis, 819

Suffrage. *See* Black suffrage; Women's suffrage

Sugar: Cuban, 638, 821; Hawaiian, 633; in post–Civil War South, 463*f*

Sugar Trust, 522, 591

Sullivan, "Big Tim," 577

Sullivan, John L., 548

Summit Tunnel, 494

Sumner, Charles, 448

Sumner, William Graham, 517

The Sun Also Rises (Hemingway), 708

The Suppression of the African Slave Trade (Du Bois), 626

Supreme Court, U.S., 752*f*; on 2000 presidential election, 928; on affirmative action, 921; on antitrust legislation, 523, 591, 615; on blacks after

Supreme Court, U.S. (continued)
Reconstruction, 477–478; Brandeis appointed to, 664; and business regulation, 521–522, 523, 751; on capital punishment, 909–910; on child labor, 605; on civil liberties, 670; on civil rights, 822; clear and present danger doctrine, 670; Clinton appointments to, 918; on colonial rights, 647; on free speech, 670; on Japanese internment, 779; on monopolies, 615; and New Deal, 751, 754–758; on oil scandal under Harding, 720; Reagan appointments to, 898; on segregation, 477–478, 822, 832; on Watergate investigation, 853, 854; on working hour legislation, 606, 698
Susman, Warren, 876f
Sweeney, Madeline Amy, 929
Syria, in Yom Kippur War, 882

Taft, Robert A., 768
Taft, William Howard, 617–618; break with Roosevelt, 619; foreign policy of, 654; as Philippines governor, 617, 647; presidency of, 617–618; in 1908 presidential election, 617; in 1912 presidential election, 620, 621m
Taft-Hartley Act, 800, 806
Taguba, Antonio M., 935f
Taiwan, 808
Taliban, 929, 931, 932
Tammany Hall, 577, 609
Tarbell, Ida, 601, 601f
Tariff(s): under Cleveland, 585; under Harrison (Benjamin), 585; in late 19th-century, 475, 502–503; post–Civil War, 465; on Puerto Rican products, 648; under Taft, 617–618; under Wilson, 623, 624
Taxation: under Bush (George H. W.), 916; and Great Depression, 731, 732; under Harding, 719–720; Mellon's program of, 719–720, 731; of property, 518; under Reagan, 895, 898; in World War I, 669, 678; in World War II, 776. See also Income tax
Teachers: college, 561; in progressive education, 563–564; women as, 533, 561
Teaford, Jon, 579f

Teapot Dome scandal, 720
Technology: impacts of, 865–866; Internet, 926–927; in mid-20th-century, 865–866
"Teddy's Bears," 612f
Telegraph: Edison and, 508; and news gathering, 557; and railroads, 505
Telephone industry, 507
Television, 858–859; and religion, 864, 896; violence on, 921–922
Teller Amendment, 644
Temperance movement, and prohibition, 704–705
Tenancy, share, 461
Tenement housing, 542–545, 546
Tennessee: Alliance movement in, 587; desegregation in, 823; evolution taught in schools of, 703
Tennessee Coal and Iron Company, 619
Tennessee Valley Authority (TVA), 745, 746m, 761
Tennis, 548, 550
"Ten percent plan," 447–448
Tenure of Office Act, 454, 455
Tepees, 482
Territorial Enterprise (newspaper), 567
Terrorism, 928–929; in 1990s, 929; after fall of Soviet Union, 928–929; in Iran-Contra arms deal, 904; in post-Reconstruction South, 464; in post–World War I period, 685; of September 11, 2001, 929–931; 2001 World Trade Center attacks, 929–931, 930f; U.S. war against, 931–932
Terry, Alfred H., 485
Tet offensive, 842
Texas: Alliance movement in, 586, 587; cattle in, 496–497; desegregation of education in, 822
Texas longhorn cattle, 496
Textbooks, post–World War I, 704
Textile industry: after Civil War, 463; cotton, 463; in post–World War I period, 729; Triangle shirtwaist factory fire, 606; women in, 532
Thernstrom, Stephen, 543f
Thirteenth Amendment: ratification of, 450; and representation, 450; southern transgressions of, 451
This Side of Paradise (Fitzgerald), 708

Thompson, Frederic, 549*f*
Thomson Steel Works, 512
Thoreau, Henry David, 554, 565
Thorpe, Jim, 700
Three-fifths Compromise, 450
Thriller (music video), 922
Thurmond, J. Strom, 805
Tilden, Samuel J., 466, 468, 469*f,*
    510–511
Tilden, William "Big Bill," 701
Tillman, "Pitchfork Ben," 645
Time (magazine), 797, 813
Titanic (film), 570*f*
Tobacco, 463, 503; in post–Civil War
    South, 463, 463*f*; in post–World War I
    period, 729
Toledo, Ohio, 603
Tolstoy, Leo Nikolayevich, 569
Tonkin incident, 838
Tontine, 516
Torture, of Iraqi prisoners, 935, 935*f*
Tourists, and destruction of buffalo, 487*f*
Towns: cattle, 490*f*; mining, 489, 491
Townsend, Francis E., 750, 753
Townsend National Weekly, 750
Toynbee Hall, 552
Trade: in 19th-century, 631; in 20th-cen-
    tury, 631; with Allies, in World War II,
    766, 768–769; cash-and-carry, 766,
    768–769; embargoes on, in 1930s,
    763, 766; lend-lease program, 769; and
    World War I, 661–664. *See also* Tariff(s)
Trade associations: New Deal and, 744; in
    post–World War I period, 729
Trade unions. *See* Labor unions
Transatlantic travel, in late 19th-century,
    537
Transcontinental railroads, 493–495,
    496*m*; competition between, 494–495;
    land-grant system and, 494; Pacific
    Railway Act and, 493–494; plans for,
    493–495; as trunk lines, 504
Transoceanic cables, 557
Transportation: freight, 505; and immi-
    gration, 537–538; in late 19th-century
    cities, 545–547; in mid-20th century,
    858; railroad competition and, 510
Triangle shirtwaist factory fire, 606
Tripp, Linda, 923
Trolley cars, 546. *See also* Streetcars

Trotter, William Monroe, 628
Trudeau, Garry, 852*f*
"True Sons of Freedom," 675*f*
Truman, Harry S., 799; atomic bomb
    and, 792; and communists in govern-
    ment, 813–814; economic policies of,
    800–801; foreign policy of, 801,
    807–808, 818–819; and Israel, 819;
    and Korean War, 808–813; at Potsdam,
    797; presidency of, 799; in 1944 presi-
    dential election, 791; in 1948 presiden-
    tial election, 804–806, 807*f*; Reagan
    compared with, 906*f*
Truman Doctrine, 802
Trunk lines, 504, 505
Trust(s), 477*f*, 512–516, 613–616; pro-
    gressivism and, 599; Roosevelt
    (Theodore) and, 612–613. *See also*
    Antitrust legislation
Tucker, Stephen, 557
Tugwell, Rexford, 738, 763
Tunney, "Gentlemen Gene," 701
Turkey, Truman Doctrine and, 802
Turner, Frederick Jackson, 565, 566*f,*
    632
Turner, Henry M., 478
Tuskegee Institute, 479, 479*f*
TVA. *See* Tennessee Valley Authority
Twain, Mark, 567–568, 708; on Gilded
    Age, 472
Tweed, William Marcy, 577–578
Tweed Ring (New York City), 466,
    577–578
Twenty-fifth Amendment, 853
Twenty-first Amendment, 741
Twenty-One Demands (1915), 659
Tydings, Millard F., 758
Tyler, Alice Kellog, 553*f*
Tyler, Elizabeth, 706
Typewriters, 503, 534

U-652 (submarine), 769
UAW. *See* United Automobile Workers
U-boat campaigns: in World War I,
    662–664, 663*f*, 665–666, 674; in
    World War II, 769
Uganda Railroad, 631
UN. *See* United Nations
Uncle Tomahawk, 869
Underwood Tariff (1913), 622

Unemployment, 532; under Clinton, 925; in Great Depression, 731, 732, 736, 761; insurance, 752; in late 19th-century, 532, 591; New Deal programs for, 745–747, 747f, 752; post–World War II, 800–801; psychological effects of, 736; in World War II, 775
The Unheralded Triumph (Teaford), 579f
Union(s), labor. *See* Labor unions
Union Cattle Company of Wyoming, 498
Union League of America, 463
Union of Russian Workers, 685
Union Pacific Railroad, 486, 487f, 493–495, 496m, 504; and Central Pacific, competition between, 494–495
Union party, 753
Union Railroad Station, Montgomery, Alabama, 506f
United Aircraft and Transport, 715
United Automobile Workers (UAW): 1937 strike by, 755; in oil crisis, 884
United Farm Workers' Organizing Committee, 869f
United Fruit Company, 655
United Kingdom. *See* Anglo-American relations; Great Britain
United Mine Workers (UMW), 1902 coal strike and, 615
United Nations (UN): charter, 794, 795; Declaration of, 795; in Korean War, 808–813; nuclear weapons and, 807; and Persian Gulf War, 914–915; and Second Iraq War, 933; Suez Canal crisis and, 819
United Nations Security Council: formation of, 795; and Korean War, 810
United States Steel, 513f
United States v. *E. C. Knight Company*, 522, 591
Universal Negro Improvement Association, 710
Universities. *See* Colleges and universities
University of Alabama, 823
University of California, 873, 921
University of Chicago, 560, 564
University of Illinois, 561
University of Michigan, 561
University of Missouri law school, 822
University of Oklahoma, 822

Urban areas. *See* Cities; Towns
U.S. Steel, 512, 523; formation of, 599; layoffs at, 902; in Taft administration, 619; in World War I, 669
U.S.A. (Dos Passos), 747–748
Utah, women's suffrage in, 609
Utilities, New Deal and, 745, 752. *See also* Electricity

Valentine's Day massacre, 705f
Valentino, Rudolph, 748
Van De Mark, Brian, 841f
Vanderbilt, "Commodore" Cornelius, 504, 519f
Vanderbilt, William, 519f, 536
Vanzetti, Bartolomeo, 707
Varieties of Religious Experience (James), 572
Vassar College, 561, 700f
Veblen, Thorstein, 562
Venezuela: border dispute with British Guiana, 637; Nixon's visit to, 821
Venture capitalists, 926
Versailles Treaty (1919), 679–683
Vesey, Denmark, 870
Veterans: benefits under Harding, 720; 1932 protest in Washington, 734; of World War II, 800–801, 872, 872f
Veterans Bureau, 719
Vetoes, presidential: by Clinton, 919; by Johnson (Andrew), 451
Vietcong, 831, 842, 846f
Viet Minh, 818
Vietnam: division of, 817–818; French in, 818
Vietnamization, 844–845
Vietnam War: costs of, 840, 849; end of, 885; under Johnson, 838–839, 839, 840m; under Kennedy, 830–831; under Nixon, 844–848, 848; opposition to, 839, 844–846; in 2004 presidential election, 935, 936; Saigon, fall of, 885
Villa, Francisco "Pancho," 659
Villard, Henry, 504
Villard, Oswald Garrison, 627
Violence: in cattle towns, 490f; popular culture and, 921–923
Virginia City, Nevada, 489
Virgin Islands, 650m
Vocational public schools, 537

Voting, in Jacksonian era. *See* Black suffrage; Women's suffrage
Voting Rights Act (1965), 838

Wade-Davis bill, 449
Wage, minimum. *See* Minimum wage
Wagner Act (1935), 751
Wald, Lillian, 552
Wallace, George C., 843
Wallace, Henry A.: in 1940 presidential election, 767; in 1944 presidential election, 791; in 1948 presidential election, 805; on Soviet Union, 794
Wallace, Henry C., 719
Wallace, Lew, 567
Walsh, Thomas J., 720
Wanamaker, John, 516
Wanghia, Treaty of (1844), 633
War Department, 668, 674
The Warfare of Science with Theology in Christendom (White), 572
War Industries Board (WIB), 668
War Mobilization, Office of, 775
Warner, Susan, 565
Warren, Earl, 822, 835
Warren Commission, 835
Warsaw Ghetto, 766*f*
Warsaw Pact, 912
Washington, Booker T., 478–480, 479*f*, 626, 628
Washington, D.C.: March on (1963), 834, 863, 920; Million Man March in (1995), 920; 2001 terrorist attack on, 930
Watergate scandal, 850–852, 853–855
Water rights, in West, 498
Watkins, Maurine, 696*f*, 697*f*
Watson, Tom, 592
Watts riots (1965), 867
Wealth: attacks on, 518–521; Long's Share Our Wealth plan and, 749; Townsend's pension plan and, 750; World War II and, 776
Wealth Against Commonwealth (Lloyd), 520, 528
Wealth of Nations (Smith), 517
Weapons: Indian vs. European/American, 485; international sale of, 763, 766, 904

Weaver, James B., 587, 589
Webb, Walter Prescott, 500
Weinberger, Caspar, 899*f*
Weinstein, Edwin, 684*f*
Wellesley College, 561
Wells Fargo, 482
West: agriculture in, 492–493; cattle ranching in, 496–500; cattle towns in, 490*f*; classification of land in, 498; and expansionism, 632; Indian wars in, 484–486; land bonanza in, 492–493; literature of, 567; mineral wealth of, 488–492; Plains Indians in, 482–483; post–Civil War, 481–482; railroads and, 493–495, 496*m*; settlement of, 481–482
Western Europe. *See* Europe
Western Traffic Association, 505
Western Union Company, 505, 507–508
West Germany, 805*m*
Westinghouse, George, 505
Westmoreland, William C., 842
Weyler, Valeriano, 638
Wharton, Edith, 708
Wheat: Civil War and, 462; in late 19th-century, 538, 585; in West, 492
Whiskey Ring affair, 465–466
White, Alfred T., 546
White, Andrew D., 579*f*
White, Richard, 566*f*
White, William Allen, 768
Whitefield, George, 551
White Government Leagues, 481
Whitewater, 916, 919
Whitman, Walt, 554
Why England Slept (Kennedy), 824
Whyo Gang, 545
WIB. *See* War Industries Board
Wichita, as cattle town, 490*f*
The Wide, Wide World (Warner), 565
Wilkins, Roy, 778
Williams, William A., 634*f*
Williams, William Appleman, 809*f*
Williamson, Joel, on Reconstruction, 457*f*
Willkie, Wendell L., 745, 768, 794
Wills, Helen, 701
Wilson, Woodrow, 531, 621–624; and blacks, 628, 674; deteriorating health of, 682, 683, 684*f*; financial reforms of,

Wilson, Woodrow (continued)
621–624; foreign policy of, 658–660;
and League of Nations, 681–683, 687;
and minority rights, 624; New
Freedom program of, 621–624, 667; in
Paris Peace Conference, 679–681;
postwar peace negotiations of,
679–681; in 1912 presidential election,
620–621, 621m, 628; in 1916 presidential election, 664–665; in 1920
presidential election, 687; vs. Senate,
681–683; World War I policies of, 662,
664–665, 668
Wimbledon, 701
Windows operating system, 926
Winning of the West (Roosevelt), 611
Winslet, Kate, 570f, 571f
Wirz, Henry, 448
Wisconsin: economy of, 502; progressivism in, 604, 607
Wllsworth, as cattle town, 490f
Woman's Home Companion, 859
Women: advertising aimed at, 700f; black,
461, 481; and dating, in post–World
War I period, 692–693; education for,
higher, 561, 561f; and Fifteenth
Amendment, 455; and Fourteenth
Amendment, 453; in Great
Depression, 736, 737f; in military, 780;
New Deal and, 759–760; in
post–World War I period, 691–692,
692–693; progressivism and, 599, 606;
in settlement house movement,
552–554; in sports, 550; World War I
and, 671; World War II and, 780–782.
See also Working women
Women's Auxiliary Army Corps, 780
Women's party, 698
Women's rights movement: in 19th-cen-
tury, 607–609; in 1960s, 878–881,
879f; higher education and, 561; 1970s
recession and, 888–890; in post–World
War I period, 692–693, 693–698;
World War I and, 671
Women's suffrage movement: Fifteenth
Amendment and, 455; Fourteenth
Amendment and, 453; in late 19th-
century, 607–609; in Progressive Era,
607–609, 608f; racial prejudice in,

625; and states, 609, 610m; after World
War I, 698; World War I and, 671
Wood, Robert E., 768
Woodrow Wilson Foundation, 723
Woods, Robert A., 553
Woodstock, 876f
Woolworth chain, 729, 832
Woolworth sit-in, 832
Work: in early 20th-century, 692; in late
19th-century, 531–532; in mid-20th
century, 836; post–World War II
changes in, 801; in World War I,
668–669. See also Labor legislation
Workers: immigrants as, 539–541; in late
19th-century, 531–532; layoffs of,
902–903; migrant, 869; in post–World
War II period, 887; in post–World War
I period, 692; progressivism and,
599–600, 602; World War I and,
668–669; World War II and, 775–776,
780–782
Worker's compensation, 606
Working class, attitudes of, 535–536
Working women: in early 20th-century,
599, 606; in late 19th-century,
532–534; in late 20th-century, 878,
888–890; in post–World War I period,
691–692, 693–698; in World War II,
780–782
Works Progress Administration (WPA),
747, 747f
World Series, 549
World Trade Center, 2001 terrorist attack
on, 929–931, 930f
World Trade Organization (WTO), 925
World War I: aftermath of, 676–678,
680m; Allied Powers in, 660; blacks
and, 671–674, 673f; casualties in, 677f;
Central Powers in, 660; civil liberty restrictions in, 669–670; economic impact of, 666–668; financing of,
668–669; mobilization for, 666–668;
opposition to, 669–670; outbreak of,
660–661; peace settlement following,
678–681; propaganda in, 669–670; sea
warfare in, 661–664, 665–666, 674;
social reforms during, 671; U.S. entry
into, 665–666; U.S. military engagements in, 674–675; U.S. neutrality in,

661–664, 665–666; Western Front in, 676*m*; women and, 671; workers in, 668–669

World War II: Allied strategy in, 782–783; atomic bomb in, 791–794; costs of, 792–793; diplomacy in, 794–797; economy during, 775–776; European theater of, 782–785, 784*m*; minorities in, 776–779; in North Atlantic, 767, 769; outbreak of, 764–767; Pacific theater of, 785–790, 790*m*; Pearl Harbor in, 772–773, 774*f*; social change in, 776; turning point in, 783–785; U.S. entry into, 773–775; before U.S. entry, 764–767; women in, 780–782

World Wide Web (WWW), 926

Worster, Donald, 566*f*

Wounded Knee, South Dakota, 870

WPA. *See* Works Progress Administration

Wright, Chauncey, 572

Wright, Frank Lloyd, 748

Wright, Orville, 715

Wright, Wilbur, 715

WTO. *See* World Trade Organization

WWW. *See* World Wide Web

Wyoming, women's suffrage in, 609

Xerox of America, 902

Yale University: football at, 550; quotas on Jews at, 691

Yalta Conference (1945), 796–797

Yamamoto, Isoroku, 789

Yankee Stadium, 702*f*

Yeltsin, Boris, 913

YMCA, 551

Yom Kippur War, 882

Yorktown (ship), 789

Youmans, Edward L., 563

Young, Andrew (Dr. Dre), 922

Young people, in post–World War I period, 692–693

Young Plan (1929), 727

Ypres, Third Battle of, 661*f*

Yugoslavia: civil war in, 913; and Greek civil war, 801

Zellweger, Renée, 696*f*

Zeta-Jones, Catherine, 696*f*

Ziegler, Ron, 852*f*

Zola, Emile, 569

ADDITIONAL TITLES
OF INTEREST

Note to Instructors: Any of these Penguin-Putnam, Inc., titles can be packaged with this book at a special discount. Contact your local Longman sales representative for details on how to create a Penguin-Putnam, Inc., Value Package.

Horatio Alger, Jr., *Ragged Dick & Struggling Upward*

Louis Auchincloss, *Woodrow Wilson*

Edward Bellamy, *Looking Backward*

Willa Cather, *O Pioneers!*

Alexis De Tocqueville, *Democracy in America*

Frederick Douglass, *Narrative of the Life of Frederick Douglass*

Gordon Hutner, *Immigrant Voices*

Martin Luther King, Jr., *Why We Can't Wait*

L. Jesse Lemisch (Editor), *Benjamin Franklin: The Autobiography & Other Writings*

Sinclair Lewis, *Babbitt*

Wendy Martin (Editor), *Colonial American Travel Narratives*

Toni Morrison, *Beloved*

Thomas Paine, *Common Sense*

Clinton Rossiter (Editor), *The Federalist Papers*

Upton Sinclair, *The Jungle*

Harriet Beecher Stowe, *Uncle Tom's Cabin*

Mark Twain, *Adventures of Huckleberry Finn*